Prisons

Prisons

*Edited by Michael Tonry
and Joan Petersilia*

Crime and Justice
A Review of Research
Edited by Michael Tonry

VOLUME **26**

The University of Chicago Press, Chicago and London

This volume was prepared under cooperative agreement no. 96-CE-VX-K001 awarded to the Castine Research Corporation by the National Institute of Justice and the Corrections Program Office, U.S. Department of Justice, under Title I of the Omnibus Crime Control and Safe Streets Act, 42 USC 3701 as amended. Points of view or opinions expressed in this volume are those of the editors or authors and do not necessarily represent the official position or policies of the U.S. Department of Justice.

The University of Chicago Press, Chicago 60637
The University of Chicago Press, Ltd., London

© 1999 by The University of Chicago
All rights reserved. Published 1999
Printed in the United States of America

ISSN: 0192-3234

ISBN: 0-226-80849-1 (cloth)
ISBN: 0-226-80850-5 (paper)

LCN: 80-642217

Contents

Preface

The number of people in, passing through, and directly affected by prisons and jails together make up the most noteworthy feature of American criminal justice policy at century's end. When a total is calculated for numbers of inmates, institutional employees, members of immediate families of both groups, and residents of communities in which correctional institutions are important employers, it is likely that tens of millions of Americans are each year directly affected by prisons and jails. One might assume that an enormous research enterprise and a substantial scholarly literature exist to inform policy making about institutions that annually shape many millions of people's lives and cost tens of billions of taxpayers' dollars. That assumption would be wrong.

In recent decades, there has been comparatively little research in the United States on prisons, and on important questions astonishingly little is known. For example, a series of self-evidently important policy questions are raised by the effects of offenders' imprisonment on their households, partners, and children and on their own later lives. The small literature that exists is fugitive and fragmentary. Because the U.S. prison population has increased by at least five times since 1972 as a result of deliberate policy decisions to increase the probability and lengths of prison sentences, it is natural to ask how on balance those decisions have affected crime rates and patterns and whether they have been cost-effective. The literatures on both subjects are tiny and contested. More sizable literatures exist on other subjects, but some are relatively old (e.g., sociological research on inmate and staff relations and subcultures) or specialized (e.g., psychological research on short- and long-term prison effects on inmates).

This volume, jointly sponsored by the National Institute of Justice (NIJ) and the Corrections Program Office (CPO) of the Office of Justice Programs of the U.S. Department of Justice, surveys current knowledge about a wide range of prison topics. The essays range from reviews of the current state-of-the-art of scholarship on prison governance and the psychological effects of imprisonment to overviews of policy developments affecting prisoners' medical care and the changing environments and challenges facing prison managers. The authors are based in the United States, Canada, and England. The process by which the essays evolved was that of every *Crime and Justice* thematic volume: a prospectus was developed at a small planning meeting attended by the editors, NIJ and CPO staff, and members of the *Crime and Justice* editorial board; papers were commissioned to agreed outlines; a conference attended by the authors, other scholars, and practitioners was convened at which initial drafts were vigorously discussed; written reports were solicited from referees; the editors, fortified by all that critical comment, prepared detailed sets of requested and proposed changes; the writers prepared final drafts; and now the book has appeared.

This volume reflects the work and ideas of many people. There could be no book without the writers, who good-naturedly put up with a lot. Everyone involved learned a great deal at the midcourse conference; as conveners we learned from all who attended, including, besides the writers, Steve Amos, Barbara Bloom, Meda Chesney-Lind, William Falcon, Mary Graham, Sally Hillsman, Susan Hunter, Pamela Lattimore, Marc Mauer, Larry Meachum, Mark H. Moore, Norval Morris, Anne Morrison Piehl, Michael E. Smith, Jeremy Travis, Christy Visher, and Edwin Zedlewski. The identities of confidential referees must remain confidential, but they know who they are and we are grateful for their help. Without much appreciated support from NIJ and CPO, and their directors Jeremy Travis and Larry Meachum, and kindly and efficient help from Mary Graham and William Falcon of NIJ's Communication Division, this book would not exist. To all of these people, who for the larger community have made possible this book and for the two of us have provided a wonderful education, we are enormously grateful. Readers will decide for themselves whether the exercise was worthwhile.

Michael Tonry
Joan Petersilia

Michael Tonry and Joan Petersilia

American Prisons at the Beginning of the Twenty-First Century

The effects of America's contemporary experiment with mass imprisonment will be clearer twenty-five years from now. The answers to some important questions, however, including whether vastly increased use of imprisonment has substantially enhanced public safety, will never be clear. The problem is one of covariance, that changes in things we measure that appear to be related to each other may not be related at all but instead may both be causally related to something else. In some northerly regions, for example, robins return from their winter vacations in February, their eggs hatch in April, and apple blossoms appear in May. It happens every year. Robins' vacation or reproductive predilections have, however, nothing to do with apple trees. Both are responding to changes in ambient temperature and climatic conditions. Apparent relations between crime and punishment may be similarly misleading.

Rising crime rates may affect imprisonment rates, or rising imprisonment may affect crime rates, or both may be affected by something else. If, for example, a broad-based, long-term change in social norms toward greater personal responsibility and respect for the interests of others were under way, it would be reasonable to predict that crime rates would fall (fewer people would choose to behave irresponsibly) and imprisonment rates would rise (many people would be more intolerant of wrongdoers and thus more inclined to punish them harshly).

Michael Tonry is director, Institute of Criminology, Cambridge University, and Sonosky Professor of Law and Public Policy, University of Minnesota Law School. Joan Petersilia is professor of criminology, law, and society, School of Social Ecology, University of California, Irvine.

Observers might well infer that increased imprisonment reduced crime rates. They might be right, or wrong, or partly right and partly wrong. The absence of a causal relationship between the activities of robins and the blossoming of trees is well understood; we understand and know how to measure changes in temperature and climate, and to predict their effects on robins and trees. Unfortunately, we do not understand what makes crime and punishment patterns change.

The world keeps changing, and it is often impossible to know why things happen when they do. The rapid increase during the 1990s in the numbers of people confined in prisons and jails coincided with falling crime rates. A cross section of lay people, public officials, and scholars believes that the deterrent and incapacitative effects of increased imprisonment caused crime rates to fall. Other cross sections of those groups believe that changes in policing strategies (e.g., community and problem-solving policing) and tactics (e.g., zero-tolerance policing) deserve substantial credit. Still others credit the robust and record-length economic expansion and related low unemployment rates of the 1990s, or they credit deeper, more fundamental, but more elusive social-structural changes that appear to be leading to falling crime rates throughout the Western world irrespective of the content or severity of countries' penal policies (Mayhew and van Dijk 1997). There are plausible cases, and plausible refutations, to be made for each of these claims. Each, no doubt, has some merit, but we will never know how to apportion credit among them or, more important, which deserve primary credit.

Likewise, whatever the future holds, we are unlikely in 2025 to know how the coming quarter century's imprisonment policies, whatever they prove to be, have affected crime rates. Imprisonment rates and numbers may continue to rise, or stabilize, or decline, or fluctuate. The current economic expansion will end, as all economic expansions do, and economic cycles will continue, as they always have. American social welfare policies will continue to be less generous than those of other Western countries, or they will move more toward the mainstream, or they will move in each direction at different times. Criminal justice policies, practices, and laws will become harsher or less harsh or will alternate. The movement toward privatization of prisons will continue, or slow, or contract, and private prison operators and employees will or will not become effective lobbyists for creation or maintenance of high-prison-use policies. And if deeper social-structural changes in American (or Western) society are primary determinants of crime-rate trends in recent years, those changes may continue or may alter direction. And something will happen to crime rates, and thoughtful people will disagree deeply about what caused what.

Nor, looking backward, is the relation between penal policy and crime rates and patterns any clearer. There is wide agreement among historians, for example, that crime rates, especially violent crime rates, fell steadily in many Western countries from early in the nineteenth century until the middle of the twentieth century, after which they began steep rises. Historians refer to this pattern as a "U-curve" or, sometimes, a (backwards) "J-curve," to make the point that twentieth-century violence rates never regained their early nineteenth-century heights. There is likewise wide agreement that crime posed vastly greater dangers to residents of early nineteenth-century cities than to residents of twentieth-century cities. But there the agreement ends.

There is no agreement on why crime rates fell for more than a century. Some argue that the increased bureaucratization of modernizing, industrializing, and centralizing countries changed socialization patterns and in effect trained people to conformity (Lane 1980, 1989, 1992; Gurr 1989a, 1989b). Some claim that religious revivalism and a moral reawakening in the nineteenth century affected basic beliefs and values and with them the socialization people received in families, schools, churches, and communities (Wilson and Hernstein 1985). Some claim that the decline was the result of a general, much longer-term "civilizing process" that has affected at least all Western societies, and to which the increased crime rates of the 1960s–1980s are simply a short-term anomaly (Elias 1978, 1982). Most strikingly, virtually no one attributes the long-term decline to changes in sentencing policies or to criminal justice innovations, even though all of the institutions of modern American criminal justice systems (professional police, imprisonment as the modal punishment, probation, parole, the reformatory, indeterminate sentencing, the juvenile court) were created between 1830 and 1900 and ubiquitous by 1930 (Rothman 1980; Friedman 1993; Walker 1998). In relation to criminal justice innovation in the nineteenth century, the absence of claims about effects on crime rates is the dog that didn't bark, and no one noticed.

All this is a pity, because prison and jail populations of the past quarter century result from conscious policy decisions by federal and state lawmakers, premised on propositions about the crime-preventive effects of harsher and more certain punishments, and the validity of those propositions is the fundamental question to be answered about the wisdom of modern penal policies. Wisdom incorporates not only knowledge and experience, however, but also values. In the end, penal policies derive from normative premises and values, and penal policies might better be served if they were openly and honestly debated in those terms.

Even if the answers to first-order questions about aggregate behavioral effects of penal policies on crime, including imprisonment policies, are probably unknowable, much more is knowable about second-order questions concerning effects of imprisonment in general, and of various prison regimes and programs in specific, on prison staff, prisoners, their families, their communities, and public spending. Surprisingly little is known, but much is knowable.

Imprisonment policies beginning in the 1970s leapt far ahead of knowledge about prisons and prisoners. Until then, the largest bodies of systematic empirical research concerning prisons consisted of a sizable but highly variable body of studies on the effectiveness of correctional treatment programs (Lipton, Martinson, and Wilks 1975), a smaller body of recidivism studies (e.g., Ohlin 1951; Glaser 1964), and a sociological literature on inmate socialization and subcultures (e.g., Clemmer 1940; Sykes 1958; Sykes and Messinger 1960; Jacobs 1977). Since then, as a result of the proliferation of criminal justice and criminology programs created in the wake of the Law Enforcement Assistance Administration, the number of researchers interested in prisons increased greatly, but the absence of sustained commitment of research funding from government agencies and foundations frustrated efforts to build a vital prisons research community. Foundations for many years exhibited little interest in research on the adult criminal justice system, including prisons and prisoners, and until recently federal research-funding agencies focused nearly all their attention on other subjects.

Nonetheless, as the essays in this volume attest, important work has been done on many prison and prison-related issues. On some topics—for example, the effectiveness of correctional treatment programs (in Canada) and prison regimes (in England)—much of the most important recent work has been done outside the United States. The essays in this volume summarize what is known about a range of important topics, and with what degree of confidence, and what should be learned next. The essays speak for themselves, so we do no more in this introduction than describe a number of issue clusters on which research sheds some light and on which more sustained and strategic research could shed much more. Prudent policy makers and practitioners presumably want to make their decisions on the basis of evidence, and there are many areas where better evidence could aid in development of better policies.

I. Collateral Effects of Imprisonment

People are placed in prisons and jails partly because of moral ideas about desert: people who do certain things, it is widely believed, deserve to be punished. However, utilitarian ideas about public safety provide at least as strong reasons for imprisonment: putting people in prison enhances public safety, it is widely believed, by incapacitating them, by rehabilitating them, by deterring them and others, and by reinforcing basic social norms about right and wrong. Put differently, when desert ideas are set aside, people sent to prison are being used as means to achievement of public ends. For both moral reasons (can using people in particular ways be morally justified?) and practical reasons (how much does using people in this way cost, does it do more good than harm, are there unintended side-effects?), we should want systematically to understand the effects of imprisonment practices and policies. Earlier we mentioned crime control effects of imprisonment. Here the subject is the collateral effects.

The literature on collateral effects is fugitive and fragmentary. At least six kinds of collateral effects can be identified. First, what are the effects of imprisonment on prisoners' later lives? Sizable economic and smaller ethnographic literatures (Fagan and Freeman 1999) convincingly show that imprisonment reduces ex-offenders' subsequent incomes and employment. A policy literature shows that various state and federal laws deny ex-offenders the right to vote or hold office in some places, the opportunity to engage in certain occupations in some places, and the right to receive various public benefits and services in some places (Fellner and Mauer 1998; Petersilia, in this volume). Various literatures show that imprisonment often leads to breakup of families and social relationships and to lessening of parental involvement with their children (Hagan and Dinovitzer, in this volume).

Second, what are the effects of imprisonment on prisoners' later physical and mental health well-being? A psychological literature on coping and adaptation in prison concludes, probably contrary to many lay people's intuitions, that even long-term imprisonment appears to have few lasting mental health effects (e.g., Adams 1992), though some researchers doubt this (Liebling, in this volume). It would be surprising if established adverse effects on income, employment, and family functioning were unrelated to former prisoners' mental and physical health. However, a serious, long-term, multiple-measure, longitudinal study of ex-offenders' lives is needed to answer such questions, and none has ever been done.

Third, what are the effects of imprisonment on offenders' spouses or partners and their children? On this subject, the literature is especially thin and fragmented, as Hagan and Dinovitzer (in this volume) show, and the most pressing task is to pull together existing knowledge in order to formulate plausible hypotheses and develop systematic research agendas. Hypotheses would presumably at least address the effects of imprisonment on the financial and social stability of prisoners' families while they were in prison and afterward, on the maintenance of prisoners' relationships with families, and on the short- and long-term well-being and social functioning of prisoners' children. These would, of course, not be simple hypotheses. No doubt sometimes families and partners benefit from the removal of abusive, disordered, or dysfunctional parents and spouses. However, given the strong negative effects on children's well-being of being raised in disadvantaged, single-parent households (Loeber and Stouthamer-Loeber 1986), the effects of imprisonment on spouses and children often are likely to be negative.

Fourth, what are the effects of imprisonment on prisoners' later crime involvement? The negative effects on ex-prisoners' incomes, employment prospects, and family involvement are predictive, according to findings from criminal careers research (Blumstein et al. 1986), of increased offending probabilities. In addition, for centuries, at least since the time of John Howard, the great eighteenth-century English prison reformer, the proposition has been put forward that prisons are "schools for crime," that younger and less experienced prisoners are socialized into antisocial and oppositional attitudes and as a result exit the prison more likely to commit crimes than when they entered. No informed person doubts that this sometimes happens and at least partly offsets any crime-reductive effects of imprisonment (Hawkins 1976). Many European scholars accept it as proven that prison is criminogenic and that prison terms should for crime-prevention reasons be avoided whenever possible (Albrecht 2000). American research on the effects of penalties typically focuses on crime reduction and only sometimes even treats crime-enhancing effects as an offset. If the criminogenic effects of imprisonment are large, contemporary research may be overlooking an important part of the crime and punishment puzzle.

Fifth, what are the collateral effects of imprisonment on the larger community? Hagan and Dinovitzer (in this issue) offer plausible hypotheses about effects of recent prison expansion on deployment of public resources (from higher education, particularly, but also other public programs and services, to prisons), on economic development (from inner cities to the usually rural communities where prisons are built), and on community cohesion (in many disadvantaged minority communities, large fractions of the young men are or have been in prison and are thereby disabled from working, parenting, marrying, or otherwise being contributing members of the community). Others have pointed out that imprisonment has become so common an experience in some communities that it may no longer carry meaningful or any stigma and thereby may lose whatever deterrent effects it would otherwise have (Nagin 1998b) or even cause prison styles and values to be exported to the outside community (Anderson 1998; Fagan and Wilkinson 1998).

Sixth, what are the immediate effects on prisoners while being confined in prison? This is the one collateral-effects subject on which there are sizable literatures: on coping and adapting generally, measured in terms of prisoners' physical and mental health (Adams 1992) and in relation to housing arrangements (Gaes 1985), and specifically on prison suicide (Liebling, in this volume).

II. Crime Control Effects of Imprisonment

The preceding discussion of research on collateral effects of imprisonment suggests that policy makers have been flying blind, making decisions costing billions of dollars and affecting millions of lives without adequate knowledge of the nature and costs of unintended side effects. A response might be that the primary goal has been to enhance public safety and, possibly regrettably but understandably, the single-minded concern has been the reduction of crime through the deterrent, incapacitative, and rehabilitative effects of increased imprisonment. The relevant literatures, however, are inconclusive, small, for the most part old, and do not provide strong support for contemporary American punishment policies. Literatures addressing four questions appear particularly relevant.

First, has increased use of imprisonment reduced crime rates through deterrence and incapacitation? Presumably most people would conclude a priori that a quarter century's quintupling of the prison and jail population must have reduced crime rates. There has, however, been relatively little research in recent years on deterrence and incapacitation effects, and most authoritative reviews of both subjects conclude that, while such effects exist, they are probably modest (Cook 1980; Nagin 1998a, 1998b). So also concluded the most famous examination of the subject, the 1978 report of the National Academy of Sciences Panel on Research on Deterrent and Incapacitative Effects (Blumstein, Cohen, and Nagin 1978). Similar conclusions were reached in successive decades by National Academy of Sciences Panels on Criminal Careers (Blumstein et al. 1986) and Understanding and Control of Violence (Reiss and Roth 1993) and by an exhaustive recent survey of research on deterrence effects commissioned by the Home Office of England and Wales (von Hirsch et al. 1998).

Second, can prisons deliver treatment programs that will enhance public safety by reducing prisoners' later recidivism? The pessimism associated with the "nothing works" findings wrongly attributed to Martinson's famous 1974 article (Martinson 1974; Lipton, Martinson, and Wilks 1975) appears to have passed, and there are grounds for cautious optimism about the positive effects, under some conditions, of some cognitive-skills, drug-treatment, vocational training, educational, and other programs in adult prisons (Gaes et al., in this volume). The conditions, however, are stringent: most notably, program eligibility must be carefully matched to prisoners' needs and risks, programs must be well implemented and adequately funded, and compatible aftercare programs in the community must sustain treatment efforts. The grounds for optimism concerning programs for young offenders and in the community are somewhat stronger (Loeber and Farrington 1998).

Third, in the aggregate, without distinguishing among deterrent, incapacitative, and rehabilitative effects, does increased use of imprisonment reduce crime rates, in general, and have the increases of recent years, in particular, done so? The prevalent answer appears to be yes (Spelman 2000), but the literature, much of it by economists, is highly technical and inaccessible to nonspecialists, mostly dates from the 1970s, and suggests that effects are much more modest than is widely understood.

Fourth, in cost-benefit terms, is increased imprisonment worth it? This is the smallest and most primitive of the prison crime-prevention effects literatures, and as yet provides few policy-relevant findings. Except for a small literature that tries to compare alternative crime-prevention programs in cost-benefit terms (e.g., Greenwood et al. 1996), the work to date is useful mostly for methodological reasons, by showing how not to pursue such inquiries. For example, the most widely publicized recent work greatly exaggerates the costs of crime by means of inflated imputed costs of victim "pain and suffering" and takes no account whatever of suffering by offenders or pains of imprisonment borne by their partners, children, or communities (Miller, Cohen, and Wiersema 1996). It may be, as Zimring and Hawkins (1991) have argued, that gross cost-benefit assessments of the effects of imprisonment require weighing of inherently incommensurable values and have reached a dead end. Recent efforts to compare the cost and benefits of alternative crime prevention policies may offer more promise (Welsh and Farrington 2000).

III. Prisoners and Prison Staff

Thirty years ago, the largest and best-known body of scholarship concerning prisons was the sociological literature on prison subcultures and the socialization of inmates into prison life. That is no longer true, as much because of the waning of that literature as because of the growth of others. Prisons have changed a great deal in the past thirty years, inmate and staff subcultures and interactions between them have changed, and the learning of earlier times may or may not still be valid but at least needs augmentation. Compared with earlier times, many prisons are much larger, inmate populations and staffs are more disproportionately black and Hispanic, many more line and management staff are women, gangs are larger and their influence more pervasive, more prison staff are unionized, a large and growing fraction of prisons is under private management, and the possibility of judicial oversight and intrusion is greater. The sentencing policy changes of the past quarter century and especially the last few years have produced larger fractions of prisoners serving very long sentences, and with them have come increased demands for medical care and other services for the aging and elderly.

The direct causes of the last quarter century's increase in imprisonment are becoming clearer. Changes in sentencing and parole policies and practices, not changes in crime rates and patterns, are the principal cause of the vastly increased numbers of people in prison and of substantially increased percentages of members of minority groups among prisoners. (What is much less clear is why policies and practices changed as they did.) Blumstein and Beck (in this volume) show that, over the past two decades, drug policies premised on incarceration of drug dealers and increased probabilities of imprisonment of those charged with crimes have been the major contributors to prison population growth. More recently, increased sentence lengths have become a major contributor. Changes in parole policies have also increased prison populations through the abolition of parole in some jurisdictions, tighter release standards that have the effect of lengthening time served, reduced tolerance of parole condition violations, and greatly increased rates of revocation and readmission to prison (Petersilia, in this volume).

Behavioral, cultural, and social changes in the larger society inevitably impinge on life inside prisons. AIDS and HIV, for example, are more prevalent inside the prisons than out. The proportions of mentally ill and defective prisoners, never small, have been augmented as a result of the 1960s and 1970s movement to deinstitutionalize many mentally ill people (Petersilia 1997a, 1997b). The civil rights and women's movements have importantly affected prisons, as has the political conservatism of recent years. Programs premised on restorative justice ideas are beginning to appear inside prison walls (Pranis 1996).

The mission for scholars of prison life is to reinvigorate that once robust subject by examining new subjects, reexamining old ones, and incorporating new ideas and theoretical perspectives. Recent work in England (Sparks, Bottoms, and Hay 1996), for example, has studied the effects of different management regimes from, among others, the procedural justice perspective that people who believe themselves to have been treated fairly and their interests to have been fairly considered are more likely to perceive the involved institutions and processes as legitimate (Tyler 1990; Braithwaite 1999).

Studies of women prisoners and life inside women's prisons continue to be conspicuously absent, including in this book. There is a small quality literature (e.g., Zedner 1995), but the recent paucity of research on life inside prisons generally has had an even more impoverishing effect on traditionally understudied subjects. Although the proportion of women to men in state and federal prisons remains small (one-fifteenth as large on June 30, 1998; Bureau of Justice Statistics 1999), the number of women prisoners has for nearly thirty years been growing faster than the number of men prisoners, and the absolute number (82,716 on June 30, 1998) is larger than the entire prison populations of France, Germany, or England.

IV. Prison Management

Prison managers, like any other managers, need systematic knowledge if they are effectively, ethically, and sensitively to do their jobs. In an important sense, the sociological and other literatures on life inside prisons mentioned in Section III, and the psychological and other literatures on how people adapt to the experience of being prisoners mentioned in Section I, are both management literatures. The English work on legitimacy and order maintenance in prison (Bottoms, in this volume), which studies prisoners, prison staff, and their interactions, all in the interest of understanding how order can be maintained in prisons, for example, is centrally concerned with management.

In practice, however, writing on management tends to come from professional managers and management consultants rather than from social and behavioral science researchers. Riveland (in this volume) provides an account of the major challenges that prison managers have faced during the past twenty-five years and how they have changed over time. A volume such as this one could have addressed any number of important challenges that contemporary prison managers face in addition to those already mentioned. Examples include the growing privatization of institutional corrections; the maturing movement for professional accreditation of prisons and prison systems; oversight of the rapid expansion in the numbers of prisons, prison staff, and prisoners; and handling of the problems created inside prisons by modern drug use patterns and policies. McDonald (in this volume) examines the nettlesome problem of health care provision inside prison and illustrates the complex lattice of management, resource, and political frameworks within which prison managers must operate.

V. The Political Economy of Prisons

No one can know what people 100 years from now will find interesting, important, or cautionary about prisons and punishment at the twentieth century's end. From our chronocentric perspective the most striking and distinctive feature of American punishment polices, both historically and comparatively, is the last quarter century's expansion in imprisonment. Older literatures attempted to explain the functions and purposes of imprisonment (Garland 1990, 1991), as have some works by historians (Foucault 1978; Ignatieff 1978; Rothman 1980), but only a small contemporary literature tries to explain the reasons why contemporary prisons policies have developed as they have. Caplow and Simon examine some of that work in this volume.

The political economy of the American prison has changed enormously over the past twenty-five years. By and large outside partisan politics before 1960, prisons and punishment policies have been political staples since the middle 1960s. Mostly immune from judicial oversight under the "hands-off" doctrine before 1970, nearly every detail of prison management came under intense and often critical scrutiny by federal judges. Nearly entirely within the authority of public officials and employees except for minor contracted services before 1975, prisons are now often managed by private corporations that operate hundreds of institutions and provide comprehensive services, such as medical care systems, to others. Although prison administrators needing to build new facilities were often before 1980 stymied by not-in-my-backyard (NIMBY) movements, communities now compete for new prison construction as local economic development initiatives. Thirty years ago, there were no labor unions for prison guards; today in at least one state, the prison guards union is a major contributor to electoral campaigns and an active lobbyist for particular penal policies.

Private-sector analysts commonly speak of the stakeholders in private businesses—managers, employees, customers, sometimes the general public. In the prisons business, where a quarter century ago the stakeholders were principally public officials and employees, prisoners, and a nebulous sense of the public interest, the stakeholders today include these but also voters, labor unions, private for-profit corporations, communities housing prisons, and the politicians, lobbyists, and political organizations that represent all these interests.

We are too close to our own times to be able to look behind crime rates and punishment policies to understand why so many people are held in American prisons and why some of them are being held for so long. Whatever the true explanations, they are much more complicated than allusions merely to rising crime rates, law-and-order politics, or a vengeful public might suggest. Researchers from many disciplines using many methods study prisons, and many more of them should do so in the future. Adding up the numbers of people admitted into or held in prisons and jails, the people who work in those institutions, the members of both groups' families, and the residents of communities housing penal institutions, tens of millions of people are directly affected by prisons. Any social institution affecting so many people should receive much more attention from scholars than prisons now do. Norval Morris has often said that prisons are a microcosm of society and that if we study them we will learn about ourselves. That is another, perhaps the best, reason for increased investment in prison research.

REFERENCES

Adams, Kenneth. 1992. "Adjusting to Prison Life." In *Crime and Justice: A Review of Research*, vol. 16, edited by Michael Tonry. Chicago: University of Chicago Press.

Albrecht, Hans-Jörg. 2000. "Post-adjudication Dispositions in Comparative Perspective." In *Sentencing and Sanctions in Western Countries*, edited by Michael Tonry and Richard Frase. New York: Oxford University Press. (Forthcoming.)

Anderson, Elijah. 1998. "The Social Ecology of Youth Violence." In *Youth Violence*, edited by Michael Tonry and Mark H. Moore. Vol. 24 of *Crime and Justice: A Review of Research*, edited by Michael Tonry. Chicago: University of Chicago Press.

Blumstein, Alfred, and Allen J. Beck. In this volume. "Population Growth in U.S. Prisons, 1980–1996."

Blumstein, Alfred, Jacqueline Cohen, and Daniel Nagin, eds. 1978. *Deterrence and Incapacitation: Estimating the Effects of Criminal Sanctions on Crime Rates.* Washington, D.C.: National Academy Press.

Blumstein, Alfred, Jacqueline Cohen, Jeffrey Roth, and Christy Visher, eds. 1986. *Criminal Careers and "Career Criminals."* Washington, D.C.: National Academy Press.

Bottoms, Anthony. In this volume. "Interpersonal Violence and Social Order in Prisons."

Braithwaite, John. 1999. "Restorative Justice: Assessing Optimistic and Pessimistic Accounts." In *Crime and Justice: A Review of Research*, vol. 25, edited by Michael Tonry. Chicago: University of Chicago Press. (Forthcoming.)

Bureau of Justice Statistics. 1999. *Prisoners and Jail Inmates at Mid-Year 1998.* Washington, D.C.: U.S. Department of Justice, Bureau of Justice Statistics.

Caplow, Theodore, and Jonathan Simon. In this volume. "Understanding Prison Policy and Population Trends."

Clemmer, Donald. 1940. *The Prison Community.* New York: Holt, Rinehart & Winston.

Cook, Philip J. 1980. "Research in Criminal Deterrence: Laying the Groundwork for the Second Decade." In *Crime and Justice: An Annual Review of Research*, vol. 2, edited by Norval Morris and Michael Tonry. Chicago: University of Chicago Press.

Elias, Norbert. 1978. *The History of Manners: The Civilising Process*, vol. 1. Oxford: Basil Blackwell. (Originally published 1939. Basel: Hans Zum Falken.)

———. 1982. *State Formation and Civilization: The Civilising Process*, vol. 2.

Oxford: Basil Blackwell. (Originally published 1939. Basel: Hans Zum Falken.)

Fagan, Jeffrey, and Richard B. Freeman. 1999. "Crime and Work." In *Crime and Justice: A Review of Research*, vol. 25, edited by Michael Tonry. Chicago: University of Chicago Press. (Forthcoming.)

Fagan, Jeffrey, and Deanna L. Wilkinson. 1998. "Guns, Youth Violence, and Social Identity in Inner Cities." In *Youth Violence*, edited by Michael Tonry and Mark H. Moore. Vol. 24 of *Crime and Justice: A Review of Research*, edited by Michael Tonry. Chicago: University of Chicago Press.

Fellner, Jamie, and Marc Mauer. 1998. "Nearly 4 Million Americans Denied Vote Because of Felony Convictions." *Overcrowded Times* 9(5):1, 6–13.

Foucault, Michel. 1978. *Discipline and Punish*. Translated by Alan Sheridan. New York: Pantheon.

Friedman, Lawrence. 1993. *Crime and Punishment in American History*. New York: Basic.

Gaes, Gerald G. 1985. "The Effects of Overcrowding in Prison." In *Crime and Justice: An Annual Review of Research*, vol. 6, edited by Michael Tonry and Norval Morris. Chicago: University of Chicago Press.

Gaes, Gerald G., Timothy J. Flanagan, Larry Motiuk, and Lynn Stewart. In this volume. "Adult Correctional Treatment."

Garland, David. 1990. *Punishment and Modern Society: A Study in Social Theory*. Oxford: Oxford University Press; Chicago: University of Chicago Press.

———. 1991. "Sociological Perspectives on Punishment." In *Crime and Justice: A Review of Research*, vol. 14, edited by Michael Tonry. Chicago: University of Chicago Press.

Glaser, Daniel. 1964. *The Effectiveness of a Prison and Parole System*. Indianapolis: Bobbs-Merrill.

Greenwood, Peter W., Karyn E. Model, C. Peter Rydell, and James Chiesa. 1996. *Diverting Children from a Life of Crime: Measuring Costs and Benefits*. Santa Monica, Calif.: Rand.

Gurr, Ted Robert. 1989*a*. "Historical Trends in Violent Crime: England, Western Europe, and the United States." In *Violence in America: The History of Crime*, vol. 1, edited by T. R. Gurr. Newbury Park, Calif.: Sage.

———, ed. 1989*b*. *Violence in America: The History of Crime*, vol. 1. Newbury Park, Calif.: Sage.

Hagan, John, and Ronit Dinovitzer. In this volume. "Collateral Consequences of Imprisonment for Children, Communities, and Prisoners."

Hawkins, Gordon. 1976. *The Prison—Policy and Practice*. Chicago: University of Chicago Press.

Ignatieff, Michael. 1978. *A Just Measure of Pain: The Penitentiary in the Industrial Revolution, 1750–1850*. New York: Pantheon.

Jacobs, James. 1977. *Stateville: The Penitentiary in Mass Society*. Chicago: University of Chicago Press.

Lane, Roger. 1980. "Urban Police and Crime in Nineteenth-Century America." In *Crime and Justice: An Annual Review of Research*, vol. 2, edited by Norval Morris and Michael Tonry. Chicago: University of Chicago Press.

———. 1989. "On the Social Meaning of Homicide Trends in America." In *Violence in America: The History of Crime*, vol. 1, edited by T. R. Gurr. Newbury Park, Calif.: Sage.

———. 1992. "Urban Police and Crime in Nineteenth-Century America." In *Modern Policing*, edited by Michael Tonry and Norval Morris. Vol. 15 of *Crime and Justice: A Review of Research*, edited by Michael Tonry. Chicago: University of Chicago Press.

Liebling, Alison. In this volume. "Prison Suicide and Prisoner Coping."

Lipton, Douglas, Robert Martinson, and Judith Wilks. 1975. *The Effectiveness of Correctional Treatment: A Survey of Correctional Treatment Evaluations*. New York: Praeger.

Loeber, Rolf, and David P. Farrington. 1998. *Serious and Violent Youthful Offenders: Risk Factors and Successful Interventions*. Newbury Park, Calif.: Sage.

Loeber, Rolf, and Magda Stouthamer-Loeber. 1986. "Family Factors as Correlates and Predictors of Juvenile Conduct Problems and Delinquency." In *Crime and Justice: An Annual Review of Research*, vol. 7, edited by Michael Tonry and Norval Morris. Chicago: University of Chicago Press.

Martinson, Robert. 1974. "What Works? Questions and Answers about Prison Reform." *Public Interest* 35(2):22–54.

Mayhew, Pat, and Jan J. M. van Dijk. 1997. *Criminal Victimisation in Eleven Industrialised Countries*. The Hague: Dutch Ministry of Justice.

McDonald, Douglas C. In this volume. "Medical Care in Prisons."

Miller, Ted R., Mark A. Cohen, and Brian Wiersema. 1996. *Victim Costs and Consequences: A New Look*. Washington, D.C.: U.S. Department of Justice, National Institute of Justice.

Nagin, Daniel S. 1998a. "Deterrence and Incapacitation." In *The Handbook of Crime and Punishment*, edited by Michael Tonry. New York: Oxford University Press.

———. 1998b. "Criminal Deterrence Research at the Outset of the Twenty-First Century." In *Crime and Justice: A Review of Research*, vol. 23, edited by Michael Tonry. Chicago: University of Chicago Press.

Ohlin, Lloyd E. 1951. *Selection for Parole: A Manual of Parole Prediction*. New York: Russell Sage.

Petersilia, Joan. 1997a. "Justice for All? Offenders with Mental Retardation and the California Corrections System." *Prison Journal* 77:355–380.

———. 1997b. "Unequal Justice? Offenders with Mental Retardation in Prison." *Corrections Management Quarterly* 1(4):35–45.

———. In this volume. "Parole and Prisoner Reentry in the United States."

Pranis, Kay. 1996. "Restorative Justice Catching on in Minnesota Corrections." *Overcrowded Times* 7(2):1, 9–11.

Reiss, Albert J., and Jeffrey Roth, eds. 1993. *Understanding and Controlling Violence*. Washington, D.C.: National Academy Press.

Riveland, Chase. In this volume. "Prison Management Trends, 1975–2025."

Rothman, David J. 1980. *Conscience and Convenience: The Asylum and Its Alternatives in Progressive America*. Boston: Little, Brown.

Sparks, R., A. E. Bottoms, and W. Hay. 1996. *Prisons and the Problem of Order.* Oxford: Clarendon.

Spelman, William. 2000. "Prisons and Crime: What Recent Studies Do (and Don't) Tell Us." In *Crime and Justice: A Review of Research*, vol. 27, edited by Michael Tonry. Chicago: University of Chicago Press. (Forthcoming.)

Sykes, Gresham. 1958. *The Society of Captives.* Princeton, N.J.: Princeton University Press.

Sykes, Gresham, and Sheldon Messinger. 1960. "The Inmate Social System." In *Theoretical Studies in the Social Organization of the Prison*, edited by Richard Cloward. New York: Social Science Research Council.

Tyler, R. T. 1990. *Why People Obey the Law.* New Haven, Conn.: Yale University Press.

von Hirsch, Andrew, Anthony Bottoms, Elizabeth Burney, and P.-O. Wikström. 1998. *Criminal Deterrence and Sentence Severity: An Analysis of Recent Research.* Oxford: Hart Press.

Walker, Samuel. 1998. *Popular Justice: A History of American Criminal Justice*, rev. ed. New York: Oxford University Press.

Welsh, Brandon C., and David P. Farrington. 2000. "Monetary Costs and Benefits of Crime Prevention Programs." In *Crime and Justice: A Review of Research*, vol. 27, edited by Michael Tonry. (Forthcoming.)

Wilson, James Q., and Richard Hernstein. 1985. *Crime and Human Nature.* New York: Simon & Schuster.

Zedner, Lucia. 1995. "Wayward Sisters: The Prison for Women." In *The Oxford History of the Prison: The Practice of Punishment in Western Society*, edited by Norval Morris and David J. Rothman.

Zimring, Franklin E., and Gordon Hawkins. 1991. *The Scale of Imprisonment.* Chicago: University of Chicago Press.

Alfred Blumstein and Allen J. Beck

Population Growth in U.S. Prisons, 1980–1996

ABSTRACT

State and federal incarceration rates grew by over 200 percent between 1980 and 1996. The dominant factor is drug offending, which grew by ten times, followed by assault and sexual assault. The growth can be partitioned among four stages: offending rates; arrests per offense; commitments to prison per arrest; and time served in prison, including time served on parole recommitments. The growth in incarceration for drugs is driven most strongly by growth in arrest rates, then by commitments per arrest; there is some increase in time served, but only in the federal system. For other offenses, there are no changes in arrests per reported offense and a net decline in offending rates. Over the full period, the growth in state incarceration for nondrug offenses is attributable entirely to sentencing increases: 42 percent to commitments per arrest and 58 percent to time-served increases. Recently, new court commitments and parole violations have flattened out; the dominant contributor to current growth for all the offenses examined is time served. Incarceration rates rose faster for women (364 percent) and minorities (184 percent for African Americans and 235 percent for Hispanics) than for men (195 percent) and non-Hispanic whites (164 percent).

The United States over the past seventy-five years has experienced a dramatic change in its use of incarceration. For the first fifty of those years, the incarceration rate was strikingly stable at approximately 110 sentenced state and federal prisoners per 100,000 U.S. residents. The

Alfred Blumstein is J. Erik Jonsson University Professor of Urban Systems and Operations Research at H. John Heinz III School of Public Policy and Management, Carnegie Mellon University, Pittsburgh, Pennsylvania. Allen J. Beck is Chief of Corrections Statistics at the Bureau of Justice Statistics, Washington, D.C. They thank Carol Zierman for her help in data analysis.

small fluctuation around that rate is shown in the "coefficient of varia-tion" (the standard deviation of that series divided by its mean), which was only 8 percent. Much of that variation was accounted for by two deviations: a rise toward the end of the Great Depression and a dip during World War II, when the nation had better uses for its young men.

That stability was sufficiently striking that it suggested a fundamen-tal phenomenon at work. The phenomenon, deriving from some ideas of Durkheim, was described by Blumstein and Cohen (1973) as a "the-ory of the stability of punishment." The basic thesis was that societies maintain a stable incarceration rate, balancing the tolerance of mar-ginal crimes against the fiscal and political costs associated with too large an incarceration rate. According to the theory, crime increases raise the threshold of the kinds of crimes and offenders perceived to warrant incarceration; crime decreases enable society to lower the threshold of appropriate crimes and offenders warranting punishment, so that more marginal offenders would then be incarcerated.

An article offering that theory was published in 1973, just as punish-ment policy in the United States initiated a radical departure from its prior stable pattern. Beginning in the early 1970s, the incarceration rate began a period of continuous growth of approximately 6.3 percent per year that has continued largely unabated to the present. The incar-ceration rate in 1997 was 445 inmates per 100,000 U.S. residents, more than four times the stable rate that had prevailed for the fifty years preceding 1973. This is shown in figure 1, which presents the U.S. in-carceration rate from 1920 to 1997.

There is no question that the nation has received some benefit from that growth in incarceration. At least for some crimes for which incar-ceration has a strong incapacitative effect, there is undoubtedly some crime reduction associated with increased incarceration. There may also be some significant deterrent effects, although those effects may be more complicated and difficult to measure (Nagin 1998).

Those benefits, however, must be weighed against the costs. The most direct component of cost is the fiscal cost borne primarily by the individual states of approximately $20,000 per prisoner per year, or a national total of nearly $25 billion for the more than 1.2 million state and federal prisoners (approximately 100,000 of whom are in the fed-eral prison system) now under state and federal incarceration.[1]

---

[1] In fiscal year 1996, states spent a total of $22.0 billion for adult institutional correc-tions, including all operating and capital expenditures and all direct and indirect expendi-

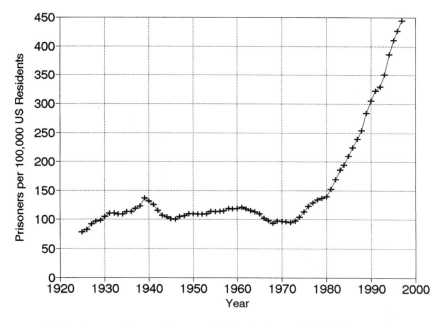

Fig. 1.—Incarceration rates for state and federal prisoners, 1925–97. Sources: Bureau of Justice Statistics (1986 for 1925–84; 1997 for 1985–95); Gilliard and Beck (1998 for 1996–97).

Those costs represent a drain on taxpayers, but they also may be seen as opportunity costs associated with other components of state budgets that have been reduced in order to accommodate the growing prison population.[2] It may well be, however, that the fiscal costs of increased incarceration are dwarfed by other costs associated with disruptions to communities from which prisoners are drawn (Lynch and Sabol 1998; Hagan, in this volume).

In this essay we examine the sources of growth in the incarceration rate during the period from 1980 to 1996. The data were collected by the Bureau of Justice Statistics (BJS) of the U.S. Department of Justice from regular surveys of state and federal prisons and were drawn from other national data sets. In examining the rising incarceration rates, we

---

tures. Dividing the operation expenditures by the average number of inmates during that year, the average cost per inmate is estimated to be $20,100 (Stephan 1999).

[2] According to annual fiscal reports issued by the National Conference of State Legislatures, state spending on higher education was the budget category experiencing the greatest reduction in state spending during the 1990s when corrections was the fastest growing budget category (Proband 1995, 1997; National Conference of State Legislatures 1998).

focus on how that growth differs across different types of crime, with particular emphasis on the six crimes that account for three-quarters of state prison populations: murder, robbery, aggravated assault, burglary, drugs, and sexual assaults. In 1980, there were 234,000 prisoners for the six offenses. By 1996, this had grown 268 percent to 860,000.

Section I examines the population growth in U.S. prisons by crime type, in particular the major growth in incarceration of drug offenders. Section II analyzes the gender, race, and Hispanic-origin components of the growth in incarceration. Section III discusses the stages of the criminal justice process that lead to an increased prison population: adult offending rates, arrests per offense, commitments to state prison per arrest, trends in time served by state prisoners, and trends in parole recommitment. Section IV analyzes the components of growth in state incarceration rates. Section V focuses on the growth in incarceration in federal prisons by crime type and allocation of growth to stages and on the growth rate for each stage in the criminal justice process. A summary is presented in Section VI.

I. Growth by Crime Type

The growth in incarceration rates has not been uniform across all the types of crime. It is widely recognized that the "drug war" has contributed to a major growth in the number of people imprisoned for drug offenses. With greater emphasis on violent crimes in recent years, there has also been a major growth in the number of violent offenders incarcerated.

The time trends from 1980 to 1996 in the incarceration rate for each of the selected crime types are presented in figure 2. The estimates here and in the following discussions of incarceration rates are based on sentenced inmates (with sentences of more than one year) per 100,000 U.S. adult population. Adults (persons aged eighteen or older) are used as the denominator because almost all (99.6 percent) of state and federal inmates are of adult age.

The most striking pattern shown in figure 2 is the growth in the incarceration of drug offenders. Over the seventeen year range of our analysis, drugs evolved from being an offense with nearly the fewest prisoners to the one with by far the most prisoners. In 1980 an estimated 23,900 people were in state and federal prisons for drug offenses, accounting for an incarceration rate of less than 15 inmates per 100,000 adults. By 1996, the drug incarceration rate had grown to 148

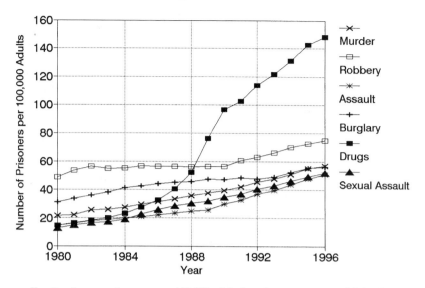

Fig. 2.—Incarceration rates per 100,000 adults by crime type, state and federal prisons combined, 1980–96. Sources: Bureau of Justice Statistics (1995*b*, table 1.9 for 1980–90; 1999*a*, tables 1.13 and 1.15 for 1990–96); Federal Bureau of Prisons (various years–*a*, table A-9 for 1980–85; various years–*b*, for 1986–89); Bureau of the Census (1993, 1996*b*).

inmates per 100,000 adults, more than ninefold, to a rate greater than that for the entire U.S. prison system in the fifty years to 1973.

Two other offenses have grown appreciably: aggravated assault (from fourteen inmates per 100,000 adults in 1980 to fifty per 100,000 in 1996) and sexual assault (from thirteen inmates per 100,000 adults to fifty-two per 100,000 in 1996), approximately a 300 percent growth for each offense. The rate for murder grew from twenty-two inmates per 100,000 adults to fifty-seven per 100,000, a growth of 164 percent. The other offense types (robbery and burglary) grew by 54 and 81 percent, respectively.

Drug offending is the major component of the overall growth. Approximately 45 percent of the growth in the total incarceration rate for these six offenses from 1980 to 1996 is attributable to the increased number of drug offenders. If all other crime types are considered, including other violent offenses (e.g., negligent manslaughter, reckless endangerment, kidnapping), other property offenses (e.g., motor-vehicle theft, fraud, arson, and larceny), and public-order offenses (e.g., drunk driving, weapons offenses, and the various nondrug vice crimes), the contribution of drug offenses to total incarceration growth is 33 percent.

II. Growth by Gender, Race, and Hispanic Origin

The growth in incarceration has been greater for women and minorities than for men and whites (table 1). Over the seventeen-year period, the incarceration rate among females rose nearly fivefold, from eleven female inmates per 100,000 resident females to fifty-one per 100,000, while the rate among males nearly tripled, from 275 male inmates per 100,000 resident males to 810 per 100,000. Despite this faster rate of growth, female inmates account for a small percent of all inmates—6.1 percent at year-end 1996, up from 3.9 percent in 1980.

Growth in incarceration was also more pronounced among blacks and Hispanics. Between 1980 and 1996, the number of sentenced prisoners (serving terms more than one year) rose by 823,000 (up 260 percent). The number of white inmates increased by 185 percent, the number of black inmates by 261 percent, and the number of Hispanic inmates by 554 percent. Hispanics were by far the fastest growing mi-

TABLE 1

Incarceration Rates in State and Federal Prisons, by Gender, Race, and Hispanic Origin, 1980 and 1996

	Number of Sentenced Prisoners*			Number of Prisoners per 100,000 Residents†		
	1980	1996	Percent Increase	1980	1996	Percent Increase
Total	315,974	1,138,984	260	139	423	204
Male	303,643	1,069,257	252	275	810	195
Female	12,331	69,727	465	11	51	364
White‡	132,600	378,000	185	73	193	164
Black‡	145,300	524,800	261	554	1,574	184
Hispanic	30,700	200,800	554	206	690	235

Sources.—Bureau of Justice Statistics (1983, 1987, 1999c); Bureau of the Census (1993, 1996a, 1996b); Gilliard and Beck (1998).

* Based on prisoners with a sentence of more than one year. The numbers for race and Hispanic origin were estimated based on the State inmate surveys in 1979 and 1997 and the federal inmate survey in 1997. Estimates have been rounded to the nearest 100.

† Based on census estimates of the U.S. resident population on July 1 of each year and adjusted for the census undercount.

‡ Excludes Hispanics.

nority group among inmates, increasing from approximately 9.7 percent of all inmates in 1980 to 17.6 percent of all inmates in 1996. At
year-end 1996, at least 200,000 Hispanics were under the jurisdiction
of state or federal prison authorities.

As a consequence of these differing rates of growth, disparities in
incarceration rates widened during the period. Relative to their numbers in the U.S. resident population, blacks were 8.2 times more likely
than whites to be in prison in 1996 (up from 7.6 in 1980), and Hispanics were 3.6 times more likely than non-Hispanic whites to be in prison
(up from 2.8). In 1996, approximately 1.6 percent of all the black residents of the United States were in a state or federal prison; the rate
was almost twice as large, 3.1 percent, for black males and, still larger,
an astonishing 8.3 percent for black males in their late twenties.[3] For
Hispanics approximately .7 percent of the total population were in
state or federal prisons in 1996, and for non-Hispanic whites approximately .2 percent of the total population were in prison (Gilliard and
Beck 1998).

An initial exploration of the six selected crime types disaggregated
by gender, race, and Hispanic origin reveals important differences in
the sources of growth among groups in state prison populations (table
2). Although data by crime type for each year by gender, race, and Hispanic origin do not exist, we have estimated these distributions for
1980 and 1996 for state prisoners.[4] We also include here for complete-
ness the other offense groups (other violent, other property, and public
order).

Among offense categories, drug offenses were the major contributors to the increases for women and blacks (increasing their incarceration at a compounded annual rate of approximately 20 percent from
1980 to 1996) and only somewhat less for males (17 percent per year)
and Hispanics (16 percent per year). Public-order offenses, largely
weapons and immigration violations, also rose sharply—representing
the second highest growth rates for women and minorities. Among

[3] The existence, causes, and implications of racial disproportionality in the U.S. criminal justice system are addressed extensively by Tonry (1995), Sampson and Lauritsen
(1997), and Lauritsen and Sampson (1998).

[4] For 1980, we used the 1979 state prison inmate survey in combination with the 1980
National Prisoner Statistics (NPS) counts to obtain these distributions. Similar distributions were estimated using stock-flow procedures that combine data from the 1991 and
1997 state inmate surveys with estimates of admissions and releases from the National
Corrections Reporting Program (NCRP), 1990–96. From these estimates, we obtained
average annual growth rates (expressed exponentially) for each group by crime type.

TABLE 2

Average Compounded Annual Rates of Growth in State Prison
Populations, by Offense, Gender, Race, and Hispanic Origin,
1980–1996

	Average Annual Percentage Increase*					
	All Inmates	Male	Female	White†	Black†	Hispanic
All offenses (%)	8.1	8.0	11.2	6.7	8.1	12.1
Six selected offenses:						
Murder	7.5	7.6	6.8	6.0	7.6	12.0
Sexual assault	10.5	10.4	14.7	12.1	7.8	12.8
Robbery	4.0	3.9	6.1	1.3	4.1	8.2
Assault	9.3	9.3	9.9	7.6	9.3	13.9
Burglary	5.0	4.9	10.8	4.3	4.9	8.0
Drugs	17.0	16.7	19.8	12.1	20.3	16.0
Other offenses:						
Other violent	4.4	4.3	4.7	4.6	2.8	8.1
Other property	7.7	7.5	8.8	6.8	7.5	13.7
Public order	11.4	11.2	16.0	10.3	11.3	15.9

Sources.—Bureau of Justice Statistics (1987; 1996a, table 1.11; 1999a, table 1.11);
Gilliard and Beck (1998).

* The compounded annual rate of growth is the percentage growth applied each year
that brings the 1980 prison population to the 1996 level for each crime type and demographic group.

† Excludes Hispanics.

whites, sexual assaults grew as rapidly as drug offenses (each up more
than 12 percent per year). Among men, sexual assaults rose by more
than 10 percent per year, followed by aggravated assaults (up 9.3 percent). For every type of crime other than drug offenses, Hispanic inmates recorded higher annual growth rates than did black or white inmates.

In absolute numbers, however, these rates have very different bases.
To measure the relative contribution of these rates to overall growth,
we partition the growth by crime type for each demographic group.
Table 3 shows that drug offenses account for the greatest share of the
total increase during the period (29 percent), followed by sexual assault
(11 percent) and murder and assault (each 10 percent). Only when all
violent offenses are combined (representing 43 percent of the growth)
is another crime category more significant than drug offenses.

The variation in prison population increases by gender, race, and

TABLE 3

Partition of the Total Growth in State Prison Population, by Offense, Gender, Race, and Hispanic Origin, 1980–1996

	All Inmates*		Male		Female		White†		Black†		Hispanic	
	Increase, 1980–96	Percent of Total	Increase, 1980–96	Percent of Total	Increase, 1980–96	Percent of Total	Increase, 1980–96	Percent of Total	Increase, 1980–96	Percent of Total	Increase, 1980–96	Percent of Total
All offenses	736,621	100	684,705	100	51,916	100	224,956	100	344,792	100	145,079	100
Six selected offenses:												
Murder	76,300	10	73,100	11	3,200	6	21,700	10	38,300	11	14,100	10
Sexual assault	80,400	11	79,600	12	800	2	46,600	21	21,800	6	8,900	6
Robbery	64,900	9	62,400	9	2,500	5	5,700	3	40,100	12	15,400	11
Assault	73,900	10	70,700	10	3,200	6	21,300	9	33,000	10	16,200	11
Burglary	59,200	8	56,700	8	2,500	5	23,500	10	23,600	7	11,000	8
Drugs	215,100	29	193,000	28	22,100	43	38,300	17	124,600	36	46,800	32
Other offenses:												
Other violent	19,300	3	17,800	3	1,500	3	8,300	4	5,200	2	4,900	3
Other property	88,000	12	77,500	11	10,500	20	36,200	16	34,800	10	15,500	11
Public order	57,800	8	53,900	8	3,900	8	24,500	11	19,900	6	11,200	8

Sources.—Bureau of Justice Statistics (1983, table 1.11; 1999a, table 1.11); Gilliard and Beck (1998).
* Based on all state inmates in custody. All data have been estimated and rounded to the nearest 100.
† Excludes Hispanics.

Hispanic origin is striking. Drug offenders account for a far greater share of the total growth among females (43 percent) than among males (28 percent). The differential is even larger between white and minority inmates: drug offenses account for 17 percent of the increase among whites compared with 36 percent among blacks and 32 percent among Hispanics.

Sexual assault is the leading source of population increase among white inmates (21 percent) but represents a relatively small component of the growth among black and Hispanic inmates (6 percent each). These differences are offset by robbery, which accounts for only 3 percent of the total growth among white inmates, but more than 10 percent of the growth among black and Hispanic inmates. Contributions to total growth by murder, assault, and burglary differed only slightly among groups.

III. Partitioning the Growth of State Incarceration Rate by Stage of the Criminal Justice Process

Growth in incarceration is typically a consequence of growth in one or more of the sequence of stages leading to an increased prison population. Those stages begin with commission of crime, which can then be followed by arrest, conviction, commitment, and time served in prison, including time served as a result of a parole violation. Changes in any or all of these stages can contribute to growth in the prison population.[5]

---

[5] Langan (1991) examined the growth in state prison population from 1974 to 1986 and found that growth to be attributable predominantly to growth in prison admissions. He found no evidence of increasing time served or a slowdown in prison releases. Thus he employed a criminal justice model limited to growth in admissions and then partitioned that growth using indirect standardization procedures. He found that the bulk of the growth in admissions was explained by increasing imprisonment rates given arrest. Cohen and Canela-Cacho (1994, pp. 307–21) looked separately at the growth in incarceration rate from 1977 to 1988 in six states (California, Florida, Michigan, New York, Pennsylvania, and Texas). They factored that growth into the same stages we consider here, with particular emphasis on changes in offending rate and in the combined effect of commitments and time served as the expected time served per adult arrest. They found that patterns do differ considerably across the states but, generally, the growth in all the states' incarceration rates is attributable to increases in commitments to prison and in time served. The Cohen and Canela-Cacho analysis is noteworthy in its analysis of the apparent paradox of relative stability in the number of crimes actually committed in the face of large increases in imprisonment. In considering the potential crime control effects of imprisonment, they accommodate both incapacitation and deterrence effects. They conclude that stability in crimes committed would be accounted for if the increases in imprisonment prevented an escalation in offending that would have accompanied increases in the size of the offender population and/or in rates of offending by active offenders.

By examining each stage of the criminal justice process separately, the contribution of each to the total growth in incarceration can be isolated. Such a partition can also provide insights into the degree to which the growth is associated with greater criminality; greater police effectiveness in arresting offenders; some combination of increased effectiveness by prosecutors and punitiveness by judges in convicting arrested offenders and sending them to prison; increases in time served once sent to prison because of longer sentences (including mandatory minimum sentences), because the parole boards or other release policies are slower in offering release or because of more aggressive policies in recommitting parolees, either for a new offense or for a technical violation. As a result of the "get tough" rhetoric that has characterized much political discussion about criminal justice policy over the past two decades, both significant growth in the likelihood of commitment to prison for those arrested and in the time served by those sent to prison might be expected.

We partition the growth for each crime type by stage by examining the time trend in each of the following: rate of reported crimes based on the Uniform Crime Reports (UCR);[6] rate of arrests per crime, based on UCR arrest reports; rate of commitments to prison per arrest, based on BJS data on admissions to state prison;[7] and time served per commitment, estimated for each year by dividing the number of prisoners (also reported by BJS) by the number of new commitments to state prison.[8] Because federal offenses and arrests are not included in the UCR, the partitioning of growth is limited to the state prison population only. Sources of growth for the federal prison population are discussed in Section V.

For each stage we graph trends over time, and these trend lines allow examination of how growth varies across the crime types. To

[6] The UCR are published annually by the Federal Bureau of Investigation as *Crime in the United States* and released in the fall of the following year. They contain detailed data on crimes reported to the police by jurisdiction and on arrests by police by crime type and demographic group.

[7] The number of new court commitments by offense by year were estimated by combining data from the BJS NCRP and NPS statistical series. For each year, the proportion of new court commitments in each offense category was multiplied by the total number of new court commitments and rounded to the nearest hundred.

[8] The offense distributions of state prisoners were estimated for 1980–96. Bureau of Justice Statistics inmate surveys provided estimates for the custody populations in 1979, 1985, and 1991. When combined with estimated counts by offense of annual admissions and releases, these surveys provide the basis for estimating the offense distributions in the other years. For details on the stock-flow estimation procedure, see Bureau of Justice Statistics (1995*a*).

provide a quantitative comparison across stages and crime types, we fit a regression line to the time series and measure the steepness of that line as an indicator of the magnitude of the growth. We analyze those trends in Section IV.

Since imprisonment almost exclusively involves adults, we are interested primarily in the adult offending rate. This is obtained by partitioning the UCR reported crime rate in proportion to the adult fraction among arrestees for that crime type. That adult fraction, shown in figure 3, varies, being lowest for burglary (averaging 63 percent) and robbery (73 percent) and highest for murder (88 percent) and drug offenses (89 percent).

The adult fraction also changes over time for the individual crime types. These variations could reflect demographic shifts; for example, there was growth in the adult fraction for burglary and robbery in the early 1980s, which may have been attributable to the transition of the peak of the baby-boom generation (cohorts born around 1960) out of the juvenile ages and into the adult ages. These variations could also be attributable to behavioral shifts in the different age groups; for example, there was a decline in the adult fraction of murders in the late 1980s, which could reflect the sharp growth in availability of guns to

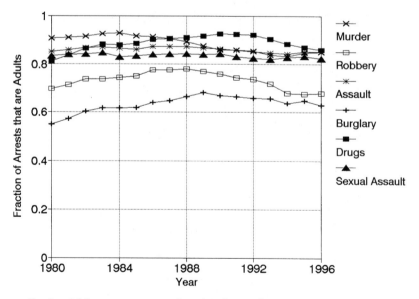

Fig. 3.—Adult arrests as a proportion of total arrests by crime type, 1980–96. Source: Federal Bureau of Investigation (1980–96).

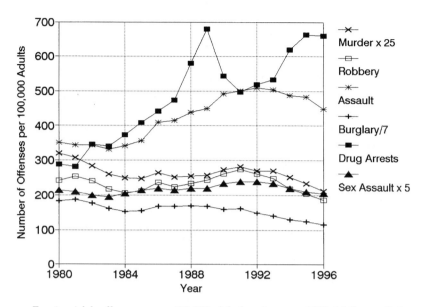

Fig. 4.—Adult offense rates per 100,000 adults by crime type, 1980–96. Source: Federal Bureau of Investigation (1980–96).

juveniles during that time (and an associated sharp increase in their homicide rate), while the homicide rate by adults was undergoing a steady decline (Blumstein 1995a; Cook and Laub 1998). These variations could also be attributable to shifting patterns of police practice; for example, adult arrests for drug offenses grew during the 1980s, when the crack epidemic flourished, and that increase in arrests may reflect a change in focus toward adults involved in crack dealing and away from juveniles involved in marijuana.

A. Adult Offending Rates

With this focus on adults we can examine the trend in the offense rate (per 100,000 U.S. adult residents) for each crime type based on UCR reports.[9] These rates are displayed in figure 4. In order to display the trend patterns of the different crimes in one figure, murder rates are multiplied by twenty-five, sex assault rates are multiplied by five,

[9] The number of adult offenses was estimated based on the total number of UCR index crimes and the number of reported arrests by age in reporting agencies in each year. For murder, forcible rape, robbery, aggravated assault, and burglary, the proportion of all arrests that were adult (ages eighteen or older) was multiplied by the total number of crimes. For drug offenses, the estimated total number of drug arrests was multiplied by the adult proportion in reporting agencies.

and burglary rates are divided by seven. Since there is no comparable independent information on trends in the rate of drug offending other than through arrest, for the drug "offense" rate we display the adult arrest rate. In order to bring the trends in the murder rate (averaging approximately 10 per 100,000) into a range that can be compared to the others, we multiply the murder rate by a factor of twenty-five. For the crime category of "sexual assault," we use forcible rape for the offending rate and for the arrest rate and expand the category to include other forms of sexual assault for commitments to prison and for time served.

The first observation from figure 4 is that only two offense types—drugs and assault—show a clear upward trend. The drug arrest rate has the sharpest growth overall; the rate rose rapidly during the 1980s, peaked in 1989, hit a trough in 1991 to 1993, and began to rise again. Because "drug offending" is measured through arrest, rather than through reported crimes as with the other crime types, and because drug arrest policies can be highly discretionary, it is difficult to distinguish how much these trends are attributable to an increase in drug offending and how much is due to changes in drug enforcement and arrest policies.[10]

The growth in aggravated assault is probably associated, at least in part, with an upward trend in the official recording of domestic assaults, especially beginning in the mid-1980s.[11] It is also possible that the inevitably subjective threshold between "aggravated" and "simple" assault in police reports to the UCR has been shifting downward, that is, that events which police in former times regarded as simple assaults are now more often categorized as aggravated assaults. There is some evidence that this downward trend is happening. In a comparison of assaults reported to the police in the UCR and reported by victims in the National Crime Victimization Survey (NCVS), Blumstein, Cohen,

---

[10] Based on reports from hospital emergency departments reported in the DAWN survey, the number of drug-related episodes increased from 323,100 in 1978 to 425,900 in 1989, fell to 371,200 in 1990, and then rose steadily to 531,800 in 1995 (Substance Abuse Mental Health Services Administration 1991, 1994).

[11] See Blumstein (1998, pp. 951–53) for an indication of the role of domestic violence in the growth of aggravated assault rates. In 1985, the ratios between arrests for aggravated assault and for homicide were rather constant at approximately 15:1 from ages eighteen through the late forties. By 1994, that same ratio prevailed until approximately age twenty-one but then increased to more than 35:1 by the thirties, as the prevalence of domestic relationships increases and the associated potential for domestic assault develops.

and Rosenfeld (1992) found that the UCR rates were lower than, but increasing toward, the NCVS rates. Also, consistent with the speculation that growth in the UCR rates may be a measurement artifact, NCVS estimates for both simple and aggravated assault, with very stable definitions in their questionnaires (until a measurement change in 1993), were very flat at a time when aggravated assault rates in the UCR were increasing.

The trends for the other crimes are much closer to each other and are much flatter. Murder and robbery, the two most serious violent crimes being considered here, track each other fairly closely and are relatively flat, following the declines in the early 1980s. Sexual assault, here measured by reports of forcible rape, follows a somewhat similar pattern.

Burglary is the only crime type with a clear downward trend, first in the early 1980s and subsequently in the 1990s. Baumer et al. (1998) attribute this to a preference for robbery over burglary by crack users: they were in a hurry to get the money to buy their drugs, and robbery offers a much shorter time interval than burglary from offense to ready cash.

B. Arrests per Offense

The conversion of an offense to an arrest depends on the identifiability of suspects and the intensity and skill of the police in pursuing a suspect. For some crimes, multiple suspects are arrested, which can raise the ratio of arrests per offense. For each offense type, the number of adult arrests in each year was estimated by multiplying the proportion of all arrests that were of adults (age eighteen or older) in agencies reporting to the UCR by the total estimated number of arrests nationwide. Figure 5 displays the ratio of reported adult arrests to reported offenses for each year and each crime type. We display here the ratio of offenses and arrests that occur in each individual year. Of course, some of the arrests in a particular year could be attributable to offenses that occurred in a previous year, and so there is no presumption of a direct link between all the offenses and all the arrests in each year. There is no line for drug offenses because we defined the offense rate to be the arrest rate, and, therefore, by definition the arrest-to-offense ratio would be 1:1.

Murder is by far the most readily solved crime, with almost one arrest per offense. In many murder cases there is an obvious suspect (e.g.,

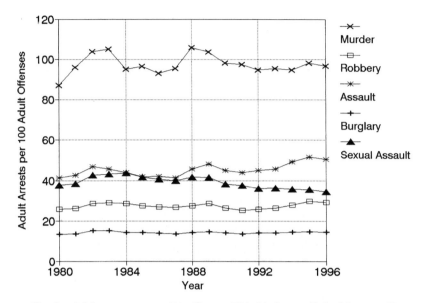

Fig. 5.—Adult arrest rate per 100 offenses, 1980–96. Source: Federal Bureau of Investigation (1980–96).

in intimate-partner homicides); sometimes, in gang homicides, there may be multiple arrests. Murder is the offense to which the greatest police resources are assigned and which often leads to intensive and long-term investigations.

Assault has the second highest ratio of arrests per offense, varying from forty-one arrests per 100 offenses in 1980 to fifty-two arrests in 1995. In assault cases the offender is often known to the victim (especially so in domestic assaults) and at least has been seen by the victim; this possibility of a positive identification enhances the likelihood of an arrest. The possibility of identification similarly enhances the prospect of an arrest for robbery. Burglaries rarely provide an opportunity for identification of a suspect and so have the lowest arrest-to-offense ratio.

The dominant picture from figure 5 is the stability of these ratios over the time period for all the crime types. In no case is there a clear trend upward or downward. If there is any notable trend, it would be associated with assault and may be indicative of the growth in police interventions in domestic assaults, where the prospect of an arrest is most likely.

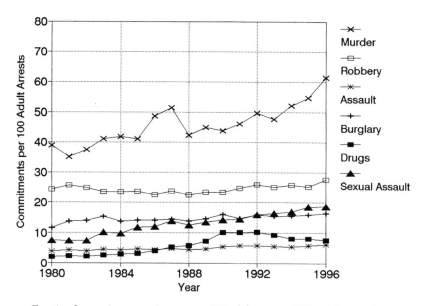

FIG. 6.—State prison commitments per 100 adult arrests, 1980–96. Sources: Bureau of Justice Statistics (1995*a*, table 4.17 for 1980–90; 1997, table 1.20 for 1991–95; various years–*a*, for 1996).

C. Commitments to State Prison per Arrest

Next, moving deeper into the criminal justice system, we consider the conversion of arrests into commitments to state prison.[12] Figure 6 presents ratios of commitments to state prison per 100 adult arrests. Any shifts in this ratio could represent a combination of changes in prosecutorial charging decisions, convictions in court (although the large majority of court outcomes are decided through guilty pleas), and sentencing decisions by judges.

Although rates of commitment per arrest for drugs are low, that offense has shown a marked increase from approximately two prison admissions per 100 arrests in 1980 to approximately ten admissions per

[12] It might be desirable to partition this transition more finely, considering prosecution and conviction stages in detail. Finding such data from the diverse information systems from fifty state courts is not feasible at this time, however. Also, not all arrests for one crime type are labeled with that crime-type designation at the time of commitment. It is possible, for example, for an aggravated assault to become a robbery or vice versa. As long as the rates at which those changes occur are fairly steady over time, the estimates of the transition rates presented here are reasonably valid. The measurements of sexual assault, in particular, are represented by crime and arrest reports of forcible rape, but by a broader class of sexual assaults in commitments to prison and in time served.

100 arrests in 1990 to 1992, a fivefold increase. It then dropped to less than eight admissions by 1996.

The ratio of commitments to arrests varies directly with the seriousness of the crime. One possible exception might be seen in assault, which is a violent crime, but with a ratio lower than the ratio for burglary. This probably reflects the diversity of the kinds of offenses that are included in arrests for aggravated assault. An "aggravated" charge can be placed on even a minor assault arrest and then dropped down during the charging process; this might be particularly common in domestic violence incidents. Victim precipitation, which can often be a consideration in an assault incident, can also be a mitigating factor that influences judgments that assaults do not warrant imprisonment.

The ratio of commitments to arrests rose sharply for all offenses other than robbery. This ratio, which may be interpreted at the offender level as the likelihood of going to prison given an arrest, rose by 257 percent for drug offenders, 149 percent for sexual assault, 57 percent for murder, 52 percent for assault, and 42 percent for burglary. Although the commitment-to-arrest ratios have all increased over time, they have fluctuated from year to year; for robbers, the ratios varied throughout the seventeen-year period and showed only a 13 percent increase.

D. Trends in Time Served by State Prisoners

Prison populations can grow because people who are committed serve longer sentences and because more people are committed. The estimate of time served in each year is based on the ratio of prisoners for each crime type to the number of new commitments.

Time served is measured much more commonly on the basis of the time served by a release cohort; any such estimate typically understates actual average time served because the releasees are more likely to be those with the shorter sentences. This is of special concern for serious offenses, which may include some very long sentences. That underestimate is most exaggerated for murder, for which many prisoners (e.g., those serving a true life sentence) never enter a release cohort. Also, such estimates are insensitive to recent changes in sentencing and release policies.[13]

In the absence of direct measures that are unbiased and sensitive to

---

[13] For an overview of the sources of distortions and misuses made of average time served in prison, see Biderman (1995).

changing sentencing policies, we use a ratio of the total prison population to new court commitments for each year.[14] This is only an indicator of time served. In periods of stability in admissions and releases, it
will equal actual time to be served by an admission cohort in each year.
In periods of steadily growing admissions, it will understate time
served, other factors being equal. In periods of declining admissions,
it will overstate time served.

Unlike the traditional measure of time served to first release, this
measure takes into account time served by prisoners who have not
been released and by those who may never be released. This measure
also includes in the prisoner counts people recommitted as parole violators with or without a new sentence and technical violators. As such,
this measure includes the time served by a growing segment of state
prisoners.[15]

Figure 7 displays the time trends in this estimate of time served. The
strongest trend here is in the murder offense, which grew from under
five years in 1980 to more than eleven years in 1996. This is probably
reflective of some combination of longer sentences for murder, more
life sentences (which would not be detected in observations of release
cohorts), greater reluctance by parole boards to release murderers, a
greater willingness to recommit them for a parole violation, and a
greater reluctance by pardons boards to commute life sentences to establish parole eligibility for lifers.[16] Time served for murder is likely to
continue to grow under the influence of cases like the Willie Horton
case, which increase officials' reluctance to risk a serious offense by

[14] For example, if there were two thousand prisoners for a particular crime type, and
one thousand prisoners were admitted each year, then the time served would be estimated as two years. This calculation is most appropriate when there are no major
changes over time in either of these rates. The previous graphs in figure 6, while they
show some trends, are not indicative of a major shift in any of the offenses other than
drugs. A similar calculation is used to monitor changes in average sentences in the
French prison population (Kensey and Tournier 1997, p. 15).

[15] New court commitments account for a steadily decreasing share of state prison admissions: 64 percent in 1996, down from 82 percent in 1980 (Beck 1999). Data from
BJS inmate surveys reflect the impact of this changing composition of admissions. In
1991, when the last survey was conducted, approximately 45 percent of state inmates
said they were either on probation or parole for a prior offense at the time of their current arrest, up from 34 percent in the 1979 survey. When translated into the number of
inmates, probation and parole violators totaled more than 356,000 state prisoners in
1991 compared with fewer than 96,000 in 1979.

[16] These trends are confirmed by the sharp decline between 1991 and 1995 in the
rates of release among murderers (Mumola and Beck 1997). During this period, the percentage discharged of all murderers in prison during the year declined by approximately
one third—from 9 percent in 1991 to 6 percent in 1995.

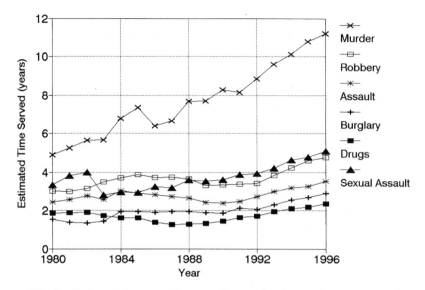

Fig. 7.—Estimated time served in state prisons, ratio of state prisoners to commitments, 1980–96. Sources: Bureau of Justice Statistics (1995*a*, table 4.17 and table 1.9 for 1980–90; 1997, table 1.20 for 1991–95; 1999*a*, table 1.13 for 1991–96; various years–*a*, for 1996).

someone they were responsible for releasing, as well as a heightened concern for public safety.

There seem also to be upward trends for other offenses, each rising steadily in the 1990s. For burglary, although time served was very flat during the 1984–90 period, since 1992 time served has increased by six months to an average of approximately two years. For sexual assault, the estimated time served rose from 3.2 years in 1987 to 5.1 in 1996. For other assaults, the upward trend began in 1990, increasing 50 percent in six years. The trend for robbery is also increasing, from an estimated 3.3 years in 1989 to 4.8 in 1996.

The pattern for drug offenses varied during the period. The ratio decreased until 1987 and then began to rise. By 1996, the estimated time served by drug offenders was 2.3 years—a full year longer than the 1.3 years recorded in 1987.

E. Trends in Parole Recommitment

The previous discussion of time served, since it is based on the ratio of prison population to number of commitments, includes not only the time served on the original sentence but also any time served following a recommitment because of a parole violation. Those violations could be either for a technical violation (i.e., violating a condition of the release, such as a prohibition on use of drugs or alcohol) or because of an arrest for a new crime. Parole decision making could thus contribute to the increases in prison population in two ways: by a delay in the first release on parole following eligibility and by an increase in returning parolees to prison following a violation, either because of a greater willingness to do so or because of an increase in the rate of violations.

The growth in the saliency of parole violation as a factor in prison populations is displayed in figure 8. Parole violation by parolees initially convicted of these six offenses constitutes approximately 70 percent of all parole violators, and that ratio is stable throughout the period. There is a clear upward trend in parole violation for all offenses, with drug offenses appearing to display the largest percentage of growth throughout the period. The large increase in the number of drug offenders returned to prison is also a reflection of the lagged effect of intense growth in the number of drug prisoners and subsequent growth in the number of paroled drug offenders.

The largest fractions of parole violators are among those initially

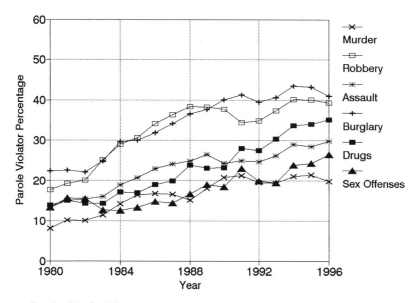

Fɪɢ. 8.—Parole violators as percentages of prison admissions, 1980–96. Sources: Bureau of Justice Statistics (1995a, table 4.17 for 1980–90; 1997, table 1.20 for 1991–95; various years–a, for 1983–96; various years–b, for 1980–82).

sentenced for burglary and robbery. They displayed large growth in the early part of the period, but the trend for robbery leveled off in 1989, and the trend for burglary leveled off after 1991. Assault displayed a slower but steadier upward growth.

The two offenses with the lowest fraction of parole violations are the violent crimes of murder and sexual assault, probably in part a reflection of the risk averseness of parole authorities as they consider offenders for release who have committed these two very prominent kinds of crimes.

Another manifestation of the increase in parole violations is that they represent an increasing fraction of all admissions to prison. This increase is reflected in figure 9, which displays the two components of prison admissions: new court commitments and parole violators. In 1980, parole violators constituted 18 percent of all admissions, and there has been steady increase to the point where they represent 35 percent of all admissions in 1996. There are no sharp differences in this trend across the offenses.

Figure 9 also shows flatness in new court commitments since 1990 and in commitment of parole violators since 1994. Despite these pat-

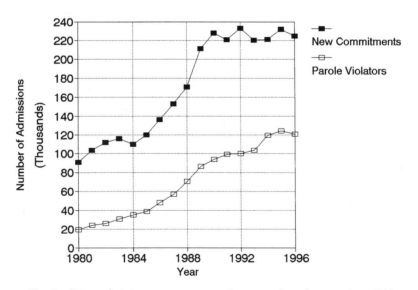

Fig. 9.—Prison admissions, new court commitments, and parole revocations, 1980–96. Sources: Bureau of Justice Statistics (1995a, table 4.17 for 1980–90; 1997, table 1.20 for 1991–95; various years–a, for 1983–96; various years–b, for 1980–82).

terns, prison populations have steadily increased, largely because of the upward trends in time served, especially in recent years, as is evident from figure 7.

IV. Analysis of the Components of Growth in State Incarceration Rates

To this point we have described changes in prison admissions relative to arrests, in sentence lengths, and in the changing mix of new court commitments and parole revocations among prison admissions. In this section we consider the relative contribution of each to overall prison population growth.

A. Analysis of Time Trends

To augment the figures shown to this point, we present in table 4 measures for each crime type of the time trend of the four components of growth in incarceration rates: offense rate, arrests per offense, commitments per arrest, and estimated time served. The measure in each entry of the table is the estimated linear time trend (the regression coefficient with time as the independent variable) as a percentage of the mean of the value over the period. Thus, for example, the commitments per 100 arrests for murder have an average upward trend of 1.15 commitments per year, which is 2.51 percent of the mean number of 45.8 commitments per 100 arrests. Nearly all the trends are statistically significant;[17] when that is not the case, the entries are designated "N.S." (not significant).

The trend in the incarceration rate for each crime type is also presented in table 4, along with the sum of the trends for the component stages. All increases are quite large, and especially that for drugs, which has increased by 13.7 percent per year. This increased rate is followed by sexual assault (8.1 percent per year), assault (7.6 percent per year), and murder (6.1 percent per year). Burglary and robbery grew at slower rates, 3.1 and 2.2 percent per year, respectively.

There is considerable diversity in the contributions of each stage to this growth. The trend in offense rate is largest for drugs—measured by arrests—at 4.8 percent per year. The only other offense rate that is growing significantly is for assault, at 2.8 percent per year. The burglary rate

---

[17] In this case, with fifteen degrees of freedom, a t-statistic greater than 2.13 indicates that the time trend is statistically significant and different from a flat trend at a 5 percent level of significance.

TABLE 4

Percentage Trends (1980–96) by Stages and Crime Types Contributing to Incarceration Rate Growth in State Prisons*

Offense Type	Offense Rate	Arrests per Offense	Commitment per Arrest	Time Served	Sum of Trends†	Incarceration Rate Trend	Mean Incarceration Rate
Murder	−1.21	N.S.‡	2.51	4.83	6.14	6.09	36.4
Robbery	N.S.‡	N.S.‡	N.S.‡	2.00	2.33	2.24	56.6
Assault	2.77	.95	2.54	1.29	7.55	7.57	27.8
Burglary	−2.17	N.S.‡	1.32	4.00	3.26	3.08	44.7
Drugs	4.80	N.A.§	8.78	N.S.‡	14.78	13.74	56.1
Sexual Assault	N.S.‡	−1.06	5.51	2.60	7.60	8.10	30.5

* The entries for the percentage trends are the coefficients of the bivariate linear regressions with time at each stage for each crime type divided by the mean incarceration rate over the 17-year period.

† The column presenting the sum of the trends is the sum of all estimated percentage trends (including those not found to be statistically significant) for all four stages; this sum is within 10 percent of the overall trend in incarceration rate.

‡ N.S. = not statistically significant at 5% level.

§ N.A. = not applicable; drug arrest rate is counted as the "offense rate."

per 100,000 adults is declining significantly, at a rate of 2.2 percent per year, and murder is declining at a rate of 1.2 percent per year.

In examining trends in rates of arrest per 100 offenses, presumably an indicator of police effectiveness in clearing crimes, two trends are statistically significant: sexual assault, which is declining, and assault, which is increasing, each at approximately 1 percent per year.

The next stage involves commitment rates of those arrested, a reflection of some combination of the effectiveness of police in accumulating evidence, prosecutors in bringing about convictions, and the punitiveness of judges in deciding on incarceration. Here, as expected, by far the largest increase (8.8 percent per year) is for drugs; this is nearly twice as large as the growth rate in drug arrests, a reflection of the growing tendency to use incarceration as a principal weapon in the "war on drugs." The growth rate in incarceration for sexual assault is strongly related to the commitment rate (up 5.5 percent per year). The increase is appreciably less for assault (2.5 percent per year), murder (2.5 percent per year), and burglary (1.3 percent per year). Robbery showed no significant trend in commitment rate per arrest.

A final indicator of the presumed toughness of the criminal justice system is time served. Murder is the offense with the strongest upward trend in time served, a 4.8 percent annual rate of increase, followed by burglary, with a 4.0 percent increase per year. The other violent offenses have smaller but significant increases in time served, sex offenses (2.6 percent), robbery (2.0 percent), and assault (1.3 percent per year).

Drugs is the one offense for which the time served trend is not statistically significant. This may seem surprising, since drug offenses displayed the strongest trends in increased commitments per arrest and in offending/arrest rate. The lack of growth in time served is not surprising, however, because the increase in the rate of commitments per arrest may bring into prison many less serious offenders who otherwise would have been placed on probation. As less serious offenders, their prison sentences are typically shorter than the average for other drug offenders. These shorter sentences keep down the average time served. Something similar happened when California dropped its indeterminate sentencing system in 1976. Under the old system, prison sentences were for "one year to the statutory maximum"; the parole agency set release dates. Unwilling to risk lengthy sentences for minor offenders whom they believed deserved short prison sentences, judges sentenced many to probation or short jail terms. Under the new determinate sentencing law, judges could know how long a prisoner would serve. Many more minor offenders were sent to prison, and average time served declined for many crimes as a result (Casper, Brereton, and Neal 1983).

These analyses demonstrate that the growing incarceration rate is a compounded effect of changes at each of the stages of the criminal justice system and that the stages displaying the upward trends vary substantially among crime types. For drugs, with the greatest growth in incarceration rate, the growth is attributable most directly to the rapid growth in the rates of arrests and commitments per arrest and not to time served. That is the clearest example of a toughening by the criminal justice system.

For sexual assault, with the second largest annual growth in incarceration rate, the greatest share of growth is linked to commitment rates. Increasing time served is also a contributing factor.

For assault, growth is predominantly attributable to an increase in reported offense rates and secondarily to growth in commitments per arrest. For burglary, the growth is primarily attributable to longer time served and secondarily attributable to an increase in commitments per arrest. For murder, the growth is entirely accounted for by the growth in time served. For robbery, with the smallest growth in incarceration rate, the growth is fully explained by the increase in time served.

It is striking that important trends in arrests per offense are virtually absent for all the offenses. Also, aside from the offense rate for drugs, which is not measured directly, the trends in offense rate are relatively small and diverse across the crime types. Two trends are not significant, one trend is positive, two trends are negative, and all trends are under 3 percent per year. This suggests that the punishment process— commitment rate and time served—will provide the strongest explanation for growth in incarceration rates.

B. Allocation of Growth Rate to Stages of the System

The sum of the component trends at each of the stages is quite close to (all within 10 percent) the trend in incarceration rate (both shown in the right portion of table 4). This, of course, is as it should be, since the selection of the stages was designed to reflect the components contributing to the total incarceration rate.

We can provide an indication of the contribution of each stage to the total growth in incarceration rate by weighting the trend for each crime type at each stage by its mean incarceration rate for the seventeen-year period (shown in the last column of table 4) and then aggregating over the crime types.[18] This weighting process leads to a percentage attribution of the contribution of each stage to the total incarceration rate as follows: offense rate (11.5 percent); arrests per offense (.5 percent); commitments per arrest (51.4 percent); time served (36.6 percent).

Of the entire growth in incarceration, only 12 percent is attributable to increased offending. There have been no important trends in arrest effectiveness. The remaining 88 percent is attributable to increases in the imposition of sanctions, primarily in the decision to incarcerate (51 percent) and secondarily in the time served by those incarcerated (37 percent).

Because the growth in drug arrests was such an important part of the growth in incarceration rate, and also because we used arrests as the indicator of offending for drugs, it is useful to examine the growth in incarceration with drug offenses omitted. In this analysis, we find a negative trend for offending rate, largely because over this period there has been a negative trend in burglary, robbery, and murder. These negative trends are partly offset by a positive trend in assault and a small positive, albeit statistically insignificant, trend in sexual assault. This result highlights the fact that the growth in drug arrests was the dominant factor in the offense rate contribution identified previously.

As a result, ignoring the negative trend in offense rate, the three remaining stages make the following contributions to the growth in incarceration rate: arrests per offense (.8 percent), commitments per arrest (41.5 percent), and time served (57.7 percent). Nearly all (over 99 percent) of the upward trend in incarceration rate is associated with the imposition of sanctions. The relative contribution of increasing rates of commitments and time served is reversed from the previous case: when drug offenses were included, the larger contributor was commitment rate, and when drug offenses are ignored, time served becomes the major contributor. This is because the trend in commitments per arrest was very high for drugs, but the trend in time served was quite small.

V. Growth of Incarceration in Federal Prisons

So far we have focused predominantly on state prison populations, since more than 90 percent of the nation's prisoners are under state

---

[18] The formula we use for the weighted trend for each stage is

$$T_k = \Sigma_j(T_{kj} * I_j),$$

where T_{kj} is the trend for crime-type j at stage k, I_j is the mean incarceration rate for crime-type j, and T_k is the weighted trend for stage k.

jurisdiction. The growth in the federal prison population has also contributed significantly to the rise in the overall U.S. prison population. Between 1980 and 1996, the federal prison population increased 333 percent, from 24,363 inmates to 105,544 inmates. This was a larger increase than for state prisoners. At year-end 1996, there were forty inmates in federal prison per 100,000 adults, up from eleven inmates per 100,000 in 1980. On average during this period, the number of federal prisoners rose by 9.6 percent per year, while state prisoners increased by 8.1 percent per year. By year-end 1996, the federal system was the third largest prison system in the nation, behind California and Texas.

The federal prison population is different from the state prison population. Demographically, the federal inmate population has a somewhat higher female percentage (7.3 percent in 1996) than the state population (6.2 percent); a higher Hispanic percentage (28 percent versus 17 percent); and a lower black non-Hispanic percentage (38 versus 47 percent). Nearly six in ten sentenced federal inmates in 1996 were in prison for a drug offense compared with two in ten state inmates. Almost all federal drug prisoners were serving time for drug trafficking, importation, or manufacturing, compared with fewer than two-thirds of the state drug prisoners. Approximately 13 percent of federal inmates had been convicted of a violent offense, primarily bank robbery, compared with 47 percent of state inmates. More than 8 percent of federal inmates were weapons offenders (comprising the second largest single crime type), compared with 2 percent of state inmates (Beck 1999).

In light of these differences, we turn our attention to identifying the factors contributing to the growth of the federal population. The data for this examination have been extracted from the BJS federal justice statistics database, which integrates data from the Executive Office for U.S. Attorneys, the Administrative Office of the U.S. Courts, and the Federal Bureau of Prisons. In examining the rising federal incarceration rates, we focus on five crime types that account for more than 85 percent of the federal prison population: robbery, fraud, drugs, weapons, and immigration violations.

A. Growth by Crime Type

The time trends from 1980 to 1996 in the incarceration rates for each of these selected crimes are presented in figure 10. As with the

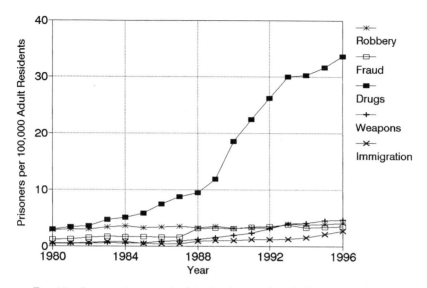

Fɪɢ. 10.—Incarceration rates in federal prisons, selected offense types, 1980–96. Sources: Federal Bureau of Prisons (various years–*a*, table A-9 for 1980–85; various years–*b*, for 1990–96); Bureau of Justice Statistics (1999*a*, table 1.15 for 1986–89); Bureau of the Census (1993, 1996*b*).

state prison population, rates are based on the number of inmates per 100,000 U.S. adult residents.

The trend lines highlight the dramatic rise in the rate of incarceration for drug offenses over the seventeen-year period. In 1980, the rate of incarceration for drugs (3.0 inmates per 100,000 adults) was similar to that for robbery (2.9 inmates per 100,000). During the early 1980s, the drug incarceration rate began to grow, more than doubling by year-end 1986. The major growth period was from 1989 through 1993, when the rate soared by 150 percent, from twelve to thirty inmates per 100,000 adult residents. By 1996, the rate was more than eleven times the rate in 1980.

The 1996 rates for the other four offenses are roughly comparable, from 2.7 inmates per 100,000 residents for immigration, to 4.7 per 100,000 residents for weapons offenses. The steady rise in the incarceration rate for weapons offenses is notable, however, rising from a very low level of 0.5 inmates per 100,000 adults in 1980 to 4.7 per 100,000 by 1996—a ninefold increase. The growth in immigration offenses was also considerable, rising from a rate of .6 inmates per 100,000 adults in 1980 to 2.7 per 100,000 in 1996, an increase of 350 percent. The incarceration rates for the other two offenses also increased, but the increases were smaller, a 41 percent growth in robbery and 192 percent increase in fraud.

The increase in drug offenders in federal prison dominates the increases for other offenses even more than at the state level. More than 75 percent of the total increase in the incarceration rate for these five crime types is attributable to the increase in drug offenders. Approximately 10 percent of the growth is attributable to the increased number of weapons offenders.

B. Allocation of the Growth of the Federal Incarceration Rate to Stages

As for the state prisoners, we can partition the growth by stage for each crime type. In the federal system, we can measure five stages, beginning with the arrest rate, followed by prosecution rate, conviction rate, commitment rate, and time served in prison.

We are unable directly to measure the offense rate, as we did using the UCR data for state offenses. Federal crimes are not reported in the UCR, though some are reported by state authorities and later determined to fall under federal jurisdiction. As a result, we begin with a proxy for arrest rate, which we measure by the number of suspects in matters concluded by U.S. attorneys per 100,000 adult residents. These suspects are involved most commonly in cases referred to the U.S. attorney by the Criminal Division of the U.S. Department of Justice; by a federal investigative agency (primarily the Drug Enforcement Administration; Federal Bureau of Investigation; Bureau of Alcohol, Tobacco, and Firearms; or Secret Service), or by a state or local law enforcement agency.

In examining trends in arrest rates, the number of drug suspects in federal criminal matters tripled during the period—rising from 5.8 per 100,000 residents in 1980 to a peak of 19.3 per 100,000 in 1992, and then dropping back to 17.0 per 100,000 in 1996. The number of suspects in weapons offenses also tripled but from a much lower base—from 1.1 per 100,000 to 3.4 per 100,000 in 1996. The number of suspects in fraud cases (which includes embezzlement, fraud, forgery, and counterfeiting) rose by more than 50 percent, from 10.1 per 100,000 to 15.6 per 100,000. For robbery and immigration, the trends were flat. These trends are displayed in figure 11.

Prosecution is the next stage. The rate of prosecution is measured by the number of suspects in cases filed in U.S. district court per 100 suspects in matters concluded by U.S. attorneys. Cases referred to the

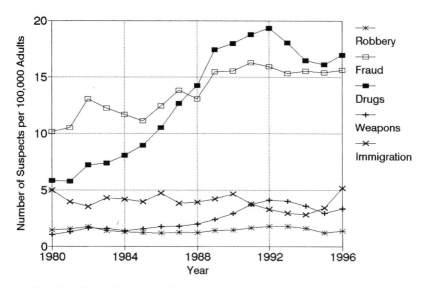

FIG. 11.—Federal "arrest rates" (rate of suspects in federal cases), 1980–96. Sources: Bureau of Justice Statistics (1990, 1996*b*, 1998, 1999*b*).

U.S. attorneys may be declined immediately, held pending further investigation, filed as a case in U.S. district courts, referred to a U.S. magistrate, or declined for prosecution. It is only those suspects in cases referred to U.S. district court that we follow to the next stage, since magistrates primarily handle misdemeanors.

The conviction stage is measured by the number of defendants convicted in U.S. district courts per 100 defendants in cases terminated. Cases may result in a conviction after a plea or a trial. Generally, the more serious the charge, the less likely defendants are to plead guilty (or nolo contendere).

Neither conviction rates nor prosecution rates have changed appreciably. Prosecution rates have, if anything, declined somewhat, perhaps because of the significant increase in the arrest workload. The mean rates of prosecution per 100 suspects for cases presented to the U.S. attorneys range from forty per 100 in immigration cases to seventy-one per 100 suspects in drug cases. The conviction rates per case prosecuted are even more stable over time, largely because they have been relatively high, ranging between eighty and ninety convictions per 100 defendants for all offense types, thus not leaving much room for increase.

The commitment rate represents the number of defendants sentenced to federal prison per 100 defendants convicted. For the federal system, we are able to disaggregate the conviction stage from the commitment stage. This contrasts with the state commitment rate, which was based on arrests, because of the difficulty of developing comparable conviction information from the fifty-one different court systems in the fifty states and the District of Columbia.

The federal commitment rate of convicted offenders, displayed in figure 12, shows more of an upward trend than the earlier court stages, but still does not grow appreciably because the earlier rates were relatively high. Robbery—predominantly bank robbery—is a prime example of this; it has hovered around ninety-five prison commitments per 100 convictions throughout the period. Even drug offenders in federal court were committed to prison over 70 percent of the time in 1980, and that rate climbed steadily to almost 90 percent in 1996. The growth was strongest from 1985 to 1990, the time of the greatest increase in crack markets and also the period of the introduction of federal sentencing guidelines, which mandated imprisonment for most drug offenses that appeared in federal court. The largest upward trend is for immigration offenses, which had a fairly steady growth in commitment rate from 46 percent to 82 percent, and weapons offenses, which grew from 59 percent to 90 percent, but most of that growth

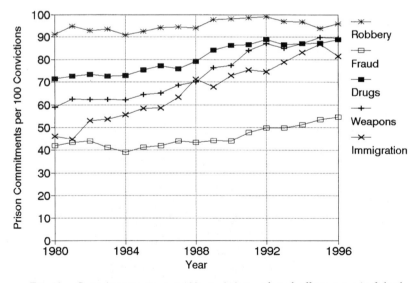

Fig. 12.—Commitment rates per 100 convictions, selected offense types in federal courts, 1980–96. Sources: Bureau of Justice Statistics (1990, 1996b, 1998, 1999b).

occurred between 1985 and 1992, the time of considerable growth in handgun homicides (Blumstein and Rosenfeld 1998).

The final stage is time served in prison, which is here measured also by the ratio of the total federal prison population to the number of new court commitments. As with the analysis of the state incarceration rates, this measure includes the time served by prisoners not yet released and those who will never be released, as well as time served by persons recommitted as parole violators. These estimates are presented in figure 13.

There is much more volatility in time served than in the measures of the federal system other than arrest. Robbery, with the largest time served, displays considerable fluctuations, but no discernible trend. By contrast, drug offenders served approximately fifteen to seventeen months until 1989, after which their sentences more than doubled to a peak of forty-four months in 1995. Similarly, the big growth in sentences for weapons offenses did not begin until 1993 and more than doubled in the four years between 1992 and 1996.

As with the state analysis, we use the data for each crime type at each stage for each year from 1980 to 1996 to estimate the time trend at

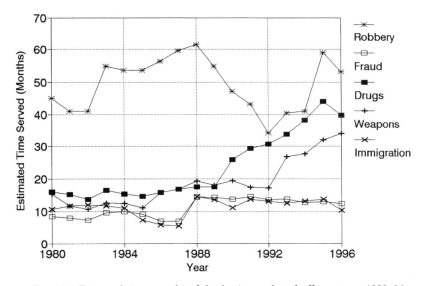

Fig. 13.—Estimated time served in federal prison, selected offense types, 1980–96. Sources: Federal Bureau of Prisons (various years–*a*, table A-9 for 1980–85; various years–*b*, for 1990–96); Bureau of Justice Statistics (1990, 1996*b*, 1998, 1999*a*, table 1.15 for 1986–89, 1999*b*).

each stage.[19] The regression coefficient of each trend is then transformed by dividing by the mean, so that the resultant coefficient can
be interpreted in terms of an annual percent change.

The results, presented in table 5, highlight the large and dramatic
changes that have occurred in the federal justice system since 1980. The
regression coefficients reveal that suspects in weapons cases increased by
7.5 percent per year, those in drug cases increased by 6.8 percent per year,
and those in fraud cases increased by 2.6 percent per year. There were no
significant trends in immigration or robbery cases.

These trends may reflect some combination of changes in underlying levels of offending, more aggressive efforts on the part of federal
investigative agencies, or an increased federalizing of these crimes
through referrals by state or local agencies. Clearly, with the surge in
suspects in drug cases, we see the combined effect of enhanced federal
law enforcement to control the importation and trafficking in illegal
drugs on the volume of cases referred to U.S. attorneys. Overall, whatever the underlying cause, the number of suspects in criminal matters
concluded by U.S. attorneys has risen by 2 percent per year since 1980.

Offsetting this growth in arrest rates was a decline in the rate of
prosecution for each crime type, except immigration violations. Although the prosecution rates fluctuated over time for each crime type,
the number prosecuted per 100 suspects in fraud and weapons cases
dropped by more than 2 percent per year, while the number in immigration cases rose by more than 2 percent. In the aggregate, the coefficient for all offenses was not statistically significant, suggesting that
federal prosecutors elected to pursue suspects in federal court at about
the same rate throughout the period.

Overall, the conviction rates were remarkably stable for all of the
five crime types. Although the number of convictions per 100 defendants in U.S. district courts was higher in 1996 (eighty-six per 100 defendants) than in 1980 (seventy-six per 100 defendants), the rate fluctuated significantly throughout the period. By crime type, there were
few differences. This suggests that the likelihood of successful prosecutions seems not to have changed, despite the rise in the number of suspects brought into the federal system.

The next stages display increases in both commitment rates and,

---

[19] Since some of these trends are not steady throughout the period (as with the time
served for drug and weapons offenses, for example), these trend estimates that are attributed to the entire period overestimate the trend during flat periods and underestimate
it during periods of rapid growth.

TABLE 5

Percentage Trends by Stages and Crime Types Contributing to Incarceration Rate Growth in Federal Prisons, 1980–1996*

	Arrest Rate†	Prosecution Rate‡	Conviction Rate§	Commitment Rate‖	Time Served#	Incarceration Rate**	Mean Incarceration Rate††
All offenses	1.99	N.S.‡‡	.47	2.58	3.76	8.10	31.81
Robbery	N.S.‡‡	−1.27	1.12	.35	N.S.‡‡	1.57	3.44
Fraud	2.65	−2.53	.71	1.76	3.74	6.93	2.51
Drugs	6.84	−1.67	.75	1.57	7.81	14.47	15.06
Weapons	7.48	−2.28	.52	2.95	6.70	15.02	1.93
Immigration	N.S.‡‡	2.40	.75	3.86	N.S.‡‡	9.50	1.06

* The entries for the percentage trends are the coefficients of the bivariate linear regressions with time at each stage for each crime type divided by the mean incarceration rate over the 17-year period.

† Suspects in matters concluded by U.S. attorneys per 100,000 adult residents.

‡ Suspects in cases filed in U.S. district courts per 100 suspects in matters concluded.

§ Defendants convicted per 100 defendants in cases terminated in U.S. district courts.

‖ Defendants sentenced to prison per 100 convictions.

Estimated by the ratio of the stock population to new court commitments.

** Federal inmates per 100,000 adult residents on July 1 of each year.

†† Mean incarceration rate, averaged over the 17 years.

‡‡ N.S. = not statistically significant at 5% level.

more strongly, in time served. This could be some combination of a similar upward trend in the states as well as the impact of changes in federal sentencing and release policies. These changes were associated with the passage of the Sentencing Reform Act of 1984 and the creation of the federal sentencing guidelines, which went into effect in late 1987.

The trend measures in table 5 reflect similar findings, though moderated somewhat due to the inclusion of the preguideline years in the estimation of the overall time trends. The largest coefficients for commitments to prison were for immigration (up 3.9 percent per year) and weapons offenses (up 3 percent per year).

Time served has the sharpest trend overall, with an annual increase estimated at 3.8 percent per year for all offenses combined. As discussed above, time served for drug offenses and for weapons offenses both rose dramatically by 7.8 and 6.7 percent per year, respectively. There was also a 3.7 percent annual increase in time served for fraud. There were no significant changes in the time served by robbers and immigration violators.

C. Allocation of the Growth Rate to Each Stage

As we did for stages in the criminal justice processing of state offenders, we can partition the total growth in federal incarceration rates by stage. Once again, we do this by weighting the trend for each crime type at each stage by the mean incarceration rate over the entire period.

The results are quite different from those we observed for the state incarceration rates. The growth for the five crime types is allocated as follows: arrest rate (38 percent); prosecutions per arrest (0 percent); convictions per prosecution (6 percent); commitments per conviction (12 percent); time served per commitment (44 percent). A large contribution, 38 percent, is attributable to increased rates of arrest, as measured by the number of suspects referred to U.S. attorneys; this is a reflection largely of the increased involvement of federal prosecutors in a variety of activities, including the inherently federal crimes as well as the drug offenses, which could be handled at either the federal or state level. The largest growth, 44 percent, is due to increases in time served by those who go to federal prisons. Increases in commitments, a major factor in the state systems, is of minor import in the federal system, probably reflecting the relative seriousness of cases that come into the federal system, with imprisonment much more often a presumption upon conviction. The other components, reflecting increases in prosecution and conviction rates, display small trends.

Although the prevalence of drug offenders among federal inmates has a dominant effect on these estimates, when we exclude drug offenders, we find some changes, but the order of importance of each stage remains unchanged: arrest rate (31 percent); prosecutions per arrest (0 percent); convictions per prosecution (11 percent); commitments per conviction (23 percent); time served per commitment (35 percent).

The contribution by the combination of commitments and time served remains approximately the same (58 percent, ignoring drugs, compared with 56 percent when drugs are included), but there has been a shift from time served to commitments in their relative contribution to the growth of federal incarceration rates. This reflects the importance of the large growth since 1990 in time served for drug offenses.

Similarly, the combined contribution of the earlier stages, arrest and conviction, remains approximately the same (42 percent without drugs compared with 44 percent when drugs are included) followed by the increased arrest rates and commitment rates. But trends in arrest rates were more salient when drugs were included, largely because of the rapid growth in drug cases filed by federal prosecutors, primarily during the 1980s. When drugs are omitted, those trends are less important, and so the contribution to the aggregate growth in the other offenses shifts somewhat to the conviction stage.

It is also striking that prosecutorial discretion in bringing cases forward has not varied and, consequently, has had no impact on growth of the federal system. But that is probably reflected in the definition of the federal "arrest rate," which reflects cases concluded by U.S. attorneys.

VI. Summary and Discussion

The United States has seen dramatic growth in its incarceration rates over the past twenty-five years—a quadrupling following a period of impressive stability for the five previous decades. The role of law enforcement in the nation's efforts to combat drug abuse has been a major contributor to that growth, to the point where the incarceration rate for drug offenses alone is now comparable to the rate that prevailed in the United States for fifty years. Drug offenders constitute 60 percent of the federal prison population and 23 percent of state prison populations. Furthermore, incarceration for drug offenses has contributed in an important way to the extreme representation of African Americans in prisons: over 8 percent of black males in their late twenties are in a state or federal prison on any given day.

In this essay, we have focused on empirically attributing responsibility for the growth in the nation's incarceration to the sequence of stages from offending patterns to arrest to prison commitment to time served in prison. Our analyses show that there has been virtually no change in police effectiveness in solving crimes (as measured by the number of arrests per crime). Aside from drug offending, which is difficult to distinguish from police pursuit of drug offenders, very little is attributable to changes in offense rates. Aggravated assault is the only one of the five offenses examined that displayed a consistent upward trend from 1980 through 1996, and much of that growth is probably due to recording domestic assaults that had previously not been recorded by the police.

The preponderance of the responsibility for prison population growth lies in the sanctioning phase, the conversion of arrests into prisoners and the time they serve in prison. For offenses other than drugs, approximately 40 percent of the growth in incarceration in state prisons is accounted for by increases in decisions to incarcerate and approximately 60 percent of the growth by increases in the time served by those sent to prison. Time served here reflects a combination of time served until first release, usually on parole, as well as subsequent time served following a parole violation. Parole violation has been an increasing factor in contributing to the growth in time served, accounting in 1996 for approximately 35 percent of all admissions to prison.

The story of drugs is quite different from that of the other offenses, which in general have seen steady upward trends, but of an appreciably smaller magnitude than drugs. The state incarceration rate (in terms of prisoners per 100,000 adult residents) for drugs has increased by a factor of ten, from twelve in 1980 to 120 in 1996, so that it is now the single largest offense category among prisoners. The growth of drug incarceration is attributable predominately to the major growth in adult drug arrest rates (which increased by a factor of 2.4 from 1980 to 1989, then declined sharply until 1991, and then rose again almost to the 1989 level by 1995). The growth in drug incarceration is also the result of the sharp increases in the conversion of drug arrests into prison sentences (increasing by a factor of five from 1980 to 1992, and then a decline to 3.6 times the 1980 level by 1996). These two factors account for almost all of the growth in drug incarceration, approximately one-third attributable to the growth in arrest and approximately two-thirds to the conversion of arrests to prisoners.

In federal prisons, drug offenses are by far the largest offense type. The story for the other offenses is quite different from that of the state prisons. The other major federal offenses are of minor import in state prisons. Even robbery, which is second only to drugs in state prisons, is distinctive in federal prisons because it involves predominantly bank robbers. The growth in the federal prison population is more evenly balanced between a growth in time served (35 percent), referrals (31 percent), and commitments per conviction (23 percent).

For the state offenses, by 1996 the rates of crime for each of the offenses considered were on the decline, new commitments to prison had been flat since 1990, new admissions of parole violators had been flat since 1994, and yet prison populations continued to increase. In recent years, only growth in time served is contributing to the growth in incarceration. Contributing to the growth in time served are more extreme sentences (e.g., under mandatory-minimum laws, sentencing enhancements, and "three-strikes" laws) and longer delays until initial release (e.g., under "truth-in-sentencing" laws).

These trends must raise concern about the benefits gained through the increase in time served. From the viewpoint of deterrence, most research has shown that between increasing the probability of commitment to prison and extending time served, the latter has the weaker deterrent effect (Blumstein, Cohen, and Nagin 1978, p. 37). From the viewpoint of incapacitation, as time served increases, the more likely it is that some individuals will be serving time after their criminal careers would have ended. These issues are particularly salient for prisoners kept incarcerated as a result of life sentences imposed under "three-strikes laws," which require dramatically extended sentences, especially for individuals whose sentencing offenses would warrant far less extreme sentences.

Our analyses also raise the question of what forces will stabilize or reverse the growth of incarceration rates. Can we expect them to continue climbing, or at some time will they reach a saturation point? It is possible that the stability we have seen since 1990 in the numbers and types of offenders sent to prison may be a leading indicator of future stability in incarceration rates. It is also conceivable that legislatures have finally reached a plateau in their desire to adopt sanctioning policies that extend the use of incarceration.

Time served is the single factor influencing prison population that has been increasing steadily during the 1990s. To the extent that political rhetoric continues to capture the public's concern in the face of reduced risks, incarceration rates might be expected to increase for some time to come. To the extent that the public displays concerns for the opportunity costs of the resources expended on incarceration (e.g., reduced money for education), then perhaps the rhetoric may cool and governors and legislators may search more seriously for other means of dealing with violators. That may involve less severe incarceration or more emphasis on intermediate punishments involving greater use of community sanctions as alternatives to incarceration (Morris and Tonry 1990). Also, the experience in California with "three-strikes laws" indicates that criminal justice systems can adapt and also moderate the impact of excessive sentencing measures.

All of these considerations inherently involve the question of the value received by the public as a result of current incarceration rates. It might have been reasonable to expect crime to have declined as a result of the quadrupling of the incarceration rate (Blumstein 1995c), but no such connection has been displayed. There certainly have been attempts to link the decline in crime during the 1990s to the growth in the prison population,[20] but any such argument must also explain why crime rates increased in the 1970s and the late 1980s while prison populations grew at the same rate as they did in the 1990s.

Of course, so complex an issue as the relationship between crime and punishment cannot be addressed through so simplistic an analysis as a negative correlation between the two very aggregated time series of crime rates and incarceration rates.[21] That has been attempted, often with significant manipulation, to make a rhetorical point.[22]

---

[20] See, e.g., Block and Twist (1994) and the commentary on their analyses by Blumstein (1995b).

[21] By comparing national imprisonment rates and crime rates at four times (1960, 1970, 1980, and 1990), a U.S. Department of Justice report (Barr 1992) asserted a strong linkage: "the increase in incarceration has been accompanied by a significant slowing of the increase in reported crime and by a decrease in estimates of total crime (reported and unreported crime combined)" (p. 2).

[22] See Block and Twist (1994), which selects an appropriate set of crimes (being sure to include burglary, which had been declining while others were increasing) and displays those along with growing incarceration rates in an "X-curve" to argue that incarceration works.

The aggregation of the two time series ignores the fact that very different factors could be affecting each one, thereby making the correlation more spurious than causal. For example, as the evidence in this essay makes clear, the growth in incarceration rate has been very strongly affected by drug enforcement policy, but drug offending does not enter into any of the measures of crime rates. Discerning the relationship between sanctioning policy and crime rates is the focus of considerable research in the areas of deterrence and incapacitation, requiring careful measurement and control for the many factors other than incarceration that affect crime rates (Blumstein, Cohen, and Nagin 1978; Cook 1980; Nagin 1998).

Furthermore, in order to establish sensible policy, benefits obtained from shifts up or down in sanctioning policy must be examined. Calling for particular attention is the massive incarceration of drug offenders, the largest group in prison. Incarceration of even three hundred thousand drug offenders does little to reduce drug sales through deterrence or incapacitation as long as the drug market can simply recruit replacements for those scared out of the business or locked away in prison (Bourgois 1989; Reuter, MacCoun, and Murphy 1990). But the analysis cannot stop there. To the extent that some of those drug offenders would have been committing other crimes on the street that are not replaced, such as interpersonal violence, their imprisonment could be contributing to the aggregate incapacitative effect of incarceration.

It is also possible that crime rates did not decrease during the 1980s while prison populations soared because the nation's level of criminality (as measured by the number of active offenders or their rate of committing crimes) would otherwise have increased during this period. If that were the case, then the growing incarceration may have kept the crime rate from ballooning dramatically. Alternatively, it could be that incarceration is far less effective than the public thinks it is or than we would all like it to be for the considerable investment it requires. People who spend time in prison have considerable difficulty functioning in the legitimate job market when they come out (Freeman 1994, 1996). These difficulties, combined with the criminal skills they develop and the connections they make while in prison, may increase the likelihood that they persist in criminal careers.

Knowledge to address these questions responsibly, especially in dealing with drug offenders, still remains unavailable. As the nation's expenditures for incarceration increases from the current level of nearly $25 billion per year, the cost of that ignorance will continue to grow. We need to know the benefits of incarceration in terms of the incapacitation and deterrence of crime. We need to find better guidance for focusing incarceration on those offenses and those offenders that represent the most serious threats and for whom incarceration will achieve the greatest crime control benefits. And we have to weigh these benefits against the number of lives disrupted (now totaling more than 1.7 million individuals in America's prisons and jails) and the families and communities—especially minority communities—disrupted by large numbers of individuals being extracted and kept in prison. Better understanding of these issues is crucial for the development of informed policy.

REFERENCES

Barr, William. 1992. *The Case for More Incarceration*. NCJ-13958. Washington, D.C.: U.S. Department of Justice, Office of Policy Development.

Baumer, Eric, Janet Lauritsen, Richard Rosenfeld, and Richard Wright. 1998. "The Influence of Crack Cocaine on Robbery, Burglary, and Homicide Rates: A Cross-City, Longitudinal Analysis." *Journal of Research in Crime and Delinquency* 35:316–40.

Beck, Allen J. 1999. "Trends in the U.S. Correctional Populations: Why Has the Number of Offenders under Supervision Tripled since 1980?" In *The Dilemmas of Corrections*, 4th ed., edited by K. Haas and G. Alpert. Prospect Heights, Ill.: Waveland.

Biderman, Albert D. "Statistics of Average Times Served in Prison Are Fallacious Indicators of Severity of Punishment." Paper prepared for the forty-seventh annual meeting of the American Society of Criminology, Boston, November 1995.

Block, Michael K., and Steven J. Twist. 1994. "Lessons from the Eighties: Incarceration Works." *Commonsense* 1(2):73–83.

Blumstein, Alfred. 1995a. "Crime and Punishment in the United States over 20 Years: A Failure of Deterrence and Incapacitation?" In *Integrating Crime Prevention Strategies: Propensity and Opportunity*, edited by Per-Olof H. Wikström, Ronald V. Clarke, and Joan McCord. Stockholm: National Crime Prevention Council of Sweden.

———. 1995b. "Youth Violence, Guns, and Illicit-Drug Markets." *Journal of Criminal Law and Criminology* 86(1):10–36.

———. 1995c. "Seeking the Connection between Crime and Punishment." *Jobs and Capital* 4(Winter):23–27.

———. 1998. "Violence Certainly Is the Problem—and Especially with Handguns." *University of Colorado Law Review* 69(4):945–67.

Blumstein, Alfred, and Jacqueline Cohen. 1973. "A Theory of the Stability of Punishment." *Journal of Criminal Law, Criminology, and Police Science* 63(2): 198–207.

Blumstein, Alfred, Jacqueline Cohen, and Daniel Nagin, eds. 1978. *Deterrence and Incapacitation: Estimating the Effects of Criminal Sanctions on Crime Rates.* Washington, D.C.: National Academy of Sciences.

Blumstein, Alfred, Jacqueline Cohen, and Richard Rosenfeld. 1992. "Trend and Deviation in Crime Rates: A Comparison of UCR and NCS Data for Burglary and Robbery." *Criminology* 29:237–63.

Blumstein, Alfred, and Richard Rosenfeld. 1998. "Explaining Recent Trends in U.S. Homicide Rates." *Journal of Criminal Law and Criminology*, 88: 1175–1216.

Bourgois, Philippe 1989. "In Search of Horatio Alger: Culture and Ideology in the Crack Economy." *Contemporary Drug Problems* 16:619–49.

Bureau of Justice Statistics. 1983. *Prisoners in State and Federal Institutions on December 31, 1981.* NCJ-86485. Washington, D.C.: U.S. Department of Justice, Bureau of Justice Statistics.

———. 1986. *State and Federal Prisoners, 1925–1985.* NCJ-102494. Washington, D.C.: U.S. Department of Justice, Bureau of Justice Statistics.

———. 1987. "Survey of Inmates in State Correctional Facilities, 1979." ICPSR 7856. A BJS data set, unpublished.

———. 1990. *Federal Criminal Case Processing, 1980–1987.* NCJ-120069. Washington, D.C.: U.S. Department of Justice, Bureau of Justice Statistics.

———. 1995a. *Correctional Populations in the United States, 1992.* NCJ-146413. Washington, D.C.: U.S. Department of Justice, Bureau of Justice Statistics.

———. 1995b. *Correctional Populations in the United States, 1993.* NCJ-156241. Washington, D.C.: U.S. Department of Justice, Bureau of Justice Statistics.

———. 1996a. *Correctional Populations in the United States, 1994.* NCJ-160091. Washington, D.C.: U.S. Department of Justice, Bureau of Justice Statistics.

———. 1996b. *Federal Criminal Case Processing, 1982–1993.* NCJ-160088. Washington, D.C.: U.S. Department of Justice, Bureau of Justice Statistics.

———. 1997. *Correctional Populations in the United States, 1995.* NCJ-163916. Washington, D.C.: U.S. Department of Justice, Bureau of Justice Statistics.

———. 1998. *Compendium of Federal Justice Statistics, 1995.* NCJ-164259. Washington, D.C.: U.S. Department of Justice, Bureau of Justice Statistics.

———. 1999a. *Correctional Populations in the United States, 1996.* NCJ-170013. Washington, D.C.: U.S. Department of Justice, Bureau of Justice Statistics.

———. 1999b. *Compendium of Federal Justice Statistics, 1996.* NCJ-172849. Washington, D.C.: U.S. Department of Justice, Bureau of Justice Statistics.

———. 1999c. "Survey of Inmates in State and Federal Correctional Facilities, 1997." A BJS data set, unpublished.

———. Various years–a. "National Corrections Reporting Program." A BJS data collection program, unpublished.

———. Various years–b. "National Prisoner Statistics, 1980–1982." NPS-2. A BJS data collection program, unpublished.

Bureau of the Census. 1993. *U.S. Population Estimates by Age, Sex, Race, and Hispanic Origin: 1980 to 1991.* P25-1095. Washington, D.C.: U.S. Government Printing Office.

———. 1996*a. Post-enumeration Survey-Based Estimates Minus Census Enumeration with Modified Age, Race, and Sex: April 1, 1990.* Statistical Information Office, Population Division, unpublished.

———. 1996*b. U.S. Population Estimates by Age, Sex, Race, and Hispanic Origin: 1990–1995.* PPL-41 (1990–95) and PPL-91 (1996). Washington, D.C.: U.S. Government Printing Office.

Casper, Jonathan D., David Brereton, and David Neal. 1983. "The California Determinate Sentencing Law." *Criminal Law Bulletin* 19:405–33.

Cohen, Jacqueline, and Jose A. Canela-Cacho. 1994. "Incarceration and Violent Crime: 1965–1988." In *Understanding and Preventing Violence*, vol. 4, *Consequences and Control*, edited by Albert J. Reiss, Jr., and Jeffrey A. Roth. Washington, D.C.: National Academy Press.

Cook, Philip. 1980. "Research in Criminal Deterrence: Laying the Groundwork for the Second Decade." In *Crime and Justice: An Annual Review of Research*, vol. 2, edited by Norval Morris and Michael Tonry. Chicago: University of Chicago Press.

Cook, Philip J., and John H. Laub. 1998. "The Social Ecology of Youth Violence." In *Youth Violence*, edited by Michael Tonry and Mark H. Moore. Vol. 24 of *Crime and Justice: A Review of Research*, edited by Michael Tonry. Chicago: University of Chicago Press.

Federal Bureau of Investigation. Various years. *Crime in the United States: Uniform Crime Reports.* Washington, D.C.: U.S. Government Printing Office.

Federal Bureau of Prisons. Various years–*a. Fiscal Year Reports.* Washington, D.C.: U.S. Department of Justice, Federal Bureau of Prisons.

———. Various years–*b.* "Key Indicators Strategic Support System." A BOP data collection, unpublished.

Freeman, Richard B. 1994. "Crime and the Job Market." National Bureau of Economic Research Working Paper no. 4910. Cambridge, Mass.: National Bureau of Economic Research.

———. 1996. "Why Do So Many Young American Men Commit Crimes and What Might We Do about It?" National Bureau of Economic Research Working Paper no. 5451. Cambridge, Mass.: National Bureau of Economic Research.

Gilliard, Darrell K., and Allen J. Beck. 1998. *Prisoners in 1997.* NCJ-170014. Washington, D.C.: U.S. Department of Justice, Bureau of Justice Statistics.

Hagan, John, and Ronit Dinovitzer. In this volume. "Collateral Consequences of Imprisonment for Children, Communities, and Prisoners."

Kensey, Annie, and Pierre Tournier. 1997. *French Prison Population.* Paris: Ministry of Justice, Directorate for Prison Administration.

Langan, Patrick A. 1991. "America's Soaring Prison Population." *Science* 251:1568–73.

Lauritsen, Janet L., and Robert J. Sampson. 1998. "Minorities, Crime, and Criminal Justice." In *The Handbook of Crime and Punishment*, edited by Michael Tonry. New York: Oxford University Press.

Lynch, James P., and William J. Sabol. 1998. "Assessing the Longer-Run Consequences of Incarceration." Paper prepared for the twentieth annual research conference of the Association for Public Policy Analysis and Management, New York, October 1998.

Morris, Norval, and Michael Tonry. 1990. *Between Prison and Probation: Intermediate Punishments in a Rational Sentencing System.* New York: Oxford University Press.

Mumola, Christopher J., and Allen J. Beck. 1997. *Prisoners in 1996.* Bureau of Justice Statistics Bulletin no. NCJ-164619. Washington, D.C.: U.S. Department of Justice, Bureau of Justice Statistics.

Nagin, Daniel S. 1998. "Criminal Deterrence Research at the Outset of the Twenty-First Century." In *Crime and Justice: A Review of Research,* vol. 23, edited by Michael Tonry. Chicago: University of Chicago Press.

National Conference of State Legislatures. 1998. *State Budget Actions—1997.* Denver: National Conference of State Legislatures.

Proband, Stan C. 1995. "Corrections Leads State Appropriation Increases for 1996." *Overcrowded Times* 6(5):4.

———. 1997. "Corrections Leads State Budget Increases in FY 1997." *Overcrowded Times* 8(4):4.

Reuter, Peter, Robert MacCoun, and Patrick Murphy. 1990. "Money from Crime: A Study of Drug Dealing in Washington, D.C." Santa Monica, Calif.: RAND Corporation.

Sampson, Robert J., and Janet L. Lauritsen. 1997. "Racial and Ethnic Disparities in Crime and Criminal Justice in the United States." In *Ethnicity, Crime, and Immigration: Comparative and Cross-National Perspectives,* edited by Michael Tonry. Vol. 21 of *Crime and Justice: A Review of Research,* edited by Michael Tonry. Chicago: University of Chicago Press.

Stephan, James J. 1999. *Expenditures for State Institutional Corrections, 1996.* Bureau of Justice Statistics Bulletin no. NCJ-172211. Washington, D.C.: U.S. Department of Justice, Bureau of Justice Statistics.

Substance Abuse and Mental Health Services Administration. Office of Applied Studies. 1991. *Annual Emergency Department Data, Data from the Drug Abuse Warning Network (DAWN),* ser. 1, no. 11-A. Rockville, Md.: U.S. Department of Health and Human Services, National Institute on Drug Abuse.

———. 1994. *Annual Emergency Department Data, Data from the Drug Abuse Warning Network (DAWN),* ser. 1, no. 14-A. Rockville, Md.: U.S. Department of Health and Human Services, National Institute on Drug Abuse.

Tonry, Michael. 1995. *Malign Neglect: Race, Crime, and Punishment in America.* New York: Oxford University Press.

Theodore Caplow and Jonathan Simon

Understanding Prison Policy and Population Trends

ABSTRACT

American incarceration numbers increased fivefold between 1973 and 1997. Changes in penal policies and practices, not changes in crime rates, are the primary explanation, but there is disagreement about the causes of penal policy changes. Two prevalent explanations are that rising crime rates led to public demand for harsher policies and that politicians used crime policy to exacerbate public fears and win electoral favor. Both have merit but either is too simple. More likely the causes are some combination of crime policy's broad public appeal in an era of fractionated politics, unintended consequences of the war on drugs, and the increased reflexivity of the justice system that, with improved accountability and efficiency, becomes a major source of demand for its penal services.

By now the image of figure 1 is a familiar one. Since the mid-1970s the national prison population has grown rapidly. In 1997, there were more than 445 adults in prison for every 100,000 residents of the United States (Gilliard and Beck 1998, p. 1). If we count jail inmates the incarceration rate was more than 645 per 100,000 residents. While the rate of increase has slowed in the 1990s, the great surge in imprisonment that began in the mid-1970s has not peaked, let alone run its course. While the eye is drawn relentlessly to that dramatic curve, it is worth pausing to consider how this pattern looked twenty years ago.

Theodore Caplow is Commonwealth Professor of Sociology at the University of Virginia. Jonathan Simon is professor of law at the University of Miami.

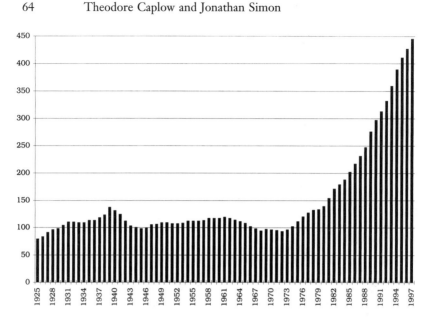

Fig. 1.—Rate of sentenced prisoners per 100,000 residents. Source: Maguire and Pastore (1997), table 6.21.

When Blumstein and Cohen (1973) wrote a famous article about American imprisonment rates in the early 1970s, they described a curve whose relatively gentle oscillations struck them as remarkable evidence that punishment was a self-regulating system. When you see what came next, you are reminded of the intrinsic limits of sociological prediction.

Still, this dramatic shift in a relatively stable long-term trend cries out for explanation and reflection. The most often heard explanations focus on the interaction of crime and politics. The view held by many political leaders and by some penal experts (DiIulio 1991; Bennett, DiIulio, and Waters 1996) points to the role of the crime waves that began in the 1960s and have kept American crime rates at elevated levels relative to earlier decades. From this perspective, the great surge of imprisonment is a response to the great surge of crime. It reflects both social outrage at crime and rational aspirations to control it. Imprisonment may not deter many criminals (DiIulio 1996), but it suppresses their criminal activity while they are confined and lessens the total social cost of crime (DiIulio and Piehl 1991).

An alternative view, virtually absent from political discourse but held by many penal experts and social scientists (Gordon 1990, 1994;

Scheingold 1991; Donziger 1996; Miller 1996; Beckett 1997; Tyler and Boeckman 1997; Currie 1998) sees the surge of imprisonment as the result of a "moral panic" (Cohen 1972; Hall, Critcher, and Jefferson 1978). According to this view, the growth of crime, real enough from the 1960s through the late 1970s, leveled off before the great surge of imprisonment began in the 1980s, and cannot explain the recent expansion of penal sanctions. Concern about the crime wave has become a symbolic vehicle to channel anxieties about social order spurred by the dismantling of racial and gender hierarchies (Beckett 1997), economic restructuring (Currie 1998), and large-scale immigration (Tyler and Boeckmann 1997). From this perspective the mobilization of laws and resources for imprisonment is political opportunism rather than rational public policy. This may be reinforced by the economic interests that have grown to serve the demand for punishment (Christie 1993; Irwin and Austin 1994; Miller 1996; Donziger 1996).

We can see these opposed positions in the ongoing debate about contemporary imprisonment policies as efforts to answer a classic sociological question, that is, What drives trends in punishment? (See Garland [1990] for an extraordinarily rich survey of the major schools of thought on this question.) The two positions bear at least a family resemblance to two important sociological approaches to punishment, one identified with the functionalist sociology of Durkheim (1933, 1983), and one related to the conflict and power perspectives in the work of Thompson (1975), Rusche and Kirchheimer (1939), and Foucault (1977).

Durkheim viewed punishment as a collective response to the violation of social norms (1933). He argued that the intensity of that response varied with the social organization and with the authoritarian character of governments (Durkheim 1983). The crime wave theory shares with Durkheim a focus on the reactions of ordinary citizens to crime, but often ignores the implications that social and political organization might have in the character of that response.[1]

Power and conflict theorists have analyzed the quantity and forms of punishment as related to the instrumental and ideological needs of governments and ruling classes. Like the power perspective, current moral panic theory emphasizes the strategies of political leaders, the

---

[1] There is some empirical evidence, for example, to suggest that support for the tough "Three Strikes" law in California was driven by concerns about the increasing cultural diversity of the state independent of views on the degree of crime threat and of social values (Tyler and Boeckmann 1997).

ideological consequences of economic restructuring, and the social control needs of postindustrial societies. Public support for punitive policies, from this perspective, may be a moral response, but the response is a political artifact.

In addition to the two opposing perspectives, a variety of other explanations have been invoked for the growth of incarceration. Some point to the growth of "the dangerous classes" (reviving the notorious nineteenth-century term for the poor) (Gordon 1994). Economic restructuring, especially the decline of well-paying but low-skilled industrial jobs, has left large numbers of uneducated young males with few job opportunities and expanded the pool of people most likely to be attracted to crime as an economic option (Currie 1998). At the same time the presence of such a pool exacerbates the tendency of the public to support coercive control strategies (Simon 1993; Gordon 1994).

Racism is another theme raised by students of the imprisonment surge (Tonry 1995; Donziger 1996; Miller 1996; Beckett 1997). It is undeniable that the incarcerated population is disproportionately composed of minorities (especially African Americans and Hispanics), and that the disproportion has increased during the period of rising imprisonment. Less clear is whether the growth of imprisonment is driven in any sense by racial animus. Tonry (1995) has suggested that penal policies leading to increasing imprisonment of minorities are a form of "malign neglect" reflecting the unintentional but foreseeable consequences of political choices. Miller (1996) suggests that pervasive racism in the law enforcement community has led to higher arrest rates for African Americans. Beckett (1997) argues that fears about crime and demands for punishment were mobilized by conservative politicians regrouping after the disaster of supporting segregation.

Another related theme is growing social distance (Black 1989, 1993). The incomes of the rich have grown much faster in the past twenty years than the incomes of poor (Greenberg and West 1998). Income inequality along with the physical separation of the poor, largely trapped in older central cities, and by the weakening or dismantling of government programs intended to reduce inequality.

In this essay, we review these arguments and provide an explanation of the growth of incarceration that ties many of these themes together. We admit in advance to a bias toward complexity in explanation. There is an illustrious tradition in sociology of interpreting changes in the prison as a reflection of overarching social trends. The rise of the prison in the nineteenth century has been interpreted as a function of

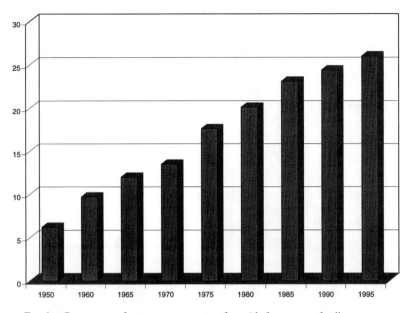

Fɪɢ. 2.—Percentage of persons over twenty-five with four years of college or more. Source: Statistical Abstracts of the United States (1996), table 242.

modernization, including the increasing economic value of human subjects (Rusche and Kirchheimer 1939); the reduced need for ritual to produce solidarity in a society characterized by an intensive division of labor (Durkheim 1933); and transformations in the technology of power through which political authority is constituted (Foucault 1977). But Garland (1990) has argued that it is a mistake to reduce our readings of punishment in society to singular social forces or processes. Punishment serves so many different functions, involves the life choices of so many different people, and bears on so many other social institutions that reductionist explanations are necessarily misleading.

Here it is useful to contemplate some other provocative time series. Figure 2 shows that the percentage of American adults who graduated from college quadrupled in the four decades between 1950 and 1990. How should we explain the great higher education boom of the past forty years? Relevant factors include the cold war, national economic planning to avoid another Depression, the need for a technically trained work force, state governments looking for ways to exercise their post-New Deal vigor, Baby Boomers pursuing the suddenly plausible ambitions that their Depression-era parents communicated to

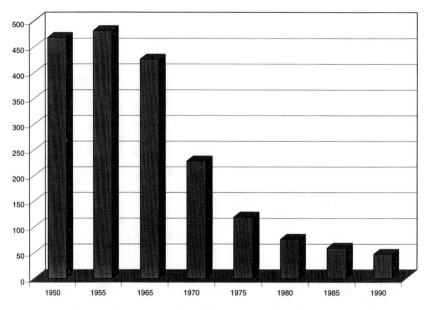

Fig. 3.—Inmates of state mental hospitals per 100,000 residents age fifteen and over. Source: Mechanic and Rochefort (1990).

them, and the work of government and financial institutions to generate the capital to build and fill hundreds of new two- and four-year colleges (Freeman 1976).

Consider Figure 3. Between 1950 and 1990, we experienced a "decarceration" boom with regard to our asylum system. The population of hospitalized mentally ill shrank from over four hundred per 100,000 adults in 1960,[2] to less than fifty. What would it take to provide a cogent explanation of this decarceration movement (see Scull 1977; Brown 1985; Torrey 1997)? Such an explanation would consider, among other factors, the changing fiscal pressures on the state, the changing social meaning of mental illness, new pharmacological options, the willingness of families to undertake greater responsibility for their mentally ill kin, and greater social tolerance for disturbed and disorderly people in public spaces.

When we examine institutional trends like the expansion of higher education we discover that the need for young people to obtain a college degree in order to improve their economic choices is no more sus-

[2] Here the rate is calculated on the denominator of adult residents rather than all residents.

ceptible to objective determination than the effects of imprisonment on crime. It is difficult to imagine that a massive state and private partnership to expand higher education could have happened without very tangible signals that college graduates would improve their lot (repeatedly confirmed by studies of average earnings of those with and without college). It is also difficult to believe that a near quadrupling of the prison population in the 1980s and 1990s could have been sustained by the states and the federal government without tangible experiences of and continuing public exposure to news about violent crime. In neither case does the reality of education or crime as public issues produce a self-realizing social initiative of the scale discussed here. While it is tempting to see in the growth of the incarceration rate, the decline of the asylum population, and the expansion of higher education a reflection of society's collective intentions, this ignores the frequency of unintended consequences (Caplow 1991). For college classrooms, missiles, asylums, or prisons to be produced, great numbers of people need to get involved for reasons independent of the general social sentiments that drive these trends.[3]

As much as possible, an interpretation of the incarceration rise should explain its rapidity, extent, and endurance. This requires us to consider what is different about America since 1980. Many of the usual suspects, including crime, unemployment, and poverty do not tightly track the path of incarceration rates (Zimring and Hawkins 1991).[4] Shifts in political ideology are also less obviously helpful than one might expect. The public desire to "get tough" with criminals is widely acknowledged, but whether one treats this as a rational response to crime, or the result of political and media manipulation, the measured desire to get tough has remained relatively constant over a period of huge growth in incarceration. The time series of responses to the question whether courts are too lenient has remained remarkably stable since 1972 (Rossi and Berk 1997, p. 7).

Shifts in basic political orientation (where Americans place themselves on a liberal/conservative spectrum) have also changed less than might be assumed (King 1997). Slightly fewer people define them-

[3] One need not assume that there is an inevitable trade-off between these but the growth of incarceration did take place during a time when the confinement of the mentally ill had been dramatically reduced and the growth of the college-bound population was flattening.

[4] One important trend that has tracked incarceration rates over the past twenty-five years is growing wealth inequality (Greenberg and West 1998). We think this plays a role in the massive increase in incarceration, but through shifts in political culture.

selves as very liberal and slightly more define themselves as very conservative on a scale of political ideology than was true in the 1960s. Somewhat more than half of survey respondents identify themselves as moderately conservative and somewhat fewer than half view themselves as moderately liberal, just as they did in the 1960s.

Our interpretation of the growth of the U.S. prison population focuses on change in three dimensions: political culture, public policy, and institutional organization.

Crime Control as a Privileged Mode of Governing. Congress has adopted crime bills in virtually every election cycle in the 1980s and 1990s (Chernoff, Kelly, and Kroger 1996). It is widely accepted that political candidates for statewide office must establish themselves as favoring more severe punishments to stand a chance of election. Between elections, crime control has also become a more salient feature of governing, with legislative bodies at all levels devoting large portions of their time and budgets to crime control measures.

We see this as a function, primarily, of two developments. First, governance measures intended to improve welfare have lost credibility. For much of the twentieth century, programs to invest capital and expertise in the education, health, and financial stability of the population enjoyed strong public support. The decline of social welfare governance is a massive subject in its own right (Weir, Orloff, and Skocpol 1988; Baldwin 1990; Burchell, Gordon, and Miller 1991; Pierson 1994; Rose 1996; Lo and Schwartz 1998). It is clear that the majority of Americans now view some of these efforts by government as more expensive than expected and less effective than hoped. Programs with an extremely broad base of beneficiaries, such as Social Security and Medicare, command more support (if not exactly confidence), but even their broad public endorsement does not extend to much expansion of benefits.

Whatever its sources, the loss of confidence in social welfare programs has removed an important set of responses that politicians (both liberals like Lyndon Johnson and conservatives like Richard Nixon) could once use to confront social problems. Moreover, the delegitimation of welfare policies has taken a heavy toll on the legitimacy of the federal government, because it was the major architect of welfare policies. For much of the twentieth century, the politics of punishment were largely subordinated to the politics of welfare. Indeed, during the era of the rehabilitative ideal (1940s–1970s) imprisonment was rationalized as a form of state benefit. The delegitimation of welfare has allowed the politics of punishment to come into its own.

A second development that seems to have raised the salience of crime control is a shift in the underlying structure of American politics—away from traditional class and ethnicity conflicts toward conflicts based on values, identity, and risk. The old politics lent itself to bargaining over resources but the new "postmaterialist" politics (Inglehart 1977, 1990) and the "new social movements" (Giddens 1991; Beck 1992) operate in terms resistant to bargaining. Conflict about abortion, gay and lesbian rights, or the death penalty are not easily compromised. Politicians seeking to build viable majorities inevitably look to the few issues that can bring people together in the new political landscape. And crime control has a presumptive validity that makes it a preferred choice. For example, in few states is there any prospect of openly negotiating a compromise on affirmative action or set-asides in public contracting, but renewed prosecutions of decades-old civil rights murders produce symbolic benefits and arouse little opposition. Not surprisingly, politicians from both parties have found a strong profile on crime issues to be indispensable.

The Unintended Consequences of the War on Drugs.   The political attractiveness of crime control is not capable of accounting for the scope and unprecedented scale of the rise in incarceration. There have been other times when crime control has emerged as a more general model for governing including the 1920s and 1930s with prohibition and gang crime, and then again in the late 1950s with the first wave of heavy narcotics law enforcement. But in neither case was there more than a moderate rise in the incarceration rate. It is possible that our current turn toward crime control governance would have produced a similar moderate rise in the incarceration rates had it not been for the rapid growth of a drug-crime economy in the 1980s.

"Tough on crime" policies produce prison population increases only to the degree that offenders are available to be imprisoned (Zimring and Hawkins 1991). The growth in nondrug crime has simply not been sufficient to sustain the rapid growth of imprisonment. By the 1970s there were already an active culture of drug use and networks of drug importation and sales in the United States, but their economic importance increased in the 1980s due to new products and distribution strategies, especially for "crack" cocaine (Chitwood, Rivers, and Inciardi 1996). This transformation in the marketing of illegal drugs coincided with political decisions to intensify the punishments for drug crimes.[5] The result was an enlargement of the population available for criminal justice processing. On any given day in any given large metropolitan area, the police can arrest as many drug offenders as they have time and resources to pursue. That is simply not true of property or violent crime. Thus while more prison time for violent crime accounts for much of the growth of incarceration, a significant portion (how much is difficult to estimate) is associated with a vector of supply with few apparent constraints. This allows growth to continue, even if at a slower pace, during cycles when for whatever reason violent crime declines (as it has lately).

Reflexivity of the Penal System. The growth of incarceration is not only dependent on positive forces, but on the weakening of those forces that act as a brake on imprisonment.[6] These include limitations on the operation of courts, community sympathy for some lawbreakers, and the ideologies of the organizations that process offenders. Foremost among these historically was the limited capacity of the justice system to absorb arrestees and keep them on track to incarceration, and the disappearance of cases along the way from arrest to imprisonment. Also important was the capacity of the correctional system to control its own population by means of parole release and revocation (Messinger et al. 1985).

Changes in the criminal justice system, beginning in the 1960s, have disabled these brakes on the growth of imprisonment, and enhanced the tendency for the system to drive its own growth, a form of institutional "reflexivity."[7] The reform of bail, indigent defense, and institutional due process, carried out by states in the 1960s and 1970s under pressure from the Supreme Court, have produced state court systems that are capable of keeping more people on line to incarceration. This means that political pressures to get tough are less likely to be ab-

[5] To some extent, to be sure, the tough new laws have been a response to the growth of drug markets, but they also reflect independent political decisions to focus on drug crimes that began even before the death of college basketball star Len Bias, which was attributed to crack cocaine, led to a media obsession with the drug over the next decade.

[6] We would like to thank David Garland for raising this issue—the brakes on incarceration—during a presentation of a draft of this chapter to the Fortunoff Colloquium at New York University Law School in February 1998.

[7] The term has been used by sociologists (Giddens 1991; Beck 1992) to describe a more general trend in postindustrial societies whereby the social institutions become increasingly focused on managing their own negative effects (industrialization creates pollution, welfare creates dependency, medical treatments produce treatment-resistant diseases, and so on).

sorbed and neutralized by bottlenecks and escape valves along the way. For those actually convicted and sentenced to prisons, a powerful feedback loop has developed between prison and correctional supervision in the community. The correctional population on supervised release has grown even faster than the prison population, but rather than operating as alternatives to prison, parole and probation increasingly return people to prison.

Beyond Crime Waves and Moral Panics.   In what follows we explore these themes in greater detail. In Section I we examine the results of the incarceration boom from a sociological perspective. In Section II we look at incarceration as a solution, not to the problem of crime per se, but to the problems of government (i.e., how to govern, what to govern, to what ends). Here we examine more closely both of the dominant explanations for the incarceration boom. Sections III and IV examine the contribution of the developments identified above in driving this trend. Section V offers concluding remarks.

I. The Results of the Imprisonment Surge

Blumstein and Beck, in this volume, have offered an analysis of the links between growth in the prison population and changes in policy at various points in the criminal justice system. In particular, they point to the increased chances of arrest for drug crimes and the increased likelihood for imprisonment if convicted of any crime. Rather than repeat their analysis this section looks briefly at the resulting accumulation of population. Who is in prison does not necessarily explain why they are there (at least in such numbers) but it may point to the social processes that led to the policies and practices that Blumstein and Beck describe.

At the end of 1997 there were 1.25 million prisoners under the jurisdiction of state and federal prison authorities, a rate of 445 prisoners for every 100,000 residents of the United States (Gilliard and Beck 1998, p. 1). Together with inmates held in jails, more than 1.7 million people were incarcerated at the end of 1997 for an incarceration rate of 645 prisoners for every 100,000 residents (p. 2) and more than 800 per 100,000 adults. At the end of 1997, more than five million persons were in the custody of the correctional system including parole, probation, and other community supervision sanctions—a little under 3 percent of the total resident population (Bureau of Justice Statistics 1998, p. 5). These figures are unprecedented in American history. The only other industrialized country with greater rates is Russia (690 per

100,000 residents) (Currie 1998, p. 15). Other countries with high incarceration rates but still well below the United States include Estonia
(270), Romania (200), Singapore (229), and South Africa (368) (Currie
1998, p. 15). Among traditional democratic countries in Europe, and
Japan, the highest rates are around 120, and the average is much lower
(Currie 1998, p. 15; see also Young and Brown [1993], showing European rates at the end of the 1980s; Kuhn [1997], showing European
rates for the early 1990s; and Stern [1998], eyewitness descriptions of
foreign prisons).

While the rate of growth has slowed some in the 1990s (Gilliard and
Beck 1998, table 2), there is no reason to expect a reversal of direction
anytime soon. Indeed, while many states stiffened their criminal penalties during the 1980s, actual time served did not rise dramatically because of various offsetting administrative measures and court orders
capping population. In the 1990s, these hidden brakes on prison population have been largely dismantled. Federal legislation has encouraged
states to adopt "truth in sentencing" laws, which typically require offenders to serve at least 85 percent of their nominal sentences.[8] Other
federal legislation attacks court ordered caps by making it harder for
federal court consent decrees to be enforced.[9] Growth in time served
is likely to sustain growth in overall prison population even if prison
admission rates should decline.

Overcrowding has become an endemic feature. As of 1997, the federal system was operating at 119 percent of capacity while the average
of state systems was at 115 percent (Gilliard and Beck 1998, p. 1).
Three states—California, Pennsylvania, and Virginia—were operating
in excess of 150 percent of capacity (Gilliard and Beck 1998, table 9).[10]
California, with the nation's largest prison population, was assessed at
206 percent of its highest measure of capacity (Gilliard and Beck 1998,
table 9). The situation seemed to be improving as of 1995, when the
last federal census of prisons was conducted, as a result of heavy investments by the states in prison construction since 1985. More than half
of all the prisons in the United States have been built within the past
twenty years (Stephan 1997, p. 6).

[8] Violent Crime Control and Law Enforcement Act of 1994, Pub. L. no. 103–322.
[9] Prison Litigation Reform Act of 1995 (PLRA), Title VIII of the Omnibus Consoli-
dated Rescissions and Appropriations Act of 1996, Pub. L. no. 104–34.
[10] Capacity is an imprecise notion. The Bureau of Justice Statistics asks states for several different measures of capacity and then compares their current population. The
numbers above are based on the highest possible measure of capacity. If a lower one is
used, twice as many states are at 150 percent or above.

With so many aspects of state budgets mandated by federal or state formulas, more money for prisons must come from borrowing, taxing, or raiding other discretionary expenditures. In nearly every state of the Union, the rising burden of prison expenditures has been met in part by cutting expenditures for higher education. From 1987 to 1995, state governments expenditures on prisons increased by 30 percent while spending on higher education fell by 18 percent (Justice Policy Institute 1997). In California, for example, the percentages of the state budget devoted to corrections and higher education were 4 and 14 percent, respectively, in 1970 and 8.5 and 12.5 percent, respectively, in 1998 (Schrag 1998, p. 95).[11] While no new campus of the University of California system has been built since the 1960s, some twenty prisons have been built since 1984 (Schrag 1998, p. 97).

The expansion of the prison population by about 300 percent, or over 800,000 souls, between 1980 and 1997 involved every one of the fifty states as well as the federal government and the District of Columbia, but with a great deal of variation. Texas held over 700 prisoners per 100,000 residents in 1997, while North Dakota held only 112 (Gilliard and Beck 1998, p. 5). California had a rate of 475 compared with 232 in Oregon. Between 1987 and 1997, the state-by-state increases in the prison population varied from a low of 25 percent in Maine to a high of 180 percent in Colorado (Gilliard and Beck 1998, p. 4).

As Zimring and Hawkins (1991) noted, there is a significant and relatively stable regional pattern to incarceration rates. The South and the West have experienced the highest growth in imprisonment, followed by the Midwest and the Northeast. In 1995, the ten highest rates in the nation were all in southern or western states, while the lowest were in midwestern and northeastern states (Morgan, Morgan, and Quitno 1996, p. 102). But the variation within regions was nearly as great: in the West, Washington and Oregon had relatively low rates of 210 and 199 prisoners per 100,000 while California and Arizona had rates of 402 and 473, respectively.[12] In the midwest, Michigan's rate of 434 contrasted with Minnesota's rate of 103 (Morgan, Morgan, and Quitno 1996, p. 102).

[11] In California, the two are on a particularly narrow collision course because state constitutional amendments have capped taxing and spending, and mandated a certain level of expenditures on K-12 public education (Schrag 1998, p. 96).

[12] This calculation excludes federal prisoners altogether, whether from the state, or confined in a federal prison there.

Who are these people? In 1996, just under half were violent offenders, 23 percent were property offenders, 23 percent were drug offenders, and another 7 percent were so-called public order offenders (Gilliard and Beck 1998, p. 11).[13] Nonviolent offenders make up a much bigger percentage of prison admissions. Of felons sent to prison by state courts in 1994, only 26 percent had been convicted of violent offenses (Langan and Brown 1997, p. 3). Property and drug offenders made up 61 percent of the prison bound, and more than 10 percent were nonviolent offenders convicted of crimes such as receiving stolen property and vandalism (Langan and Brown 1997, p. 3). Since violent offenders generally receive longer sentences than nonviolent offenders do, they constitute a larger proportion of a prison's resident population at any given moment than of its intake population.

Prisoners are also more likely than not to be repeat players to the criminal justice system. Only 38 percent of state prison inmates in the 1991 survey were experiencing prison for the first time, only 19 percent were serving their first criminal sentence of any kind (Beck et al. 1993, p. 11). This reflects sentencing procedures that punish previous convictions by increasing the likelihood and length of imprisonment. First offenders manage to escape incarceration some of the time, even for serious offenses. Nonconfinement sentences went to 3 percent of murderers, 13 percent of robbers, 25 percent of burglars, and 29 percent of drug traffickers convicted in state courts in 1994; most were first offenders. At the other end of the scale, some repeat offenders received life sentences for simple assault, burglary, or drug possession.

As always before, the occupants of our prisons today are overwhelmingly male. Although the female prison population has been growing faster than the total prison population for some years, it still made up only 6.4 percent of the total in 1997 (Gilliard and Beck 1998, p. 3). The proportion of women in local jails is considerably higher but still came to only 12 percent in 1996. Women commit many fewer offenses, are less likely to be charged when they do, and receive shorter sentences if convicted.

It is not surprising that most prisoners are recruited from the ranks of the poor, the uneducated, and the unaffiliated, as is normal every-

---

[13] This relies on state counts. A 1991 survey of state prison inmates calculated that only 45 percent were serving sentences for violent offenses (Beck et al. 1993). It is possible that the percentage of violent offenders is going up as longer sentences make themselves felt on the mix in prison.

where and always. In the most recent Bureau of Justice Statistics survey of state prison inmates, the median preincarceration income of prisoners during their last full year of freedom was barely a third of the national median income for year-round full-time workers (Beck et al. 1993). Only 34 percent of prisoners said they had completed high school (Beck et al. 1993, p. 3) compared to approximately 79 percent of the national population. Fewer than one in five were married (Beck et al. 1993, p. 3), less than half the rate for the general population of comparable age.[14] Thirty-seven percent had an immediate family member who had served time, including 7 percent who had a parent and 31 percent who had a brother who had served time (Beck et al. 1993, p. 9). Despite massive growth in prison admissions, these factors have not changed significantly since earlier surveys. The prison seems to be absorbing more of its traditional constituency of lower-class males than before, but it is not pursuing new targets.

African-American overrepresentation is a long-term feature of the U.S. prison system, but it seems to have been exacerbated by the rapid growth of the 1980s and 1990s (Tonry 1995, chap. 2). In 1960, 37 percent of prison inmates were African American. At the end of 1995, 48 percent of U.S. prisoners were African American (Bureau of Justice Statistics 1997a, p. 91).[15] When the Bureau of Justice Statistics estimated lifetime incarceration risks based on 1991 rates of incarceration, they found that 29 percent of African-American males, 16 percent of Hispanic males, and 4 percent of white males would be expected to serve time in prison within their lifetime (Bonczar and Beck 1997, p. 1). It has been estimated that over 30 percent of African-American males between the ages of nineteen and twenty-nine were in some sector of criminal justice custody as of 1994 (Mauer 1997). In inner cities with heavy poverty zones, such as Washington, D.C., and Baltimore, more than 50 percent of young African-American men were in the criminal justice system (Miller 1997a, 1997b). African-American women were also comparably disproportionately represented in prison, although on a much lower absolute level.

---

[14] They were otherwise disadvantaged as well. More than half had grown up without fathers (as many of their children will also). More than a third had an immediate family member who had served time. More than a quarter had parents or guardians who drank heavily.

[15] Hispanics, a category that can include African Americans and whites, made up 15 percent of the prison population in 1995 (Bureau of Justice Statistics 1997a, p. 94).

II. Governing through Crime

Crime control has acquired a new importance among the strategies available to government for confronting the complex array of domestic (and foreign) problems facing the United States. Political leaders at all levels of government in the 1990s recognize that their public commitment to punitive policies against crime is vital to election. To talk about crime control as governance in this respect does not imply that public support for crime control is irrational or the product of artful manipulation. For any kind of risk to become a major source of public concern it helps greatly for it to have some objective reality, either in incidence or severity, that captures the imagination of the public. But this objective foundation can never fully account for an end product like imprisonment. Knowing that chemical contamination of former factory sites is a real problem does not tell us whether public policies committing us to spend billions of dollars to restore the site to a normal condition are rational. Likewise, whether the current level of imprisonment in the United States is or is not optimal is a difficult question for experts to answer.

Crime control has been an enduring source of popular legitimacy for state and local governments in the United States. In the twentieth century, crime control has also emerged as a source of legitimacy for the federal government as well, with gangsters and prohibition during the 1920s (Ruth 1996), street crime and terrorism in the 1970s, and drugs in the 1980s and 1990s (Wright 1995). Historically, American political culture appears to favor crime control as a mode of governing because of the strength of individual responsibility as a dominant virtue (Scheingold 1991). American crime policy has also been more open to pressure from public opinion than is the case in other liberal democracies. Savelsberg (1994) compared American and German policy discussions of crime and found that far more attention is given to popular views in America than in Germany. German crime policy tends to be set by bargaining within a relatively insulated set of governmental bureaucracies with little direct accountability to the electorate. In the United States, at least in recent years, crime policy has been influenced by elected legislators and executives.

But if Americans are pulling politicians toward more and more punitive policies, the functionaries of the state may have their own reasons to favor crime control as a mode of governance. Looking broadly at advanced liberal societies including the United States, Garland (1996) suggests that the growth of punishment at the end of the century reflects the relative weakness of the state. The contemporary state finds itself rather routinely confronted with failure, and its most refined twentieth-century techniques of government—welfare, redistribution, and regulation—no longer seem to work well. The effect of such state interventions on the well being of national economies is increasingly viewed as unfavorable. Belief in the self-regulatory capacity of markets, restored to a kind of orthodoxy in Western societies that have not experienced a market collapse in more than half a century, has generated pressure to trim government growth and privatize public services. Globalization of the economy has limited the capacity of national governments to deploy effective countercyclical controls. Finally surges in crime, experienced not just in the United States, but in most of the advanced industrial societies, have diminished the prestige of governments in their most traditional function of maintaining civil order. In the face of losses in its perceived competence, purposes, and boundaries, the state finds the intensification of crime control attractive. Punishment invokes a primordial understanding of state power that remains highly credible. Imprisonment, especially when promoted as incapacitation, is something government knows it can accomplish.

These arguments shed important light on the American experience with the growth of imprisonment over the last quarter century, but none seems complete. The individualistic and populist aspects of American culture existed for a long time. If punishment compensates for a weaker overall state, it is hard to see why the United States would be so much more prone to punish than are other Western democracies. The forces which are undermining the traditional position of the national state are if anything less severe for the United States, with its huge economy and singular military position.

Nevertheless, it is noteworthy that the past twenty-five years have seen an unprecedented expansion of the role of the federal government with very mixed results. And for largely unrelated reasons, American politics since the 1960s have moved away from traditional class and regional conflicts, toward conflicts about "values." The former divisions have not disappeared, but have been submerged under new issues. Political campaigns are now won by finding themes that attract and link minorities with strong value-based identities. Crime control has come to be a rare source of agreement in a factionalized public.

A. Welfare and Government's Crisis of Confidence

In 1960, huge areas of collective action were outside the federal orbit—health care, education, street crime, civil litigation, infant care, occupational safety, personnel procedures, the regulation of sexual relationships, child care, environmental protection, music and art, historic preservation, the content of advertising, the design of consumer products, the menus of school lunches, the smoking habits of the population, the labeling of used cars, the grading practices of colleges. Today all of them are subject to federal oversight. Whatever the merits of these myriad interventions they have worked a constitutional transformation in American politics. A vast range of issues now implicate federal authority.

The expanded terrain of the federal government has coincided with a catastrophic decline in the public's confidence in the capacities of government. It is startling to consider just how much this has changed since the mid-1960s. In response to the survey question, "How much of the time do you trust the government in Washington to do the right thing," 76 percent of a national sample in 1964 answered "just about always" or "most of the time." When the same question was put to a similar sample in 1995, only 25 percent gave that answer (Pearlstein 1996). Indeed, a 1996 survey showed solid majorities of respondents agreeing with a whole gamut of disgruntled statements: (1) the federal government controls too much of our daily lives (62 percent); (2) our system of government is good but the people running it are incompetent (66 percent); (3) most elected officials don't care what people like me think (69 percent); (4) our leaders are more concerned with managing their images than with solving the nation's problems (79 percent); (5) most politicians are more interested in winning elections than in doing what is right (80 percent); (6) our government is pretty much run by a few big interests looking out for themselves (81 percent); and (7) people in government waste a lot of the money we pay in taxes (91 percent).

While some of the government's efforts at social amelioration, for example, Social Security, are seen as successful and enjoy wide support, many others are perceived as failures (Murray 1984; Wattenberg 1995).[16] In a relatively short span of time, large portions of the public became convinced that however attractive government programs

---

[16] This view of welfare has been forcefully contested by scholars but there is little doubt that it has largely prevailed in public opinion.

might sound, in practice they would be incompetently implemented and reward the wrong people for doing the wrong things. This includes not only government aid to the poor (which has received the most critical scrutiny) but also efforts to improve education, promote job training, provide affordable housing, and assure retirement benefits. This was apparent in the 1993 debate on health care reform where despite high levels of public support for general health coverage, the involvement of the federal government in such a program was the source of vulnerability that opponents were able most effectively to exploit. Thus for politicians, especially federal politicians, seeking to fill the rather large role in public life that the federal government has staked out for itself in the late twentieth century, there is a limited range of governmental strategies available. State governments enjoy somewhat higher esteem, but they too are limited in their ability to mount new social programs in the face of a public that regards such efforts as likely to be wasteful and counterproductive (Dionne 1991).

The impact of this shift in sentiment has been felt broadly across the spectrum of policy formation. The discrediting of welfare initiatives has closed off a broad range of options for addressing the threats to social order that every modern government confronts. Crime and punishment have become important vehicles for doing the work of politics precisely because the major alternatives have been moved off the table.

B. Crime and the New Politics

We often talk as if the center dominated U.S. politics, but today's center is little more than a floating set of preferences on a vast range of issues charted by polls and pundits. Instead, our politics has moved farther away from the center once defined by key issues of economic and national security and toward a borderland of values and identity based politics (Wattenberg 1995). Today, public discourse is dominated by culture wars, including controversies over abortion, affirmative action, mass immigration, school prayer, capital punishment, animal rights, and assisted suicide (Wattenberg 1995). These issues have long been part of American politics, but rarely have they enjoyed as much political influence as now. They have not abolished traditional American divisions about wealth and national security, but displaced them in public discourse.

The United States is hardly unique in this. Sociologists and political scientists studying postindustrial societies have been pointing to profound changes in the sources of political mobilization and identity since the 1970s (Inglehart 1977, 1990; Giddens 1991; Beck 1992). In the early 1970s, the central issues of political concern in all these countries remained the classic ones of economic and military security. Since then, largely through a process of generational change, increasingly large portions of European and American publics bring to politics what has been described as "postmaterialist" values, including concerns with the environment, public morality, and quality of life (Inglehart 1990). These changes have altered the traditional right-to-left political spectrum that defined politics in most industrial democracies during most of the twentieth century. In place of broad divisions based on issues of wealth and national security, publics are divided by innumerable value conflicts. Moreover, while traditional publics were dominated by elites who could effectively represent them in bargaining at the center, social movements have become increasingly skilled in political participation from the grassroots. Thus minority factions are less likely to be submerged in the grand compromises of politics, and more likely to make themselves directly visible to political leaders, what Inglehart (1990, p. 335) describes as a shift from "elite directed" to "elite directing" politics. These new social movements have not replaced the traditional parties that have anchored politics in most Western democracies, but have rendered their underlying support increasingly unreliable.

It is clear that these well-documented transformations in political identity and participation pose tremendous challenges to the forging of the majority coalitions necessary to legislate and govern. The value conflicts that most potently mobilize publics today do not lend themselves to the logrolling and bargaining that were characteristic of traditional American politics. Rather than seeking a bigger piece of the pie for people like themselves, members of the new social movements invite people to join the fight of good against evil. To antiabortion activists, abortion is cold-blooded murder; to their adversaries, the right to abortion secures women's ownership of their own bodies. To advocates of strict gun control, the private possession of firearms is a wicked aberration; to their adversaries, it is the keystone of liberty. The well-organized pressure groups that represent such interests have few lateral mechanisms of coordination outside of the federal courts and Congress. Nor do they have many incentives to cooperate in making government more effective. This makes coalition building and the effective implementation of policies more and more difficult.

The relationship of the new politics to crime is not obvious. Most students of this shift have focused on postmaterialist values of the left, for example, ecology (Douglas and Wildavsky 1982), feminism, and peace movements (Beck 1992). Crime control is often presumed to be a traditional conservative political value along with economic and military security (Inglehart 1990). No doubt many people who value crime control efforts by government do so for the promise of security for their lives and property. But it is clear that crime as a political issue is increasingly linked to values rather than to materialist choices. Unlike most values issues of the left or right, crime control seems to cut across the political spectrum. That is why those most supportive of punitive policies are not necessarily those who face the greatest crime risks. That is also why crime has become a key issue on both the left and the right. That is why election campaigns continue to focus on crime and punishment issues even when opposing candidates agree in their support of punitive anticrime measures.[17] Faced with voters who split on so many issues and who are profoundly skeptical about the ability of government to improve their lives through welfare-oriented interventions, the mode of governing that commands the broadest support—punitiveness toward criminal offenders—is understandably precious.

C. Crime Control as a Value

In recent years, a number of social movements have grown up around crime, including Mothers against Drunk Driving, the feminist movements against rape and domestic violence, and popular mobilizations around punitive policies like "Three Strikes and You're Out." But if crime is the explicit subject of some movements, it is well suited to appeal to groups primarily mobilized along other axes. Historically, conservative politicians were initially responsible for promoting crime as a political issue (Chernoff et al. 1996; Beckett 1997). For conservatives, crime as a values issue has proved a potent tonic. It provided a compelling representation of the cost of liberal "permissiveness." It also provided a critical defense against the potentially devastating effects of having been on the wrong side of the civil rights issue during

---

[17] During the 1998 gubernatorial campaign in California, the death penalty (along with abortion) emerged as key issues. There was a difference on abortion between the two contenders, but both candidates strongly supported the death penalty. It remained a focus of competition however. Campaign professionals defend the relevance of this kind of campaign as legitimate. In the words of one Republican expert: "We in society have sort of chosen the death penalty as a symbol of crime and abortion as a social issue. From that, the discussion gets into what each of them are about. What the voter is really looking for is what kind of a person is the candidate—a look into the soul of the candidate" (Decker 1998).

the 1960s when a clear moral consensus formed against race discrimination. But the origin of something is often a misleading indicator of its significance. Crime control has clearly emerged as an effective mobilizing issue for liberals.

This is true for centrist Democrats, such as Bill Clinton, who have been able to take the crime issue away from the right in some recent elections (Wattenberg 1995; Chernoff et al. 1996). But it is also true for groups farther to the left, including feminists, gays and lesbians, and empowerment movements of racial and ethnic minorities. These are groups whose members have experienced victimization of a sort that is not only metaphorically related to crime. Justice is an ambiguous term, and while historically many on the left have viewed it in welfare terms, punitive justice provides an alternative. Not surprisingly, hate crimes and domestic violence have become priority issues for these constituencies (Jacobs and Potter 1998).

If the postmaterialist politics tends toward issues of good and evil, crime is a natural metaphor for evil. In their insightful analysis of the antinuclear power wing of the environmental movement, Mary Douglas and Aaron Wildavsky (1982) argued the ecology movement of the 1970s reflected a popular concern with moral pollution for which environmental contamination was a perfect metaphor. Like witchcraft in the seventeenth century and communist subversion in the twentieth century, environmental pollution was presented as invisible, unavoidable, and irreversible (Douglas and Wildavsky 1982).

More than a decade and half later, the environmental movement remains an important force in the new political landscape, although not the dominant one that Douglas and Wildavsky thought it might become.[18] Instead the postmaterialist value that has been most successful in dominating political discourse has been crime control. In ways that closely track Douglas and Wildavsky's analysis, crime in contemporary public discourse is the "pollution" issue of the 1980s and 1990s. Crime is portrayed as stealthy. It operates through deception or surprise. It is envisioned as unavoidable. Criminologists routinely note that many violent crime victims know their assailants, and could choose to avoid them, but media attention is attracted by incidents of random violence. Likewise "stranger rape" dominates the popular image of rape, even though studies indicate that rape commonly occurs among family and

---

[18] Recent elections have shown that while environmentalism may not dominate the political agenda of Americans, a majority of American voters are turned off by candidates who appear expressly antienvironmental.

friends (Estrich 1987). Crime is also portrayed as irreversible in its effects. The damage to the victim of violent crime is, by general consent, very difficult or impossible to overcome fully. Although the damage of most property offenses can be reversed by insurance, the public is much more concerned with violent crime precisely because it poses risks of permanent harm. Not surprisingly most political mobilization against crime targets violent crime, even if the same policies affect property offenders (Miller 1996).

D. Drugs and Kids: Moral Panics and Crime Control Values

"Moral panics" occur when policies are made in response to particular crimes that have captured the public imagination (Cohen 1972; Hall, Critcher, and Jefferson 1978). Sexually tinged homicides have long been triggers for such panics (Jenkins 1998, p. 10).[19] The term implies a "wave of irrational public fear" (Jenkins 1998, p. 6), or a response "out of all proportion to the actual threat offered" (Hall, Critcher, and Jefferson 1978, p. 16). But as we suggested above, the boundaries of rationality are never easy to draw in responding to serious social problems. One need not assume that the American response to crime has been wholly irrational to believe particular crimes signal a threat to the fundamental moral order of society. Two types of criminality that currently provoke moral panic are drug trafficking and child abuse. Since the 1970s, both topics have caused high levels of public concern with notable peaks (on drugs, see Gordon 1994; Beckett 1997; on child abuse, see Jenkins 1998).

The focus of drug concern in America is on marijuana, heroin, cocaine, and an assortment of stimulants and hallucinogens with varied pharmacological effects. We say more below about the effect of the war on drugs on the growth of the prison population (as do Blumstein and Beck, in this volume). Here we want to point to features of the moral panic about drugs that help explain the priority of crime control as governance. Drugs as a form of criminality exemplify the features that make crime such a compelling source of "pollution" in contemporary society, that is, invisibility, unavoidability, and irreversibility. Drugs operate invisibly. Parents and employers have been encouraged

---

[19] Evans (1996, p. 592) provides a fascinating picture of a moral panic over sex murders in Weimar Germany that helped feed fascist sentiments. Examples are multiple and across time. Only recently the government of Belgium was severely challenged by accusations of bungling a case in which a young girl was kidnapped for sexual purposes and killed.

to fear that their children and employees may be using drugs with dire consequences that only emerge when a crime or accident takes place. (This has in turn led to a market for drug testing.) Drug use may begin by choice, but a major part of the lore of drugs is that addiction follows and makes continued use involuntary and unavoidable. Drugs are also portrayed as irreversible. In much drug education and public service advertising, drugs are portrayed as so irresistibly attractive that a single taste usually leads to lifelong addiction and that users destroy their health and their minds.[20] This picture may be overdrawn but it drives public policy.

Because much of the contemporary moral panic about drugs has been about children (crack babies, addicted students), it is linked to another moral panic that has gathered force in the same years concerning the abuse, and especially the sexual abuse, of children. Beginning in the 1980s a growing sensitivity to persistent child abuse within families has converged with a host of related problems, including missing children, sexually abused children, and especially horrific cases in which children are taken, sexually abused, and killed (Best 1990; Forst and Blomquist 1991; Nathan and Snedeker 1995; Costin, Krager, and Stoesz 1996; Jenkins 1998). While some elements are also found in other societies, the panic about children has been almost exclusively American. Even more than drugs, the physical and sexual abuse of children is thought to lead to irreversible damage. Frightening cases greet us in the newspaper often enough to suggest that such events are becoming more frequent, although statistics fail to confirm the supposed trend. Child deaths classified as homicides (an admittedly imperfect measure) have remained stable at a very low level for the past thirty years (averaging about one thousand cases per year among children under ten in the entire United States) (Gilbert 1995).[21] As with drug abuse, clinical findings of damage are easy to find in a handful of extreme cases. But the scope of the panic and resulting laws has ensnared a far wider range of conduct. Invisibility, unavoidability, and irreversibility take on heightened dimensions with children. They cannot be expected to perceive even visible threats, or make sensible voluntary

---

[20] The federal government has recently entered into a remarkable relationship with a public service advertising consortium, the Partnership for a Drug Free America, to place high quality and extremely aggressive antidrug ads, largely aimed at parents of children, on prime time television.

[21] Jenkins reports that about nine hundred children under the age of twelve were killed each year between 1980 and 1994 with no upward trend (Jenkins 1998, p. 10).

decisions, and damage to the young psyche or body is assumed to have lasting consequences.

We think these topics have been important not because they contribute to the growth of imprisonment directly (although drugs are a major source of imprisonment), but because as key images in public discourse about crime, they have contributed to the selection of crime as an issue for value-oriented politics. Not only have they captured a share of public attention out of all proportion to their share of the overall crime problem, but they fix the larger moral features of crime. Burglaries and robberies do not easily lend themselves to the metaphors of ritual contamination,[22] but drug trafficking and child abuse carry evocative images of moral depravity. The high rates at which arrestees are found to test positive for drugs helps tie property crime to that contamination. Likewise some of the most widely publicized child murder cases, like that of Polly Klaas, have involved repeat offenders, which helps tie all ex-prisoners to the potential for the most horrendous of violent crimes (Jenkins 1998).

E. Moral Panic or Crime Wave?

For many observers the key question is whether the historic rise in incarceration should be seen largely as a response to the great crime wave that occurred between 1965 and 1980. Those who think so tend to dismiss discussion of the politics of crime as elitist. Those who disagree, view the politics of crime as a manipulative effort by politicians to accomplish short-term goals with little heed to long-term consequences. We think the explanation for the surge in incarceration rates must address the politics of crime, but most existing explanations do not acknowledge the deeper changes in American political culture that make crime so productive politically. Just as Douglas and Wildavsky (1982) argued that the reality of the threat posed by environmental pollution was both necessary and insufficient to account for its prominence as a mobilizing force in politics during the 1970s, we think the crime threat is both necessary and insufficient to account for the incarceration rise of the 1980s and 1990s.

A great surge of violent crime did take place in the United States between 1967 and 1975, when the number of murders, rapes, robberies, and aggravated assaults reported to the police increased by 91 per-

---

[22] But see Rock (1986), p. 38, noting the widely circulated rumors in Britain that burglars defecate in the houses they invade, which Rock links to the pollution idea.

cent in only eight years. After a brief interruption, violent crime continued to rise until 1980 before leveling off, dropping in the early 1980s, rising again in the late 1980s, and declining again after 1992 (Boggess and Bound 1993; Currie 1998, p. 22). The total inmate population, which had declined from 211,000 in 1965 to 196,000 in 1970, then rose back to 240,000 in 1975 (Maguire and Pastore 1998). Thereafter, the rates of all index crimes leveled off while the incarceration rate began its spectacular climb into unfamiliar territory.

But the wave's most important effects may have been on our views about government. Garland (1996) argued that the international crime waves of the 1960s and 1970s helped diminish the prestige of national governments all over the industrial world, by calling into question their capacity to maintain social order. The increase of crime rates at a time of increasing government efforts to help the poor undermined many of the traditional arguments for welfare, and helped confirm the view of many conservatives that efforts to help the poor only made things worse by eliminating incentives to self improvement. This is not the place to determine whether the crime wave was caused by expansions in welfare programs or simply coincided with them. The important point is that in addition to the direct links between high rates of crime (especially violent crime) and demands for punitive governmental responses, the crime wave may have indirectly diminished the prestige of welfare-oriented government. It also raised the priority of crime in everyday life and our customary practices (e.g., locking doors, not walking through certain areas) (Garland, n.d.). Even if the crime rate should continue its recent decline and reach new lows, these enduring changes in the priority of crime control in everyday life will probably sustain a continued demand for strict crime control policies.

The average citizen's fear of being victimized by strangers is not unrealistic. According to the National Victimization Survey, one in seventeen males over twelve was victimized by a reportable felony (excluding homicide) in 1994 (Bureau of Justice Statistics 1997b, p. v). Urban dwellers know that there are some neighborhoods where they walk at risk at any time and many more where they cannot walk at night. Nearly half of the respondents to the General Social Survey locate such places within a mile of their homes (Davis and Smith 1994). American victimization rates are not, contrary to popular belief, extraordinary compared with Europe, but violent crime is more prevalent here, and lethal violence extraordinarily so (Zimring and Hawkins 1997; Langan and Farrington 1998). For those who live in affluent suburbs and gated communities, the personal risks are slight but the fear is no less acute.[23]

The sense of being embattled by crime is partially explainable by the fact that Americans spend a large fraction of their time in the virtual world of television where crime is more ubiquitous, consequential, and violent than in the real world. Television news programs are obsessed with crime. Local news broadcasts routinely feature the local crime of the day, easy to identify and report, sure to attract viewer interest. National broadcast news focuses on celebrity crimes and trials; the O. J. Simpson case dominated the networks for more than a year. Television fiction is equally obsessed. Murder and robbery account for nearly a quarter of all television crimes (Surette 1992). In the virtual world, people in all contexts are potentially violent. Bankers plan murders. Schoolteachers kidnap their pupils. Crimes are serious and well planned. And the perpetrators, when unmasked, are revealed as thoroughly evil.

F. The Dangerous Classes

Every highly stratified society regards its least favored stratum as a source of disorder and contamination requiring careful management. The greater the social and cultural distance that separates the underprivileged from the main body of society, the more punitive that management is likely to be. The class that most white Americans identify as dangerous consists largely of African Americans and Hispanics (especially Mexican-Americans, and Puerto Ricans), living in largely segregated districts in large metropolitan areas, and characterized by poverty, high unemployment, single-parent families, disorderly schools, and high levels of interpersonal violence. A history of prejudice, combined with a constant display of grim social images through the media, has fostered a sense that members of these communities are uniformly dangerous. Most of the government programs directed toward such communities, including welfare, foster care, school busing, and public housing, are widely resented (Wattenberg 1995; Gilens 1996). But law enforcement and incarceration, which target these communities while identifying them as contaminating, are more favorably regarded by the general public (Wattenberg 1995).

Given this background it is tempting to view the growth of incarcer-

[23] As in Tom Wolfe's 1987 novel *Bonfire of the Vanities*, in which a rich Manhattanite takes a wrong turn off a highway into a dangerous neighborhood and is hopelessly entangled in crime.

ation in the 1980s and 1990s as a product of America's complex class and racial politics. While the classic forms of animus against African Americans and other minorities show signs of abating, fear and loathing of the "underclass" in the inner cities seems to have hardened (Schuman, Steeh, and Bobo 1985; Jaynes and Williams 1989; Jackman 1994; Hochschild 1995; McDaniel 1995; Gilens 1996). The period of rapid growth in incarceration rates has seen a significant increase in the proportion of minorities in the inmate population (Tonry 1995), especially among drug offenders, the fastest growing segment of that population (Blumstein and Beck, in this volume).

Among criminological observers there have been two basic explanatory narratives. One takes the predominance of African Americans and Hispanics in the correctional population as a direct consequence of their disproportionate criminal activity. Research in the early 1980s showed that as much as 80 percent of the racial discrepancies in imprisonment rates could be accounted for by the racial distribution of perpetrators in the National Victimization Surveys.[24] In the 1994 survey, for example, over 50 percent of respondents who had been robbed identified their assailant or assailants as African American (Maguire and Pastore 1997, tables 3.28, 3.30). Additional support comes from recent studies of street gang activity showing that street gangs have spread from the major metropolitan centers to many smaller cities, that they routinely engage in criminal activities, and that they are predominantly African American (Klein 1995; Decker and Van Winkle 1996). Moreover, studies of felony sentences seem to show that racial disparity in sentencing is minimal and disappearing (Blumstein 1982; Klein, Turner, and Petersilia 1988). This narrative does not propose any particular explanation for the concentration of crimes likely to lead to imprisonment among African Americans and other minorities, but it treats the racial composition of the prison population as more or less in balance with the pattern of offending.

The other approach emphasizes enduring sources of discrimination in the criminal justice system that promote the incarceration of African Americans and Hispanics in several ways. Although the public fears vi-

---

[24] Perhaps the most often cited piece of research is Blumstein (1982). Blumstein was careful to note that significance of the unexplained 20 percent of the variation. His more recent research suggests that the strong association between imprisonment rates and victim reports had weakened slightly in the late 1980s and early 1990s, largely as a result of the increasing role of drug offenses in prison admissions (Blumstein 1993).

olent and consequential criminal incidents, of the kind that are repeated endlessly in the virtual world of television, the great majority
of criminal convictions are for essentially trivial offenses (Miller 1996,
p. 19). Despite efforts to limit discretion in the interest of fighting discrimination (Walker 1993), the broad inventory of minor offenses
available to the police leaves much discretion in place. Given the undeniable history of discriminatory application of the criminal law to minorities, it is not implausible that some police continue to use arrests
against those elements of the population whom they dislike and fear,
and for whom little public outcry can be expected.[25] Even though such
trivial offenses rarely lead directly to prison, they become part of an
offender's record and raise the odds that subsequent contacts with the
police or the courts will lead to harsher treatment. An arrest record is
relevant to probable-cause determinations for police searches and seizures. Prior convictions for petty offenses can tip sentencing decisions
from probation to prison. In the aggregate and over time, a systematic
effect of subjecting African Americans to greater scrutiny for minor offenses will produce effects in the imprisonment rates (although how
much of the racial disproportion they account for would be difficult to
estimate).

It is undeniable that some white Americans were pleased to see the
benefits of the civil rights movement and affirmative action partly can-
celed by the rise in the incarceration of African Americans, but there
is no evidence that such bigotry drives the trend.[26] We think the rise
in incarceration is better understood as the product of forces independent of racism but which have interacted with America's unfinished
agenda of racial equality. Indeed, it is possible to view the increased
demonization of criminals as a reflection of the decline of classic racial
animus. For much of American history it was taken for granted that

[25] The Supreme Court has declined in recent years to increase monitoring of potentially discriminatory discretion by police, see *Whren v. United States*, 116 S.Ct. 1769
(1996) (refusing to question the legitimacy of pretextual stops as long as the officer was
aware of facts sufficient to justify a traffic stop); *United States v. Armstrong*, 517 U.S. 456
(1996) (setting high initial showing for defense to make a selective prosecution claim
against the prosecution).
[26] Some scholars have found an association between punitive attitudes and racial discrimination (Stinchcombe et al. 1980), but that does not mean punitive attitudes are necessarily or commonly proxies for racism. Likewise, there is evidence that crime as a political issue was promoted aggressively by politicians from the South seeking to expand
their political base for resistance to the civil rights movement (Beckett 1997). But neither
of these facts really proves that the dynamics of American racial formation provide the
key impetus to the incarceration explosion.

the state should govern for the benefit of white Christian men and their legitimate families. The criminal law was always part of that sanctioning system, and until the threshold of our era, it routinely punished miscegenation and illegitimacy while protecting male violence in the home. One of the distinctive changes of recent decades has been the divorce of government from this implicit racial communitarianism. Driven by the courts and by elite public opinion, the same government that formerly supported white and male domination now vigorously opposes gender and ethnic discrimination. In this climate, the traditional moral stigma attached to crime has become one of the few areas where the state can openly signal its sympathy with majoritarian moral values. As Gaubatz (1995) noted in her study of popular views of crime, criminals are the only remaining minority that it is acceptable to hate.

But while we doubt racism has driven the rise in incarceration, we acknowledge that the rise of punitive governance cannot be separated from popular racial associations with crime and punishment (Mendelberg 1997). The delegitimation of welfare strategies, which we view as critical to the priority of punishment, is rooted in part in racial assumptions about the beneficiaries of government social programs (Gilens 1996). But the priority of punishment also derives from the reconfiguration of politics around values issues, a shift that seems to have no direct link to our history of racism. Indeed the rise of identity politics in the civil rights community exemplifies this reconfiguration.

If race does not drive the rise of incarceration, the effects of this trend on minorities is one of its most disturbing implications. The large number of African American adult males either confined or disadvantaged in the labor market by being ex-prisoners means that a large proportion of African-American women must go without husbands and many who do marry cannot expect much financial or moral support. This is having drastic effects on family life in inner-city African-American communities. Some scholars even suggest that the capacity of these communities to suppress crime by informal means has been undermined by the removal of so many actors from the scene (Meares 1998). Even without intentional harm, the racial consequences of these policies are too serious to ignore. Indeed, if these consequences are ignored after becoming apparent they may become, in some sense, retroactively intentional or at least a form of "malign neglect" (Tonry 1995). A recent and glaring example was in 1995 when Congress rejected the U.S. Sentencing Commission's recommendation on diminishing the racially sensitive disparity between punishments for possessing crack and possessing powder cocaine.

III. The War on Drugs

In the preceding section we examined the intensification of public demands for punitive justice. Such demands always exist in modern democracies, but in the United States in the past two decades they have reached a rare peak, observable in the public discourse on crime, in the resources allocated to building and staffing prisons, and in the severity of criminal sanctions. American society in the late twentieth century has developed a political culture in which crime occupies a central place, but that political culture does not provide a complete account of the unprecedented rise in incarceration. As Zimring and Hawkins point out (1991, p. 126), there is no necessary relationship between popular political mobilization around law and order and the accumulation of people in prison. The country has seen similar episodes before without a sustained growth in incarceration rates. In the early 1920s, public alarm over radical immigrants and Prohibition-related violence combined with the increase in automobiles and personal consumption to drive an earlier incarceration boom (Walker 1998, pp. 157–58). Imprisonment rates rose from 79 per 100,000 residents in 1925 to a peak of 110 in 1931 (see fig. 1). But the growth of the prison rate from trough to peak represented only a 40 percent increase. Although Prohibition ended in the early 1930s, a second peak occurred later in the decade (Walker 1998, pp. 157–58). The second panic was fed by the Depression and well-publicized crimes such as the Lindbergh kidnapping, which intensified federal efforts in crime control (Friedman 1993, pp. 266–67). After peaking at 137 in 1939, the incarceration rate declined and remained low until the beginning of the current rise. The 1939 rate was not matched until 1980 (fig. 1).

For political mobilization around law and order to produce a sustained increase in imprisonment, other conditions must be present. A key condition is a large pool of offenders available to be imprisoned. America's crime surge in the late 1960s increased the supply of burglars, robbers, and other serious felons, and sentencing changes in the 1980s led to a much greater portion of those convicted receiving imprisonment than before (Blumstein and Beck, in this volume). But even a dramatic shift in the punitiveness toward ordinary felons could not have quadrupled the prison population. The large-scale imprisonment of drug offenders has become a major factor in the rise in incarceration (Donziger 1996; Miller 1996; Blumstein and Beck, in this volume). The expansion of criminal sanctions for drug crimes began in the 1970s but picked up speed after President Reagan's election in 1980. The punitive response to drugs has been so potent that drug trafficking can lead to longer prison sentences than for homicide. More importantly, the rise of a large retail drug sales force in the 1980s and 1990s has furnished a nearly unlimited pool of offenders.

A. The Economic Base

None of the index crimes is especially lucrative. Murder and rape seldom pay. The average monetary yield of robberies and burglaries is very low—much lower than average losses to victims (Gottfredson and Hirschi 1990, pp. 25–31). The maintenance of a large criminal population requires a better resource base than street crime. Prohibition, of course, assured a generous cash flow, but only for a few years. Gambling—especially the numbers game and illegal bookmaking—were the main sources of underworld income until driven out of business by state lotteries, Indian casinos, and off-track betting. Meanwhile, prostitution ceased to generate much protection income. Extortion still thrives in some localities but is highly vulnerable to energetic prosecution. Drug smuggling and trafficking are the only activities capable of providing a solid economic base for a large criminal population under current conditions. The initial cost of goods is low and law enforcement efforts sustain high retail prices and guarantee extraordinary profit margins (Reuter and Kleiman 1986).

Prior to 1980, the relatively small market for hard drugs and the ease with which marijuana could be domestically produced limited the scale of drug enterprises. The introduction of crack cocaine in the mid-1980s changed all that. It created a market far larger than those for previously available drugs (including heroin in the 1960s and 1970s). It was retailed more openly and on a larger scale than other drugs. Crack created large numbers of job openings for low-paid retail sellers and assistants at a time when youth unemployment was high in the inner cities. Although such work is less lucrative than is commonly believed (Reuter, MacCoun, and Murphy 1990), the paucity of other alternatives, and the relative social benefits compared with other work in the low end of the service sector (McDonalds, Burger King) produced an apparently inexhaustible supply of new recruits to replace those imprisoned or killed. The drug economy has spillover effects, like the popularity of being armed[27] that may independently raise the odds of imprisonment.

The economic base provided by drug trafficking has enabled street gangs—almost exclusively African American except in a few cities—to flourish as never before, to expand in size and diversify their activities, and to spread from the major urban centers to smaller cities and towns (Klein 1995; Decker and Van Winkle 1996). Few of them seem to specialize in drug trafficking but most are somewhat involved. Their recreational, protective, and combative activities typically involve the versatile participation of gang members, individually and in groups, in drug transactions and in street crimes ranging from vandalism to murder.

Under our criminal justice system the penalty for a criminal offense is jointly determined by the severity of the offense, as defined by statute, and the criminal history of the defendant. First offenders are treated rather leniently; even for relatively serious crimes, many first offenders are sentenced to probation rather than imprisonment. Subsequent convictions bring sentences of increasing severity. Sometimes, under the new regime of mandatory penalties, life sentences without possibility of parole are handed down for such offenses as shoplifting and drug possession.

Thus in the early stages of a criminal career, the system offers some possibility of escape. Although the median age of felony perpetrators is about nineteen, the median age of first prison commitment is about twenty-five. But once incarcerated, the individual's opportunities for education, employment, military service, political participation, or any other lawful activity, are so drastically curtailed that further convictions are the normal expectation. Incarceration fixes the stamp of a criminal career (Freeman 1996). Men who complete a prison term have a better than two-thirds chance of being arrested for a new felony within four years (Conklin 1998, pp. 516–17). Those released on probation and parole have a better than even chance of being returned to prison for violations of probation or parole (more on that shortly). And those incarcerated without a drug habit are likely to acquire one in

---

[27] Blumstein has argued that this had important ripple effects among young persons not directly involved in drug trafficking who nonetheless have armed themselves to keep up with their peers who are (Blumstein 1996). Between 1985 and 1992, the portion of prison admissions from weapons offenses went from 1.8 percent of state prison admissions to 2.4 percent, and from 4.9 percent of federal prison admissions, to 10.2 percent (Bureau of Justice Statistics 1995).

confinement. The spoiling of identity is a gradual process but in most cases inexorable. It accounts for the extraordinary proportion of the African-American male population that has become criminalized since 1980.

B. Police Prosperity

Economically disadvantaged minority youth are not the only group attracted by drug markets: they alter the incentives and practices of law enforcement agencies as well. Because inner-city cocaine markets are often public and visible, and because mere possession has become a serious offense, police and other agents have had a far easier time making arrests than in any other law enforcement sector. In effect, the police in any large city in the United States can make as many drug arrests on any given day as departmental resources will allow. That is not possible for crimes like robbery and burglary.

Since arrests have historically been the most valued marker of police success, the opportunities provided by narcotics may already distort police priorities. But the allocation of large federal bloc grants to local drug efforts and the practice of asset forfeiture have provided law enforcement agencies and even individual officers a direct financial stake in drug arrests unmatched by any other kind of crime threat (Blumenson and Nilsen 1998, p. 40). On the darker side, their intervention in a market where all transactions are in cash and huge amounts of cash are passed from hand to hand, provides opportunities for corrupt enrichment unlike anything seen before. Few law enforcement agencies—federal, state, or local—have been untainted by drug money.

The drug economy and the war on drugs have produced a kind of substitute economy for the populations most affected by the shrinkage of the low-skilled industrial labor market in the United States. Both the drug trade and law enforcement (and also correctional employment) offer job opportunities to those without college educations (or in the case of the drug trade, without high school educations) with better financial compensation than other low-skilled employment can offer. Moreover, these jobs offer prestige (in their communities), excitement, and a space for the kind of aggressive masculinity that was tolerated in the old industrial jobs but is discouraged in the service economy.[28]

---

[28] Feminist theorists might find here an important way in which the society continues to subsidize male identities.

IV. The Increasing Reflexivity of the U.S. Penal System

The war on drugs has produced a new and seemingly endless supply of potential prisoners. But the rapidity with which the prison population has grown suggests that other factors are at work within the criminal justice system itself. The formal institutional structure of criminal justice looks much the same as it did at the end of the 1920s (police, courts, corrections, etc.), but fundamental changes in organization and program have taken place, most of them since 1970 (Cohen 1995; Feeley and Simon 1992; Walker 1993). In 1960, most of the criminal justice system at the state and local levels was organized in a pre-bureaucratic manner with highly personalistic executives, few rules, and many forms of exchange with the environment. By the late 1980s, this had changed. In many parts of the system, agencies have become fully modernized.

Sociologists such as Luhman (1985), Giddens (1991), and Beck (1992) have recently focused attention on reflexivity as a central feature of institutional practice in advanced liberal and industrial societies like the United States and Western Europe. Reflexivity describes the tendency of individuals, institutions, and whole societies to be mobilized by the collateral consequences of their own purposeful actions. Thus Beck (1992) argues that the struggle over the distribution of wealth, so central to the politics of modernizing societies, is being joined by the struggle over the distribution of the risks created by wealth-producing activities. Advanced societies find their politics increasingly focused on threats to social stability arising from their own political and economic practices, including environmental degradation, welfare dependency, and the dissolution of families. As Beck notes: "Modernization is becoming *reflexive*; it is becoming its own theme. Questions of development and employment of technologies (in the realms of nature, society and the personality) are being eclipsed by questions of the political and economic 'management' of the risks of actually or potentially utilized technologies—discovering, administering, acknowledging, avoiding or concealing such hazards with respect to specially defined horizons of relevance. The promise of security grows with the risks and destruction and must be reaffirmed over and over again to an alert and critical public through cosmetic or real interventions in the techno-economic development" (p. 21).

The primary social institutions put in place from the middle of the nineteenth century to respond to the problems of industrialization have themselves become sources of threat in the late twentieth century.

Mass education, welfare, social insurance, liberal liability rules, and economic regulation—the triumphs of progressive government—are now seen as the source of problems like the underclass and declining personal responsibility. The prison was one of the first institutions consciously designed to cope with the problems of what would come to be called modernization (Rothman 1972). From the start its reflexive potential was already visible. As the penitentiary developed, it created a shadow population of ex-prisoners, those "recidivists" who have haunted us for more than a century. The visibility of failure engendered numerous efforts at reform. From early on, the prison has been proposed as the solution to the problem it seems to create (Foucault 1977). But two developments in the twentieth century have accentuated this. First, a series of reforms aimed at improving the fairness of the system has operated to make the criminal justice system more efficient with the result that it can be far more responsive to pressures for growth than it might have been in the past. Second, the creation of large populations under correctional supervision in the community provides a supply of potential prisoners who can be handled faster and less expensively than in the ordinary criminal process.

A. Taming the System and Growing It

Using terms such as "the new penology" (Feeley and Simon 1992, 1994; Simon and Feeley 1995) and "managerialism" (Bottoms 1994), some observers claim that criminal justice institutions, especially the penal system, are now less focused on transforming criminal subjects and more focused on managing a seemingly permanent criminal population. Moving away from the nineteenth-and twentieth-century aspirations to individualization, normalization, and community benefits, contemporary penal policy is oriented to efficient control of the populations that flow through its institutions. These institutions are becoming more reflexive in the sense that they respond more and more to their own initiatives.

One sign of this transformation is visible in the heightened rationality of criminal justice. In his aptly titled book *Taming the System*, Walker (1993) traces a number of reforms at different levels of the criminal justice system aimed at greater control of discretion. These reforms have increased the inherent reflexivity of the penal enterprise both by making it easier to keep larger numbers of people under correctional supervision, and by intensifying the accountability of decision makers for the conduct of this enlarged population.

Law contributes to reflexivity generally (Luhman 1985) by creating feedback loops between the operation of an institution and its responses. This has been a major factor in the criminal justice system. For example, the rise of successful civil suits against police for violation of constitutional rights has encouraged the rise of what some experts call "passive policing," whereby more and more management attention is devoted to monitoring police action and discouraging conduct likely to provoke litigation (Langan and Farrington 1998, p. 11). Law has played a crucial role in bringing about rationalization in each segment of criminal justice since the 1960s.

The legal initiatives to reform state criminal justice agencies since the 1960s are one of the great success stories of twentieth-century government (Walker 1993; for a contrary view see Rosenberg 1991). Ironically, the chief initiatives that have increased the reflexivity of the criminal justice system have come from both liberals and conservatives (Walker 1993). Most of them have been pursued because of substantive issues that had relatively little to do with the overall scale or severity of punishment.

B. Bail Reform

Much of the emphasis today is on the use of administrative detention for explicit crime prevention purposes. In 1992, nearly a third of federal defendants were subjected to preventive detention under the Bail Reform Act of 1984 (Maguire and Pastore 1995, p. 442). But even so, detention levels are lower than they were a generation ago. Cash bail was a crucial choke point in the old system. Reformers at the time complained that it resulted in large numbers of indigent arrestees being held prior to trial simply because of their inability to raise the 5 or 10 percent cash payment required for commercial bail in those days (President's Commission on Law Enforcement and Administration of Justice 1967, pp. 130–31). In 1962, more than half of all arrestees were not released on bail. In many states, more than 60 percent of arrestees were not released (the median was 56 percent) (Silverstein 1965, pp. 7–8). In 1992, about two-thirds of all state court defendants in the seventy-five largest counties in the United States were released prior to the disposition of their cases, most of them on a noncash basis (Bureau of Justice Statistics 1994, p. 2). While we cannot calculate the precise effect without far more information, releasing a larger proportion of offenders pretrial allows the system to extend the time permitted to resolve the case and thus keep more cases in the queue toward conviction.[29] Not all of these cases result in prison time, but they often increase the chances of going to prison next time.

C. Right to Counsel

The right to counsel has also enlarged the managerial capacity of the criminal justice system. Typically it is assumed that the right to counsel raises the odds of dismissal or acquittal if charged at trial rather than a guilty plea or conviction without counsel. This does occur. But overall capacity of the system to process cases efficiently may increase with more adequate representation.[30] Judges and prosecutors have long recognized that the unrepresented defendant can prove extremely difficult to manage. Public defenders or court-appointed counsel are crucial members of the court work group. Their organizational incentives are to aid in the goal of smoothly processing cases—incentives that sometimes conflict with a defense counsel's ethical duties of representation (Blumberg 1967).

In 1962, fewer than half of defendants in state courts had assigned counsel or public defenders (the median was 43 percent) (Silverstein 1965, p. 8). In 1992, about 80 percent of the defendants in the seventy-five largest counties in the United States were so represented (Smith and DeFrances 1996, p. 1). It is highly likely that the extension of counsel for the indigent has increased the chances that those wrongly accused will have their charges dismissed or be acquitted. It is probably also true, however, that many of those factually guilty are moved through to conviction more rapidly and reliably.

D. Administrative Due Process

The due process revolution[31] has also been counted among the legal changes that made crime control less effective after the 1960s (Wilson 1983). However, it has almost surely increased the tendency of the system to establish formal custody over individuals and thus subject them

[29] Offenders denied bail have the recourse of demanding a speedy trial. While there are disadvantages for the defense in moving quickly to trial, too many such speedy trials would clearly strain the system or require major investment in courts and court personnel. It is noteworthy that spending on courts increased 177 percent between 1982 and 1993 but spending on corrections increased 253 percent, suggesting that the rise in incarceration has been carried out in a manner which has achieved economies in the use of courts (Maguire and Pastore 1998, table 1.2).

[30] Especially when one considers that the sorts of charges flushed out by the involvement of counsel will be weak cases and that there is a surplus of cases to charge.

[31] The expansion of procedural rights against police searches and seizures and procedural due process generally, as in *Mathews v. Eldridge*, 424 U.S. 319 (1976).

to further monitoring and potential punishment. Before the 1970s, both police and correctional agents used their arrest powers combined with the absence of any pressure to file charges quickly to administer short-term jail time as a quasi-informal punishment. Due process rights have made that tactic more difficult to use. Incarceration, even for relatively short periods, triggers the application of procedural rights that require the government to make a definitive decision whether to process the case forward. Police and correctional agents are forced to choose earlier whether or not to seek a formal sanction against an accused. This may in some cases result in a decision against arrest, but we suspect that far more often it results in a decision to move forward (Simon 1993, pp. 119–22). In short, due process raises the costs of informal sanctioning. In a system that is prepared to respond even to relatively minor violations with incarceration, the cost of formality is more incarceration.

Due process reforms have made the criminal justice system better and fairer in many respects. As a collateral (and almost certainly unintentional) result, they have also made the system more responsive to political pressure and flexible. This does not determine the direction of change. Under different political and social conditions, that flexibility might be used to reduce the prison population. One might predict that greater systemic rationality would make the system more stable, since the greater degree of administrative control would support management's interest in predictability and smooth functioning. But here reflexivity works at cross-purposes with other aspects of rationalization. The measures that allow the system to process its criminal subjects with greater efficiency and precision also compel it to confront regular evidence of its failures.[32] This is exacerbated in the American context by a criminal justice system that has always been highly vulnerable to populist pressures. Indeed, many of the recent administrative reforms have shifted discretion toward those agents of the system most sensitive to populist pressures, especially prosecutors and legislators.

[32] This was always a feature of parole systems but less critically so than when administrative procedures were less rigorous and the insulation from populist political pressures was thicker than it is today. For example, in an era when it was difficult to track parolees after they left prison it was easy to count as successes those who did not show up again in court. In contrast, contemporary parole, with far greater capacities to track its subjects, is far better at discovering violations. The taming of the system has in large part been a story of increasing internal auditing capacity. These failures demand responses and responses that may become the subject of populist political concern. This encourages officials to respond (often with imprisonment). Thus the paradox that the better managed these systems are, the more they seem to fail.

E. The Transformation of Parole and Probation into Imprisonment Systems

Perhaps the most important source of reflexivity in the criminal justice system is the changing function of parole and probation (Messinger et al. 1985; Simon 1993). While receiving far less public attention, probation and parole populations have grown along with the prison population. Between 1985 and 1995, the prison population increased by 121 percent, while probationers increased by 57 percent, and parolees by 133 percent (Bureau of Justice Statistics 1997a, p. 5). At one time, probation and parole operated as alternatives to imprisonment by providing correctional supervision in the community. Since the 1980s, however, parole and probation have become an increasing source of prison admissions. Rather than operate as alternatives to, or exits from, the prison system, both are becoming alternative routes to prison (Simon 1993, pp. 205–29).

The development of parole in the early twentieth century greatly increased the reflexivity of the prison. Parole gave prison officials a means of controlling the size of the inmate population when dozens of local judges did the sentencing. In a study of California prisons during the twentieth century, Messinger (1969) found a constant struggle by the department of corrections to increase its influence over the parole release function as a way of handling population stress. Parole revocation, the power to return parolees back to prison for committing new crimes or for violating the rules of parole, provided a less visible device for managing prison populations.[33] But until the 1980s, the contribution of parole revocations to prison admissions was modest compared to new commitments coming from the courts.[34]

F. Community Supervision as Source of Prison Admissions

That changed in the 1980s. The function of channeling people to prison increasingly took precedence over the provision of rehabilitative support. Parole and probation as sources of prison admissions have become almost as important as the court system itself. In the Bureau of

[33] In a series of fascinating papers written in the late 1960s, department criminologists Robison and Takagi argued that parole revocation rates were largely a function of variation among parole agents and units, and thus dominated by parole organization (part of the department of corrections; see Robison and Takagi 1968; Robison 1969).

[34] Except for brief surges in the mid 1960s and mid 1970s, the rate of parolees returning to prison in California (by either court action or administrative action) remained under 20 percent. In the 1980s and 1990s, it climbed to above 40 percent (Simon 1993, pp. 206–9).

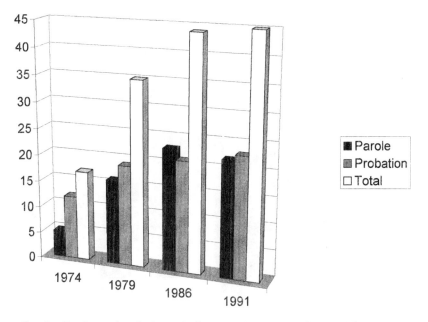

Fɪɢ. 4.—Parolees and probationers in the state prison surveys. Source: Cohen (1995)

Justice Statistics' 1991 survey of state prison inmates (Beck et al. 1993), 45 percent of prisoners had been on parole or probation before their current incarceration. Figure 4 compares the 1991 figures to those calculated from similar surveys in 1974, 1979, and 1986 (Cohen 1995). The number of prisoners who were previously on parole or probation has nearly tripled. Parole's contribution to the prison population has grown especially fast. In 1974, only 5 percent of surveyed prisoners had been on parole prior to their current incarceration; by 1991, the figure was 22 percent, more than four times the earlier level. Probation violators were 12 percent of the prison population in 1974 and 20 percent in 1991.

As figure 5 shows, persons on parole or conditional release (not including probation) and returned to prison for violating that status, have accounted for an increasing proportion of prison admissions throughout the century, but especially since the early 1980s (Cohen 1995, p. 4, app. 2). The Bureau of Justice Statistics found that from 1975 to 1991 the number of parole or probation violators entering prison grew at twice the rate of ordinary admissions (Cohen 1995, p. 1).

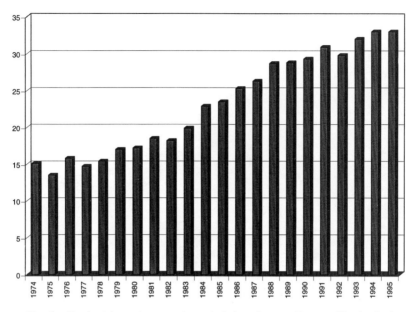

Fig. 5.—Parole violators in state prison admissions. Sources: Bureau of Justice Statistics (1997*a*); Cohen (1995), app. 2.

Figure 6 shows that this story is more complicated when states are considered individually.[35] For all states, the percentage of parolees among those admitted to prison climbed from 12 percent in 1974, to 24 percent in 1986, to 33 percent in 1995.[36] In California over the same period, parolees went from 19 percent, to 49 percent, to 60 percent of prison admissions. Among the five largest state parole populations, only New York had a smaller percentage of parolees among prison admissions in 1995 than in 1974. In Pennsylvania and Texas the rise has been especially substantial.

G. Shortening the Feedback Loop

Parole and probation make the system much more reflexive because they shorten the feedback loop between prison and the community.

[35] Surveys of prison population tend to understate the role of parole and probation in prison admissions since these returnees usually have shorter sentences and are thus less likely to be present than offenders with convictions for violent felonies.

[36] On our reading of the Bureau of Justice Statistics data, this does not include probationers who are included among the court commitments. We have not found a way to separate them out and add them to the parole population but we estimate that it would bring admissions closer to 50 percent.

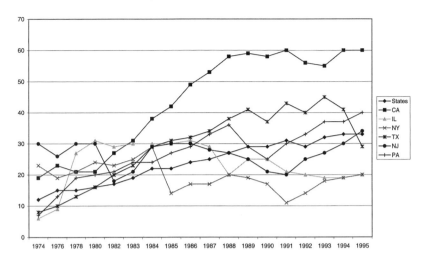

Fig. 6.—Parole violators as a percentage of prison admissions. Sources: Maguire and Flanagan (1991); Maguire, Pastore, and Flanagan (1993); Simon (1993); Maguire and Pastore (1998).

First, parole and probation make it easier for law enforcement and prosecutors to discover offenses and convict offenders. Second, administrative revocation permits the return of the subject to prison more easily than could be done through the courts. Third, parole and probation agents can also seek return for technical violations of the conditions of release for which there are no sanctions in criminal law. All this means that the defendant on parole or probation can be sent to prison more quickly and easily than the defendant with no criminal justice status. In a study of felony defendants in the seventy-five largest counties, just over one-third of felony defendants were detained in custody prior to final disposition of their case: 68 percent of parolees, and 56 percent of those on probation were detained (Bureau of Justice Statistics 1994, p. 6). Pretrial release has long been seen as providing significant advantages to those defendants who receive it. Only 45 percent of felony defendants who obtained pretrial release were convicted in contrast to 70 percent of those denied releases (Bureau of Justice Statistics 1994, p. 13). Nineteen percent of felony defendants who had been given pretrial release received a prison sentence when convicted, but more than twice as many detained defendants were imprisoned (Bureau of Justice Statistics 1994, p. 13).

Indeed, if a defendant violates parole or probation, return to prison may be by revocation, that is, an administrative proceeding far less protective of defendants than the adjudicatory route. Parole and probation also have a considerable influence over the discovery of violations. By routinely administering drug tests, and by being able to ignore the Fourth Amendment limitations on searches and seizures, parole and probation officers have advantages in law enforcement that are not available to police.[37] Thus parole and probation practices influence the level of criminality the system confronts. Not only can the administrative procedures available to parole and probation officers accelerate the speed of imprisonment, but also these low-friction procedures can feed the perception that criminality is spiraling out of control.

None of this is very surprising. Parole and probation were justified historically as a means of effective surveillance over risky former offenders, with the object of returning to prison those posing a threat to the community. But historically these powers were coupled with strong internal pressures to work with offenders in the community and to reserve reimprisonment for those posing a serious threat to the community (Simon 1993). Indeed, the Supreme Court in *Morrissey v. Brewer* (408 U.S. 471 [1972]) limited the application of full adversary rights to parolees and probationers facing revocation on the grounds that parole and probation authorities, unlike prosecutors, have strong incentives to exercise their discretion for the benefit of their subjects. That has changed dramatically in the 1980s and 1990s.

As the prison population grows, it is probably inevitable that a larger proportion of the total pool of criminals will be on parole or probation. Thus even if there were no change in the rate at which parole and probation systems returned their subjects to prison, we would expect the proportion of prison admissions coming from parole and probation to go up. There is reason, however, to believe that policies (often informal) have changed to make return to prison even more likely. Reflecting the internal narratives of parole agencies, and the growing political pressure for imprisonment, revocation rates have gone up nationally and in many of the largest states since the 1970s. Although we have not developed better tools for predicting future dangerous criminality, with rehabilitation discredited, and strong political support for reimprisonment, parole and probation agents tend to return offenders to prison for less serious activity than in the past.

---

[37] The Supreme Court will soon decide whether the exclusionary rule applies in parole or probation revocation hearings. See *Pennsylvania Board of Probation and Parole v. Scott*, no. 97-581, 66, *United States Law Week* 3283.

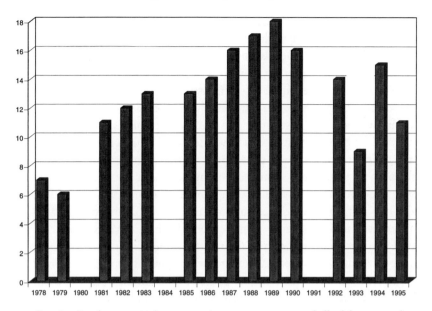

FIG. 7.—Parolees returned to state prison as a percentage of all adults on parole. Sources: *Sourcebook of Criminal Justice Statistics* (1990–97); Simon (1993).

Figure 7 shows the total number of parolees or conditional release violators returned to prison as a percentage of all persons on parole or conditional release in that year.[38] State parole and conditional release systems have increased the rate at which they return their subjects to prison from 7 percent in 1978 to 11 percent in 1995. The rate went as high as 18 percent in the late 1980s. Some states have experienced particularly strong trends. California, with the nation's largest parole system, doubled its revocation rate during the 1980s.

Returns to prison are at their most reflexive when administrative procedures are used to accomplish imprisonment. These procedures carry no automatic right to counsel, minimal confrontation rights, and a lower standard of proof. In California, the rate of parolees returning through new court commitments and through administrative revocation was about even during the 1970s. By the mid 1980s, more than

[38] This is a conservative calculation since it defines the relevant parole population as each person on parole on January 1 of each year, plus all persons added to parole during the rest of the calendar year. Of the 368,746 adults leaving state parole or community release status in 1995, nearly 42 percent were being reincarcerated (Bureau of Justice Statistics 1997*a*, table 6.5).

three times as many parolees were returning through revocation (Simon 1993, p. 206, figure based on Messinger et al. 1985).

During the 1980s, there seems to have been an increasing tendency for parole and probation systems to return their subjects to prison and to do so using more expedited administrative procedures. Assessment of the net effect depends in part on whether parole and probation revocation is simply substituting for the more cumbersome process of convicting the same person of a new offense. To the degree that parole and probation systems are generating violations that return people to prison who would not be subject to imprisonment for any new crime, the reflexivity of the system is compounded considerably.

The California experience suggests that in the course of the 1980s a growing number of revocations reflected both new crimes that might have resulted in imprisonment even without the administrative process and violations that were less likely to be prosecuted or not even cognizable under the regular criminal process. Thus Simon (1993, p. 246) found that the percentage of parolees returned to prison by revocation for violence more than doubled from 2.4 in 1971–72 to 5.4 in 1987, and property offenses quintupled from one percent to 5.4 percent. Drug offenses, likewise, increased from 2.7 percent to 7.2 percent. These are acts that quite likely would have resulted in imprisonment for a recently released prisoner even if no parole system existed. But the single largest category of violations in 1987 was "technical" violations, which were mainly violations of the conditions of parole that do not correspond to the other criminal categories (violence, property, and drugs). In 1971–72, a negligible .04 percent of parolees were returned to prison for technical violations. In 1987, nearly 10 percent were returned to prison for technical violations.

The 1991 Bureau of Justice Statistics survey of state inmates provides support for the proposition that technical violations of parole and probation have become a major route to prison.[39] Overall, 10.5 percent of all inmates in 1991 were there for violating a technical condition of parole and probation without having been convicted of a new crime (Cohen 1995, p. 1). Of inmates who had been on parole or probation, more than three-quarters were convicted of a new crime while 25 percent of probation violators and 20 percent of parole violators were

---

[39] The overall tone of Cohen (1995) is very much to the contrary. The publication seeks to emphasize that most parole and probation violators are there for a new and often serious crime. That is correct but the fact that as many as 10 percent of all prison inmates are there for technical violations of parole and probation is substantial.

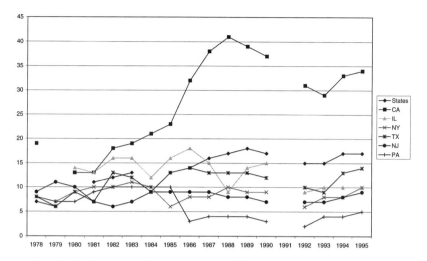

Fig. 8.—Parolees returned as a percentage of all persons on parole. Sources: *Correctional Populations in the United States* (1990–95); Simon (1993).

there for technical violations alone (Cohen 1995, p. 2).[40] Many of these technical violators were returned to prison for acts that would not be cognizable as crimes. Among parole violators, 10 percent had a revocation hearing for failing a drug test (regular submission of drug tests is a frequent condition of parole). Among parole and probation violators, 36 percent had a revocation hearing for failure to report for supervision or for "absconding."[41] Because the Bureau of Justice Statistics survey data included detailed information about parole and probation violators for the first time in 1991, we cannot know whether there is an increasing trend toward technical violations.

Reflexivity does not inevitably lead to increased incarceration. The same administrative capacity that drives imprisonment today could potentially be used to divert parole and probation violators away from prison. Indeed, as figure 8 shows, several of the states with large parole populations decreased their revocation rates during the late 1980s or early 1990s as the weight of the incarceration boom began to press on state budgets. California is a case in point. Between 1990 and 1993,

[40] The Bureau of Justice Statistics notes that 87 percent of the technical probation violators and 43 percent of the technical parole violators had been arrested for some crime other than violation (Cohen 1995, p. 2). Arrest, of course, is not a reliable indicator of guilt.

[41] Absconding usually involves willful avoidance of parole or probation supervision, including failing to show up for meetings and evading contact with agents.

California's revocation rate dropped from over 40 to under 30 percent.[42] This was at least in part the result of administrative strategies designed to balance the organizational incentives toward revocation with incentives for effective surveillance.

This strategy was introduced in memoranda and amended procedures that sought to harness the reflexivity of the system to retard growth. For example, parole supervision units all over the state were provided with statistical information about their revocation rates in comparison with other units. Without any change in formal policies, outlier units began to bring their rates closer to the statewide norms.

In 1994, political pressure began to mount. Right-wing newspapers in coalition with sheriffs, district attorneys, and parole agent union leaders, helped to mobilize a media panic about parole decision making. These reports claimed that as many as ten persons had been murdered by parolees whose paroles would have already been revoked under previous practice. The Democrats picked up the issue, including the nominee for governor, Kathleen Brown, who promised if elected to immediately imprison any parolee who violated parole conditions. Without any official change in policy (there never was much of an official policy to begin with), the department changed direction. The revocation rate shot up significantly by the end of 1994 and has remained high.

V. Conclusion

We have tried to suggest that the rise in incarceration is a result of independent but interactive factors. First, crime control has emerged as a privileged function of government. To an extraordinary degree the rhetoric of punishment is being drawn on to resolve basic administrative problems. In Florida, for example, a successful 1998 ballot proposal shifted financial responsibilities for trial courts from counties to the state government. The move had been long sought by public administrators and was widely supported by liberals and conservatives alike. Despite that, it was promoted in commercial messages that featured the families of murder victims bemoaning that the death penalty could not be pursued in their loved one's case because the county just could not afford the capital prosecution. When it comes to domestic

---

[42] California figures show an even steeper drop from nearly 60 percent to just under 40 percent. These figures were made available to one of the authors in his capacity as an expert witness in *Cervantes v. California*, a federal civil rights suit challenging parole revocation practices in the state.

policy at least, crime control has become the dominant model for governing.[43]

Second, the intensification of the war on drugs in the early 1980s coincided with the introduction of crack cocaine and the ensuing creation of an illegal mass market. That produces a virtually limitless supply of candidates for imprisonment. Moreover, they are available for apprehension on an ongoing basis without any need for complainants, and in a way that is largely self-financing from confiscations.

Third, the penal system has become more reflexive in that reforms introduced since the 1960s have made it more responsive to political pressures for growth and capable of handling such growth. The penal system maintains large populations of offenders under conditions that make the discovery (and in some sense the production) of large numbers of violations inevitable.

Governing through crime and the reflexivity of the criminal justice system have clear parallels in other advanced industrial societies, although in different ways and to different degrees. The war on drugs is largely an American situation (although one which we are aggressively seeking to export). For reasons imperfectly addressed here, these elements have interacted in a uniquely powerful way in the United States.

We are not abolitionists. The prison offers a potentially humane and legal way to address violent offenders that society must be protected from. Indeed, the twentieth century has given us plenty of other examples of how societies can deal with populations they deem troubling, including killing fields, deportation camps, and death squads. From its start, the promise of the prison was its ability to secure and punish without extraordinary measures or cruelties. It remains a potential locus of accountability and human rights.

The historically unprecedented incarceration rates of the past two decades tell a different story. We believe that they carry serious risks for American society, regardless of whether they can be shown to have lowered crime rates at the margins. No comparable society has ever tried to govern itself with such a large percentage of its adults in cor-

---

[43] Some have compared the current imprisonment build-up to the role the cold war played in the United States from the 1940s through the 1980s. We find that analogy helpful when it highlights the breadth of terrain across which one should look for effects. The cold war provided careers and ways of life, generated many cultural responses, modeled approaches to governing which spread to other fields, and linked levels of government and different centers of power (e.g., unions and political parties). Crime control works in many of the same ways to effectuate government. Less clear is the question of scale.

rectional custody. It is difficult to assess the long-term consequences of this move. Imprisonment has always harmed a prisoner's future prospects, but its consequences seem to be becoming more dire as the labor market for low-skilled workers worsens and the fear of crime itself marks former prisoners as unemployable (Freeman 1996; Beckett and Western 1997).[44] Just as important is the question of how a large population of former prisoners will affect the communities in which they live. A recent hate crime in Texas, in which an African-American man was dragged to his death tied to a car driven by several whites, sparked comparisons to the worst racial violence of the early 1960s (Hart 1998). The killers developed their racist attitudes in the Texas Department of Corrections where they had participated in a white supremacist gang. What will it mean to have exposed millions of less than stable adults to such ideas and practices?

The incarceration rate can be expected to continue to rise for some time, even if the crime rate continues to decline. The political dynamics that have made crime control such a good platform for politicians reflect long-term changes in U.S. political culture. Less clear is whether some of the brakes that once constrained cycles of governing through crime in the United States may begin to be felt. One traditional brake was popular sympathy for some law breakers. There are stirrings of such populist responses in America's inner cities (Butler 1995). Another brake is resistance from prison managers to increasing the population. As suggested by the California experience above, there may be lots of ways that mid-level penal managers can slow the growth of the prison population even without changing official policies.

Perhaps the most important brake is the potential demand of voters for other kinds of public goods like education. As state governments look for revenues to pay for these new initiatives, the corrections budget is almost an inevitable place to look (Petersilia 1997). Despite the great political appeal for being punitive, solutions that promise administrative savings by moving offenders from prisons to less expensive alternatives are also attractive to voters. The pressure to combine these imperatives has already produced heavy investment in "boot camps" (Little Hoover Commission 1995) and has led some to call for greater use of shame sanctions (Kahan 1996). There are signs in several states of just this kind of change. In Wisconsin, Republican Governor

---

[44] The recent high-growth rate of the U.S. economy may offer more hopeful prospects for prisoners. In Texas, prisons held a successful series of job fairs with employers quite interested in lining up those soon to be released.

Tommy Thompson has quietly encouraged plans to channel nonviolent offenders out of prison and into community supervision (Wisconsin Governor's Task Force on Sentencing and Corrections 1996). Similar proposals have been made for California (Petersilia 1997; Little Hoover Commission 1998).

REFERENCES

Baldwin, Peter. 1990. *The Politics of Social Solidarity: Class Bases of the European Welfare State.* Cambridge: Cambridge University Press.

Beck, Allen J., Darrell Gilliard, Lawrence Greenfeld, Caroline Harlow, Thomas Hester, Louis Jankowski, Tracy Snell, James Stephan, and Danielle Morton. 1993. *Survey of State Prison Inmates, 1991.* Washington, D.C.: U.S. Department of Justice.

Beck, Ulrich. 1992. *Risk Society: Towards a New Modernity.* London: Sage.

Beckett, Katherine. 1997. *Making Crime Pay: Law and Order in Contemporary American Politics.* New York: Oxford University Press.

Beckett, Katherine, and Bruce Western. 1997. "The Penal System as Labor Market Institution: Jobs and Jails, 1980–95." *Overcrowded Times* 8(6):1, 9–13.

Bennett, William J., John J. DiIulio, and John P. Waters. 1996. *Body Count: Moral Poverty—and How to Win America's War against Crime and Drugs.* New York: Simon & Schuster.

Best, Joel. 1990. *Threatened Children.* Chicago: University of Chicago Press.

Black, Donald. 1989. *Sociological Justice.* New York: Oxford University Press.

———. 1993. *The Social Structure of Right and Wrong.* San Diego, Calif.: Academic Press.

Blumberg, Abraham. 1967. "The Practice of Law as a Confidence Game: Organizational Cooptation of a Profession." *Law and Society Review* 1:15–39.

Blumenson, Eric, and Eva Nilsen. 1998. "Policing for Profit: The Drug War's Hidden Economic Agenda." *University of Chicago Law Review* 65:35–113.

Blumstein, Alfred. 1982. "On the Racial Disproportionality of United States Prison Populations." *Journal of Criminal Law and Criminology* 73:1259–81.

———. 1993. "Racial Disproportionality Revisited." *University of Colorado Law Review* 64:743–60.

———. 1996. "Interview, Alfred Blumstein: Youth, Guns and the Drug Trade." *Drug Policy Letter* (Summer), pp. 28–30.

Blumstein, Alfred, and Allen J. Beck. In this volume. "Population Growth in U.S. Prisons, 1980–1996."

Blumstein, Alfred, and Jacqueline Cohen. 1973. "A Theory of the Stability of Punishment." *Journal of Criminal Law and Criminology* 64:198–207.

Boggess, Scott, and John Bound. 1993. "Did Criminal Activity Increase during the 1980s? Comparisons across Data Sources." Working Paper no. 4431. Cambridge, Mass.: National Bureau of Economic Research.

Bonczar, Thomas P., and Allen J. Beck. 1997. *Lifetime Likelihood of Going to State or Federal Prison.* Washington, D.C.: U.S. Department of Justice.

Bottoms, Anthony. 1995. "The Philosophy and Politics of Punishment and Sentencing." In *The Politics of Sentencing Reform,* edited by Chris Clarkson and Rod Morgan. New York: Oxford University Press.

Brown, Phil. 1985. *The Transfer of Care: Psychiatric Deinstitutionalization and Its Aftermath.* Boston: Routledge & Kegan Paul.

Burchell, Graham, Colin Gordon, and Peter Miller. 1991. *The Foucault Effect: Studies in Governmentality.* Chicago: University of Chicago Press.

Bureau of Justice Statistics. 1994. *Pretrial Release of Felony Defendants, 1992.* Washington, D.C.: U.S. Department of Justice, Bureau of Justice Statistics. Internet edition: www.ojp.usdoj.gov/pub/bjs/ascii/nprp92.txt.

———. 1995. *Weapons Offenses and Offenders.* NCJ-155284. Washington, D.C.: U.S. Department of Justice, Bureau of Justice Statistics.

———. 1997a. *Correctional Populations in the United States, 1995.* Washington, D.C.: U.S. Department of Justice, Bureau of Justice Statistics.

———. 1997b. *Criminal Victimization in the United States, 1994.* Washington, D.C.: U.S. Department of Justice, Bureau of Justice Statistics.

———. 1998. "Nation's Probation and Parole Population Reached New High Last Year." Press release, August 16, 1998. Washington, D.C.: U.S. Department of Justice, Bureau of Justice Statistics.

Butler, Paul. 1995. "Racially Based Jury Nullification: Black Power in the Criminal Justice System." *Yale Law Journal* 105:677–725.

Caplow, Theodore. 1991. *Perverse Incentives: The Neglect of Social Technology in the Public Sector.* Westport, Conn.: Praeger.

Chernoff, Harry A., Christopher M. Kelly, and John R. Kroger. 1996. "The Politics of Crime." *Harvard Journal on Legislation* 33:527–78.

Chitwood, Dale D., James E. Rivers, and James A. Inciardi. 1996. *The American Pipe Dream: Crack Cocaine and the Inner City.* Ft. Worth, Tex.: Harcourt, Brace.

Christie, Nils. 1993. *Crime Control as Industry.* London: Routledge.

Cohen, Robyn. 1995. *Probation and Parole Violators in State Prison, 1991.* Washington, D.C.: U.S. Department of Justice.

Cohen, Stanley. 1972. *Folk Devils and Moral Panics.* Oxford: Blackwell.

———. 1985. *Visions of Social Control.* New York: Polity.

Conklin, John F. 1998. *Criminology,* 6th ed. Boston: Allyn & Bacon.

Correctional Populations in the United States. 1990–95. Washington, D.C.: U.S. Department of Justice, Bureau of Justice Statistics.

Costin, Lela, Howard Krager, and David Stoesz. 1996. *The Politics of Child Abuse in America.* New York: Oxford University Press.

Currie, Elliott. 1998. *Crime and Punishment in America.* New York: Metropolitan Books.

Davis, James A., and Tom W. Smith. 1994. *General Social Surveys, 1972–1994.* Question 233. Chicago: National Opinion Research Center.

Decker, Cathleen. 1998. "Lack of Defining Issues Hampers Davis, Lungren Campaign." *Los Angeles Times* (August 23), p. A3.

Decker, Scott H., and Barrik Van Winkle. 1996. *Life in the Gang: Family, Friends and Violence.* Cambridge: Cambridge University Press.

DiIulio, John. 1991. *No Escape: The Future of American Corrections.* New York: Basic Books.

———. 1996. "Help Wanted: Economists, Crime and Public Policy." *Journal of Economic Perspectives* 10:3–24.

DiIulio, John J., and Anne Morrison Piehl. 1991. "Does Prison Pay? The Stormy National Debate over the Cost-Effectiveness of Imprisonment." *Brookings Review* 9:28–35.

Dionne, E. J., Jr. 1991. *Why Americans Hate Politics.* New York: Simon & Schuster.

Donziger, Steven R., ed. 1996. *The Real War on Crime: The Report of the National Criminal Justice Commission.* New York: HarperPerennial.

Douglas, Mary, and Aaron Wildavsky. 1982. *Risk and Culture.* Berkeley: University of California Press.

Durkheim, Emile. 1933. *The Division of Labor in Society.* New York: Free Press.

———. 1983. "Two Laws of Penal Evolution," translated by T. Anthony Jones and Andrew Scull. In *Durkheim and the Law,* edited by Stephen Lukes and Andrew Scull. Oxford: Blackwell. (Originally published 1901, translated 1973.)

Estrich, Susan. 1987. *Real Rape.* Cambridge, Mass.: Harvard University Press.

Evans, Richard. 1996. *Rituals of Retribution: Capital Punishment in Germany, 1600–1987.* New York: Oxford University Press.

Feeley, Malcolm, and Jonathan Simon. 1992. "The New Penology: Notes on the Emerging Strategy of Corrections and Its Implications." *Criminology* 30:449–74.

———. 1994. "Actuarial Justice: Power/Knowledge in Contemporary Criminal Justice." In *The Future of Criminology,* edited by David Nelkin. London: Sage.

Forst, Martin, and Martha-Elin Blomquist. 1991. *Missing Children: Rhetoric and Reality.* Toronto: Lexington Books.

Foucault, Michel. 1977. *Discipline and Punish: The Birth of the Prison.* Translated by Robert Hurley. New York: Pantheon.

Freeman, Richard B. 1976. *The Overeducated American.* New York: Academic Press.

———. 1996. *Why Do So Many Young American Men Commit Crimes and What Might We Do about It?* Working Paper no. 5451. Cambridge, Mass.: National Bureau of Economic Research.

Friedman, Lawrence M. 1993. *Crime and Punishment in American History.* New York: Basic.

Garland, David. n.d. "Crime Control and Culture." Unpublished manuscript. New York: New York University School of Law.

———. 1990. *Punishment and Modern Society.* Chicago: University of Chicago Press.

————. 1996. "The Limits of the Sovereign State: Strategies of Crime Control in Contemporary Society." *British Journal of Criminology* 36:445–71.

Gaubatz, Kathlyn. 1995. *Crime in the Public Mind*. Ann Arbor: University of Michigan Press.

Giddens, Anthony. 1991. *The Consequences of Modernity*. Stanford, Calif.: Stanford University Press.

Gilbert, Neil. 1995. "Miscounting Social Ills." In *Fraud and Fallible Judgment*, edited by Nathaniel J. Pallone and James J. Hennessey. New Brunswick, N.J.: Transaction.

Gilens, Martin. 1996. " 'Race Coding' and White Opposition to Welfare." *American Political Science Review* 90:593–604.

Gilliard, Darrell K., and Allen J. Beck. 1998. *Prisoners in 1997*. Washington, D.C.: U.S. Department of Justice, Bureau of Justice Statistics.

Gordon, Diana. 1990. *The Justice Juggernaut: Fighting Crime, Controlling Citizens*. New Brunswick, N.J.: Rutgers University Press.

————. 1994. *The Return of the Dangerous Classes: Drug Prohibition and Policy Politics*. New York: Norton.

Gottfredson, Michael R., and Travis Hirschi. 1990. *A General Theory of Crime*. Stanford, Calif.: Stanford University Press.

Greenberg, David F., and Valery West. 1998. "The Persistent Significance of Race: Growth in State Prison Populations." Paper presented at the fiftieth annual meeting of the American Society of Criminology, Washington, D.C., November.

Hall, Stuart, Chas Critcher, and Tony Jefferson. 1978. *Policing the Crisis*. Basingstoke: Macmillan.

Hart, Lianne. 1998. "Three Charged in Texas after Black Man's Grisly Death Crime: Victim Was Dragged behind Pick-Up Truck and Torn Apart." *Los Angeles Times* (June 10), p. A1.

Hochschild, Jennifer L. 1995. *Facing Up to the American Dream: Race, Class, and the Soul of the Nation*. Princeton, N.J.: Princeton University Press.

Inglehart, Ronald. 1977. *The Silent Revolution: Changing Values and Political Styles among Western Publics*. Princeton, N.J.: Princeton University Press.

————. 1990. *Culture Shift in Advanced Industrial Society*. Princeton, N.J.: Princeton University Press.

Irwin, John, and James Austin. 1994. *It's about Time: America's Imprisonment Binge*. Belmont, Calif.: Wadsworth.

Jackman, Mary R. 1994. *The Velvet Glove: Paternalism and Conflict in Gender, Class, and Race Relations*. Berkeley and Los Angeles: University of California Press.

Jacobs, James B., and Kimberly Potter. 1998. *Hate Crimes: Criminal Law and Identity Politics*. New York: Oxford University Press.

Jaynes, Gerald David, and Robin W. Williams, Jr., eds. 1989. *A Common Destiny: Blacks and American Society*. Washington, D.C.: National Academy Press.

Jenkins, Philip. 1998. *Moral Panic: Changing Concepts of the Child Molester in Modern America*. New Haven, Conn.: Yale University Press.

Justice Policy Institute. 1997. "More Is Spent on New Prisons than Colleges." *Washington Post* (February 24), p. A8.

Kahan, Dan. 1996. "What Do Alternative Sanctions Mean?" *University of Chicago Law Review* 63:591–653.

King, David C. 1997. "The Polarization of American Political Parties and Mistrust of Government." Politics Research Group Working Papers. Cambridge, Mass.: Harvard University, Kennedy School of Government. Available online at www.ksg.harvard.edu/prg/king/polar.html.

Klein, Malcolm W. 1995. *The American Street Gang: Its Nature, Prevalence and Control.* New York: Oxford University Press.

Klein, Susan P., Susan Turner, and Joan Petersilia. 1988. *Racial Equity in Sentencing.* RAND Report no. R-3599-RC. Santa Monica, Calif.: RAND.

Kuhn, Andrè. 1997. "Prison Populations in Western Europe." In *Sentencing Reform in Overcrowded Times: A Comparative Perspective,* edited by Michael Tonry and Kathleen Hatlestad. New York: Oxford University Press.

Langan, Patrick A., and Jodi M. Brown. 1997. *Felony Sentences in the United States, 1994.* Washington, D.C.: U.S. Department of Justice, Bureau of Justice Statistics.

Langan, Patrick A., and David P. Farrington. 1998. *Crime and Justice in the United States and in England and Wales, 1981–96.* Washington, D.C.: U.S. Department of Justice, Bureau of Justice Statistics.

Little Hoover Commission. 1995. *Boot Camps: An Evolving Alternative to the Traditional Prison.* Report no. 128. Sacramento, Calif.: Little Hoover Commission, January.

———. 1998. *Beyond Bars: Correctional Reforms to Lower Prison Costs and Reduce Crime.* Report no. 144. Sacramento, Calif.: Little Hoover Commission. Available online at http://www.lhc.ca.gov./lhcdir/144/TC144.html.

Lo, Clarence Y. H., and Michael Schwartz. 1998. *Social Policy and the Conservative Agenda.* Malden, Mass.: Blackwell.

Luhman, Niklas. 1985. *Ecological Communication.* Translated by John Bednarz, Jr. Chicago: University of Chicago Press.

Maguire, Kathleen, and Timothy J. Flanagan. 1991. *Sourcebook of Criminal Justice Statistics, 1990.* Washington, D.C.: U.S. Department of Justice, Bureau of Justice Statistics.

Maguire, Kathleen, and Ann L. Pastore. 1995. *Sourcebook of Criminal Justice Statistics, 1994.* Washington, D.C.: U.S. Department of Justice, Bureau of Justice Statistics.

———. 1997. *Sourcebook of Criminal Justice Statistics, 1996.* Washington, D.C.: U.S. Department of Justice, Bureau of Justice Statistics.

———. 1998. *Sourcebook of Criminal Justice Statistics, 1997.* Washington, D.C.: U.S. Department of Justice, Bureau of Justice Statistics.

Maguire, Kathleen, Ann L. Pastore, and Timothy J. Flanagan. 1993. *Sourcebook of Criminal Justice Statistics, 1992.* Washington, D.C.: U.S. Department of Justice, Bureau of Justice Statistics.

Mauer, Marc. 1997. "Young Black Men and the Criminal Justice System." In *Sentencing Reform in Overcrowded Times: A Comparative Perspective,* edited by

Michael Tonry and Kathleen Hatlestad. New York: Oxford University Press.

McDaniel, Antonio. 1995. "The Dynamic Racial Composition of the United States." *Daedalus* 124 (Winter): 183–89.

Meares, Tracey. 1998. "Place and Crime." *Chicago-Kent Law Review* 73:669–704.

Mechanic, D., and D. A. Rochefort. 1990. "Deinstitutionalization: An Appraisal of Reform." *Annual Review of Sociology* 16:301–27.

Mendelberg, Tali. 1997. "Executing Hortons: Racial Crime in the 1988 Presidential Campaign." *Public Opinion Quarterly* 61:134–57.

Messinger, Sheldon. 1969. "Strategies of Control." Ph.D. dissertation, University of California, Los Angeles.

Messinger, Sheldon L., John E. Berecochea, Richard A. Berk, and David Rauma. 1988. *Parolees Returned to Prison and the California Prison Population.* Sacramento, Calif.: Bureau of Criminal Statistics.

Messinger, Sheldon L., John E. Berecochea, David Rauma, and Richard Berk. 1985. "The Foundations of Parole in California." *Law and Society Review* 19:69–106.

Miller, Jerome. 1996. *Search and Destroy: African-American Males in the Criminal Justice System.* Cambridge: Cambridge University Press.

———. 1997a. "Forty-Two Percent of Black D.C. Males, Ages Eighteen to Thirty-Five under Criminal Justice System Control." In *Sentencing Reform in Overcrowded Times: A Comparative Perspective*, edited by Michael Tonry and Kathleen Hatlestad. New York: Oxford University Press.

———. 1997b. "Fifty-Six Percent of Young Black Males in Baltimore under Criminal Justice System Control." In *Sentencing Reform in Overcrowded Times: A Comparative Perspective*, edited by Michael Tonry and Kathleen Hatlestad. New York: Oxford University Press.

Morgan, Kathleen O'Leary, Scott Morgan, and Neal Quitno. 1996. *Crime State Rankings, 1996: Crime in the 50 States.* Lawrence, Kans.: Morgan Quitno Press.

Murray, Charles. 1984. *Losing Ground: American Social Policy, 1950–1980.* New York: Basic Books.

Nathan, Debbie, and Michael Snedeker. 1995. *Satan's Silence.* New York: Basic Books.

Pearlstein, Steven. 1996. "Angry Female Voters a Growing Force. Reality Check: The Politics of Mistrust." *Washington Post* (January 30), p. A1.

Petersilia, Joan. 1997. "Diverting Nonviolent Prisoners to Intermediate Sanctions." *Corrections Management Quarterly* 1:1–15.

Pierson, Paul. 1994. *Dismantling the Welfare State: Reagan, Thatcher and the Politics of Retrenchment.* Cambridge: Cambridge University Press.

President's Commission on Law Enforcement and Administration of Justice. 1967. *The Challenge of Crime in a Free Society.* Washington D.C.: U.S. Government Printing Office.

Reuter, Peter, and Mark A. R. Kleiman. 1986. "Risks and Prices: An Economic Analysis of Drug Enforcement." In *Crime and Justice: An Annual Review of*

Research, vol. 7, edited by Michael Tonry and Norval Morris. Chicago: University of Chicago Press.

Reuter, Peter, Robert MacCoun, and Patrick Murphy. 1990. *Money from Crime: A Study of Drug Dealing in Washington, D.C.* Santa Monica, Calif.: RAND.

Robison, James O. 1969. "It's Time to Stop Counting." Technical Suppl. no. 2: "Assembly Report on the Costs and Effects of the California Criminal Justice System." Sacramento: California State Assembly.

Robison, James O., and Paul Takagi. 1968. *Case Decisions in a State Parole System.* Sacramento: California Department of Corrections.

Rock, Paul. 1986. "Society's Attitude to the Victim." In *From Crime Policy to Victim Policy: Reorienting the Justice System*, edited by Essat A. Fattah. New York: St. Martin's.

Rose, Nikolas. 1996. "Governing 'Advanced' Liberal Democracies." In *Foucault and Political Reason: Liberalism, Neo-Liberalism and Rationalities of Government*, edited by Andrew Barry, Thomas Osborne, and Nikolas Rose. Chicago: University of Chicago Press.

Rosenberg, Gerald N. 1991. *The Hollow Hope: Can Courts Bring About Social Change?* Chicago: University of Chicago Press.

Rossi, Peter H., and Richard A. Berk. 1997. *Just Punishments: Federal Guidelines and Public Views.* New York: Aldine de Gruyter.

Rothman, David J. 1972. *The Discovery of the Asylum.* Boston: Little, Brown.

Rusche, Georg, and Otto Kirchheimer. 1939. *Punishment and Social Structure.* New York: Columbia University Press.

Ruth, David J. 1996. *Inventing the Public Enemy: The Gangster in American Culture, 1918–1934.* Chicago: University of Chicago Press.

Savelsberg, Joachim. 1994. "Knowledge, Domination, and Criminal Punishment." *American Journal of Sociology* 99:911–43.

Scheingold, Stuart A. 1991. *The Politics of Street Crime: Criminal Process and Cultural Obsession.* Philadelphia: Temple University Press.

Schrag, Peter. 1998. *Paradise Lost: California's Experience, America's Future.* New York: New Press.

Schuman, Howard, Charlotte Steeh, and Lawrence Bobo. 1985. *Racial Attitudes in America: Trends and Interpretations.* Cambridge, Mass.: Harvard University Press.

Scull, Andrew. 1977. *Decarceration: Community Treatment and the Deviant, a Radical View.* Englewood Cliffs, N.J.: Prentice Hall.

Silverstein, Lee. 1965. *Defense of the Poor in Criminal Cases in American State Courts.* Chicago: American Bar Foundation.

Simon, Jonathan. 1993. *Poor Discipline: Parole and the Social Control of the Underclass, 1890–1990.* Chicago: University of Chicago Press.

Simon, Jonathan, and Malcolm Feeley. 1995. "True Crime: The New Penology and Public Discourse on Crime." In *Punishment and Social Control: Essays in Honor of Sheldon Messinger*, edited by Thomas G. Blomberg and Stanley Cohen. New York: Aldine de Gruyter.

Smith, Steven K., and Carol J. DeFrances. 1996. *Selected Findings, Indigent De-*

fense. NCJ-158909. Washington, D.C.: U.S. Department of Justice, Bureau of Justice Statistics.

Sourcebook of Criminal Justice Statistics. 1990–97. Washington, D.C.: U.S. Department of Justice, Bureau of Justice Statistics.

Stephan, James J. 1997. *Census of State and Federal Correctional Facilities, 1995.* Washington, D.C.: U.S. Department of Justice.

Stern, Vivian. 1998. *A Sin against the Future: Imprisonment in the World.* Boston: Northeastern University Press.

Stinchcombe, Arthur L., Rebecca Adams, Carol A. Heimer, Kim Lane Scheppele, Tom W. Smith, and D. Garth Taylor. 1980. *Crime and Punishment— Changing Attitudes in America.* NORC Series in Social Research. San Francisco: Jossey-Bass.

Surette, Ray. 1992. *Media, Crime, and Criminal Justice: Images and Realities.* Pacific Grove, Calif.: Brooks/Cole.

Thompson, E. P. 1975. *Whigs and Hunters: The Origins of the Black Act.* New York: Pantheon.

Tonry, Michael. 1995. *Malign Neglect: Race, Crime, and Punishment in America.* New York: Oxford University Press.

Torrey, E. Fuller. 1997. *Out of the Shadows: Confronting America's Mental Illness Crisis.* New York: Wiley.

Tyler, Tom R., and Robert J. Boeckmann. 1997. "Three Strikes and You Are Out, but Why? The Psychology of Public Support for Punishing Rule Breakers." *Law and Society Review* 31:237–64.

Walker, Samuel. 1993. *Taming the System: The Control of Discretion in Criminal Justice, 1950–1990.* New York: Oxford University Press.

———. 1998. *Popular Justice: A History of Criminal Justice,* 2d ed. New York: Oxford University Press.

Wattenberg, Ben J. 1995. *Values Matter Most.* New York: Free Press.

Weir, Margaret, Anne Shola Orloff, and Theda Skocpol. 1988. *The Politics of Social Policy in the United States.* Princeton, N.J.: Princeton University Press.

Wilson, James Q. 1983. *Thinking about Crime,* 2d ed. New York: Basic Books.

Wisconsin Governor's Task Force on Sentencing and Corrections. 1996. "Final Report (12/17/96)." Reprinted in *Overcrowded Times* 7(6):5–17.

Wolfe, Tom. 1987. *Bonfire of the Vanities.* New York: Farrar Straus & Giroux.

Wright, Stuart A. 1995. *Armageddon in Waco: Critical Perspectives on the Branch Davidian Conflict.* Chicago: University of Chicago Press.

Young, Warren, and Mark Brown. 1993. "Cross-National Comparisons of Imprisonment." In *Crime and Justice: A Review of Research,* vol. 17, edited by Michael Tonry. Chicago: University of Chicago Press.

Zimring, Franklin, and Gordon Hawkins. 1991. *The Scale of Punishment.* Chicago: University of Chicago Press.

———. 1997. *Crime Is Not the Problem: Lethal Violence in America.* New York: Oxford University Press.

John Hagan and Ronit Dinovitzer

Collateral Consequences of Imprisonment for Children, Communities, and Prisoners

ABSTRACT

Analyses of the effects of America's experiment with vastly increased use
of imprisonment as a penal sanction typically focus on crime reduction
and public spending. Little attention has been paid to collateral effects.
Imprisonment significantly reduces later employment rates and incomes
of exprisoners. In many urban communities, large fractions of young men
attain prison records and are thus made less able to contribute to their
communities and families. Less is known about the effects of a parent's
imprisonment on children's development, though mainstream theories
provide grounds for predicting those effects are substantial and deleterious.
Until research begins to shed light on these questions, penal policy will
continue to be set in ignorance of important ramifications of alternate
policy options.

We are at a crossing point in American crime and punishment: rates
of imprisonment are increasing at the same time that rates of crime are
decreasing. Some argue this is exactly as it should be, and that increased investment in prisons is being repaid in benefits of reduced
crime. Yet if this is so, the benefits of imprisonment are less certain
and slower in arriving than expected, and few may realize the full extent of the costs. This last possibility seems especially likely when we
take into account collateral costs and consequences of imprisonment
that may be especially consequential for children of imprisoned parents
who are already at risk as a result of growing up and coming of age in
disadvantaged communities.

John Hagan is University Professor in the department of sociology and the faculty of
law at the University of Toronto. Ronit Dinovitzer is a doctoral candidate in sociology
at the University of Toronto.

The collateral costs of imprisonment may be extensive. The most obvious concern is that the effects of imprisonment damage the human and social capital of those who are incarcerated, their families, and their communities, including the detrimental impact of imprisoning parents on their children. Less obvious concerns involve foregone opportunities to invest in schools and the selective direction of existing and new resources away from minority to majority group communities where prisons are being built and operated. More specifically, imprisonment may engender negative consequences for offenders whose employment prospects after release are diminished; for families who suffer losses both emotional and financial; for children who suffer emotional and behavioral problems due to the loss of a parent, financial strain, and possible displacement into the care of others; for communities whose stability is threatened due to the loss of working males; and for other social institutions that are affected by the budgetary constraints imposed by the increases in spending on incarceration.

This essay considers this collection of costs. It begins and ends with a consideration of the impact of the imprisonment of parents on children, noting that this may be the least understood and most consequential implication of the high reliance on incarceration in America. Because we are concerned that the impact on children is the most serious result of the growing reliance on imprisonment, we begin in Section I by first outlining theoretical perspectives that can inform our understanding of the effects of parental incarceration on children. In Section II, we briefly survey the extent of incarceration, the costs of corrections, and the implications of this spending for other sectors of the economy. In Section III, the consequences of incarceration in terms of human and social capital are considered and the implications for work and families, and the effects thus far observed in research on the children of incarcerated parents. A particular goal of the essay is to stimulate more systematic research on this last topic, and to this end the essay concludes in Section IV with specific proposals for how research on children of imprisoned parents can be carried out most effectively. This research is needed to assess more systematically the losses in human and social capital that the largest and most racially concentrated imprisonment in the history of this country is having on a future generation of children. Until this research is undertaken in a serious and systematic way, the potential impact of the incarceration of parents on children will remain an unrecognized and therefore neglected consideration in the policy framework that surrounds the increased reliance on imprisonment in America.

I. Theoretical Background of Parenting and
Prison Research

There obviously are cases involving the incarceration of negligent, violent, and abusive parents where the imprisonment of the parents benefits children by removing serious risks of current and future harm. But how often is this the case? How often and to what extent is parental imprisonment beneficial or detrimental to children? The imprisonment of parents may more often be a traumatic life event that initiates or intensifies rather than reduces the problems of the involved children. Thus even in problem-plagued families the incarceration of a parent may only add to the difficulties faced by children. Imprisonment of a parent can alter the prospects of the family in a number of significant ways that are anticipated in the literature on single parenthood (see McLanahan and Sandefur 1994), with the trauma of parental imprisonment having possible economic and socioemotional ramifications.

Removal of one parent from participation in a child's life can have severe implications for the child's social capital—the resources that can be drawn on to facilitate relationships and initiatives, "making possible the achievement of certain ends" (Coleman 1990, p. 302). Portes (1998, p. 6) defines social capital in terms of "the ability of actors to secure benefits by virtue of membership in social networks or other social structures." The effects of diminished social capital can be observed in the loss of its functions. For example, the loss of social capital can be recognized in the ways in which disruptions in families are dysfunctional for children. Associated sociological and criminological theories point to three prominent ways in which the effects of parental imprisonment on the social capital of children might be understood. These involve the strains of economic deprivation, the loss of parental socialization through role modeling, support, and supervision, and the stigma and shame of societal labeling. For ease of reference, we call these the *strain*, *socialization*, and *stigmatization* perspectives.

As formulated, these perspectives all involve assumptions about the ways in which parental adversity can deplete the human and social capital resources of the family. However, we also consider below an alternative version of the strain perspective that adopts the assumption that the imprisoned parent poses a drain or threat to the human and social capital of the family. And we also introduce a selection perspective that considers predisposing processes that may lead children to follow imprisoned parents into crime and result in other threats to their social well-being. As noted at the outset of this section and in the alternative version of the strain perspective outlined below, if these selection processes are sufficiently problematic, they might be mitigated by the removal of troublesome parents. However, we hypothesize that imprisonment more often intensifies the problems caused by a dysfunctional parent. Knowing if and when either of these possible outcomes is the case is obviously important for policy as well as for theoretical reasons, and can only be determined through the kinds of research reviewed and proposed in later sections of this essay.

A. The Strain Perspective

If a subsequently imprisoned parent previously contributes positively to the family, the imprisonment of that parent may result in economic deprivation and resulting strains that affect children. Positive contributions by a subsequently imprisoned parent may not always have involved the parents maintaining an intact household. Many nonresident parents, even many never-married and absent parents, maintain frequent contact with their children, and much of the variation in the nature of the parental contribution may have to do with the form and quality of family relationships rather than with the legal and residential nature of the relationship. The quantity and quality of these relationships need to be measured directly.

Direct effects of economic deprivation on children are emphasized in the classical opportunity and strain theories of crime and deviance (Merton 1938; Cloward and Ohlin 1960; Messner and Rosenfeld 1993). The effects of economic deprivation can be indirect as well as direct, involving not only the loss of income-related opportunities that the imprisoned parent may have provided, but also the input that parent may have made to family life more generally (McLanahan and Bumpass 1988).

In terms of human and social capital, remaining single parents simply may have less money and time to invest in their children (McLanahan and Sandefur 1994). In turn, older children may have to assume unexpected role responsibilities, for example, caring for younger children, and they may also be diverted from school and into early or unplanned labor force participation in order to reduce demands on or to supplement household income. Alternatively, these youth may be pushed toward the underground economy and its criminal activities, or toward early marriage and parenthood as means of escaping the disrupted family of origin (Hagan and Wheaton 1993).

However, it must also be acknowledged that there is an alternative possible strain theory of the effects of parental imprisonment on children, and this theory makes opposite predictions from the perspective just noted. This version of strain theory begins from the awareness that imprisonment is sometimes a means by which families encourage the court to remove a parent who has "burned through" the supportive capacity of the family, often as a result of idleness or negligence, and sometimes through violence and abuse (see Simon 1993). Such a parent is a drain or threat rather than an asset to the family.

This second version of strain theory is quite different from the first in that imprisonment is seen as a potential source of relief from difficulties associated with the removed parent. This version of strain theory underlines the importance of knowing the prior relationship between an offender and his family that predates imprisonment. It is possible that both versions of strain theory operate, and that in the aggregate they cancel one another's effects. However, we hypothesize that it is more likely imprisonment is harmful to children even in dysfunctional families, because imprisonment will more often compound than mitigate preexisting family problems. Furthermore, once the parent is removed from the household, the quality of the alternative care arrangements for the children may be inadequate, further compounding the trauma of separation. This possibility is developed further in the discussion of the socialization and stigmatization perspectives that follow.

B. The Socialization Perspective

Again assuming the imprisoned parent previously contributed positively to the life of the family, imprisonment can deprive the family of an important resource for the socialization of the child. Sociological and criminological theories commonly emphasize the importance of parental supervision, role models, and support in the childhood socialization process. This perspective is reflected most prominently in control theories of crime and deviance. The most prominent version of control theory maintains that even parents and siblings who are oriented to criminal activities can often steer younger family members in prosocial directions (Hirschi 1969). The most important contemporary application of control theory in the study of crime is the longitudinal research of Sampson and Laub (1993), which emphasizes that the so-cial control of children by parents is an important source of social capi-tal that persists in its influence throughout the life course (also Hagan and Parker 1997).

The loss of a parent from the family can influence children in a vari-ety of ways. The impact may involve not only the loss of the supervi-sion, support, and role model of the absent parent, but also the in-creased salience of the remaining parent, for example, as a model of single parenthood, and through a strengthening of the role of peers (McLanahan and Bumpass 1988). Control and socialization theories tend to see children as situated in a struggle of allegiances between family and peers, with the absence of a parent shifting the balance of this struggle in favor of antisocial peers. That the parent is absent for crime-related reasons may reasonably intensify this concern although, as noted above, it remains an unresolved question how different kinds of criminal parents actually influence their children.

C. The Stigmatization Perspective

Criminologists have paid particular attention to the theoretical im-plications of imprisonment as a form of stigma that attaches to individ-uals and the groups to which they belong, in this case including most notably their families. The stigma of criminalization is another source of the depletion of the social capital of children (Hagan and Palloni 1990; Hagan 1991). Braithwaite (1989) draws an important distinction between the kind of stigma imposed by imprisonment and alternative processes of "reintegrative shaming." While the stigma of imprison-ment is intended to result in exclusion from the social group, reinte-grative shaming includes rituals of reacceptance and reabsorption that are designed to encourage resumption of life in the group. Well-func-tioning families are prominent sites of reintegrative shaming, but Braithwaite's point is that this kind of response to antisocial behaviors can be adopted in broader societal settings as well.

Historically, the development of probation and parole was intended to offer the prospect of reintegration to criminal offenders as alterna-tives to the stigma of imprisonment (Rothman 1980); but this use of probation and parole is less common today than it was in the past (Si-mon 1993). In the absence of efforts to encourage reacceptance and reabsorption, the stigma of imprisonment risks not only making par-ents into outlaws, but their children as well. The processes by which this may occur are only beginning to be understood.

Scheff and Retzinger (1991) suggest that the kind of stigmatization experience that Braithwaite associates with imprisonment can cause angry and defiant responses involving feelings of unacknowledged shame and rejection. These feelings and responses to stigmatization may affect not only the parents who are imprisoned, but also their children. Scheff writes of such experiences that "when there is a real and/or imagined rejection . . . the deference-emotion system may show a malign form, a chain reaction of shame and anger" (Scheff 1988, p. 397).

Scheff and Retzinger go on to note that schools, parents, employers, and fellow citizens increasingly recognize large numbers of highly "touchy," angry young people ready to punish any available target in response to perceived insults of the past, which may include the stigmatization experienced as children of incarcerated parents (1991, p. 65). In developing a defiance theory of criminal sanctions, Sherman suggests that "a great deal of evidence suggests that the best name for this proud and angry emotion—and the retaliation it causes against vicarious victims—is defiance" (1993, p. 459).

The emotions that can surround a traumatic experience such as the imprisonment of a parent can be linked into sequential analyses of stressful life events and turning points and transitions in the life course (Hagan and McCarthy 1997a, 1997b). From this perspective, the imprisonment of a parent represents one kind of event that can combine with other adverse life experiences in influencing longer-term life outcomes. For example, Rutter discusses chains of adversity in the life cycle (see also Caspi and Elder 1988) and suggests that "the impact of some factor in childhood may lie less in the immediate behavioral change it brings about than in the fact that it sets in motion a chain reaction in which one 'bad' thing leads to another" (Rutter 1989, p. 27). Rutter further observes that "antisocial behavior . . . will influence later environments through the societal responses it induces— such as custodial or correctional actions that may serve both to 'label' and to strengthen antisocial peer group influences" (1989, p. 42).

Peggy Thoits similarly points to multiplicative processes that can compound additive effects of stressful life events. She observes that "a person who has experienced one event may react with even more distress to a second . . . ; to the person, life might seem to be spiraling out of control. This would produce [an] . . . interaction between event occurrences; two or more events would result in more distress than would be expected from the simple sum of their singular effects"

(Thoits 1983, p. 69). Thoits goes on to describe a vulnerability model in which early stressful events set the foundation for adverse reactions to subsequent events. In this model, "predispositions are remote, enduring physiological and psychological characteristics that . . . enhance . . . the impacts of current life experiences" (1983, p. 80). The stigma of having a parent incarcerated is a likely candidate for inclusion in such a vulnerability model.

D. The Selection Perspective

Finally, it is crucial that the above perspectives be assessed in relation to what we have called the selection perspective. This perspective assumes that imprisoned parents and their children are already different from parents and their children who are not imprisoned, prior to the imposition of a prison sentence. The likelihood that this is the case is reflected in the commission of and conviction for the crime that leads to incarceration.

Note that differences that predate parental incarceration may derive from a mixture of genetic and social factors that accumulate up to the point of parental imprisonment. These factors may include patterns of negligence, violence, and abuse noted in the alternative version of strain theory discussed above. It is crucial that these predetermining differences be taken into account in assessing effects of parental imprisonment. As noted at earlier points in our discussion, these predetermining differences may often interact with responses to them, such as imprisonment. It is fair to say that we know little about the additive or multiplicative ways in which parental imprisonment may be causally linked to changes in the well-being of children. We lack full answers even to the basic question whether in the aggregate the children of imprisoned parents are less well off than children of parents who do not experience imprisonment.

Assuming an absence of good answers, we should ask: Are the children of imprisoned children also less well off than children of parents who do not experience imprisonment and who have similar background characteristics, including prior family relationships, race, gender, income, and education? And if so, would children of imprisoned parents do better if their parents were given a noncustodial sentence? Finally, can we further specify kinds of children and circumstances that combine with imprisonment to produce the most and least harmful effects on children? In particular, it is likely important to know whether the consequences of incarcerating mothers and fathers differ, and whether this varies according to the sole or combined role they play in supporting and caring for their children. These questions become progressively more challenging to answer, yet they are questions that judges regularly encounter in making sentencing decisions involving parents.

We have now introduced the major theoretical perspectives that can inform our thinking about the effects of imprisoning parents on children. These effects occur within the larger context of the extent to which imprisonment is used as a criminal sanction. Before further considering the effects of imprisonment it is important to establish just how extensive our reliance on incarceration has become in the United States, and how its effects may be felt outside as well as inside the family.

II. Calculating Costs and Consequences

From the outset we must acknowledge that it is a challenging task to establish exact trends in American imprisonment for use as a baseline in assessing the collateral consequences of incarceration. Most developed countries have more centralized systems of imprisonment than the United States. In the United States less serious and unconvicted offenders frequently are kept in local jails, making it difficult to be sure just how many Americans are incarcerated at any given time.

Despite this difficulty, the Bureau of Justice Statistics offers a regular report of the number of prisoners under the jurisdiction of federal or state correctional authorities. These data indicate that at year-end 1997, the U.S. incarceration rate was 645 persons in jail or prison per 100,000 residents (Bureau of Justice Statistics 1998b). Cross-national comparisons reveal that U.S. incarceration rates are far higher than those of other industrial democracies, whose rates are in the range of 55–130 per 100,000 of population (Mauer 1997). Moreover, the U.S. rate of incarceration has grown at a decade long rate of about 7 percent a year, more than doubling the 1985 figure of 744,208, so that in 1997 there were about 1.7 million Americans in jail and prison (Bureau of Justice Statistics 1997, 1998b). At this rate of growth, the American incarcerated population will easily exceed two million by the millennium.

Incarceration rates have not varied in clear or close connection to crime rates. Although the consensus of criminologists is that less serious crimes such as theft and burglary are difficult if not impossible to count accurately, there nonetheless is some evidence from the National Crime Victimization Survey that theft and burglary began to de-

crease in the late 1970s, about five years after imprisonment rates
started their sharp ascent; police statistics indicate that property crimes
actually increased during these years (Maguire and Pastore 1997;
Rand, Lynch, and Cantor 1997). Meanwhile, the victim survey data indicate that more serious violent crimes, which presumably are more
accurately reported, started to decline in the early 1980s, rose again
after 1986, and did not start to clearly decline again until the early to
middle 1990s, about twenty years after the spike upward in imprisonment; police data on violent victimization indicate a fairly similar pattern. Divergence between crime rates and incarceration rates is indicated by several studies based on official data and survey data (Bureau
of Justice Statistics 1998a; see also Lynch and Sabol 1997).

It is estimated that the cost of corrections in the U.S. is now about
$32 billion a year (Maguire and Pastore 1997). So if there is a deterrent
or incapacitative effect of incarceration in America, it is a product of a
huge and long-term investment. The number of beds in state and federal penitentiaries increased 41 percent to 976,000 in the first half of
this decade, while the number of correctional employees jumped 31
percent to 347,320 (Bureau of Justice Statistics 1997). This investment
is so extensive that several large states now spend as much or more
money to incarcerate young adults than to educate their college-age
citizens (Ambrosio and Schiraldi 1997). From the 1980s through the
late 1990s, corrections spending has grown at a faster rate than any
other state spending category, with state corrections budgets almost
tripling, increasing from $7 billion in 1986 to more than $20 billion
in 1996 (Eckl 1998, p. 30; see also Eckl 1994).

This growth in spending on prisons is almost certainly related to a
decline in growth of spending in other areas. California built about a
prison a year, every year, for the past two decades, while in the same
period it added only one new university (Ambrosio and Schiraldi
1997). The chancellor of the California State University System recently noted that his state is spending about $6,000 a year per college
student, compared to about $34,000 a year per prison inmate (cited in
Butterfield 1997). Similar trends are noted in other states, with the
budget for Florida's department of corrections increasing $450 million
between 1992 and 1994, an increase greater than Florida's university
system received in the ten previous years (Ambrosio and Schiraldi
1997). Overall, state corrections spending increased 1,200 percent between 1973 and 1993, while spending on higher education increased
only 419 percent (Ambrosio and Schiraldi 1997).

These data confirm that we are spending escalating amounts of money to combat a crime problem that may finally be in decline, for reasons that may or may not include the increased use of imprisonment. Citizens in some states are showing signs of reluctance to pay the escalating costs of prisons, in ways that bear some resemblance to earlier rebellions against rising costs of education. A recent survey in California indicates that, by a margin of five to one, Californians would prefer to invest in prevention than in incarceration (California Center for Health Improvement 1997). National surveys indicate that only 31 percent of the public favor an increase in taxes to build more prisons, while the percentage of those who think that too much is being spent on crime control is slowly creeping up from around 4 percent in the 1980s to 7 percent in 1996 (Maguire and Pastore 1997; see also Ambrosio and Schiraldi 1997). This suggestion of a modest but rising disenchantment with imprisonment probably results from the fact that trade-offs between imprisonment and education are becoming too dramatic to ignore (Arum 1997). A nascent awareness of these trade-offs is the beginning of a realization of the high collateral costs of relying on imprisonment as a response to problems of crime.

The dilemma is that given fiscal constraints on governments, when we invest in prisons we often in effect make choices to disinvest in other social institutions as well as in the individuals who would otherwise receive assistance from them (Chambliss 1994; Hagan 1994). The collateral costs of this disinvestment are social as well as economic, and they especially involve the communities and children from which and whom inmates are taken.

III. Collateral Costs in Human and Social Capital

We have pointed to a glaring cost in human capital that can result from increased spending on prisons: the withdrawal of money from educational institutions charged with the responsibility for building human capital through the transmission of knowledge and skills to students. The related concept of social capital is useful in extending our understanding to less tangible and often less directly measurable collateral costs of imprisonment.

Social capital results from membership in social networks or other social structures (Portes 1998, p. 6). Imprisonment can swiftly and irreparably alter the social networks and structures to which inmates, and those to whom they are connected, belong. When incarceration is a rare or infrequent event within a social group, the change in social networks caused by imprisonment may be mainly a problem for the individuals involved. However, when imprisonment becomes more common and widely expected in a social group, the changes in social networks and structures may often become damaging for the group more generally.

Moore (1991) illustrates the loss of social capital in communities by describing how Chicano gangs formed and reproduced in prison spill over in their effects on the street. This spillover occurs through communication back and forth between the prison and the street, and through the eventual return of imprisoned gang members to the community of origin. A result is that both while these gang members are in prison and when they return to the street, the community at large loses cohesion and capacity to be relied on in ways that characterized earlier periods. In this way and others, the social capital not only of individuals but also of entire communities is placed at risk (see Rose and Clear 1998). These radiating effects of the increased use of imprisonment have special significance for members of minority communities in America.

An important feature of the concept of social capital is its sensitivity to the differential access minority and nonminority youth have to opportunities as a result of social connections to other individuals through social structures, especially the family and work settings that form the framework of local communities (Loury 1977, 1992). Investments in prisons uniquely dissipate the limited social capital available to children who live in already disadvantaged communities, diverting and redirecting resources and opportunities away from these young people.

This regressive, redistributive process is observable at the macrolevel when comparisons are made between the communities from which prisoners typically come in America, and the locations of the new prison settings to which they go. Towns across America now compete as sites for new prison construction and the jobs they bring, much as towns for a longer period of time have vied with one another for automotive plants and other sources of new community investment (Nadel 1995). Prisons can bring a flow of new jobs to a community, and in this way increases in imprisonment are the resource base of a new growth industry in America (California Journal 1995; Lotke 1996; Swope 1998).

New structures of opportunity are built around the construction and operation of prisons, creating sources of economic and social capital in the host community, as old and new social networks become ports of entry into the new economy of the prison. Of course, the inmates of American prisons are taken in great disproportion from disadvantaged minority communities. Currently about half the prison inmates in the United States are African American (Bureau of Justice Statistics 1998*b*); considering the impact of incarceration for these inmates' families is especially important (King 1993). On any given day, it is estimated that nearly one in every three African-American males between twenty and twenty-nine years of age is on probation or parole or in jail or prison— that is, under supervision of the criminal justice system (Mauer and Huling 1995; Tonry 1995, tables 1–3).

Simon (1993) notes that criminal justice supervision is the most frequent exposure to government institutions for many if not most adults in American ghettos, a circumstance that amounts to "governing through crime" (Simon 1997). A reflection of the resulting salience of penal sanctions for these ghetto communities is that children in them are more likely to know someone who has been involved in the criminal justice system than to know someone who is employed in a profession, such as law or medicine (Case and Katz 1991).

Furthermore, some have argued that there has been a diffusion of prison culture to the street which has important ramifications for adolescents. For example, the style of dress popularized in the "hip hop" culture of baggy jeans and denim work shirts is a derivation from prison dress. This dissemination process may involve an anticipatory socialization of adolescents through gangs in the community for the culture of prisons, as illustrated in Vigil's (1988) ethnography of Chicano gangs in Chicago. This "prisonization" (also Moore 1996) of street life has extended beyond physical presentation, in the form of dress and appearance, to attitudes and behaviors. As large numbers of inmates return to their communities, so too does the prison subculture, which, Moore (1996, p. 73) cautions, may be "intensely hostile to established authority."

It is a cruel irony that when young minority males are taken from their communities and imprisoned, they become a novel resource in the investment/disinvestment equation that shifts resources from one location to another, disadvantaging the minority community to the relative advantage of another community, usually in a majority group setting (Clear 1996; Moore 1996). The potential input of new resources is well recognized in the communities that compete for new prisons (McDonald 1989, cited in Clear 1996). However, the social and economic consequences of the outflow of resources is not nearly so well understood in relation to the family and work environments that in better circumstances would serve as structural cornerstones in the minority communities from which inmates are taken (see Rose and Clear 1998).

A. Work, Families, and Imprisonment

The effects of incarceration on the family and community are entangled with the issue of employment. Offenders work in both the legal and illegal sectors of the economy. Their incarceration impinges not only on their families' finances—their removal also results in the loss of a working male from that community and may produce a concomitant rise in community instability. The short- and long-term negative effects of imprisonment on future earnings and employment are outlined in this section, with an emphasis on the finding that exoffenders confront a long-term reduced prospect of stable employment and adequate earnings over their life course. The impact of unstable employment and low earnings on the families and children of offenders, as well as on their communities, must therefore be considered.

Social scientists are only beginning to investigate seriously the dynamics of work in disadvantaged communities. As they do so, they are finding that these communities are far more complicated than is commonly assumed. An important insight into the complexity of these work environments has involved the realization that individuals often work simultaneously in both criminal and more conventional forms of employment (Hagedorn 1994; Sanchez-Jankowski 1995; Hagan and McCarthy 1997a). More than half of state prison inmates are found to be employed at the time of their arrest (Bureau of Justice Statistics 1993). The reality, Fagan and Freeman (1999) observe, is that "many offenders drift back and forth over time between legal and illegal work."

The overlapping nature of crime and work has important implications for our understanding of the collateral consequences of imprisonment for communities and families. These implications arise because offenders who are employed in more conventional work often contribute in positive ways to their communities and families. Added to this, it must be acknowledged that criminal activity also generates wealth, sometimes in the redistributive fashion of bringing income into a community from the outside, for example, through the cross-community drug trade.

Sullivan (1989) estimates that criminally active, working-age males in a minority neighborhood he studied generated about $12,000 of income in a given year. Sullivan emphasizes that this economic activity is a mixed benefit for disadvantaged communities, in that added unwanted behaviors may also be brought into the community; however, insofar as there is a net positive balance in the redistribution of resources, removal of these working age youth from the community is a collateral cost of imprisonment. Meanwhile, it is also important to keep in mind that most of those who are imprisoned will in any case ultimately return to the communities from which they come. For example, while possibly overstating the numbers, it is estimated that 80 percent of the inmates in one large New York City institution come from and return to just seven communities in New York City (Clines 1992). Meanwhile, between 1985 and 1992, 37 percent of all persons admitted into state prison in California were from Los Angeles County, which comprised only 12 percent of the state's total population; and the city of Baltimore contributed more than 50 percent of Maryland's prison admissions, but only 15 percent of the state's population (see also Lynch and Sabol 1997). Removing these individuals from their communities may typically be little more than a temporary measure.

It also bears emphasis that removing youth from their positions in the legal and illegal economy can have a negative kind of churning effect in working class labor markets, increasing community instability. This effect partly operates through a queuing process involving vacancy chains for demand-driven illegal work (Hagan 1993). For example, since the demand for drugs does not cease with the removal of a runner or even a dealer from the drug trade, when one criminal is removed from this economic chain, another new participant will usually take over the vacant role (Blumstein 1993).

The vacancy chain model may be a more common pattern in the drug economy than in sectors of the legal economy, where jobs are more likely to be left unfilled and where employers may simply conclude that it is impossible to find sufficiently durable employees to continue doing business. This is one part of a process that Wilson (1996) captures in the title of his book, *When Work Disappears*. Many minority ghettos in America have lost the workforce that is necessary to sustain viable labor market activity. Illegal work is often most of what remains, a situation Anderson (1990) illuminates in his description of the minority drug trade as the American ghetto's version of an employment agency.

The further impact of imprisonment on many minority youth and their families and communities becomes apparent in recent studies which consider the later life employment records of former prison inmates (Freeman 1992; Sampson and Laub 1993; Laub and Sampson 1995; Needels 1996). These studies make the point that imprisonment is a part of a process through which minority males in particular become embedded in social networks of crime that lead away from opportunities for legal work (Hagan 1993; Sampson and Laub 1993). At the same time that imprisonment weakens links into legal employment for these youth, the effect of the prison inmate culture is to strengthen their connection into gangs and the criminal underworld more generally (Hunt et al. 1993; Moore 1996).

The problem is that legal and illegal forms of work each create their own chainlike possibilities for further engagement and activity. Granovetter (1974) has made this point about legal jobs, noting that it is often the first job that establishes a mobility ladder within the same and adjoining occupational networks. The chances of moving onward and upward in a labor market increase as a function of learning and being exposed to the new opportunities that employment in a work sector brings. Unfortunately, this is no less true of illegal work than it is of legal employment, and as individuals become involved in one or the other kind of setting, it is opportunities within that sector that are enhanced (Hagan 1993; Hagan and McCarthy 1997*a*). Imprisonment can be a particularly consequential event in this kind of employment history. A number of studies now confirm that as time spent in prison increases, net of other background factors and involvements, the subsequent likelihood of disengagement from the legal economy increases. This is not surprising given that even those who do not have criminal records have difficulty finding employment. Hagan (1991), using data from a thirteen-year panel study, and Grogger (1995), analyzing arrest data from the California Justice Department's Adult Criminal Justice Statistical System and earnings records from the California Employment Development Department, have demonstrated that even being charged and arrested are detrimental in the near term for occupational outcomes and earnings.

Conviction and imprisonment have also been established to have a more permanent effect on legal earnings (Freeman 1992; Sampson and Laub 1993). For example, Freeman's (1992, p. 220) analysis of the Boston Youth Survey indicated that youths who were incarcerated had "exceptionally" low chances of employment; similarly, his analysis

(1992, p. 217) of the National Longitudinal Survey of Youth revealed that men who had been in jail or on probation experienced "massive long-term effects on employment." Sampson and Laub (1993) found that unstable employment and higher likelihoods of welfare dependency characterized the lives of the delinquent boys in the Gluecks's prospective sample of five hundred delinquents and five hundred non-delinquents. Moreover, juvenile incarceration was found to have an indirect effect on the incidence of future crime, because "incarceration appears to cut off opportunities and prospects for stable employment . . . [and] . . . job stability in turn has importance in explaining later crime" (Laub and Sampson 1995, p. 256). Other data indicate that while more than half of state prisoners are employed before going to jail, only about one-fifth of those on parole are employed following imprisonment (Irwin and Austin 1994). The long-term individual, family, and community repercussions of imprisonment for employability and earnings deserve further consideration.

We have now considered a range of research suggesting the kinds of effects imprisonment has on work, families, and communities in general, providing a background for our consideration, more specifically of the effects this imprisonment may have through parents on their children.

B. The Children of Imprisoned Parents

It should not come as a surprise that the presence of parents in U.S. prison populations is growing, although relatively little attention has been given to this. This change is a result of the increasing reliance on incarceration as a criminal sanction described earlier in this essay, for women as well as men. A survey by the Bureau of Justice Statistics (1993) reveals that about two-thirds of incarcerated women and more than one-half of incarcerated men are parents of children under eighteen years of age. Recent estimates show that more than 1.5 million children have a parent who is incarcerated in the United States (Bloom 1993; Johnston 1995*b*, p. 62), and many more children will have a parent incarcerated during a period of their lives. This grim reality should be a major policy concern because the imprisonment of parents, as noted in the theories reviewed at the outset of this essay, can severely diminish the economic and social capital on which families and communities depend to raise children successfully (see Sampson 1992; Hagan 1994). Studies of the families of incarcerated parents indicate that the family left behind usually suffers financial difficulties (Bloom and

Steinhart 1993). The financial difficulties and loss of a parent precipitate a range of emotional and psychological problems that affect these children, including educational failures, aggression, depression, and withdrawal (see generally, Johnston 1995*b*). Especially in disadvantaged minority communities, the children of this prison generation form a high-risk link to the future.

Although relatively little attention has been given to the consequences of criminal sanctioning for families and children, much research has focused on recidivism rates among those who have been incarcerated (see, e.g., Clear et al. 1988) and on issues of deterrence and incapacitation more generally (see, e.g., Blumstein, Cohen, and Nagin 1978). The results of this research do not seem especially encouraging, and experts remain uncertain about the relationship between punishment policy and crime rates (Reiss and Roth 1993; Tonry 1995; Lynch and Sabol 1997; Blumstein 1998; Bureau of Justice Statistics 1998*a*). A disturbing possibility raised by this literature is that offenders may defy as often as they defer to criminal sanctions (Sherman 1993).

The massive spending on penal sanctioning can be placed in a broader and more meaningful context if it is considered in terms of the indirect effects these sanctions have on the children of incarcerated parents. As Phillips and Bloom (1998, p. 539) note, "by getting tough on crime, the United States has also gotten tough on children." While we have acknowledged that it is undoubtedly the case that some unknown number of families benefits from the elimination of a dangerous or burdensome parent's incarceration, it may more often be the case that a father or mother's imprisonment can be the final, lethal blow to an already weakened family structure (Adalist-Estrin 1994; Women's Prison Association 1995).

The growth in the imprisonment of both men and women implies consequences for children who lose a parent to the criminal justice system.

1. *Incarcerated Fathers.*   In 1991, it was estimated that male inmates were fathers of more than 770,00 children under age eighteen, and that about one-third of all incarcerated men with children had two or more children under age eighteen (Bureau of Justice Statistics 1993). The effects of imprisonment for men as economic actors was considered in some detail earlier, but their removal from social roles in their families and communities deserves further consideration. Many young males who are involved in crime bring legal as well as illegal income into the settings in which they live, and they may contribute in other ways to

these settings. For example, even when they are not resident in their children's homes, these fathers may often contribute not only income but also child care and social support to the resident parent (Bureau of Justice Statistics 1993; Hairston 1998).

Although the literature on nonresident fathers is not large, it is suggestive (Garfinkel, McLanahan, and Hanson 1998). The ethnographic work in this area indicates that nonresident minority fathers often make informal contributions to their children, for example, by buying toys and diapers or providing babysitting services, and in other ways demonstrating that paternity is significant to them, even when this role emphasizes emotional support and guidance more than economic responsibility (Furstenberg, Sherwood, and Sullivan 1992; Edin 1995).

Edin and Lein's (1997) intensive interviews with 379 low-income single mothers found that about one-third of the mothers on welfare and over 40 percent of the mothers who worked received cash support from a child's father. Furthermore, Decker and Van Winkle's (1996) ethnography of gang members found that all but one of the gang members who had children but did not live with them saw their children every day or nearly every day. Evidence of fathers' involvement with their children has also emerged from studies of incarcerated parents. A study of 188 fathers in a maximum-security prison in New York reported that over 74 percent of fathers lived with their child before they were incarcerated and 75 percent reported that they spent a lot of time with their children prior to their incarceration (Lanier 1993). Other studies suggest lower rates of residency with children prior to incarceration, in the area of 50 percent (Bureau of Justice Statistics 1993), but such studies often further indicate that these fathers contribute to the financial support of at least one of their children (Hairston 1995, 1998). Studies also suggest that incarcerated men with children usually wish to maintain their social status as fathers, indicating a desire to strengthen their parenting skills (Hairston 1989, 1998), expressing feelings of closeness with their children (Carlson and Cervera 1991), and expecting to live with their children after their release (Lanier 1991).

The imprisonment of a father who was residing with his family means that the family's status changes, at least temporarily, into a single parent family (Lowenstein 1986), and the impact on children of the loss of a father due to incarceration often mirrors the symptoms of children in single-parent families who have lost their fathers due to death or divorce (see, e.g., Moerk 1973; Lowenstein 1986). Often the family faces a new array of issues, such as financial instability, and the emotional and psychological impacts on the children and spouse due to this separation (Schneller 1975; Ferraro et al. 1983; Lowenstein 1986; Fishman 1990). Interviews with the families of fifty-eight men incarcerated in a maximum security institution in Arizona revealed that 92 percent of the families experienced financial problems due to the father's absence (Ferraro et al. 1983); similarly, interviews with small samples of women in the United States and in the United Kingdom highlight the severe financial strain faced by these families (Fishman 1990; Davis 1992). Girshik (1996, p. 59) reports that "besides losing the economic contribution of her husband, a wife may lose her job due to the stigma of being married to a prisoner." Studies also suggest that once a spouse is imprisoned, couples are more likely to divorce, meaning that the temporary separation may become permanent (Hairston 1991a; Girshik 1996). The problems faced by the remaining family members often endure, becoming long term and chronic.

A question that this emerging literature on nonresident fathers clearly must address is whether these parents are a positive influence when they are involved in their children's families. Garfinkel, McLanahan, and Hanson (1998, p. 8) answer this question affirmatively: "With respect to the mental health and problem behavior of nonresident fathers, the ethnographies suggest that while many young fathers have trouble holding a job and may even spend time in jail, most have something to offer their children. The overwhelming impression of these young men conveyed by the literature is one of immaturity and irresponsibility rather than pathology or dangerousness. Indeed many of the fathers who are not paying child support are maintaining contact with their children and are still involved with the mothers, although often intermittently."

The possibility that even nonresident and criminally active fathers are nonetheless net contributors to family and community life therefore at least requires serious research attention.

2. *Incarcerated Mothers.* The incarceration of mothers is becoming an increasingly important issue as greater numbers of women are being imprisoned. This section charts trends in the growth of women's imprisonment, and then highlights some of the major issues resulting from their incarceration, including the custodial arrangements for the child when the mother is removed from the home, the difficulties faced by the substitute parents, and the potential parenting problems faced by women on their release from state custody.

Women represent a small part of the prison population, still less than 10 percent, but this share is increasing as the relative growth of the female prison population is outpacing the proportionate growth of the male prison population (Bureau of Justice Statistics 1998*b*). A comparative sense of relative change in male and female imprisonment is reflected by the fact that between 1980 and 1993, the U.S. male prison population grew by about 200 percent, while the female prison population grew by more than 350 percent (Beck and Gilliard 1995). Incarceration more often is being used, for longer terms, and with declining prospects of parole, partly because federal sentencing guidelines in particular have reduced the discretion of judges to impose noncustodial sentences. These guidelines have especially increased the incarceration of women for economic offenses and drug crimes; between 1990 and 1996, the number of female inmates serving time for drug offenses grew by over 100 percent, compared to a 55 percent increase for men (Bureau of Justice Statistics 1998*b*). Sentencing guidelines leave judges reduced room for treating family responsibilities as a mitigating circumstance that encourages probation as an alternative to prison; although this affects fathers as well as mothers, it has resulted in bigger changes for mothers (Raeder 1995).

As a result, where women formerly were more likely to receive probation and short prison sentences than men, they are now more vulnerable to imprisonment (cf. Daly 1994). Chief Judge Julian Abele Cook, Jr., of the U.S. District Court in the eastern district of Michigan, illustrates this point by recounting his sentencing of a mother of two children who was pregnant with a third and sought lenient treatment based on her special circumstances (Cook 1995). This woman was minimally involved as a "coconspirator" in a drug sale. Judge Cook did not treat the parental responsibilities of the mother in the above case as extraordinary. He reasoned that "to grant (her) request would have the practical effect of establishing a precedent whereby the recent birth of a baby, coupled with the fear of being unable to identify an 'adequate' family member to care for the minor children, would form the basis for vacating a term of incarceration in favor of probation" (Cook 1995, p. 146). Since Judge Cook did not find these circumstances extraordinary, he concluded that he had to impose the prison sentence that the guidelines indicated. "I thought the guidelines gave me little, if any, choice," writes Judge Cook, "other than to impose incarceration—a penalty that, in all probability, I would not have imposed in the absence of the compelling language in the statute" (1995, p. 146).

Yet, there is also a more general belief in the literature on sentencing that women receive lenient treatment relative to men, and that they in particular are less vulnerable to incarceration (see Nagel and Johnson 1994). Furthermore, there are also suggestions that prosecutors offer more beneficial plea agreements to women than to men (Coughenour 1995, p. 142). However, there is better reason to believe that women received lenient treatment in the preguidelines era than now. That is, while judges may once have been inclined to restrict the use of incarceration with both men and women who had family responsibilities (Daly 1987), sentencing reforms and guidelines have made this less likely (Daly 1994). In the more recent era, judges seem to be leaning toward imposing the same standards on men and women by disregarding the greater responsibilities of women for children in families (Daly 1995). The result is that the number of mothers of children who are being incarcerated is growing. Judges (e.g., Wald 1995) and researchers (Newton, Glazer, and Blackwell 1995) increasingly express concern about this.

A particular concern is that this trend of increasing imprisonment of parents is building without an empirical base of knowledge about its collateral consequences for children. That a large number of parents are being imprisoned (McGowan and Blumenthal 1978) implies that there is a neglected class of young people whose lives are disrupted and damaged by their separation from imprisoned mothers and fathers (Bloom 1993). Especially, but not exclusively, when a mother is incarcerated it is often uncertain who will care for her children (Johnston 1995a). Because there are fewer prisons for women, women are at increased risk of being incarcerated at a greater distance from their children than are men. Coughenour (1995, p. 143) reports that due to the scarcity of federal prisons for women, an average female inmate is more than 160 miles farther from her family than a male inmate. Studies indicate that at least half the children of imprisoned mothers have either not seen or not visited their mothers since incarceration (Zalba 1964; Hairston 1991b; Bloom and Steinhart 1993; Bureau of Justice Statistics 1994). This low rate of contact may have further negative consequences given that the maintenance of strong family relationships during incarceration may lower recidivism rates, and that "on the whole, prison inmates with family ties during imprisonment do better on release than those without them" (Hairston 1991a, p. 99; see also Hale 1988; Couturier 1995).

A number of other important factors differentiate the experiences of incarcerated mothers from those of incarcerated fathers. Imprisoned mothers are more likely than imprisoned fathers to believe that their children are not happy (Koban 1983). Furthermore, since incarcerated mothers are more likely to be living with their children prior to their arrest than are incarcerated fathers, the incarceration of mothers puts their children at greater risk (Koban 1983). Single women are at increased risk of termination of their parental rights as a result of their incarceration (Smith and Elstein 1994, app. A; Genty 1995). Furthermore, the incarceration of a mother usually means that the child has to be removed from the home and placed with relatives or in foster care, with siblings sometimes being separated in order to accommodate the new arrangements (Stanton 1980; Koban 1983; Johnston 1995a). When children's mothers are incarcerated, their children are most likely to live with their grandparents and other relatives or friends rather than with their fathers (Raeder 1995, p. 159); a recent report indicates that half of the children of women inmates under the age of eighteen live with their grandparents (Bureau of Justice Statistics 1994), with a number of other studies corroborating this finding (Baunach 1985; LaPoint, Pickett, and Harris 1985; Hairston 1991b; Bloom and Steinhart 1993; Singer et al. 1995).

Yet, when fathers are incarcerated, their children usually remain living with their mothers, with less consequent disruption in the children's lives (Koban 1983; Hairston 1995). A recent survey indicates that while 90 percent of male inmates' children were living with the child's mother, only a quarter of the female inmates reported that the child lived with his or her father (Bureau of Justice Statistics 1993). Moreover, Koban's (1983, p. 178) research cautions that "women were disadvantaged by their dependency on an extended network of relatives, friends and social agencies for contact with their children while men could rely on the child's mother."

Meanwhile, substitute parents not only bear unexpected burdens, they also confront unique kinds of problems (see, e.g., Hungerford 1993; Barnhill 1996). In general, they are eligible for fewer benefits and receive less support than nonrelative caregivers (Phillips and Bloom 1998). One study reports that two-thirds of the caregivers to children of imprisoned mothers did not have the financial support needed to meet the necessary expenses of the child (Bloom and Steinhart 1993; see also Hungerford 1993). Furthermore, the quality of care received by the children while in caregivers' custody is unknown. While LaPoint, Pickett, and Harris (1985) report that 82 percent of the caregivers in their sample were rated as providing a high quality of care, Hungerford found that "in most cases, the caretakers are poorly educated and do not exhibit prosocial parenting skills in watching the children" (1993, p. 130). These disparate findings suggest that further studies should be undertaken in order to assess the quality of care received by the children of incarcerated parents.

Despite the separation from their children, and the relocation of their children to other households, studies indicate that the majority of imprisoned mothers expect to resume their parenting role and reside with their children after their release—even though it is uncertain what percentage of women actually do so (Koban 1983; Baunach 1985; Hairston 1991b; Bloom and Steinhart 1993). Katz (1998, p. 502) points out that resuming the parenting role may be difficult for women who have been in jail, since they "frequently do not provide the drug treatment or parenting classes most women must complete before they can reunify their families. Further, upon release, women often have difficulty finding services such as housing, employment or child care that would allow them to care for their children" (see also Smith and Elstein 1994, pp. 272–80). The same holds true for women in prison. Based on a study of women in prisons, Baunach (1985) cautions that the loss of imprisoned mothers' daily contact with their children and the subsequent loss of parental skills is coupled with feelings of inadequacy regarding their parental authority. This often makes the desire of these mothers for reunion with their children shortly after release an unrealistic goal. Finally, although many women's families received state support prior to their incarceration, on their release they face even more serious financial difficulties in trying to support their families, with many unable to find employment (Stanton 1980). As Browne (1989, p. 219) concludes, incarcerated mothers "are a group at risk for future parental difficulties."

The effects of imprisonment on children therefore may last far beyond their parents' incarceration. This brings us, then, to the perhaps key research question to be asked: What is the impact of the imprisonment of parents on children?

C. Prior Studies of the Children of Imprisoned Parents

Despite the theories with which this essay began, relatively little is actually known about the causal role that the penal sanctioning of parents plays in children's lives, alone or in combination with other experiences and events in the lives of these children (Gabel 1992). For example, little is known about how this causal influence may vary with the prior and continuing relationship between the parents, the race and gender of the parents, the prior and continuing relationships of parents with their children, the gender or age of the children, and the class and community circumstances from which the imprisoned parents and children come. Nonetheless, there is speculation that the consequences of imprisoning parents can be substantial, especially when mothers are involved: "The children of women in prison have a greater tendency to exhibit many of the problems that generally accompany parental absence including: low self-esteem, impaired achievement motivation and poor peer relations. In addition, these children contend with feelings like anxiety, shame, sadness, grief, social isolation and guilt. The children will often withdraw and regress developmentally, exhibiting behaviors of younger children, like bedwetting. . . . As the children reach adolescence, they may begin to act out in anti-social ways. Searching for attention, pre-teens and teens are at high risk for delinquency, drug addiction and gang involvement" (Women's Prison Association 1995, p. 9).

However, there have been relatively few studies of prisoners' families, and very few studies that examine the children of prisoners specifically (but see, e.g., Hungerford 1993; Johnston 1995b), even though research in this area began early in this century. The first of these studies focused on the financial troubles and adjustments of these families, which were found to be severe (Bloodgood 1928; Sacks 1938; see also Morris 1965; Ferraro et al. 1983). Gabel (1992) identifies several other themes in the evolution of this research literature as it relates to children, including the deception and trauma surrounding the separation from the imprisoned parent, caretaking problems, stigma, and antisocial behavior (see also Bakker, Morris, and Janus 1978; Fritsch and Burkhead 1981; Swan 1981; Lowenstein 1986). Perhaps the best known of this work is done by Sack and colleagues, who studied clinical and nonclinical samples of the children of incarcerated parents (Sack, Seidler, and Thomas 1976; Sack 1977). Sack's (1977) clinical observations of six families in which the father was imprisoned revealed that the children were preoccupied with the loss of their fathers and had a pervading sense of sadness; many suffered from separation anxiety. Sack (1977) also noted that the change in family dynamics led in some cases to rebelliousness in the child, manifested by truancy and problems at school.

A more recent study by Kampfner compared children of incarcerated mothers to a control group of children from similar high-risk backgrounds whose mothers were not in prison. Significant differences between the samples were found, with the children of imprisoned mothers reporting long-term recall of the trauma of separation from their mothers; these children were also more likely to report an absence of emotional support: "They could not identify people who might be sources of support, and they felt that they had no one with whom they could talk about their mothers" (1995, p. 94). Drawing on observations of fifty children who visited their mothers in prison, and interviews with a smaller subsample, Kampfner notes that a number of these children displayed several symptoms of posttraumatic stress disorder, namely: depression, feelings of anger and guilt, flashbacks about their mothers' crimes or arrests, and the experience of hearing their mothers' voices. Kampfner (1995, p. 97) concludes that "the traumas that these children experience due to an early separation from their primary caregiver and the difficult life that follows impact their mental health." A further study of incarcerated mothers by Hungerford (1993) found that the effects of parental incarceration on children varied by age and gender; it was especially the older children who suffered from fatalism and feelings of helplessness, and the male children were likely to mask their feelings of depression through aggression and violence.

A number of studies, based on indirect parental reports of their children's behavior and direct contact with children of incarcerated parents, also have documented adverse effects due to parental incarceration. These studies report negative outcomes, including a range of behavioral problems (Fritsch and Burkhead 1981; LaPoint, Pickett, and Harris 1985; Lowenstein 1986; Bloom and Steinhart 1993); school-related difficulties (Stanton 1980; Fishman 1990; Bloom and Steinhart 1993; Hungerford 1993; Kampfner 1995); depression (Shaw 1992; Hungerford 1993; Kampfner 1995); low self-esteem (Stanton 1980); aggressive behavior (Sack 1977; Baunach 1985); and general emotional dysfunction (Lowenstein 1986; Fishman 1990).

A further finding of special concern involves the intergenerational transmission of risks of imprisonment. Johnston (1995b, p. 84) reports that "parental crime, arrests, and incarceration interfere with the ability of children to successfully master developmental tasks and to overcome the effects of enduring trauma, parent-child separation, and an inadequate quality of care. The combination of these effects produces serious long-term outcomes, including intergenerational incarceration." One study suggests that children of incarcerated parents may be six times more likely than their counterparts to become incarcerated (Barnhill and Dressel 1991, as cited in Moses 1995; see also Johnston 1995*b*, p. 67). In Hungerford's (1993) sample of children of incarcerated mothers, 40 percent of the boys aged twelve to seventeen were delinquent, while the rate of teenage pregnancy among female children was 60 percent. Finally, the Survey of Youth in Custody conducted by the Bureau of Justice Statistics (1988) found that more than half of all the juveniles and young adults studied reported a family member who had served time in jail or prison, with 25 percent reporting that their father had been incarcerated some time in the past.

The intergenerational relationship of parental incarceration and youth crime is explored in Hagan and Palloni's (1990) reanalysis of London panel data. Drawing on the stigmatization theory introduced early in this essay, Hagan and Palloni (1990, p. 292) report that "there is an intergenerational interaction effect of the labeling of parents and sons on subsequent delinquent and criminal behavior." The stigmatizing effects of parental incarceration need to be more fully explored (see also, Lowenstein 1986; Johnston 1995*b*, p. 83; Rowe and Farrington 1997).

The ways in which parental imprisonment can affect children are probably as varied as the range of parental influences on delinquency. The research literature identifies numerous family factors that affect juvenile delinquency. Thus Loeber and Stouthamer-Loeber's (1986) comprehensive meta-analysis of these factors indicates that lack of parental involvement with their children, lax parental supervision, parental rejection, unstable parental marital relationships, and parental criminality are consistent predictors of juvenile conduct problems and delinquency; weaker predictors include parental discipline style, parental health, and parental absence. Furthermore, as Larzelere and Patterson (1990) demonstrate, quality of parenting can mediate the effects of family socioeconomic status on adolescent delinquency, with poor parental monitoring and discipline style related to increased delinquency in thirteen-year-old boys. Even the simple presence or absence of parents may be related to rates of delinquency. Harper and McLanahan's (1998) longitudinal study of 6,300 males between the ages of fourteen and twenty-two found that the absence of fathers doubled the odds of a boy's future incarceration, net of parental education, family income, urban residence, race, and being born to a teen mother. In sum, these findings highlight the importance of parental involvement in children's lives and the negative consequences of poor parenting. The implication is that relations between imprisonment and these aspects of parenting should be systematically considered in future research.

Finally, a few studies suggest that the adverse effects of parental incarceration on children may vary depending on whether it is the mother or father who is removed from the household (Koban 1983). When mothers are incarcerated, children often are relocated to another home, and in such instances the loss of a parent results in the loss of the child's primary parental figure. One study comparing the effects of the loss of a mother to the loss of a father found that while male and female prisoners reported the same number of problems per child, the type of problems differed (Fritsch and Burkhead 1981). Fathers reported discipline-related problems, such as drug and alcohol use and school truancy, while mothers noted that their children "withdrew" as a result of their incarceration, crying a lot, daydreaming, and suffering academically.

The effects of imprisonment on children can be especially apparent in the transition from adolescence to adulthood (see generally Thornberry 1997; Jessor 1998). Elijah Anderson (1990) emphasizes that the presence of "old heads" in the traditional black community has been integral to the successful transition to adulthood, for both boys and girls; yet, with the increase in community instability due to crime and unemployment, the positive influence of "old heads" has declined as both they and the adolescents have disengaged from mentoring relationships. Drawing from the more general literature on the transition from adolescence to adulthood, it would seem that variation in the well-being of the children of imprisoned parents may include not only involvement in delinquency and crime (Sampson and Laub 1997), but also educational failure, precocious sexuality, premature departures from home, early childbearing and marriage, and idleness linked to joblessness (Anderson 1990; Hagan and McCarthy 1997; Matsueda and Heimer 1997; Graber, Brooks-Gunn, and Galen 1998). In addition, the signs of such impending problems should be apparent earlier in life (Matsueda and Heimer 1997). The higher-risk prospects of the children of imprisoned parents are likely to be anticipated in earlier behaviors during childhood (see, e.g., Johnston 1995b). The following section outlines a research agenda that can address this range of possibilities and concerns.

IV. Requirements of a Meaningful Research Design

Granting the significance of the questions thus far raised with regard to the well-being of the children of imprisoned parents, and lacking research to answer these questions more systematically, it may be useful to suggest some of the parameters of the further work that needs to be initiated. Ideally, in answering the questions set out above, one might imagine a research design in which parents were randomly assigned to prison and noncustodial sentences in a social experiment that allowed a clear indication of the causal effects of imprisonment on the children of the incarcerated parents. However, criminal statutes, sentencing guidelines, and ethical prohibitions make this kind of social experiment uncommon and unlikely. The moral and policy imperatives of the criminal justice system strongly discourage randomly sending some convicted offenders to prison, while others are selected randomly for more lenient noncustodial treatment. In place of a randomized experimental design, the research that can best inform us about the effects of parental imprisonment on children will need to address a number of concerns, some of which go beyond the common requirements associated with nonexperimental designs.

First, this research will want to address the impact of parental imprisonment on children of various ages, from childhood through adolescence. This is a challenging requirement, since children confront quite different problems at different ages and stages, and this makes it more difficult to design a common measurement strategy for the children of imprisoned parents included in the research.

Second, the research will need to include guardians and step-parents as well as resident and nonresident biological parents. Essentially, the problem is one of representing the full variety of imprisoned and unimprisoned parents who participate in children's lives. Over time and across families and communities, this variety is extensive.

Third, the research should include parents who receive noncustodial as well as prison sentences, so that it is possible to make comparisons of outcomes with parents who are as much as possible like imprisoned parents, except for the incarceration experience.

Fourth, the research will be more useful if it includes the possibility of panel measurement before and after the imprisonment of a parent, to allow the near-term assessment of effects of parental imprisonment, along with the added possibility of future tracing of the involved children to determine longer-term outcomes during their transitions to adulthood.

Fifth, the research needs to incorporate comprehensive and detailed measurement of background differences between imprisoned and unimprisoned families and their children, so that it is possible to perform an analysis that takes into account the ways in which these two groups of families vary from one another prior to the imprisonment of a parent.

Most of the above requirements are connected to the need to control for prior background differences in family circumstances associated with the imprisonment of parents. Parents who are imprisoned probably are more likely previously to have left their families and to have difficulties with the remaining parent and children in these families, including problems of violence and conflict; these families may also be more likely to have added social and economic problems prior to imprisonment. Several features of an effective research design can address this issue.

First, we can make extensive use of statistical controls for differences prior to sentencing between children of parents sentenced to prison and to noncustodial sentences. This information can be obtained from unofficial surveys and official police and court sources. For example, presentence report interviews with parents who are both imprisoned and unimprisoned offer useful opportunities for cross-validation and multiple measurement of family background differences. Differences in the well-being of children of imprisoned parents that withstand these statistical controls for preexisting differences are more likely to be attributable to the effects of imprisonment.

Second, statistical models that combine information on the decision about which offenders are sent to prison, with outcome measures of the well-being of involved children, can establish further information on the boundaries of the possible added influence of unmeasured differences between the families of parents who do and do not experience imprisonment (Manski et al. 1992). These estimates can add confidence to our knowledge of the likely range of the impact of parental imprisonment on the well-being of involved children.

Third, measures of well-being gathered on the same children after sentencing of their parents to prison can be analyzed in relation to the same measures before sentencing to assess changes over time and in response to the sentence imposed. This analysis of change can take advantage of the fact that the same children of the same family backgrounds are involved, in effect using the subjects as their own controls for background differences, so that the analysis of within child variation is a control for these differences.

Fourth, information gathered over time in panel interviews with the unsentenced parents after sentencing can be used to explore the sources of change in family circumstances and childhood experiences that might explain differences in outcomes that persist in the above models. For example, the economic strain perspective outlined above proposes that changes in the financial resources of families who have had a parent imprisoned will explain declines in the well-being of children. Such changes in financial resources can be measured over time in the panel interviews, and these measured changes can be introduced into the analyses to determine whether this variation accounts for differences in child well-being.

Fifth, it will be useful to include added data on pairs of siblings with the same parents in the research design. This can be done simply by asking interviewed parents to provide data on more than one of their children. Since siblings of the same parents can vary, for example, in gender and age, while sharing a common family history, differences in their well-being after sentencing can be attributed to causes other than pure family selection (see Hauser and Mossel 1985).

A. Measuring Gender Specific Antisocial Behavior of Children and Adolescents

One challenge in researching effects of parental imprisonment on children will involve implementing a unified measurement scheme for identifying problems that parental imprisonment may cause from childhood through adolescence. Over the longer term we expect that these problems may be especially apparent as youth make the transition to adulthood, as they fail and withdraw from school, abandon their families of origin, enter into early parenthood and marriage, and encounter problems of joblessness. However, the antecedents of these problematic outcomes should be apparent earlier in the life cycle, and research on the effects of parental imprisonment will be more compelling if we can identify the precursors of these later outcomes. Parents or parent substitutes living with these children are an important source of information about their early problems, especially as approaching difficulties are signaled in common problem behaviors. These problems may further vary by gender, and our measurement tools should therefore be broad enough to capture these differences.

One effective way to tap this information about the problems of children could build on the use of a child behavior checklist of the kind designed by Achenbach and Edelbrock (1979) for use with parents and teachers. Designs that include both parent and teacher measures will be more compelling in providing multiple sources of measurement.

Since many criminological researchers may be unfamiliar with the child behavior checklist, we provide a brief introduction here.

The checklist items refer to specific syndromes of problem behaviors. Lizotte et al. (1992) indicate that these reported behaviors load onto nine narrow-band behavior problem scales, which in turn are divided into three broad dimensions that are designated as externalizing scales—aggressive, delinquent, and hyperactive; internalizing scales—immature, obsessive-compulsive, schizoid, somatic complaints, and uncommunicative; and a mixed scale—hostile-withdrawal. The checklist is often used as a diagnostic tool to identify children who fall at the behavioral extremes on these scales and are of clinical concern, and the externalizing scales noted above have recently been demonstrated by Lizotte et al. (1992) to be highly predictive of involvement in delinquency, as indicated in widely used self-report scales of delinquency.

An attractive feature of the checklist's inclusion of externalizing and internalizing scales is the likelihood that this can capture variation not only across ages, but also in the possibly different responses of girls and boys to the imprisonment of a parent. There is a tendency in the kind of research we are proposing to concentrate on the effects of parental absence on boys. McLanahan and Sandefur note the tendency to adopt this view in research on the effects of single parenthood on children, but they also emphasize that the effects are often just as significant for girls, although manifested in different ways. They note that "boys tend to express their feelings by acting out, whereas girls tend to hide their feelings inside" (1994, p. 56). Use of behavioral measures like the Achenbach Checklist can provide a test of this possibility, thus broadening the opportunities to consider the specific consequences of mother and father absence due to imprisonment on sons and daughters.

B. Losing Generations

Although most Americans may have come to accept that high levels of imprisonment are an unchangeable cost of living in our society, they might be less inclined to do so if more was known about the collateral and unanticipated costs of imprisonment, especially for the children of incarcerated parents. The implication of not having better and more systematic research on the collateral effects of imprisonment is that we are making penal policy in a less than fully, indeed poorly, informed fashion. Neglecting to initiate and sustain systematic research on the effects of imprisoning parents on children is the metaphorical equivalent of making penal policy blindfolded. We have considered some of the less direct but still highly consequential costs of imprisonment, including the diversion and direction of funds for prisons away from schools and from minority communities, the damaging effects of imprisonment on employment prospects, and the detrimental impact of imprisoning parents on their children. The latter impact on a new generation of children is perhaps the least understood consequence of imprisonment. We have spelled out the kind of research that is required to establish more fully the consequences for children of a growing concentration of high levels of imprisonment on young minority men and women who are parents.

The "children of the prison generation" are coming of age in communities that are increasingly recognized as high-risk settings. A National Research Council (1993) report, *Losing Generations*, stresses that "high-risk settings do not just happen: they are the result of policies and choices that cumulatively determine whether families will have adequate incomes, whether neighborhoods will be safe or dangerous, whether schools will be capable of teaching, whether health care will be available—in short, whether young people will be helped or hindered while growing up" (1993, pp. vii–viii). Said slightly differently, the degree of risk that these communities present to young people is greatly influenced by the choices we make to invest government resources in various ways.

The decision to so extensively invest in and rely on imprisonment as a solution to crime problems has unnoticed costs and consequences that we are only beginning to understand. A better understanding of these costs, especially as these costs are imposed on the children of incarcerated parents, requires a far more systematic research base than we have yet established. This research requires before and after measures of parent and child attitudes and behaviors in panel designs that, ideally, will also include data collection from teachers, and from the young people themselves, as they become old enough to self-report their own experiences and activities. This research will be expensive, if it is to effectively meet all of the needs outlined above, and this work may therefore require partnerships between government and foundation funding sources. Yet it also must be noted that this investment is actually very small relative to the current risks and costs of America's reliance on imprisonment as the increasingly common sanction of choice.

It is not at all clear that this increased use of imprisonment has reduced levels of risk in endangered communities. Indeed, consideration of collateral consequences of imprisonment suggests that these risks

have increased. It is almost certainly the case that within the most endangered minority communities the perception of risk, especially for
young people, has increased. There is great need for research that addresses these perceptions and the questions they raise.

REFERENCES

Achenbach, T. M., and C. S. Edelbrock. 1979. "The Child Behavior Profile:
    II. Boys Aged 12–16 and Girls Aged 6–11 and 12–16." *Journal of Consulting
    and Clinical Psychology* 47:223–33.
Adalist-Estrin, Ann. 1994. "Family Support and Criminal Justice." In *Putting
    Families First: America's Family Support Movement and the Challenge of Change*,
    edited by S. L. Kagan and B. Weissbourd. San Francisco: Jossey-Bass.
Ambrosio, Tara-Jen, and Vincent Schiraldi. 1997. "From Classrooms to Cell
    Blocks: A National Perspective." Washington, D.C.: Justice Policy Institute.
Anderson, Elijah. 1990. *Street Wise: Race, Class and Change in an Urban Com-
    munity*. Chicago: University of Chicago Press.
Arum, Richard. 1997. "Schools or Prisons? The Effects of High School Edu-
    cation on the Risk of Incarceration." Essay presented at the American So-
    ciological Association Meeting, Toronto, August.
Bakker, L. J., B. A. Morris, and L. M. Janus. 1978. "Hidden Victims of
    Crime." *Social Work* 23:143–48.
Barnhill, Sandra. 1996. "Three Generations at Risk: Imprisoned Women,
    Their Children, and Grandmother Caregivers." *Generations* 20:39–40.
Baunach, Phyllis Jo. 1985. *Mothers in Prison*. New Brunswick, N.J.: Transac-
    tion Books.
Beck, Allen J., and Darrell Gilliard. 1995. *Prisoners in 1994*. Washington, D.C.:
    U.S. Department of Justice, Bureau of Justice Statistics.
Bloodgood, R. 1928. "Welfare of Prisoners' Families in Kentucky." Publica-
    tion no. 182. Washington, D.C.: U.S. Department of Labor, Children's Bu-
    reau.
Bloom, Barbara. 1993. "Why Punish the Children? A Reappraisal of the Chil-
    dren of Incarcerated Mothers in America." *IARCA Journal* 6:14–17.
Bloom, Barbara, and David Steinhart. 1993. *Why Punish the Children? A Reap-
    praisal of the Children of Incarcerated Mothers in America*. San Francisco: Na-
    tional Council on Crime and Delinquency.
Blumstein, Alfred. 1993. "Making Rationality Relevant." *Criminology* 31:1–16.
———. 1998. "U.S. Criminal Justice Conundrum: Rising Prison Populations
    and Stable Crime Rates." *Crime and Delinquency* 44:127–35.
Blumstein, Alfred, Jacqueline Cohen, and Daniel Nagin, eds. 1978. *Deterrence
    and Incapacitation: Estimating the Effects of Criminal Sanctions on Crime Rates*.
    Washington, D.C.: National Academy of Sciences.

Braithwaite, John. 1989. *Crime, Shame, and Reintegration*. Melbourne: Cambridge University Press.

Browne, Dorothy. 1989. "Incarcerated Mothers and Parenting." *Journal of Family Violence* 4:211–21.

Bureau of Justice Statistics. 1988. *Survey of Youth in Custody, 1987*. Washington, D.C.: U.S. Department of Justice, Bureau of Justice Statistics.

———. 1993. *Survey of State Prison Inmates, 1991*. Washington, D.C.: U.S. Department of Justice, Bureau of Justice Statistics.

———. 1994. *Women in Prison: Survey of State Prison Inmates, 1991*. Washington, D.C.: U.S. Department of Justice, Bureau of Justice Statistics.

———. 1997. *Census of State and Federal Correctional Facilities*. Washington, D.C.: U.S. Department of Justice, Bureau of Justice Statistics.

———. 1998*a*. *Crime and Justice in the United States and in England and Wales, 1981–96*. Washington, D.C.: U.S. Department of Justice, Bureau of Justice Statistics.

———. 1998*b*. *Prisoners in 1997*. Washington, D.C.: U.S. Department of Justice, Bureau of Justice Statistics.

Butterfield, Fox. 1997. "Crime Keeps on Falling, but Prisons Keep on Filling." *New York Times* (September 28), sec. 4, p. 1.

California Center for Health Improvement. 1997. "Invest in Kids—Californians Support New Approach to Prevent Youth Violence." Sacramento: California Center for Health Improvement.

California Journal. 1995. "The Prison Industrial Complex." (October 1).

Carlson, Bonnie, and Neil Cervera. 1991. "Inmates and Their Families." *Criminal Justice and Behavior* 18:318–31.

Case, A. C., and L. F. Katz. 1991. *The Company You Keep: The Effects of Family and Neighborhood on Disadvantaged Youths*. Cambridge, Mass: National Bureau of Economic Research.

Caspi, A., and Glen Elder. 1988. "Emergent Family Patterns: The Intergenerational Construction of Problem Behaviors and Relationships." In *Relationships within Families: Mutual Influences*, edited by R. A. Hinde and J. Stevenson-Hinde. Oxford: Clarendon.

Chambliss, William J. 1994. "Policing the Ghetto Underclass: The Politics of Law and Law Enforcement." *Social Problems* 41:177–94.

Clear, T. R., C. A. Shapiro, S. Flynn, and E. Chayet. 1988. *Final Report of the Probation Development Project*. New Brunswick, N.J.: Rutgers University Program Resources Center.

Clear, Todd. 1996. "Backfire: When Incarceration Increases Crime." In *The Unintended Consequences of Incarceration*, commissioned by the Vera Institute of Justice. New York: Vera Institute of Justice.

Clines, Francis X. 1992. "Ex-Inmates Urge Return to Areas of Crime to Help." *New York Times* (December 23), p. A1.

Cloward, Richard, and Lloyd Ohlin. 1960. *Delinquency and Opportunity: A Theory of Delinquent Gangs*. New York: Free Press.

Coleman, James S. 1990. *Foundations of Social Theory*. Cambridge, Mass.: Harvard University Press.

Cook, Jr., Julian Abele. 1995. "Family Responsibility." *Federal Sentencing Reporter* 8:145–47.

Coughenour, John C. 1995. "Separate and Unequal: Women in the Federal Criminal Justice System." *Federal Sentencing Reporter* 8:142–44.

Couturier, Lance C. 1995. "Inmates Benefit from Family Services Programs." *Corrections Today* 57:102–7.

Daly, Kathleen. 1987. "Discrimination in the Criminal Courts: Family, Gender, and the Problem of Equal Treatment." *Social Forces* 66:152–75.

———. 1994. *Gender, Crime, and Punishment.* New Haven, Conn.: Yale University Press.

———. 1995. "Gender and Sentencing: What We Know and Don't Know from Empirical Research." *Federal Sentencing Reporter* 8:163–68.

Davis, Ann. 1992. "Men's Imprisonment: The Financial Cost to Women and Children." In *Prisoners' Children: What Are the Issues?* edited by R. Shaw. London: Routledge.

Decker, Scott H., and Barrik Van Winkle. 1996. *Life in the Gang: Family, Friends and Violence.* New York: Cambridge University Press.

Eckl, Corina. 1994. "Playing Hardball with Criminals." *State Legislatures* 20:14–19.

———. 1998. "The Cost of Corrections." *State Legislatures* 24:30–33.

Edin, Kathryn. 1995. "Single Mothers and Child Support: The Possibilities and Limits of Child Support Policy." *Children and Youth Services Review* 17:203–30.

Edin, Kathryn, and Laura Lein. 1997. "Work, Welfare, and Single Mothers' Economic Survival Strategies." *American Sociological Review* 62:253–66.

Fagan, Jeffrey, and Richard B. Freeman. 1999. "Crime and Work." In *Crime and Justice: A Review of Research,* vol. 25, edited by Michael Tonry. Chicago: University of Chicago Press.

Ferraro, K., J. Johnson, S. Jorgensen, and F. G. Bolton. 1983. "Problems of Prisoners' Families: The Hidden Costs of Imprisonment." *Journal of Family Issues* 4:575–91.

Fishman, Laura T. 1990. *Women at the Wall: A Study of Prisoners' Wives Doing Time on the Outside.* Albany, N.Y.: SUNY Press.

Freeman, Richard. 1992 . "Crime and the Economic Status of Disadvantaged Young Men." In *Urban Labor Markets and Job Opportunities,* edited by George Peterson and Wayne Vroman. Washington, D.C.: Urban Institute Press.

Fritsch, T. A., and J. D. Burkhead. 1981. "Behavioral Reactions of Children to Parental Absence due to Imprisonment." *Family Relations* 30:83–88.

Furstenberg, Frank, Kay Sherwood, and Mercer Sullivan. 1992. *Caring and Pain: What Fathers and Mothers Say about Child Support.* New York: Manpower Demonstration Research Corporation.

Gabel, Stewart. 1992. "Behavioral Problems in Some of Incarcerated or Otherwise Absent Fathers: The Issue of Separation." *Family Process* 31:303–14.

Garfinkel, Irwin, Sara McLanahan, and Thomas L. Hanson. 1998. "A Patchwork Portrait of Nonresident Fathers." Working Paper no. 98–25. Princeton, N.J.: Princeton University.

Genty, Philip M. 1995. "Termination of Parental Rights among Prisoners." In *Children of Incarcerated Parents*, edited by K. Gable and D. Johnston. New York: Lexington Books.

Girshik, Lori B. 1996. *Soledad Women: Wives of Prisoners Speak Out.* Westport, Conn.: Praeger.

Graber, Julia A., Jeanne Brooks-Gunn, and Britt R. Galen. 1998. "Betwixt and Between: Sexuality in the Context of Adolescent Transitions." In *New Perspectives on Adolescent Risk Behavior*, edited by R. Jessor. New York: Cambridge University Press.

Granovetter, Mark. 1974. *Getting a Job: A Study of Contacts and Careers.* Cambridge, Mass.: Harvard University Press.

Grogger, Jeffrey. 1995. "The Effects of Arrest on the Employment and Earnings of Young Men." *Quarterly Journal of Economics* 110:51–72.

Hagan, John. 1991. "Destiny and Drift: Subcultural Preferences, Status Attainments and the Risks and Rewards of Youth." *American Sociological Review* 56:567–82.

———. 1993. "The Social Embeddedness of Crime and Unemployment." *Criminology* 31:465–91.

———. 1994. *Crime and Disrepute.* Thousand Oaks, Calif.: Pine Forge Press.

Hagan, John, and Bill McCarthy. 1997*a*. *Mean Streets.* New York: Cambridge University Press.

———. 1997*b*. "Intergenerational Sanction Sequences and Trajectories of Street-Crime Amplification." In *Stress and Adversity over the Life Course*, edited by Ian H. Gotlib and Blair Wheaton. New York: Cambridge University Press.

Hagan, John, and Alberto Palloni. 1990. "The Social Reproduction of a Criminal Class in Working Class London, circa 1950–80." *American Journal of Sociology* 96:265–99.

Hagan, John, and Patricia Parker. 1997. "Rebellion in the Classroom: A Life Course Capitalization Theory of Intergenerational Delinquency Causation." Paper presented at the forty-ninth annual meeting of the American Society of Criminology, San Diego, November.

Hagan, John, and Blair Wheaton. 1993. "The Search for Adolescent Role Exits and the Transition to Adulthood." *Social Forces* 71:955–80.

Hagedorn, John. 1994. "Neighborhoods, Markets, and Gang Drug Organizations." *Journal of Research in Crime and Delinquency* 31:264–94.

Hairston, Creasie Finney. 1989. "Men in Prison: Family Characteristics and Parenting Views." *Journal of Offender Counseling, Services and Rehabilitation* 14:23–30.

———. 1991*a*. "Family Ties during Imprisonment: Important to Whom and for What?" *Journal of Sociology and Social Welfare* 18:87–104.

———. 1991*b*. "Mothers in Jail: Parent-Child Separation and Jail Visitation." *Affilia* 6:9–27.

———. 1995. "Fathers in Prison." In *Children of Incarcerated Parents*, edited by K. Gabel and D. Johnston. New York: Lexington Books.

———. 1998. "The Forgotten Parent: Understanding the Forces That Influence Incarcerated Fathers' Relationships with Their Children." *Child Welfare* 77:617–39.

Hale, Donna C. 1988. "The Impact of Mothers' Incarceration on the Family System: Research and Recommendations." *Marriage and Family Review* 12:143–54.

Harper, Cynthia C., and Sarah McLanahan. 1998. "Father Absence and Youth Crime." Paper presented at the annual meeting of the American Sociological Association, San Francisco, August.

Hauser, Robert, and Peter Mossel. 1985. "Fraternal Resemblance in Educational Attainment and Occupational Status." *American Journal of Sociology* 91:650–73.

Hirschi, Travis. 1969. *Causes of Delinquency.* Berkeley: University of California Press.

Hungerford, Gregory Patrick. 1993. "The Children of Inmate Mothers: An Exploratory Study of Children, Caretakers, and Inmate Mothers in Ohio." Ph.D. dissertation, Ohio State University, College of Social Work.

Hunt, Geoffrey, Stephanie Riegel, Thomas Morales, and Dan Waldorf. 1993. "Changes in Prison Culture: Prison Gangs and the Case of the 'Pepsi Generation.'" *Social Problems* 40:398–409.

Irwin, John, and James Austin. 1994. *It's about Time.* Belmont, Calif: Wadsworth.

Jessor, Richard, ed. 1998. *Adolescent Risk Behavior.* New York: Cambridge University Press.

Johnston, Denise. 1995*a*. "The Care and Placement of Prisoners' Children." In *Children of Incarcerated Parents*, edited by K. Gabel and D. Johnston. New York: Lexington Books.

———. 1995*b*. "Effects of Parental Incarceration." In *Children of Incarcerated Parents*, edited by K. Gabel and D. Johnston. New York: Lexington Books.

Kampfner, Christina Jose. 1995. "Post-traumatic Stress Reactions of Children of Imprisoned Mothers." In *Children of Incarcerated Parents*, edited by K. Gabel and D. Johnston. New York: Lexington Books.

Katz, Pamela Covington. 1998. "Supporting Families and Children of Mothers in Jail: An Integrated Child Welfare and Criminal Justice Strategy." *Child Welfare* 77:495–511.

King, Anthony. 1993. "The Impact of Incarceration on African American Families: Implications for Practice." *Families in Society: The Journal of Contemporary Human Services* 74:145–53.

Koban, Linda Abram. 1983. "Parents in Prison: A Comparative Analysis of the Effects of Incarceration on the Families of Men and Women." *Research in Law, Deviance and Social Control* 5:171–83.

Lanier, C. S. 1991. "Dimensions of Father-Child Interaction in a New York State Prison Population." *Journal of Offender Rehabilitation* 16:27–42.

———. 1993. "Affective States of Fathers in Prison." *Justice Quarterly* 10:49–66.

LaPoint, Velma, Marilyn Oliver Pickett, and Beverly Fairley Harris. 1985. "Enforced Family Separation: A Descriptive Analysis of Some Experiences of Children of Black Imprisoned Mothers." In *Beginnings: The Social and Affective Development of Black Children*, edited by M. B. Spencer, G. K. Brookins, and W. R. Allen. Hillsdale, N.J.: Erlbaum.

Larzelere, Robert E., and Gerald R. Patterson. 1990. "Parental Management: Mediator of the Effect of Socioeconomic Status on Early Delinquency." *Criminology* 28:301–23.

Laub, John H., and Robert J. Sampson. 1995. "The Long-Term Effect of Punitive Discipline." In *Coercion and Punishment in Long-Term Perspectives*, edited by J. McCord. New York: Cambridge University Press.

Lizotte, Alan, Deborah Chard-Wierschem, Rolf Loeber, and Susan Stern. 1992. "A Shortened Child Behavior Checklist for Delinquency Studies." *Journal of Quantitative Criminology* 8:233–45.

Loeber, Rolf, and Magda Stouthamer-Loeber. 1986. "Family Factors as Correlates and Predictors of Juvenile Conduct Problems and Delinquency." In *Crime and Justice: An Annual Review of Research*, vol. 7, edited by Michael Tonry and Norval Morris. Chicago: University of Chicago Press.

Lotke, Eric. 1996. "The Prison-Industrial Complex." *Multinational Monitor* (November), pp. 18–22.

Loury, G. 1977. "A Dynamic Theory of Racial Income Differences." In *Women, Minorities and Employment Discrimination*, edited by P. A. Wallace and A. LeMund. Lexington, Mass.: Lexington Books.

———. 1992. "The Economics of Discrimination: Getting to the Core of the Problem." *Harvard Journal for African American Public Policy* 1:91–110.

Lowenstein, Ariela. 1986. "Temporary Single Parenthood: The Case of Prisoners' Families." *Family Relations* 35:379–85.

Lynch, James P., and William J. Sabol. 1997. "Did Getting Tough on Crime Pay?" Washington, D.C.: Urban Institute.

Maguire, Kathleen, and Ann L. Pastore, eds. 1997. *Sourcebook of Criminal Justice Statistics, 1996*. Washington, D.C.: U.S. Department of Justice, Bureau of Justice Statistics. Available online at http://www.albany.edu/sourcebook.

Manski, Charles, Gary Sandefur, Sara McLanahan, and Daniel Powers. 1992. "Alternative Estimates of the Effect of Family Structure during Adolescence on High School Graduation." *Journal of the American Statistical Association* 87:23–37.

Matsueda, Ross L., and Karen Heimer. 1997. "A Symbolic Interactionist Theory of Role-Transitions, Role-Commitments, and Delinquency." In *Developmental Theories of Crime and Delinquency*, edited by T. P. Thornberry. New Brunswick, N.J.: Transaction.

Mauer, Marc. 1997. *Americans behind Bars: U.S. and International Use of Incarceration, 1995*. Washington, D.C.: Sentencing Project.

Mauer, Marc, and Tracy Huling. 1995. *Young Black Americans and the Criminal Justice System: Five Years Later*. Washington, D.C.: Sentencing Project.

McGowan, B. G., and K. C. Blumenthal. 1978. *Why Punish Children?* Washington, D.C.: National Council on Crime and Delinquency.

McLanahan, Sara, and Larry Bumpass. 1988. "Intergenerational Consequences of Family Disruption." *American Journal of Sociology* 94:130–52.

McLanahan, Sara, and Gary Sandefur. 1994. *Growing Up with a Single Parent: What Hurts, What Helps*. Cambridge, Mass.: Harvard University Press.

Merton, Robert. 1938. "Social Structure and Anomie." *American Sociological Review* 3:672–82.

Messner, Steven, and Richard Rosenfeld. 1993. *Crime and the American Dream.* Belmont, Calif.: Wadsworth.

Moerk, Ernst L. 1973. "Like Father Like Son: Imprisonment and the Psychological Adjustment of Sons." *Journal of Youth and Adolescence* 2:303–12.

Moore, Joan. 1991. *Going Down to the Barrio: Homeboys and Homegirls in Change.* Philadelphia: Temple University Press.

———. 1996. "Bearing the Burden: How Incarceration Policies Weaken Inner-City Communities." In *The Unintended Consequences of Incarceration,* commissioned by the Vera Institute of Justice. New York: Vera Institute of Justice.

Morris, Pauline. 1965. *Prisoners and Their Families.* London: Allen & Unwin.

Moses, Marilyn C. 1995. *Keeping Incarcerated Mothers and Their Daughters Together: Girl Scouts beyond Bars.* Washington, D.C.: U.S. Department of Justice, National Institute of Justice.

Nadel, Barbara A. 1995. "Prison Sightings." *Planning* 61:14–9.

Nagel, Ilene, and Barry Johnson. 1994. "The Role of Gender in a Structured Sentencing System: Equal Treatment, Policy Choices, and the Sentencing of Female Offenders under the United States Sentencing Guidelines." *Journal of Criminal Law and Criminology* 85:181–221.

National Research Council. 1993. *Losing Generations: Adolescents in High Risk Settings.* Washington, D.C.: National Academy Press.

Needels, Karen E. 1996. "Go Directly to Jail and Do Not Collect? A Long-Term Study of Recidivism, Employment, and Earnings Patterns among Prison Releasees." *Journal of Research in Crime and Delinquency* 33:471–96.

Newton, Phyllis J., Jill Glazer, and Kevin Blackwell. 1995. "Gender, Individuality, and the Federal Sentencing Guidelines." *Federal Sentencing Reporter* 8:148–53.

Phillips, Susan, and Barbara Bloom. 1998. "In Whose Best Interest? The Impact of Changing Public Policy on Relatives Caring for Children with Incarcerated Parents." *Child Welfare* 77:531–41.

Portes, Alejandro. 1998. "Social Capital: Its Origins and Applications in Modern Sociology." *Annual Review of Sociology* 24:1–24.

Raeder, Myrna S. 1995. "The Forgotten Offender: The Effect of the Sentencing Guidelines and Mandatory Minimums on Women and Their Children." *Federal Sentencing Reporter* 8:157–62.

Rand, Michael, James Lynch, and David Cantor. 1997. *Criminal Victimization, 1973–95.* Washington, D.C.: U.S. Department of Justice, Bureau of Justice Statistics.

Reiss, Jr., Albert J., and Jeffrey A. Roth, eds. 1993. *Understanding and Preventing Violence.* Washington, D.C.: National Academy Press.

Rose, Dina R., and Todd R. Clear. 1998. "Incarceration, Social Capital, and Crime: Implications for Social Disorganization Theory." *Criminology* 36:441–79.

Rothman, David. 1980. *Conscience and Convenience: The Asylum and Its Alternatives in Progressive America.* Boston: Little, Brown.

Rowe, David C., and David P. Farrington. 1997. "The Familial Transmission of Criminal Convictions." *Criminology* 35:177–201.

Rutter, Michael. 1989. "Pathways from Childhood to Adult Life." *Journal of Child Psychology and Psychiatry* 30:25–31.

Sack, W. H. 1977. "Children of Imprisoned Fathers." *Psychiatry* 40:163–74.

Sack, W. H., J. Seidler, and S. Thomas. 1976. "The Children of Imprisoned Parents: A Psychosocial Exploration." *American Journal of Orthopsychiatry* 46:618–28.

Sacks, J. 1938. "The Social and Economic Adjustments of the Families of a Selected Group of Imprisoned Felons." Master's thesis, American Catholic University, School of Social Work.

Sampson, Robert. 1992. "Family Management and Child Development: Insights from Social Disorganization Theory." *Advances in Criminological Theory* 3:63–93.

Sampson, Robert, and John Laub. 1993. *Crime in the Making*. Cambridge, Mass.: Harvard University Press.

———. 1997. "A Life-Course Theory of Cumulative Disadvantage and the Stability of Delinquency." In *Developmental Theories of Crime and Delinquency*, edited by T. P. Thornberry. New Brunswick, N.J.: Transaction.

Sanchez-Jankowski, Martin. 1995. "Ethnography, Inequality, and Crime in the Low-Income Community." In *Crime and Inequality*, edited by John Hagan and Ruth Peterson. Stanford, Calif.: Stanford University Press.

Scheff, Thomas. 1988. "Shame and Conformity: The Deference-Emotion System." *American Sociological Review* 53:395–406.

Scheff, Thomas, and Suzanne Retzinger. 1991. *Emotions and Violence: Shame and Rage in Destructive Conflicts*. Lexington, Mass.: Lexington Books.

Schneller, Donald P. 1975. "Prisoners' Families: A Study of Some Social and Psychological Effects of Incarceration on the Families of Negro Prisoners." *Criminology* 12:402–12.

Shaw, Roger. 1992. "Imprisoned Fathers and the Orphans of Justice." In *Prisoners' Children: What Are the Issues?* edited by R. Shaw. London: Routledge.

Sherman, Lawrence. 1993. "Defiance, Deterrence, and Irrelevance: A Theory of the Criminal Sanction." *Journal of Research in Crime and Delinquency* 30:445–73.

Simon, Jonathan. 1993. *Poor Discipline: Parole and the Social Control of the Underclass, 1890–1990*. Chicago: University of Chicago Press.

———. 1997. "Governing through Crime in a Democratic Society." Paper presented at the American Sociological Association meeting, Toronto, August.

Singer, Mark I., Janet Bussey, Li-Yu Song, and Lisa Lunghofer. 1995. "The Psychosocial Issues of Women Serving Time in Jail." *Social Work* 40:103–13.

Smith, Barbara E., and Sharon Goretsky Elstein. 1994. *Children on Hold: Improving the Response to Children Whose Parents Are Arrested and Incarcerated*. Washington, D.C.: American Bar Association, Center on Children and the Law.

Stanton, Ann M. 1980. *When Mothers Go to Jail*. Lexington, Mass.: Lexington Books.

Sullivan, Mercer. 1989. *Getting Paid: Youth Crime and Work in the Inner City*. Ithaca, N.Y.: Cornell University Press.

Swan, A. 1981. *Families of Black Prisoners: Survival and Progress.* Boston: G. K. Hill.

Swope, Christopher. 1998. "The Inmate Bazaar." *Governing Magazine* (October), p. 18.

Thoits, Peggy. 1983. "Dimensions of Life Events That Influence Psychological Distress: An Evaluation and Synthesis of the Literature." In *Psychosocial Distress: Trends in Theory and Research,* edited by Howard Kaplan. New York: Academic.

Thornberry, Terence P., ed. 1997. *Developmental Theories of Crime and Delinquency.* New Brunswick, N.J.: Transaction.

Tonry, Michael. 1995. *Malign Neglect—Race, Crime, and Punishment in America.* New York: Oxford University Press.

Vigil, James Diego. 1988. *Barrio Gangs: Street Life and Identity in Southern California.* Austin: University of Texas Press.

Wald, Patricia M. 1995. " 'What about the Kids?' Parenting Issues in Sentencing." *Federal Sentencing Reporter* 8:137–41.

Wilson, William J. 1996. *When Work Disappears: The World of the New Urban Poor.* New York: Knopf.

Women's Prison Association. 1995. *Breaking the Cycle of Despair: Children of Incarcerated Mothers.* New York: Women's Prison Association.

Zalba, S. 1964. *Women Prisoners and Their Families.* Sacramento: California Department of Social Welfare and Department of Corrections.

Chase Riveland

Prison Management Trends, 1975–2025

ABSTRACT

Prison administration in this country has changed dramatically in recent years. Twenty-five years ago, the warden was the overseer of an attempt to achieve reformation of character through isolation, hard work, and repentance. Today's superintendent must manage complex personnel systems, overcrowded institutions, and technological advances in a context of increased public and political scrutiny and close legal oversight. No one twenty-five years ago could have foreseen massive involvement of federal courts in prison oversight, rapid recent proliferation of private prisons, or politicization of criminal justice policy. The most important challenges for the next quarter century are probably as unforeseeable as were the most important in the past quarter century.

During the past twenty-five years, the administration of prisons in this country has changed considerably. The challenges presented by increasing numbers of people entering the nation's prisons and jails, increased use and criminalization of illegal drugs, privatization of prisons, politicization of crime, and advent of the "technology era" have profoundly influenced today's prison administrators, compared with those of the early 1970s. Prisons and prison systems are much larger today. Prisons are increasingly filling up with disproportionate numbers of minority inmates—particularly black and Hispanic inmates. Prison gangs have emerged with new power and influence in many jurisdictions, challenging the ability of prison administrators to control the prison environment.

This essay, drawing on my own experience administering prisons

Chase Riveland is former secretary of corrections in Washington State and Colorado.

and prison systems, and the views of seven nationally known correctional administrators, describes many of the changes in prison administration over the past one-quarter decade and explores some implications for the next quarter century.

As a former director of two state correctional agencies and a long-term employee of a third, I have lived through the evolution of prison administration over the past quarter century. My views were formed by experiences gained at specific times at those agencies. The recollections of other corrections officials are based on their "place and time" experiences. The next few paragraphs sketch the history of imprisonment in America. Much more detailed accounts can be found in *The Oxford History of the Prison* (Morris and Rothman 1995).

America's history with prisoners began in the early 1600s when England transported hundreds of "banished" convicts to the Virginia colonies, a practice that continued until the late 1700s. Early colonial punishments of criminals were similar to those long used by our European ancestors: public humiliation, whipping, branding, banishment, and hanging. Legal codes were dominantly constructed to reflect the religious principles of the time, particularly as articulated in Anglican traditions. Deviance was seen as an inherent part of human nature, and retribution and punishment the dominant goals in responding to those so judged.

In the 1800s, as America became larger, more complex, and more heterogeneous, many responsibilities previously handled by neighborhoods and communities became the province of the state. One of these was for dealing with those convicted of crimes. As structures were built to incarcerate those violating the laws of the time, the country began to develop its reliance on prisons as a primary response to crime. Early prisons in this country focused on improving the moral attributes of those incarcerated and also served as places for punishment. The assumption was that crime could be eliminated if offenders were isolated from bad influences, engaged in labor, and encouraged to repent.

The advent of the concept of penitentiaries in the early 1800s in several eastern states stressed isolation (generally known as the Pennsylvania system) and was generally based on Quaker principles of silent contemplation leading to penitence. This was followed somewhat later by the introduction of the New York or Auburn system in which inmates stayed in single cells at night but were placed with other inmates in workshops during the day. Discipline, however, was strict, with silence, the lockstep, tight control, and routine being a major part of the regimen.

The later 1800s experienced the rise of "reformatories" and with them the creation of indeterminate sentences, parole, and rehabilitative programs. Reformatories were built to house younger offenders, usually sixteen to twenty-three years old. Many eventually became adult prisons. Because of a recent trend to place younger and younger persons in adult correctional systems, some jurisdictions are again revisiting the concept of separate prisons for young inmates.

Reformatories became the core elements of "indeterminate sentencing," the ubiquitous system of sentencing and corrections in the United States from early in the twentieth century until the mid-1970s (Blumstein et al. 1983, chap. 3). These were followed in the early 1900s by what generally are referred to as "progressive reforms," which suggested that crime was caused by social and biological influences rather than moral deviancy and that each individual offender required a unique response (Rothman 1980). In the 1930s, the "medical model" began to emerge with its emphasis on diagnosis and treatment of each inmate during the period of incarceration.

During the 1940s and the 1950s, there were relatively minor changes in prison administration, but an influx of federal money beginning in the late 1960s (from the Law Enforcement Administration Act) encouraged a range of new programs, many highlighting the concept of prisoner reintegration.

The 1970s was a period in which the value of prisons and the "treatment" approaches that evolved with the medical model were questioned. Alternatives to incarceration and community programs were commonly stressed. The civil unrest during this era resulted in challenges to many prevalent attitudes and practices around issues of race relations, poverty, and the role and treatment of women. The influence on prison administration was also dramatic.

This article discusses the evolution of prison administration over the past twenty-five years in Section I. Section II draws on the experience of seven present or former correctional administrators, and my own, and reflects on the events, influences, and occurrences in prison administration over the past quarter of a century. Section III presents predictions about likely developments in prison administration between the present and the year 2025. Section IV offers concluding remarks.

I. Prison Administration: 1975–97

During the 1960s and the early 1970s the activism in our communities also entered our prison gates, radically altering the manner in which prisons would—indeed could—be managed. Civil rights and liberties litigation that was so successful in addressing the abuse of civil liberties in the communities became the tool to challenge the administration of prisons (Jacobs 1980). The action and authority of prison wardens and correctional administrators was repeatedly challenged across the country with the federal courts playing an expanding role in defining and redefining the rights of those who were incarcerated. The courts gave new definition to the right to due process in disciplinary actions, the right to the practice or observance of religion, the right to have and communicate with an attorney, and the right to sue without retaliation—among others. Many past practices were examined by the courts and in many instances eliminated or radically changed. Those of a corporal or harsh nature were particularly vulnerable.

During the mid- and late 1970s the major thrust in litigation shifted from challenges highlighting civil rights issues to challenges to overall conditions of confinement. The Attica prison riot of 1971 drew national attention to the issue of prison overcrowding and the conditions inside prisons. Although prison disturbances had occurred in other jurisdictions, none had been so deadly as Attica, nor so heavily covered by the media. The problems and forces that led to the Attica uprising also existed in many other prisons across the country. The Attica event caused public officials and prison administrators to take closer looks at conditions in their own institutions. The involvement of the federal courts in civil rights litigation in the 1960s and early 1970s became the instrument for challenging the conditions of the nation's prisons.

Many institutions—and sometimes entire correctional systems—found themselves operating under the directions, orders, and limitations of the federal courts. Many prison administrators at institutional and system levels found it easier and less costly to sign consent agreements or decrees than to resist litigation. By 1980, more than two-thirds of the states in the country had one or more prisons operating under some form of federal court oversight.

Correctional administrators, wardens, governors, and state legislators often resisted the assertion of authority over prisons by the courts. Correctional administrators often resented their loss of power, and elected officials resented the amount of money required to satisfy the courts' orders, or to fulfill the terms of a consent agreement. Prison administrators often found themselves in a dilemma. Although they resented the loss of power, they also found that they were the beneficiaries of more resources than they traditionally had had to operate their prisons. Indeed, they discovered that their institutions became safer and easier to run when overcrowding was mitigated, programs and work opportunities were expanded, health and mental health services were improved, and many other improvements occurred.

During the early and mid-1970s, several jurisdictions enacted "community corrections acts" based on the premise that certain types of offenders could best be managed and treated in the community from which they came. Community corrections also stressed reintegration into community settings of those released from prison. It was commonly believed that prisons should be reserved predominantly for violent offenders or chronic recidivists. That belief also generally incorporated the idea that money would be saved by avoiding the construction of costly institutions and that at least a portion of those savings could be directed to local levels to operate community programs.

Robert Martinson (1974), in his influential article summarizing findings of a comprehensive analysis of research on the effectiveness of correctional treatment programs (Lipton, Martinson, and Wilks 1975), was commonly understood to have concluded "nothing works" in reducing recidivism. As correctional budgets rose over the next twenty years, this "finding" became a mantra for many policy makers whose dominant desire was to save money.[1]

The late 1970s and early 1980s were a period in which many prisons and many correctional systems remained involved in litigation. Building new facilities was not uncommon, particularly in those jurisdictions required by the courts to relieve overcrowding in existing prisons. The rate of building during this period was modest, however, compared to that experienced in the late 1980s and the 1990s (Bureau of Justice Statistics 1997a).

Several jurisdictions in the mid-1970s began to replace indeterminate sentencing systems with determinate or presumptive systems. The general philosophical base for those supporting the determinate mod-

---

[1] The field of corrections is one of the few that measures itself by its failures—recidivism. Welfare reduction programs measure themselves by the number of people successfully placed in jobs, doctors by the number of patients successfully treated, etc. Corrections measures itself by the number of released inmates who fail to stay out of prison or the number of parolees and probationers who are revoked, etc.

els was that achievement of equity, parity, proportionality, and certainty would be enhanced by such an approach. Many of these systems also included mechanisms to attempt to match the number of persons being incarcerated to the available prison capacity (Tonry 1996, chaps. 1, 3).

In many of the early determinate or presumptive sentencing states, incarceration rates initially did recede, particularly in jurisdictions that experienced retroactive application of the new sentences to those inmates incarcerated under previous sentencing laws.

Crime rates during this time were at a record high and growing sharply, the nation's concern over a real or perceived sharp increase in illegal drugs was receiving political attention, and the demographic trends produced an unprecedentedly large proportion of the population in their high-crime ages of mid-teens through mid-twenties (Farrington 1986).

The constant media attention to crime and the recognition by elected officials that "tough on crime" was a lucrative—and possibly necessary—position to take led to passage of a growing number of laws during the 1980s and into the 1990s that required prison sentences for crimes previously sanctioned by nonincarcerative sentences, lengthened sentences for existing crimes, or both. Many prison systems bore the effects of legislative bodies enacting harsh penalties for the "crime of the year"—year after year. In the late 1980s and early 1990s, sentences were frequently enhanced accompanied by laws bearing such sound-bite titles as: "Three Strikes and You're Out" and "Hard Time for Armed Crime" (both initiatives originated in Washington state, but were replicated in many other jurisdictions). Many such laws greatly enhanced the length of sentences, in some instances requiring life in prison without parole. The general philosophy behind most sentencing changes in the late 1980s and 1990s has been to promote punishment and incapacitation (or arguably revenge) as the primary purposes for prison sentences.

The major driver of greatly increased prison populations across the country during this period was an increase in law enforcement attention to illegal drugs and related increases in sentence severity, particularly for crack cocaine offenses, although increased penalties for trafficking in other drugs and longer sentences for violent and sex offenders also occurred in most jurisdictions. The approach taken by most jurisdictions, including the federal government, was to imprison increasingly large numbers of persons arrested for possession, possession with intent to sell, or sale of drugs. Many sentences for drug crimes were made mandatory and frequently for much longer terms than had previously been the case.

The net effect of all of these influences has been a rapid increase in prison and jail populations at the federal, state, and local levels. Bureau of Justice Statistics figures for the period of 1985–95 reflect an increase of 590,952 prison inmates and 255,000 jail inmates, for an average annual increase of 8.3 percent in prison inmates and 7 percent in jail inmates (Bureau of Justice Statistics 1997*b*).

Massive construction projects have been the norm in most jurisdictions, although seldom at a rate capable of keeping up with prison population growth. Bureau of Justice Statistics data show that rated capacity of state correctional facilities rose by 40 percent between mid-1990 and mid-1995, while inmate populations rose 43 percent. The total number of state and federal correctional facilities increased by 17 percent. Facilities holding 2,500 inmates or more increased 108 percent; those holding between 1,000 and 2,500 inmates increased by 65 percent; and the number of maximum security facilities rose by 27 percent (Bureau of Justice Statistics 1997*b*).

Congress, intruding in an area (criminal justice and sentencing) that typically has been within the purview of state and local governments, committed billions of federal dollars (the 1995 Violent Offender/ Truth in Sentencing Act) to encourage states to expand their prisons or build new ones and to enact laws that mitigate inmate legal rights and remove resources for inmate education.

As prison populations in most jurisdictions have risen—so too have the proposed options to expensive prison construction. "Build cheaper," privatization, boot camps, chain gangs, and "take away privileges and amenities" have all had their proponents among elected officials.

Prisons have been viewed by communities in many jurisdictions across the country as a means of economic development. Some communities have built prisons, or encouraged private prison operators to build prisons, on the speculation that they would be able to find "customers" if they had an available facility. In most instances they have been correct. States facing overcrowded conditions ship prisoners to other jurisdictions hundreds and even thousands of miles away (examples included Alaska sending prisoners to a privately operated facility in Arizona, Wisconsin to a facility in Texas, and Hawaii sending prisoners to a private prison in New Mexico).

Overcrowding remains rampant in many prisons across the country, yet the litigation relief valve used so effectively during the late 1960s through the early 1990s has been weakened by the passage in Congress of the Prison Litigation Relief Act (Bronstein and Gainsborough 1996). The effects of this legislation remain to be seen.

Prison and correctional agency budgets are consuming increasingly larger portions of state general fund budgets (this also being true of most counties), in many states competing with other critical governmental services, such as education (National Conference of State Legislatures 1997). Recent media reports indicate that the higher education budget in the state of California has decreased by 3 percent over the last five years, while the state's corrections budget has increased by 60 percent. Similar patterns exist in other jurisdictions.

Prison administrators, whether superintendents or wardens at the institution level, or directors or commissioners at the state level, have been vulnerable to the same pressures, influences, trends, and fads as individuals and communities within our society. Economic, social, political, and legal trends in our communities generally have significant influences on prison administration.

As one example, the diseases that afflicted American communities during the past quarter decade have presented significant challenges to prison administrators. HIV-AIDS, tuberculosis, and hepatitis all required prison administrators to assume responsibility for identification, treatment, prevention, and control of these diseases—much as in the community. Prison administrators had also to deal with the issues of segregating these populations—or not; whether those with the disease should be identified to staff or prisoners; and fear on the part of inmates and staff of diseases and those afflicted by them.

From 1975 to present, the nation has gone through profound changes politically, economically, and socially. As the nation's priorities have changed, so have those of our prison administrators. They have had to adapt to the influences from "outside of the walls," often finding that those influences become concentrated problems when confronted in the prison setting.

II. Remembering Prison Administration: 1975–97

Different experiences, in different places, lead to different memories and observations. Seven respected correctional administrators who were active during some or all the time from 1975 to 1997 agreed to be interviewed regarding their observations on changes in prison administration during that time. All were directors or commissioners of a state or federal correctional agency. They are Norman Carlson, former director of the Federal Bureau of Prisons; Tom Coughlin, former director of the New York Department of Corrections; Joseph Lehman, secretary of the Washington State Department of Corrections; Kenneth McGinnis, former director of the Michigan Department of Corrections; James Spalding, director of the Idaho Department of Corrections; Reginald Wilkinson, director of the Ohio Department of Rehabilitation and Correction; and Frank Wood, former director of the Minnesota Department of Corrections. Many served as directors or commissioners in several jurisdictions, most served as superintendent or warden of a prison and held other correctional positions at various times. Each was asked the following questions regarding changes in prison administration from 1975 to 1997, and subsequently about the likely effects of the past on prison administration in coming years:

1. During the twenty-two years from 1975 to 1997, administration of prisons has changed dramatically. What major differences, based on your experience, do you see between administration of prisons today and in 1975?
2. Robert Martinson's article "What Works—Questions and Answers about Prison Reform" was published in 1974, calling into question the "rehabilitation model" of corrections. Do you feel that this affected prison administration? If so, how?
3. The United States incarceration rate doubled between 1979 and 1989. What effects has that trend had on prison administration?
4. What influences have affected prison administration as a result of judicial intervention from 1975 to the present?
5. Prevalence of illegal substances in prisons is reportedly much greater today than in 1975. What impact has that had on prison administration?
6. What other changes have you seen in prison administration during the past twenty-two years and what do you think created those changes?
7. Looking to 2025, what changes in prison administration do you foresee?
8. What influences do you think will have the greatest impact on prison administration in the future?

9. What effects do you expect the growing trend toward "privatization" to have on prison administration?
10. What other observations do you have?

A. During the Twenty-Two Years from 1975 to 1997, Administration of Prisons Has Changed Dramatically. What Major Differences, Based on Your Experience, Do You See between Administration of Prisons Today and in 1975?

Norman Carlson: "Much of the way we administer our prisons today is predicated on our reaction to the events at Attica in 1971. Prior to Attica most prisons were run similarly to the Auburn system. Attica alerted us to the fact that we now had a different composition of inmates and that their attitudes were different. We began to change the way we operated our prisons and paid attention to many things we had previously taken for granted. The second major difference between today's prison environment is the politicization of corrections. Elected officials have found corrections and prisons to be attractive, safe subjects to campaign on."

Tom Coughlin: "The experience in New York in 1975 was colored by Attica. Governor Carey and subsequently Governor Cuomo wanted to assure that nothing like Attica happened in New York again. From that point on we single-celled nearly all inmates, and had nearly full employment or school assignments. There is little institutional memory in New York today of Attica, neither in corrections nor among elected officials. This may not bode well for the future."

Joseph Lehman: "In the seventies institutions were closed entities. 'Out of sight-out of mind' was the norm. The internal focus was on the individual management of inmates, 'changing the offender,' and from the inmates' perspective 'doing your own time.' There was little interest or involvement by policy makers and little involvement or scrutiny on the part of the public. Abuses did take place in our prisons. During the late seventies and early eighties, the courts took over as the major influence in prison administration. In the 1990s the policy makers took over from the courts. One impact is that this makes prisons and how they operate more visible to the public and under regular scrutiny. Prison administrators today are—by necessity—more focused on broader policy issues."

Kenneth McGinnis: "Two major influences have occurred during this time frame. First, the intervention of the courts in the 1970s turned around how prisons and correctional systems were administered, this influence remaining strong into the mid-1980s. In some instances this was direct intervention on the part of the courts, in some instances simply the fear of their involvement. This brought about a remarkable improvement in the professionalism of correctional staff. It brought about significant changes in health care in prisons, due process, and most importantly, the accountability of prison administrators. Secondly, the legislative and media interest and involvement from the mid-eighties on has been a major change from the seventies. They had no interest before, now prisons are one of the hottest political topics."

James Spalding: "We went through serious periods of unrest in the seventies. The riots made us know that the old ways of doing things weren't working. Then the courts came in bringing the 'due process movement.' Other things began to change for prison administrators. The big industrial plants we used to run—such as making shoes and canning—were no longer profitable. We had to try to create jobs through small shops, such as small engine repair. We saw—as a result of the courts becoming involved— an improvement in classification, work programs, education, and health care. Stability was experienced from the mid-1980s on, but then overcrowding became a constant challenge again."

Reginald Wilkinson: "Today we are responsible for not only more—but a larger percentage of—taxpayers' dollars. The autonomy of corrections has diminished over the years. Wardens are no longer omnipotent administrators. Correctional staff are more professional and sophisticated. This has been necessary in order to survive. Wardens and correctional administrators are more policy oriented today than in the 1970s."

Frank Wood: "There is a lot in the day-to-day operations of individual prisons that hasn't changed that much. However, in the 1970s we experienced disturbances, homicides, and general unrest. All authority was being challenged. As a result of that there was a general attitude of wanting to reform the prisons—to make them better. They—the elected officials— listened to you. There was a receptive climate for resources. There was little demagoguery and many people felt that prisons weren't the only answer. Now we are faced with some people who are political opportunists who almost have a 'love affair' with prisons. Some do not mind distorting facts, in turn fueling the fears of the public. We have moved now from crowded prisons to overcrowded prisons in most parts of the country. This of course puts much greater stress on prison administrators. There are some people who not only want to incarcerate people, but then want to poke sticks at them while they're in. They think the job of being a correctional administrator is to make life miserable for inmates. There will be a reaction to all of this meanness."

In many ways prisons have come full circle from twenty-five years ago. As mentioned by several of the correctional administrators, the riot at Attica had profound effects on prison administration. It highlighted the negative effects that overcrowding, unfavorable conditions, racial imbalance, lack of meaningful activity, and apathy can have in a prison setting. It emphatically demonstrated that the civil rights movement of the 1960s was having a significant influence on the prison environment. At the time of the Attica riots, many prisons operated under substantially similar conditions.

As the courts entered the prison administration arena from the mid-1970s through the mid-1980s, setting new standards of acceptable physical and operational conditions (or in some cases describing nonacceptable conditions), conditions in many prisons across the country improved. Many jurisdictions made substantial improvements voluntarily in attempting to ward off the intrusion of the courts.

During this period, professional standards were developed and adopted by many jurisdictions and training of correctional staff improved. Policies and procedures were refined, and new management tools such as classification systems were developed or enhanced.

Today, however, many of the positive changes that have occurred in the nation's prisons during this quarter decade are in some jeopardy. According to Bureau of Justice Statistics data, prison populations between 1985 and 1995 alone grew 121.2 percent (from 487,593 to 1,078,545). This rapid growth in the number of people incarcerated has resulted in many American prisons being as overcrowded, or more, than in the 1970s (Bureau of Justice Statistics 1997*b*).

Idleness has long been a major threat to the orderly operation of prisons (it certainly was a contributing factor at Attica) and is a reality in many of our prisons today. Work and educational opportunities have frequently not kept pace with population growth, and in some instances have been intentionally reduced, most frequently due to the actions of legislative bodies. Access to courts previously available to inmates to challenge conditions of confinement has been limited by congressional passage of the Prison Litigation Reform Act, and in some jurisdictions by changes in state laws. Public sentiment and political rhetoric have often limited prison administrators' ability to manage overcrowded prisons in ways and with tools that sound professional judgment suggests are appropriate. Weights, televisions, and other "amenities" have been removed from prisons in many jurisdictions. Overcrowded prisons frequently have not been provided sufficient additional staff to handle the excess population. Some of the volatile conditions that existed in the 1970s exist today.

Many jurisdictions during the past quarter decade, having learned from Attica and the civil rights movement, paid close attention to the distinctive needs of minority inmates. "Black history clubs" and other ethnicity-based clubs appeared. Training for staff in relating to those of different ethnicity and cultures evolved. Segregation practices in many prisons were called into question. Greater attention was paid to the recruitment and hiring of minority staff.

The changes during that period were not only about race and ethnicity, but also about gender. Women, who traditionally held few jobs inside male prisons, have not only become a significant part of the custody work force in most jurisdictions, but increasingly represent larger percentages of all other positions—including administration. For example, in 1997, six of nine major institutions in the Washington State Department of Corrections were headed by female superintendents. The Bureau of Justice Statistics reported that the number of females on prison payrolls rose 60 percent between 1990 and 1995 alone (compared with 29 percent for males). Females made up nearly a third of all correctional staff by 1995 (Bureau of Justice Statistics 1997b).

The introduction of women into the internal operation of male prisons resulted in new challenges: some real, some perceived. Many questioned the ability of women correctional officers to meet the physical standards expected of correctional officers. The introduction of women into the work force in prison created staff-staff and staff-inmate relationship challenges to a degree not previously experienced. Sexual harassment issues in the workplace became quite common. The "male-exclusive" domain was no more. Most thoughtful prison administrators, however, believe that any real problems were heavily offset by creation of a more "normative" environment in the prison setting.

Gender also became more significant during the past quarter century in relation to the inmate population. Although remaining but a small percentage of total prison populations, the number of women in prisons in this country has risen significantly and faster than the increase in male prisoners. The Bureau of Justice Statistics reports that between 1985 and 1995 the incarceration rate for female inmates jumped from 17 per 100,000 to 48 per 100,000 (Bureau of Justice Statistics 1997*b*). There are several reasons for this increase. The use, possession, and sale of illegal drugs is not gender specific. Women have fallen victim to the increased number and lengths of drug-violation sentence enhancements at a rate greater than men. Jurisdictions that adopted presumptive or determinate sentencing de facto created gender neutrality in the sentencing of women committing the same crimes as men; since women in many jurisdictions typically received, all else being equal, less severe sentences than men, "equality" had the effect of making women's sentences harsher. The evolution of the women's movement and women's rights resulted in more women in the workplace, and therefore in more places where crime is committed, than was previously the case.

The increase in the number of incarcerated women was also accompanied by legal challenges across the country regarding the availability and comparability of programs and services available to women prisoners relative to those for men. This, of course, challenged (and challenges yet) prison administrators to devote "disproportionate" financial resources to women's prisons in order to satisfy the "parity" challenges. Despite the relatively greater increase in the number of women inmates, they constitute fewer than 7 percent of prisoners in 1997. The much larger number of men in prison permits economies of scale in programming and facilities that are often not possible in typically much smaller women's institutions.

It may well be that coming years will present some of the same challenges to prison administrators that were faced in the 1970s and 1980s. Are there things we learned during the past twenty-five years that we should remember?

B. *Robert Martinson's Article "What Works? Questions and Answers about Prison Reform" Was Published in 1974, Calling into Question the "Rehabilitation Model" of Corrections. Do You Feel That This Affected Prison Administration? If So, How?*

Norman Carlson: "It did have an impact on prison administrators. It suggested, as was also stated by other criminal justice authors of the day, that confinement goals and rehabilitation goals may inherently be in conflict. Quite honestly, many of us felt that many of the programs we had been providing were not working. It was, however, not intellectually wise to speak out and publicly question all we had been doing.

We did begin to ask more questions about how we were using our resources."

Tom Coughlin: "In a way I think he was right. The word rehabilitation assumes that the inmate was OK at some point in time and that he/she simply has to be returned to that status. I found few inmates that came from a healthy, normal background.

"We tried to focus on basic life skills, with a significant emphasis on reading and English skills. In prison administration we missed anticipating the cultural changes that would affect us in the 1970s which included a predominantly black population. We are now moving to a predominantly brown, and frequently non-English speaking, population. We should try to anticipate this cultural change in our prisons and be more thoughtful on what our responses to this change may be."

Joseph Lehman: "I think the impact was greater in community corrections than in prisons. It created a long-lasting erosion in programs. The impact continues on into the 1990s and gives further credence to the 'get tough' proponents. It supports widening the I/we gap. It does leverage the necessity of managing correctional systems today from a research base."

Kenneth McGinnis: "I think it did create a big shift initially from the medical model to the reintegration model. Then many of the reintegration programs were challenged by Willie Horton. Willie Horton brought corrections into the political arena in a big way. Any correctional program now continually asks: 'Do we have any Willie Hortons?'"

James Spalding: "Up to 1975 we weren't sure who was running the operation. Hundreds of volunteers were in and out of the institutions—inmates were given a great deal of freedom and latitude. We still haven't done a good job of looking at 'what works.' When we run programs without knowing if they work it causes expectations to run too high. We need to lower expectations. We have seen a reduction in programs due to the attitude that nothing works and because of that gap between expectations and results."

Reginald Wilkinson: "Actually, it was probably prophetic as to 'what works.' The American Correctional Association and National Governor's Association are now asking that same question. We need to invest in more research. There probably are things we are doing that don't work—but they are imbedded in our culture. We can't have rehabilitation or retribution individually, we need balance. Restoration is the new wrinkle."

Frank Wood: "Its major impact was a negative one. Some jurisdictions dismantled most of their programs as a result of what that study was interpreted to have said."

Several themes are offered by the prison administrators. First is the suggestion that prison administrators must move beyond the suggestion that "nothing works" to an agenda of finding out "what does work?" As flawed as Martinson's own research may have been, the field of corrections desperately is in need of evaluation and research that will allow for a better targeting of available resources. As funding of prisons and prison systems becomes strained, prison administrators are constantly being called on to justify existing programs and continually are searching for programs that can stand the test of cost-benefit analysis.

Unfortunately, policy makers and corrections professionals too frequently lock into a "one-size-fits-all" agenda. We suggest that education is the solution, when probably it is an intervention that will significantly affect a specific segment of the population but not other segments. The same is probably true of sex-offender treatment programs, vocational programs, substance abuse treatment programs, and cognitive programs. The field sorely needs research and evaluation that not only tells us "what works" but also "who it works on."

In the last few years a growing portion of the corrections community has begun a discussion of "what works," with numerous professional conferences adopting that phrase as a theme for their gatherings. Much of this trend has been related to the need to justify program expenditures on such things as education or drug treatment to politically elected funding bodies, or to attempt to resist the imposition by those same bodies of programs such as boot camps that professionals find questionable.

Generally missing from this type of discussion, at least in the political arena, is the need to have a significant amount of programming available in prisons—regardless of the rehabilitative value of the programming. Idle prisoners often become troublesome prisoners. No matter whether the programming is education, jobs, or other activities, a certain amount is essential to the safe and humane operation of a prison. If that programming can be targeted to the inmates whom it will most benefit, then resource expenditures and human benefit can be optimized.

Arguably, over the past twenty-five years, prison administrators often either chose or were forced to "throw the baby out with the bath water." The medical model suggesting that criminal behavior can be diagnosed and treated, although dated, still has applicability for populations of mentally ill offenders and offenders with addictions. These two populations have become a significant portion of today's prison populations due to the "deinstitutionalization" of mental health institutions and increased use of illegal substances.

The reintegration model, although set back by the saga of Willie Horton and other highly publicized cases, remains a desirable manner of prison release for a select number of inmates to maximize their potential of making the transition from prison to successful community life.

New programs adopted by many jurisdictions in recent years such as cognitive therapies, anger management, and substance abuse treatment show some promise, but still await validation by rigorous evaluations. There seems to be a lack of clarity even among corrections professionals concerning the premises that should guide execution of the various responsibilities that prisons are to fulfill. Even for those prison administrators who continue to value rehabilitation, burgeoning numbers of inmates combined with dwindling resources make the achievement of that goal increasingly unlikely.

C. The United States Incarceration Rate Doubled between 1979 and 1989. What Effects Has That Trend Had on Prison Administration?

Norman Carlson: "The enormous growth in our prison populations in the 1980s escalated and exasperated all the problems we had. It had a profound impact on us and the operation of our institutions. Probably the most serious impact was that our rates of violence went up in our prisons. With all of the crowding it made it more difficult to manage correctional institutions as safely as we would like to. Crowding creates unsafe situations for staff and inmates alike."

Tom Coughlin: "The initial impact was two-fold: First, how to build and secondly, what to build. Many prison and corrections administrators had little experience in building, certainly not in the volume that the numbers were requiring. The question then was what to build. New York began receiving large numbers of second time nonviolent felons. We didn't need maximum security prisons for them. We decided to build mostly medium security beds. We built over 45,000 of them over the next several years."

Joseph Lehman: "As populations in prisons increased—frequently resulting in overcrowding—resources began eroding. More emphasis was placed on security and control than on programming. Prison administrators at the institution and central office levels had to pay more attention to keeping the lid on—even as programs disappeared."

Tom McGinnis: "One impact is that it has made us better managers. The spiraling costs of corrections forced us to do things we didn't think we could do. We double bunked places we didn't think we could. We were pushed to levels of creativity and innovation that surpassed anything we had previously experienced. We became more businesslike and focused more on management. We paid more attention to how we handled our resources. This continues to be a focus for prison managers today."

James Spalding: "We simply—around the country—weren't ready for the increase in numbers. The continual increase in the number of inmates and constant overcrowding has been the largest problem since the mid-1980s. It has created the perception among corrections staff that things are worse than in the 1970s—even if they aren't."

Reginald Wilkinson: "It created an enormous impact on correctional budgets. Budgets doubled—then doubled again. By necessity we had to make our agencies and prisons much more businesslike. We began paying attention to things like benchmarking, quality improvement, and improving our image. Most of all the expectations for fiscal accountability rose significantly among legislators, governors, the public, and among corrections managers themselves."

Frank Wood: "It has been devastating. We have continued on a spiral of incarcerating people in this country who simply do not need to be in prison. It has forced us to spend time and resources trying to figure out how to manage large numbers of people rather than improving what we do with those that need to be or should be in prison."

The prison administrators discuss several things that have occurred as a result of the massive increase in the nation's prison populations. They mention overcrowding, increased violence in prisons, fiscal impact, major building programs, a requirement to manage in a more businesslike manner, and the imprisonment of people who do not need to be there.

The effects of these developments are probably felt to varying degrees by each jurisdiction in the country. Building new prisons and expanding existing ones generally has occurred only after existing prisons have become overcrowded. Billions of dollars have been spent by local, state, and federal correctional agencies in the construction of prisons—with major burdens of debt service and operating costs yet to come.

The private sector began finding a lucrative market for its facilities as many jurisdictions simply have not been able to maintain funding and construction schedules congruent with population increases (Harding 1998). Many governmental entities and private companies began building prisons on "spec," assuming that "if you build them, they will come." For the most part that old saying has proven to be true.

The fiscal effects of expanding and building prisons have not yet fully been felt. The long-term costs of operating the prisons will far exceed their capital costs, with many jurisdictions only recently beginning to realize the extent to which the original capital investment drives a significantly greater operating cost. Annual operating costs typically run $20,000–$30,000 per prisoner. Compared with typical construction costs of $50,000–$100,000 per bed, cumulative operating costs equal construction costs within a few years, and continue thereafter indefinitely. In many states the growth in corrections budgets has been the largest in percentage terms, or nearly the largest, of any component or agency in the state budget. The National Conference of State Legislatures reported estimated state spending for corrections (state systems) between Fiscal Years 1997 and 1998 was 5.1 percent. Nineteen states reported a greater than 10 percent increase, nine greater than 15 percent, and four greater than 20 percent (National Conference of State Legislatures 1997; Proband 1998).

With significant and continuing need for more money, prisons and corrections became more visible to legislative bodies, to governors, and to the media. Traditional justifications for resource needs were often no longer sufficient. Therefore the comments that prison administrators had to become more "business-like" in recent years are at least partly related to external demands by policy makers and chief executives to demonstrate and explain this significant consumption of fiscal resources in the operation of prisons. Certainly, the challenge presented by privatization of prisons added to this pressure to be "more like business."

Overcrowding has been experienced by nearly every prison system. Some have experienced only short-term overcrowding, others have been severely overcrowded for extended periods of time. Bureau of Justice Statistics data indicate that as of December 31, 1997, state prisons were operating between 15 percent and 24 percent above capacity, while federal prisons were operating at 119 percent of capacity (Bureau of Justice Statistics 1998).

Indeed, the definitions of "prison capacity" have undergone revision in many jurisdictions in the last ten years or so. For example, Washington State traditionally used the term "design capacity" to describe the optimal number of inmates that should be housed in a given prison. This was the number of prisoners a prison was intended to house when it was built. In the mid-1980s, as the prison population was growing quickly, the term "operational capacity" was used to describe the number of inmates a prison could hold considering cell size, program space available, environmental limitations, and other physical factors. Any population placed in a prison beyond the "operational capacity" was considered an emergency population. Professional standards, such as those issued by the American Correctional Association, also became more flexible to allow for crowded conditions. Existing prisons became larger as renovations and additions became a faster and frequently less costly way to achieve new capacity than building new prisons. New prisons being built frequently have been much larger than their predecessors. This general increase in prison size, although generally resulting in decreased per-inmate cost, may have unintended effects in the long run. The "depersonalization" (among staff as well as inmates) that results from very large prisons may prove an important and troubling unintended consequence.

One of the most difficult effects of this massive growth in incarceration to evaluate is its human impact. As larger numbers of our citizens experience imprisonment, what will the effects be on them, their families, and their communities? Will the allegiances and influences of prison gangs continue to have major influence after the inmate's release? Will the growing numbers of correctional staff become major lobbying groups or special interest groups at local, state, or federal levels? Will the disproportionate representation of minorities in our prison population result in future litigation or disturbances?

D. What Influences Have Affected Prison Administration as a Result of Judicial Intervention from 1975 to the Present?

Norman Carlson: "The courts spearheaded the positive changes that were made in prisons during those years. They forced legislative bodies at the state and federal levels to face up to the problems in the prisons. It forced administrators to try to anticipate what needed to be done. We tried to stay ahead of the curve and make changes before we were challenged in court."

Tom Coughlin: "Judicial intervention was never a major problem in New York state. Attica occurred before the period of intense judicial activism and it had a more profound effect on making changes in the system than the courts. Judicial intervention did obviously have a significant impact across the country. It was a major force in changing unacceptable correctional practices."

Joseph Lehman: "The involvement of the courts had a major influence on prison administration—both in reality and in perception. It did correct some real abuses as well as improve the overall operations of prisons. It not only forced prison administration to meet constitutional minima, but leveraged greatly enhanced professionalism at all levels of prison administration. That influence continues on with us today."

Kenneth McGinnis: "Judicial intervention allowed us to access resources that previously had not been available. It also forced us to put a new and increased emphasis on policy and procedures. The move from a verbal environment to a written policy and procedure environment had a lot to do with enhancing the professionalism at all levels of corrections. Although bothersome at the time, the early day court involvement was probably necessary and certainly critical to changes that needed to be made."

James Spalding: "In the 1970s we set ourselves up for judicial intervention. The 'liberal community' decided to experiment with the way we ran our prisons. The pendulum swung too far and we lost control of our institutions. We panicked and actually forced intervention on the part of the courts. There were abuses such as correctional officers medicating inmates, extremely long periods of segregation, and unbridled use of force. The end result was twenty years of litigation. Now we know how things need to work—we may not have made those advances without the courts."

Reginald Wilkinson: "Certainly there were some devastating situations and events in the seventies, particularly post-Attica, that required court intervention and things have improved. But at times the court went too far and ignored internal remedies. Many jurisdictions also entered into consent decrees too readily and made them open-ended, with no end times. This kept many prisons and even entire systems under court control even after the abuses and problems were long gone. Frivolous lawsuits became an enormous problem, only tapering off recently."

Frank Wood: "The intervention by the courts was very positive. It dragged many prisons and entire correctional systems into the twentieth century. It created a forum to consider and force change. Many of the very positive changes that we have seen occur in our prisons over the past fifteen years never would have occurred without the involvement, or at least the threat of involvement of the courts."

Court involvement in the operation of prisons, particularly by the federal courts, was generally seen by the prison administrators as having a favorable impact on the nation's prisons. The courts determined what minimum standards had to be met by prison administrators in order to operate a constitutionally sufficient prison. Those administrators not directly responsible for the operation of the prisons at the time the courts became involved frequently "inherited" existing court orders or consent decrees as they were promoted to positions of greater authority or moved to new jurisdictions controlled by such instruments.

Many improvements are apparent as a result of court intervention during that period (see, e.g., Jacobs 1980). Physical facilities and hygiene were improved. New classification systems were developed. Activity levels, recreation, and educational programming were enhanced. Standards for air movement, food preparation, and service were clarified. Safety for inmates and staff was generally improved. Access to lawyers and courts was directed and defined. Staff training, policies, and procedures were improved. Through court orders or consent decrees or actions taken to avoid court involvement, corrections systems around the country made significant changes in the physical environments and operations of prisons. Certainly, some think the courts "went too far." They would say that the reportedly large number of frivolous inmate lawsuits has simply been a symptom of excess. Yet, such massive changes, in most prisons in the country, probably would not have occurred without judicial intervention.

A National Center for State Courts bulletin entitled "Caseload Highlights" reports that "in the 1960s, when the U.S. Supreme Court first established that prisoners had constitutional rights, there were few Section 1983 lawsuits filed in U.S. District Courts. The Administrative Office of the U.S. Courts reported only 218 cases nationally in 1966, the first year Section 1983 lawsuits were recorded as a specific category of litigation" (National Center for State Courts 1998).

The scope of such litigation expanded in the 1970s, and the number of lawsuits jumped. That same report indicates that Section 1983 lawsuits shot up from 3,348 in 1972 to 41,952 in 1996. Prison populations rose by 902,246 inmates during that same period, accounting for at least some of the growth in lawsuits. Prison systems had a variety of legal access mechanisms, ranging from provision of attorneys to providing access to law libraries. Many inmates became quite proficient and knowledgeable about the law, spawning a series of "jailhouse lawyers" around the country. This resulted in a flood of litigation being filed in federal courts around the country, much of it found by the courts to not have merit.

The notoriety of frivolous lawsuits, played up by the media and "outraged" politicians, was a major factor in the marketing and passage of the Prisoner Litigation Reform Act in April 1996 (Bronstein and Gainsborough 1996). Yet the more ominous portions of the act are those that may provide a chilling effect on inmate access to the courts. The act limits the number of consecutive filings that an inmate may file, requires the inmate to prove physical injury, and requires the inmate to pay a filing fee. Section 1983 lawsuits dropped from 41,000 in 1996 to around 27,000 in 1997.

Personal interviews with inmates convince me that the requirements for filing fees are in and of themselves having that effect—even when the issues inmates want to raise are quite legitimate. The effect the act will have on existing court orders and consent agreements remains to be seen, as do its effects on future potential settlements.

The real question for the future is, If inmates do not feel they have adequate access to raise their issues in court, how will they respond to conditions that are less than humane? My years as a prison administrator lead me to believe prisoners will find a way to respond.

E. Prevalence of Illegal Substances in Prison Is Reportedly Much Greater Today than in 1975. What Impact Has That Had on Prison Administration?

Norman Carlson: "Drugs in our institutions were the cause of many of our operational problems. I do think the problem has been more pervasive in recent years than it was years ago. When we had violent incidents, frequently drugs were behind it. The fighting for control of the drug trade—inside and outside of the institution—created a lot of the violence we experienced."

Tom Coughlin: "If it weren't for drugs, and laws affecting those who possess or sell drugs, the New York prison system would have half the inmates they have today. In New York the severe sentences for drug offenders were initially enacted to predominantly deal with heroin, and to a lesser degree marijuana offenders. No one at the time anticipated the impact that the emergence of cocaine and crack cocaine would have when the sentences were applied to those convicted of possession or sale of them. One good thing did evolve out of all of that. As policy makers became aware of the large number of drug offenders that were going to prison they also began to realize that there was little drug-treatment available in the community. They then appropriated large amounts of money for drug treatment in the prisons in New York. By 1988 we had nearly 25,000 drug-treatment beds available in the New York state correctional system. In some instances entire institutions were devoted to drug treatment."

Joseph Lehman: "I am not sure that there are more drugs in our prisons today; in fact I think there are less. Several years ago we began placing a greater emphasis on drug detection. Unfortunately, it frequently had to be done by diverting resources from other areas. We also spent more time scrutinizing staff, raising interesting work-force issues. Today's technologies allow us to detect illegal drugs much more readily than we could before. I think this has created a significant deterrent effect."

Kenneth McGinnis: "I do think drugs in prison are more prevalent now than in 1975, however, much of it simply replaced 'hooch' [homemade alcohol]. Drugs represent one of the greatest risks to prison administrators. It is tied up with power struggles, gambling, gangs, and attempts to compromise staff. The new technologies help us control it. Urine testing is essential and we spend millions of dollars doing it. It is also critical to assure prosecution—for inmates or staff—for possession or introduction of drugs in the prison setting."

James Spalding: "I don't agree that there are more drugs in prisons today than in 1975. In fact I think they are less of a problem today than then. The technology helps us do a better job. We do a lot of drug testing and the monitoring and taping of telephone conversations has a big impact on drug use and trafficking. The increased availability of drug treatment in prisons also helps. In 1975 we were more punitive than corrective about drug use."

Reginald Wilkinson: "In the past we frequently ignored or denied the influence of drugs. I don't think they are more prevalent today than in 1975. We have a zero tolerance policy for drugs today in Ohio. We randomly test inmates and staff. We use urine testing, drug dogs, and phone monitoring. These weren't available in 1975."

Frank Wood: "I think there were more drugs inside our prisons in 1975. There were more visitors and volunteers allowed access to the inside of our institutions then. There were banquets, self-help groups, and many other groups that had access with much less security or control. Telephone monitoring, urine testing and other technologies have created a dramatic reduction in the use of drugs in prisons. In many institutions today—those that prohibit smoking and tobacco—cigarettes are more of a problem than drugs."

The interviewees' views are mixed concerning the importance of drugs in prisons today compared with 1975. Most point to the use of "new" technologies such as telephone monitoring, drug testing, and drug dogs as having a significant effect on controlling the presence of and introduction of drugs into prisons. Any candid prison administrator, however, will admit that the effort to control illegal substances (or even legal substances, as in prisons that ban tobacco) is unending.

The market value of drugs inside a prison is easily ten to thirty times what it would be on the street, creating an environment in which individuals and inmate groups and gangs battle for control of the market. The potentially high financial return also makes some staff and visitors vulnerable to being co-opted into participating in the drug trade.

That drugs are so desirable is in part because of the extremely high percentage of inmates who were substance abusers before coming to prison. The Bureau of Justice Statistics reports that 17 percent of state inmates in 1991 reported committing their crimes to support their drug use and that 28 percent of violent offenders, 35 percent of property offenders, and 37 percent of drug offenders were under the influence of drugs at the time they committed their crimes (Bureau of Justice Statistics 1994). Addiction does not disappear when people enter the prison door.

Most administrators would also assert that there are not enough drug-treatment resources available in the prison setting (they would also likely add that this is true in our communities as well). The reality then is that prison administrators face the same dilemma dealing with substance abuse that our communities face: should the drug problem be dealt with by controlling the supply, the demand, or some combination of both? Traditionally, the results have been not dissimilar to the results in our communities. It is easier politically to obtain resources to try to control the supply. Many millions of dollars more are spent trying to prevent drugs from crossing our borders and enforcing drug laws than is spent on treatment in our communities. The same is true of prison administrators' attempts to keep drugs from passing through their prison gates, which consumes many more resources than are devoted to drug treatment. Our prisons are microcosms of our communities—with many of the same problems, challenges, and solutions.

*F. What Other Changes Have You Seen in Prison Administration during
    the Past Twenty-Two Years and What Do You Think Created Those
    Changes?*

Norman Carlson: "In recent years our prisons have been much more open than they were in the 1970s. They are more open to the media and the public. This again is at least partially due to the courts. In the early days no one came into our institutions unless we invited them. Inmates never wrote to the press or called them with their problems or allegations. The openness has been healthy. Once the press saw what was going on and that it wasn't something mysterious or bad they became less interested. The overall acceptance of what we do has improved."

Tom Coughlin: "The professionalization of correctional employees, particularly at the line level, has been one of the biggest and most important changes since the 1970s. The union movement helped open up what had been a very top-down, paramilitary organization. More involvement in the operations of the prisons coupled with more and better training have all contributed to this very important improvement."

Joseph Lehman: "The tenure of prisons administrators has changed significantly. Wardens and state directors seem to have much shorter periods of service than was the case in the 1970s. It would seem to be but one indicator of how political this business has become."

Kenneth McGinnis: "The focus now is on punitiveness, and has increasingly moved in that direction since Willie Horton, and the attendant politicization of the prison business. Historically there was little interest or review of prison operations. Now there is a great deal of oversight—by the legislature, the media, and the general public."

James Spalding: "In the 1970s, we were dealing primarily with the internal environment in our institutions and agencies. Today our time is spent increasingly with the external environment. The media, legislature, and external interest groups all have major influence on prison operations. The scrutiny of our prison budgets is also unparalleled."

Reginald Wilkinson: "One of the most significant changes from the 1970s is that more people know and get involved in the prisons business—we are no longer a 'secret society.' The public understands us better. The media understands us better. Some of this is due to our opening up through advisory committees, marketing, etc. We also have more external influences: media, taxpayers, victims groups, the legislature, and other special interest groups."

Frank Wood: "The overcrowding that exists now, particularly in prisons that are multioccupancy, is in many instances worse than we had years ago. High costs and lack of political will contribute to this. Continued multioccupancy poses a threat as it allows the predators to exploit and intimidate other inmates and it is difficult for staff to control it. Down the road we will pay."

Most correctional administrators recognize the intensified focus on prisons and prison administration during the past twenty-five years. Certainly the image of Willie Horton brought intense scrutiny of release laws, policies, and programs, and dramatized the political advantage of being tough on crime and criminals. Fueled at the time by a rising crime rate, enhanced media attention to crime stories, and increased availability and use of drugs, politicians found that it was not only helpful to call for tougher penalties, but essential to their political aspirations.

Most state legislatures revised penalties for drug offenses in the 1980s, followed by penalties for sex offenses, followed by penalties for use of guns during the commission of a crime. Not only were many public officials fighting to sponsor new "tough on crime" bills, but often policy makers who did not personally support the proposed bills believed that they could not vote against them for fear that it would be used against them in their next campaign.

Not to be outdone by the states, many congressional candidates began to campaign on crime issues, and Congress itself began passing new and tougher crime legislation. It reinstated the federal death penalty and expanded the list of crimes to which it would apply. It passed tougher drug laws and lengthened sentences under those laws. It tried to influence states into greater use of incarceration by the passage of the Truth in Sentencing/Violent Offender Incarceration Act. This act, which pays states money if they meet certain formula-driven criteria (such as a requirement that 85 percent of the sentence for certain violent crimes must be served in order to qualify), arguably sets the tone for the country that incarceration should be the dominant response to crime.

As federal and state prisons filled, and construction and operating costs mounted, the visibility of the prison "business" increased proportionately. More communities found prisons being built in their midst—with many communities, for economic reasons, competing for the privilege. Increasing numbers of people were hired as correctional staff. Private companies began competing with each other and with public agencies for the right to run prisons.

The large sums of money involved in building and operating facilities for these expanding populations focused attention on prison budgets as never before. As money was diverted from other essential public services, such as education and the environment, elected officials began to demand more spartan prison conditions. The internal operations of state prisons were scrutinized by legislative budget staff and legislators alike, with the net result often being attempts to micromanage prisons and prison systems.

The media became enthralled with "innovative" correctional programs such as boot camps and chain gangs. Research findings on whether they were effective were ignored or dismissed; their political attractiveness was the persuasive determinant of whether they were established.

During this period, prison administrators were confronted with massive increases in their budgets for health care (McDonald, in this volume). As was true in the nation in general, the treatments available increased radically, and the cost of that health care increased substantially. Health-care cost-containment efforts varied by jurisdiction, but included privately provided health-care services, telemedicine, restrictions of types of treatment provided, and charges to inmates for health-care visits.

Mental health services also placed a heavy demand on prison resources. The nationwide deinstitutionalization of mental hospitals in the late 1960s and 1970s, and the subsequent governmental failure to make treatment resources available in the community to treat the mentally ill, has resulted in many of those persons being handled by the criminal justice system. Many end up in prison. Issues of adequate mental health treatment feature in many federal lawsuits about prison conditions, making provision of those services a constant challenge for prison administrators.

During this period too, the influx of prison gangs has been a major management challenge for prison administrators. With some differences between jurisdictions, the gangs generally form along racial lines and compete for control of contraband, drugs, and sex. Prison administrators have taken different approaches to attempt to mitigate or control gangs and gang members, with dispersion throughout a prison or prison system being the most common approach. In recent years some correctional systems have began placing the most dangerous of the gang members (typically called security threat groups) into administrative segregation, separating them almost totally from the general population of the prisons.

Emerging during this time also has been the "supermax" prison. Deriving from examples provided by Federal Bureau of Prisons facilities at Alcatraz and subsequently Marion, numerous states now have either built or are planning to build these types of prisons. Purportedly used to remove from the general population those inmates who present the greatest threats to the safety or orderly operation of the prison or prison system (or present a major escape risk), these facilities are characterized by extreme control measures. Generally, the inmate in a "supermax" prison is not allowed contact with other inmates and receives most services (including food, laundry, commissary, and programs, if any) in their cells. They are allowed out of their cells only in restraints and accompanied by two or more correctional officers.

The effects of these facilities are not well known. The human impact on inmates and staff has had little examination, and there has been little litigation that assesses whether their operation meets constitutional minimum standards. Proponents argue that such facilities reduce violence against staff and inmates in the general prison population. Critics state that they constitute cruel and unusual punishment, are inhumane, and violate minimum standards of decency.

III. Prison Administration in 2025

Criminal justice policy, including prisons policy, has changed repeatedly over the past 125 years and enormously over the past twenty-five years. While sometimes, in some contexts, the past is the best predictor of the future, that does not appear to be true of prison management. The seven administrators were asked a number of questions that required them to predict future developments.

A. Looking to 2025, What Changes in Prison Administration Do You Foresee?

Norman Carlson: "The economic realities will hit everyone between now and 2025, maybe sooner than later. It will result in policy changes. It may not reverse everything that has happened, but it may lessen the rate of increase in prison populations. We probably will not see the double-digit increases we have seen in the recent past. The economics of prison operations will force major change on corrections."

Tom Coughlin: "In 1981, I organized the Governor's Conference on Crime for Governor Carey. Part of the agenda was to discuss whether New York should consider moving from indeterminate sentencing to determinate sentencing. In doing some research for the conference I found a conference report from a similar governor's conference held in 1934. The minutes from that conference stated that the debate was over whether they should consider moving from their sentencing system of the time (determinate), to an indeterminate system. The message I gained from this experience is that ' . . . if you stand in one place long enough—it will all come back.' In year 2025, brilliant ideas of the past will come back again. I also believe that the present radical expenditures on corrections—mostly on prisons—will end when the negative impacts on schools and transportation are great enough."

Joseph Lehman: "I believe that prison administrators will continue to be challenged by staff boundary issues—issues of discrimination, harassment, and inmate/staff relationships. I think there will be a continuation of the emerging interest in 'What Works' and research-based practice and programs. I believe the public interest in government— accountable government—will continue, with that accountability measured in outcomes rather than process. The question for prison administrators is whether they will lead that effort or be defensive and led. We also must assume that some impossible-to-predict event or events may well shape that future."

Kenneth McGinnis: "I think that by 2025 we will see widespread privatization of prisons and corrections in general. I think there will be vouchers that a person convicted of crimes can use to gain access to either a public or privately operated facility. This vouchering will also be very prevalent among community alternative and treatment programs allowing an individual to pick from a variety of programs and setting up market-like competition. The major investment already being made in technology will continue. Cost will be driving policy in 2025."

James Spalding: "I think we will see an increased reliance on technology in the administration of prisons. Not only will management be more dependent on technology, but inmates will be increasingly monitored by technology. As we become more sophisticated in the information we are able to gather we will be able to make data-driven decisions about individual inmate placements, as well as about overall operations. I also believe we will see more centralization of functions, partially due to fiscal concerns and partially due to the need for more consistent control."

Reginald Wilkinson: "In 2025, prison inmate populations will be more heavily concentrated with inmates who need heavier custody—violent, career criminal, and predatory inmates. Corrections officials will become more sophisticated in handling offenders and there will be more community involvement in doing so. Nonviolent and nondangerous offenders will be handled in the community. New technologies and reformed policy thinking will make this possible."

Frank Wood: "We won't be able to pay the bill in 2025 for the policies we have created today. The enormous cost of operating the prisons required by today's sentencing policies will finally bring us to our senses. Our prisons then will be reserved for those 'we are afraid of' rather than those we are simply 'mad at.'"

Ignoring the inevitable unpredictable events that will occur over the next twenty-five years to shape prison administration, there are several areas sorely in need of change, some trends starting to emerge, and some unmet needs begging for solutions.

Classification of prisoners is critical to sound prison administration, yet few advances have been made since the near universal adoption of objective classification systems by most jurisdictions ten to fifteen years ago. Sophistication of classification instruments and procedures is essential to providing a safe prison environment, maintaining the population in the most efficient manner possible in both capital and operating costs, mitigating the likelihood of escape, and placing inmates in facilities and programs that will best address their needs. Much work needs to be done in combining appropriate psychological testing and existing and new research with new predictive instruments that allow more finely tailored decision-making about placement of inmates in prisons.

Likewise, research may provide some answers as to the most appropriate sentences for individual offenders or groups of offenders. Although determinate, presumptive, and mandatory minimum sentences offer the advantages of equity and parity for those convicted of the same crime, some offenders reach an optimal point at which their punishment has been sufficient, and their access to programs sufficient for them to be released safely. Retaining them longer may hinder their chances for a subsequent successful adjustment.

Use of existing and yet-to-be developed technologies will be part of the prison administrator's challenge during the next twenty-five years. Some technologies will be used simply for efficiency reasons, others to enhance the quality or efficiency of services. Already being employed are telemedicine technologies, electronic identification technologies, and remote tracking technologies. With the continued application and improvement of information systems, the prison administrator will have an enormous amount of information available to assist in these efforts to focus resources to permit their most effective and efficient application.

Certainly the use of fiscal resources will be a continuing political issue, particularly when, as inevitably it will, the nation's economy flattens or recedes. Prison operating budgets continue to increase, not only because of increasing numbers of inmates, but also because of escalation in staffing costs, health-care costs, and goods and services costs. Many jurisdictions will be paying substantial amounts far into the future for debt service on bonding for prison construction.

The role of the private sector in the operation of prisons appears likely to persist—and probably to grow. Much debate has occurred on the question whether these private corrections companies will lobby in the future for more and longer prison sentences in order to maintain their "customer base."

B. What Influences Do You Think Will Have the Greatest Impact on Prison Administration in the Future?

Norman Carlson: "In addition to the economics, demographics could have an almost countervailing influence on prisons and prison populations. The large number of people in the age-at-risk cohort could make our crime rates, and in turn, our prison populations go up."

Tom Coughlin: "Our failure to remember our failures of the past and what it took to fix them will be an influence. It will lead us to repeat many of those mistakes and unfortunately probably with similar results."

Joseph Lehman: "I think we will see new partnerships develop between corrections, the community, and other entities. I am particularly intrigued by the models offered by community policing. Community corrections and law enforcement partnering together could well create new paradigms, moving away from the tough approach to one of prevention and community involvement. The role of victims groups and other community organizations will become more pronounced."

Kenneth McGinnis: "Economics of prisons, corrections, and criminal justice will have the greatest influence. The high cost of what we are doing will possibly cause our criminal justice policies to 'swing back' a bit between now and the year 2025."

James Spalding: "The major influence on prison administration will be money. It will dictate the quality of the operations in our prisons for many years to come as well as providing the biggest challenge for prison and correctional administrators."

Reginald Wilkinson: "A major change by 2025 will be the full involvement of our communities in corrections. They won't simply be vicariously involved—we'll invite them in and open up the system. We'll ask for advice from the business community. Research will drive our behaviors and decisions. We will get rid of nonworking programs. We will be much more sophisticated, based on research findings, in how we deal with special populations such as mentally ill offenders, youth, the elderly offenders, etc."

Frank Wood: "Economics will have the greatest influence on prison administration between now and 2025. It will force changes at the federal, state, and local levels. We'll have to cut through the 'smoke and mirrors' of present-day policies and rethink and revise our approaches to the use of prisons. Many of the institutions built in recent years will be closed and the impact on the economy of local communities will be severe, not unlike the closure of mental hospitals in years past."

Most of the administrators project that the sentencing policies of the last several years and the enormous fiscal bow-wave they push into the future will at some point require that sentencing policies be reconsidered. It would be admirable if those policies were revisited because our society is simply dismayed at the large number of citizens being incarcerated and at the highly disproportionate number of minorities included in those numbers. The Bureau of Justice Statistics recently reported that, if incarceration rates remain unchanged, an estimated one in every twenty persons (5.1 percent) will serve time in a prison in their lifetime; that men (9 percent) are over eight times more likely than women (1.1 percent) to be incarcerated in prison at least once in their lives; that among men, blacks (28.5 percent) are about twice as likely as Hispanics (16.0 percent) and six times more likely than whites (4.4 percent) to be admitted to prison during their lives; that among women, 3.6 percent of blacks, 1.5 percent of Hispanics, and 0.5 percent of whites will enter prison at least once. If rates of incarceration and mortality rates recorded in 1991 remain unchanged, an estimated 1.1 percent of all persons born today will go to prison by the time they are age twenty, 3.3 percent by the time they are thirty, and 4.4 percent by the time they are forty (Bureau of Justice Statistics 1997b).

Conventional wisdom and history suggest that our society will not change its sentencing policies out of dismay over figures such as those previously noted. Rather, it is more likely that the projections of most of the interviewees are correct—such changes will occur because of economic pressures.

The predictions by several administrators that communities will become more involved in prisons, corrections, and criminal justice appear sound. A number of indicators substantiate those predictions. The success of community-policing programs in many jurisdictions and growing interest in restorative and community-justice programs may well be the genesis of a trend that could result in a paradigm shift in this country. Perhaps crime, like politics, is local.

Unknown now are what the ramifications of recent welfare reforms will be for crime rates or prison populations. Other influences may include changes in the nation's economy, advancing technologies and medical/mental health treatments, changing approaches to illegal drugs, and new diseases.

C. What Effects Do You Expect the Growing Trend toward "Privatization" to Have on Prison Administration?

Norman Carlson: "I think the competition it is creating is very healthy. It sends a clear message to labor organizations that there are other options out there. It sounds an alert to everyone in public corrections that they must be competitive, or alternatives can be exercised."

Tom Coughlin: "I think that privatized services as part of a prison operation, such as medical services, food services, and others, works well. Often in these specialty areas the private sector can do much better than government. I think these types of arrangements will continue and grow. It is my opinion that anything that the private sector can do government can do and at the same cost. The public sector simply has to manage as wisely as the private sector. I do not believe, as some people do, that the private sector will take over a major share of the prison business, or run entire systems."

Joseph Lehman: "I think the pressure to privatize the building and operation of prisons will continue and probably increase. In the long term, privatization is not a solution for our problems—any more than any other singular proposal. I think our correctional agencies and prisons will increasingly operate more like private companies. By 2025, we may also see some hybrid organizations—combinations of private and public organizations arranged in ways we haven't thought of yet. This would allow taking advantage of the strengths of each."

Kenneth McGinnis: "Privatization has been touted as a panacea by politicians and the media. It obviously is not a panacea. It is generally sold as being able to 'save money.' In the long term, I don't think that will be the case. As the pressure to privatize continues, the labor organizations will take an increasingly active role in opposition."

James Spalding: "We've created an environment that makes privatization of prisons very attractive and it won't be stopped. We've created such big bureaucracies in the public sector that we set up a perfect environment for private sector competition. At this point I don't think it is an issue of whether the private sector can do the job better or not—it's a matter of real or perceived financial savings. Prison administrators have to learn how to effectively monitor the private operations and learn how to make it work. In the long term, learning ways to assure accountability is critical."

Reginald Wilkinson: "I don't see the trend toward privatization diminishing, although I think that we will become more sophisticated in managing those relationships. The scrutiny of the private operations will increase. However, the cheaper way in may not be the cheaper way out. The whole privatization thing isn't new—we've been outsourcing for years. New ways of outsourcing in the future may include contracting with local government for correctional services including for prison space, as well as with nonprofit organizations for prisons."

Frank Wood: "I have some strong concerns about the delegation of governmental responsibility to someone with a financial interest in the results. Most people supporting privatization because they think it is cheaper don't realize that frequently the companies are responding with 'loss leaders' in order to get their foot in the door. Over the long haul I don't think they can sustain those savings, as the dominant cost—generally over 80 percent—of operating a prison is the cost of staff. There is little saving potential in the remaining 20 percent. I am also concerned that the corporate world will have increasing influence on correctional and sentencing policy—either directly or indirectly, with the profit motive being their major motive for involvement."

The trend line certainly suggests continued growth of the numbers of privately operated prisons. A recent report from the Private Corrections Project of the University of Florida documents current trends. In 1988 there were fewer than 5,000 privately operated, secure prison beds available in the country; by year-end 1997 there were nearly 107,000 beds. Two privately operated companies operated 101 separate prisons. At year-end 1997, Texas alone had 27,139 privately operated secure prison beds, four states had more than 5,000, and eight states had more than 2,000. Using a conservative trend line, the same group projects that by year-end 1998 there will be over 136,480 privately operated secure prison beds and over 323,919 by year-end 2002 (Bollinger and Thomas 1998).

The desirability of this trend remains hotly debated, but there appears to be no barrier to its continuation on the horizon. Some of the questions regularly debated concern comparative cost, quality, liability, delegation of power to a private company, and legality (depending on the jurisdiction). One unanswered question that will be answered in the next twenty-five years is, Will private, for-profit companies, lobby for more onerous sentencing laws simply to continue the growth in their "customer base"?

D. What Other Observations Do You Have?

Norman Carlson: "I find it interesting that few elected officials in the pre-1970s had much real interest in the corrections business. Attica changed all of that. But, many of the persons who are wardens today were in high school in 1971 [when Attica occurred] and have no real memory of it."

Tom Coughlin: "I remain concerned that we will forget the lessons of the past. We will then have a very painful relearning period to go through."

Joseph Lehman: "We face some big choices between now and year 2025. Our national and state sentencing and correctional policies will evolve into something very different. Our communities will—and should—play a bigger role in that evolution. Our correctional agencies and leaders should look for new paradigms in providing correctional services."

Kenneth McGinnis: "We are much better off today than twenty-five years ago. We have more resources to do the job today than then. Our staff have a much higher degree of professionalism, our managers are better, and training has improved drastically in quality and quantity. I would hope that the next twenty-five years would bring as much improvement again."

James Spalding: "Prison administrators in the future are going to have to be flexible. They are going to have to ask the hard questions and are going to be asked the hard questions."

Reginald Wilkinson: "Prison administrators need to think seriously about what the future will look like. They can't just let things happen—they must have some influence in shaping that future. They will need to develop new partnerships with higher education, business, other public agencies, etc."

Frank Wood: "There will be three major challenges for prison administrators in the future: first, the growing influence of correctional labor organizations and the disproportionate impact they can have politically; second, the elected officials who are political opportunists— willing to forgo sound policy and facts for the chance to gain visibility; and lastly, privatization."

The administrators collectively suggest that two critical things should be kept in mind by the prison administrators of the future.

First, the lessons of the past should not be lost or ignored. The events and challenges of the future may not be the same as those of the past, but the lessons of the past can at least alert future administrators to likely future challenges and be instructive to efforts to find solutions.

Second, it is important for prison administrators of the future to try to shape the future, to anticipate as many events and new challenges as possible, and to involve a wider, more diverse group of actors in the prison administration business.

IV. Conclusion

These seven administrators remember the many challenges to corrections and prison administration during the 1970s, 1980s, and 1990s. They are astute in drawing on their experiences to forecast future issues and challenges. They remember some different things and some things differently, probably due to their serving in different systems, in different geographic areas, and in different positions. Yet many of their observations are similar.

Today the influences on prison administration across the country are similar, as are the challenges. If we look ahead twenty-five years, we may assume that today's problems will be the major drivers of tomorrow's problems.

It might be interesting to step back for a moment to the year 1970, a time of comparatively stable prison populations. Would we then have been able to predict the effects that inner-city disturbances would have on the environments and administration of prisons? Would we be able to predict nationwide involvement of the courts in determining the manner in which inmates would be treated and how our prisons would be operated? Would we have predicted that such an awesome event as Attica would occur in a prison in this country? Would we possibly forecast the unprecedented growth in prison populations in the 1980s and 1990s, and the attendant massive prison building boom?

Would we have guessed that a single Massachusetts prisoner on furlough, highlighted in a presidential campaign, would have a long-lasting impact on correctional and sentencing policy? Would we have forecast that private companies would be operating major prison facilities? Would we have predicted that prisons in the 1990s would be filled with extremely high percentages of drug offenders, and that cocaine and crack cocaine would be the substances most frequently abused, possessed, and sold? Would we have guessed that state legislators would sponsor bills and have lengthy debates about weight lifting in prisons, or televisions in prisons, or a return to chain gangs? Would we have projected that the U.S. Congress would commit billions of dollars to encourage the states to assure that their inmates serve at least 85 percent of their sentences? Would we have anticipated the enormous expenditures on health care that correctional systems would incur because of aging correctional populations and requirements for sound medical care from the courts? The answer to most of those questions is probably "no."

If we would have had difficulty in 1970 in anticipating the events that have shaped the administration of prisons in the past quarter century, it must give us pause in contemplating the events, circumstances, and pressures that will influence corrections and prisons over the next twenty-five years.

With continued and growing economic disparities between those living in our suburbs and those living in our inner cities, will we once again live through social disruption in our cities and subsequently in our prisons? Will the effects of significant cuts in who is eligible for welfare and for how long influence the number of persons who participate in criminal activity—and are therefore potential prison candidates? Will state and local governments be financially able to sustain the operation of the many jails and correctional facilities built in the 1980s and 1990s?

Demographics, particularly the relative size of birth cohorts, have long had a direct relationship to the size of our prison populations. What impact will the "baby boom echo" have on prison populations? Similar questions can be asked about the influence of high divorce rates, improved health care resulting in longer lives, the increasing proportion of our population that is black, Hispanic, or Asian, and the increasing proportion of women at all levels in our work force.

Drugs have been a significant influence on our prison population during the 1980s and 1990s. Will society become more tolerant and support legalization of some or all drugs, or will some new drug—possibly even more addictive than crack cocaine—cause even greater human destruction and once again increase levels of incarceration? Will new methods of drug treatment, more effective than present-day treatments, be developed or will chemicals that fully eliminate the desire for drugs be available?

The move from the industrial age to the information/technology age has already created major changes in our society. What effects will the continuation of that trend have on corrections and prison operations? Will global positioning technology have application either in our prisons or as a means of tracking offenders in the community? Will other new surveillance techniques be available? Will the ability to gather, collate, and analyze data more easily enhance research and allow us to know "what works"? Will private corporations operate entire correctional systems or will some event eliminate them from the correctional field entirely?

As influential as the courts have been in the last twenty-five years in changing the administration of prisons, what role will they play between now and 2025? Will they determine that the disproportionate representation of minorities in our prisons is a form of discrimination or that a sentence of life without parole for crimes less than the most heinous does not meet a test of proportionality or that banishment to space is an acceptable penalty for some crimes? Will they redefine dangerousness so that much larger numbers of persons can be civilly committed for life or will they deinstitutionalize prisons much as happened with the mentally ill in the 1970s?

What events both within and outside of our prisons will shape our sentencing policies and the way we operate our prisons? Is there a new version of Willie Horton out there? Wars, riots in prisons, and even natural disasters have historically had an impact on prison administration nationwide. How many—if any—of these will occur between now and 2025? Will the demands of international human rights organizations pressure us to lower our incarceration rates, or will those in other countries match ours?

Will the organization of prison administration change to a national prison system that handles all convicted prisoners, or to a regional system in which states share facilities, or will communities assume greater responsibility for their citizens who violate their laws?

Based on the seven correctional administrators' observations of the changes they perceived from 1975 to 1997, the single conclusion that I can offer about prison administration in 2025 is that it "will not be the same."

REFERENCES

Blumstein, Alfred, Jacqueline Cohen, Susan E. Martin, and Michael Tonry, eds. 1983. *Research on Sentencing: The Search for Reform.* Washington, D.C.: National Academy Press.

Bollinger, Dianne, and Charles W. Thomas. 1998. *Private Adult Correctional Facility Census: A Year-End Census.* Gainesville: University of Florida, Private Corrections Project.

Bronstein, Alvin J., and Jenni Gainsborough. 1996. "Prison Litigation: Past, Present, and Future." *Overcrowded Times* 7(3):1, 15–18, 20.

Bureau of Justice Statistics. 1994. *Fact Sheet: Drug-Related Crime.* Washington, D.C.: U.S. Department of Justice, Bureau of Justice Statistics.

———. 1997a. *Census of State and Federal Correctional Facilities, 1995.* Washington, D.C.: U.S. Department of Justice, Bureau of Justice Statistics.

———. 1997b. *Correctional Populations in the United States, 1995.* Washington, D.C.: U.S. Department of Justice, Bureau of Justice Statistics.

———.1997c. *Lifetime Likelihood of Going to State or Federal Prison.* Washington, D.C.: U.S. Department of Justice, Bureau of Justice Statistics.

———. 1998. *Prison and Jail Inmates at Mid-year 1997.* Washington, D.C.: U.S. Department of Justice, Bureau of Justice Statistics.

Farrington, David P. 1986. "Age and Crime." In *Crime and Justice: An Annual Review of Research*, vol. 7, edited by Michael Tonry and Norval Morris. Chicago: University of Chicago Press.

Harding, Richard. 1998. "Private Prisons." In *The Handbook of Crime and Punishment*, edited by Michael Tonry. New York: Oxford University Press.

Jacobs, James B. 1980. "The Prisoners' Rights Movement and Its Impacts, 1960–80." In *Crime and Justice: An Annual Review of Research*, vol. 2, edited by Norval Morris and Michael Tonry. Chicago: University of Chicago Press.

Lipton, D., R. Martinson, and J. Wilks. 1975. *The Effectiveness of Correctional Treatment*. New York: Praeger.

Martinson, R. 1974. "What Works? Questions and Answers about Prison Reform." *Public Interest* 35:22–45.

McDonald, Douglas C. In this volume. "Medical Care in Prisons."

Morris, Norval, and David J. Rothman, eds. 1995. *The Oxford History of the Prison: The Practice of Punishment in Western Society*. New York: Oxford University Press.

National Center for State Courts. 1998. "Prisoner Litigation in Relation to Prisoner Population." *Caseload Highlights* 4(2):1–6.

National Conference of State Legislatures. 1997. *State Budget Actions, 1997*. Denver: National Conference of State Legislatures.

Proband, Stan C. "Corrections Leads State Budget Increases in FY 97." *Overcrowded Times* 8(4):4.

Rothman, David. 1980. *Conscience and Convenience*. Boston: Little, Brown.

Tonry, Michael. 1996. *Sentencing Matters*. New York: Oxford University Press.

Anthony E. Bottoms

Interpersonal Violence and Social Order in Prisons

ABSTRACT

The incidence of acts of interpersonal violence in prisons is influenced by the characteristics of inmates but also by aspects of the prison environment and by the continual dynamic interaction between prisoners, prison staff, and the physical and social context within which they are placed. Enhanced physical restrictions can often reduce levels of violence due to restrictions on opportunity but may also sometimes lead to a loss of legitimacy that can escalate violence. Previously understudied aspects of prison social life include routines and staff-prisoner relationships, both of which are central to the maintenance of everyday social order. Prisoner-staff assaults are particularly associated with the potential "friction points" of the prison regime and the prison day, but some officers seem more skilled at handling these friction points in ways that avoid violence. The study of prisoner-prisoner violence presents a paradox, with a frequently described pervasiveness of the rule of force within inmate society yet also surprisingly high levels of day-to-day prisoner safety: explaining this paradox is a key issue for future research.

For analytical purposes, the topic of prison violence has been usefully divided by Braswell, Montgomery, and Lombardo (1994) into two main types of behavior, namely "interpersonal violence" and "collec-

Anthony E. Bottoms is Wolfson Professor of Criminology at the Institute of Criminology, University of Cambridge. Grateful acknowledgment is made for intellectual stimulus from colleagues working on Cambridge-based prison research projects, especially Will Hay, Alison Liebling, and Richard Sparks. Parts of the introduction and Section IV of this essay are adapted and developed from A. E. Bottoms and R. Sparks, "How Is Order in Prisons Maintained?" in *Security, Justice and Order in Prison: Developing Perspectives*, edited by A. Liebling (Cambridge: University of Cambridge, Institute of Criminology, 1997). Kimmett Edgar of Oxford University made valuable comments on an earlier draft of Section VI.

tive violence." These authors do not, however, address the important question: What primarily distinguishes these two categories?

The kernel of the answer to this question, I suggest, lies in the relationship between prison violence and the social order of the prison. When so-called collective violence occurs, it brings with it *a significant breakdown in the normal patterns of social order in the institution*—a breakdown that is seen most spectacularly, of course, in major prison riots such as those at Attica, New York, in 1970 and Santa Fe, New Mexico, in 1980. By contrast, when people speak of "interpersonal violence," they refer to violent events that take place *within the everyday frameworks of the prison's social order*. Such events, although occurring within "everyday frameworks," can of course be extremely serious; they might involve, for example, a homicidal assault or a major injury, and they might generate considerable fear among at least some prisoners and some staff. Yet, notwithstanding the very serious character of some interpersonal violence, it differs from collective violence in that it poses no decisive challenge to the continued smooth functioning of the prison *as an organization:*[1]

> Organizations (offices, factories, schools, hospitals, prisons) direct the activities of their members via the precise control of time; their hierarchies are reflected and sustained in their "zoning" of space; they monitor their own activities through surveillance, considered both as the collation and storage of information (files, records, inventories, accounts) and through direct "supervision," especially of subordinate members. Organizations use "specially designed locales" (Giddens 1987, p. 157) to facilitate their continuous activity. Such buildings (of which prisons are an obvious instance . . .) are "power containers: physical settings which through the interaction of setting and social conduct generate administrative power" (Giddens 1987, p. 157). (Sparks, Bottoms, and Hay 1996, pp. 75–76)

---

[1] Three qualifications to this statement are required in the interests of full accuracy. First, interpersonal violence, especially if serious, does produce some temporary disturbance to some aspects of the prison's social order. Second, it follows that the distinction between "collective violence" and "interpersonal violence," though clear in most contexts, will be difficult to apply to some intermediate incidents. Third, it must be pointed out that even in the case of major riots, the authorities always eventually regain control of the prison—even if this process takes several weeks (see Woolf [1991] on the disturbances in England at Manchester Prison and elsewhere in 1990).

This essay does not discuss collective violence in prisons, a topic that would merit a separate review essay.[2] Rather, the focus here is on interpersonal violence in prisons—on prisoners assaulting prisoners and prisoners assaulting staff members.[3] Following the line of thought sketched above, the essay seeks to understand interpersonal violence within the framework of the prison's everyday social functioning. Of course, interpersonal violent acts are committed by individuals (or by individuals acting in small groups), and it is always important to consider the background characteristics, the life histories, and the current emotional states of those who assault. (This is especially the case in the prison setting, since prisons by definition contain a disproportionate number of individuals who can reasonably be described as "violence-prone.") Yet interpersonal prison violence, although always committed by individuals, also always occurs *within the social context of daily prison life;* and prisons, as the quotation above will already have made clear, are in a very real sense "special places" (Bottoms and Sparks 1997, p. 16). It follows that, in discussing interpersonal prison violence, some close attention needs to be paid to the social organization of the prison, as well as to the characteristics and histories of individual prisoners.

Prisons are special places, with a special kind of social organization, in at least six senses. These are as follows:

First, as Goffman (1961) famously observed, prisons are, in common with other kinds of organizations such as boarding schools, mental hospitals, barracks, and monasteries, total institutions. That is to say, in such institutions people ("inmates") regularly sleep, eat, work, and play on the same premises in a process that might be described as "batch living." Hence, such institutions have a tendency to encompass the lives of their inmates "to a degree discontinuously greater" than other social institutions, a discontinuity that is "often built right into the physical plant" through features such as "high walls, barbed wire . . . or moors" (Goffman 1961, p. 4). These important observations, however, need qualification in two senses. First, while all "total institu-

---

[2] For discussions of collective violence in prisons, see, e.g., Useem and Kimball (1989), R. Adams (1992), Colvin (1992), and sec. III of Braswell, Montgomery, and Lombardo (1994).

[3] There is, of course, a third type of prison interpersonal violence, namely staff members assaulting prisoners. This is an important topic, but it raises a distinct set of issues, which for reasons of space cannot be tackled here. For discussions of staff violence to prisoners see, e.g., Marquart (1986); chaps. 8, 10, and 11 in Braswell, Montgomery, and Lombardo (1994); Human Rights Watch (1996).

tions" share certain common characteristics, it does not follow that they are all identical—clearly, there are some significant and easily identified differences between barracks, monasteries, and prisons. Moreover, Goffman's use of the adjective "total," although graphic and making an important point, is potentially misleading. Now that we live in a globalized, media-dominated age (where, e.g., in-cell televisions are no longer a rarity in prisons) it is easy to see that total institutions are not as "total," nor as impervious to external influences, as the terminology might seem to imply. Although prisons were almost certainly more "total" in the past, the reality is that they have always been, to some extent, influenced by the sociopolitical milieu in which they are set (for an extended discussion of this point see Jacobs 1977).

Second, unlike some total institutions, prisons are, in a real sense, *punitive establishments.* Liberal penologists have often declared, following Alexander Paterson (see Ruck 1951) that offenders are sent to prison "as a punishment, and not for punishment." But not even the most liberal penologist would deny that imprisonment is part of a country's *penal system* (note the adjective "penal"); and any penal system has among its features both the prevention of crime (through general deterrence, incapacitation, and so on) and the imposition of censure on convicted criminals (see von Hirsch 1993). Prisoners themselves are acutely aware of these matters. As King (1985, p. 187) once bluntly observed: "For as long as we have prisons . . . then we will continue to hold prisoners against their will. *At bottom that is what it is about"* (emphasis added).

Third, as in other organizations ("total" or otherwise), within prisons there is a special internal organization of both *space and time.* There are routine practices—for example, of feeding, work, educational opportunities, recreation, and locking up—that take place at scheduled times and in scheduled places. These routines create a patterning of the day, and different "atmospheres" or "social climates" in different locations (or at different times of the day in the same location), focused around a particular activity. Such patterning and social climates bite deeply into the everyday consciousness of both custodians and captives; and they can vary substantially in different prisons.[4]

---

[4] See, e.g., the comment by the English Research and Advisory Group on the Long-Term Prison System that one important element in a prison regime is its *"degree of structure . . .* by [which] we mean the degree to which prisoners are free to make choices about their use of time and space. The degree of structure present in regimes varies considerably from one type of establishment to another throughout the prison system. Local prisons, for example, are characterised by a highly structured regime where particular

Fourth, it follows from the above that, as in other organizations, the reiteration of a *daily routine* is central to the prison's nature as an institution. The British sociologist Giddens (1984, 1987) has argued persuasively that everyone's daily life contains a significant element of routine, and that social theorists need to pay close attention both to how everyday routines structure and sustain social institutions over time,[5] *and* to how individuals assimilate new routines and, in time, are thus enabled to cope with many aspects of contemporary life by developing everyday skills that they hardly realize they have.[6] Since most prisons have a more pronounced daily routine than other social institutions, it is not surprising that all of these features can easily be uncovered, in any prison setting, by a careful observer. Yet the importance of routines, though not absent from the research literature on prisons, has been insufficiently analyzed by most prison scholars, particularly given that this is such a prominent feature of every prisoner's and every prison officer's daily life. However, none of the above should be read as an assertion that prison life (or social life in other contexts) is *nothing but* the orderly repetition of routines. People are not automata. And sometimes, routines will be resented or rebelled against by those who are subjected to them: though on closer examination, as we shall see later in this essay, such rebellions themselves sometimes prove to have at least a partially patterned or predictable character (e.g., some moments in the daily routine seem particularly likely to be subject to challenge and possible disruption).

Fifth, there is the complex issue of *staff-prisoner relationships*. As Sykes (1958) indicated in his early and classic book *The Society of Captives*, once permanent solitary confinement has been eschewed by a prison system, and the prisoners are allowed some degree of "association" (as English prison administrators still call it), it follows that the

---

pre-determined activities take place at particular pre-determined times and in particular pre-determined places. By comparison, prisoners in a dispersal prison have a much greater degree of choice about how and where they spend their time" (Home Office 1987, para. 82; emphasis in original).

[5] For example, the daily reproduction of the social institution of the school is achieved by, among other processes, routine actions in thousands of households every morning, with parents ensuring that their children have all the appropriate accessories (coat, lunch, schoolbooks, etc.), and then bundling them into the car or toward the school bus.

[6] For example, driving a car requires much concentration for the new driver, but skillful driving can be accomplished almost subconsciously by the experienced motorist. This latter kind of activity is usefully called "practical consciousness" by Giddens: he argues that actions of this sort are "not directly motivated," but rather consist "of all the things that actors know tacitly about how to 'go on' in the contexts of social life, without being able to give them direct discursive expression" (Giddens 1984, p. xxiii).

prison becomes, in miniature, a kind of castelike social system, with two main sets of players: the captors and the captives. But, for prison officers, all this creates some difficulties. It is they who must ensure that the daily social routines are followed, and that the business of the prison day follows a smooth and orderly progression. (In a very real sense, a prison officer's day can be said to have been "successful" when the day's routines have been accomplished, the prisoners are all safely locked in their cells, and *nothing untoward has happened all day*.) Yet for prison officers to achieve these "orderly progressions" is by no means simple. The routines are prescribed (see above), but it is prison officers who must persuade prisoners to follow these routines. And they must do this notwithstanding that the prisoners are in prison against their will; that (at least in most day-to-day situations) prisoners heavily out-number prison officers; and that, to many prisoners, the incentives or disincentives (rewards and punishments) that the prison system offers have little real meaning. Sykes's conclusion, reaffirmed by many schol-ars since his day, was that the guards have to resort to many small "ac-commodations"[7] to get the job done. Subsequent researchers have also observed the very real interpersonal skills intuitively deployed by many basic-grade prison officers in such contexts (perhaps, e.g., in defusing a potentially very tense situation in a cell block over a new directive from the prison's governor; see generally Sparks, Bottoms, and Hay 1996; Liebling and Price 1999). It follows from all this that the mainte-nance of order in a prison never just "happens," and nothing (certainly not simple repression) guarantees its continuity. If "order" of some sort exists in most prisons (and it does), then it is something that is accomplished by people (especially prison officers) as an outcome of certain distinct kinds of work. All such work is skilled and knowledge-able activity. It requires personal agency, even though many of the ac-tions involved (more especially the routinized ones) are in the sphere of "practical consciousness" (see n. 6) rather than being carefully cal-culated or deliberated-over. Identifiable special measures directed spe-cifically toward keeping or restoring "control" in a particular prison may indeed be part-and-parcel of the work of accomplishing order, but they are emphatically not the whole of it. Rather, order in prisons is to a large extent achieved through the subtle interplay of relationships

---

[7] Sykes calls these accommodations "corruptions," but the use of this term seems dis-tracting and rather misleading: see Sparks, Bottoms, and Hay (1996), p. 42.

between prison officers and prisoners, as they work their way through the prison day. Thus we ultimately cannot understand day-to-day order in prisons unless we understand both the prison's daily routines and the interpersonal (but structured) relationships that grow up around them.

Sixth, prisons are, by their nature, restricted *geographical locales*, or *places*. This is a point that is too often overlooked, both in the academic literature, and by senior managers in prison headquarters who can on occasion become overly preoccupied with abstract management systems. But on the ground, in any given prison, a shrewd observer often notices that the prison walls do not simply surround those people (staff and prisoners) who are there at a given moment. Rather, the walls *contain a whole history*. For example, an in-depth study of two English maximum–security prisons was conducted by a research team that included the present author (Sparks, Bottoms, and Hay 1996). These two prisons had, at that time, very different regimes. One prison, Long Lartin, had for special historical reasons evolved a somewhat relaxed supervisory style, perhaps epitomized by the remark of a previous governor that "you may have to lose some control in order to gain control" (quoted in Bottoms and Light 1987, p. 15). Over time, this supervisory style had won very substantial support and loyalty from the uniformed officers in the prison, who referred to it proudly as the "Long Lartin ethos." The other prison, Albany, had suffered two major crises of control in fairly quick succession; and these setbacks had very seriously eroded the professional self-confidence of the frontline staff, who argued strongly that the only way for the prison to regain and retain firm control was to adopt a deliberately restrictive regime. No incoming governor of Long Lartin, whatever his/her preferred management style, could afford to ignore the "Long Lartin ethos," and the uniformed staff's loyalty to it, which significantly influenced many day-to-day staff-prisoner interactions in the cell blocks and elsewhere. No incoming governor of Albany, whatever his/her preferred management style, could afford to ignore the uniformed staff's fearful and demoralized state, based directly on the prison's recent history. Any seasoned observer of prisons will be able to recall other situations where a particular prison's recent (or even not-so-recent) history has been similarly important because of key memories and perceptions of staff, or prisoners, or both. As Giddens (1984, p. 367) neatly puts it, in such contexts we have to take account of the fact that "the continuity of the biography of the individual is expressed in, and also expresses, [elements of] institutional reproduction."[8]

As later sections of this essay will indicate, it has now become something of a commonplace in the research literature on prisons to say that interpersonal violence can only properly be understood by an "interactionist" approach, that is to say an approach that takes into account not only the characteristics of individual prisoners, and not only the nature of the prison environment (as exemplified in the six points made above), but also what Wright (1991a, p. 217) has called "the fit between person and environment" (or, in the less mechanical language that I would prefer, the continual dynamic process of interaction between the prisoners, the staff, and the environment they both inhabit). Yet when we turn to the world of prison policy documents, matters are often very different. As King and McDermott (1990, p. 449) have observed, official discourse on prison control problems "sometimes pays lip-service to the capacity of the system to generate its own trouble," yet in practice it "falls back time and again on a model that locates trouble primarily in the dispositions of individual prisoners."[9] One reason for such a disjunction is, perhaps, that prison scholars have failed adequately to develop socially contextualized accounts of prison violence that make real connections to the lived daily experience of prison administrators. Researchers speak of "interactionist" approaches, but they have rarely addressed the minutiae of the average prison day, or considered in detail how violence can arise within this social order.

This essay is intended, in part, to redress this balance. While providing a general (and, I hope, fair) overview of the literature on prison interpersonal violence, there is a special emphasis on understanding such violence within the context of the everyday social order of prisons as organizations. This emphasis derives from the research, mentioned above, into two contrasting English maximum-security prisons (see Sparks, Bottoms, and Hay 1996, where a fuller theoretical elaboration of some aspects of this approach may also be found).

In pursuit of these aims, the remainder of this essay is organized in

---

[8] The original quotation refers to "the continuity of institutional reproduction." I have amended this because, as the Albany example shows, elements of institutional reproduction that deliberately reject past practices may also be attributable to the continuity of the biography of individuals.

[9] A notable exception to this generalization, in England, was the major report on prison disturbances published a year after King and McDermott had made their comment; see Woolf (1991).

the following way. Section I asks what interpersonal prison violence is, how it can be measured, and how frequently it occurs. Section II considers the evidence relating to some basic possible correlates of interpersonal prison violence, such as age, gender, race, and sentence conditions. Section III assesses what convincing evidence we have that a prison's environmental conditions (to use a very all-encompassing term) do indeed have an influence on the level and the types of interpersonal violence. Section IV then asks the too-often ignored question as to how daily social order is in fact maintained in most prisons most of the time. After this somewhat elaborate (but, I would argue, necessary) set of maneuvers, we are in a better position to consider interpersonal prison violence "in the round." The remaining two sections then focus briefly on the two main types of interpersonal prison violence, asking what can be freshly learned about them from the approach that this essay recommends, and what gaps in our knowledge remain. Section V addresses prisoner-staff violence from this perspective, while Section VI considers prisoner-prisoner violence.

I. How Much Interpersonal Prison Violence?

One needs only to pose seriously the question, "How much prison violence?" to realize that there are no easy answers. Davies (1982, p. 150) provides a useful starting point in suggesting how difficult it is to define what is or is not a violent incident in the prison context. As he puts it: "There are degrees of aggression and violence which lie on a continuum, for example: shouting, 'squaring up,' pushing or shoving, slapping, scratching, butting, punching, biting, elbowing, kneeing, kicking, knifing, shooting, (causing an explosion). In prison, an inmate might find himself on a violence disciplinary report for virtually any of these activities, from pushing to knifing inclusive."

Nor do the definitional problems stop there. For even if, in a particular situation, there is an admitted use of force (e.g., a slap or a punch), it can often be argued that the force used was justified—for example, an inmate might say he/she used force in self-defense, or a guard might say he/she used force as a necessary tactic, and to a reasonable extent, to quell an infractious prisoner. There is also the further complicating issue of nonphysical types of victimization. Bowker (1980), in an influential early study, identified four types of victimization among prisoners, namely physical victimization, psychological victimization, economic victimization, and social victimization. It is not hard to appreciate that, to a prisoner, some kinds of continuous economic or psychological victimization could be more hurtful than, say, a single physical slap. (Very similar issues arise when considering victimization and abuse within family and spousal contexts. See, e.g., Bijleveld 1998; van Dijk et al. 1998.)

In this essay, in order to keep the scope of the discussion within reasonable limits, I shall confine the analysis to *the unjustified use of, and threats of, actual physical force in prison*. But this initial definitional step is only a beginning. Accurately measuring prison violence, so defined, poses many further problems—not least since anyone with any knowledge of prisons knows that a considerable proportion of assaults and physical threats are known only to the parties concerned, and therefore do not find their way into the official prison assault figures.

In considering the measurement of international variations in community crime rates, Lynch (1995, p. 21) makes the following pragmatic and sensible suggestion about data sources: "Police statistics should be used for comparing crimes that are known to be well reported to the police and that are consistently well reported across nations. This includes homicide, motor vehicle theft, and burglaries involving forcible entry. Victim surveys should be used for comparing classes of crime that are not well reported to the police."

Following this advice, obviously one should use victim surveys to assess the levels of most interpersonal violence in prisons, since prison assaults are certainly not "well reported" to the authorities, and nor, probably, are they "consistently . . . reported" in different prisons. Unfortunately, for the purposes of the present essay, such a conclusion is of limited assistance, because victim surveys are at present not at all well developed in the prisons context (see further below). As for Lynch's first category of crimes (i.e., those where the use of official data would apparently be appropriate because of high and consistent reporting and recording), there are few types of incident in the prison setting that are at present known to fall within such a definition. An obvious possible candidate is prison homicide—but, as we shall see, the extent and the technical quality of the data available on this topic is at present quite limited. Thus the question "How much prison violence?" can, at this time, be answered only very tentatively and approximately.

A. Studies of Physical Victimization in Prisons

As far as I am aware, the jurisdiction that, at present, has the most extensive available set of information on physical victimization in prisons is England and Wales. I shall, therefore, begin with a description

TABLE 1

Recorded Disciplinary Offenses of Assault and Fighting in Prison Service Establishments Housing Male Prisoners, England and Wales, 1990–96 (Rates per 1,000 Inmate Population)

	1990	1991	1992	1993	1994	1995	1996
A. Assaults on staff:							
All establishments	37	42	48	60	61	50	39
Local prisons	42	48	55	74	81	71	56
Open prisons	3	0	5	3	3	1	2
Closed training prisons	33	33	40	43	42	34	26
YOIs	43	47	55	64	66	63	49
Remand centers	76	121	110	137	106	83	57
B. Assaults on inmates:							
All establishments	30	33	33	41	39	38	34
Local prisons	32	33	31	38	41	43	36
Open prisons	2	3	4	2	4	3	3
Closed training prisons	17	18	17	19	18	15	15
YOIs	120	118	140	146	151	153	168
Remand centers	159	182	189	211	175	206	184
C. Fighting:							
All establishments	93	91	95	104	101	93	89
Local prisons	83	84	88	93	93	96	94
Open prisons	12	8	7	8	4	4	4
Closed training prisons	71	55	55	54	49	53	47
YOIs	383	375	416	497	501	462	526
Remand centers	439	523	499	518	522	473	437

Source.—Data are derived from relevant annual volumes of *Statistics of Offences against Prison Discipline and Punishments in England and Wales.*

Note.—YOIs = young offender institutions.

of what is known from these British sources. As will be seen, making sense of the available data is far from straightforward.

In England and Wales, the prison authorities are by statute required to publish annually a statistical return of all the recorded disciplinary offenses in every prison. Recorded data for assaults and fighting in male prisons since 1990, with a breakdown by type of prison, are given in table 1. These data show that, overall, in 1996 there was a rate of thirty-nine per thousand inmate population for prisoner–staff assaults, thirty-four per thousand for prisoner-prisoner assaults, and eighty-nine per thousand for offenses of fighting.[10] However, further examination of table 1 shows first, interesting changes over time (with rates

[10] In principle, an "assault" is unjustified violence by one person on another; and "fighting" is a bilateral or multilateral physical conflict, in which no one party is necessarily the aggressor. Obviously, in practice the distinction is not at all clear-cut.

peaking in 1993–94), and second, some marked variations by types of institution.[11] On the latter point, open prisons have very low rates for all three offenses. The two kinds of establishments for persons aged under twenty-one (YOIs and remand centers) have much higher rates than the adult prisons both for inmate-inmate assaults and (especially) for fighting. Adult closed prisons (i.e., local prisons and closed training prisons) have more recorded inmate-staff assaults than inmate-inmate assaults; but in the institutions for young offenders (YOIs and remand centers) this pattern is reversed. These are intriguing apparent differences, yet, from these data alone, there is no way of judging whether the picture they present is a valid one, or how far it is a product of, for example, differential use of discretion by prison staff in different kinds of establishment.

In 1991, in England and Wales, the first National Prison Survey (NPS) was conducted, with a random sample of all prisoners being interviewed on a range of topics, including the prison regime (work and education programs, etc.), relationships with prison officers, and preparations for release (for sentenced prisoners near release). The response rate for the survey was very good (90 percent). In the NPS, one question was asked on prison assaults: this was a simple yes/no question, inquiring "Have you been physically assaulted in any way by another inmate in the last six months"?[12] Overall, 9 percent of prisoners responded affirmatively to this question (Dodd and Hunter 1992, p. 54); however, there was a marked skew by age, with 15 percent of under-twenty-one's saying they had been assaulted, as compared with only 4 percent of prisoners over fifty.[13] But if we try to compare these data with those in table 1, we immediately run into difficulties. The NPS statistics are *prevalence* data only, with no follow-up question be-

[11] In England, there is no distinction between "jails" and "prisons," and the U.K. government is responsible for all custodial establishments for persons aged fifteen and over. The main types of institution are: (1) for those under twenty-one, "remand centers" (for those not yet sentenced) and "young offender institutions" or "YOIs"; (2) for adults, local prisons (holding remands and short sentence prisoners), and a variety of "training prisons" of ascending degrees of security, namely "open prisons" (for category D inmates who can be trusted not to escape); category C training prisons; category B training prisons; and maximum-security prisons holding category A prisoners (known as "dispersal prisons").

[12] For those who had been incarcerated on this occasion for less than six months, interviewers were instructed to substitute the words "since you have been in prison," in place of "in the last six months."

[13] These data include responses by female prisoners, but these constituted only 6 percent of the sample, reflecting their proportion in the prison population. See further Subsec. II*E* below.

ing asked about the frequency of recent assaults; but the information in table 1 is incidence data. At first sight, the overall NPS prevalence figure for inmate assault seems to be just under three times higher than the official 1991 inmate-inmate incidence data (90 vs. 33). However, this may not be accurate, because some incidents classed as assaults by NPS respondents might have been prosecuted, in the prison disciplinary code, as "fighting" (see n. 10). The total incidence figure for 1991 for inmate-inmate assaults *plus* fighting is 124 per thousand inmates: this is nearly 40 percent higher than the NPS prevalence rate, though the difference could of course be attributable to repeat victimization.

In the late 1980s, King and McDermott (1995) carried out a major study of many aspects of prison regimes in England, focusing on five adult prisons (though they did not write up their full results until after publication of the NPS). King and McDermott had distributed self-completion questionnaires to inmates in all their prisons, but they took this step only "at the very end of the fieldwork in each prison when both the researchers personally, and the aims of the research, were well known" (King and McDermott 1995, pp. 20–21). Over eleven hundred usable questionnaires were received. No formal data on response rates are given, but it can reasonably be inferred that the rate of completed responses in most of the prisons was substantially lower than in the NPS.[14] Overall, King and McDermott report that 12.5 percent of their sample said they had been assaulted *at some time while in their current prisons;* 6.8 percent of respondents claimed to have been sexually attacked; and 33 percent said they had been threatened with violence. The prevalence figures for assaults (sexual and otherwise) are obviously higher than those for adults in the NPS, but exact comparisons are impossible because of the different time frames used in the two surveys (for a detailed discussion on this point, see King and McDermott 1995, p. 120). There is also the separate and complex issue of the very different methodologies adopted in the two studies.[15]

---

[14] Approximate response rates can be calculated from the numbers of completed questionnaires, plus the data given by the authors on intended sample coverage (p. 21n.) and the average daily population (ADP) in each prison (pp. 17–19). On this basis, four of the prisons had response rates between 45 percent and 53 percent, while the fifth (the local prison) had a response rate of 80 percent.

[15] The National Prison Survey used an interview approach, but with interviewers meeting the prisoner-respondent for the first time in the survey context (as with most surveys of the general population). King and McDermott (see text) had deliberately tried to build up a degree of personal trust before distributing their questionnaires; but they preferred to rely on prisoners completing their own written responses, rather than an interview format.

TABLE 2

Self-Reported Victimization Prevalence Rates in Current Prison
for Three Kinds of Violent Incident in Five English Prisons
for Adult Males, 1985–86 (Percent)

	Prevalence of Victimization for:			
	Assaults	Sex Attacks	Threats of Violence	Sample N
Local prison: remand prisoners	10	5	35	211
Local prison: sentenced prisoners	7	3	26	201
Open prison	2	3	14	168
Closed training prison (category C)	10	7	36	269
Closed training prison (category B)	22	12	43	156
Closed training prison (maximum security)	30	13	49	155
Overall percent figure	13	7	33	1,160

SOURCE.—King and McDermott (1995), table 3.1 (p. 122).

In the King-McDermott research, the prevalence rates for all three
types of violent incident varied substantially by prison—for assaults,
for example, from 2 percent in an open prison to 30 percent in a maximum security training prison (see table 2). Most of these differences
are encouragingly consistent with the variations in the official data
shown in table 1; but the data for the local prison in the King-
McDermott study are unfortunately much harder to interpret.[16]

Fieldwork for a further research study was carried out in England in
1994–95; unlike the previous surveys, the principal topic of the research was on this occasion victimization and bullying in institutions.
The study, by researchers from Oxford University, was carried out in
two adult prisons holding sentenced offenders (one category B; one
category C; see n. 11 above), and two YOIs, one of which also func-
tioned as a Remand Center (see O'Donnell and Edgar 1996a, 1996b,
1998a, 1998b). Like King and McDermott, the Oxford researchers

[16] The authors note that "the victimization rates for both remand and convicted prisoners in Birmingham were somewhat lower than we had expected," a result that they
attributed to the substantially lower number of hours that prisoners spent out of their
cells in this prison (as in most local prisons in England) (King and McDermott 1995,
pp. 121–23). However, this suggestion, while valid in itself, does not take account of the
fact that Birmingham, unlike most of the prisons in the King-McDermott study, had a
substantial proportion of its population sharing cells. Cell sharing also potentially facili-
tates assaults, and there were suggestions in an earlier study of Birmingham Prison that
in-cell assaults occurred quite frequently (Davies 1982).

TABLE 3

One-Month Self-Reported Victimization Rates for Three Kinds
of Incident in Four English Prison Service Establishments
for Males, 1994–95 (Percent)

	YOI plus Remands	Small YOI	Adult Closed Training (Category C)	Adult Closed Training (Category B)
Assault:				
None	68	74	83	80
One/two	28	24	16	19
More often	4	1	1	1
Robbery/extortion:				
None	89	92	98	95
One/two	7	5	1	4
More often	4	3	0	2
Threats of violence:				
None	54	60	75	73
One/two	38	37	23	24
More often	8	3	2	3
Sample N	650	185	213	518

Source.—O'Donnell and Edgar (1998*a*), pp. 26, 28, 30.
Note.—All percents sum to 100. YOI = youth offender institution.

chose to rely on a prisoners' written self-completion questionnaire as
their main quantitative data source; but in the Oxford study, the questionnaires were apparently completed under more controlled conditions,[17] and the survey response rate was substantially higher than in
the King-McDermott research (90 percent, identical to that for the
NPS).

The Oxford study focused specifically on six particular types of victimization, each of which was described on the questionnaire in ordinary language. Three of these six related to violence or threats of violence, and respondents were asked to state whether they had been
victimized during the last month for each incident type. The main results for the three types of violent victimization are shown in table 3.

[17] After an extensive period of qualitative fieldwork in each establishment, O'Donnell
and Edgar made personal visits to prisoners while they were locked in their cells, explaining the purpose of the research and its confidentiality. They then left the inmate
with a victimization questionnaire, returning after half an hour to collect it. If there were
any blank sections, the prisoner was encouraged to complete the questionnaire, and usually did so.

For each incident type, the first row of table 3 gives the percentage claiming no victimization. From the obverse of these figures, one can derive prevalence data comparable with the NPS and the King-McDermott study, though for the much shorter time period of one month. As may be seen, for assaults in the young offender establishments the claimed victimization prevalence rate is over 25 percent in both institutions in a one-month period (cf. the NPS figure of 15 percent for prisoners under twenty-one, in a six-month period). For sentenced adult offenders, the prevalence rate for assaults in the O'Donnell-Edgar study was lower than for the young prisoners, but was still close to 20 percent. A comparison with the prevalence rates in the King-McDermott study, for the same types of adult prison, is particularly interesting given the apparent similarity of the methodology employed in the two studies:

> *Category B Prison:*
>   King-McDermott:
>   22 percent prevalence (any time in this prison)
>   O'Donnell-Edgar:
>   20 percent prevalence (in last month)
> *Category C Prison:*
>   King-McDermott:
>   10 percent prevalence (any time in this prison)
>   O'Donnell-Edgar:
>   17 percent prevalence (in last month)

Clearly, the O'Donnell-Edgar figures are, prima facie, substantially the higher. However, adequate reconciliation of the figures in the two studies poses difficult questions, including methodological issues.[18]

The O'Donnell-Edgar study is the first published prison victimization study in England to have considered issues of *incidence* as well as *prevalence*. However, the question of incidence was operationalized in the research only in an imprecise fashion. (Respondents who claimed any victimization in the last month were asked whether this had hap-

---

[18] Apart from the difference in response rates, one other relevant factor is that, in both surveys, the researchers asked about inmates' level of victimizing behavior, as well as about victimization. In the King-McDermott study, it was reported that "prisoners were, understandably, somewhat more reluctant to report" predatory behavior (p. 125); however, in the O'Donnell-Edgar study admitted levels of victimizing behavior were in general very similar to self-reported levels of victimization (O'Donnell and Edgar 1998a, chap. 3).

pened, within that time frame, "once or twice," or more often.) Relevant data are given in table 3. Among all victimized respondents, the proportion claiming multiple victimization (three times or more in the last month) was particularly high for robbery/extortion in the two young offender institutions (4 percent among 11 percent victimized in one establishment; 3 percent among 8 percent victimized in the other). This finding is of particular interest, because in the Oxford research, robbery was the type of violent victimization with substantially the lowest prevalence rates. In other words, robbery/extortion was, in this study, the rarest type of violent victimization, *but in young offender institutions it was also the kind of violent victimization whose victims were, proportionately, most likely to be repeatedly victimized.* These data are interestingly congruent with other analyses in the O'Donnell-Edgar study, concerning the extent of the overlap between victims and victimizers. Both for assaults and for threats of violence, there was a substantial element of *mutuality* in the data: being a victim of these offenses was strongly associated with being a victimizer also. But for robbery, the pattern was quite different—"those who were robbed did not rob others" (O'Donnell and Edgar 1996*b*, p. 3). For this offense, it seemed, there was little mutuality—rather, the few who were victimized could be victimized frequently, and they did not attack others in reply.

Although it is important not to read too much into one exploratory study, the apparent differences in the O'Donnell-Edgar research between more and less "mutual" prison victimization seems well worth much fuller exploration in a range of different prison contexts. I shall return to this theme in Section VI below.

After recently reviewing the rather limited number of prison victimization studies carried out in North America, Maitland and Sluder (1998, p. 57) commented that there has been a strong tendency in such research "to operationalize victimization narrowly, with many scales composed of only three or four items . . . [and] focused on a few forms of physical victimization." As will be clear from the preceding account, this conclusion also holds true, to a substantial extent, for Britain. Hence, there is a very strong case for a much fuller development and use of victim survey methodology in the prisons context in the future.[19] In any such development, careful note should be taken of the many methodological lessons to be learned from the now extensive literature

---

[19] As well as other possible methods for uncovering "hidden violence," such as the analysis of prison medical records (on which see Davies 1982).

on victim surveys on crime in ordinary residential communities (see, e.g., Maung [1995] on the British Crime Survey).

Among the published North American prison victimization studies, one of the most interesting is Cooley's (1993) research in five adult male Canadian Federal prisons (though the total sample in this research was small: $N = 117$). Unlike any of the British researchers previously discussed, Cooley employed what has become, in general criminological research, the standard approach in victim survey methodology, namely an interview-based approach, using a Victimization Screening Schedule, and, where appropriate, Incident Report Forms (see Maung 1995). Cooley asked his respondents to recall prison victimizations over a twelve-month period, for which period he had access to the official disciplinary data for the five institutions studied. For assaults and fights, victim survey data were more than three times higher than the official rates (Cooley 1993, p. 489), though multiple victimizations were rarer than might reasonably have been expected in a twelve-month time frame. By contrast, in a study of young prisoners (mean age 21) in a Midwestern U.S. state, Maitland and Sluder (1998) found what must be regarded as relatively low prevalence rates for some kinds of victimization, but also data suggesting that "a significant proportion of prisoners are subjected to multiple forms of victimization" (p. 64).[20]

A substantial number of the published studies on interpersonal prison violence rely only or mainly on recorded disciplinary incidents from official files. It is very clear (see the preceding discussion) that such data often substantially understate the extent of violent victimization among inmates. But it is also important to glean what we can from the research literature about known biases (or lack of bias) in the recorded data—that is, to consider what evidence there is that some kinds of incident, or attacks against certain sorts of victims, are particularly likely or unlikely to find their way into the official data sources. In such an analysis, there are of course two particularly important "filtering points" to consider—first, the extent to which inmates are willing to report victimizations, and second, the extent to which staff may differentially report or record certain incidents.

---

[20] Maitland and Sluder collected prevalence data only, but did so on a wide range of fourteen items about victimization experiences (see their table 3). "Multiple victimization," in their study, refers to inmates reporting several different kinds of victimization while serving their current term of imprisonment: the researchers found that 69 percent of the sample had experienced *at least ten* of the fourteen listed kinds of victimization (p. 64).

As regards the reporting of violence to the authorities by inmates, all sources seem to agree (though sometimes only with anecdotal evidence) that this is rare. At the same time, it is clear that action of this kind is sometimes taken by prisoners, and there would be merit in a more systematic exploration of this phenomenon. O'Donnell and Edgar (1998a, pp. 41–42) touch on this issue briefly, with evidence that between 10 percent and 20 percent of victims of assaults and threats, among both adults and young prisoners, were prepared to make a formal complaint to the authorities about the incident. These authors point out, however, that prisoners who do make complaints in this way have to be prepared, potentially, to have their identity discovered by other inmates. Given that there is a strong subcultural norm against "grassing" (i.e., acting as an informer), the possibility of such discovery means that making a formal complaint is often an inmate's last resort—as one prisoner put it, when asked whether he had informed the authorities: "Not yet, but I might have to." Those who made formal complaints also had to accept the possibility that this might result in their being transferred to another institution, in the interests of their own safety (even though this second prison might be less geographically convenient for family visits, and/or have a less agreeable regime).

What of the filtering process exercised by prison staff in respect of reporting prisoner assaults? We will return to this issue again in Section V, but for the moment it can be noted that the research literature contains several examples of differential responses by staff to known institutional misconduct by inmates, and these differences will obviously potentially affect the statistical distribution in any sample of officially recorded prison violence. Perhaps most importantly for present purposes, there is some suggestive research evidence of a differential staff response by the prisoner's race and by institutional classification.

Both these variables were found to be relevant in a small study ($N = 84$) by Silberman (1995) in a male maximum-security prison in the United States. In the prison studied ("Central"), a classification system known as the Adult Internal Management System (AIMS) was used (see Quay 1984). This system is designed to differentiate prisoners who are aggressive and independent (known as "heavies"), from those who are passive and dependent ("lights"), and those who fall into neither of these categories ("moderates"). According to self-reported aggressive behavior scales applied by the researcher, heavies had, in Central, threatened or assaulted others (inmates and staff) significantly more often than moderates or lights. But, Silberman additionally reports, the detection rate for assaults was higher among heavies because they were subjected to closer official surveillance (p. 93). Hence, the much higher officially recorded assault rate among heavies partly reflected actual inmate behavior, but was also partly an artefact of prison management practices that generated higher detection. Turning to race, self-reported assaultiveness was similar between black and white prisoners, but blacks were significantly more likely to have been officially cited for assault. This differential treatment, however, seemed not to be attributable to "overt racial bias" (p. 105), but rather to the fact that black prisoners were more likely than whites to be labeled as heavies by the AIMS classification system, and were consequently subject to closer surveillance by guards.[21]

Silberman's results on race are not dissimilar to those found in an earlier and much-cited article by Poole and Regoli (1980). That study had found that whites and blacks were equally likely to engage in prison rule-breaking activity (not simply assaults), but that blacks were more likely to be officially reported for rule infractions. Moreover, a prior record of official disciplinary action was shown to be strongly related to the decision to take official action in the case of blacks, while prior record exerted "no measurable effects" (p. 942) in the citation of whites. In short, there was a "cumulative labeling effect" (p. 943) that acted to the detriment of blacks. In part, the authors suggest, these cumulative effects might be the product of institutional processes: "Prior official reactions may lead guards to a pattern of closer surveillance of labeled inmates. This greater vigilance is likely to result in more frequent detection of infractions" (p. 943).

While processes of the above kind have not been unambiguously demonstrated in the research literature in studies with large samples, nevertheless it is clear that cumulative labeling effects of the kind described are possible. Researchers cannot, therefore, at present reasonably rule out the existence of such effects; and one of the challenges for future research in this area is to investigate such possible processes more thoroughly.

In addition to factors of the above kind, formal citation for prisoner-prisoner assaults can potentially vary by the personal attitudes of indi-

[21] However, as Silberman (1995) notes, the AIMS classification depends heavily on prior criminal justice records (for any stage of processing from arrest onward) and on social factors such as employment histories and family status. Consequently, "the differential treatment of black prisoners at Central is primarily a consequence of racial bias in society as a whole, rather than policies generated at this institution" (p. 95).

vidual prison officers. For example, from a questionnaire study of correctional officers in Texas, Eigenberg (1994) developed as a dependent variable a nine-item scale measuring officers' willingness to respond officially to prisoner rape. The independent variables that were most strongly associated with this scale were first, attitudes toward appropriate "social distance" between officers and prisoners (those who maintained less social distance and a more rehabilitative approach to prisoners were more willing to react officially to prisoner rape); and second, attitudes toward women (those who endorsed a more conservative, home-based role for women in society were less likely to respond officially to prisoner rape, perhaps because they were also more willing to endorse stereotypical beliefs about the nature of the act of rape).

B. Prison Homicides

Many jurisdictions have reassuringly low rates of homicide victimization among prisoners, and where this is so, assessing any kind of time-trend in prison homicide rates is statistically hazardous.

By comparison with other jurisdictions, the United States has a relatively high prison homicide rate, but unfortunately it is not possible from the available sources to derive fully accurate figures over time. For the period before 1978, only data from occasional (although thorough) national surveys can be adduced. Since 1978, there has been a regularly reported figure for sentenced prisoners whose deaths were "caused by another," but (see the "Note on Sources" attached to table 4) a few of the deaths included in these totals are not homicides; moreover, since the late 1980s a number of jurisdictions have not sent in returns.

The data shown in table 4 are therefore clearly imperfect. Nevertheless, they do reveal a general pattern that is probably accurate. The rate of inmate homicides per ten thousand prisoners shows a curvilinear pattern: it apparently increased sharply in the 1970s, and then steadily declined, eventually falling well below its 1960s levels. The pattern is so pronounced that it probably cannot be attributed to the known weaknesses in the data set.

I shall return in Section III to possible reasons for this apparent pattern. For the moment, however, one important point is worth noting. A possible explanation of the observed homicide time-trend relates to the use of the death penalty in the United States, since there was a de facto moratorium on executions from 1967 onward (Bedau 1982,

TABLE 4

Imputed Inmate Homicide Victimizations among Sentenced
Prisoners in the United States, 1965–94

Year	Imputed no. of Inmate Homicides	Rate per 10,000 prisoners	Jurisdictions Not Reporting
1965	53	25	5
1973	124	61	0
1974	114	52	6
1975	110	46	6
1978	89	30	0
1979	84	28	0
1980	127*	40	0
1983	86	21	0
1984	128†	29	0
1986	100	19	1
1987	91	16	2
1988	67	11	4
1989	67	10	4
1990	49	7	3
1991	62	8	5
1992	67	8	6
1994	68	7	3

SOURCES.—Data on imputed homicide victimizations in this table have been derived from a number of sources, listed below. Data from sources (i)–(iii) inclusive include only inmate-inmate homicides; but source (iv) uses a wider definition: (i) for 1965, from Sellin (1967); (ii) for 1973, from Sylvester, Reed and Nelson (1977); (iii) for 1974 and 1975, from a special survey reported in the *Sourcebook of Criminal Justice Statistics 1978*, p. 641; (iv) for 1978 onward, from the annual tables, reported in successive *Sourcebooks of Criminal Justice Statistics*, identifying causes of death among sentenced prisoners. The data given are for deaths "caused by another," which explanatory notes in the *Sourcebook* indicate incorporates "all inmates whose deaths were caused accidentally or intentionally by another inmate or by prison personnel."

* This figure includes thirty-nine cases from New Mexico. A total of thirty-three inmates were killed in the Santa Fe riot in New Mexico in 1980 (see Colvin 1992).

† This figure includes 25 inmate homicides in Texas, which can be attributed to the special events in the Texas prison system at that time (see Crouch and Marquart 1989, chap. 7).

pp. 24–25), with a resumption of executions only in the 1980s. However, an explanation of this kind is made harder to sustain by the fact that cross-sectional comparisons of prison homicides in jurisdictions with and without the death penalty have revealed no discernible effects of an apparently deterrent kind (Wolfson 1982; Bedau 1997, pp. 176–77). As Bedau (p. 177) notes, the available data on this point are not conclusive, but they are suggestive.

II. Some Basic Features of Interpersonal Prison Violence
In this section, data on some of the main possible correlates of interpersonal prison violence are presented as an essential background to the discussion in later sections. As other reviewers have already thoroughly covered some of this ground, the treatment of certain topics within this section is relatively brief, and readers are referred to the cited sources for more detailed analyses.

In reviewing research results of this kind, it is necessary to refer to studies relating to prisons in several different jurisdictions. The details of the day-to-day social settings in such prisons can vary substantially, and (see the later sections of this essay) such settings may sometimes substantially influence levels of prison violence. These issues should be borne in mind as caveats in considering the research results here cited.

A. Age
One of the most consistently established correlates of interpersonal prison violence is that, in general, younger inmates are more often the perpetrators of such violence (for literature citations see, e.g., Goetting and Howsen 1986, pp. 51–52; Ditchfield 1990, pp. 48–55; K. Adams 1992, pp. 202–3; and for a recent time-series analysis, see Walters 1998).

Among the more interesting analyses of this issue is that by MacKenzie (1987), conducted in four medium and maximum security prisons for males in three U.S. states. MacKenzie used three measures of conflict/aggression for each prisoner: a self-reported scale (Inmate Conflicts) designed to measure the amount of conflict the respondent had with other prisoners; another self-reported scale (Guard Conflicts) designed to measure conflicts with guards; and the officially recorded number of (Major Misconduct) tickets for the inmate in question. For inmates aged twenty or over, seven separate age-bands were identified (the oldest being 50+), and all three of the conflict measures showed a significant decline in rates from younger to older age-bands. However, the speed of decline differed: the Major Misconduct scale dropped rapidly from age twenty to age thirty to thirty-four, and slowly thereafter; but Inmate Conflicts and Guard Conflicts dropped only slowly in the twenties. A related finding was that an "assertiveness" measure was strongly correlated with individuals' Inmate Conflict and Guard Conflict scores at all ages, but the relationship between assertiveness and individuals' Major Misconduct tickets was limited to those under thirty. Separate analyses of anxiety suggested that these differences between younger and older prisoners were not accounted for by differential stress levels or by differential ability to cope when under stress. Rather, the younger inmates seemed to be willing to "act out" their assertiveness more freely and with less inhibitions, so acquiring more tickets for Major Misconduct—or, as Kenneth Adams (1992, p. 302) puts it when discussing this study, perhaps younger inmates tend to resolve their conflicts "in ways that are demonstrably visible and that advertise toughness and strength."[22] These are intriguing results that deserve research replication. One implication of the results is to emphasize again that one cannot necessarily treat recorded prison disciplinary infractions as a valid measure of aggression, even in comparative analyses between groups of prisoners within the same institutions.

The research literature additionally suggests that younger inmates are more likely to be victimized in the prison context than are older inmates (see, e.g., Cooley 1993; O'Donnell and Edgar 1998a). However, in interpreting this finding one needs to bear in mind that frequently in prison systems younger inmates are placed in separate, age-segregated institutions or housing blocks.

B. Race

Findings on race and the commission of interpersonal prison violence have been mixed (see, e.g., Ellis, Grasmick, and Gilman 1974; Petersilia 1983; K. Adams 1992, pp. 301–2). The most recent, and very large-scale study was conducted by Harer and Steffensmeier (1996), using data for male prisoners in the federal prison system (inmate $N = 24{,}000$). This study is particularly notable for two reasons. First, the

---

[22] This pattern was even more evident in the small group ($N = 31$) of inmates aged nineteen or less in the MacKenzie study. This group had much the highest rate of Major Misconduct tickets of any age group, but their Inmate Conflict and Guard Conflict scores were lower than those of the twenty to twenty-four year age group.

authors were interested in the question of the effects of race net of controls, and they introduced many more control variables than do most comparable analyses. Second, the research focused on two separate dependent variables, namely "prison violence" and "prison alcohol/drug violations," with differing results: black inmates were found, after applying statistical controls, to have higher prison interpersonal violence rates than whites, but lower rates of alcohol/drug misconduct.[23] These results are interpreted by the researchers as supportive of a racially based "subculture of violence" thesis—a subculture which, it is suggested, has been developed in the outside community, and then "imported" into the prison by black inmates. However, such an interpretation depends crucially on the assumption, explicitly made by the authors, that at least in the federal prison system official rates of misconduct "reflect real differences in behavior and are not simply a product of discretionary sanctioning practices on the part of prison staff" (p. 330). But this seems a very bold assumption—not least in the light of the research discussed at the end of Section I.4 above.

Research results on the relationship between race and victimization in prison, using victim survey data, are sparse. However, O'Donnell and Edgar (1996a, tables A and B), in their English study, found different results for adult prisoners and for young offender institutions: for adults, there was no significant difference in victimization by ethnic group, but among young prisoners, whites and Asians were significantly more likely to be victimized than were blacks. In their U.S. victimization study among younger prisoners, Maitland and Sluder (1998, tables 7–9) similarly found that whites had significantly higher victimization rates than nonwhites.

C. Criminal and Social History

There are two main considerations regarding the histories of those who resort to violence in prisons: criminal history and mental illness or disturbance. As regards criminal history, the research studies are not consistent in their results. However, as Kenneth Adams (1992) summarizes, with the exception of those convicted of homicide, most studies suggest that "violent offenders tend to have higher prison infraction rates than nonviolent offenders" (p. 305). But in interpreting this finding, it is important to recall the apparently paramount importance of

[23] To simplify the analysis, Harer and Steffensmeier excluded from their sample non-U.S. citizens and persons from ethnic groups other than blacks and whites, e.g., Hispanics.

young age, a variable that shows a much stronger correlation with prison violence (whatever measure of such violence is adopted). Hence studies of the criminal history of perpetrators of prison violence that do not control for age are of limited value.

In a cross-sectional study of 942 inmates from ten prisons in New York State, Wright (1991b) found that, as well as being younger, those found guilty of any assault in prison "tend to have histories of unemployment, are less educated . . . are more likely to be single [and] were incarcerated for the first time at a younger age" (p. 12). As Wright points out, these data are consistent with the social histories described by Irwin (1970) for what he calls "state-raised youth": that is, persistent young offenders with relatively unstable social lives, who made an early start to their criminal careers, and have spent a disproportionate amount of time in children's homes and/or state institutions for juvenile offenders. Such a description is, of course, also very familiar from the results found for persistent offenders in criminal career research (for a summary, see, e.g., Farrington 1997).

Given the high "dark figure" for prison violence, one point that is crucially raised by research results of the above kind is: How representative are those officially identified as having committed prison violence of the broader universe of those who at some time have resorted to such violence? Here, the fact of a high dark figure for violent incidents in prison does not necessarily invalidate the representativeness of studies of the characteristics of a sample of identified offenders. For example, in a Danish self-report study among school children, Balvig (1988) reported that although only one in ten of relatively serious delinquent incidents had led to the offender being identified by the police, nevertheless, 90 percent of all those who had committed such offences with any frequency had been caught and identified as an "official" offender on at least one occasion. Given such a factual constellation, if the characteristics of identified offenders differ significantly from those of the population as a whole, some reasonable validity might be inferred for the statistical differences found.

Kenneth Adams (1992) offers a very different argument, which seeks to establish especially the validity of data on the characteristics of repeat offenders against the prison disciplinary code: "While an occasional misbehavior report cannot be accorded much significance as an adjustment problem, frequent or systematic violations of prison rules are much less ambiguous signs of adjustment difficulties, especially when the focus is on extreme or chronic offenders. . . . [This argument] is reinforced further by the implausibility of describing inmate misbehavior as constructive problem-solving efforts to deal with one's situation given that the formal disciplinary process carries serious adverse consequences for the inmate" (pp. 296–97).

Two comments may be made about this approach. First, a data source on rule infractions (in the present context, especially aggressive rule-infractions) has, by a subtle shift, been called into service as an indicator of "adjustment problems." This "adjustment," however, is assessed only from the viewpoint of the authorities, and does not take into account the possibly very different demands on the inmate to adjust to the subcultural world of inmate life (Silberman 1995, p. 27; see also Sec. VI below). Second, and more important, in a context where the vast majority of violent acts are apparently undetected, it should be clear that those who are formally identified as repeat offenders may well be atypical of the larger universe of those who are prepared, when occasion demands, to resort to violence to achieve their own ends. For example, a research focus on *formally identified repeat offenders* will very likely overstate the proportionate significance, within the universe of interpersonal prison violence, of those whose violence is less calculated and is thus more associated with emotional or mental health problems. Given this background, the important and detailed work of Toch and Adams (1989), which pays special attention to a smallish group of so-called DDIs, or "disturbed-disruptive inmates," needs to be read with some care. DDIs undoubtedly exist, and form a significant element within the total picture of prison violence; but a focus on official data sources on repeat offenders will almost certainly lead to disproportionate attention being focused on the DDI group.

Given the above comments, it is particularly important to note that there is some evidence of heightened psychiatric impairment even among general samples of those who have *any record of prison violence* (see, e.g., Wright 1991*b*; K. Adams 1992, pp. 306–8). Perhaps the study of greatest interest in this regard is Baskin, Sommers, and Steadman's (1991) analysis of over three thousand prisoners in New York State, where the sampling procedures specifically excluded those inmates housed in special mental health housing units. The researchers developed three simple scales to measure psychiatric impairment while in prison: these were labeled respectively as "confusion," "depression," and "manifest symptomatology" (for the scales used, see appendix A of the cited source). The dependent variables used in the analysis were yes/no measures of four types of prison violence within the last ninety days, as assessed by prison case managers: these were violence to another prisoner, violence to prison staff, destruction of prison property, and "violence to self" (attempted suicide or self-harm). In a multivariate analysis, controlling for age, race, gender, and criminal history, and so on, the confusion scale was found to be strongly statistically associated with both violence to prisoners and violence to staff, while the depression scale was, not unexpectedly, even more closely associated with violence to self. There is, therefore, some reasonable general evidence of a link between emotional disorder and interpersonal prison violence, though as will become clear in Section III, other variables are certainly also very important in influencing this kind of behavior.

D. Sentence Variables

Two variables relating to general administrative dimensions of the inmate's prison experience have been especially studied for their possible association with interpersonal prison violence: they are the inmate's security level and the phase of his or her sentence.

Research studies have consistently shown that rates of prison violence are higher in maximum-security than in lower-security prisons (for an example, see the data in table 2, from King and McDermott's [1995] inmate questionnaire). Data such as this, however, are in themselves of limited value, since obviously prisoners considered to be more "difficult" may be placed in higher custody levels, and it might therefore simply be the combined individual effects of "difficult prisoners" that are being measured. Some analyses have, therefore, attempted to assess the importance of security level while controlling for various individual-level variables (see, e.g., Mandaraka-Sheppard 1986; Baskin, Sommers, and Steadman 1991; Wright 1991a; Cooley 1993). These studies have used different individual-level variables as controls and also different measures of prison violence (official and self-reported); but all have found higher security levels to be associated with greater violence. It is therefore possible, as Wright (1991a, p. 235) puts it, that "more structured, more authoritarian settings may engender more disruptive behavior. This finding is consistent with the literature on environmental effects, which suggests that the more control inmates feel they exercise within their settings, the less likely they are to experience adjustment problems."

Care must be taken, however, before firmly accepting such a conclusion. Although the cited studies each control for some individual-level effects, they may not control either for sufficient numbers of such variables or for various possible interactive effects (see further Subsec. IV*D* below).

When we turn to the literature on phase of sentence, we find a much more variegated picture. A number of writers have found that predatory aggression appears to peak relatively early in the inmate's sentence, and then decline—a pattern found particularly strongly among younger prisoners (see, e.g., Toch and Adams 1989, and the discussion of various studies in K. Adams 1992). If this is a true finding, it has at least two possible interpretations: first, that the majority of prisoners "learn to adapt successfully to the prison setting" (K. Adams 1992, p. 331); or second, that inmates far away in time from their potential parole dates may feel less inhibited about prison offending (see, e.g., Ellis, Grasmick, and Gilman 1974). However, it is also notable that the studies finding an "early in sentence" effect tend overwhelmingly to be based on official indices of the commission of prison violence. Hence it is of special interest that Wright (1991*a*, p. 235) found, in multivariate analyses with the same sample of prisoners, that: using official data, newly arrived prisoners had higher infraction rates than longer-serving inmates; but using self-reports of aggressive behavior, "time incarcerated" did not appear in the multivariate model. The implication of these results is, as Wright points out, that "shorter and longer-term inmates do not have different actual rates of aggressiveness, but that the responsiveness of the system determines who will be charged with rule infractions" (p. 235). If this interpretation is valid, then clearly it is also of some potential relevance that: the Toch-Adams study found a much stronger "time-decline" effect for younger inmates than for adults, and that MacKenzie (1987) found that younger prisoners in her sample showed greater disjunction between official infraction rates and self-reported measures of Prisoner Conflict and Guard Conflict (see the discussion in Subsec. *A* above).

A few studies have also examined violent victimization by time in sentence, with equally inconclusive results. Thus, for example, Cooley (1993), in his Canadian study, found that those who were victimized were more likely to be in the early stages of their sentence, but this finding has not been replicated in other studies (e.g., Wooldredge 1994; O'Donnell and Edgar 1996*a*, 1996*b*).

In summary, therefore, the inmate's security level has been shown by research to be consistently related to prison violence, though the interpretation of this finding is not clear-cut. By contrast, the research evidence on prison violence and time in sentence must at present be regarded as very uncertain.

E. Gender

The available data on interpersonal prison violence and gender are sparse, but also quite provocative. As is well known, in general studies of crime commission in the community, males consistently appear to offend more often than females, especially for certain kinds of offense, including violence; and these gender differences are generally replicated by self-report studies, at least for offenses of any seriousness (see, e.g., Graham and Bowling 1995).

Some aspects of the data on interpersonal prison violence fully conform to this pattern. For example, very few prison homicides involve women as either assailants or victims: of the 374 imputed homicides of sentenced prisoners in the United States from 1986 to 1990 inclusive (see table 4), only two occurred in women's prisons. Similarly, in the Baskin, Sommers, and Steadman (1991) study in New York State, it was noted that "the frequency of recorded incidents of prison violence during the ninety-day period under study varied greatly by gender" (p. 276), in the expected direction.

But results of this kind are by no means universal in the literature. For example, in England recorded data for prison assaults and fighting are substantially higher, overall, in women's prisons than in male institutions (see table 5); and in the English NPS similar proportions of female and male prisoners said they had been assaulted in the last six months.[24] An analogous North American study, using official data for all prison infractions, is that by Tischler and Marquart (1989) in Texas, which found that "females . . . did not differ from males on the total number of offenses committed, nor did they differ with respect to the number of serious infractions" (p. 512).[25]

Once again, the data patterns are inconclusive; but from the available evidence it seems to be at least possible that, while serious violence in women's prisons is rare (cf. the homicide data), minor violence

[24] This result is not reported in the official publication on the NPS (see Dodd and Hunter 1992, chap. 5). I am indebted to John Ditchfield of the Home Office Research and Statistics Directorate for obtaining this information for me.

[25] There were also some qualitative differences within these general results. In particular, "male inmates were more likely to direct an attack towards correctional staff members; females were more likely to attack one another physically, with and without weapons" (p. 512).

TABLE 5

Comparison of Male and Female Establishments: Recorded
Disciplinary Offenses of Assault and Fighting, England and Wales,
1990–96 (Rates per 1,000 Inmate Population)

	1990	1991	1992	1993	1994	1995	1996
A. Assaults on staff:							
Male establishments	37	42	48	60	61	50	39
Female establishments	137	126	137	162	144	131	115
B. Assaults on inmates:							
Male establishments	30	33	33	41	39	38	34
Female establishments	55	47	74	86	77	77	59
C. Fighting:							
Male establishments	93	91	95	104	101	93	89
Female establishments	141	123	136	140	181	158	150

SOURCES.—Data are derived from relevant annual volumes of *Statistics of Offences
against Prison Discipline and Punishments in England and Wales.*

is not. If further studies were to support such a conclusion, then this
would provide strong prima facie evidence of an environmental effect,
with the transition from the outside community to the prison tending
to heighten levels of women's minor violence, at least as compared
with those of men. I shall return to this point in Section III below,
when discussing the results of the multivariate study by Mandaraka-
Sheppard (1986).

III. Do Environmental Factors Affect Prison Violence?

A main feature of the analysis in this essay (see the Introduction) is to
attempt to set interpersonal prison violence within the context of daily
social order in prisons. But, as a preliminary to such an analysis, we
must first consider what convincing evidence there is that variables
connected to the prison's environment (in the broadest sense of that
term) do indeed influence the amount and type of violence.

A useful starting point is Wright and Goodstein's (1989) essay of a
decade ago on correctional environments. As these writers point out,
three broad groups of prison environment studies can usefully be dis-
tinguished, namely: (i) those focusing on the physical characteristics of
the prison environment, such as architecture and the degree of crowding in the institution; (ii) transactional studies, mostly by social psychologists, focusing on "interactions between people and events or
settings and . . . the social ecology of these person/environment trans-

actions" (p. 259); and (iii) studies that do not focus on the prison environment directly but instead infer an environmental effect from empirical analyses of prison system policy changes and their intended and unintended consequences. I shall adopt a similar framework for analysis in this section, though the three types of studies will be considered in a different order than in the Wright-Goodstein review. Additionally, the third category will be expanded to include studies that draw conclusions inferring environmental effects from radical changes in prisoners' environments occurring other than as a result of alterations in prison system policies.

A. Studies Inferring Environmental Effects on Prison Violence

The essential common characteristic of this first kind of research study is that a feature or features of the environment of a given prisoner changes substantially, and then a before-and-after analysis of the transition is conducted. From such an analysis, environmental effects may then be inferred, though obviously there are a number of potential threats to the validity of any such conclusion (see, generally, Cook and Campbell 1979).

A particularly interesting analysis of this kind was conducted by Cooke (1989) at the so-called Special Unit in Barlinnie Prison, Glasgow, Scotland (see also, more generally, Cooke 1991). The Special Unit, now closed, was in its day a famous separate enclave within Barlinnie Prison, reserved for a very small number of male long-term prisoners who had proved very disruptive in the main prison system. The unit was originally designed on "therapeutic community" lines (see, e.g., Jones 1968), to which it subsequently did not adhere in full; nevertheless, the notion of "the community" within the unit (embracing both inmates and staff) remained an important organizing concept, and "community meetings" were regularly held (see Whatmore [1987] for a brief description of the unit; Boyle [1984] for an inmate's account; and Bottomley, Liebling, and Sparks [1994] for a qualitative research assessment). Another extremely important feature of life in the unit was its high level of privileges, which were significantly greater than those available to other long-term inmates in Scotland.[26] Special Unit

---

[26] Many observers have commented on the paradox whereby some of the most disruptive prisoners in the Scottish system received, in the Special Unit, a particularly generous level of privileges. However, the smallness of the Special Unit, and the complexities of the administrative systems involved, made it virtually impossible for any prisoner successfully to plan to reach the Unit by a program of disruption.

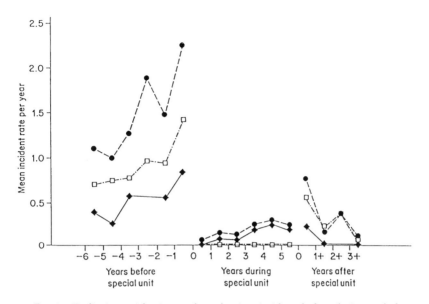

Fig. 1.—Barlinnie special unit: assaults and serious incidents before, during, and after time in unit. Solid circles = total number of incidents; open squares = number of individuals assaulted; solid diamonds = number of serious incidents. Source: Cooke (1989), used with permission.

privileges included virtually unlimited visiting facilities for families and friends, the right not to work if one did not wish to do so, the opportunity to cook and eat nonprison food, and access to in-cell television. Of these, it is quite clear that the visiting privilege was particularly valued by prisoners, not least because Barlinnie Prison is situated in the heart of Glasgow, Scotland's largest and most criminal city, and visiting was therefore relatively easy and convenient for the families of most of the unit's prisoners.

Cooke (1989) showed that for individual prisoners, the level of assaults and other serious incidents committed by residents in the Special Unit was markedly lower than for the same inmates in the years in prison immediately before their unit experience. Moreover, as can be seen in figure 1, average violence levels dropped very sharply on entering the unit, prima facie suggesting a situational or environmental explanation for the change in behavior (i.e., living conditions in the unit were radically different from those in the main prison system, and this change, it was suggested, significantly affected prisoners' behavior). Cooke argued that a main situational factor in operation was that of greater autonomy for the prisoner; that is, prisoners had much more say in their choice of daily activities in the unit than in mainstream prisons and more say also about the way that the unit was run.[27] A further situational mechanism suggested by Cooke (1989, p. 141), and which others would probably regard as more important than the autonomy factor, relates to incentives and disincentives: that is, prisoners greatly preferred the Special Unit environment (especially the visits) to that of ordinary prisons, and they were well aware that the unit had a strict rule disallowing physical violence, serious breach of which would result in immediate expulsion back to the "mainstream." Thus the total environmental context might well provide a powerful disincentive to act violently, though in the absence of more detailed research data this point cannot be definitively established.[28]

Two other studies from which environmental effects on prisoners' behavior have been inferred relate to important policy changes in the 1970s and 1980s in two states, California and Texas.

In the early 1970s, violence in Californian prisons reached what the state's Department of Corrections described as "intolerable" levels. Tighter security was therefore ordered at all twelve state adult prisons from a given date, to include "lockdowns" at the four maximum-security prisons. Bidna (1975) carried out a before-and-after analysis of prison violence in California at this time. The tighter security policies apparently had some success, since there was a significant decline in the overall rate of stabbings from time 1 to time 2.[29] Moreover, there was a change in the pattern of stabbings: fewer stabbings in time 2 involved heavy weapons, and stabbings perpetrated by cliques or with a racial basis proportionately declined, while those arising from personal conflicts proportionately rose. One could reasonably infer from these data that more restrictive management policies had reduced the opportunities for stabbings and for the acquisition of heavy weapons, and had

---

[27] There was also a very rapid grievance procedure available: any member of the community with a grievance could at any time call a "community meeting," which it was expected that everyone (officers and prisoners) would attend.

[28] In the longer term, however, Cooke argued that more normative factors came into play, as the unit's nonviolent philosophy and encouragement of prisoners' self-fulfillment via various individual programs, were gradually internalized by the prisoners. Cooke (1989) believes that such processes help to explain the lower long-term violence rates of the Special Unit sample (i.e., when they returned to the mainstream prison system: see fig. 1), though he carried out no empirical investigation to test this hypothesis.

[29] Bidna selected two particular indices of prison violence, namely stabbings and assaults on staff, on the grounds that "few if any" of such events are likely to go unrecorded. This is an incorrect assumption as regards assaults on staff (see Sec. V), so I have not here discussed Bidna's results relating to this offense.

also restricted the extent to which cliques and racial groups could effectively combine to perpetrate stabbings. Further analysis, however,
revealed a less successful outcome for one group of prisoners. There
was a marked change in the location of stabbings from time 1 to time
2: the rate of stabbings per 100 inmates in general prison locations declined by over half, while the rate of stabbings in "special security
housing" doubled. The more restrictive policy was therefore apparently unsuccessful in the "special security" locations, though the research was unable to investigate in detail why this was so. Bidna (1975,
pp. 42–43) speculates that the increases were perhaps due to a more
violent group of prisoners in the security units, but on the facts this
seems unlikely.[30] An alternative possible explanation was also raised by
the author, namely that "with limited exercise available in security
units, the energies and tensions which inmates formerly released in
general population exercise periods and other available diversions may
have found an outlet in violent activity" (p. 43). I shall return to this
suggestion at a later point in this essay.

The Texas Department of Corrections had, up to the 1980s, operated a control system that relied heavily on two strategies: the unofficial use of force by guards (Marquart 1986), and the so-called building
tender (BT) system, whereby certain inmates were selected as "trust-
ies" and were assigned various officer-like functions such as being
turnkeys or bookkeepers. In certain circumstances, BTs were given the
authority to "break up inmate fights, give orders to the other inmates
[and] perform head counts" (Crouch and Marquart 1989, pp. 187–88).
Perhaps unsurprisingly, those inmates selected as BTs were very predominantly whites. Following intervention by the U.S. federal courts,
the BT system had to be completely dismantled and the abuse of force
by guards curbed. The immediate result, researchers found, was an
"authority vacuum" (Crouch and Marquart 1989, p. 185), in which
prisoner violence rapidly escalated—in 1984, for example, there were
an unprecedented twenty-five inmate homicides (see explanatory note
to table 4), rising to twenty-seven in 1985. Several proffered explanations for this change, such as the arrival of a different kind of inmate,

---

[30] During the period from time 1 to time 2, there was an overall increase in the prison
population in California, and also (as a result of the restrictive management policies) a
higher proportion of prisoners were sent to special security housing. One might reasonably expect (although Bidna does not discuss the point) that given such circumstances
the average "prespecial housing" profile for time 1 special housing inmates would be
more serious than at time 2 (i.e., the time 1 inmates were a smaller and more extreme
group).

were discounted for various reasons by the researchers evaluating the changes (Crouch and Marquart 1989, pp. 196–98). Instead, after examining various pieces of detailed evidence, these authors offer what they regard as a much more adequate explanation, based on the changing nature of the social order in Texas prisons:

> The court-ordered reforms dissolved the inmate power structure that had for so long been controlled and defined by the authorities. Dominant convicts soon emerged and filled the authority vacuum left by the building tenders and by a [now] seemingly powerless security force. The transition in control precipitated a crisis in [inmate] self-protection. While some inmates succumbed to the advances of the stronger aggressive prisoners, others secured weapons. Weapons were increasingly involved in disputes. . . . These conditions offered fertile ground for the growth of prison gangs . . . [and] the gangs that emerged have been responsible for a disproportionate amount of prison violence. (Crouch and Marquart 1989, p. 220)

By 1986, however, the evidence suggested that matters had changed again. A recovery of confidence by staff, plus the extensive use of administrative segregation, helped the Texas Department of Corrections to establish "a new prison order," which in time produced a marked reduction in deaths and injuries (Crouch and Marquart 1989, chap. 8). Thus indicators of prison violence levels in Texas had, over time, followed a bell-shaped curve, not dissimilar to that found for prison homicides in the United States as a whole (table 4). It is therefore tempting to wonder whether the U.S. prison homicide trends in table 4 can have a similar explanation, given the liberalization of many state prison systems in the late 1960s and early 1970s (following the civil rights protests of the 1960s, and the courts' abandonment of the traditional "hands-off" doctrine for prison litigation); and given also the subsequent establishment of a "new prison professionalism," spearheaded initially by the activities of the American Correctional Association from the late 1970s (Silberman 1995, pp. 120–26). But for the moment, these suggestions must be regarded only as speculative.

None of the three case studies considered in this subsection provides irrefutable evidence of an environmental effect on interpersonal prison violence. But the authors of each of the three studies postulates the radical environmental changes described as being, in each case, the most adequate explanation of the changed patterns of violence observed. The three studies taken together thus seem to provide powerful evidence that changed prison environments can indeed affect levels of interpersonal violence.

B. Physical Characteristics of the Prison Environment

As is well known, in the field of criminal policy powerful voices have been raised, backed by strong research evidence, in favor of so-called situational crime prevention, a strategy that focuses especially on the manipulation of the physical environment so as to reduce the opportunities for crime (see, e.g., Clarke 1995). Among the particular strategies suggested by advocates of situational crime prevention are "target-hardening" and "target removal"; restricting access to the potential target by restraints on the movements of potential offenders, and restricting access to the means of committing crime, such as the availability of potential weapons (guns, knives, etc).

It is not at all surprising that prison officials have for many years been deploying various kinds of "situational crime prevention" in the prisons context, without calling them by that name (see, generally, Bottoms, Hay, and Sparks 1990). It is also not surprising that the research evidence continues to suggest that some of the physical characteristics of particular prisons, and their permitted routines, may indeed enhance the opportunities for various kinds of infraction of the prison rules, including physical violence. We have already encountered this in reverse in Bidna's California study: the more restrictive security policy seemed to reduce the opportunities both for stabbings in general and for the development of gangs and cliques in particular. Very similar implications emerged from the detailed study of Long Lartin prison, England (Sparks, Bottoms, and Hay 1996). As mentioned in a previous section, Long Lartin had enjoyed a traditionally liberal regime policy for a maximum security prison; and detailed contrast with another maximum security prison (Albany) showed, for example, that Long Lartin had much more liberal rules about informal inmate association and movements, including the official approval of so-called cell association (two or more prisoners meeting informally in an inmate's cell). These enhanced freedoms were greatly prized by most Long Lartin prisoners; but they had a "down side." Inmates' qualitative evidence, as well as some quantitative evidence relating to the use of alarm bells in the prison and the number of head injuries treated in the prison hospital (Sparks, Bottoms, and Hay 1996, pp. 259–62), all suggested that the considerable freedom of movement and association in Long Lartin was sometimes abused by some prisoners to "settle a score" by violent means. When this occurred, it was not at all difficult for the aggressor to choose a location that was poorly supervised—and the existence of cell association certainly made this choice easier, given the particular architectural design of the cell blocks in Long Lartin.[31] Moreover, the substantially greater freedom of movement and association in Long Lartin apparently facilitated the establishment of a more complex set of inmate social networks in Long Lartin than in Albany, including the easier development of gangs and cliques. These more complex social networks were empirically reflected in the kinds of violent incident that came to official notice in Long Lartin (Sparks, Bottoms, and Hay 1996, chap. 7; note again the close congruence with the results from Bidna's earlier Californian research).

Other data are also congruent with the potential importance of an "opportunity" dimension in prison violence. For example, in England prison regimes were liberalized, with more time out of cell in the early 1990s, and then tightened again in mid-decade: official assault rates rose and then fell correspondingly (see table 1). Or again, in the recent Oxford study, and taking the four studied institutions together, the shower areas were regarded by prisoners as the most unsafe part of the prison, because of the opportunities they provided for undetected attacks (see O'Donnell and Edgar 1999, table 4). Yet one must also be careful not to infer, from results such as these, that the existence of certain physical characteristics in a prison will automatically promote violence. Within the boundaries of the Barlinnie Special Unit (see Cooke 1989), for example, prisoners had significantly more freedom of movement and association than they did even at Long Lartin; yet violence levels in the unit were very low (see Subsec. A). I shall return to this apparent paradox in Section IV.

Awareness of the potential importance of the "opportunity" factor in the genesis of prison violence has led to the so-called new generation of prison architecture (see, e.g., Home Office 1985). In a nutshell, such architecture seeks to incorporate desirable features of situational crime prevention into prison design. Such features may include: separated smallish housing units, each with its own exercise area; security corridors linking housing units, but with barrier gates to isolate hous-

---

[31] There were six cell blocks at Long Lartin, each containing three "spurs" set at ninety degrees to the next spur; staff operated from the landing where the three spurs met.

ing units in an emergency and a separate corridor to which staff only have access; cells within housing units placed around a living area, so that officers operating informally in the living area have a clear sight of all cell entrances (unlike in the traditional "corridor design"; see fig. 2); and a special attempt to "normalize" the atmosphere and expectations of the housing units, and other facilities, by, for example, replacing "barred doors . . . with wooden ones [and] concrete floors with carpets" (Wener 1994, p. 2).

Typically, "new generation" architecture has been implemented hand-in-hand with a so-called direct supervision management model, which "had as its basic tenet the notion that visual contact—even if omnipresent—was in itself insufficient for adequate supervision. Rather, it proposed placing officers in direct contact with inmates to facilitate closer observation and communication. The officer's job was no longer to watch and respond to inmate problems, but to predict and prevent them . . . One physical implication of this model was the elimination of the traditional enclosed officer station" (Wener 1994, p. 2).

As will be noted, there are several different conceptual strands within the "direct supervision" package. Among these are, especially, the reduction of opportunities for inmate-inmate violence in unsupervised or poorly supervised space, so creating a safer environment; the deliberate manipulation of the symbolic features of the environment, so that the reduced-opportunity physical design does not feel oppressive to inmates;[32] and the development of a proactive, preventive role and style for basic-grade prison staff.

The research evidence on the direct supervision approach is suggestive but not conclusive. As Wener (1994, p. 3) notes, there is some evidence that the approach reduces prison violence, and this evidence "comes from anecdotal [accounts] . . . , survey research (Farbstein and Wener 1989) and individual and comparative case studies (Wener, Frazier, and Farbstein 1985)." But apart from the usual methodological difficulties in evaluation studies, a complicating factor in this instance is that individual institutions' implementation of the "direct su-

[32] Additionally, within the direct-supervision approach, emphasis is placed on giving prisoners as much *autonomy* and *choice* as possible, consistently with the maintenance of a safe environment. It is interesting that at the Wolds private prison in England, which adopted a direct supervision approach in a building with a more traditional prison design, the initially granted level of inmate autonomy had to be restricted because of behavior such as cell theft and "taxing" (extracting goods/money through threats; see James et al. 1997, pp. 70–71).

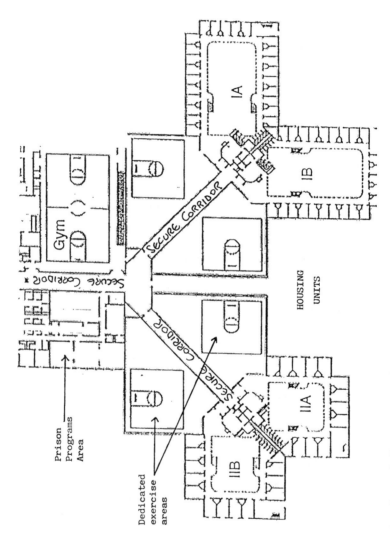

Fig. 2.—Floor plan of part of a "new generation design" prison. Source: Adapted from part of floor plan of Norfolk County Sheriff's Correctional Center, Mass., as illustrated in Farbstein, Liebert, and Sigurdson (1996, p. 15).

pervision" style has varied substantially in detail, and this has resulted in emphasis being differentially placed, in different prisons, on one or more of the varying conceptual strands within "direct supervision" (see, e.g., Farbstein, Liebert, and Sigurdson 1996). Hence, it is not always easy to know from the published studies exactly what it is that has been evaluated.

Before concluding this subsection, one other physical characteristic of the prison environment should be mentioned, especially because it has featured fairly prominently in the previous literature on prison violence—namely, overcrowding. Extensive citations to relevant publications will be found in the detailed overview of overcrowding research by Gaes (1994). In the section of this overview dealing with overcrowding and violence, Gaes makes two linked central points. The first is that the results of the empirical studies on crowding and violence are inconsistent and one reason for this inconsistency is that "researchers have failed to examine the proximal causes of violence as well as the formal mechanisms that prison administrators use to control or limit violence" (p. 329). The second point is that there has been insufficient adequate theorization, and theory testing, in this field. For example, it is a basic assumption of much crowding research that the effects of crowding are mediated through stress and the consequences of stress, but most researchers have "failed to do strong tests of these theoretical assumptions" (p. 337). Gaes's strong emphasis in these conclusions is thus both on the importance of theory and on the importance of detailed studies of how violence actually emerges in day-to-day prison life. These emphases are highly congruent with the basic framework and assumptions of the present essay.

C. Transactional and Interactive Analyses of Prison Violence

In prison sociology, there is a famous and extended debate between the so-called deprivation and importation models. The deprivation model argues, essentially, that inmates' adaptation to the prison, and the development of inmate subcultures, arises as a response to what Sykes (1958) called "the pains of imprisonment"—the deprivation of liberty, goods, and services; personal autonomy; personal security; and heterosexual relationships. The "importation" model, by contrast, argues that prisoner adaptations and subcultures are primarily influenced by what the prisoner brings into the institution: personal history, informal links with particular social groups, formal affiliations with organized crime syndicates, and so on. The generally agreed resolution of this debate has been that both preprison socialization experiences and the experiences of imprisonment (including deprivation), together with important extraprison influences during one's prison stay (e.g., major events in a prisoner's family life), all in fact influence prisoner adaptations (see, e.g., Thomas, Peterson, and Zingraff 1978; Goodstein and Wright 1989). The reasons for this conclusion are, in retrospect, really rather obvious. As Porporino and Zamble (1984, p. 409) put it in a slightly different context: "Generally speaking, there are few attitudinal or behavioral dispositions that are so powerful as to totally determine actions in all situations, and few environmental events which can compel identical responses from people with varying dispositions. We would expect that the interaction between the individual and his environment would be the most powerful determinant of behavior."

Within the more restricted field of prison violence studies very similar conclusions have been reached. This body of research literature therefore adds to the cumulative evidence, as previously described in this and earlier sections, that emphasizes the importance of a full study of the prison's daily environment when analyzing interpersonal prison violence. I shall illustrate the contribution of this kind of approach by discussing one little-known publication (an English study by Mandaraka-Sheppard) and one very well-known strand of American research work (deriving especially from the contributions of Toch and Wright).

Mandaraka-Sheppard (1986) studied the dynamics of inmate aggression in six English prisons for women. For present purposes, central attention focuses on the researcher's "physical violence" scale, which was a self-reported behavior scale with a five-point range, tested for its reliability and validity (pp. 62–63). The "violence" items were, in substance, mostly relatively minor events, such as "fighting with a group of inmates," "fighting with staff," and "throwing things at inmates during an argument." The author's eventual composite multivariate analysis (see her chap. 7) suggested that institutional variables accounted for the bulk of the statistical variance in the physical violence scale, though of course these institutional variables were themselves not necessarily uninfluenced by preprison characteristics. To give a specific example, within the composite analysis one of the variables correlating most strongly with "physical violence level" was an institutional variable measuring "defiant or compliant attitude to present prison" (see Mandaraka-Sheppard 1986, chap. 4). A significant proportion of the variance in prisoners' defiance-compliance scores was statistically explained by preprison variables such as age (older inmates were less defiant) and what was labeled as a "potency" score (roughly, hard/masculine vs. soft/feminine; the latter were less defiant). But, even when these preprison variables had been taken into account, there was a very specifically prison-focused dimension that was reflected in the defiance/compliance scores. As Mandaraka-Sheppard put it, the implication was that "although compliant inmates in the context of prisons are likely to be inmates who are older, rated as less potent [etc.] . . . yet there will still be non-compliant inmates from these categories (i.e., older, [less potent] etc.) *if the institution is lacking in order, [is] preventing autonomy of inmates, and is using severe punishments*" (p. 189, emphasis added).

In other words, Mandaraka-Sheppard found truly interactive effects between preprison and institutional variables, and both kinds of effect were clearly related to the physical violence scale used.

Comparing this study with others in the literature, it can be said to show particularly clearly and decisively the apparent importance of institutional variables. As the author put it, within her study "institutional characteristics appear to exert an independent (i.e., direct) influence upon misbehavior within the prison" (p. 191). The apparent special clarity of these "environmental" effects within this research project might possibly be related to the fact that the six prisons studied were women's prisons, and the "violence" was substantively relatively minor. For it could be the case that, given women's low preprison violence levels, their institutional violence is more likely than that of men to be especially influenced by their prison environment. It could also be the case that minor institutional violence is more likely to be particularly influenced by environmental factors. These are matters that deserve fuller exploration in future research.

In a seminal text, Toch (1977) analyzed nine hundred interviews with prisoners in five New York State maximum-security prisons, focusing on the problems prisoners faced in confronting incarceration. Content analysis yielded eight separate dimensions of prisoner concerns about life in prison, namely privacy, safety, structure, support, emotional feedback, social stimulation, activity, and freedom. Subsequently, Toch developed a questionnaire (the Prison Preference Inventory or PPI) to tap the individual's preferences, needs, or concerns relating to these eight dimensions; and Wright (1985) developed a separate instrument (the Prison Environment Inventory or PEI) to assess institutional environments along the same dimensions. Kenneth Adams (1992, pp. 318–24) provides an excellent summary of work in this tradition. Briefly, Toch (1977) initially demonstrated that individual prisoners varied in their environmental preferences or needs (e.g., older inmates valued structure and placed less emphasis on freedom, but younger inmates especially valued freedom). In a subsequent series of studies, Wright (see esp. Wright 1991*a*, 1991*b*) examined the relationship between the actual prison environment and inmate adjustment to prison. Two of Wright's variables are of special interest here—namely, those of self-reported aggression ("external problems") and prison victimization (suffering injury or being taken advantage of, i.e., "physical problems"). For both measures, Wright (1991*a*) found that not only individual characteristics, and, not only environmental characteristics, but also measures focusing on "the fit between person and environment" were significantly related to the dependent variable.

There is thus a consistent message from these and other studies that researchers into interpersonal prison violence who approach their task with a less than fully interactive framework (i.e., focusing on the individual *and* the environment, *and* on the way that the individual reacts to the specific environment) will have provided an incomplete picture.

Yet some anxieties remain about the Toch-Wright approach, which is in danger of presenting too static a picture. To speak of "the fit between person and environment," as Wright does, suggests first, that "person" and "environment" are two readily separable categories, and second, that a particular environment will "fit" a particular type of prisoner, tout court. Such an approach fails to take the "interactionist" or "transactionalist" approach to its logical conclusion, namely that persons adapt to, and change in, environments, and that social environments are always shaped by human contributions. Hence, there is no static "fit," but rather a series of continual interactions and transactions. As Wener (1994, p. 4) has usefully put it, following his extensive studies of physical environments in prisons, it looks as if the most appropriate conceptual framework will make three key assumptions, namely: "It is artificial to separate the psychological and organizational aspects of the setting—they are mutually dependent and important; the setting's effect on violence is in part mediated by the way in which inmates perceive and respond to their situation; and individual characteristics of inmates, such as personality and psychopathology, may in some cases lead directly to violent behavior, *but [they] also affect, and are affected by other aspects of the setting*" (emphasis added).

Much recent work in social theory, such as "structuration theory" (see Giddens 1984, applied in the prisons context by Sparks, Bottoms, and Hay 1996) conveys exactly the same message.

D. Conclusions and Implications

Criticisms can of course always be made of the validity or generalizability of particular research studies. But there seems little doubt, from the research reviewed in this section, that Kenneth Adams (1992) was right to conclude that, taken together, the evidence is clear: "*Inmates behave differently in different prison settings*" (p. 315).

What is not yet so clear is whether prison administrators have really grasped the implications of this conclusion, but those implications must surely include the following: first, that when high levels of interpersonal prison violence occur, officials seeking causes and remedies must look hard at the prison environment and at prison management practices, as well as at the problems posed by particular high-profile inmates; and second, that attempts to predict "troublesome inmates" (through "risk profiles" and the like), will always be imperfect, for the research evidence is clear that " 'troublesomeness' and similar concepts are not just naturally occurring phenomena, carried around by individuals as a set of characteristics, identifiable in advance and just waiting to erupt" (King and McDermott 1990, p. 453).

Even researchers sympathetic to an environmental approach can easily fall into the trap identified by King and McDermott in this last quotation. For example, we have seen that Bidna (1975), in his important early article on environmental changes in California, postulated that, given the limited opportunities for physical exercise in special security housing units, perhaps inmates in such units—after the state-imposed restrictions—channeled "the energy and tensions which [they] formerly released in the general population exercise periods into violent activity" (p. 43). But to speak in this manner is to adopt a kind of "hydraulic" theory of violence in which individuals have a "violence potential" that must be actualized or else sublimated in physical exercise. Among other things, this excludes the meaning of a given environment to participants and the way they themselves shape, mold, and sometimes transform that environment. A more subtle approach than this is needed; and the argument of this essay is that appropriate subtlety is unattainable unless we pay close attention to the day-to-day life of prisons.

IV. How Is Order Maintained in Prisons?

The central focus of this essay is on interpersonal prison violence, not collective violence; and we have noted (see the Introduction) that the distinguishing feature of interpersonal prison violence is that it takes place within the normal social frameworks of the day-to-day functioning of the prison. Cressey (1961, p. 2) famously commented that "one of the most amazing things about prisons is that they 'work' at all." Despite all the disadvantages that prison administrators face (e.g., they are dealing with some of the most violent and recalcitrant members of the general population, who are in prison against their will, and who heavily outnumber the guard force), the fact is that, in Cressey's words, "the social system which is a prison does not degenerate into a chaotic mess of social relations which have no order and make no sense."

If, therefore, we are to pursue a fully interactive approach to interpersonal prison violence (see Sec. III), it is vital at this point in the argument to "reverse the lens" away from a concentration on prison violence per se, and to consider instead, in Cressey's language, that "amazing thing" about prisons—that most of the time they are *not* places that "have no order and make no sense."

A. Maintaining Social Order

Quite often, prison administrators speak of the "problems of control" in prisons. Inmates, however, tend to be uncomfortable with this language (which has rather obviously sprung from the particular preoccupations of those with official responsibilities in the criminal justice system). By contrast, prisoners are much more receptive to the concept of "order" in prisons, for most of them positively value an orderly framework, both to the prison day, and to the idea of progression through a prison sentence. Order and predictability make it easier to "do your time."[33]

Building on these ideas, in *Prisons and the Problem of Order* (Sparks, Bottoms, and Hay 1996, p. 119) we offered formal definitions of "order" and "control" in the prisons context, as follows:

> *Order*: an orderly situation is any long-standing pattern of social relations (characterized by a minimum level of respect for persons)

---

[33] Indeed, one of the mechanisms used in concentration camps to destabilize inmates psychologically was to alter the camp regime at very regular intervals, perhaps daily. Routines thus have the effect of assisting everyone—in and out of prisons—to maintain what Giddens (1984) describes as a level of "ontological security" in day-to-day living.

in which the expectations that participants have of one another are commonly met, though not necessarily without contestation. Order can also, in part, be defined negatively as the absence of violence, overt conflict or the imminent threat of the chaotic breakdown of social routines.

Control: the use of routines and of a variety of formal and informal practices—especially, but not only, sanctions—which assist in the maintenance of order, whether or not they are recognized as doing so.

Thus, in the prisons context, "order" is a dynamic social equilibrium, while "control" is, in effect, a set of strategies or tactics used by prison administrators to achieve order.

Two things follow. First, there are many different kinds of possible social order in prisons—a fact that was obvious to us as researchers, faced with studying two of the seven maximum-security institutions (or "dispersal prisons") within the English prison system, and realizing quickly that these two prisons (Albany and Long Lartin) had radically different regimes and radically different staff philosophies (see earlier discussion). Second, if the focus is—as I am contending it should be—on "order" and "dynamic social equilibrium," then the prison researcher's focus of attention needs to be much wider than the prison itself. Manifestly, there is a "problem of order" in outside society as well as in the prison, and this general problem of order has been widely reflected upon by sociologists and by political philosophers (see generally Wrong 1994).

Wrong offers a self-confessedly simplified but heuristically very useful characterization of three major approaches to the problem of order in classical political philosophy: "Hobbes's solution was coercive, Locke's stressed mutual self-interest, and the Rousseau of *The Social Contract* gave primacy to normative consensus" (p. 9).

Wrong goes on to complain—rightly—that too often only one or other of these three approaches has been emphasized by analysts of social order. Hence, he argues, normatively oriented sociologists have placed too much reliance on norms and values; some traditions in political thought have tended to exaggerate the role of force, coercion, and constraint; and economists have "notoriously overstressed economic interest." But when one looks at empirical social realities, there is no particular justification for giving primacy to one of these approaches, since none of them "precludes or subsumes the others, but

A.	INSTRUMENTAL/PRUDENTIAL	1.	Incentives
		2.	Disincentives
B.	NORMATIVE	1.	Normative Consensus/ Acceptance
		2.	Legitimacy
C.	CONSTRAINT-BASED	1.	Physical Restrictions on Individual
		2.	Restrictions on Access to Target
		3.	Structural Constraints

Fig. 3.—Reasons for social/legal compliance. Source: author

. . . on the contrary, all three may operate conjointly in concrete human societies" (p. 9).

This is an extremely valuable insight. So let us pursue Wrong's threefold classification, conjointly with the emphasis of this section on *order* rather than *disorder*. We can then quickly identify the fact that each of the main classical approaches to order—the normative, the coercive, and the instrumental—can lead, in a given situation, to what may seem to a given social actor to be rather compelling reasons for complying with a particular set of rules or expectations. This possible list of main reasons for social and legal compliance is set out schematically in figure 3.

As figure 3 shows, from an instrumental or prudential perspective, two simple reasons for compliance may operate—incentives and disincentives. Both may, of course, be relevant in the prison context, as some prisoners' reactions to parole incentives, and to threats of punishment, readily demonstrate. The second perspective on compliance—the normative approach—likewise contains two main reasons for compliance, but these need a little more explanation. The first is normative consensus or acceptance: for example, within an Orthodox Jewish extended family there may be a unanimous consensus on strict observance of the Sabbath. In such a context, no one forces the family members to comply with the rules about what may and may not be done on the Sabbath (hence, coercion is absent), nor do incentives and disincentives predominate (though they may certainly be present if, e.g., disobedience might entail ostracism by the family). Rather, the predominant reason for observance is family members' acceptance of the truth of Orthodox Judaism and their individual and joint commitment to the normative prescriptions that this religion expects its adherents to observe. And despite the moral pluralism of the late twentieth century, there remains much normative consensus in contemporary societies—for example, a consensus against killing others and burgling others' homes. Much socialization (in families, schools, and communities) attempts to inculcate such norms in the young and to reinforce symbolically the importance of the moral values that the norms embody.

The other reason for compliance, from within a normative framework, is *legitimacy*—that is, compliance with a rule because it has been promulgated by a person or body with legitimate authority, acting in a proper way to exercise that authority. Hence, some people might obey the speed limit on a motorway, not because they are normatively committed to it (they might prefer a much higher limit), but because the speed limit has been set by the appropriate legal authorities within a democratic state.[34]

In prisons, normative reasons for compliance may seem at first sight to be of little relevance—approaches based on incentives/disincentives, and/or on coercion and constraint, might seem to be much more to the point. To the contrary, as I shall argue in the next subsection, legitimacy in particular is of crucial importance in securing compliance in the prisons context.

The third main approach to compliance is that based on coercion and constraint. Some reasons for compliance, within this approach, are physical—a prisoner locked alone in his cell cannot assault anyone; or a group of prisoners wishing to gain access to their personal files may find that the security restrictions surrounding the file store make the task of breaking into the store impossible. The final reason for compliance within this framework is subtly different, and is best called "structural constraint." In society at large structural constraints vary enormously, but their distinguishing feature is that they in effect compel

[34] Indeed, the law's perceived legitimacy may induce persons to obey even where they regard the particular directive as being positively objectionable. For example, in Britain some of those who in the late 1980s disagreed on moral grounds with the then newly enacted Community Charge ("Poll Tax") nevertheless felt bound to comply because the tax constituted a validly enacted measure of a democratically elected government.

the obedience of the subject, not through the rational calculus of self-interest (incentives and disincentives), nor through any kind of normative commitment on the part of the subject, but simply through the weight of the power relations involved and/or through resignation to the fact that "this is the way things are round here," and they cannot be changed.[35] So stated, it is not hard to see that structural constraints may operate in the prisons context.

B. Legitimacy

In England, the prestigious Woolf Inquiry into the disturbances at Manchester Prison and elsewhere in 1990 took the view that a widespread sense of *injustice* among prisoners about their general treatment in prison was causally implicated in the scale of the disorders (see, e.g., Woolf 1991, paras. 9.24, 14.437–38). "Injustice" was a term used by Lord Justice Woolf in a rather broad way, to include the basic "quality of life" for prisoners (adequate living quarters, food, and so on), various informal aspects of inmate life (including the manner of prisoners' treatment at the hands of staff), and formal procedures (such as the disciplinary and grievance systems).

Woolf did not use the term "legitimacy," but in the debates following publication of the Woolf Report, my colleagues and I took the view that, if indeed "justice" does help to sustain order in prisons (as Woolf proposed) then it does so because of the contribution that it makes to the legitimation of the prison authorities and the prison regime in the eyes of the prisoners. In our analysis, the acquiescence or otherwise of prisoners to the kinds of authority claimed or exercised over them by officials is a variable matter, centered around a complex matrix of interactions between prisoners' expectations of their captivity, and the reality of that captivity. In particular, the core issue is whether, judged by the reasonable standards of the wider community in which the prison is set, prisoners come to see the behavior of their custodians as being justifiable, comprehensible, consistent and hence *fair*—or, alternatively, unwarranted, arbitrary, capricious, and overweening (for fuller analyses, see Sparks and Bottoms 1995; Sparks, Bottoms, and Hay 1996).

---

[35] The distinction between structural constraint and normative consensus is in principle conceptually clear, but in practice may be difficult to draw. For example, in a traditional society some women may conform to prescribed gender roles because they are strongly normatively committed to them; others may conform only because of structural constraint; others may analyze their conformity as containing some element both of structural constraint and of normative commitment.

	Criteria of legitimacy	Corresponding form of non-legitimate power
1.	Conformity to rules (legal validity)	Illegitimacy (breach of rules)
2.	Justifiability of rules in terms of shared beliefs	Legitimacy deficit (discrepancy between rules and supporting shared beliefs, absence of shared beliefs)
3.	Legitimation through expressed consent	Delegitimation (withdrawal of consent)

FIG. 4.—Beetham's dimensions of legitimacy. Source: Beetham (1991), p. 20

A main theoretical source drawn on in our analysis is that of the political theorist Beetham (1991). Beetham argues that virtually all systems of power relations, including ones which are quite autocratic, stand in need of legitimation. Conversely, they encounter particular kinds of problems when power is exercised in nonlegitimate ways (see fig. 4).

As figure 4 shows, Beetham identifies three separate (but of course interconnected) "dimensions" of legitimacy, which roughly correspond to the traditional preoccupations of three different academic specialisms that have considered legitimacy as a concept. The three "dimensions" are thus respectively of special interest to lawyers (Has power been legally acquired, and is it being exercised within the law?), to political philosophers (Are the power relations at issue morally justifiable?), and finally, to social scientists (What are the actual beliefs of subjects about issues of legitimacy in that particular society?) (Beetham 1991, p. 4 ff.). This scheme usefully reminds us that formal legality is only one aspect of legitimacy, and is not on its own a sufficient criterion of it, in prisons as elsewhere. Legitimacy also requires that office holders (such as wardens and prison officers) act fairly; and that they can and do justify what they do to those who are affected by their decisions and practices (such as prisoners and their families), thus heightening the likelihood that their authority will be assented to.

Empirical support for this last point comes from the work of Tyler (1990). Using data from a panel study of Chicago citizens' encounters with the police and courts, Tyler argues that people are generally more concerned with issues of *procedural fairness* (Has their case or situation been treated in a fair way? Are like cases treated similarly? and so on), and of the *manner* of their treatment (e.g., Are they accorded respect by police in on-street encounters?) than they are with the outcome of their own case tout court. In Tyler's view, in "special communities" (like prisons) where news travels fast and people know each others' business, such niceties matter all the more.[36] Tyler's argument is that people view their encounters with authority as "information about the group that the authority represents and to which the parties to the dispute or allocation belong" (Tyler 1990, p. 175). Hence, every transaction with an authority figure raises questions that extend "far beyond those connected with the issue to be decided" (p. 175). Such issues include "representation, neutrality, bias, honesty, quality of decision, and consistency" (p. 175) and more generally of esteem. In short, we can postulate from Tyler's work—when we extrapolate from it into the prison context—that *ordinary everyday encounters between staff and prisoners can have crucial implications for the nature of the power relations in the prison, and to the validity of the staff's claims to justified authority—* that is, to legitimacy. This view has been further supported by more recent research work, including work in English prisons (see, e.g., James et al. 1997; Paternoster et al. 1997; Liebling and Price 1999).

One final point about legitimacy must be made. It has been challengingly put to me that to emphasize legitimation within the framework of order maintenance in prison is ultimately simply a recipe for "being nice" to prisoners, "giving them everything they want," and, in some versions "appeasing them." (For a full discussion of this important objection, see Sparks, Bottoms, and Hay 1996, pp. 329–36.) But, on careful examination, that proves not to be the case. To emphasize legitimation is, certainly, to emphasize the general moral obligation on those in power to consider the consequences of their decisions for those under their care, and to be able to give a morally justifiable account of those decisions. But that does not entail giving assent to every far-fetched request made by prisoners. However, straying, in one's

[36] Specifically, Tyler (1990) argues, from the data in his panel study, that *fair procedures* were more important to respondents than fair *outcomes*, partly because of lack of knowledge of outcomes in cases other than their own. Moreover, generally speaking, even if "unfavorable *outcomes* are delivered through *procedures viewed as fair*, the unfavorable outcomes *do not harm the legitimacy* of legal authorities" (p. 107, emphasis added). In "special communities," where people know each others' business, outcomes are more likely to be generally known, *but so is the way that the authorities treat fellow-subjects*; hence, consistency of procedural treatment can, in such communities, be added to the list of other dimensions of procedural fairness (e.g., the politeness, apparent honesty, and ethicality of officials in their encounters with citizens; pp. 153–54).

prison decision making, too far from the generally accepted moral code of a society may ultimately have severely practical consequences for prison order. One implication of the emphasis on legitimacy is that *if one is unable to provide, on reasonable request, a morally justifiable account of decisions made, then this may ultimately be instrumental in producing just the kinds of disorders that wardens and staff want to avoid.*

C. Social Order in Prisons

From the arguments of the two previous subsections, we can now postulate a theoretical model as to how order in prisons is maintained (see fig. 5). The model takes as given that some characteristics of the inmate population, such as age, will be relevant to the degree of potential disruptiveness within the establishment (box 4). Seven main additional variables are then identified as relevant to order maintenance. Five of these are based on reasons for social/legal compliance, as identified in figure 3 (boxes 1, 2, 3, 5, and 6). The two remaining variables relate to the key mediating role of the staff (box 8) and the sometimes considerable importance, in the prisons context, of specific incidents and their consequences (box 7).

The model is based on research findings, and especially on a linked series of studies carried out at Cambridge University in recent years, (see, e.g., Ahmad 1996; Sparks, Bottoms, and Hay 1996; Liebling et al. 1999; Liebling and Price 1999). It is, however, far from a final product. Rather, it should be regarded as a heuristic model, developed from existing research, but requiring further and more explicit testing and refinement.

In more detail, the main factors postulated as relevant to the maintenance of order in prisons can be described as follows (the numbers given refer to the box numbers in fig. 5).

1. *Legitimation (Leading to Assent: 1A).*   This concept has been outlined above. Within box 1 of figure 5, three different dimensions of legitimacy in prisons are identified, namely the perceived fairness of the staff, the perceived fairness of various regime features (such as visits, search policies, time out of cell, etc.), and distributive fairness (based on perceptions of formal procedures such as the discipline and complaints mechanisms). This very useful threefold understanding of fairness in prisons is derived from Ahmad's (1996) pioneering research study of inmates' perceptions of fairness. Among other things, Ahmad found that prisoners did not make simple blanket judgments about fairness or unfairness, but rather drew distinctions between different

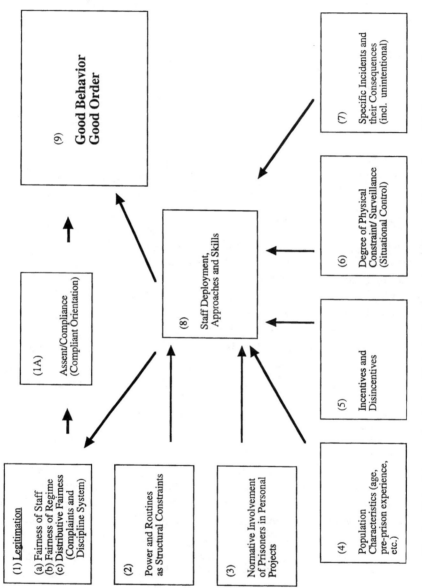

Fig. 5.—Maintaining good order/good behavior in prisons: a speculative and interactive model. Source: author

aspects of their prison experience (e.g., a particular inmate might regard the uniformed staff as generally very fair in a given prison, while regarding the time allowed out of cell as moderately fair, and the searching policies as unfair).

2. *Power and Routines as Structural Constraints.*   The concept of legitimation refers, in the prisons context, to inmates' normative judgments on some aspects of their incarceration. But compliance may, obviously, also be achieved in prisons through structural constraints, with no necessary element of normative acceptance by inmates. One element of such constraint will be the obviously displayed power of the state, represented in prisons by the prison staff (and by prisoners' knowledge that staff can be heavily reinforced by the police, and if necessary the military, in an emergency). Another element of structural constraint is, however, the prison routine itself. Routines are a very prominent feature of prison life (see the Introduction). They clearly assist prison staff effectively to fulfill some of the prison's essential tasks of "self-maintenance" (Sykes 1958) but they also carry some benefits for inmates in providing an element of predictability to prison life. Thus prisoners' largely subconscious acquiescence to the prison's routines constitutes an element of structural constraint which helps to achieve overall order in the prison.

3. *Normative Involvement in Projects.*   More rarely, some prisoners become strongly committed to prison projects of one kind or another (e.g., an educational course or some recreational activity such as weightlifting) that provides them with a real involvement in the goals of at least some staff in the prison. Such an involvement may have the effect of aiding the overall maintenance of order in the institution (cf. Hirschi 1969).

5. *Incentives and Disincentives.*   Some "carrot-and-stick" techniques are, of course, a standard feature of virtually all prison regimes, although the emphasis on them varies from jurisdiction to jurisdiction. Incentives and disincentives certainly sometimes work in reducing prison violence—see, for example, Ellis, Grasmick, and Gilman (1974) on the importance for prison violence of a prisoner's proximity or otherwise to his parole date. That example, however, also illustrates another very important aspect of incentives and disincentives, and one that is apparent in the outside world as well as in prisons (see von Hirsch et al. 1999): namely, that incentives work better if they are linked in some meaningful way to the subject's normative commitments. Thus in the outside world those with strong normative links to

law-abiding communities have been shown to be more easily deterrable than persons without such links. Similarly, the parole incentive can be expected to be of significantly more relevance to the prisoner with strong family ties.[37]

6. *Degree of Physical Constraint.* We have seen in a previous section, from research such as that of Bidna (1975), that enhanced physical constraints can sometimes operate to reduce prison violence. Paradoxically, however, enhanced restraints can sometimes actually *encourage* violence as a form of rebellion against the degree of constraint imposed by the authorities. I return to this paradox in Subsec. *D* below.

7. *Specific Incidents.* I noted in the introduction to this essay that prisons are places that, to an extent, can have an importance within the meaning structure and biographical continuities of individuals. A consequence of this fact is that a particular major incident in a prison (e.g., a fire started by an inmate, in which some staff members become trapped, and for a while placed in real danger) can have social reverberations and consequences in that institution for a lengthy period of time. The incident will help to shape the consciousness of key players in the prison social world, and will probably be referred to again and again in future debates on the theme of order in that particular prison.

8. *Staff Deployment, Approaches, and Skills.* The final dimension represented in figure 5 relates to the role of the prison staff. The importance of this dimension was again demonstrated in Ahmad's (1996) research, where the author considered that the single most important empirical result of his study was the centrality of prisoners' perceptions of staff fairness: "Perceived unfairness of staff is a problem that affects not just the relationship between prisoners and staff, but all other aspects of prison life, including perception of fairness of [various aspects of] the regime, and satisfaction with complaints and grievances. . . . [For example], the data suggest that if staff are perceived as fair, prisoners will perceive the overall prison [experience] as fair even though

---

[37] Incentives approaches in prisons are, however, not always successful. For example, in English prisons in the 1990s a new "Incentives and Earned Privileges" (IEP) scheme was introduced, with the aim of improving prisoner behavior through enhanced incentives for good conduct. A research evaluation showed that, at least in the early days of the scheme, its effect in changing behavior was minimal, notwithstanding that most prisoners agreed in principle with the incentives philosophy. A main reason for the disappointing result regarding behavior was that the IEP scheme was seen by most prisoners as having, in practice, reduced fairness levels in the prison (e.g., because IEP enhanced staff discretion, and this discretion was sometimes seen as having been exercised arbitrarily). See Liebling et al. (1999).

they may not be satisfied with specific aspects of the regime and their perceived fairness" (Ahmad 1996, pp. 246, 241).

Thus, as suggested in the heuristic model shown in figure 5, staff approaches and skills can in a real sense act as a mediating force between some of the other factors shown (e.g., the degree of physical constraint and surveillance) and the eventual outcome of good or bad prisoner behavior. For a fuller discussion of this key role of the prison staff in the maintenance of order, see Liebling and Price (1999).

As previously indicated, the model shown in figure 5 requires further testing and refinement. But for the moment, it perhaps brings coherently together some of our understandings, based on existing research into the problems of prison order and prison violence.

It should finally be emphasized that this heuristic model should be seen as potentially *fully interactive*, especially as regards the key dimension of legitimacy: for example, an officious emphasis by staff on physical constraints may have a cost in terms of legitimacy. This point is developed more fully in the next subsection.

D. Tensions for Prison Administrators

If the model suggested in the previous subsection has validity, then it might also be of relevance to prison administrators in considering possible "control strategies" intended to strengthen the sense of order in the institution.

Pursuing this line of thought, toward the end of *Prisons and the Problem of Order* we set up a speculative model of some styles of prison control, focused on prison regimes that were known to us through our own or others' research (see Sparks, Bottoms, and Hay 1996, p. 328). Part of that speculative model is presented here as figure 6: included in this figure are the researchers' suggestions about how one might appropriately describe aspects of the regimes of four prisons, namely Albany, Long Lartin, Barlinnie Special Unit, and Marion (the former end-of-the-line penitentiary in the U.S. Federal system; see Ward 1987).

What figure 6 very well illustrates is that within the interactive model presented in figure 5 there can be some real tensions for prison administrators. In particular, it is striking when considering the "plus" and "minus" notations in the first two rows of figure 6 that there seems to be a very real tension between the dimensions of "legitimacy" and of "physical control." A loosening of physical restrictions will probably be appreciated by most prisoners and may therefore enhance the per-

	MARION	ALBANY (main)	LONG LARTIN	BARLINNIE Sp. Unit
Level of situational control	+++	+	—	— —
Legitimacy	— — —	— (disputed)	+ (disputed)	++
Model of social control delivery	redundant?	'rule of rules' routinization good service	civility/discretion routinization privileged status	autonomy participation
Status of prisoner	dangerous object	dangerous subject	thinking agent (some dangerous)	participant

Fig. 6.—A speculative model of some styles of prison control. Source: Adapted from Sparks, Bottoms, and Hay (1996), p. 328.

ceived legitimacy of the regime. But it may easily also create more areas in the prison, at more times, that are unsupervised by staff, and therefore provide many more opportunities for hidden violence.[38] Conversely, to impose additional physical restrictions, especially of a severe character, will almost certainly lead to a legitimacy deficit; and that deficit may well in the end play itself out in enhanced violence. This is consistent with Wright's (1991a, p. 235) comment, noted earlier, that "more structured, more authoritarian settings may engender more disruptive behavior." Although the matter cannot now be established with certainty, mechanisms such as these seem to be the most plausible explanation of Bidna's results (see Subsec. IIIA above). In the general housing units in Californian prisons, it appears likely that the enhanced physical restrictions reduced violence as a result of enhanced situational control. But in the special security housing, the allocation of more inmates to this status, plus enhanced physical restrictions within the units, seems likely to have led to a severe legitimacy deficit, leading to enhanced violence.

[38] As previously noted, however, low situational control can coexist with low violence levels, if other mechanisms for securing compliance are in operation—as in Barlinnie Special Unit.

If these speculations have merit, the final question that they raise is, obviously, whether it is in fact possible to create a prison regime that imposes tight situational controls without loss of legitimacy. The likeliest way of achieving this, within our present knowledge, seems likely to lie with the "new generation architecture plus direct supervision" package, if implemented in an appropriate way.[39] Unfortunately, most writers on direct supervision have not considered the relevant issues using this set of concepts. However, an optimistic answer to the question posed above is perhaps suggested by King's (1991) careful comparative analysis of two high-security prisons, Gartree in England and Oak Park Heights in Minnesota, the latter built to "new generation" specifications. Although prison violence levels are generally higher in the United States than in Britain, and although the population profiles of the two prisons did not particularly suggest that Gartree had the more difficult group of inmates, nevertheless, the self-reported victimization levels in Oak Park Heights were only a third of those in Gartree, using the same research instrument in both prisons (King 1991; see also King and McDermott 1995, pp. 123–24).

V. Prisoner-Staff Violence
Patterns of prisoner assaults against prison staff have been studied less fully than prisoner-prisoner assaults. But much can be learned from the few research studies that are available.

A. Environmental and Social Context
Atlas (1983) studied the sites of recorded assaults in four Florida prisons, distinguishing between inmate-inmate and inmate-staff assaults. Among other variables, he considered whether the site of the assault was in an area of the prison that was directly supervised, or had only limited staff supervision. Reworking the data in his table 4, an interesting pattern emerges. Most recorded assaults of all kinds took place in areas of only limited supervision. However, while only 10 percent of recorded inmate-inmate assaults were in areas of direct supervision, that was true of 20 percent of inmate-staff assaults. Because so many unreported prisoner-prisoner assaults occur out of sight of staff, it seems very unlikely that this difference is an artefact of reporting and recording processes; and if that is correct, then an initial point to note

---

[39] Though this does not always occur in practice—see, e.g., Farbstein, Liebert, and Sigurdson (1996); and James et al. (1997).

is that prisoner-staff assaults are more likely than prisoner-prisoner assaults to be *public events.*

Other analyses of the physical location of prisoner-staff assaults suggest that they take place disproportionately often in inmates' residential areas, and in special security housing units; by contrast, other areas of the prison (gym/recreation areas, workshops, and so on) are underrepresented (Kratcoski 1988; Light 1991; Sparks, Bottoms, and Hay 1996, pp. 234–35).

Light (1991) carried out a content analysis of official records relating to nearly seven hundred prisoner-staff assaults in New York State; in particular, he studied what he described as the "themes" of the assaults, that is, the immediate context within which they had taken place. In the cases where a theme could be identified from the records, six contexts were dominant and they accounted for over four-fifths of the cases. These contexts were (in decreasing order of frequency): (i) *Officer's Command* (assault on officer following explicit command to inmate); (ii) *Protest* (assault occurs because inmate considers himself to be the victim of unjust or inconsistent treatment by a staff member); (iii) *Search* (assault occurring during search of a prisoner's body or cell, excluding specific contraband searches); (iv) *Inmates' Fighting* (assault on officer intervening in fight between inmates); (v) *Movement* (assault during movement of inmates from one part of the prison to another); and (vi) *Contraband* (assault consequent upon a staff member suspecting inmate of possessing contraband items).

Examining and reflecting on these categories, several relevant issues emerge. First, in several of the categories the assault has arisen in circumstances where formal legal *power* is being explicitly asserted by the officer—by the issuing of a command, by undertaking a search, or by an interaction concerning alleged contraband. It is, of course, central to a prison's social system that, formally speaking, prison officers have extensive powers over inmates. But, as we have seen in the Introduction, most prison officers most of the time choose to avoid overt displays of power and instead rely on staff-prisoner relationships and on some limited "accommodations" to get them (and the prisoners) through the prison day. On occasions, however, the officer feels that power has to be asserted—and perhaps at these times assaults on the officer may be most likely to occur. Naturally, different officers may choose to "draw the line" in this way at different threshold-points (see Subsec. *B* below) and with varying personal styles (Liebling and Price 1999).

Two other apparent themes arise from Light's categorization (see above), namely *routines* and *legitimacy*. The "protest" category speaks for itself as an illustration of the importance of dimensions of legitimacy within the prison (see Sec. IV above). The "movement" category is an illustration of violence arising directly out of aspects of the prison's daily routine (see further below), and the "inmates' fighting" category exemplifies the hazards to which prison officers may be subject in carrying out their routine tasks, in this case their role of "peacekeeper" between inmates (cf. Liebling and Price 1999).

The themes of *power* and *routines* are further illustrated by some data on the timing of recorded disciplinary offenses (including assaults) at Albany Prison, England, in 1988 (see Sparks, Bottoms, and Hay 1996, pp. 233–36). Four particular moments of the prison day were found to be especially associated with recorded disciplinary incidents: these were "morning unlock" (when prisoners are woken and expected to begin the day's routine), the start of the morning (0900 hours) and afternoon (1415 hours) work periods (when prisoners are moved from cell blocks to workshops), and evening lockup. Between them, these four very short periods of the day, each lasting about ten minutes, accounted for 25 percent of all the prison's recorded disciplinary incidents, thus confirming "conventional wisdom in prisons . . . that incidents are most likely to occur at particular moments such as unlock and 'bang-up' " (Sparks, Bottoms, and Hay 1996, p. 235).

From these various data sources a clear pattern emerges. Prisoner-staff assaults, it seems, are mostly not random events, but are very disproportionately likely to occur at what might be described as the "rubbing-points" of the prison's social order, that is, at particular moments of the daily routine such as unlock and the movement to work, during particular routines such as searches, and on particular occasions when the officer decides that power has to be asserted (by a command or a contraband search). But individual officers may handle these "critical events" very differently from one another.

B. Officers' Age and Experience

In the late 1980s, Kratcoski (1988) carried out a small study of two American correctional facilities (one federal, one state), and discovered that more experienced prison officers (in terms of length of service in the job) were proportionately less likely to be the victims of recorded prisoner-staff assaults. Very similar results were reported in England at about the same time, in a study of a large local prison (Davies and Burgess 1988).

More recently, the British researcher Ditchfield (1997) has carried out two more extensive statistical studies on this issue. The first study examined data on recorded prisoner-staff assaults in all male closed establishments in England and Wales (Ditchfield 1997, pp. 1–11), while the second study reanalyzed data from a 1994 survey of basic-grade prison officers ($N = 1,800$) which had included a yes/no question on whether the officer had been assaulted in the past six months (Ditchfield 1997, pp. 42–46).

In the first study, a regression analysis was carried out on an institutional basis, with the rate of prisoner-staff assaults in each prison as the dependent variable. In the final regression model covering all establishments, "staff age" in the prison (i.e., percentage of older/younger staff in the prison) "emerged as the best predictor of assault rates" (p. 1) outstripping even average inmate age. However, in this study Ditchfield also included variables relating to staff experience. He found that age and length of experience were almost equally predictive of recorded prisoner-staff assaults, and thus more or less interchangeable in the various statistical models; hence he preferred to speak of an "age/experience factor." Interestingly, when particular types of prison were separately analyzed, low-security (category C) institutions constituted an exception to these general patterns, with "staff age/experience" failing to emerge as significantly related to prisoner-staff assault levels.

In Ditchfield's second study, the age/experience factor was again highly significant. However, as this was an individually based rather than an institutional data set, it was possible to carry out a more refined disaggregation of the age/experience issue. This analysis produced an interactive result. For young officers (under thirty), length of experience seemed to have no effect on whether the officer said he or she had been assaulted (though regardless of length of experience, self-reported assault victimizations were highest in this younger age group). There was a slight experience effect for officers aged thirty to thirty-nine; but in older officers (forty plus) there was a marked experience dimension, with the more experienced officers reporting lower assault rates. These intriguing results suggest that age per se (with concomitantly limited life experience) may be the key variable for officers under thirty, but for those above that age lack of experience in the job might be of greater importance. Clearly, however, this single result should not be taken as definitive, especially as the dependent variable used in the second study was a simple dichotomized one (whether assaulted in the past six months).

With the exception of Ditchfield's second study, all the research on the age/experience issue has used data relating to *formally recorded assaults* on prison staff.[40] Using such data, the lower assault rate for older/more experienced staff could reflect either or both of the following: greater interpersonal skills in older/more experienced officers, so that such officers are better able to prevent conflict-laden situations from erupting into physical violence; a similar actual rate of assault in the different groups, but a greater propensity on the part of the younger/less experienced staff to place prisoners on formal disciplinary reports for more minor assaults (arising, perhaps, from a lower level of confidence in their own authority).

Clearly, both these possibilities have some intuitive plausibility. But Ditchfield's second study—based on self-reported victimizations by officers—perhaps provides some evidence that the results of the studies using formal assault rates are not simply the product of differential reporting and recording practices.[41]

Further research on these issues is obviously required. In the meantime, however, it is worth noting that results of the above kind can have clear practical consequences for prison managers. Thus, for example, in a longitudinal analysis of recorded assaults against prison officers in England in the period 1988–93, Ditchfield (1997, pp. 37–42) found that during these years the proportion of uniformed prison staff under thirty in the English prison service increased sharply (from 16.5 percent to 28 percent), and hence that "a significant proportion of the increased rate of assaults on staff since 1988–89 has been caused by the exceptionally large increase in the numbers of young and inexperienced staff joining the service" (p. vii).[42]

C. Conclusions

Although research on prisoner-staff violence is underdeveloped, it seems clear from the available literature that this kind of behavior is

---

[40] It is also possible that the respondents to the staff survey (used in Ditchfield's second study) had formally recorded assaults principally in mind.

[41] Though see n. 40 above.

[42] In a recent time-series analysis in Canada, Walters (1998) found that, at an aggregate level within the prison system as a whole, mean length of service by staff was *positively* associated with violence levels. Walters seeks to interpret this result in systemic terms, but the mechanisms that might be involved are not altogether clear.

Anthony E. Bottoms

intimately bound up with the core issues of *daily routines* and of *staff-prisoner relationships* to which attention was drawn in the Introduction to this essay. There is some evidence that such assaults are closely connected to the potential "friction points" of the prison regime (e.g., searches) and of the prison day (e.g., morning unlock). But there is also evidence that some officers may be more skilled than others in handling these "friction points," and that officers' age and prior experience may be key variables in this regard. There is, further, at least a hint (in Ditchfield's 1997 finding about minimum-security prisons) that skilled officer handling of friction points may be of less practical significance for the assault levels in low-security prisons, perhaps because the regimes in such prisons have fewer potential friction points. There is clearly here a rich seam for future research, which should be intimately linked to the understudied but important topic of staff-prisoner relationships in prisons (see Liebling and Price 1999).

VI. Prisoner-Prisoner Violence

Part of the aim of this essay is to consider interpersonal prison violence within the daily frameworks of the prison social order. From such a perspective, when we turn from prisoner-staff to prisoner-prisoner interpersonal violence, we move—at least to some extent—into a different social world. This is the social world of the prisoner subculture, of shifting alliances between groups of prisoners and of antagonisms that may culminate in a serious assault in an unsupervised place. Indeed, some have portrayed the prisoners' hidden world as akin to a Hobbesian "state of nature," and a "war of every man against every man":

> For WARRE, consisteth not in Battell onely, or the act of fighting; but in a tract of time, wherein the Will to contend by Battell is sufficiently known. . . . For as the nature of Foule weather, lyeth not in a showre or two of rain; but in an inclination thereto of many dayes together; So *the nature of War, consisteth not in actuall fighting; but in the known disposition thereto, during all the time there is no assurance to the contrary.* . . .
>
> In such condition, there is no place for Industry; because the fruit thereof is uncertain: and consequently no Culture of the Earth, no Navigation, . . . ; no Arts; no Letters; no Society; and *which is worst of all, continuall feare, and danger of violent death;* and the life of man, solitary, poore, nasty, brutish, and short. (Hobbes 1973, pp. 64–65, emphasis added)

There are in the prisons literature anecdotal accounts, seemingly carrying a ring of validity, that paint a picture of inmate society very close to Hobbes's nightmarish vision. Lowman (1986), for example, comments that "even the most naive of new inmates soon come to realise the pervasiveness of the rule of force" (p. 255) in the prisoners' world, and he offers a harrowing real-life example of the kind of social choices and pressures that may be forced on prisoners (p. 256).

And yet there is a paradox. Some recent researchers have carried out surveys of prisoners' sense of safety, with surprisingly positive results. King and McDermott (1995, pp. 141–42), for example, asked their sample of prisoners to rate in general terms how safe or dangerous was the prison in which they were located. For all five prisons taken together, the mean response (on a five-point scale from −2 [very dangerous] to +2 [very safe]) was +0.45, though these scores did vary substantially by prison.[43] O'Donnell and Edgar (1996a, 1999) in their Oxford study, asked the rather more specific question whether their respondent-prisoners felt safe from assault, and received positive answers from 60 percent or more in all four of the institutions they studied, despite the high self-reported victimization rates in these institutions (see table 3).[44]

How can we explain this apparent paradox (hereafter referred to as the "safety paradox")—of the frequently described "pervasiveness of the rule of force" in the inmate world, as against apparently much more positive answers to questions on safety? No definitive answers to this question can be offered in the present state of the research evidence, but some suggestive pointers may be available.

A. Basic Aspects of the Inmate Experience

We may begin with two apparently near-universally agreed points about the inmate experience. The first of these relates to the dominant norms of the inmate world, the second to the dangerousness of certain locations.

Lowman (1986, pp. 254–55) speaks of "two disciplines" in prison— the discipline of the officials and the discipline of the inmate world.

[43] The "most unsafe" prisons were the local prison (Birmingham) and the maximum security training prison: both had mean scores in the minus range.

[44] The O'Donnell-Edgar study did include a catergory B prison with some of the functions of a local prison, but it did not include a maximum security prison (cf. n. 43 above). It is also worth observing that in the NPS, even higher overall safety levels were reported (Dodd and Hunter 1992), but this could be a methodological artefact arising from reluctance to admit lack of safety in prison to an unknown interviewer.

Contrary to Foucault's (1977) perception, Lowman argues that the surveillance of officials "is nothing compared to that exercised by inmates over each other" for, except when locked alone in a single cell, "one is never beyond the scrutiny of inmate eyes." Moreover, many of those eyes belong to people who advocate "the use of physical violence as the ultimate resolution to all conflict," in a value system that is truly based on machismo (p. 248; see also Toch 1997, chap. 21 on "hyper-masculinity and prison violence").[45] While detailed accounts of inmate value systems in the research literature vary, and there is also some evidence that such systems may differ in different types of institution, yet there are very few prison scholars who would argue that Lowman's portrayal of the core values of the inmate world is fundamentally mis-conceived.

Lowman further points out that, for prisoners, "quite frequently custodial staff are out of sight" (pp. 254–55); and it is this that makes certain locations in the prison seem so potentially dangerous (on this, see e.g., O'Donnell and Edgar 1999). There can be no reasonable doubt that "out of sight" locations exist in most prisons and that they are an obvious target area for prisoners wanting to settle conflicts by force.

Yet we must also note a third fact about the experience of being a prisoner. While most new prisoners (especially first-timers) are disoriented and fearful on arrival in the prison, there is now substantial research evidence that over time they gradually work out ways of coping with this strange social world (see, e.g., Ericson 1975; Zamble and Porporino 1988; Liebling and Krarup 1993). As far as I am aware, no surveys of prisoners' feelings of safety have yet analyzed such perceptions by phase of custody, but one might reasonably hypothesize from the above-cited literature that this might be a relevant variable. One might also expect, for the same reasons, that indices of violence and victimization might vary with phase of custody, though as we have seen (Subsec. IID above) the existing data on this point are at present very inconclusive.

What is clearly lacking is adequate longitudinal data on how, as their sentence progresses, prisoners view the surveillance and demands of other inmates and their own ability to remain safe in this world. Nor

[45] Obviously these remarks are made in the context of prisons for males. The literature on violence in women's prisons (see Subsec. IIE above) is not sufficiently well developed to be able to say with any confidence how far such comments would also hold true in that different context.

do we know much about the changing patterns of friendships and alliances that prisoners enter into as time goes on. Without such data, our knowledge of prisoner-prisoner violence and the "safety paradox" mentioned in the introduction to this section, will necessarily remain incomplete.

B. Personal Protection Strategies

Since there is no doubt that many prisoners face potential dangers from at least some other prisoners, analyses of inmates' personal protection strategies seem to be called for in any full account of prisoner-prisoner violence. Again, however, the literature on this topic is sparse (though see esp. McCorkle 1992).

Broadly, there seem to be several main kinds of personal protection strategies available to prisoners. They include the following: (1) *withdrawal* (avoid certain activities or certain areas of the prison, spend more time in cell, etc.), (2) *seek support from other inmates* (e.g., from one's own home town), (3) *seek support or formal protection from staff*, (4) *"suspended identity" and temporary manipulation of self-image* (attempt, at least to an extent, to suspend one's preprison identity and to construct an inauthentic prison identity through impression management, e.g., by appearing more "macho" than one really is), (5) *utilization of skills* (make available to other inmates any special skills that one possesses—e.g., well-educated prisoners helping others to frame petitions), (6) *passive-aggressive protection* (e.g., acquire homemade weapons and make clear to other prisoners that one has done so), and (7) *preemptive strike* (in McCorkle's research [1992, p. 166], a number of prisoners suggested to the researcher that " 'getting tough' often requires more than 'tough talk' "; for a full analysis of a preemptive strike of this kind ["Incident LL1"] in a maximum-security prison, see Sparks, Bottoms, and Hay [1996], pp. 239, 253–55).

McCorkle's (1992) evidence, based on a study in Tennessee, was that individual prisoners might often adopt several different personal protection strategies at various points in their sentence. But two broad styles of personal protection tended to predominate: namely "withdrawal/avoidance," a strategy especially adopted by fearful, older, and socially isolated inmates; and "aggressive and proactive techniques," especially adopted by younger inmates. Unfortunately, however, McCorkle did not include all of the above-listed strategies within his research framework; in particular, he omitted the "suspended identity" approach. Empirical support for the adoption of "suspended identity" strategies by prisoners has been provided by Schmid and Jones (1991), who argue that by embracing this approach "inmates are able to forestall more radical identity change and to maintain a general sense of identity continuity for most of their prison careers" (p. 415). It is therefore at least possible that the adoption of impression management techniques of this sort may help prisoners to feel safe in prisons, despite the apparent "pervasiveness of the rule of force" in the culture around them. However, at present such a suggestion must remain speculative.

We noted in the previous subsection some research evidence to the effect that prisoners, from a position of initial disorientation, gradually develop ways of coping with the social world of the prison. There is no evidence, at present, concerning the extent to which prisoners' personal protection styles may alter as these "prison coping strategies" gradually gain ground, but this topic also would appear to be worthy of future exploration.

C. Daily Routines and Daily Choices

From one perspective, being a prisoner among prisoners is a lifestyle that requires continual choices. Do I try to be friendly to Inmate X or to avoid him? If I am waiting to use the telephone and another prisoner seeks to usurp my place in the line, what do I do? Do I shout insults at other prisoners to show that I am "one of the lads," even if I might receive a mild assault in response? (see, generally, Edgar and O'Donnell 1998).

Choices of this kind are clearly relevant to the incidence of prisoner-prisoner violence. McCorkle (1992) usefully reminds us that many physical assaults between prisoners "follow challenges to machismo, strivings for status, or disreputable dealings on the sub rosa economy" (p. 170). Hence, choosing to engage such activities will, prima facie, increase the risk of violent victimization; yet some striving for status or machismo often seems to the individual inmate to be necessary for survival in the inmate world (on this paradox, see further Edgar and O'Donnell [1998]). By contrast, continual withdrawal from challenges to status or machismo might well be "interpreted by aggressive inmates as signs of weakness and vulnerability," so that those who "opt out" in this way "risk being assigned to a pool of victims who can easily be robbed . . . or dominated" (McCorkle 1992, p. 170).

These dilemmas posed by McCorkle take us back to the very important distinction, made by O'Donnell and Edgar, and supported in their data, between "mutual victimization" (those who were victims *and* aggressors in different assault incidents) and "vulnerable victimization" (those who were repeatedly victimized without retaliation) (see also Edgar and O'Donnell 1998). We lack research evidence on this point, but from an analytic standpoint it would seem that avoidance of the "vulnerable victim" status must rank as the highest priority for comfortable survival in the inmate world. If that is right, then successful "survival strategies" inevitably seem to court some risk of violent victimization. But a crucial and so far unasked question seems to be, Is it in fact possible to minimize one's participation in activities that risk violent victimization (such as striving for status or sub rosa trading) while at the same time also avoiding the potential label of "vulnerable victim"? Clearly, this kind of "tightrope-walking" will not be easy to accomplish, but how many prisoners in fact successfully achieve it? Such questions seem directly relevant to the "safety paradox" posed at the beginning of this section.

D. Social Order and the Inmate World

At this point in the argument, it is worth returning to the broader dimensions of order maintenance in prisons, previously discussed in Section IV above. The analysis in Section IV explicitly included the official power structure of the prison and interactions between staff and prisoners as key elements in overall order maintenance. But, as Cohen (1976) has usefully pointed out, within the more limited framework of the inmates' social world, some different considerations may apply when analyzing order. Most people, Cohen argues, if they are the victim of a criminal or civil wrong, turn naturally to the official agencies (police, courts, etc.) to obtain justice. But there are some social contexts in which, when one is wronged, "the prevailing attitude and practice [in seeking redress] is some form of self-help or private vengeance" (p. 12). There is widespread evidence, in the prisons literature, of prisoners' reluctance to turn immediately to staff when victimized by other prisoners. Hence, alongside the broader questions of order maintenance in prison (see Sec. IV above), for a full explanation of prisoner-prisoner violence one also has to consider the question of social order within those parts of the inmate world that are based on "private justice" and thus have only a partial connection to the official structures.

Systems of private justice may sometimes be based on normative consensus within a cohesive social group as is the case, for example, in many religious communities. But in a social context such as the prisoner community, where one has a "preference for private justice," as Cohen puts it, together with a notable lack of social cohesion in certain respects,[46] then it is easy to see that the use or threat of violence may become socially endemic. In truth, in such a social context violence has for some actors a degree of positive social utility: "violence may be used to establish, assert, and restore relationships, especially relationships of dominance, where these relationships have been threatened by challenges, by failure to exhibit appropriate deference, [or] by assertions of autonomy incompatible with the demands of the relationship" (Cohen 1976, p. 4).

It is worth reexamining the conceptual scheme of Section IV (see esp. figs. 3 and 5), with the specific context of the prisoners' world in mind. In figure 5, box 8 ("staff deployment, approaches, and skills") occupies a central mediating position, but such influences are, at least in a direct sense, largely absent in the inmates' own social world (though see Subsec. VIE below). Moreover, within the prisoners' world there is little compliance based on legitimacy, for few (if any) prisoners are recognized as having legitimate authority (as opposed to coercive authority) over their peers. Hence, within the prisoners' own world there is a variant kind of social order existing within the broader social order of the prison and unusually weighted toward coercive power and towards instrumental/prudential reasons for compliance. Not surprisingly, in such a social world violence is never far below the surface.

In Section IVC above, the definition of "order" given by Sparks, Bottoms, and Hay (1996, p. 119) was quoted. The first part of that definition characterizes order as "any long-standing pattern of social relations . . . in which the expectations that participants have of one another are commonly met, though not necessarily without contestation." The literature on inmate subcultures in prisons has consistently suggested that there is a kind of social order, in this sense, within the prisoners' own world: that is to say, there is a kind of patterning of

---

[46] Most inmates do normatively assent to certain values such as the "preference for private justice" itself. Some sociological research studies (such as that of Sykes [1958]) have emphasized the pressures within inmate society toward the adoption of a value stance of "inmate solidarity," but even such analyses readily concede that in practice the inmate world contains many individuals who do not act fully in accordance with the code of "solidarity" (see e.g., Sykes [1958], chap. 5, on the various "argot roles" in the prison he studied).

social relationships and some common understandings about how to "go on" in this social milieu, so that, to an extent at least, mutual expectations are "commonly met."[47] Hence, the evidence that we have about the prisoners' own world suggests both that it is a special kind of social context unusually weighted toward coercive power and that it nevertheless frequently contains elements of predictability and order. These considerations seem highly relevant to the "safety paradox" posed in the introduction to this section, though no studies yet exist that analyze the safety paradox in these terms.

E. The Role of the Prison Staff

There is sometimes a tendency, when discussing prisoner-prisoner violence, to assume that this topic can be appropriately discussed with only minimal reference to the official routines and management of the prison. But such an assumption is false, as is evidenced by—in different ways—the Texas experience of the 1980s and the literature on new generation architecture and direct supervision (see Sec. III above). In Texas, management changes forced on the department of corrections by the courts led, indirectly and temporarily, to a massive increase in inmates' acquisition of makeshift weapons for self-protection and violence. Management changes designed to calm the system then achieved a reduction of this kind of personal protection strategy. In new generation prisons, the different physical layout and recommended management style could and should lead to the custodial staff being out of sight of the inmates far less often than in most traditional prisons, which obviously might well have effects on prisoner-prisoner violence. All this being the case, general questions relating to the maintenance of order in prisons (see Sec. IV above) are by no means irrelevant to issues of prisoner-prisoner assault but are in fact integrally related to them—even if, when discussing prisoner-prisoner assaults, one also has to take account of certain special features of the inmate social world.

Since it seems therefore that changing the official routines or management of the prison can indeed indirectly affect prisoner-prisoner violence levels, there is a concomitant challenge to prison administrators to consider how they might best achieve reductions in prisoner-prisoner violence by thoughtful management changes.

---

[47] For a brief overview of the literature on the sociology of prisons, with references, see Sparks, Bottoms, and Hay (1996), chap. 2.

REFERENCES

Adams, K. 1992. "Adjusting to Prison Life." In *Crime and Justice: A Review of Research*, vol. 16, edited by Michael Tonry. Chicago: University of Chicago Press.

Adams, R. 1992. *Prison Riots in Britain and in the U.S.A.* London: Macmillan.

Ahmad, S. 1996. "Fairness in Prison." Ph.D. dissertation, University of Cambridge.

Atlas, R. 1983. "Crime Site Selection for Assaults in Four Florida Prisons." *Prison Journal* 53:59–72.

Balvig, F. 1988. *Delinquent and Not-Delinquent Youth: A Study on Self-Reported Delinquency among Youth in a Metropolitan Suburb in Denmark* (Kriminalistisk Instituts Stencilserie no. 43). Copenhagen: University of Copenhagen, Institute of Criminal Science.

Baskin, D. R., I. Sommers, and H. J. Steadman. 1991. "Assessing the Impact of Psychiatric Impairment on Prison Violence." *Journal of Criminal Justice* 19:271–80.

Bedau, H. A. 1982. "Background and Developments." In *The Death Penalty in America*, 3d ed., edited by H. A. Bedau. New York: Oxford University Press.

———. 1997. "Prison Homicides, Recidivist Murder and Life Imprisonment." In *The Death Penalty in America: Current Controversies*, edited by H. A. Bedau. New York: Oxford University Press.

Beetham, D. 1991. *The Legitimation of Power.* London: Macmillan.

Bidna, H. 1975. "Effects of Increased Security on Prison Violence." *Journal of Criminal Justice* 3:33–46.

Bijleveld, C. C. J. H. 1998. "Methodological Issues in the Study of Domestic Violence Prevalence." *European Journal on Criminal Policy and Research* 6:607–15.

Bottomley, K., A. Liebling, and R. Sparks. 1994. "Barlinnie Special Unit and Shotts Unit: An Assessment." Occasional Paper no. 7/1994. Edinburgh: Scottish Prison Service.

Bottoms, A. E., W. Hay, and R. Sparks. 1990. "Situational and Social Approaches to the Prevention of Disorder in Long-Term Prisons." *Prison Journal* 80:83–95.

Bottoms, A. E., and R. Light, eds. 1987. *Problems of Long-Term Imprisonment.* Aldershot: Gower.

Bottoms, A. E., and R. Sparks. 1997. "How Is Order in Prisons Maintained?" In *Security, Justice and Order in Prison: Developing Perspectives*, edited by A. Liebling. Cambridge: University of Cambridge, Institute of Criminology.

Bowker, L. 1980. *Prison Victimization.* New York: Elsevier.

Boyle, J. 1984. *The Pain of Confinement.* London: Canongate.

Braswell, M. C., R. H. Montgomery, Jr., and L. X. Lombardo, eds. 1994. *Prison Violence in America*, 2d ed. Cincinnati: Anderson.

Clarke, R. V. 1995. "Situational Crime Prevention." In *Building a Safer Society: Strategic Approaches to Crime Prevention*, edited by M. Tonry and D. P. Farrington. Vol. 19 of *Crime and Justice: A Review of Research*, edited by M. Tonry. Chicago: University of Chicago Press.

Cohen, A. K. 1976. "Prison Violence: A Sociological Perspecitve." In *Prison Violence*, edited by A. K. Cohen, G. F. Cole, and R. G. Bailey. Lexington, Mass.: D. C. Heath & Co.

Colvin, M. 1992. *The Penitentiary in Crisis: From Accommodation to Riot in New Mexico*. Albany, N.Y.: SUNY Press.

Cook, T. D., and D. T. Campbell. 1979. *Quasi-experimentation: Design and Analysis Issues for Field Settings*. Boston: Houghton Mifflin.

Cooke, D. J. 1989. "Containing Violent Prisoners: An Analysis of the Barlinnie Special Unit." *British Journal of Criminology* 29:129–43.

———. 1991. "Violence in Prisons: The Influence of Regime Factors." *Howard Journal of Criminal Justice* 30:95–107.

Cooley, D. 1993. "Criminal Victimization in Male Federal Prisons." *Canadian Journal of Criminology* 35:479–95.

Cressey, D. R., ed. 1961. *The Prison: Studies in Institutional Organization and Change*. New York: Holt, Rinehart, & Winston.

Crouch, B. M., and J. W. Marquart. 1989. *An Appeal to Justice: Litigated Reform of Texas Prisons*. Austin: University of Texas Press.

Davies, W. 1982. "Violence in Prisons." In *Developments in the Study of Criminal Behaviour*, vol. 2, edited by P. Feldman. Chichester: Wiley.

Davies, W., and P. W. Burgess. 1988. "Prison Officers' Experience as a Predictor of Risk of Attack: An Analysis within the British Prison System." *Medicine, Science and the Law* 28:135–38.

Ditchfield, J. 1990. *Control in Prisons: A Review of the Literature*. Home Office Research Study no. 118. London: H.M. Stationery Office.

———. 1997. "Assaults on Staff in Male Closed Establishments: A Statistical Study." Home Office Research and Statistics Directorate Internal Paper. Unpublished manuscript. London: Home Office.

Dodd, T., and P. Hunter. 1992. *The National Prison Survey, 1991*. London: H.M. Stationery Office.

Edgar, K., and I. O'Donnell. 1998. "Assault in Prison: The 'Victim's' Contribution." *British Journal of Criminology* 38:635–50.

Eigenberg, H. M. 1994. "Rape in Male Prisons: Examining the Relationship between Correctional Officers' Attitudes toward Male Rape and Their Willingness to Respond to Acts of Rape." In *Prison Violence in America*, 2d ed., edited by M. C. Braswell, R. H. Montgomery, Jr., and L. X. Lombardo. Cincinnati: Anderson.

Ellis, D., H. G. Grasmick, and B. Gilman. 1974. "Violence in Prisons: A Sociological Analysis." *American Journal of Sociology* 80:16–43.

Ericson, R. V. 1975. *Young Offenders and Their Social World*. Farnborough: Saxon House.

Farbstein, J. D., D. Liebert, and H. Sigurdson. 1996. *Audits of Podular Direct-Supervision Jails*. Washington, D.C.: National Institute of Corrections.

Farbstein, J. D., and R. Wener. 1989. *A Comparison of Direct and Indirect Supervision Correctional Facilities*. Washington, D.C.: National Institute of Corrections.

Farrington, D. P. 1997. "Human Development and Criminal Careers." In *The*

Oxford Handbook of Criminology, 2d ed., edited by M. Maguire, R. Morgan, and R. Reiner. Oxford: Clarendon.

Foucault, M. 1977. *Discipline and Punish: The Birth of the Prison*. London: Allen Lane.

Gaes, G. 1994. "Prison Crowding Research Re-examined." *Prison Journal* 74:329–63.

Giddens, A. 1984. *The Constitution of Society*. Cambridge: Polity.

———. 1987. *Social Theory and Modern Sociology*. Cambridge: Polity.

Goetting, A., and R. M. Howsen. 1986. "Correlates of Prisoner Misconduct." *Journal of Quantitative Criminology* 2:49–67.

Goffman, E. 1961. *Asylums*. Garden City, N.Y.: Anchor Books.

Goodstein, L., and K. N. Wright. 1989. "Inmate Adjustment to Prison." In *The American Prison: Issues in Research and Policy*, edited by L. Goodstein and D. L. MacKenzie. New York: Plenum.

Graham, J., and B. Bowling. 1995. *Young People and Crime*. Home Office Research Study no. 145. London: Home Office.

Harer, M. D., and D. J. Steffensmeier. 1996. "Race and Prison Violence." *Criminology* 34:323–55.

Hirschi, T. 1969. *Causes of Delinquency*. Berkeley: University of California Press.

Hobbes, T. 1973. *Leviathan*. Everyman's Library edition. London: Dent. (Originally published 1651.)

Home Office. 1985. *New Directions in Prison Design*. London: H.M. Stationery Office.

———. 1987. *Special Units for Long-Term Prisoners: A Report by the Research and Advisory Group of the Long-Term Prison System*. London: H.M. Stationery Office.

Human Rights Watch. 1996. *All Too Familiar: Sexual Abuse of Women in U.S. State Prisons*. New York: Human Rights Watch.

Irwin, J. 1970. *The Felon*. Englewood Cliffs, N.J.: Prentice-Hall.

Jacobs, James B. 1977. *Stateville: The Penitentiary in Mass Society*. Chicago: University of Chicago Press.

James, A. L., A. K. Bottomley, A. Liebling, and E. Clare. 1997. *Privatising Prisons: Rhetoric and Reality*. London: Sage.

Jones, M. 1968. *Social Psychiatry in Practice: The Idea of the Therapeutic Community*. Harmondsworth: Penguin.

King, R. 1985. "Control in Prisons." In *Accountability and Prisons*, edited by M. Maguire, J. Vagg, and R. Morgan. London: Tavistock.

———. 1991. "Maximum Security Custody in Britain and the USA: A Study of Gartree and Oak Park Heights." *British Journal of Criminology* 31:126–52.

King, R. D., and K. McDermott. 1990. " 'My Geranium Is Subversive': Notes on the Management of Trouble in Prisons." *British Journal of Sociology* 41:445–71.

———. 1995. *The State of Our Prisons*. Oxford: Clarendon.

Kratcoski, P. C. 1988. "The Implications of Research Explaining Prison Violence and Disruption." *Federal Probation* 52(1):27–32.

Liebling, A., and H. Krarup. 1993. *Suicide Attempts and Self-Injury in Male Prisons*. London: Home Office.

Liebling, A., G. Muir, G. Rose, and A. Bottoms. 1999. "Incentives and Earned Privileges for Prisoners: An Evaluation." Research Findings no. 87. London: Home Office.

Liebling, A., and D. Price. 1999. *An Exploration of Staff-Prisoner Relationships at HMP Whitemoor*. London: Prison Service.

Light, S. C. 1991. "Assaults on Prison Officers: Interactional Themes." *Justice Quarterly* 8:243–61.

Lowman, J. 1986. "Images of Discipline in Prison." In *The Social Dimensions of Law*, edited by N. Boyd. Scarborough: Prentice-Hall Canada.

Lynch, J. 1995. "Crime in International Perspective." In *Crime*, edited by J. Q. Wilson and J. Petersilia. San Francisco: ICS.

MacKenzie, D. L. 1987. "Age and Adjustment to Prison: Interactions with Attitudes and Anxiety." *Criminal Justice and Behavior* 14:427–47.

Maitland, A. S., and R. D. Sluder. 1998. "Victimization and Youthful Prison Inmates: An Empirical Analysis." *Prison Journal* 78:55–73.

Mandaraka-Sheppard, A. 1986. *The Dynamics of Aggression in Women's Prisons in England*. Aldershot: Gower.

Marquart, J. W. 1986. "Prison Guards and the Use of Physical Coercion as a Mechanism of Prisoner Control." *Criminology* 24:347–66.

Maung, N. A. 1995. "Survey Design and Interpretation of the British Crime Survey." In *Interpreting Crime Statistics*, edited by M. A. Walker. Oxford: Clarendon.

McCorkle, R. C. 1992. "Personal Precautions to Violence in Prison." *Criminal Justice and Behavior* 19:160–73.

O'Donnell, I., and K. Edgar. 1996*a*. "The Extent and Dynamics of Victimization in Prisons." Research Report to the Home Office. Unpublished manuscript. Oxford: University of Oxford Centre for Criminological Research.

———. 1996*b*. "Victimization in Prisons." Research Findings no. 37. London: Home Office, Research and Statistics Directorate.

———. 1998*a*. "Bullying in Prisons." Occasional Paper no. 18. Oxford: University of Oxford Centre for Criminological Research.

———. 1998*b*. "Routine Victimization in Prisons." *Howard Journal of Criminal Justice* 37:266–79.

———. 1999. "Fear in Prison." *Prison Journal*, vol. 79 (forthcoming).

Paternoster, R., R. Brame, R. Bachman, and L. W. Sherman. 1997. "Do Fair Procedures Matter? The Effect of Procedural Justice on Spouse Assault." *Law and Society Review* 31:163–204.

Petersilia, J. 1983. *Racial Disparities in the Criminal Justice System*. Santa Monica, Calif: Rand.

Poole, E. D., and R. M. Regoli. 1980. "Race, Institutional Rule Breaking and Disciplinary Response: A Study of Discretionary Decision Making in Prison." *Law and Society Review* 14:931–46.

Porporino, F. J., and E. Zamble. 1984. "Coping with Imprisonment." *Canadian Journal of Criminology* 26:403–22.

Quay, H. C. 1984. *Managing Adult Inmates*. College Park, Md.: American Correctional Association.

Ruck, S. K. 1951. *Paterson on Prisons*. London: Muller.

Schmid, T. J., and R. S. Jones. 1991. "Suspended Identity: Identity Transformation in a Maximum Security Prison." *Symbolic Interaction* 14:415–32.

Sellin, T. 1967. "Prison Homicides." In *Capital Punishment*, edited by T. Sellin. New York: Harper & Row.

Silberman, M. 1995. *A World of Violence: Corrections in America*. Belmont, Calif.: Wadsworth.

Sourcebook of Criminal Justice Statistics. Various years. Washington, D.C.: U.S. Department of Justice, Bureau of Justice Statistics.

Sparks, R., and A. E. Bottoms. 1995. "Legitimacy and Order in Prisons." *British Journal of Sociology* 46:45–62.

Sparks, R., A. E. Bottoms, and W. Hay. 1996. *Prisons and the Problem of Order*. Oxford: Clarendon.

Statistics of Offences against Prison Discipline and Punishments in England and Wales. Various years. London: H.M. Stationery Office.

Sykes, G. M. 1958. *The Society of Captives*. Princeton, N.J.: Princeton University Press.

Sylvester, S. F., J. H. Reed, and D. O. Nelson. 1977. *Prison Homicide*. New York: Spectrum.

Thomas, C. W., D. Petersen, and R. Zingraff. 1978. "Structural and Social Psychological Correlates of Prisonization." *Criminology* 16:383–93.

Tischler, C. A., and J. W. Marquart. 1989. "Analysis of Disciplinary Infraction Rates among Female and Male Inmates." *Journal of Criminal Justice* 17:507–13.

Toch, H. 1977. *Living in Prison: The Ecology of Survival*. New York: Free Press.

———. 1997. *Corrections: A Humanistic Approach*. Guilderland, N.Y.: Harrow & Heston.

Toch, H., and K. Adams. 1989. *Coping: Maladaptation in Prisons*. New Brunswick, N.J.: Transaction.

Tyler, R. T. 1990. *Why People Obey the Law*. New Haven, Conn.: Yale University Press.

Useem, B., and P. A. Kimball. 1989. *States of Siege: U.S. Prison Riots, 1971–1986*. New York: Oxford University Press.

van Dijk, T., S. Flight, E. Oppenhuis, and B. Duesmann. 1998. "Domestic Violence: A National Study of the Nature, Size and Effects of Domestic Violence in the Netherlands." *European Journal on Criminal Policy and Research* 6:7–35.

von Hirsch, A. 1993. *Censure and Sanctions*. Oxford: Clarendon.

von Hirsch, A., A. E. Bottoms, E. Burney, and P.-O. Wikström. 1999. *Criminal Deterrence and Sentence Severity*. Oxford: Hart.

Walters, G. D. 1998. "Time Series and Correlational Analyses of Inmate-Initiated Assaultive Incidents in a Large Correctional System." *International Journal of Offender Therapy and Comparative Criminology* 42:124–32.

Ward, D. 1987. "Control Strategies for Problem Prisoners in American Prison

Systems." In *Problems of Long-Term Imprisonment*, edited by A. E. Bottoms and R. Light. Aldershot: Gower.

Wener, R. 1994. "An Environmental Model of Violence in Institutional Settings." Division 34 Presidential Address, American Psychological Association. *Division 34 Newsletter* (October 14).

Wener, R., W. Frazier, and J. Farbstein. 1985. "Three Generations of Evaluation and Design of Correctional Facilities." *Environment and Behavior* 17:71–95.

Whatmore, P. B. 1987. "Barlinnie Special Unit: An Insider's View." In *Problems of Long-Term Imprisonment*, edited by A. E. Bottoms and R. Light. Aldershot: Gower.

Wolfson, W. P. 1982. "The Deterrent Effect of the Death Penalty upon Prison Murder." In *The Death Penalty in America*, 3d ed., edited by H. A. Bedau. New York: Oxford University Press.

Wooldredge, J. D. 1994. "Inmate Crime and Victimization in a Southwestern Correctional Facility." *Journal of Criminal Justice* 22:367–81.

Woolf, Lord Justice. 1991. *Prison Disturbances April, 1990*. London: H.M. Stationery Office.

Wright, K. 1985. "Developing the Prison Environment Inventory." *Journal of Research in Crime and Delinquency* 22:257–77.

Wright, K. N. 1991*a*. "A Study of Individual, Environmental and Interactive Effects in Explaining Adjustment to Prison." *Justice Quarterly* 8:217–42.

———. 1991*b*. "The Violent and Victimized in the Male Prison." *Journal of Offender Rehabilitation* 16:1–25.

Wright, K. N., and L. Goodstein. 1989. "Correctional Environments." In *The American Prison: Issues in Research and Policy*, edited by L. Goodstein and D. L. MacKenzie. New York: Plenum.

Wrong, D. 1994. *The Problem of Order: What Unites and Divides Society*. Cambridge, Mass.: Harvard University Press.

Zamble, E., and F. J. Porporino. 1988. *Coping, Behavior and Adaptation in Prison Inmates*. New York: Springer-Verlag.

Alison Liebling

Prison Suicide and Prisoner Coping

ABSTRACT

An exploration of prison suicide can offer a variety of significant insights.
It can help in the development of suicide prevention policy, but may also
help in the broader understanding of the nature of prisons. There is an
"additional strain" of imprisonment, and identifiable groups of prisoners
are especially susceptible to it. There are discontinuities between the
literature on adjustment to imprisonment and the literature on suicides in
prison. Bringing together the separate literatures on coping, on suicide,
and on the prison experience strengthens our appreciation of the distress
suffered in prison and some of the reasons for it. The figures show
relatively high and increasing rates of prison suicides, particularly among
sentenced, and notably, life-sentence prisoners. Our profile of the suicidal
prisoner is incomplete and biased. Different types of prison suicide can be
identified, and problems of coping with various aspects of imprisonment
take on special significance for some of these groups. Apparently mundane
(or routine) features of the prison world can make huge demands on
limited coping resources.

> For prisoners . . . the death rate from suicide . . . is over
> four times as great. . . . Is this increased incidence of suicide
> also a direct effect of the prison environment; or is it due
> to the fact that persons with marked suicidal tendency are

Alison Liebling is a senior research associate at the Institute of Criminology, University of Cambridge, United Kingdom. The author thanks Anthony Bottoms for encouraging her to accept this commission and for clarifying her thoughts. Grateful thanks are also due to Andrew von Hirsch, Michael Tonry, Timothy Flanagan, Joan Petersilia, Hans Toch, and two anonymous reviewers for helpful comments. Thanks are also due to the Economic and Social Research Council for financial support (grant no. H52427001594). Previous versions of some material appeared in Liebling (1992, 1993, 1995, 1997, and 1998). The author is grateful to the publishers for permission to reproduce these materials in revised form here.

more liable to be imprisoned for crime? This question cannot be definitely answered from the statistical evidence before us, although, in the circumstances of the case, there can be little doubt as to what the correct answer should be. We know that the suicidal act does require a certain conjunction of favourable conditions for its successful accomplishment; and that these conditions would be least likely found in the prison environment, which, with its constant supervision of, and restrictions upon, a prisoner's actions, operates in every direction against his committing suicide easily. Consequently, we should assume that the greater the intensity of the suicidal tendency, the less would be the likelihood of the suicidal act deferred until a time particularly unfavourable for its consummation; but on the other hand, we would conjecture that, among persons possessing an equal tendency to commit suicide, the additional strain of imprisonment would inevitably lead to an increased desire of death among suicides. (GORING, *The English Convict* [1913], p. 152)

No . . . I wasn't on my own, I was in a cell with somebody else. He's in the hospital now with his nerves [laughs]—I must have lost nearly all my blood. (PRISONER)

It is like the blood is doing the crying for me. . . . It's not a cry for help. It's a cry of pain. (PRISONER)

It was serious and not serious at the same time. It relieves the depression, releases it. Outside, I'd go out and get into trouble. In here, your head just gets in bits. (PRISONER)

Psychological research has concluded that the effects of imprisonment are largely minimal (Banister et al. 1973; Bolton et al. 1976; Bukstel and Kilmann 1980; Walker 1983, 1987) or that prisoners cope surprisingly well (Richards 1978; Sapsford 1978, 1983; Zamble and Porporino 1988) despite an initial period of disorientation and serious anxieties about family and friends. These studies have also concluded that ex-prisoners are typically able to resettle after an initial period of restlessness on release (Coker and Martin 1983). Specific concerns such as overcrowding (see Gaes 1985) have been investigated in some detail, and concerns have been raised about the findings reported in some studies that high degrees of sustained overcrowding contribute to higher rates of disciplinary infractions, illness complaints, and more deaths. Social density (number of occupants in housing quarters) has been found to have more negative effects than spatial density (space per person) (see McCain, Cox, and Paulus 1980; Cox, Paulus, and McCain 1984; Gaes 1985). On the whole, psychological research has characterized the experience of imprisonment as little worse than a period of "deep freeze" (cf. Zamble and Porporino 1988)—albeit a "deep freeze" imposed on people who are often poor copers to begin with.

The sociological literature by contrast has represented the power of institutions as brutal, mortifying, and damaging (see especially Sykes 1958; Goffman 1968; Cohen and Taylor 1972), but these studies have been subject to methodological criticism and accusations of ideological bias (see Sapsford 1978; Walker 1987). The "pains" identified by these studies, which remain largely omitted from or unsubstantiated by psychological research, include fear of breakdown (Cohen and Taylor 1972), fear of contamination, and loss of "self." Sykes argued that the pains of imprisonment include the deprivation of liberty (resulting in lost emotional relationships, loneliness, and boredom), the deprivation of goods and services, the deprivation of heterosexual relationships, the deprivation of autonomy, and the deprivation of security (enforced association with other unpredictable prisoners, causing fear and anxiety) (Sykes 1958, pp. 63–78). These deprivations can constitute a serious attack on the personality and on self-esteem. The prisoner loses society's trust, the status of citizenship, and material possessions, which might constitute a large part of the individual's self-perception. The prisoner is figuratively "castrated," and the minutiae of life are regulated with a "bureaucratic indifference" to individual need and worth:

Imprisonment, then, is painful. The pains of imprisonment, however, cannot be viewed as being limited to the loss of physical liberty. The significant hurts lie in the frustrations or deprivations which attend the withdrawal of freedom, such as the lack of heterosexual relationships, isolation from the free community, the withholding of goods and services, and so on. And however painful these frustrations or deprivations may be in the immediate terms of thwarted goals, discomfort, boredom, and loneliness, they carry a more profound hurt as a set of threats or attacks which are directed against the very foundations of the prisoner's being. The individual's picture of himself as a person of value . . . begins to waver and grow dim. Society did not plan this onslaught, it is true, and society may even "point with pride" to its humanity in the modern treatment of the criminal. But the pains of imprisonment remain and it is imperative that we recognise them, for they provide the energy for the society of captives as a system of action. (Sykes 1958, pp. 78–79)

Reconciling these apparent contradictions in research on the effects of imprisonment can be achieved by addressing the question of suicide in prison. Prison suicide rates are high, and research on the causes of such disproportionate rates suggests that the experience of imprisonment is far from neutral. Studies of suicide in prison suggest that surviving prison demands a set of resources that are often in short supply. Pressures of isolation, inactivity, regulation, loss of control, and unpredictability cause considerable distress, particularly at certain stages of custody. The experience of imprisonment can be corrosive and demanding, particularly for vulnerable groups of prisoners.

Hay and Sparks characterize the "effects debate" about imprisonment as sterile (1992, p. 302). The operationalization of harm has been poor (Liebling 1992), and the focus of almost all the research has been on long-term prisoners because of an assumption that any harmful effects—if such exist—will be curvilinear, increasing with length of time in custody. However, there are several flaws in this latter argument and in the studies that have been built on it. The impact of custody is extreme at early stages: this is reflected in suicide rates and absconding figures (see, e.g., Ericson 1975; Sapsford 1983). It has been established that the early period of confinement subjects prisoners to a great deal of stress and a feeling of disorientation. It may be assumed that this early experience of imprisonment is especially true for first-time prisoners. Suicides early in custody also occur among persistent prisoners, and as this article shows, rapid return to prison may be an indicator of poor coping rather than a sign of indifference to the impact of imprisonment. Research shows that in time prisoners may adjust and cope, and thus generally do not suffer from long-term deterioration. Their styles of coping, and the social life that emerges in the process of coping has been the subject of interesting theoretical and sociological study (see Toch, Adams, and Grant 1989; Adams 1992). Prisoners who die by suicide do not, of course, appear in such "long-term" samples, nor do those who "exit" the prison experience by other means—for example, by transfer to psychiatric hospitals or by natural death. At the end of a substantial period of imprisonment, those who are left are the survivors. (This may, however, include prisoners who have made un-successful suicide attempts.) None of the existing longitudinal studies of the effects of imprisonment estimate the extent of attrition from long-term entry cohorts by these means.

Many detailed studies have been carried out on the effects of imprisonment. Psychologists and criminologists have concluded their investigations with the following sorts of statements: "Research in British prisons—chiefly by psychologists—has done much to deflate the sweeping exaggerations—chiefly by sociologists—about the ill effects of normal incarceration" (Walker 1987). By contrast, Bukstel and Kilmann in their review article found from the available evidence that "confinement in penal isolation awaiting execution was quite stressful" (Bukstel and Kilmann 1980, p. 478).

These sorts of conclusions—and bland understatements—illustrate the failure of research on the effects of prison life to ask the right questions or to ask in an appropriate kind of way how imprisonment is experienced. Research methods typically employed have not tapped the subjective, cognitive, or affective contributions prisoners make to their own experiences of prison. Answering this question, "Is prison harmful?" is—at least in part—a matter of empathy or "appreciative understanding." These dimensions of the human experience do not contradict the research principles of rigor, care, or the need for empirical evidence. Prison research (particularly prison suicide research, but also most major studies on the effects of imprisonment) have largely proceeded without sufficient affective understanding, in deference to record-based measurement. Such studies rarely follow prisoners after release, and they rarely investigate psychological or emotional distress and disability (Grounds 1996). They look instead at skills and personality traits, omitting to consider those who have not survived (or who have almost not survived) the prison experience. It is by this route that such research has been able to conclude that imprisonment is not harmful. Studies that employ criteria of harm-as-deterioration, and deterioration as permanent negative change in IQ, cognitive functioning, or other such skills are seriously limited. Suicide does not require a permanent drop in such measurable psychological constructs. Pain is a harm that psychological scales have so far failed to reflect. Damage may be immediate, and cumulative, and yet independent of the amount of time spent in custody. Repeated short periods of custody may engender at least as much "risk" and pain as one long sentence. This issue of the cumulative effects of imprisonment is complex and needs further exploration (see, e.g., Sampson and Laub's study of the cumulative effects of custody on reconviction [1993] and von Hirsch [1993] on "proportionality" and the differential impact of sentences on considerations of deterrence).

There is a second major difficulty with previous studies. Prison is not a uniform experience. Studies have tended to take large undifferentiated samples and to look for general patterns that omit the experience of particular groups and individuals. They have tended to omit specific groups (such as women, the young, prisoners segregated for their own protection, those spending long periods of time in segregation units for disciplinary reasons, etc.). As this article shows, particular groups may be especially vulnerable to suicide in prison. Their experience of imprisonment is qualitatively different from others' experience. Methodological failure satisfactorily to consider prisoners' own accounts of the prison experience, and the differences between prisoner groups, have resulted in the sterility to which Hay and Sparks refer.

The study of suicide in prison reveals that imprisonment is selectively directed at vulnerable groups, that the experience of imprisonment can be deceptively difficult and unpredictable, and that it may have devastating psychological consequences. Approaches to prevention should place due emphasis on alternatives to custody and general regime measures and should not focus exclusively on medical or psychiatric strategies of identification. Constructive regimes that provide activity, opportunities for change, contact, and support may offset some of the worst aspects of prison life. Coping with prison is a major, private, and individual struggle that, for some, is unbearable. The adaptation literature seriously underestimates the degree of anguish experienced by many prisoners through their own efforts to keep anguish and distress under control (Gallo and Ruggiero 1991). Coping, in other words, is partial, unstable, and arduous.

This article aims to consider the existing literature on prison suicide and to link this literature with current knowledge about coping with prison and the nature of the prison experience. Is there an "additional strain" of imprisonment, and if so, which prisoners are most susceptible to it? How does research on prison suicide assist in the broader search for understanding the nature of prisons? The article assesses current understanding of the nature and causes of suicide in prison, explores the validity of current studies and their relevance to the general field of prisons research, and considers the problems faced by prison staff in the management and prevention of suicides in custody.

This article is divided into four sections. Section I considers prison suicide rates, profiles of prisoner suicides and attempted suicides, and
some of the reasons for both. Section II reexamines the concepts of
coping, and not coping, and shows how this helps understanding both
vulnerability to suicide and the nature of the prison experience. Section
III considers implications for policy, in particular, the concept of risk
management. The final section considers the implications of this re-
conceptualization of the significance of prison suicide for prison studies. I draw mainly on the English-language literature, although inevitably given my personal experience, most of the examples given are
English.

I. Prison Suicide

This section considers the problem of measuring suicide rates and reviews the literature on prison suicide profiles. It shows that aggregate
prison suicide rates require careful scrutiny and that our profile of the
suicidal prisoner is incomplete and biased. Different types of prison
suicide can be identified, and problems of coping with various aspects
of imprisonment take on special significance for some of these groups.
It argues that there are important links between suicide and attempted
suicide, and it redresses the omission in many studies (and the serious
underestimation) of suicides among women in prison.

A. The Problem of Measurement

> There is an important distinction between the knowledge
> that someone . . . probably . . . committed suicide, and the
> *legal requirement* that one be *sure* that he . . . both intended
> the outcome, and had the capacity to take the action. In a
> court of law, one must be satisfied of the *intent* and of the
> *capacity*. A suicide is—historically—the murder of oneself,
> and the law requires it to mean just that. (CORONER, cited
> in LIEBLING [1992], pp. 83–84)

One of the major limitations in research on suicide in general, and
perhaps in particular on suicides in prison, is the unreliability of figures
on suicide. Official figures, prison service files, and other sources of
recorded information provide the sources for much current understanding of suicide and suicide attempts in prison. Few studies reflect
critically on this information as a data source, yet there are serious
doubts about its validity, about recording practice and file content.

Many factors play an important role in the recording of such information, including preparation for inquests, the availability of time, training, staff priorities, and staffing levels.

Official suicide figures and records, based as they are on the outcomes of coroners' inquests, provide an inadequate data source for any analysis of rates or explanations of suicides in prison. Since 1990, the English Prison Service has been publishing figures for all self-inflicted deaths in addition to those defined as suicide at inquests. Also since 1990, several prison services (e.g., in the United Kingdom and Australia) and many of those engaged in research have tended to use "self-inflicted deaths," including those that did not attract suicide verdicts at inquests. A study by Dooley in the United Kingdom shows how "probable suicides" receiving other verdicts (such as "open," "misadventure," or "accidental") differ in significant respects from prison suicides receiving a suicide verdict (Dooley 1990*b*). In his study of 346 nonnatural deaths in prison between 1972 and 1987, those self-inflicted deaths not receiving suicide verdicts at inquests were more likely to be female, young, to die by means other than hanging, to have injured themselves before, and to have occurred during the day (Dooley 1990*b*; see also Liebling 1992, pp. 82–93). In other words, only those suicides that "look like" suicides (i.e., that fulfill prior expectations) are recorded as suicides. This limits the validity of research that takes such selective information as its starting point, as sociological critiques of suicide in the community have demonstrated (see, e.g., Douglas 1967; Atkinson 1982; Taylor 1982). As Stengel argued, "Doctors and prison officers are not unbiased in these cases. It would not be surprising if, unconsciously, they preferred to blame misadventure for a death which could possibly have been prevented by them, had they taken a different view of the situation" (1971, p. 14).

Our profile of the prison suicide may therefore be biased and incomplete. As with most statistical information on which criminological research is based, the requirements for recording such information are unrelated to the requirements of research: they are collected for another purpose (Kitsuse and Cicourel 1963). Even suicides, so often taken to be "unequivocal," cannot be assumed to be so.

A further problem inherent in record-based research is the unreliability of the information available in case records. File information may be incomplete (Dooley 1990*a*), incorrect (Dooley 1990*b*, 1990*c*), or selective (see also Griffiths and Rundle 1976; Zamble and Porporino 1988). Files may contain contradictory information, and it is apparent that an inmate's understanding of events and decisions (which usually go unrecorded) may be different from those recorded in his or her file. Record-based studies miss a great deal of valuable information relating to suicidal activities in prison and the context in which they arise. Certain situational or institutional factors may appear in documentary material available to the researcher, such as the extent of overcrowding, hours spent out of cell, the prisoner's location, the ratio of staff to inmates, and so on. But this conception of the prison as a series of identifiable and recordable institutional variables is seriously limited, as other areas of prison research illustrate (McDermott and King 1988). Organizational and relational aspects of the prison (such as how prisoners are treated, how staff "deliver" regimes, etc.) are as real and important in terms of life inside as are visible and quantifiable factors such as hours out of cell, timing in sentence, and so on. The prison itself "does" very little in terms of its impact on prisoners: "the prison itself does not do anything . . . it just sits there. What really matters are the 'subtle specifics of each prisoner's participation in prison life' " (Wormith and Porporino 1984, p. 427).

What goes on in prison may be unavailable in any form of documentation, however carefully collected, and despite the increasing volume and availability of this sort of material. Similar criticisms of retrospective, record-based suicide, and suicide attempt research can be found in studies in the community (Hawton and Catalan 1987). Record-based information may be incomplete, biased, and unreliable (Liebling 1992).

Using official figures, then, for explanations of suicide, can be hazardous. Exploring epidemiological trends may be less hazardous, as recording differences between countries (and groups) tend to remain relatively stable over time. A World Health Organization working group found on careful examination of the evidence that official suicide statistics could be used for trend analysis (see Rutter and Smith 1995). I consider aggregate rates and prison suicide trends in the next section.

B. Aggregate Prison Suicide Rates

Most studies of prison suicide rates (except for the United States) do not separate remand (jail) populations from sentenced populations. Almost all studies find that the suicide rates of prisoners on remand or awaiting trial and sentenced prisoners are similarly high, once reception figures are taken into account. More than half of all prison suicides in any one year in all jurisdictions occur among sentenced prisoners (see Backett 1987; Dooley 1990*a*; Liebling and Krarup 1993; Towl

1997). It is consistently found in international studies of prison suicide that suicide rates calculated on the basis of average daily population (ADP) are at least four times higher than suicide rates for the general community (these studies are not generally controlled for composition, however; see below). Most of the studies looking at prison suicide rates over time in the United Kingdom (e.g., 1972–98) and elsewhere show an increase in the rate of prison suicides over and above any rate of increase in the ADP or in the number of receptions. Many show an increase in the ratio of suicides in prison to those in the community.

Despite being the most widely used base from which to calculate prison suicide rates, there are difficulties in using ADP as the base from which to make comparisons with the general community. (For a more detailed review of the complex arguments relating to the calculation of prison suicide rates, see O'Mahony [1994].) Some consideration of the reception rate and the length of stay (or "exposure-to-risk") of prisoners should be included in any calculation of the relative rates of suicides in prison, particularly in the light of what is known about the higher risk of suicide in the early days of custody (Ericson 1975; Topp 1979; Sapsford 1983; Thornton et al. 1984; Backett 1987; Dooley 1990*a*; see also, on coping difficulties, Zamble and Porporino [1988]). Demographic differences between the populations in prison and the community (e.g., age, other sociodemographic characteristics, and gender) must also be taken into account. Only one study (in the United States) compares prison suicide rates based on "person-years-at risk" with the general population equivalent rate adjusted by age, sex, and race. This study found that the prison suicide rate is higher than the rate for the equivalent general population, but by a slightly smaller ratio than that reported in most recent studies (Winfree 1985). This type of calculation has not been carried out in the United Kingdom, and many of the studies carried out are therefore using unsatisfactory figures.

Recent studies carried out in the United Kingdom and elsewhere do show that prison suicide rates are increasing over time faster than the increase in either reception rates or ADP and that suicides in prison occur more frequently than might be expected from the age and other demographic characteristics of the prison population (Correctional Service of Canada 1981; Special Commission to Investigate Suicide in Municipal Detention Centers 1984; Hatty and Walker 1986; Bernheim 1987; Dooley 1990*a*). In 1997–98 there were seventy-two suicides in prisons in England and Wales, which had an average prison

TABLE 1

Self-Inflicted Death Rates in Prison in England and Wales,
Scotland, and Australia

	N	Average Prison Population	Average Suicide Rate (per 100,000)
England/Wales:			
1983–86	101	44,950	56
1987–90	181	47,700	95
1991–94	192	45,675	105
1995–96	123 (246)	53,150	116
Scotland:			
1980–83	12	4,830	62
1984–87	23	5,265	109
1988–91	20	4,930	101
1992–93	14	5,447	128
Australia:			
1987–90	80	12,320	162
1991–94	81	14,613	139
1995–96	50 (100)	16,165	155

Sources.—Suicide Awareness Support Unit, United Kingdom; McDonald (1988).

population of 62,500 prisoners (Prison Service 1998). This resulted in a prison suicide rate of around 120 suicides per 100,000 citizens. The suicide rate among young males (under twenty-five years old) in the community—the closest comparative statistic available—in England and Wales during 1996 was around seventeen per 100,000 (Samaritans 1997; see also Rutter and Smith 1995). Suicide rates in other jurisdictions are similarly high, compared with expected rates, suggesting that prison suicides can only partly be accounted for by the selective demographic nature of prison populations. Vulnerability and prison-induced distress (Backett 1987, 1988) may also play a part.

Table 1 shows increases in the rate of prison suicide against ADPs of prisons in England and Wales, Scotland, and Australia. It is interesting to note that a temporary reduction in the prison suicide rate occurred in Australia during the early 1990s (perhaps related to activities following the Royal Commission into Aboriginal Deaths in Custody; see McDonald [1994, 1998] for useful reviews).

Table 2 shows international prison suicides rates based on ADP. All studies show elevated rates compared with rates in the community (by

TABLE 2
International Prison Suicide Rates

	Rate per 100,000	
	Most Recent	Previous Studies (pre-1991)
Australia	155	(90–180)
Canada	94	(120)
Denmark	19	. . .
England and Wales	116	(56)
France	. . .	43–169
Netherlands	105	. . .
New Zealand	89	. . .
Scotland	128	(52)
United States	140–200	200

SOURCES.—Hayes (1983); Anno (1985); Hatty and Walker (1986); Backett (1987); Bernheim (1987); Dooley (1990a); Rowan (1994, 1997).

a factor of three to ten; see Hatty and Walker 1986; Backett 1987; Dooley 1990a; Rowan 1994).

Crighton and Towl (1997) reviewed two samples of self-inflicted deaths in prisons in England and Wales during 1988–90 and 1994–95 (one hundred and ninety-seven deaths, respectively), comparing them for changes over time. They found (as do all studies) that suicides consistently occur at a disproportionate rate among remand prisoners (prisoners awaiting trial), but that there has recently been a larger increase in suicides among sentenced prisoners. Life-sentence prisoners have a particularly high rate of suicide, despite relatively small absolute numbers (260 per 100,000 ADP in 1994–95 in the United Kingdom; Crighton and Towl 1997, p. 15). Although there has been a marked increase in the numbers of prisoners identified as at increased risk of suicide, the majority of those who complete suicide are not identified in advance. Most of those who kill themselves do not have a history of psychiatric intervention. Almost half of the deaths occur within one month of reception into custody. White and Asian prisoners show similar rates of suicide, while black prisoners show lower rates.

There is some evidence of a slowdown in the rate of increase in prison suicides in the United Kingdom since 1996 (Tilt 1998), in many states in the United States (Rowan 1994; Hayes 1995), and in Australia (McDonald 1998). There is also some evidence that reductions in prison suicide rates can be achieved through prevention strategies, increased awareness, decarceration, and bail programs (Hayes 1995; Rowan 1998).

A more careful analysis of suicide rates both in and out of prison should be a prerequisite of future research. It is also important to consider whether prison suicides differ in qualitative respects from suicides in the general community.

C. The Prison Suicide Profile

The earliest studies of prison suicide in the United Kingdom were carried out by prison medical officers, who began the search for a profile of the "suicidal inmate" in their capacity as medical inspectors of prisons, whose annual reports considered mortality statistics (see Gover 1880; Smalley 1911; Goring 1913; Topp 1979; and reviews by Liebling 1992; Liebling and Ward 1995). This approach set the tone for most subsequent studies of prison suicide, which have been retrospective profile accounts based on small numbers of inmates (e.g., Danto 1973; Hankoff 1980). Because a death had occurred, medical knowledge was sought (Liebling and Ward 1995). All of these early studies observed that prison suicide accounted for a disproportionate number of deaths and proposed that the demographic profile of the prison population could account for this (for more detail, see Sim 1990; Sim and Ward 1994). There were anxieties that prison regimes contributed to some of the deaths—in which case the fine balance between deterrence and reform was wrong. Prison chaplains were held to possess greater knowledge than most about prisoners' mental states and their possible motivations for suicide. The chaplain at Clerkenwell (London's main remand prison in 1881; cited and paraphrased in Anderson [1987], p. 320) considered that "suicide, like every other kind of sin, crime and misery, was caused by intemperance, impurity, laziness, and bad temper, and nothing else" (quoted in Liebling and Ward 1995, p. 124). Attempted suicide was punished as a crime (so that a handful of prisoners were serving sentences as a result of attempted suicide in the community) and as a prison disciplinary offense until 1961. The growth of the power of medical officers (and the parallel decline in the power of chaplains) influenced an important assumption enshrined in suicide prevention procedures and in most studies that suicide was a medical (specifically, psychiatric) problem. The profile research approach grew out of this perception. This approach remained a powerful part of official thinking about suicide until the late 1980s (see Liebling and Ward 1995). Important changes have taken place in some respects since then. A psychiatrist asked to investigate a series of young prisoner suicides in Scotland in 1985 concluded that "this is not a psychiatric problem, it's a management problem" (Scottish Home and Health Department 1985). For a review, see Liebling (1992).

Prison suicides "represent a profile which is distinct from the population of suicides generally, but little different from that of the general prison population" (Hankoff 1980, p. 166). Studies conclude overall that the suicide rate in prison is disproportionately high, that most completed prison suicides are male, that a disproportionate number are on remand at the time of death, that a third have a history of in-patient psychiatric treatment, that lifers are overrepresented, that most have previous convictions, and that 40 percent have been seen by a doctor in the week preceding death (see Topp 1979; Backett 1987; Dooley 1990a). Most completed suicides are accomplished by hanging, many have injured themselves before (often in custody), many have serious drug and alcohol problems, and many completed prison suicides are accomplished by the young (age range: 20–34) (Topp 1979; Backett 1987; Dooley 1990a; see also, Lloyd 1990; Liebling 1992). About a third of all prison suicides occur very early in custody (within the first week). It is significant, in particular, that a history of psychiatric treatment is less likely among prison suicides than among those in the community (Backett 1987, 1988). Only one-third of prison suicides are found to have a psychiatric history, as opposed to 80–90 percent of suicides in the general community (Backett 1987; Dooley 1990a; see also Barraclough et al. 1974; Barraclough and Hughes 1987). A high proportion are found to have psychological difficulties falling short of a formal psychiatric diagnosis, such as alcohol or drug problems, personality disorders or borderline personality disorders, self-reported anxiety and depression (see, e.g., Skegg and Cox 1993). This has important implications for prevention strategies, which have historically treated suicide risk as an exclusively medical or psychiatric problem.

Prison suicides are found to be younger than suicides in the community, reflecting the relatively young age profile of the prison population. The proportion of female suicides in prison is found to be proportionate to their numbers in the population (see Liebling [1994] and below). Ethnic minorities are represented in the prison suicide statistics proportionate to their numbers in the prison population in the United Kingdom (which vastly overrepresent ethnic minority groups in custody, of course) and disproportionately in some jurisdictions (e.g., in Australia, see McDonald 1998). Being married does not exclude a prisoner from suicide, although it does operate as a protective factor. Isolation from relationships or a breakdown in communication may be more important overall than marital status. The constellation of factors relating family history to vulnerability to suicide out of prison have not been applied to research on prisoner suicide. This is despite the known high levels of family breakdown and discord reported among prisoner populations.

Offense history may be related to prison suicide, but research results are contradictory. Studies disagree as to whether completed prison suicides are more likely to have been convicted of acquisitive crimes or crimes of violence.

Inevitably, the profile approach to prison suicide seeks predictive risk factors. Risk factors identified in the literature include the use of drugs (both before and during custody), and problems with alcohol use, particularly among those suicides that occur early in a period of custody. Just as outside, almost half of all prison suicides are found to have a history of self-injury or previous suicide attempts. A quarter have injured themselves in custody before.

Over time, as an increasing number of studies were carried out, it became clear that situational factors were easier to identify than individual factors in the prediction of suicide in prison. Research results illustrated that predicting who might abscond was more difficult than predicting when such absconding might occur (Clarke and Martin 1971; Banks, Mayhew, and Sapsford 1975; Laycock 1977). The same was true of prison suicides (Liebling 1992). Most suicides occur by hanging and at night. A slightly disproportionate number occur at the weekend, during the summer months (when staffing and activity levels are low), and during the early stages of custody (both before and after trial). A disproportionate number of suicides occur in special locations, such as health care centers, the segregation or punishment block, and other areas of seclusion. Overcrowding may exacerbate problems contributing to suicide risk among the vulnerable, such as lack of access to medical and other specialist care, increased misconduct and assault rates, lack of time spent in activity, lack of clothing and food, unwanted interactions, feelings of helplessness, and rapidly changing hierarchies among inmates (see Liebling 1992).

The apparent motivation for prison suicide appears to be fear or loss: fear of other inmates, of the consequences of one's crime, of imprisonment, and the loss of a significant relationship. Shame, guilt, and psychiatric disorder play a relatively minor role (numerically) for the younger sentenced prisoner (Liebling 1992). The most common emotion in suicides outside is hopelessness or helplessness, intense anguish, or "ennui" (see Beck et al. 1974; Diekstra 1987; Maltsberger and Goldblatt 1996). Prison-induced distress may be seen as a continuum that may contribute to suicide, particularly if a certain threshold is exceeded (Backett 1987). Where this threshold lies will depend on the coping skills and resources of particular inmates. Repeated disruptions and stresses may be as damaging as one particularly stressful experience.

1. *Suicide among Remand/Pretrial Prisoners.* One of the most consistent findings of research is that a disproportionate number of suicides occur among remand (jail) prisoners or early in custody (Topp 1979; Backett 1987; Dooley 1990*a*; Lloyd 1990; Liebling 1992). The high number of receptions arriving at remand centers does mean that far more prisoners are exposed to risk during what is arguably an extremely stressful stage of custody. Studies suggest that the disproportionate rate of suicides during the remand period is in part due to the greater number of prisoners exposed to risk (Crighton and Towl 1997). Other factors may contribute to an excess, however. These factors may include the stressful nature of early confinement, the tension and uncertainty of the pretrial phase, the proximity of the offense, overcrowding and staff shortages, the instability of a continually changing inmate population, and the high proportion of mentally disordered prisoners on remand. Alcohol and drug dependence play an important role, particularly among those suicides that occur within the first twenty-four hours of reception into custody. This group of suicides, who are a major cause for concern in jails and police lockups, have a literature of their own and are not the primary focus of this chapter. (For more detail, see, e.g., Danto 1973; Flaherty 1980; Hayes 1983; Hayes and Rowan 1988). Evidence suggests that the rate of prison suicides is at least as high as the rate of remand/jail suicides and may be increasing at a faster rate (see table 3).

2. *Suicides among Prisoners under Age Twenty-One.* In the United Kingdom, suicides among prisoners under age 21 have been a major cause for concern. Studies have linked these suicides in particular to bullying, inactivity, and lack of contact with families (see esp. Grindrod and Black 1989; Liebling 1992; Davies 1994). A group of thirty-one prison suicides under age twenty-one were identified in a study of all prison suicides occurring in England and Wales between 1972 and 1987; and a comparison made with the general pool of prisoner suicides (see Dooley [1990*a*] for the original study and Liebling [1992]

TABLE 3

Self-Inflicted Deaths per 100,000 ADP and per 100,000 Receptions

	Rate per Annum	ADP 1989*/1994	Rate per 100,000 ADP	Receptions	Rate per 100,000 Receptions
1988–90:					
Sentenced	20	36,700	54	72,912	27
Remand (untried)	21	8,672	242	56,687	37
Convicted unsentenced	5	1,727	290	16,589	30
1994–95:					
Sentenced	34	34,505	99	79,251	43
Remand (untried)	21	9,196	290	54,157	39
Convicted unsentenced	6	3,188	188	32,751	18

Source.—Crighton and Towl (1997), p. 14.

Note.—ADP = average daily population.

*The average daily population for 1989 was taken from the House of Commons (1990, 1996).

for the analysis). The following results were found: Young prisoner suicides were more likely to cluster in particular establishments than were other prison suicides (partly because young prisoners are more likely to be accommodated in particular establishments or wings; young prisoners may also be more susceptible to imitation; see Phillips 1974; Lester and Danto 1993). They were more likely to be charged with or convicted of property offenses. They were likely to be serving slightly shorter terms and to end their lives within one month or at most one year of reception into custody. Young prisoners who committed suicide were even less likely to have received psychiatric treatment (13 percent as opposed to one-third of all prison suicides), and they were slightly more likely than all prison suicides to have injured themselves before. They were slightly more likely to die between midnight and 8 A.M. Almost half of these suicides were attributed to prison pressures (Liebling 1992).

Several studies also support the argument that the under-twenty-one age group differ from adults and may have a different susceptibility to suicide in prison (see Flaherty 1980, 1983; Scottish Home and Health Department 1985; see also Grindrod and Black 1989; Home Office 1990). Their offenses are less serious (usually property offenses), their suicide attempts are more frequent, and within an establishment, such attempts are more likely to occur in clusters. The young offender with a history of convictions for property offenses who is single, with no job or family support, and with a history of self-injury is found in other studies to stand out as a frequent type of prison suicide (e.g., Hatty and Walker 1986). Their need for support is intense, and their reactions to distress impulsive. Young prisoners may be particularly susceptible to threats or attacks from others, having few of the resources and skills necessary to avert such behavior. Rates of bullying and victimization in young offender establishments and in prisons that accommodate young offenders are high and may be increasing (Johnson 1978; McGurk and McDougal 1986; Shine, Wilson, and Hammond 1990). Young prisoner suicides may be more "situation specific" than adult suicides in prison. The term "young," however, can apply in this context to prisoners up to the age of about twenty-six to thirty, as many studies suggest that this highly situational susceptibility does not end at age twenty-one (Liebling 1992; Liebling and Krarup 1993; see also Hatty and Walker 1986).

There are useful lessons to be learned from the search for a profile of a suicidal prisoner. However, there are flaws in the "single profile" approach. It may be more helpful to regard prison suicides as hetero-geneous—consisting of different types (e.g., lifers, the psychiatrically ill, and younger prisoners with mainly property offense convictions), with different offense and demographic profiles, slightly different his-tories, and disparate motivations for suicide. These groups are not mu-tually exclusive. Removing a distinct group of prisoners facing homi-cide charges (therefore facing life sentences) from the total pool of prison suicides results in a slightly different criminal justice profile for other types of prison suicide.

3. *Flaws in the Single Profile Approach.* One of the problems with previous attempts to seek a profile of "the suicidal prisoner" is that treating all prison suicides as a single problem with a single profile and explanation is misleading. At least three distinct types of prison suicide can be identified in the literature (and would be recognized by most professionals working in prison). These are life-sentence prisoners (or domestic homicide charge cases facing life sentences), the psychiatri-cally ill, and "poor copers."[1] Such a differentiated typology may have important policy implications, both in terms of developing appropriate prevention strategies in prison and in reflecting on broader criminal justice policies and practices.

Table 4 is a conceptual, heuristic typology, compiled from data col-lected by the Suicide Awareness Support Unit in the United Kingdom on completed self-inflicted deaths in prisons in England and Wales be-tween 1987 and 1993.[2] Looking at the deaths individually, and catego-rizing them as shown in table 4 demonstrates this distinction. The three groups—life-/long-sentence prisoners, the psychiatrically ill, and "poor copers" each have a different profile; with regard to the age, his-tory, possible motivation, and the types of situational factors that ap-pear to contribute to their deaths, from the available information. Sep-arating these types of prison suicides illustrates that treating them as a homogenous group masks important features of each type.

First, long-sentence prisoner suicides (that include a high propor-tion of domestic homicide cases and that may include for the purposes of this category prisoners on remand but facing life or long sentences)

---

[1] Hatty and Walker did carry out a cluster analysis in their study of deaths in Austra-lian prisons (1986). They identified several distinguishable groups: the violent, the "unfit to plead," and the young prisoner with property convictions. Danto (1973) has also de-scribed different suicidal "types," although his typology is based on very small numbers.

[2] A group working in Prison Service Headquarters whose role is to support establish-ments facing inquests, to collect and disseminate information about suicides in prison, and to carry out and steer research.

TABLE 4

Prison Suicide: A Typology

	Life and Very Long Sentence Prisoners (1)	Psychiatrically Ill (2)	Poor Copers (3)
Motivation	Guilt/no future	Alienation, loss of self-control, fear/ helplessness	Fear/helplessness, distress/isolation
Age	30+	30+	16–30
Proportion of total	5–20 percent	10–22 percent*	30–45 percent +
Relevance of situation	Chronic	Varied	Acute
History of previous self-injury	Low	Medium	High
Features	Often (76%)† on remand, after midnight; some well into sentence	Psychiatric history present; single; no fixed abode	Often more typical of prison population, i.e., acquisitive offenses

*13 percent for young offenders under age 21.
†Dooley 1990a.

tend to be older than average. Some take their lives significantly later during their sentences. Links have long been established between domestic homicide and suicide before arrest (West 1982). Including this group of prison suicides in a general profile may distort the profile toward violent offenses and longer sentences. Removing them and treating them as a group enables one to regard their particular circumstances more appropriately.

Second, the psychiatrically ill. Again, it is well established that there is a strong association between psychiatric illness and suicide (Barraclough and Hughes 1987; Sainsbury 1988). This is especially true of those with a diagnosis of schizophrenia, but those with other psychiatric diagnoses are also disproportionately represented in the suicide figures. There is also an established link between the closure of psychiatric institutions and increases in suicides in prison among this population (Skegg and Cox 1993).

Finally, the group that this article characterizes as "poor copers." This group are the most significant in relation to the prison experience, as they resemble other prisoners most closely. They are arguably the most preventable group, despite being perhaps the most difficult to identify. It is important to note that the "poor copers" or vulnerable constitute the most numerous group of prison suicides and that the significance of the immediate prison situation may be most acute in these cases. It is also important to note that more of this group have attempted suicide or injured themselves before.

4. *Prediction and Control Populations.* Finally, in relation to the "profile" approach to prison suicide, there is an argument that a preoccupation with the "individual" is conceptually limited. This has been raised in other areas of prison research: "This 'individualization of blame,' together with allegations or assumptions of 'pathology' in the etiology/motivation of disruptive behavior undoubtedly appeals to popular stereotypes and mirrors a similar long and now somewhat discredited theme in the history of criminological theory; from Lombroso in the nineteenth century to 'dangerous offender/sexual psychopath' legislation in the second half of the twentieth century" (Bottomley 1990, p. 12).

Most prison suicide studies do not include control data from the general population or from the prison population from which suicides and suicide attempters are drawn. Thus it is impossible to know whether characteristics found to be associated with prison suicides and suicide attempters are simply reflections of the characteristics of the general prison population. Where profiles are drawn up, they are only weakly predictive, thus diverting attention away from many at-risk inmates who do not share the typical characteristics of a suicide. The individual prediction approach to research has not succeeded in either understanding or preventing suicide. Recognizing vulnerability, so that it can be understood (rather than simply predicted), may be more useful. Profiles drawn up in the course of research on prison suicide should be explanatory, aiding in the development of preventive measures, rather than exclusively predictive. The search for the single suicidal profile dominated research until quite recently and has restricted theoretical approaches to the problem.

D. Suicide and Attempted Suicide

> I wanted someone to stop me. But no-one stopped me. So
> I carried on. (PRISONER)

No fully reliable figures on attempted suicide and self-injury exist, either in prison or in the community. Suicide attempt forms, on which annual figures and most research on suicide attempts in custody have been based, are infrequently and haphazardly completed (Tumim 1990). Part of the problem lies in the uncertainty over what actually constitutes a suicide attempt. This issue has never been satisfactorily resolved, and definitions continue to differ. No guidance is given to prison medical officers regarding a suitable operational definition, and no consensus exists as to what might constitute a "genuine" suicide attempt. There may be factors discouraging staff from raising the relevant forms every time an incident occurs: the wish to keep incidents out of the "attempted suicide" figures, the time involved, the dislike of complex forms, and the possibly limited amount of information available on the prisoner concerned. There are serious difficulties inherent in relying on statistical information alone when trying to assess the incidence of attempted suicide in prison (the same can be said of other types of behavior such as assaults, cell thefts, etc.).

In the community, attempted suicide and self-injury have typically been treated as separate phenomena having a limited association with completed suicide. This is despite the existence of evidence that such a separation is artificial (see, e.g., Stengel and Cook 1958; Stengel 1971; Kreitman 1977; Morgan 1979) and follow-up studies of suicide attempts showing up to thirty times greater risk of suicide than in the general population. Studies of suicides and suicide attempts in prison often seek differences between populations who engage in these supposedly distinct behaviors (e.g., Phillips 1986; Griffiths 1990). The causes of the two behaviors are in fact found to be similar. Acts of self-injury, like suicide attempts and suicides, are associated with feelings of melancholy tinged with self-contempt (Cooper 1971), depression, self-doubt, and the search for relief (Toch 1975; Liebling 1992). They are acts of "dead-end desperation," expressing, "an intolerable emptiness, helplessness, tension . . . a demand for release and escape at all costs" (Toch 1975, p. 40).

The populations involved overlap considerably, completed suicides often having a history of attempted suicide or self-injury. Half of all those who die by suicide in prison have injured themselves before—a third in prison (Dooley 1990a). In addition, in the controlled environment of the prison, many potentially lethal suicide attempts are prevented by chance intervention. The relationship between the two is complex and has been largely neglected or oversimplified in research, both in prison and in the community. It may be useful to see suicide— both in action and intent—as a continuum. Self-injury may be the first overt symptom of a level of distress only steps away from a final act of despair (see fig. 1; also see Liebling 1992, pp. 59–67; and Sparks 1994, p. 83).

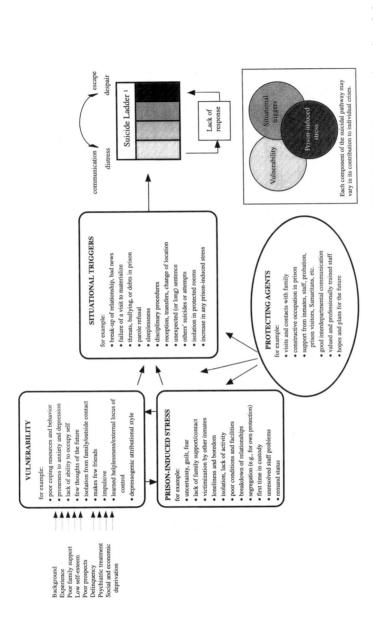

FIG. 1.—Toward a theoretical model of the prisoner's pathway to suicide. The "Suicide Ladder" (cf. Eldrid 1988) indicates a pathway from feelings and thoughts of suicide, through self-injury and failed suicide attempts, to completed suicide. The inmate may be propelled along the continuum of suicidal action by the (lack of) institutional response.

Several studies have been carried out on attempted suicide and self-harm in prison (Johnson 1976; Johnson and Toch 1982; Phillips 1986; Power and Spencer 1987; Wool and Dooley 1987; Thornton 1990; Liebling 1992; Liebling and Krarup 1993). Many recent studies see attempted suicide as an indication of low coping resources and destructive behavior patterns that render the individuals concerned especially vulnerable to suicide (see Liebling 1992; see also Toch 1975; Zamble and Porporino 1988). Stengel identified the "appeal function" of suicide attempts (Stengel 1970, 1971).[3] If there is no response to what can be seen as a "last ditch" effort to change an unbearable environment, suicide may be extremely likely. Self-injury can incorporate a vast spectrum of "harm" to the self, and there is no direct relationship between level of harm or seriousness of injury and the level of intent reported.

Self-injury and suicide can be, then, "expressions of a common suicidal process" (Goldney and Burvil 1980, p. 2). The continuities between them (particularly in terms of motivation, causes, and prevention) may be far more important than their differences (see Liebling [1992], pp. 62–67, for a review). Both may be reactive rather than purposive (or, e.g., "manipulative"), to be impulsive rather than planned. When asked, "Did you think about it before you did it?" prisoners say, "I didn't plan it. I didn't think about it, but I knew it was coming; do you know what I mean?" (see Liebling 1992). It is important to inquire why the behavior occurred rather than what it was intended to achieve (Wicks 1974). Both may contain the cognitive ambivalence expressed by suicide attempters who live (see Diekstra 1987). Responding at the first step and providing alternatives—and support, and solutions—may divert prisoners from the destructive route along which they are setting (see, e.g., Shepherd 1991). There are convincing arguments, then, for studying suicide attempts in prison as a way of understanding completed suicide in prison (see Liebling 1992; Lester and Danto 1993).

E. The Gender Myth and Prison Suicide

> You feel relief—and then disgust. It's like the blood from
> the injury is doing the crying for me; "letting" out the pain.
> (YOUNG WOMAN PRISONER)

---

[3] He did not consider the limited "appeal effect" of attempted suicide: there seems to be an inverse relationship between the "appeal function" attributed to a suicide attempt and its "appeal effect" on others ("if it was seeking to communicate or to achieve change, then it was manipulative").

At first, I was repulsed by the very idea, when I saw other inmates who'd done it. Then one day I'd been locked up in strips, everything was getting on top of me. I'd had a bad letter from home, I wasn't getting any visits. I'd been thinking about the consequences of what I'd done. I was depressed. I hit out at the window—smashed it. I was shocked—but felt, for the first time, an inner peace, as though I was released from all the strain. (YOUNG WOMAN PRISONER)

There is a myth in prison research that women are overrepresented in the self-injury figures and underrepresented in suicide rates. The first half of the myth has some evidence to support it. The second half does not. Women in prison far outnumber men in terms of the number of incidents of self-injury per head of population. Cookson found that self-injury occurred in individual women's prisons at a rate of at least 1.5 incidents per week (Cookson 1977, p. 335). This was a cautious estimate at best. There may be a core group of women in one prison who account for most of the incidents that occur. Twenty or thirty incidents of "cutting" during one sentence is not unusual for particular women prisoners. Self-injury is more common among younger than older women (particularly up to about age twenty-six), and it is associated with low self-esteem. Research in the community suggests that women show less suicidal intent than men, the ratio of self-injury to suicide being much higher among women (Birtchnell and Alacron 1971; Stephens 1987; Lester and Gatto 1989).

The rate of suicide among women prisoners, however, has been seriously underestimated (Liebling 1994). The relatively small numbers of women in prison (an average of 4–5 percent in all countries, although this is increasing) leads to their neglect in several important ways, but failure to consider the specific question of suicide among women prisoners has led to several misapprehensions. Few official publications about suicides in prison include women, and most studies argue that one of the most important risk factors associated with suicide both in prison and in the community is being male (Home Office 1986). In fact, the suicide rate for women prisoners may be as high as the suicide rate for male prisoners. This would be highly unexpected, given the disproportionate male to female ratio for suicides in the community (suicides by men outnumber suicides by women by a factor of 2.5 to 1; see Birtchnell and Alacron 1971; Stephens 1987; Lester and Gatto 1989; Rutter and Smith 1995). Apparent suicides by women prisoners may be significantly less likely to receive suicide verdicts at inquests (see Dooley 1990*b*; Liebling 1994; and below). They may instead attract verdicts such as "misadventure," "accidental," or "open" more frequently, as a result of assumptions of low intent. The suicide rate by women prisoners may be subject to large fluctuations. This is because of small numbers, which normally creates greater instability in statistical rates over time. (There is a general problem of studying low base rate events; Cookson and Williams 1990.) One study showed that if suicides and self-inflicted deaths were used as the baseline from which to calculate suicide rates, then the suicide rate for male and female prisoners was identical (Liebling 1994). This unexpected finding—that the suicide rates for male and female prisoners may be the same—requires explanation, given the disproportionate rates in the community. There are two possibilities: the greater vulnerability of the female prison population and the specific impact of imprisonment on women.

It is apparent that the female prison population differs from the male prison population generally in important respects. The size of the female prison population has been increasing faster than the male population in the United Kingdom; a higher proportion of women prisoners are on remand; women tend to be serving shorter sentences, and they are less recidivist; a far higher proportion of women prisoners are drawn from ethnic minorities, their average age is higher, and they have a lower number of previous convictions (Morgan 1997, p. 1155). A study of young women prisoners carried out in the United Kingdom found that women prisoners differed from male prisoners in several respects. This youthful group were significantly more likely to have been convicted of violent or drug-related offenses, robbery, and arson; they tended to be older than young male prisoners at first conviction and often had fewer previous convictions (Liebling 1992). They were less likely to have been living with or in touch with their parents before custody but had been living on their own or with friends. More than a third had children. They were more likely than young male prisoners to have received in-patient psychiatric care. They were far more likely to have been sexually abused (one-third), almost exclusively by male members of the family (Liebling 1992). They were also more likely to have experienced violence at home. Many of the young women had been involved in fighting at school, and many reported having used a wide range of drugs.

There is some evidence that the female prison population has a higher level of psychiatric or borderline psychiatric disorder (although this finding may be seriously compounded by labeling: women prisoners tending to attract higher levels of psychiatric attention and pathologizing of their behavior; Allen 1987). The extremely high levels of sexual and physical abuse may render the female prisoner population especially vulnerable—they may be especially vulnerable to "control" (see below). This raises the second possibility—that the experience of imprisonment for women is qualitatively different.

There may be gender-specific effects of custody on women, particularly among women with children. Almost half of the women in prison have dependent children (Walmsley, Howard, and White 1992). Individual cases of suicide by women prisoners tend to be linked to the removal of children into care; or the use of drugs and its specific consequences for the future of the child.

Liebling (1992) found that women suffered particularly from problems associated with family and outside contacts. Decreasing contact with—or interest in—the outside world was an indication of suicide risk. In general, women prisoners were more likely than male prisoners to want to share prison accommodation and to make friends while in prison (rather than meet "mates" they already knew from outside). They reported fewer difficulties with other women but were more likely to be seen as a "disciplinary problem" within prison. They were more likely to have spent time in solitary confinement and to have been referred to the doctor or psychiatrist. They reported more problems relating to visits and more anxiety associated with visits, feeling more depressed afterwards. They spent more time thinking about their families. They often wanted to change something personal about themselves and were more likely to talk to someone in prison if they had problems. They were especially more likely than male prisoners to turn to staff when they needed help. They found the lack of freedom and lack of access to their families by far the worst aspects of imprisonment (Liebling 1992; see also Lyon 1994).

Self-injury is often an attempt to communicate intolerable distress. Feelings of helplessness and uncertainty may precipitate self-injury (Cookson 1977). Jack (1992) argues in his study of *Women and Attempted Suicide* that women may be more predisposed to feelings of (learned) helplessness than men. Women are found to be more driven by present feelings (such as feeling lonely or unwanted) than with feelings about the past (e.g., feeling ashamed or that they had failed in life). Other studies show that women are more likely to suffer from depression, lack of self-worth, and from a low sense of their "locus of control" (ability to affect their environment) (see Brown and Harris 1978; Jack 1992).

Coid and his colleagues carried out a detailed study of women self-injurers in Holloway prison (Wilkins and Coid 1991; Coid et al. 1992). Most of the women self-harmers injured themselves many times. They described a progressive buildup of symptoms of anxiety, dysphoria (unpleasant depressed feelings), irritability, and feelings of emptiness before the injury. Twelve percent said they intended to kill themselves. The remainder described wanting to relieve tension, anger, and feelings of depression. Those women who injured themselves were more likely than other prisoners to have been convicted of offenses of violence or property damage, to have received psychiatric treatment, and to have received a diagnosis of (borderline) personality disorder. They were more likely to have a history of alcohol abuse, disorders of appetite, and other "impulse" disorders. The extent of family disruption and physical and sexual abuse in their histories was "depressingly high" (Coid et al. 1992).

Of those women who injured themselves while in prison in the Liebling (1992) study, a quarter did not describe what they had done as a suicide attempt. However, several of those women who had not injured themselves, but who were randomly selected for interview as part of the comparison group, reported having thought about suicide at some stage during custody. Women thought depression was the main cause of suicide in prison. Young men thought not being able to handle the sentence was the main cause. Most of the women who injured themselves cut their arms, although some also cut their legs and faces. None of the young men cut their faces. In addition to these cuts (which they bitterly regretted), two women had also scarred their faces with scouring pads. Two of the three women who cut their faces asked the interviewer whether she thought the scars would heal and whether it spoiled their appearance (Liebling 1992). One woman cut herself all over her body, including her face, when she caught sight of herself in a mirror after a visit with her daughter. She had been in the segregation unit for several weeks; her hair had dried out; it showed dye growing out at the roots and her legs were (she said) "shapeless" after so long without proper exercise. The significance of gender, appearance, and the body, and their relation to imprisonment is a topic worthy of study in its own right (see, e.g., Howe 1994).

More of the women than men carried out their injuries in a dormitory, sometimes in the company of others (Liebling 1992). The battle to eliminate potential "implements" (glass, laces, plaster from the walls, etc.) between staff and prisoners became fierce at times. All of the incidents occurred after 4 P.M. All of the women who had carried out an injury reported that they had done so impulsively. Many of the women felt they would repeat their injuries.

There may be, then, a "tension-relieving" aspect to self-harm. This has important implications for prison regime design as well as for individual preventive measures. Young women as a group may be extremely vulnerable and may need to be helped to develop alternative (or, at first, supplementary) ways of coping with unmanageable feelings, whose origins often lie in their severely troubled histories. Situational triggers may include cancellations of parole or home leave, receiving distressing or incomplete news, removal of a cell mate, an unwanted transfer, or problems with children and contact with family. Women who injure themselves often also become involved in disciplinary infractions in prison, are more likely to have received psychiatric treatment, and to have injured themselves before (Liebling 1992).

Research on self-injuring women in prison has tended to focus on the pathological and psychiatric aspects of their behavior (see Allen 1987; Coid et al. 1992; Jack 1992). This can be explained partly by the tendency to medicalize women's problems and their criminality (Dobash, Dobash, and Gutteridge 1986; Sim 1990; Howe 1994) but also partly by real differences between male and female prisoners. Few studies seek to understand deliberate self-harm as a response to and expression of pain, which may occur well within the boundaries of "normal mental health." Women themselves say, "Self-harm is a way of *controlling* anger and pain. . . . You *can feel* physical pain. It is easier to cope with than emotional pain. . . . Self-harm is a way of expressing that hurt. How else do you say, 'Inside, I feel like my *soul* is dying'?" (Consumers of the Mental Health Services 1989).

Aggregate prison suicide figures show relatively high and, in places, increasing rates of prison suicides. This may be particularly the case among sentenced and, notably, life-sentence prisoners. Prison suicide figures require careful scrutiny, however. Our profile of the suicidal prisoner is incomplete and biased. Different types of prison suicide can be identified, and problems of coping with various aspects of imprisonment take on special significance for some of these groups. Suicide and self-injury may constitute a response (or a "solution") to painful feelings. Both men and women who self-harm are at increased risk of suicide. The possibility that suicide rates for men and for women in custody are similar is worthy of further investigation.

II. Prison Suicide and Prisoner Coping: A Reexamination

This section considers the existing literature on prisoner coping and adaptation, showing how an application of the coping model to prisoners at risk of suicide can account for differences between at-risk prisoners and prisoners who do not appear to be at risk of suicide. Bringing together the (typically separate) literatures on coping, on suicide, and on the prison experience strengthen our appreciation of the distress suffered in prison and some of the reasons for it.

A. Prisoner Coping[4]

An important study of coping behavior in prison argues that the interaction between situational and environmental factors and the inmate's coping ability will be a crucial determinant of prison behavior (Zamble and Porporino 1988). Coping ability is related to other aspects of lifestyle, such as the use of time and relationships with others (Zamble and Porporino 1988). Self-destructive inmates have been shown to have sharply limited coping and problem-solving skills (Toch, Adams, and Grant 1989), living a loose, impulsive, and unstructured life outside. Poor coping is associated with instability in relationships and residence, with low proportions of time spent in work and directed activities and with lack of planning and infrequent thoughts of the future (Zamble and Porporino 1988). Others have identified the significance of coping to prison life (Backett 1988; Toch, Adams, and Grant 1989; and see review by Adams [1992]). Although, as I argue in this article, there are important links between poor coping in the community and poor coping in prison, there may also be some important differences between the precise range of coping skills required for survival in the community and the specific coping skills required for survival in prison. The material reviewed here raises doubts about the popular assumption that some prisoners may prefer prison because they cope better with institutional life than with "freedom."

Most studies of coping behavior in prison have tended to take general prisoner samples as their starting point. Prisoners may, however, be differentiated according to the extent of this poor coping ability;

---

[4] Coping is a mixture of thoughts and actions; individuals' coping styles and abilities can vary over time, and coping can be seen as a mediator of emotion (Folkman and Lazarus 1991).

those inmates least able to cope with the special environment of a prison will be those most at risk of suicidal thoughts and actions during a sentence. Zamble and Porporino show that depression in prison is associated less with background factors or expected variables such as sentence length or current offense than with cognitive appraisals such as reported problems, feelings of boredom, and expectations of the future (1988). As Sapsford argued, research needs to look more closely at attitudes and beliefs; what prisoners "do" and what they "think" (1983, p. 5). It is only through the use of long, semistructured interviews that this type of information can be sought.

Research projects carried out in this way have explored differences between prisoners who make suicide attempts and comparison groups drawn from the general prison population (Liebling 1992; Liebling and Krarup 1993). Major differences in inmates' coping styles, and a relationship between "poor coping" ability and suicide attempts have been found (see Shepherd 1991; Liebling 1992; Liebling and Krarup 1993; see also Livingstone 1994; Blud 1995). In two of the first such studies carried out in the United Kingdom, few differences emerged between suicide attempters and nonsuicide attempters in relation to criminal justice variables (Liebling 1992; Liebling and Krarup 1993). Suicide attempters were found to have slightly more previous convictions. They had spent less time at liberty between sentences, suggesting poorer coping in the community, and had slightly poorer future prospects. Family backgrounds were unstable for both groups of prisoners, but a higher level of family violence (particularly witnessed) and (psychiatric) pathology was reported by the suicide attempters (Liebling 1992; Liebling and Krarup 1993).

In relation to their backgrounds, suicide attempters were found to have fewer qualifications from school than comparison groups. This is particularly significant as few were able to read and write without difficulty. They were frequent truants (although only marginally more than comparison groups), and they were significantly more likely to have been involved in violence at school, including having been the victims of bullying. They were more likely to have been in local authority care, and this was slightly more likely to have been for family or behavioral problems than for offending behavior alone. They were more likely to have received psychiatric treatment, both in and out of hospital, and they were more likely to report major alcohol and drug problems. More of the suicide attempters had injured themselves before coming into custody; only a quarter had not injured themselves in any way before their sentence. On a range of background characteristics, then, suicide attempters could be differentiated from comparison groups, using a dimensional approach.

Most of the differences between suicide attempters and others were found in relation to their accounts of the prison experience. Suicide attempters were more likely than comparison groups to have spent time in custody before trial and to be at their current establishment as the result of a transfer. They were more likely to prefer to share a cell rather than live in a single cell. A large group were averse to physical education, which was rare among comparison groups. Suicide attempters were slightly less likely to describe any of their fellow inmates as "friends"; and those they did describe as friends, they were more likely to have met in prison than outside, unlike their contemporaries, who were almost as likely to know people from outside. Suicide attempters described themselves as more isolated or alone in the prison, and they were far more likely to report difficulties with other inmates. They had more complaints about the disciplinary system, feeling it to be less fair, and—perhaps related to this—they were far more likely to have spent time in seclusion or protective custody (which may involve varying levels of isolation or association during the day), for a variety of reasons including both punishment and suicide risk. These differences have been confirmed by further studies investigating links between suicide attempts and the experience of prison (Livingstone 1994, 1997; Blud 1995). These findings relate clearly to coping styles and have important implications for treatment, research, and prevention.

The view of prisoners as either internal or external expressers of disturbance is not confirmed by research, as in both studies, more of the suicide attempters also had disciplinary problems within the institution. This finding has also been reported by Toch, Adams, and Grant (1989). More of the suicide attempters had been referred to a doctor since coming in on reception, and more had been referred to, or were currently seeing, a visiting psychiatrist. Far more of the suicide attempt group reported current problems, and these were more likely to be prison problems or a combination of inside and outside problems. Suicide attempters received fewer visits, wrote fewer letters, and missed specific people (family members or friends) more. They had slightly less contact from the probation service, fewer finding their contacts useful. They kept in touch with the outside slightly less and found it marginally harder to keep in touch with the world outside, preferring to forget it, even if in the end, they could not.

In a Swedish study, Bondeson showed that over 80 percent of inmates in all types of penal establishments reported feeling more irritable, more anxious, more depressed, and more apathetic in prison than they did outside (Bondeson 1989, p. 75). The prison experience may be differentially perceived, however. The level of significance of some of the differences between suicide attempters and comparison groups in relation to their experiences of imprisonment are important. Suicide attempters in the two studies carried out in the United Kingdom were more likely to spend the time in their cells doing nothing; fewer would (could) read or write, or do anything else (draw, make matchstick models, engage in other hobbies, etc.). On a constructed variable, "active" (i.e., could the prisoners actively or constructively occupy themselves while locked in their cells?), significantly fewer of the suicide attempters could do so to any extent (46 percent, compared with 90 percent of the comparison group; $p < .0001$; see Liebling 1991, 1992). This particular group of responses relating to how time is spent in cells has important implications for suicide prevention procedures. It is also important in relation to understanding of prisoner coping. Suicide attempters spent significantly more time in their cells and were far more likely to feel bored than were other prisoners. They got more bored as the sentence went on, could think of less ways of relieving this, and were more likely to do something negative or destructive as a result (Liebling 1992; Liebling and Krarup 1993).

More of the suicide attempters wanted to change something personal about themselves (e.g., give up drugs, reorganize their lives, "sort their heads out"; Liebling 1991, pp. 215–16); they were more likely to daydream, were less hopeful about their release, had far more problems sleeping at night, and predictably, were more likely to have had more serious thoughts of suicide during the sentence or to describe themselves as having attempted suicide (Liebling 1992). They were more likely to perceive others' attempts as serious. They reported having found the prison experience more difficult, were more likely to have found being "banged up" the main problem of imprisonment, and they scored higher on a hopelessness scale (Beck et al. 1974; Liebling 1992; Liebling and Krarup 1993).

The most significant point to emerge from the responses to questions about the experience of imprisonment was the consistency with which prison suicide attempters were (and felt) worse off than their fellow prisoners in terms of the availability and desirability of work, education, physical education, and other methods of occupation and distraction. They did not see as many opportunities for themselves in prison, nor did they seem able to make constructive use of their time. The combination of practical constraints and their own lethargy left them helpless and resourceless in the face of hours of unfilled time. Suicide attempters appeared to be less able to occupy themselves when locked in their cells. They felt more bored, did less, ruminated on their problems, became more bored as the sentence went on, and yet spent more time in their cells. This is a "vulnerability factor" in prison research that has not been satisfactorily explored and yet which is clearly related to the concept of coping. If some prisoners cannot read or write, and spend so much time staring at four walls, the inability to relieve this prison pressure could contribute directly to the crossing of a threshold that otherwise may never have been reached. It is their inability to occupy themselves constructively, combined with enforced idleness (Home Office 1990), isolation, and forced contemplation, that increases their vulnerability to both impulsive acts of self-harm and suicidal thoughts.

The theoretical model toward which this analysis is moving provides an understanding of coping and vulnerability (see fig. 1). This specific type of vulnerability may precede many prisoner suicides. It may constitute part of a suicidal process, in which the prison situation plays a crucial role in exposing the lack of coping resources inmates have. Of equal relevance to policy and understanding are the immediate (precipitating) and background (distal) situational factors provoking such distress. Inactivity is a central variable in this context. Can analysis move toward a link between what is known about vulnerability to suicide, what is known about prison suicide, and the experience of prison?

B. Suicide, Prison, and "The Cry of Pain"

> To understand the vulnerability to suicide is to understand
> the psychology of despair. (MALTSBERGER 1986, p. 1)

Suicide can be seen as having three main causes, which coincide: lack of strong social bonds and support, lack of meaning, and suffering (see, e.g., Maris 1981; Diekstra and Hawton 1987; Shneidman 1993). There has been a marked cross-national increase in suicide among young males in the general population, mainly from lower social classes (Kreitman, Carstairs, and Duffy 1991; Rutter and Smith 1995). Risk factors among young people include depression, conduct disorders, and substance misuse. Explanations for suicide include the rising divorce rate and changes in family structure, geographical mobility (leading to lack of support, fragile relationships), unemployment, disempowerment, and decreased religious affiliation (e.g., Rutter and Smith 1995). These variables explain the lack of social bonds and the lack of meaning. Durkheim used the term "anomie" to describe social "detachment" or disintegration. The more strongly any individual is integrated into a social group (such as a close knit family or religious group), the less likely they are to commit suicide (Durkheim 1952). Researchers are relatively knowledgeable about the lack of social bonds and the lack of social meaning—incidentally, also thought to be responsible for much crime (see, e.g., Sampson and Laub 1993).

Less is known about suffering. There is evidence to suggest that some people can summon the resources to cope with adversity and that others have more limited access to such resources. Some individuals may fail to realize or be able to sustain the bonds that connect them to other people, even if those bonds are there. It is the combination of poor circumstances and few resources to sustain the individual that leads to suicide. Prisoners may as a group be especially vulnerable to suicide and to all the other risk factors that can lead to suicide, such as unemployment, family breakdown, poor relationships generally, abuse of drugs, and involvement in criminal justice. What is the—as yet almost unexplored—connection between the "known about" risk factors and the "less known about" experience of despair?

The risk factors associated with suicide in the community are highly prevalent among prisoners. Factors found to predict suicide and suicide attempts in the general population include previous suicide attempts; a diagnosis of personality disorder; alcohol misuse; previous psychiatric treatment; unemployment; low social class/economic status; drug abuse; a criminal record; violence; being single, widowed or divorced; being a white male; problems of affective control (anger, impulsivity); and suicide in the family (see, e.g., Maris 1981; Barraclough and Hughes 1987; Diekstra and Hawton 1987; Sainsbury 1988; Rutter and Smith 1995; Williams 1997). Studies of suicide attempts in the community have found that coping styles are significantly associated with suicide (Beck et al. 1979; Rotharum-Borus et al. 1990). Suicidal individuals report significantly fewer alternatives for solving problems, have negative attributional styles, engage in fewer activities, and ruminate more on problems than controls (see Rotharum-Borus et al. 1990).

Large groups among prisoner populations share those characteristics associated with increased suicide risk in the community: adverse life events, negative interpersonal relationships, experiences of violence and other forms of abuse, social and economic disadvantage, alcohol and drug addiction, early contact with criminal justice agencies, poor educational and employment history, low self-esteem, poor problem-solving ability, learned helplessness, and low motivational drive (see, e.g., Zamble and Porporino 1988; Walmsley, Howard, and White 1992; Liebling and Krarup 1993). Arguably, the prison population is carefully (but, of course, unintentionally) selected to be at risk of suicide. Two studies in the United Kingdom found that 17–18 percent of prisoners reported having thought about suicide while in custody (Liebling 1992; Liebling and Krarup 1993) (compared to 8.9 percent of the general population, according to other studies).

The impact of these features of a life history on the psychological circumstances and emotional state of the individual is rarely addressed. The situational aspects of suicide in prison (such as bullying, lack of activity, isolation, the breakdown of relationships, parole refusal, an unexpected sentence or change in location, etc.) may be crucial in the onset of suicidal thoughts for particular groups. What matters most is how these experiences are interpreted and experienced subjectively by the prisoner. The most common idea verbalized after a suicide attempt is "the situation was so unbearable, I had to do something and I didn't know what else to do."

What is it to experience the "unbearable"? Often there are multiple "motivations" that can include the above, as well as wanting to die, wanting to escape, wanting to get relief, communicating desperate feelings, and trying to change a situation. These are not mutually exclusive.

Williams argues in his study of suicide in the community that those suffering from personality disorders, or those attracting diagnoses of borderline personality disorders, may be especially at risk of suicide (see Williams 1997; see also Adler and Buie 1979). As argued earlier, a disproportionate number of prisoner suicides are found to have diagnoses of personality disorder and borderline personality disorder. Borderline patients suffer from affective instability; that is, they may feel "at the mercy" of powerful feelings. They tend to have a history of self-damaging acts and damaging relationships, chronic feelings of emptiness and boredom, intolerance of being alone, and they may have brief dissociative episodes, often associated with flashbacks of physical or sexual abuse (Williams 1997). Evidence shows that between 4 and 10 percent will eventually kill themselves, although up to half may attempt suicide at some stage in their lives.

The sort of suffering reported by those who go on to kill themselves, or who have made determined attempts, involves feelings of uncontrollability, helplessness, and powerlessness (Abramson, Seligman, and Teasdale 1978; Beck 1979; Seligman 1992). This is one reason why changing circumstances (even a change in location) in prison can be so devastating. These feelings—of upset mood, anger, anxiety, and confusion—occur against a background condition of low self-esteem or a feeling that one is not deserving of care; problems in integrating with others and in achieving a sense of fulfillment from life. Williams argues that the pain of these acute feelings when they occur are like the expressed pain of an animal caught in a trap. The animal lets out a squeal—the squeal is a cry of pain; it communicates the pain; it represents an attempt to escape from the snare, but it is primarily an expression of pain and fear (Williams 1997).

Williams has found that those at risk of suicide are vulnerable to acute sensations of pain and despair for particular reasons. Suicide attempters appear to attribute problems in their lives to global and stable causes; that is, they are pessimistic about themselves and their capacity to make life or their relationships better (Williams 1997). This is consistent with a theory of learned helplessness, or external locus of control, where reactions to stressors may be especially negative (see Rotharum-Borus et al. 1990). Their main problems in living are interpersonal as a result of underlying emotional and cognitive maps (Beck 1979).

Locus of control theory (a version of social learning theory), first fully developed by Rotter (1966), asserts that individuals differ along a continuum as regards the perceived influence of "their own actions . . . in maximizing good outcomes and minimizing bad outcomes" (Baron and Byrne 1991, p. 511). Some believe that their own actions can play a very large part in shaping outcomes: these individuals are said to have an internal locus of control. At the other extreme, others believe that what happens to them depends very largely on luck, fate, and other uncontrollable features of the external environment: these individuals are said to have an external locus of control. There is consistent empirical support in the research literature for the contention that "working class" individuals (those with low socioeconomic status) and those with low educational attainment are more likely to have an external locus of control (see Baron and Byrne 1991; Jack 1992; see also Brown and Harris 1978; Monat and Lazarus 1991; Seligman 1992; Williams 1997). Those with high internal locus of control will "prepare for mastery," seeking information, learning, and using information once it is acquired, using feedback and exerting greater control and effort in their activities. Those with low internal control (but high external control) may trust the environment less, expect little success, and use information less "strategically" in their own favor. This is highly significant in relation to other areas of prison life (such as response to punishments, privileges, and rewards; see Liebling et al. 1997), but for purposes of this article, it is the relationship between perceptions of control and the experience of despair that are of most interest.

Williams found that people who have made suicide attempts are more passive and less active in their problem solving; they show more avoidance; they judge their problems more negatively than others might; and importantly, when asked to retrieve memories of events from their past, they tend to remember their past negatively and in a summarized, overgeneral way (Rotharum-Borus et al. 1990; Williams 1997). They think far less into the future, and what little thinking about the future is engaged in is lacking in positive events. Highly hopeless people tend to lack short-term routines, as well as long-term plans and goals. Their emotions and lives are experienced as chaotic and full of anguish. This is highly significant in prison, where routine takes on a special significance (see Sparks, Bottoms, and Hay 1996; and below).

Their relationships with the world—especially with significant others or those who come to represent significant others—tend to degenerate into hostility, demandingness, and conflict, or eventually, into apathy. They are poor regulators of emotion, and they experience instability, impulsivity, and anger to intolerable degrees (Williams 1997). They are prone to perceive abandonment and rejection even where it does not exist and to react as though any experienced abandonment were already complete at its first sign. Their behavior toward others may range from clinging to rejecting in a moment (Williams 1997, pp. 91–99; see also Adler and Buie 1979). Feelings of distress, aloneness, and rage, and of wanting to punish others for abandoning them are common. These feelings are usually linked to earlier experiences of loss and abandonment, when the vulnerability and aloneness were real and were experienced as literally life threatening. If individuals' self-perception is of low status, of being a failure, being "rejectable," they may "invent for themselves a punitive environment" (Williams 1997, p. 149). Many "disruptive" prisoners match this profile (see, e.g., Toch, Adams, and Grant 1989). Such feelings of worthlessness, uselessness, inferiority, and powerlessness can lie behind lack of interest in engaging in activities or social relationships—the psychological "anomie" of feeling isolated and excluded, different, and unworthy (Rotharum-Borus et al. 1990; Williams 1997).

This insight can be applied to the question of coping with the prison experience. Prison is a "critical situation" (Bettleheim 1960; Giddens 1984), a radical shattering of continuity and routine—both integral to the survival of the personality (Giddens 1984, pp. 60–61).[5] Prison disrupts accustomed forms of life, sweeping away an already fragile sense of trust, tearing apart families and friends, requiring a kind of psychological distancing from oneself that is in itself damaging. Prison has been described as a dislocation, shown to have similarities with those overwhelming dislocations experienced by victims of disaster or trauma, leading to severe problems of relatedness and identity (Grounds 1996).[6] Such trauma produces intense fear and helplessness, sometimes overwhelming an individual's psychological coping mechanisms.[7] Traumatic experiences seem incomprehensible, shattering one's assumptions about the world; they can rupture attachments to others and can leave individuals with a constant sense of threat. It has been shown that widely different kinds of trauma can produce a similar set of clinical symptoms, including severe difficulties in forming—or reforming—relationships. The key to traumatic experiences seems to be that they are uncontrollable, incomprehensible, and intense; control over one's fate is swept away. It is this question of control, wielded by an unpredictable and external "other" or "others," that seems to do damage.

[5] Bettleheim describes the conscious efforts made by concentration camp survivors "not to observe" or "not to know" in situations where survival depended on such "not knowing" (see Sutton 1995, pp. 147–49). Survivors of other forms of trauma (e.g., sexual abuse) describe the same mechanism, although the "not knowing" process might be unconscious, a natural ego defense mechanism against unbearable attacks. Both processes have damaging consequences for future psychological health, leading to feelings of unreality and depression.

[6] "We find ourselves in an extreme situation when we are suddenly catapulted into a set of conditions where our old adaptive mechanisms and values do not apply any more and when some of them may even endanger the life they were meant to protect" (Sutton 1995, p. 153; see also Bettleheim 1979).

[7] Again, while this account may have a particular relevance to first-time prisoners, it would be premature to assume that repeat prisoners are not also vulnerable to these experiences. The suicide figures would suggest that rapid reconviction and repeat imprisonment do increase vulnerability (Liebling 1992).

Control in prison can be at once strictly routinized and erratic. The unpredictability of life in prison, under the deceptive aura of apparent (but highly selective) predictability, is one of its most acute pains. Prisoners prefer order, consistency, and predictability to instability and change. Perhaps this is some beginning of an explanation for the deeply felt need for order, justice, and consistency reported by prisoners (see, e.g., Ahmad 1995; Sparks, Bottoms, and Hay 1996). Prisoners respond extremely negatively to sudden or unexplained changes to routines and rules. Giddens describes a state of "ontological insecurity," where the future is impossible to plan, and all tasks seem senseless.[8] Prisoners' accounts of radical changes in policy (e.g., swiftly introduced new restrictions on temporary release in the United Kingdom), the changing of parole eligibility, the experience of sudden transfers, and the discretion invested in staff, have analogies with these accounts. Prisoners describe separation from families as one of the greatest sources of distress. This is a clearly identifiable and powerful source of pain. Another less clearly documented and articulated source of distress is the loss of the capacity to act, the loss of self brought about by regulation and discipline, the "afflictive control" exerted in order to reform (Gallo and Ruggiero 1991). As discussed above, Sykes and others did describe precisely this aspect of the prison experience. The subjective significance of routine and unpredictability—and the extreme but dual nature of the reality of prison (certainty and uncertainty, routine and disruption, control and chaos)—has not received serious criminological attention since. Again, survivors of concentration camp experiences say that "only prisoners who managed to maintain some small sphere of control in their daily lives, which they still regarded as their 'own,' were able to survive" (Giddens 1984, p. 63).

It is significant that research has shown that those prisoners who find themselves able to exert control over their lives in prison are more likely to recover from suicidal feelings (Dexter 1993). Some prisoners forgo the possibility of obtaining parole because the experience of permitting unpredictable choices to be made about one's life is intolerable (i.e., they cannot face submitting themselves to the uncertainty of the selection process). It is especially intolerable if life has exposed them to such threatening experiences before.

---

[8] Bettleheim, who shared Giddens's concern for order and freedom from arbitrary power, was writing about concentration camps. Giddens was drawing on Bettleheim in

In order to survive, and to address the unbearable anxiety experienced at such a loss of control, prisoners sometimes forgo their orientation to the outside world and turn inward, reconstituting themselves as agents by integrating themselves deeply into prison life, participating in its rituals, and chastising the staff for not following the rules (Mathiesen 1965). Psychological survival may require such adaptation. Is it so surprising that prisoners begin to exert control over each other and that those over whom random violence and control is exerted find the experience catastrophic? Surviving prison requires a form of self-regulation (see Garland 1997)—a certain amount of distress is caused by "the effort to keep distress itself under control" (Gallo and Ruggiero 1991, p. 280). Gallo and Ruggiero described custody as "a factory for the manufacture of handicaps," a world of "de-communication" and aggression (1991, p. 283). Prisoners live in a constant state of anxiety, fearing violence or deterioration (Cohen and Taylor 1972), or more discipline. Why did Foucault, Giddens, and others never apply their theoretical ideas to observational study of the inner life of prisons? A rigorous research agenda must operationalize both quantifiable regime characteristics and these subjective feelings of distress and powerlessness, and should aim to consider attempts made by prisoners to manage their emotions (see, e.g., Roger 1997).

The topics of suicide and suicide attempts are not unusual subjects for discussion among prisoners. There exist a series of explanations for and opinions about these activities that all inmates share. A language (argot) is perceptible: he's slashed up, she's "cut-up" again, he's got "tram-lines," they "topped themselves." More suicide attempters see self-inflicted injuries by other prisoners as "serious," suggesting that the generally hostile and negative attitudes toward suicide attempters found among prisoners and some staff mask empathetic feelings among "those who know" (Liebling 1992).

Most of the existing studies of suicides in prison have failed to answer the question, why do prisoners commit suicide? Many did not pose the question in this way but restricted their studies to the establishment of risk profiles. Any satisfactory model needs to address individual and situational factors, interactions between these variables and the meanings attributed to environments and to actions taken. If asked,

---

his more general theory of the significance of routine, predictability, and structure for identity and social life (see Giddens 1984, 1991).

those who attempt suicide in prison say "they do it because it's too much pressure on them, it gets to them and that, they're sick of being locked up, and they're sick of taking orders, and they're sick of no-one caring. . . . It does your head in, doesn't it? Completely" (suicide attempter).

When asked about specific triggers or events that might have provoked their attempts or injuries, almost a third of suicide attempters (30 percent) said there had been some problem with other inmates before the incident: threats, bullying, teasing, or arguments (Liebling 1992). Prison pressures were most often chosen from a list of alternative problems that might have precipitated the suicide attempt. Twenty-two percent of prison suicide attempters said they had recently received a long or unexpected sentence; a quarter had recently been punished or segregated; 12 percent had received (or were expecting) a "Dear John" letter; 8 percent had either been transferred or moved from one location in the prison to another; and 4 percent had received a parole refusal (Liebling 1992). The attempts or thoughts were usually brought about by identifiable problems. Ten percent of suicide attempters said that the major motivation was an outside problem, usually to do with family or girlfriend/boyfriend. Almost a third said it was a prison problem (Liebling 1992; see also Backett 1987; Dooley 1990a): "Being padded up on my own, it was a bit hard, I felt depressed and all that, there was no-one there to talk to, and I was scared, I just didn't want to be on my own."

Over half mentioned motivations that were a combination of problems inside and outside of prison: "I just couldn't do any more time in prison, and I didn't know if my girlfriend would visit on Saturday, and . . . you know, I'd just had it."

Many of their own explanations for the suicide attempt differed from those found in their prison records. It was not unusual for prisoners to express feelings during the interview of having been under pressure to "tell the doctor what he wanted to know": ("I had to say that, you know? It's what they want you to say . . . I couldn't answer their questions . . . I didn't know what to say."). Prison suicide notes expressed anger and resignation, and were concerned with lack of contact and concern. The most frequent sentiment indicated was "I've had enough."

When prisoners are asked, in the context of a long, semistructured interview, "Would you say, then, that you had ever had serious thoughts of suicide on this sentence, and if so why?" their responses are often fluent: "It was everything—my brother's death, the sentence, my family, worrying if everything was going to be all right, prison—it was everything—even being in prison. . . . Loneliness . . . it's a very lonely place. . . . You just feel that there's no hope, when you're banged up just looking at four walls. . . . It was the sentence . . . how long it was, feeling down."

Many mention isolation, not being able to turn to anyone, not feeling like anyone cares: "People just haven't got time for me." "Did you tell anyone?" "I thought the screws or probation might laugh at me." "No-one will talk to you, it's mad, it was doing my head in. No-one asked me about it—they did ask me why I'd done it, I didn't want to say aught because, you know, I didn't want to tell them the reasons because I knew they'd just shove me back in the strip cells."

The precise reasons can be varied; sometimes they are specific, and sometimes they seem impossible to define: "I don't know . . . I was just fed up at the time, just a build up of things. I didn't think, I just did it."

The feelings expressed, however, are common: "I just felt so helpless. . . . I just felt that there was nothing. . . . There was no-one to talk to."

The prison suicide attempter is vulnerable in many respects. He or she is "a lonely child without friends and without firm ties" (Rood de boer 1978) who does not feel safe or loved (Bowlby 1965; Diekstra 1987). Difficulties in communication and isolation expose this resourcelessness. In prison, this vulnerability is crucial.

The trigger for a suicide attempt in prison might consist of something that, in the eyes of staff (and in the eyes of many) appears relatively trivial: a threat by other inmates, a bad letter, a visit that does not materialize, too much time alone, a sleepless night. But the context for this precipitant is an emotional state of despair. The threshold at which prison-induced distress becomes unbearable varies according to the vulnerability (or the coping ability) of the prisoner, as shown in figure 1. As argued above, the pains of imprisonment may vary according to the inmate's situation as well as his or her resources (see also Toch 1975).

Prisoners attempting suicide in custody share certain characteristics that distinguish them to some extent from the rest of the inmate population. These characteristics are shared by only a proportion of those who attempt suicide, and they may also be shared by many prisoners who do not (Liebling 1992). A profile of the vulnerable inmate can be constructed: this profile should not be regarded as a predictive tool, but as an aid to understanding. (There is a widely held assumption explicit in prison suicide prevention procedures that suicides can be predicted and action taken to avert them. This assumption is of crucial importance at inquests and may influence the verdict. The extent to which individual suicides are in fact predictable remains a complex and confused issue. Prison staff tend to assume that "genuine" suicides will never be predicted. Both assumptions are flawed. It is likely that certain types of suicide are more predictable and preventable than others.) The lack of coping resources and ability provides a useful way of conceptualizing these findings (see the appendix).

This is a very particular form of poor coping. There are other ways not to cope in prison (including being aggressive or disruptive), although these are not mutually exclusive. It is the resourcelessness and emptiness of their lives that distinguishes those vulnerable to suicide from those less vulnerable: the degree of deprivation and the scale of their problems. They show a "psychological anomie." Unable to help themselves, and receiving little support from elsewhere, their actions are desperate expressions of unhappiness (Rood de Boer 1978). The suicide attempt, and all that comes before it, is a declaration of bankruptcy, of "psychic collapse and hopelessness or impotence" (Diekstra and Hawton 1987, p. 44; see also Toch, Adams, and Grant 1989). The "cognitive triad" of self, the future, and the environment are all negative (Beck 1979, pp. 11–12). The contribution of isolation in stripped conditions, the boredom and inactivity of a stagnant regime, the removal from sources of support, and the exposure to uncertainty and constraint cannot lead to the reconstruction of the self, the future, or this environment (Liebling 1992).

C. Toward a Theory of Prison Suicide

Most of the available studies fail to incorporate, develop, or test a theoretical model of prisoner suicide. Two notable exceptions are the study by Hatty and Walker (1986) and the study by Kennedy (1984). Hatty and Walker suggest that the "importation" and "deprivation" theses have implicitly organized studies of the causes of prison suicide (Hatty and Walker 1986; see also Clemmer [1940], Sykes [1958], Sykes and Messinger [1960] on the "deprivation thesis," and Irwin [1970] and Jacobs [1977] on "importation"). The deprivation model assumes that prisons are total institutions and that its social life arises from its deprivations. The importation model argues that the walls are more permeable and that its social life is "imported" via the characteristics of its inmates. They conclude that insufficient data exist to validate either approach but argue that some integration of the two approaches is necessary (e.g., Thomas and Petersen 1977). Kennedy argued that the concept of "prisonization" could be applied to those suicides occurring early in custody (Kennedy 1984; see also Clemmer 1940). The elevated levels of anxiety and depression associated with the transition from street to jail may be especially likely to precipitate suicide. Once the prisoner adjusts, this "transition trauma" diminishes. Anxiety levels may increase again toward the end of a sentence, although levels of depression may be slightly lower. Both applications of sociological ideas to the prison suicide problem raise interesting possibilities, but neither approach incorporates the "duality" of agency and structure necessary to explanation (Giddens 1984): the prisoners' subjectivity is missing.

There are clearly difficulties in developing a satisfactory theoretical model of suicide in prison. Such a model would need to take account of the structural context in which prison populations are produced, the structural environments of prisons, and the lived experiences of the prisoner. A general theory of prison suicide should (at least) be formulated that is capable of addressing individual, situational, and "interactive" dimensions of the problem. Identifying and understanding vulnerability, and then returning to the prison experience and showing how vulnerable prisoners may be "tested" by such an environment takes one further than concepts like "prisonization" on their own. Research reviewed in this essay shows that vulnerable groups of prisoners have different experiences and perceive their situation differently, often finding themselves worse off than others in terms of their contacts with outside and many aspects of their daily life inside.

The studies of coping and prisoner suicide already referred to have attempted to generate a theoretical model of vulnerability to suicide (see Liebling 1992; Liebling and Krarup 1993). This model is further developed here (see fig. 1). Suicidal behavior and intent may each be viewed as a continuum along which the vulnerable may quickly progress (O'Mahony 1990). Self-injury, once accomplished, increases the risk of suicide by a factor of between ten and one hundred (Kreitman 1988; Pallis 1988). Inquiring into the reasons for self-injury (particularly where the stated intention is suicide) is a valid route toward understanding the pathway to suicide. Looking at the overlap between these traditionally distinct concepts provides a clearer understanding of suicide risk than looking at either behavior alone or at the distinctions between them.

Contributory factors may include the disruption of relationships, lack of communication and support, bullying, threats, fear and violence, uncertainty, isolation, boredom, "enforced idleness," insomnia, and the prospect of a long or meaningless sentence devoid of future hopes or plans.

Inmates who do nothing during the day, or sleep through hours of inactivity, become restless and anxious at night. Common feelings of hopelessness, helplessness, loneliness, isolation, depression, and boredom are expressed by those who come close to the suicidal act. Many unseen features of the prison experience have a direct bearing on the buildup of suicidal feelings. For prisoners with fewer coping resources, aspects of the prison situation may be particularly important. Younger prisoner suicides may be less likely to resemble suicides in the community and are even less likely to show evidence of psychiatric illness than other prison suicides. The role of imitation, boredom, and bullying may be of particular concern in young offender institutions and remand centers or wings (Lester and Danto 1993). It may also be that the threshold at which suicide is reached is lowered by the presence of others who make suicide attempts. Prison pressures for younger offenders may include physical, economic, and psychological victimization (cf. Bowker 1980). With no escape route, legitimate or illegitimate, suicide becomes an alternative to distress. The impulsivity of young prisoner suicide attempts may persuade staff that they are not "serious and genuine" attempts. Such an assumption is wrong. The most common motivation for suicide attempts is a mixture of escape and communication. As Hawton and Catalan found in their study of suicide attempts among adolescents, what is being communicated is the declaration that "things got so unbearable, I didn't know what else to do" (Hawton and Catalan 1987, p. 44). Those who are most at risk are those who cannot generate their own solutions to problems. This is what it means to be "vulnerable to suicide."

It is the combined effects of feelings of hopelessness, their histories, their current situation, and the fact that they cannot generate solutions to that situation or find others to help them generate solutions that propel prisoners toward suicide. Situational triggers or provoking agents may be decisive in a suicide attempt at different thresholds, depending on both the prisoner's vulnerability, and the level of stress he or she experiences. These situations include inactivity, lack of or dwindling contact and support from outside, pressures from other inmates, and lack of support in prison. Different sets of circumstances can produce many outcomes. Those inmates who are most vulnerable often find themselves subject to the worst stresses in prison. They are more likely to be isolated, to be without activity, and to be without contact from home. Those inmates who are least resourceful are exposed to the most severe provoking agents. These constellations of variables are interacting: poor family support may act as a predisposing factor, rendering the inmate vulnerable to feelings of anxiety and low self-esteem; it may also provide a situational stress, as promised visits fail to materialize. Likewise, fear may act as a prison-induced stress (Adler 1994), increasing at particular times, perhaps ultimately providing the final catalyst to suicidal action once a particular threshold is reached. The ability to cope with imprisonment varies between inmates and is amenable to simple investigation by prison officers.

The above account calls into question any conception of prisoner suicide as an exclusively or predominantly psychiatric problem. A move away from the medical model of the earliest studies has been reflected in more recent prevention programs (see, e.g., Prison Service 1994). Suicide in prison is—at least in part—a problem of coping and of psychological distress. The main solution currently offered by medical resources for being unable to cope is the option of temporary sanctuary in a hospital. Nonmedical solutions must be part of any effective suicide prevention strategy.

Figure 2 shows how different groups of prisoners, at different stages of custody, may enter "the pathway to suicide" in different ways or at different places. A differentiated model of suicide, which can distinguish between, for example, jail populations and prison/sentenced populations, has the potential to radically improve our understanding. Links can be drawn between what is known about suicide and suicide attempts among these different groups and other studies of prison life and prisoner populations. In a study of suicide attempts in sixteen prison establishments in England and Wales (Liebling and Krarup 1993), different types of suicidal pathways were identified. These prisoners' suicide attempts seemed to be related to slightly different features of their personal histories and prison experience, such as prisoners in pretrial confinement, long-termers, the young, first-timers, and

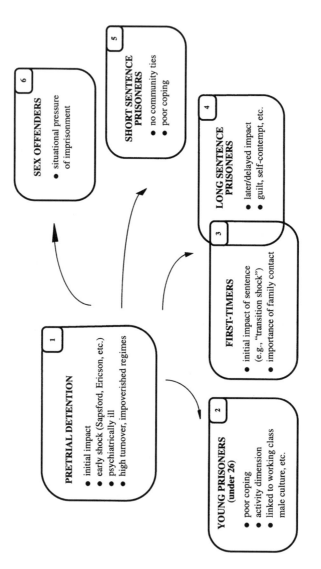

1
PRETRIAL DETENTION

- initial impact
- early shock (Sapsford, Ericson, etc.)
- psychiatrically ill
- high turnover, impoverished regimes

2
YOUNG PRISONERS (under 26)

- poor coping
- activity dimension
- linked to working class male culture, etc.

3
FIRST-TIMERS

- initial impact of sentence (e.g., "transition shock")
- importance of family contact

4
LONG SENTENCE PRISONERS

- later/delayed impact
- guilt, self-contempt, etc.

5
SHORT SENTENCE PRISONERS

- no community ties
- poor coping

6
SEX OFFENDERS

- situational pressure of imprisonment

Fig. 2.—A differentiated model of prison suicide vulnerability

those on Rule 43 (administrative segregation for their own protection). Figure 2 illustrates the main distinctions between these groups (which may overlap; for more detail, see Liebling and Krarup [1993]). What the figure shows is that the nature (and degree) of suicide risk in different establishments may vary according to the populations concerned. These distinctions are generalizations only and may serve as guides to risk management rather than "predictors."

As seen in the diagram, pretrial detainees may be especially at risk, particularly in the very early stages of their time in custody (i.e., within the first seven days). This is in part because that population contains all the most vulnerable groups (the young, first-timers, the psychiatrically ill, etc.) at a highly stressful time, under difficult circumstances, when the uncertainties of charge, conviction, sentence, family contact, and allocation are at their greatest, and when feelings of guilt and shame may be acute. "Family problems" can be especially distressing at this stage, and at-risk prisoners in jail expressed having problems with other prisoners and not knowing how to get problems solved. For young prisoners under the age of twenty-six, it is the prison situation that is particularly important. Compared to older prisoners at risk of suicide, younger prisoners are less likely to be suffering from psychiatric illnesses or from problems relating to shame and guilt. They may be unable to cope with the prison environment, often having problem histories (such as violence at home, sexual abuse, being bullied at school, etc.). They may be especially dependent on activity, structure, and contact with family, staff, and others (i.e., "sustaining external resources"), and may be especially prone to boredom and/or bullying. Their need for support is marked, and their reactions to distress may be impulsive. First-timers expressed severe difficulties in dealing with custody (many reported having been devastated by receiving a sentence). Among the first-timers, those who attempted suicide were significantly younger and had fewer previous convictions than their peers (Liebling and Krarup 1993). Their relative youth and inexperience meant that they were particularly dependent on (and therefore vulnerable to) outside contacts. Suicide attempts were more likely to occur at the weekends (e.g., after visits). Short-term prisoners at risk of suicide showed distinct problems relating to lack of community ties and release plans. This group was most likely to have received news of separation or divorce, had few plans for employment or accommodation, and had few family ties. Among long-term prisoners, suicide attempters were significantly more concerned about losing contact with their families. They were more likely to be receiving treatment for depression, and they regarded staff as less helpful than their peers did. Suicide attempts occurred much longer after arrival than among other groups, and they had often been planned over long periods. Clearly, the sex-offender population is a highly vulnerable population, their protected status reflecting the particular pressures of the prison environment for this group. The suicide attempters in this group had the most troubled histories and were most likely to have injured themselves before. They were most likely to report difficulties with staff and other prisoners.

What this account suggests is that exploring accounts of suicide and suicide attempts in prison can aid in understanding how the prison environment can be experienced as traumatic and overwhelming for many, with those who die by suicide existing at the extreme end of a "continuum" of intolerable affect. To recap:

1. Those who are vulnerable have specific vulnerabilities while in the community. They have few external and personal resources.

2. These deficits then lead to poor general adjustment in prison; particularly to quasi-depressive features of apathy, inactivity, sleeplessness, rumination, and so on.

3. The prison experience generates an extraordinary set of special pressures and traumas for this population. The vulnerable are much less well situated to cope with these pressures, and they may be exposed to greater pressures because they are least likely to "glean" jobs and courses, they may become the targets of others' aggression, and so on.

This account shows how apparently mundane (or routine) features of the prison world can make huge demands on limited "coping" resources.

III. Implications for Policy

This section considers implications of the above account of coping and vulnerability to suicide for policy, in particular, for the concept of risk identification and management, which has limitations. It looks at prevention strategies aimed at the reduction of suicides in prison, arguing that carefully focused training can improve knowledge and attitudes, and that clearer understanding of the nature of the prison experience should be emphasized.

A. Risk Identification

There are two problems with the "risk identification" approach to suicide. One is practical—few improvements have been achieved in the identification of those at risk of suicide (Topp 1979; Dooley 1990a; Crighton and Towl 1997). The numbers of "false negatives" (prisoners at risk who are not identified) and "false positives" (inmates wrongly thought to be at risk) are unacceptably high. The distinction drawn in Section III between understanding and prediction is important here. There are major unpleasant consequences of being falsely identified, both for the individual and the institution, particularly when risk identification (and not risk reduction) forms the main strategic approach to suicide prevention. The problems of small numbers pose difficulties in any risk assessment. Suicide is a classic example of this general problem. Figures 1 and 2 show how complex the pathway to suicide can be. Inmates can enter and leave it at any point and as a result of vulnerability, prison-induced distress, or situational triggers, to very different degrees. Suicide risk is not a fixed characteristic of the individual. The second problem is theoretical and explains some of the difficulties with the first: this is an era of risk and risk management (e.g., Beck 1992; Sparks 1997). There are limitations to its usefulness and dangers in many of its assumptions. The "risk society" is a way of thinking; risk is linked to fear and blame (Douglas 1992); risk calculations assume predictable (rational) human behavior; they are always based on insufficient information (Sparks 1997). A risk strategy can result in defensive behavior by staff: it is a defensive strategy. The benefits of a "risk climate," however, are that institutions are persuaded to become reflexive, self-critical, and responsive, and to develop systematic ways of dealing with perceived risk. This can be an effective spur to improved practices.

It is possible, based on the review of research summarized here, to begin to formulate a new conception of suicide risk that may be seen as complementary to the traditional profile approach to prevention. The conventional profile suffers from several limitations; the most important of which is its failure to identify individual inmates who may go on to make a suicide attempt. Based as it is on limited statistical probabilities, many of those inmates who are especially vulnerable to suicidal thoughts in prison will not be identified by its narrow parameters. Nor will these "typical characteristics" necessarily distinguish individuals at high risk of suicide from the rest of the prison population, many of whom share those characteristics found to be associated with suicide on the outside. It has been argued in several studies that the prison population is a particularly "suicide-prone" group. This is a result of inmates' propensity to show those risk characteristics associated with suicide outside, and because of the poor coping skills and the limited future prospects shown by many prisoners. The evidence for this can be seen throughout in their lack of any constructive use made of either idle or occupied time. Opportunities are missed, nothing is planned, and consequently, the sentence is lived in the present. For most inmates, prison serves no purpose and provides no support.

A better understanding of risk should be based on the notion of vulnerability to suicide. Staff with current training in the identification of risk see it as a specialist skill that they learn to carry out as a separate and distinct part of their work. This rather limited and unsuccessful notion of risk identification should be rethought: Inmates can and will participate in their own risk assessment; they may indicate their own vulnerability, admit their current problems, and even attempt to avoid some of the stresses leading to suicidal feelings in custody. Suicide risk may be reframed in terms of inmates' coping ability; it is indicated in indirect ways by evidence of poor coping in other areas of prison life. In order to assess this ability, or its absence, staff should be engaged in the process of listening and communicating. The questions, "What do you do when you're locked in your cell?" and, "What sort of plans do you have for when you get out?" may be better questions and may be more accurately answered than, "Are you feeling suicidal"? These are the sort of questions that personal officers (or other prison officers) could pursue, without having to concern themselves exclusively with the question of suicide. The proportion of suicide attempters who disliked physical education in my study (Liebling 1992), for example, may have been expressing difficulties with other inmates or an inability to achieve the level of activity expected of other inmates. An attitude toward an everyday prison feature may indicate other important feelings. Prison officers could be encouraged to make these sorts of inquiries as part of their general welfare role, taking an interest in all inmates without concentrating exclusively on the suicidal. As part of a series of related questions, officers could look for signs and symptoms at least, of stress, or an inability to cope.

Lack of contacts with outside, or lack of interest in the outside world, are already well-established indicators of risk. Visits and contacts are evidently an important area for inmates, whether they are receiving them or not. Lack of socialization within the prison may be another indicator of risk, particularly if the inmate has few friends inside, spends a lot of time on his own, has difficulties with other inmates, or knows few other inmates from his own area. Importantly, inmates who present disciplinary problems to the staff cannot be assumed to be (just) manipulative, or obvious troublemakers (Toch, Adams, and Grant 1989). Their disciplinary problems may be another feature of the difficulties they are experiencing in coping with prison.

The essential difference between the concepts of "risk" and "vulnerability" are, then, that risk is probabilistic and static; it is based on factors external to the prisoners (e.g., previous history), and it neglects regime features. Vulnerability, on the contrary, has to include the prisoner's subjective (and affective) state; it is dynamic, and it incorporates a regime dimension. It makes clear that the process of identifying vulnerability is not enough. The assessment of vulnerability poses a question: what then to do with the vulnerable prisoner, or the poorest copers. Identification does not comprise a solution in itself, just as isolation in stripped conditions fails to address the problem of suicidal feelings. At present, at worst, inmates at risk of suicide are moved between health care centers and wings, or between different prisons, with neither doctors nor prison officers feeling that the problem belongs in their hands. The practical implications of this state of affairs have been seen in lack of care verdicts returned by inquest juries. A view of suicide risk as either present or absent, as either the psychiatrist's problem or "one for the discipline staff," is inadequate. A paper by Towl and Hudson on risk assessment and management begins with a useful warning about dividing populations into "at risk" and "not at risk" when serious errors can be made and suicide risk can fluctuate along a continuum. "Risk has a dynamic quality" (Towl and Hudson 1997, p. 61). Maltsberger argues that the search for prediction should be replaced by a search for "alertness" to the danger of the possibility of suicide (1986). Given the difficulties of risk identification, proactive management approaches and regime-level improvements should form part of any comprehensive suicide awareness strategy. It is to these sorts of preventive measures that this section now turns.

B. Preventive Measures

Recent research by Cutler, Bailey, and Dexter, on evaluating suicide awareness training for prison staff demonstrated that carefully focused training can improve both knowledge and attitudes among both uniformed and nonuniformed staff (1997). It is also clear from research on situational prevention that constraints and opportunities matter (Clarke and Lester 1989).

Policy on suicide prevention in prisons in the United Kingdom has until recently been informed largely by studies of those risk factors found to be associated with suicide risk on the outside (such as previous psychiatric treatment, depression, alcohol abuse, and social isolation). In prison, many of these characteristics are exhibited by a large proportion of the inmate population, thus detracting from the relevance of such factors in providing an indication of suicide risk. There may be other important factors in the prison situation, for particular groups of prisoners, and as argued above, a different conception of risk is required. Considerable progress has been made in the United Kingdom and elsewhere in developing suicide prevention strategies, improving training, and developing multidisciplinary teams with responsibility for the implementation and review of policy for prisoners at risk of suicide (Office of Corrections Resource Centre 1988; Basedow 1990; Northern Ireland Prison Service 1990; Biles and MacDonald 1992; Prison Service 1992a, 1992b, 1994; Scottish Prison Service 1992; see also Hayes 1994; Rowan 1994) in response to increasing suicide rates in prison. Research commissioned by the Home Office and the Scottish Office in the United Kingdom (Dooley 1990a, 1990b; Lloyd 1990; Liebling 1992; Liebling and Krarup 1993; Gunn 1995; Biggam and Power 1997), several significant reviews of current procedures (Scottish Home and Health Department 1985; Backett 1987; Home Office 1990; O'Mahony 1990), and several other jurisdictions (Hatty and Walker 1986; Green et al. 1993) together confirm a growing awareness of the potential impact of prison regimes, staff training, and carefully planned suicide prevention procedures on minimizing the likelihood of suicide (Hopes and Shaull 1986; Cox et al. 1987; Ramsay, Tanney, and Searle 1987; Backett 1988; Bagshaw 1988; Rowan 1994). Thorough induction procedures based on alertness to vulnerability are helpful (see Blud 1995), provided support is on offer for those identified as "at risk." Staff require clear guidance, workable instructions, and support in order to deal effectively with suicidal prisoners. Clearer understanding of the nature of the prison experience, the vulnerability of the prison population, and the importance of diversity should be emphasized. In the event of a completed suicide, adequate postincident support, prompt communication with families, and confident preparation for inquests can minimize the damage done to staff and prisoner morale, thus reducing the likelihood of further suicides in establishments (see Langlay and Bayatti 1984; Liebling 1992; Prison Service 1994; Ward and Coles 1994).

Distinctions should be drawn between sentenced prisoners and those in pretrial detention, whose populations may be distinct in their levels of psychiatric morbidity in addition to the crucial difference between the population in the stage of custody that they experience. The adult male remand population has a high prevalence of psychiatric disorder, including schizophrenia, alcoholism, depression, and other problems that are related to suicide (Gunn, Maden, and Swinton 1991). Many may be in prison for the preparation of medical reports for the courts because of suspected psychiatric disturbance. The sentenced population, however, shows relatively low levels of depressive illness and schizophrenia—conditions known to be associated with increased suicide risk—while problems such as drug abuse, personality disorder, and sexual disorders are high (Gunn, Maden, and Swinton 1991). Psychiatric explanations may contribute to the suicide figures among remand prisoners to a greater degree than among the sentenced population. A psychiatric assessment may be more relevant for remand prisoners thought to be at risk of suicide than for sentenced prisoners showing evidence of psychological distress rather than psychiatric illness. General health screening may be more appropriate for sentenced prisoners.

It may be that distinctions should be drawn between short- and long-sentence prisoners, and between young prisoners and adults, in the formulation of suicide prevention policies. Procedures that stress interaction and support should supplement identification and assessment systems that prevent by physical restraint. In addition to prerelease courses, inmates should be offered coping-skills courses that address pretrial, sentence, and postrelease survival. Legitimate alternatives to self-injury should be provided and made obvious to inmates experiencing difficulties. Under no circumstances should the response to a suicide attempt be punitive: isolation in stripped conditions is sometimes assumed by inmates to be a punishment for their behavior. Staff training should supplement the identification of risk factors with a thorough discussion of the meaning of a suicide attempt and the reframing of the concept of risk. To attribute a unitary meaning to these acts (i.e., attention seeking) is potentially dangerous and misleading. Training should be aimed at encouraging all staff to appreciate the complexity of such behavior and its possible causes and motivations, which are multiple. It should be stressed that so-called attention-seeking behavior often precedes suicide.

Most evaluation studies of treatment and training in suicide prevention in the prison context (of which there are few in the United Kingdom) show that therapeutic intervention is both possible and effective (Wicks 1972; Jenkins, Heidemann, and Powell 1982; Hopes and Shaull 1986; Sperbeck and Parlour 1986; Ramsay, Tanney, and Searle 1987). The authors of these studies also agree that more systematic research is needed on suicide attempters in the prison setting. The use of behavioral contracts, psychological counseling and support, and a change of environment, including movement to a different wing or to shared accommodation, have all been shown to contribute to recovery from suicidal feelings (Sperbeck and Parlour 1986; Ramsay, Tanney, and Searle 1987). Prisoners may have distinct and individual needs. There seems to be a case for making available, for those who wish to undertake them, courses on problem solving, coping skills, tackling offending behavior, addressing motivation, and emotion control. There is a case for developing innovative methods of psychological support. As indicated in studies carried out in the community (e.g., Hawton and Catalan 1987), different groups of prisoners are found to respond to different types of treatment. Prisoners should not be isolated in response to suicidal feelings as they do not cope well in single cells (Sperbeck and Parlour 1986). Good morale among staff is essential to successful treatment (Langlay and Bayatti 1984; Scottish Home and Health Department 1985; Sainsbury 1988; Bluglass 1990).

Listener schemes ("buddy" schemes in the United States), whereby inmates are trained (e.g., by the Samaritans) to act as "listeners" in confidence to other inmates in distress, sometimes in specially prepared rooms, have been evaluated positively (Davies 1994) and are shown to have favorable effects on rates of suicide and self-harm, on staff-prisoner relationships, and on the role of others in the prison. A study of young prisoners showed that good staff-prisoner relationships led to significantly reduced levels of anxiety and depression (Biggam and Power 1997).

Clearly, frequent or current referrals to the doctor or psychiatrist indicate possible problems, but far more significant is the finding that, when asked, suicide attempters report far more problems than their contemporaries, often relating to the prison situation or a combination of inside and outside problems (Liebling 1992; Liebling and Krarup

1993). This suggests that, given a willing ear, inmates may indicate their own vulnerability. The listening ear needs to recognize and acknowledges these signs as signs of risk—or as "cries of pain." Having serious problems sleeping at night, daydreaming, signs of hopelessness, and viewing others' self-injury as serious and genuine, could all be indicators of the risk of "the onset of a suicidal crisis," particularly if these immediate responses have a context of poor release plans and hopes, few outside contacts, and disappointments in relationships. Protective responses to suicide attempts include offering support, allowing the expression of feelings, resolving personal problems, a high level of involvement with the woman concerned, and practical help (Liebling 1992). What women prisoners who attempted suicide said they wanted in response to their "cries for help" or "cries of pain" was as follows: "We want *nurturing* . . . we want to *talk* . . . we want to take the pain away . . . we want to feel clean, and loveable. We want to be mothered . . . we want carers who may not understand, but who can *accept* . . . a chance to scream, to shout, to cry. . . . We just want to be listened to . . . by another human being."

Staff also require effective support and training in the management of self-injury, which can be extremely distressing, both at the time and subsequently. The fear of self-injury causes enormous anxiety among staff (Liebling 1990).

Much can be learned from community studies in the search for preventive approaches to vulnerability in prison. Proper clinical assessment takes time (Hawton and Catalan 1987), negative attitudes from staff interfere with recovery (Hawton and Catalan 1987; Morgan 1979), nonmedically qualified staff can assess the state of the patient as well as medical staff (Gardner et al. 1982), and patients will report their own problems and may participate in the provision of appropriate treatment. Cognitive or group therapy is found to be an effective method of treatment with some (Sainsbury 1988), and trained prison staff can be very effective agents of therapy as they are in daily contact with prisoners. Staff should be encouraged to "engage in casual and frequent conversations with inmates, since these may often reveal cognitive and affective suicidal cues" (Sperbeck and Parlour 1986, p. 97). If memory and the future are key problems, sensitive and realistic sentence planning could actually address the question of survival. Prisons, and prison staff, need to be encouraged to develop a tolerance for anguish—to allow talk of despair. The best help for an individual feeling suicidal is not " 'how do you, I, or we make it all different,' since often we cannot, but 'how do you, I, we, take care of you just now?' " (Williams 1997, p. 227). Staff need careful training, support, and taking care of themselves. Studies suggest that "high self-esteem" among prison staff may be linked to good overall job performance and can contribute to lower suicide rates (Rowan 1998). A minimal requirement should be an orientation to prison life that respects and assists the individual. Respect for the individual requires hope, for "we are not what we appear, but what we are becoming; and if that is truly what we are, no penal system is fully just which treats us as anything else" (Bedson, cited in James 1990, pp. 43–44; see also Bottoms 1990).

Prisons differ. They differ in the extent to which they resemble the deliberately destructive institutions described by Bettleheim, Goffman, and others in the many powerful studies of "total institutions" available. Prisons are less deliberately destructive than concentration camps; and their propensity to damage (or sometimes, to repair) may vary in important ways. It is important that one understand the nature of this difference between individual establishments and establish the reasons for it. Not enough is known about why some prisons offer fewer "invitations to suicide" than others. Why is one prison (or often, one wing) better than another? Why do staff behave sensitively and professionally in one establishment and with indifference in another? Prisons could learn more from each other, and from research on prisons that permit, or encourage survival.

IV. Implications for Prison Studies

There are several implications of the above account of prison suicide research for the broader field of prisons studies. These are the neglect of prison suicide in sociological studies of prison, implications for the "effects" debate and understanding of the prison experience, the methodological lessons to be learned from prison suicide research, the (unexplored) links between prison suicide research and studies of criminal careers, and the significance of prison staff.

A. The Neglect of Suicide in General Studies of Prison

In the general field of prisons research, prisoner suicide has barely featured. In the classic Clemmer-Sykes-Jacobs tradition, despite powerful accounts of "the pains of imprisonment," there is no account of suicide. One can only speculate as to the reasons for its neglect in otherwise thorough and imaginative studies of prison life—its hidden nature, assumptions sociologists make about its "medical" status, or the "individual" nature of the suicidal process, the pain of the topic, its lack of "attraction" compared to problems of violence to others, disturbances, and so on, or perhaps the methodological difficulties associated with its study. As this essay has tried to show, suicide is a sociological phenomenon, with a rich tradition of sociological analysis in the community. Much of this analysis could be "brought in" to prison, but has not been. Looking at prison suicide in this way helps in understanding the impact of control in prison: at once deceptively predictable and yet unpredictable (e.g., see Price and Liebling [1998] on the use of staff discretion), with devastating psychological consequences. Surely, no significant conclusions can be drawn about prison and the interactions between individuals who are imprisoned and their environment without considering suicide. It raises some of the most important questions about prison in a particularly acute form. How does one describe and understand the social world of a prison? What is the relevance of "anomie" to prison life? of power and powerlessness? of control and self-control? What is the role of prison staff, and what difficulties do they face in their work? How does one understand prisons in their social context? As I argue below, prison suicide may also have a relevance to broader criminological questions, such as the study of criminal careers.

B. Implications for the "Effects of Imprisonment" Debate

The effects literature is without a sufficient affective dimension. Fear, anxiety, loneliness, trauma, depression, injustice, powerlessness, violence, rejection, and uncertainty are all part of the experience of prison. It is this "hidden," but everywhere apparent, feature of prison life that medical officers, psychologists, and others have failed to measure or take seriously. Sociologists of prison life knew it was there, but have to date largely failed to convince others in a sufficiently methodologically convincing way that pain is a harm. It is increasingly recognized in other spheres (especially in psychoanalysis and psychiatry) that pain damages. Suicide is perhaps its most dramatic outcome, but there are many other consequences: increased aggression, bitterness, spiralling violence, and the erosion of any capacity to love. Is there a deep unwillingness to consider this unwelcome (or is it unwelcome?) feature of imprisonment? It stands awkwardly next to the belief that "prison works." It may be the apparent failure of the sociology of imprisonment to engage with relevant psychological research that has deprived critical sociological analysis of the prison of one of its most powerful tools. That this harm is without any legitimate justification leaves staff, prisoners, and policy makers confused. Who are the prison population? How do they live the imprisonment experience—or fail to live it? What are the intended effects of imprisonment?

In the debate over the effects of imprisonment (see esp. Walker [1983, 1987] and the review by Bukstel and Kilmann [1980]), it should be noted that those prisoners who have died by suicide have never had a voice in such studies. The operational measures of "harm" in such studies have been inadequate, failing to take into account the subjective world of prisoners. Suicides are disproportionately likely early in custody (see Backett 1987; Dooley 1990a; Liebling 1992) just as absconding (see Clarke and Martin 1971; Sinclair 1971; Banks, Mayhew, and Sapsford 1975; Laycock 1977) and extreme anxiety (Ericson 1975; Sapsford 1978, 1983) were found to be. The "pains of imprisonment" may be concentrated at particular points in time: arrival, parole refusal, following a visit, at weekends, at night, or among particular groups within the prison population (see Sykes 1958; Cohen and Taylor 1972; Ericson 1975; Home Office 1986). These findings are illustrated in the suicide figures (see Lloyd 1990; Liebling 1992) and in what is known about suicide attempts (Liebling 1992; Liebling and Krarup 1993). Most prisoners "cope" (cf. Johnson and Toch 1982; Sapsford 1983; Zamble and Porporino 1988; Toch, Adams, and Grant 1989), but only just, and not all prisoners are able to do so (Liebling 1992; Liebling and Krarup 1993). Prison is not a uniform experience—its effects have been underestimated by research that has taken average populations as its base line and insensitive measures of pain as its tools. Evidence suggests that the pains of imprisonment are tragically underestimated. Researchers may not be asking the right questions, either of prison or of those imprisoned. For some, prisons may contain "invitations to suicide" (Williams 1997, p. 196).

C. Methodological Lessons

Prison suicide research has remained isolated from advances made in other areas of prison research and from sociological critiques. Historically, the study of prison suicide reflects some of the methodological tensions of much of criminology: the medical model, the prediction approach, sociological critique, and the absence of theory in otherwise useful administrative studies. The role of individual factors has always been prominent: psychiatric explanations have been assumed to play a major role in accounts of suicides both in and out of prison. Research in prison sociology first indicated the importance of environmental variables in understanding issues such as absconding, riots, and disturbances, but a broader and more critical sociology was also available long before it was applied to the study of prison suicide. The "new realist" preference for interactive explanations is now perceptible (see Young 1997), as prisons and corrections services struggle with increasing suicide rates, some jurisdictions manage to reduce their figures and enhance the skills of their staff, and better quality data is available on both aggregate suicide rates, individual cases, and "the meaning of imprisonment." Suicide as a topic is notoriously amenable to projection. In the absence of the subject, the deceased becomes the object of others' assumptions, fears, and constructions. In such a field, but in prisons research more generally, it is essential that the voices of prisoners and staff are heard. The methodologies developed in prisons suicide studies have important implications for future research. The pains of imprisonment are many and varied. They are also, often, hidden. It is not so much to the visible eye or the measuring instrument that they are perceptible but to the "informed heart" (Bettleheim 1960). Among those who have taken their own lives are Bruno Bettleheim, Arthur Koestler, Primo Levi, Virginia Woolf, Sylvia Plath, and Ernest Hemingway. All were gifted and creative commentators on the human condition, whose wisdom is widely acknowledged. As Bettleheim said after his experiences in concentration camps, to have survived is to be wealthy. Those who have attempted suicide in prison possess a wealth of knowledge about the prison experience. Their accounts constitute an important part of the truth about prison. Research and policy should take account of what they have to say.

Research should approach official data with caution; recorded rates and official files require critical evaluation. Sensitive interviewing of prisoners who have survived suicide attempts, and of control groups, focusing on the experience of imprisonment and on coping behavior, should continue. The research methods employed in such investigations should be sufficiently "grounded" to permit the prison experience to emerge. Generally speaking, sociological accounts of prison life have reflected the "real world" lives of prisoners (and occasionally those of staff) more deeply than psychological and medical studies (although exceptions can be found; e.g., Sapsford 1983; Zamble and Porporino 1988). Both strategies are required in order to temper the damaging claims of the selectively informed on both sides of the methodological divide. Particular prisoner groups: for example, prisoners not physically attempting suicide but expressing suicidal thoughts and the specific question of suicides among life-sentence prisoners could be addressed. Future research is required on long-term outcomes, on prisoners who successfully recover from suicidal crises, and on those who go on to repeat their attempts. More work is needed on differences between males and females in the development and expression of suicidal feelings (see Liebling 1992, chap. 7). The role of appeals against conviction and sentence in first sustaining and then dashing hope during a long-prison sentence should be explored. A closer study of suicide verdicts and of inquest procedures—particularly of differences in proceedings and outcomes between cases of apparently self-inflicted deaths in custody and those in the community—would provide an important context in which prison suicide figures could be properly understood (see Liebling 1992, chap. 4). Research is urgently required on treatment methods, on staff training, and on comparisons between prisons. What this essay argues above all is, first, that prison suicides should be considered sociologically, and, second, that the affective dimension of the prison experience should be included in studies of the prison.

D. Links between Prison Suicide and Criminal Careers

There are implicit and unexplored links between the poor coping or vulnerability model of prisoner suicide developed in this review essay and the concept of "vulnerability to reconviction" developed in studies of criminal careers (Farrington 1997). It is significant that those prisoners who had attempted suicide in prison were significantly more likely to have returned to prison quickly between sentences (Liebling 1992). Criminal career research has identified a core group of persistent male offenders whose offending begins early, is frequent and serious in nature, and who are rapidly reconvicted (e.g., Blumstein et al. 1986; Farrington and West 1990; Farrington and Wikström 1993; Farrington 1994; Burnett 1996). These offenders, who typically constitute approximately 5–6 percent of known offenders are responsible for at least half of all known offenses (Wolfgang, Figlio, and Sellin 1972; West and Farrington 1977; Home Office 1987; Wikström 1990; Farrington 1994). Farrington has demonstrated how such persistent offenders' careers are often preceded and then accompanied by a broader range of antisocial or dysfunctional behaviors that may include aggression and bullying, cruelty to animals, frequent lying, and frequent truancy in childhood, followed by heavy drinking, the frequent use of prohibited drugs, poor job performance, failure to maintain close personal relationships, recklessness, and low frustration tolerance in later adolescence and early adulthood (Farrington 1994, pp. 28–29; see also Farrington and West 1977). These measures tend to be associated with high impulsivity, poor concentration, low empathy and poor abstract thinking (e.g., Farrington 1994). Such an underlying and continuous "syndrome" of conduct disorder has been associated with persistent or chronic offending and rapid reconviction in numerous studies (Robins and Rutter 1990; review article by Farrington [1994]) and has been shown to persist into adulthood as "adult social dysfunction in areas of work and social and sexual relationships" (Robins 1990; Zoccolillo et al. 1992; Farrington 1994, p. 31, 1997). The factors most frequently associated with the development of such a syndrome are poor (lax, aggressive, or rejecting) parenting, conflict in the home, having criminal parental or sibling models, low family income, poor housing, and low school attainment (e.g., West and Farrington 1977; McCord 1982; Fergusson, Horwood, and Lynskey 1992; Farrington 1994). These variables are all found to contribute independently to the development of delinquency, but they may also coincide and be interrelated (Farrington 1994, pp. 61, 78).

Criminal career research has thus identified a core group of offenders who are most vulnerable to rapid reconviction as a result of impulsive and antisocial behavior that is rooted in a complex constellation of personal, family, and social disadvantages. There is also increasing interest in relating these individual differences to area context (Farrington, Sampson, and Wikström 1993). It is a significant omission that criminal career studies have not considered suicide and attempted suicide, or affective aspects of offenders' lives, despite high rates of suicide among offenders (e.g., Akhurst, Brown, and Wessley 1995).

Research on suicide and suicide attempts in prison has also identified a vulnerable group, with many overlapping characteristics, as described above. They share some of the background disadvantages and present behavioral and affective problems, and may share an elevated risk of rapid reconviction. There is a need for further theoretical and empirical investigation of these previously unidentified links between vulnerability to suicide and to offending and reconviction. There may be important continuities (but there may also be some important discontinuities) between these apparently overlapping groups, particularly in relation to affect, emotion control, substance use, impulsivity, risk taking, and thinking styles (see, e.g., McMurran, Hodge, and Hollin

1997).[9] Such a study could bring together the two previously conceptually distinct areas of criminological research on prison suicide and criminal careers, as well as considering the implications of these topics for the development of regimes in prisons.[10]

E. The Significance of Prison Staff

Appreciating the problems faced by staff in the management and prevention of suicides in prison is crucially important. This review essay has not included a discussion of prison staff. Their problems and concerns are addressed elsewhere (Liebling 1992; Liebling and Krarup 1993; Price and Liebling 1998). Apart from feeling inadequately prepared to deal with the problem in the way they are asked to (by identifying risk factors and referring the inmate to the hospital), prison staff also perceive major problems of cooperation and communication between departments. They feel inadequately trained and yet see themselves as held accountable for decisions they make about potential suicide risks. They have no say in decisions to return an inmate thought to be at risk of suicide from the hospital back to the wing. Completed suicides occurring on wings may be bitterly resented by those who discover the body, particularly among staff members who had been seeking some support for the inmate. If there are nonmedical aspects to suicide in custody, nonmedical staff should be more directly involved in prevention policy. However, they need training and support in order to embrace this responsibility confidently.

What is clear from the research reviewed in this chapter is that staff matter. They have a crucial role to play in the quality of life in prison. Good relationships with staff can insulate prisoners against suicidal feelings (Biggam and Power 1997). Prison staff "embody" the regime

---

[9] The overlap can be conceived as the homicide-suicide, aggressive-depressive, or disruptive-disturbed dimension identified in several studies (e.g., Toch, Adams, and Grant 1989). See also Freud (1917) and others on the turning of aggression against the self and the many studies of aggression in suicide to follow (e.g., the collection by Maltsberger and Goldblatt [1996]). Few have studied the counterside to this duality, that is, the presence of depression in aggression and offending (although see Thornton 1990).

[10] A literature review is under way on the linkages between vulnerability to suicide and propensity to reoffend, together with a reinvestigation of the results of the two previous prison suicide projects carried out by the author and colleagues in the light of the reoffending findings to emerge from the Cambridge Study in Delinquent Development, the leading British study of the development of criminal careers (see, e.g., Farrington 1994). This will enable a detailed exploration of the related concepts of vulnerability to suicide and to reconviction identified above. This work is being conducted as part of an Economic and Social Research Council Post-Doctoral Research Fellowship.

of a prison, determining by their every interaction with prisoners the perceived fairness of prison life (Bottoms and Rose 1998; Price and Liebling 1998).

An exploration of prison suicide can offer a variety of significant insights. It can help in the development of suicide prevention policy, but may also help in the broader understanding of the nature of prisons.

APPENDIX

Suicide in Prison: A Vulnerability Profile[11]

Criminal Justice History:
  Many previous convictions
  Short periods in the community

Background:
  No qualifications/poor reading ability
  Frequent truancy
  Bullied at school
  Family and behavior problems (leading to care)
  Major drink and drug use/dependence
  Witnessed or experienced family violence
  Previous suicide attempts

Experience of Prison and Coping with Custody:
  Inactive in cell
  Cannot relieve boredom
  Avoidance of physical education/other activities
  Few friends in prison
  Difficulties with other inmates
  Disciplinary problem
  Experience of segregation/solitary confinement
  Frequent/recent referral to medical services
  Reports current problems
  Problems sleeping
  Finds prison (and "being banged up") difficult
  Feelings of hopelessness
  Not hopeful about release

Family and Outside Contact:
  Few or unreliable visits
  Writes few letters
  Misses family
  Little contact from probation
  Finds thinking of outside difficult

[11] Based on Liebling (1992).

REFERENCES

Abramson, L. Y., M. E. P. Seligman, and J. D. Teasdale. 1978. "Learned Helplessness in Humans: Critique and Reformulation." *Journal of Abnormal Psychology* 87:49–74.

Adams, K. 1992. "Adjusting to Prison Life." In *Crime and Justice: A Review of Research*, vol. 16, edited by Michael Tonry. Chicago: University of Chicago Press.

Adler, G., and D. H. Buie. 1979. "Aloneness and Borderline Psychopathology: The Possible Relevance of Childhood Development Issues." *International Journal of Psychoanalysis* 60:83–96.

Adler, J. 1994. *Fear in Prison*. London: Prison Reform Trust.

Ahmad, S. 1995. "Fairness in Prison." Ph.D. thesis, Cambridge University.

Akhurst, M., I. Brown, and S. Wessley. 1995. *A Study of the Prevalence of Self-Harm Behaviour among Offenders Supervised by the Probation Service*. Leeds: West Yorkshire Probation Service.

Allen, H. 1987. *Justice Unbalanced: Gender, Psychiatry and Judicial Decisions*. Milton Keynes, England: Open University Press.

Anderson, O. 1987. *Suicide in Victorian and Edwardian England*. Oxford: Clarendon.

Anno, B. Jaye. 1985. "Patterns of Suicide in the Texas Department of Corrections." *Journal of Prison and Jail Health* 5:82–93.

Atkinson, J. M. 1982. *Discovering Suicide: Studies in the Social Organisation of Sudden Death*, 2d ed. London: Macmillan.

Backett, S. 1987. "Suicides in Scottish Prisons." *British Journal of Psychiatry* 151:218–21.

———. 1988. "Suicide and Stress in Prison." In *Imprisonment Today*, edited by S. Backett, J. McNeil, and A. Yellowlees. London: Macmillan.

Bagshaw, M. 1988. "Suicide Prevention Training: Lessons from the Corrections Service of Canada." *Prison Service Journal* 70:5–6.

Banister, P. A., F. V. Smith, K. J. Heskin, and N. Bolton. 1973. "Psychological Correlates of Long-Term Imprisonment. I. Cognitive Variables." *British Journal of Criminology* 13:312–22.

Banks, C., P. Mayhew, and R. Sapsford. 1975. *Absconding from Open Prisons*. Home Office Research Studies, vol. 26. London: H.M. Stationery Office.

Basedow, M. 1990. *A Review of Suicide Prevention Procedures Used by New South Wales Police Department*. Sydney: New South Wales Police Research Department.

Baron, R., and D. Byrne. 1991. *Social Psychology*, 6th ed. Boston: Allyn & Bacon.

Barraclough, B. M., J. Bunch, B. Nelson, and P. Sainsbury. 1974. "A Hundred Cases of Suicide: Clinical Aspects." *British Journal of Psychiatry* 125:355–73.

Barraclough, B. M., and J. Hughes. 1987. *Suicide: Clinical and Epidemiological Studies*. London: Croom Helm.

Beck, A. T. 1979. *Cognitive Therapy and Emotional Disorders*. New York: New American Library.

Beck, A. T., with G. Emery and B. F. Shaw. 1979. *Cognitive Therapy of Depression*. New York: Guilford.

Beck, A. T., A. Weissman, D. Lester, and L. Trexler. 1974. "The Measurement of Pessimism: The Hopelessness Scale." *Journal of Clinical and Consulting Psychology* 42:861–65.

Beck, U. 1992. *Risk Society*. London: Sage.

Bernheim, J. C. 1987. *Les suicides en prison*. Canada: Les Editions du Meridian.

Bettleheim, B. 1960. *The Informed Heart: A Study of the Psychological Consequences of Living under Extreme Fear and Terror*. New York: Free Press.

———. 1979. *Surviving and Other Essays*. New York: Thames & Hudson.

Biggam, F. H., and K. G. Power. 1997. "Social Support and Psychological Distress in a Group of Incarcerated Young Offenders." *International Journal of Offender Therapy and Comparative Criminology* 41:213–30.

Biles, D., and D. MacDonald. 1992. *Deaths in Custody in Australia, 1980–1989: The Research Papers of the Criminology Unit of the Royal Commission into Aboriginal Deaths in Custody*. Canberra: Australian Institute of Criminology.

Birtchnell, J., and J. Alacron. 1971. "The Motivation and Emotional State of 91 Cases of Attempted Suicide." *British Journal of Medical Psychology* 44:45–52.

Blud, L. 1995. "The Development of a Young Offender Institution Induction Checklist for Vulnerable Prisoners." Unpublished manuscript. London: H.M. Prison Service Psychology Department.

Bluglass, R. 1990. "Recruitment and Training of Prison Doctors." *British Medical Journal* 301:249–50.

Blumstein, A., J. Cohen, J. Roth, and C. Visher, eds. 1986. *Criminal Careers and "Career Criminals."* Vol. 1. Washington, D.C.: National Academy Press.

Bolton, N., F. V. Smith, K. J. Heskin, and P. A. Banister. 1976. "Psychological Correlates of Long-Term Imprisonment. IV. A Longitudinal Analysis." *British Journal of Criminology* 16:38–47.

Bondeson, U. V. 1989. *Prisoners in Prison Societies*. New Brunswick, N.J.: Transaction.

Bottomley, A. Keith. 1990. "Lord Justice Woolf's Inquiry into Prison Disturbances." Unpublished manuscript. Hull: University of Hull.

Bottoms, A. E. 1990. "The Aims of Imprisonment." In *Justice, Guilt and Forgiveness in the Penal System*, edited by D. Garland. Occasional Paper no. 18. Edinburgh: University of Edinburgh, Centre for Theology and Public Issues.

Bottoms, A. E., and G. Rose. 1998. "The Importance of Staff Prisoner Relationships: Results from a Study in Three Prisons." In *Staff Prisoner Relationships: A Review of the Literature*, edited by D. Price and A. Liebling. Home Office Report. London: H.M. Stationery Office.

Bowker, L. H. 1980. *Prison Victimization*. New York: Elsevier.

Bowlby, J. 1965. *Child Care and the Growth of Love*. Middlesex: Penguin.

Brown, G. W., and T. Harris. 1978. *Social Origins of Depression: A Study of Psychiatric Disorder in Women*. London: Tavistock.

Bukstel, L. H., and P. R. Kilmann. 1980. "Psychological Effects of Imprisonment on Confined Individuals." *Psychological Bulletin* 88(2):469–93.

Burnett, R. 1996. "The Dynamics of Recidivism." Report submitted to the Home Office, London.

Clarke, R. V., and D. Lester. 1989. *Suicide: Closing the Exits*. New York: Springer.

Clarke, R. V. G., and D. N. Martin. 1971. *Absconding from Approved Schools.* Home Office Research Studies, vol. 12. London: H.M. Stationery Office.

Clemmer, D. 1940. *The Prison Community.* New York: Holt, Rinehart, & Winston.

Cohen, S., and L. Taylor. 1972. *Psychological Survival.* Harmondsworth: Penguin.

Coid, J., J. Wilkins, B. Coid, and B. Everitt. 1992. "Self-Mutilation in Female Remanded Prisoners. II. A Cluster Analytic Approach towards Identification of a Behavioural Syndrome." *Criminal Behaviour and Mental Health* 2:1–14.

Coker, J., and J. P. Martin. 1983. *Licensed to Live.* Oxford: Blackwell.

Consumers of the Mental Health Services. 1989. Unpublished proceedings of the conference "Consumers of the Mental Health Services," London.

Cookson, H. M. 1977. "A Survey of Self-Injury in a Closed Prison for Women." *British Journal of Criminology* 17(4):332–47.

Cookson, H. M., and M. Williams. 1990. *Assessing the Statistical Significance of Rare Events.* Directorate of Psychological Services Report, ser. 1, no. 33. London: Home Office.

Cooper, H. H. A. 1971. "Self-Mutilation by Peruvian Prisoners." *International Journal of Offender Therapy and Comparative Criminology* 15(3):180–88.

Correctional Service of Canada. 1981. *Self-Inflicted Injuries and Suicides.* Canada: Bureau of Management Consulting.

Cox, J. F., D. W. McCarty, G. Landsberg, and M. P. Pavarati. 1987. *The Mental Health Resource Handbook for Human Service Personnel Serving the Local Correctional Population.* New York: New York Office of Mental Health.

Cox, V. C., P. Paulus, and G. McCain. 1984. "Prison Crowding Research: The Relevance for Prison Housing Standards and a General Approach regarding Crowding Phenomena." *American Psychologist* 39(10):1148–60.

Crighton, D., and G. Towl. 1997. "Self-Inflicted Deaths in Prisons in England and Wales: An Analysis of the Data for 1988–90 and 1994–95." In *Suicide and Self-Injury in Prisons: Research Directions in the 1990s,* edited by G. Towl. Issues in Criminological and Legal Psychology, no. 28. Leicester: British Psychological Society.

Cutler, J., J. Bailey, and P. Dexter. 1997. "Suicide Awareness Training for Prison Staff: An Evaluation." In *Suicide and Self-Injury in Prisons: Research Directions in the 1990s,* edited by G. Towl. Issues in Criminological and Legal Psychology, no. 28. Leicester: British Psychological Society.

Danto, B., ed. 1973. *Jail House Blues: Studies of Suicidal Behavior in Jail and Prison.* Orchard Lake, Mich.: Epic.

Davies, B. 1994. "The Swansea Listener Scheme: Views from the Prison Landings." *Howard Journal* 33(2):125–36.

Dexter, P. 1993. *Suicide Attempts at Highpoint Prison.* M.Sc. thesis, Birbeck College, Psychology Department, London.

Diekstra, R. E. W. 1987. "Renee: Chronicle of a Misspent Life, and Renee or the Complex Dynamics of Adolescent Suicide." In *Suicide in Adolescence,* edited by R. E. W. Diekstra and K. Hawton. Dordrecht: Martinus Nijhoff.

Diekstra, R. E. W., and K. Hawton, eds. 1987. *Suicide in Adolescence.* Dordrecht: Martinus Nijhoff.

Dobash, R. P., R. E. Dobash, and S. Gutteridge. 1986. *The Imprisonment of Women.* Oxford: Blackwell.

Dooley, E. 1990*a.* "Prison Suicide in England and Wales, 1972–1987." *British Journal of Psychiatry* 156:40–45.

———. 1990*b.* "Non-natural Deaths in Prison." *British Journal of Criminology* 30:229–34.

———. 1990*c.* "Deaths in Custody." Seminar given to Institute of Criminology, Cambridge, February.

Douglas, J. 1967. *The Social Meanings of Suicide.* London: Routledge.

Douglas, M. 1992. *Risk and Blame: Essays in Cultural Theory.* London: Routledge.

Durkheim, E. 1952. *Suicide.* New York: Free Press.

Eldrid, J. 1988. *Caring for the Suicidal.* London: Constable.

Ericson, R. V. 1975. *Young Offenders and Their Social Work.* Lexington, Mass.: Lexington Books.

Farrington, David. 1994. "Human Development and Criminal Careers." In *The Oxford Handbook of Criminology*, edited by M. MacGuire, M. Morgan, and R. Reiner. Oxford: Oxford University Press.

———. 1997. "Human Development and Criminal Careers." In *The Oxford Handbook of Criminology*, 2d ed., edited by M. MacGuire, M. Morgan, and R. Reiner. Oxford: Oxford University Press.

Farrington, D., R. Sampson, and P.-O. Wikström, eds. 1993. *Integrating Individual and Ecological Aspects of Crime.* Stockholm: National Council for Crime Prevention.

Farrington, David, and Donald West. 1977. *The Delinquent Way of Life.* London: Heinemann.

———. 1990. "The Cambridge Study in Delinquent Development: A Long Term Follow-Up of 411 London Males." In *Criminality: Personality, Behaviour and Life History*, edited by H. J. Kerner and G. Kaiser. Berlin: Springer.

Farrington, D., and P.-O. Wikström. 1993. "Criminal Careers in London and Stockholm: A Cross-National Comparative Study." In *Research on Human Development and Criminal Behaviour*, edited by E. Weitekamp and H. J. Kerner. Dordrecht: Kluwer.

Fergusson, D. M., L. J. Horwood, and M. T. Lynskey. 1992. "Family Change, Parental Discord and Early Offending." *Journal of Child Psychology and Psychiatry* 33:1059–75.

Flaherty, M. G. 1980. *An Assessment of the National Incidence of Juvenile Suicide in Adult Jails, Lock-Ups and Juvenile Detention Centres.* Urbana-Champaign: University of Illinois Press.

———. 1983. *The National Incidence of Juvenile Suicide in Adult Jails, Lock-Ups and Juvenile Detention Centres.* Urbana-Champaign: University of Illinois Press.

Folkman, S., and R. S. Lazarus. 1991. "Coping and Emotion." In *Stress and Coping: An Anthology*, edited by A. Monat and R. S. Lazarus. New York: Columbia University Press.

Freud, S. 1917. *Mourning and Melancholia.* London: Hogarth.

Gaes, Gerald G. 1985. "The Effects of Overcrowding in Prison." In *Crime and*

Justice: An Annual Review of Research, vol. 6, edited by Michael Tonry and Norval Morris. Chicago: University of Chicago Press.

Gallo, E., and V. Ruggiero. 1991. "The Immaterial Prison: Custody as a Factory for the Manufacture of Handicaps." *International Journal for the Sociology of Law* (19):273–91.

Gardner, R., R. Hanka, S. J. Roberts, J. M. Allon Smith, A. A. Kings, and R. Nicholson. 1982. "Psychological and Social Evaluation in Cases of Deliberate Self-Poisoning Seen in an Accident Department." *British Medical Journal* 284:491–93.

Garland, D. 1997. " 'Governmentality' and the Problem of Crime: Foucault, Criminology, Sociology." *Theoretical Criminology* 1:173–214.

Giddens, A. 1984. *The Constitution of Society.* Cambridge: Polity.

———. 1991. *The Consequences of Modernity.* Cambridge: Polity.

Goffman, E. 1968. *Asylums.* London: Penguin.

Goldney, R. D., and P. W. Burvil. 1980. "Trends in Suicidal Behaviour and Its Management." *Australian and New Zealand Journal of Psychiatry* 14:1–15.

Goring, C. 1913. *The English Convict.* London: H.M. Stationery Office.

Gover, R. M. 1880. "Notes by the Medical Inspector." In *Prison Commission Annual Report, 1880,* app. 19. London: H.M. Stationery Office.

Green, C., K. Kendall, G. Andre, T. Looman, and N. Polvi. 1993. "A Study of 133 Suicides among Canadian Federal Prisoners." *Medicine, Science and the Law* 2:121–27.

Griffiths, A. W. 1990. "Correlates of Suicidal History in Male Prisoners." *Medicine, Science and the Law* 30(3):217–18.

Griffiths, A. W., and A. T. Rundle. 1976. "A Survey of Male Prisoners." *British Journal of Criminology* 16:352–66.

Grindrod, H., and G. Black. 1989. *Suicides at Leeds Prison: An Enquiry into the Deaths of Five Teenagers during 1988/9.* London: Howard League for Penal Reform.

Grounds, A. 1996. "Psychiatric Morbidity amongst Long-Term Prisoners and Their Families." Unpublished manuscript. Cambridge: Institute of Criminology.

Gunn, J. 1995. "Suicides in Scottish Prisons." Unpublished study. Edinburgh: Scottish Office.

Gunn, J., T. Maden, and M. Swinton. 1991. *Mentally Disordered Prisoners.* London: Home Office.

Hankoff, L. D. 1980. "Prisoner Suicide." *International Journal of Offender Therapy and Comparative Criminology* 24(2):162–66.

Hatty, S. E., and J. R. Walker. 1986. *A National Study of Deaths in Australian Prisons.* Canberra: Australian Centre of Criminology.

Hawton, K., and J. Catalan. 1987. *Attempted Suicide: A Practical Guide to Its Nature and Management,* 2d ed. Oxford: Oxford University Press.

Hay, W., and R. Sparks. 1992. "Vulnerable Prisoners: Risk in Long-Term Prisons." In *Criminal Justice: Theory and Practice,* edited by A. K. Bottomley, A. J. Fowles, and R. Reiner. London: British Society of Criminology.

Hayes, L. 1983. "And Darkness Closes In: A National Study of Jail Suicides." *Criminal Justice Behaviour* 10:461–84.

———. 1994. "Jail Suicide Prevention in the USA: Yesterday, Today and To-morrow." In *Death in Custody: International Perspectives*, edited by A. Lie-bling and T. Ward. London: Whiting & Birch.

———. 1995. *Prison Suicide: An Overview and Guide to Prevention.* Washing-ton, D.C.: U.S. Department of Justice, National Institute of Corrections.

Hayes, L., and J. Rowan. 1988. *National Study of Jail Suicides: Seven Years Later.* Alexandria, Va.: National Center on Institutions and Alternatives.

Home Office. 1986. *Report of the Working Group on Suicide Prevention.* London: H.M. Stationery Office.

———. 1987. *Criminal Careers of Those Born in 1953: Persistent Offenders and Desistance.* Home Office Statistical Bulletin no. 35/87. London: Home Of-fice.

———. 1990. *Report on a Review by Her Majesty's Chief Inspector of Prisons for England and Wales of Suicide and Self-Harm in Prison Service Establishments in England and Wales.* London: H.M. Stationery Office.

Hopes, B., and R. Shaull. 1986. "Jail Suicide Prevention: Effective Programs Can Save Lives." *Corrections Today* 48(8):64–70.

House of Commons. 1990. *Prison Statistics: England and Wales.* Cmnd. 1800.

———. 1996. *Prison Statistics: England and Wales.* Cmnd. 3086.

Howe, A. 1994. *Punish and Critique: Towards a Feminist Analysis of Penality.* London: Routledge.

Irwin, J. 1970. *The Felon.* Englewood Cliffs, N.J.: Prentice-Hall.

Jack, R. 1992. *Women and Attempted Suicide.* Hove: Erlbaum.

Jacobs, James B. 1977. *Stateville: The Penitentiary in Mass Society.* Chicago: Uni-versity of Chicago Press.

James, J. T. L. 1990. *A Living Tradition: Penitentiary Chaplaincy.* Ottawa: Cor-rectional Service of Canada.

Jenkins, R. L., P. H. Heidemann, and S. Powell. 1982. "The Risk and Preven-tion of Suicide in Residential Treatment of Adolescents." *Juvenile and Fam-ily Court Journal* 33(2):11–16.

Johnson, R. 1976. *Culture and Crisis in Confinement.* Lexington: Heath.

———. 1978. "Youth in Crisis: Dimensions of Self-Destructive Conduct among Adolescent Prisoners." *Adolescence* 1(51):461–82.

Johnson, R., and H. Toch. 1982. *The Pains of Imprisonment.* California: Sage.

Kennedy, D. B. 1984. "A Theory of Suicide While in Police Custody." *Journal of Police Science and Administration* 12(2):191–200.

Kitsuse, J. L., and A. V. Cicourel. 1963. "A Note on the Uses of Official Sta-tistics." *Social Problems* 11:131–39.

Kreitman, N., ed. 1977. *Parasuicide.* London: Wiley.

———. 1988. "Some General Observations on Suicide in Psychiatric Pa-tients." In *The Clinical Management of Suicide Risk*, edited by H. G. Morgan. London: Royal Society of Medicine Press.

Kreitman, N., V. Carstairs, and J. Duffy. 1991. "Association of Age and Social Class with Suicide among Men in Great Britain." *Journal of Epidemiology and Community Health* 45:195–202.

Langlay, G. E., and N. N. Bayatti. 1984. "Suicide in Exe Vale Hospital, 1972–1981." *British Journal of Psychiatry* 145:463–67.

Laycock, G. K. 1977. *Absconding from Borstals*. Home Office Research Study, vol. 41. London: H.M. Stationery Office.

Lester, D., and B. Danto. 1993. *Suicide behind Bars: Prediction and Prevention*. Philadelphia: Charles Press.

Lester, D., and J. Gatto. 1989. "Self-Destructive Tendencies and Depression as Predictors of Suicidal Ideation in Teenagers." *Journal of Adolescence* 12:221–23.

Liebling, A. 1991. "Suicide and Self-Injury amongst Young Offenders in Custody." Ph.D. dissertation, University of Cambridge.

———. 1992. *Suicides in Prison*. London: Routledge.

———. 1993. "Suicides in Young Prisoners: A Summary." *Death Studies* 17: 381–409.

———. 1994. "Suicides amongst Women Prisoners." *Howard Journal* 33(1):1–9.

———. 1995. "Vulnerability and Prison Suicide." *British Journal of Criminology* 35:173–87.

———. 1997. "Risk and Prison Suicide." In *Good Practice in Risk Assessment and Risk Management: Protection, Rights and Responsibilities*, edited by H. Kemshall and J. Pritchard. London: Jessica Kingsley.

———. 1998. "Prison Suicide and the Nature of Imprisonment." In *Deaths of Offenders: The Hidden Side of Justice*, edited by A. Liebling. Winchester: Waterside.

Liebling, A., and H. Krarup. 1993. *Suicide Attempts in Male Prisons*. London: Home Office.

Liebling, A., G. Muir, G. Rose, and A. E. Bottoms. 1997. "An Evaluation of Incentives and Earned Privileges." Final report submitted to the Home Office, London.

Liebling, A., and T. Ward, eds. 1994. *Deaths in Custody: International Perspectives*. London: Whiting & Birch.

———. 1995. "Prison Doctors and Prison Suicide Research." In *The Health of Prisoners*, edited by R. Creese, W. F. Bynm, and J. Bearn. London: CLIO MEDICA.

Liebling, H. 1990. "A Study of Anxiety Levels in Female Prison Officers Working in Different Levels of Security and Female Hostel Staff." M.Phil. thesis, University of Edinburgh, Psychology Department.

Livingstone, M. 1994. "Self-Injurious Behaviour in Prisoners." Ph.D. dissertation, University of Leeds, Psychology Department.

———. 1997. "A Review of the Literature on Self-Injurious Behaviour amongst Prisoners." In *Suicide and Self-Injury in Prisons: Research Directions in the 1990s*, edited by G. Towl. Issues in Criminological and Legal Psychology, no. 28. Leicester: British Psychological Society.

Lloyd, C. 1990. *Suicide in Prison: A Literature Review*. Home Office Research Study no. 115. London: Home Office Research and Planning Unit.

Lyon, Juliet. 1994. "Adolescents Who Offend: An Applied Research Project." Paper presented at the Conference of European Association for Research on Adolescence, Stockholm.

Maltsberger, J. T. 1986. *Suicide Risk: The Formulation of Clinical Judgment*. New York: New York University Press.

Maltsberger, J. T., and M. J. Goldblatt. 1996. *Essential Papers on Suicide*. New York: New York University Press.

Maris, R. W. 1981. *Pathways to Suicide: A Survey of Self-Destructive Behaviours*. Baltimore: Johns Hopkins University Press.

Mathiesen, T. 1965. *The Defences of the Weak: A Sociological Study of a Norwegian Correctional Institution*. London: Tavistock.

McCain, G., V. C. Cox, and P. B. Paulus. 1980. *The Effects of Prison Crowding on Inmate Behaviour*. Washington, D.C.: National Institute of Justice.

McCord, J. 1982. "A Longitudinal View of the Relationship between Paternal Absence and Crime." In *Abnormal Offenders, Delinquency and the Criminal Justice System*, edited by J. Gunn and D. P. Farrington. Chichester: Wiley.

McDermott, K., and R. D. King. 1988. "Mind Games." *British Journal of Criminology* 28:357–78.

McDonald, D. 1994. "Australian Deaths in Custody: The Impact of the Royal Commission into Aboriginal Deaths in Custody." In *Deaths in Custody: Caring for People at Risk*, edited by A. Liebling. Bournmouth: Whiting & Birch.

———. 1998. "Man Passeth Away like a Shadow: Deaths Associated with the Australian Criminal Justice System, Six Years after the Royal Commission into Aboriginal Deaths in Custody." In *Deaths of Offenders: The Hidden Side of Justice*, edited by A. Liebling. Winchester: Waterside.

McGurk, B. J., and C. McDougal. 1986. *The Prevention of Bullying among Incarcerated Delinquents*. DPS Report, ser. 11, no. 114, restricted circulation. London: Directorate of Psychology Services.

McMurran, M., J. Hodge, and C. Hollin. 1997. "Current Issues in the Treatment of Addiction and Crime." In *Addicted to Crime?* Wiley Series in Offender Rehabilitation, edited by J. E. Hodge, M. McMurran, and C. R. Hollin. West Sussex: Wiley.

Monat, A., and R. S. Lazarus. 1991. *Stress and Coping: An Anthology*. New York: Columbia University Press.

Morgan, H. G. 1979. *Deathwishes: The Understanding and Management of Deliberate Self-Harm*. Chichester: Wiley.

Morgan, R. 1997. "Imprisonment: Current Concerns and a Brief History." In *The Oxford Handbook of Criminology*, edited by M. MacGuire, R. Morgan, and R. Reiner. Oxford: Oxford University Press.

Northern Ireland Prison Service. 1990. "Inmate Suicide: An Awareness and Prevention Manual." Belfast: Northern Ireland Office.

Office of Corrections Resource Centre. 1988. *Suicide and Other Deaths in Prisons including Victorian Results from the National Deaths in Corrections Study Research Unit*. Victoria: Office of Corrections.

O'Mahony, P. 1990. "A Review of the Problem of Prison Suicide." Unpublished report (restricted circulation), Dublin.

———. 1994. "Prison Suicide Rates: What Do They Mean?" In *Death in Custody: International Perspectives*, edited by A. Liebling and T. Ward. London: Whiting & Birch.

Pallis, D. J. 1988. "Open Forum Discussion." In *The Clinical Management of Suicide Risk*, edited by H. G. Morgan. London: Royal Society of Medicine Press.

Phillips, D. P. 1974. "The Influence of Suggestion on Suicide: Substantive and Theoretical Implications of the Werther Effect." *American Sociological Review* 39:340–54.

Phillips, M. 1986. *Suicide and Attempted Suicide in Brixton Prison*. London: Directorate of Psychological Services Report.

Power, K. G., and A. P. Spencer. 1987. "Parasuicidal Behaviour of Detained Scottish Young Offenders." *International Journal of Offender Therapy and Comparative Criminology* 31:227–35.

Price, D., and A. Liebling. 1998. "Staff Prisoner Relationships: A Review of the Literature." Report submitted to Home Office, London.

Prison Service. 1992*a*. *Report of the Work of the Prison Service, April 1990– March 1991*. London: H.M. Stationery Office.

———. 1992*b*. "The Way Forward: Caring for Prisoners at Risk of Suicide and Self-Injury." Information paper. London: Home Office.

———. 1994. *Caring for the Suicidal in Custody: A Training Pack*. London: Home Office.

———. 1998. *Business Plan, 1998–1999*. London: H.M. Stationery Office.

Ramsay, R. F., B. L. Tanney, and C. A. Searle. 1987. "Suicide Prevention in High-Risk Prison Populations." *Canadian Journal of Criminology* 29:295– 307.

Richards, M. 1978. "The Experience of Long-Term Imprisonment." *British Journal Of Criminology* 18:162–69.

Robins, L. N. 1990. "Conduct Disorder." *Journal of Child Psychology and Psychiatry* 32:193–212.

Robins, L. N., and M. Rutter, eds. 1990. *Straight and Devious Pathways from Childhood to Adulthood*. Cambridge: Cambridge University Press.

Roger, D. 1997. "Crime and Emotion Control." In *Addicted to Crime?* edited by M. McMurran, J. Hodge, and C. Hollin. Chichester: Wiley.

Rood de Boer, M. 1978. "Children's Suicide." In *Family Violence: An International and Interdisciplinary Study*, edited by J. M. Eekelaar and S. M. Katz. Toronto: Butterworths.

Rotharum-Borus, M. J., P. D. Trautman, S. C. Dopkins, and P. E. Shrout. 1990. "Cognitive Style and Pleasant Activities among Female Adolescent Suicide Attempters." *Journal of Consulting and Clinical Psychology* 58:554– 61.

Rotter, J. B. 1966. "Generalised Expectancies for Internal versus External Control of Reinforcement." *Psychological Monographs*, vol. 80, no. 609.

Rowan, J. 1994. "The Prevention of Suicide in Custody." In *Deaths in Custody: An International Conference*, edited by A. Liebling and T. Ward. London: Whiting & Birch.

———. 1998. "Who Is Safer in Male Maximum Security Prisons?" *The Keepers Voice*. www.acsp.uic.edu.

Rutter, H., and D. Smith. 1995. *Psychosocial Problems in Young People: Time Trends and Their Causes*. Chichester: Wiley & Sons.

Sainsbury, R. 1988. "Suicide Prevention—an Overview." In *The Clinical Management of Suicide Risk*, edited by H. G. Morgan. London: Royal Society of Medicine Press.

Samaritans. 1997. *Annual Report of the Samaritans.* London: Samaritans.

Sampson, R. J., and J. H. Laub. 1993. *Crime in the Making: Pathways and Turning Points through Life.* Cambridge, Mass.: Harvard University Press.

Sapsford, R. 1978. "Life Sentence Prisoners." *British Journal of Criminology* 18:128–45.

———. 1983. *Life Sentence Prisoners.* Milton Keynes: Open University Press.

Scottish Home and Health Department. 1985. *Report of the Review of Suicide Precautions at H.M. Detention Centre and Young Offenders Institution, Glenochil.* Edinburgh: H.M. Stationery Office.

Scottish Prison Service. 1992. *Suicide Prevention Strategy.* Edinburgh: Scottish Prison Service.

Seligman, M. E. D. 1992. *Helplessness: On Depression, Development and Death.* New York: W. H. Freeman. (Originally published 1975. San Francisco: W. H. Freeman.)

Shepherd, S. 1991. "A Brief Group Cognitive-Behavioural Intervention for Anxiety and Depression with Young Offenders in Custody." M.Sc. thesis, Birkbeck College, London.

Shine, J., R. Wilson, and D. Hammond. 1990. "Understanding and Controlling Violence in a Long-Term Young Offender Institution." In *Proceedings from Psychologists Conference 1989*, edited by N. L. Fludger and I. R. Simmons, pp. 115–32. Directorate of Psychological Services Report, ser. 1, no. 34. London: Home Office, Prison Department.

Shneidman, E. 1993. "Suicide as Psychache." *Journal of Nervous and Mental Disease* 181:147–49.

Sim, J. 1990. *Medical Power in Prisons: The Prison Medical Service in England: 1774–1989.* Milton Keynes: Open University Press.

Sim, J., and T. Ward. 1994. "The Magistrate of the Poor? Coroners and Deaths in Custody in Nineteenth Century England." In *Legal Medicine in History*, edited by M. J. Clarke and C. Crawford. Cambridge: Cambridge University Press.

Sinclair, I. 1971. *Hostels for Probationers.* Home Office Research Studies no. 6. London: H.M. Stationery Office.

Skegg, K., and B. Cox. 1993. "Suicide in Custody: Occurrence in Maori and Non-Maori New Zealanders." *New Zealand Medical Journal* 106(948):1–3.

Smalley, H. 1911. "Report by the Medical Inspector." In *Report by the Prison Commissioners*, edited by The Prison Commission. London: H.M. Stationery Office.

Sparks, J. R. 1994. "*Suicides in Prison* by Alison Liebling—a Review." *British Journal of Criminology* 34:82–84.

Sparks, R. 1997. "Recent Social Theory and the Study of Crime." In *The Oxford Handbook of Criminology*, edited by M. MacGuire, R. Morgan, and R. Reiner. Oxford: Oxford University Press.

Sparks, R., A. Bottoms, and W. Hay. 1996. *Prisons and the Problem of Order.* Oxford: Clarendon.

Special Commission to Investigate Suicide in Municipal Detention Centers. 1984. *Final Report—Suicide in Massachusetts Lockups, 1973–1984*. Boston: Special Commission to Investigate Suicide in Municipal Detention Centers.

Sperbeck, D. J., and R. R. Parlour. 1986. "Screening and Managing Suicidal Prisoners." *Corrective and Social Psychiatry* 32(3):95–98.

Stengel, E. 1970. "Attempted Suicide (Letter)." *British Journal of Psychiatry* 116:237–38.

———. 1971. "Suicide in Prison: The Gesture and the Risk." *Prison Service Journal* 2:13–14.

Stengel, E., and N. Cook. 1958. *Attempted Suicide: Its Social Significance and Its Effects*. London: Chapman & Hall.

Stephens, J. 1987. "Cheap Thrills and Humble Pie: The Adolescence of Female Suicide Attempters." *Suicide and Life-Threatening Behaviour* 12(2):107–18.

Sutton, N. 1995. *Bruno Bettleheim: The Other Side of Madness*. London: Duckworth.

Sykes, G. 1958. *The Society of Captives*. Princeton, N.J.: Princeton University Press.

Sykes, G., and S. Messinger. 1960. "The Inmate Social System." In *Theoretical Studies in Social Organization of the Prison*, edited by R. Cloward. New York: Social Science Research Council.

Taylor, S. 1982. *Durkheim and the Study of Suicide*. London: Macmillan.

Thomas, C. W., and D. M. Petersen. 1977. *Prison Organization and Inmate Subcultures*. Indianapolis: Bobbs Merrill.

Thornton, D. 1990. "Depression, Self-Injury and Attempted Suicide amongst the YOI Population." In *Proceedings of the Prison Psychologists' Conference*, edited by N. L. Fludger and I. P. Simmons, pp. 47–55. Directorate of Psychological Services Report, ser. 1, no. 43. London: Home Office, Prison Department.

Thornton, D., L. Curran, D. Grayson, and V. Holloway. 1984. *Tougher Regimes in Detention Centres: Report of an Evaluation by the Young Offender Psychology Unit*. London: H.M. Stationery Office.

Tilt, R. 1998. "Address to Prison Service Conference." Unpublished manuscript. Harrogate: Prison Service of England and Wales.

Toch, H. 1975. *Men in Crisis: Human Breakdowns in Prisons*. New York: Aldine.

Toch, H., K. Adams, and D. Grant. 1989. *Coping: Maladaptation in Prisons*. New Brunswick, N.J.: Transaction.

Topp, D. O. 1979. "Suicide in Prison." *British Journal of Criminology* 143:24–27.

Towl, G., ed. 1997. *Suicide and Self-Injury in Prisons: Research Directions in the 1990s*. Issues in Criminological and Legal Psychology, no. 28. Leicester: British Psychological Society.

Towl, G., and D. Hudson. 1997. "Risk Assessment and Management of the Suicidal." In *Suicide and Self-Injury in Prisons: Research Directions in the 1990s*, edited by G. Towl. Issues in Criminological and Legal Psychology, no. 28. Leicester: British Psychological Society.

Tumim, S. 1990. *Report of a Review by Her Majesty's Chief Inspector of Prisons for*

England and Wales of Suicide and Self-Harm in Prison Service Establishments in England and Wales. London: H.M. Stationery Office.

von Hirsch, A. 1993. *Censure and Sanctions.* Oxford: Clarendon.

Walker, N. 1983. "The Side-Effects of Incarceration." *British Journal of Criminology* 23:61–71.

———. 1987. "The Unwanted Effects of Long-Term Imprisonment." In *Problems of Long-Term Imprisonment,* edited by A. E. Bottoms and R. Light. Aldershot: Gower.

Walmsley, R., L. Howard, and S. White. 1992. *The National Prison Survey 1991: Main Findings.* London: H.M. Stationery Office.

Ward, T., and D. Coles. 1994. "Failure Stories: Prison Suicides and How Not to Prevent Them." In *Deaths in Custody: International Perspectives,* edited by A. Liebling and T. Ward. London: Whiting & Birch.

West, D. 1982. *Delinquency: Its Roots, Careers and Prospects.* London: Heinemann.

West, D., and D. P. Farrington. 1977. *The Delinquent Way of Life.* London: Heinemann.

Wicks, R. J. 1972. "Suicide Prevention: A Brief for Corrections Officers." *Federal Probation* 36:29–31.

———. 1974. "Suicidal Manipulators in the Penal Setting." *Chitty's Law Journal* 22(7):249–50.

Wikström, Per-Olaf. 1990. "Age and Crime in a Stockholm Cohort." *Journal of Quantitative Criminology* 6:61–84.

Wilkins, J., and J. Coid. 1991. "Self-Mutilation in Female Remanded Prisoners. I. An Indicator of Severe Pathology." *Criminal Behaviour and Mental Health* 1:247–67.

Williams, M. 1997. *A Cry of Pain: Understanding Suicide and Self-Harm.* London: Penguin.

Winfree, L. T. 1985. "American Jail Death-Rates: A Comparison of the 1978 and 1983 Jail Census Data." Paper presented at the thirty-seventh annual meeting of the American Society of Criminology, San Diego, Calif., November.

Wolfgang, M. E., R. M. Figlio, and T. Sellin. 1972. *Delinquency in a Birth Cohort.* Chicago: University of Chicago Press.

Wool, R., and E. Dooley. 1987. "A Study of Attempted Suicides in Prisons." *Medicine, Science and the Law* 27:297–301.

Wormith, J. S., and F. J. Porporino. 1984. "The Controversy over the Effects of Long-Term Incarceration." *Canadian Journal of Criminology* 26(4):423–38.

Young, J. 1997. "Left Realist Criminology: Radical in Its Analysis, Realist in Its Policy." In *The Oxford Handbook of Criminology,* 2d ed., edited by M. MacGuire, R. Morgan, and R. Reiner. Oxford: Oxford University Press.

Zamble, E., and F. J. Porporino. 1988. *Coping, Behaviour and Adaptation in Prison Inmates.* New York: Springer.

Zoccolillo, M., A. Pickles, D. Quinton, and M. Rutter. 1992. "The Outcome of Childhood Conduct Disorder: Implications for Defining Adult Personality Disorder and Conduct Disorder." *Psychological Medicine* 22:971–86.

Gerald G. Gaes, Timothy J. Flanagan,
Laurence L. Motiuk, and Lynn Stewart

Adult Correctional
Treatment

ABSTRACT

Adult correctional treatment is effective in reducing criminal recidivism.
Meta-analyses of adult and juvenile correctional interventions demonstrate
that juvenile interventions are more effective than those designed for
adults. Behavioral/cognitive treatments, on average, produce larger effects
than other treatments. Analyses of specific treatment domains indicate
effective interventions. Cognitive skills training seems successful with
adult probationers and specific subgroups of offenders. Intensive, in-prison
drug treatment is effective, especially when combined with community
aftercare. Education, vocational training, and prison labor programs have
modest effects on reducing criminal recidivism and increase positive
behavior in prison. Evidence on sex offender treatment interventions is
less positive, probably because the target population is heterogeneous and
treatments need to be tailored to specific offender deficits.

Most correctional treatments for adult prisoners probably have modest
positive effects. Juvenile interventions seem to have stronger effects.
Behavioral and cognitive skills training seems to hold the most promise. Interventions in combination (multimodal treatments) probably
work better than those in isolation. If successful programs are to be
replicated, they should be replicated intact, without modification, and

Gerald G. Gaes is director of research, Federal Bureau of Prisons. Timothy J. Flanagan is vice president for academic affairs, State University of New York at Brockport.
Laurence L. Motiuk is director general of research, Correctional Service Canada. Lynn
Stewart is manager of Living Skills and Family Violence Prevention Programs at Correctional Service Canada. The opinions expressed in this essay by Gerald G. Gaes are
solely those of the author and are not intended to represent the policies or practices of
the Federal Bureau of Prisons or the U.S. Department of Justice. The opinions expressed by Larry Motiuk and Lynn Stewart are solely theirs and are not intended to
represent the policies or practices of Correctional Service Canada.

with extensive monitoring. Cognitive skills programs are relatively in-
expensive and can be seen as a foundation that can be used in conjunction with most other approaches. Intensive in-prison drug treatment
programs for adults seem to work; however, they also seem to require
extension of treatment into the community, both during supervision
and, in some cases, after supervision has ended. Work, vocational
training, and education have modest effects on adult postrelease behavior; however, these programs also seem to have salutary effects on behavior in prison while prisoners are participating in them. While there
is some evidence that treatments for sex offenders are effective, of the
substantive areas we examined, it was the most perplexing and the most
difficult about which to draw any conclusions. Although there have
been significant advances in theoretical approaches to treatment, and
a new tool—meta-analysis—can be used to summarize research and
deduce principles across different types of interventions, there are still
too many flawed intervention studies. They are flawed in essentially
the same ways as they were when the watershed reviews by Martinson
(1974), Lipton, Martinson, and Wilks (1975), and Sechrest, White, and
Brown (1979) were published.

A great deal of the most recent research on adult and juvenile interventions is based on a theoretical perspective developed by Canadian
researchers. Don Andrews and his colleagues (e.g., Andrews et al.
1990; Andrews and Bonta 1994) have produced a psychological model
for understanding behavioral change in offenders. In Section I of this
essay, we briefly examine this model, since it is used by many researchers in their analyses and explanations of treatment effects. In Section
II, we review the results of all of the meta-analyses of correctional
treatment done thus far. We summarize this research and discuss some
of the problems and contradictions of treatment meta-analyses. The
next four sections of this essay cover several well-defined domains of
adult intervention: cognitive skills training (Sec. III), intensive in-
prison drug treatment (Sec. IV), educational instruction and vocational
and industrial training (Sec. V), and sex-offender treatment (Sec. VI).
There are, of course, other rehabilitation domains such as anger management, group and individual counseling, psychotherapy, and values
training, to mention a few. Since it was impossible to cover all types
of programs individually, we elected to offer a general critique of the
intervention literature and to use these critical principles in an assessment of specific rehabilitative subdomains. Section VII discusses some
of the remaining problems in the theoretical principles of behavior

change and explains strong inference designs, that is, designs that evaluate the mechanisms of change in a treatment study. Finally, Section VIII summarizes the analysis and offers suggestions for future research.

Throughout this essay, we use the terms *rehabilitation, treatment,* and *intervention* as synonyms. The definition of *rehabilitation* proposed by The National Academy of Sciences Panel on Rehabilitative Techniques seems particularly appropriate since it has broad scope. "*Rehabilitation is the result of any planned intervention that reduces an offender's further criminal activity. . . . The effects of maturation and the effects associated with 'fear' or 'intimidation' are excluded*" (italicized in original, Sechrest, White, and Brown 1979, pp. 4–5).

I. Principles of Correctional Treatment

The principles of treatment intervention that we outline below derive from the work of Gendreau and Ross (1987), Andrews (1989, 1995, 1996), Andrews and Bonta (1994), and Antonowicz and Ross (1994). In addition, work by Palmer (1975, 1992), Lipsey (1989, 1992, 1995), Loesel (1995*a*, 1995*b*, 1996), and McGuire (1995*b*) are also important foundations for these principles. These principles represent the most coherent approach to treatment now available. Although the principles need further theoretical development and explication, most can be readily translated into testable hypotheses and meet the scientific requirement of refutability.

Criminogenic Needs: Intervention Efforts Must Be Linked to Criminogenic Characteristics. Human deficits that are directly related to the propensity to commit crime are referred to as criminogenic needs. These include procriminal attitudes, procriminal associates, impulsivity, weak socialization, below average verbal intelligence, a taste for risk, weak problem-solving and self-control skills, early onset of antisocial behavior, poor parental practices, and deficits in educational, vocational, and employment skills (Andrews 1995). Static characteristics such as age, race, and gender are important only as boundary conditions that determine which interventions work for which demographic subgroups. This principle implies that we understand individual-based attributes that determine the propensity to commit crime. It also assumes valid and reliable measurement of these needs. Most intervention research, however, rarely reports client needs except by implication. If a treatment is designed to address a deficit, then it is assumed that the need exists rather than measuring the need prior to and after treatment.

Multimodal Programs: All Criminogenic Deficits Should Be Treated. If an individual has multiple deficits that, in combination, increase the propensity toward crime, these deficits must all be addressed. The unstated assumption is that researchers can assess the deficits adequately and determine the proper sequencing of treatments. Are there, for example, rudimentary cognitive and emotional deficits that must be addressed before other treatment techniques can be implemented? There is not a great deal of multimodal research examining treatment combinations, much less their appropriate sequencing.

Responsivity: Treatment Providers Should Match Client Learning Styles with Staff Teaching Styles.   Programs must be tailored to the specific needs and learning styles of their clients. The unstated assumption is that we understand and measure learning and teaching styles so that matching can be implemented. Typically, responsivity is inferred from the success or failure of a program rather than by measuring or experimenting with staff and client characteristics. Of all the intervention propositions, the responsivity principle seems the most obvious, yet the most tautological.

Risk Differentiation: Higher-Risk Clients Are More Likely to Benefit from Treatment Than Are Lower-Risk Clients; the Highest Level of Treatment Intensity Should Be Used for the Highest-Risk Clients.   This principle also implies that there may be a small set of very high-risk clients who are not amenable to treatment or who are treatable only with great difficulty. The effect of the risk principle may be modest. Although client characteristics, such as risk, do affect treatment outcomes, meta-analyses of juvenile interventions indicate that treatment seems to be more influential than client characteristics (Lipsey 1995). In some treatment domains, lower-risk probationers seem to benefit more than do higher-risk prisoners. In the drug abuse treatment literature, the most dependent drug users benefit far less from the same treatment than do more moderate drug abusers. In one sense, the risk principle is a restatement of the needs principle. The riskiest clients are typically those with the most needs.

Skills Oriented and Cognitive-Behavioral Treatments: Treatment Providers Should Use Programs That Teach Clients Skills That Allow Them to Understand and Resist Antisocial Behavior.   Treatment should involve effective social learning principles in order to model and shape prosocial behavior. The most comprehensive meta-analyses support this principle.

Program Implementation and Continuity of Care: Clients Should Be Treated in Well-Supported Programs.   The best intervention will fail if there are insufficient funds or if there is a lack of commitment from treatment staff, administrators, or support staff. This is especially true if a program is conducted within an institutional setting primarily designed for custody purposes. Community settings may be more appropriate. This principle raises the question of the suitability of prison environments for successful treatments. Some interventions may be more effective after offenders have been released under supervision. This does not mean we should vitiate prison programs, since they also have a positive effect on inmate behavior. However, the principle does imply a need for better coordination between prison and community supervision programs. Treatments initiated in institutions will be more successful if there is continued care in the community. Aftercare is more effective if it is a continuation of the type of treatment delivered in the institutional setting.

Dosage: Interventions Should Be Comprehensive and of Sufficient Duration (Sufficient Dosage). While it is difficult to disagree with this principle, it is another matter to test optimal dosage amounts. Unlike clinical trials of medications, few studies of correctional treatments examine optimal or sufficient levels. This is further complicated by the varying need levels of clients. Thus dosage requires fine calibration of the client and of the treatment.

Researcher Involvement: Researchers Should Be Involved in Both Program Development and Evaluation. Lipsey's meta-analysis (1995) showed that studies that involved researchers directly in program design and development had larger effects. Lipsey cautioned that researcher involvement could be interpreted as experimenter bias, that is, that the success of a program may merely be an artifact of the researcher's participation. However, he also argued that since smaller research studies yielded larger effects, the overarching principle is one of treatment integrity. Researchers can enhance the integrity of a program, if it is not delivered to a large number of people or at a large number of sites. One possibility is that both program integrity and researcher bias occur at the same time. Unfortunately, while both determinants produce a greater treatment effect, only treatment integrity yields an unbiased result. We argue below (Sec. II) that program evaluations conducted by researchers testing their own theoretical proposals need safeguards against possible experimenter bias.

These principles form the basis of a psychological model of behavioral change. While other social sciences predict behavioral change on the basis of structural, cultural, or economic principles, those ideas are not easy to translate into individual-based intervention strategies. Many psychologists believe that behavior results from interactions between predispositions and situations, with situation defined in structural, cultural, or economic terms. One limitation of the psychological perspective is that there may be many contexts in which behavioral changes, despite the best treatments, are limited by structural and cultural obstacles beyond the control of the treatment provider.

II. Meta-analyses of Treatment Research

A series of meta-analyses of the treatment literature has attracted widespread attention. Prior to the development and acceptance of meta-analysis, reviews of research typically assessed each study carefully and then tallied those that supported a theoretical perspective against those that did not. A major weakness of "vote counting" was that it did not allow studies to be summarized mathematically. Studies with large samples were typically weighted as if they were as important as studies with small samples. Thus a treatment effect observed on ten clients was treated as being as important as a treatment effect observed on 1,000 clients. In contrast, meta-analysis is based on a common metric, called an effect size, that is standardized and is used to represent the results from each study (see especially Cooper and Hedges 1994a).

To be included in a meta-analysis, a study must provide sufficient information for calculation of the effect size. The researcher assigns a value to the influence of the independent variable on the outcome being studied. For example, one common metric often chosen is correlation. If treatment has an effect in a given study, then that effect can be summarized by the correlation between the treatment and the study outcome. If a study has a very large sample size, that correlation can be given a higher weight than correlations in studies having smaller samples. Both the average effect of all of the studies or the distribution can be analyzed. In the latter case, the researcher can isolate the studies with the most typical, the largest, or the smallest effects.

Although the main purpose of a meta-analysis is to calculate the effect size for each study of the treatment under consideration, the technique has more value when other measures are coded that allow interpretations of the precise meaning of the results of the research synthesis. Measures of study methodology, treatment type, sample characteristics, and other variables can set the boundary conditions of a treatment. These measures are called moderator variables. They are important in suggesting not only the limiting conditions of a treatment but also future directions of possible theoretical interest. A meta-analysis can be conducted on a sample of studies in much the same way as an analysis of a sample of subjects. Instead of variables representing subject characteristics, a meta-analysis includes moderator variables that indicate specific conditions related to variations in treatment effects. This approach provides a much more rigorous and systematic analysis of effects, their causes, and their limiting conditions.

Although meta-analysis has gained wide appeal and is used extensively in medicine, education, and social science, certain precautions are necessary. Although meta-analysis improves the rigor of research reviews, the results must be evaluated under the same scientific standards that would be used with any primary research or secondary summarization of that research (Hall et al. 1994). The same questions apply. Do the results make theoretical sense? Is there consistency across different meta-analyses, especially meta-analyses of the same set of studies? Are there reasons to suspect that some fundamental bias broadly underlies the results of a particular research domain? The best meta-analyses are designed to minimize these problems by selecting the better-designed studies and by coding methods variables that indicate when conclusions are more likely to be artifactual than real.

In the next subsection of this essay, we examine the meta-analytic studies of correctional treatment. We describe what they imply about effective juvenile and adult interventions. Readers interested in the more troublesome conceptual and methodological problems with this literature will find them addressed in the appendix.

A. Current Meta-analyses

Lipton et al. (1998) identified twenty-eight reviews of the intervention literature; about half were meta-analyses. These studies are depicted in table 1. Loesel (1995a) has published a review of meta-analyses of correctional treatment; he summarized thirteen meta-analyses. Some meta-analyses focus on a specific intervention subset. For example, Tobler's (1986) was on youth drug prevention programs. Mayer et al. (1986) examined juvenile social learning treatment. Garrett (1985) examined the effect of residential treatment for adjudicated juveniles.

Table 1 also shows the number of studies analyzed and whether the study population was juvenile or adult. Most of the meta-analyses were based on the juvenile intervention literature. Lipsey's (1992, 1995) analyses of juvenile interventions supersede, and are inclusive of, almost all of the other meta-analyses of juvenile interventions. He col-

TABLE 1

Meta-analyses of Juvenile and Adult Correctional Treatment

Study	Number of Studies Included in the Meta-analysis	Juvenile	Adult
Andrews et al. (1990)	80	Yes	Yes
Garrett (1985)	111	Yes	No
Gensheimer et al. (1986)	44	Yes	No
Gottshalk et al. (1987a)	90	Yes	No
Gottshalk et al. (1987b)	25	Yes	No
Izzo and Ross (1990)	46	Yes	No
Lipsey (1992, 1995)	443	Yes	No
CDATE—Lipton et al. (1998)	900	Yes	Yes
Loesel, Koferl, and Weber (1987); Loesel and Koferl (1989); Loesel (1993)	8	No	No
Mayer et al. (1986)	34	Yes	No
Redondo, Garrido, and Sanchez-Meca (1996)	57	No	Yes
Roberts and Camasso (1991)	46	Yes	No
Tobler (1986)	143	Yes	No
Whitehead and Lab (1989)	50	Yes	No

lected juvenile intervention studies from English-speaking countries, published and unpublished, produced between 1950 and 1991. He analyzed 443 of the most rigorously designed studies that used recidivism as an outcome. Not only does Lipsey's analysis cover most of the studies included in other meta-analyses of juvenile treatments, it also has the most thorough assessment of moderator variables.

The CDATE project (Lipton et al. 1998) will be the most comprehensive review and research synthesis of correctional treatment ever undertaken. The project will include juvenile and adult intervention studies from any source country, published and unpublished, produced between 1968 and 1997. Of the 1,500 studies included in the CDATE project thus far, 900 used recidivism as an outcome. The preliminary findings reported by Lipton et al. (1998) are based on 226 juvenile studies and 261 adult studies.

B. Meta-analytic Findings from the Treatment Literature

Lipsey's analysis of over 400 studies representing juvenile delinquency interventions has been the most comprehensive published meta-analysis of treatment to date. After controlling for differences in study methodology, Lipsey found a substantial effect due to treatment variations. Treatment in public facilities, custodial institutions, and the juvenile justice system produced smaller effects than treatment in community settings. Treatment that was behavioral, skill-oriented, or multimodal (using more than one treatment approach) was associated with larger effect sizes than treatment that was based on deterrence, family counseling, group counseling, or individual counseling. Because the treatment effect depended on whether the treatment was delivered in a juvenile justice or community setting, conclusions have to be qualified accordingly. For example, employment training had the highest average effect size when delivered in the juvenile justice setting. When delivered in nonjuvenile justice settings, it had a negative effect size, indicating that the intervention increased delinquency.

At face value, Lipsey's results are encouraging, especially for juvenile justice interventions. By developing a large set of methods variables, Lipsey showed how variation in treatment effects reflects variations in the quality of the research methods. He also showed that despite this method variation, juvenile correctional treatments produced dramatic effects.

Because the CDATE project (Lipton et al. 1998) includes both juvenile and adult interventions, we can begin to see emerging differences between these two realms. Preliminary data indicate that cognitive/behavioral treatment, on average, produces larger effects than interventions characterized as punishment, intensive community supervision, educational training, substance abuse, or group counseling. The CDATE data also show, with a few exceptions, that randomized designs produce smaller effects than nonrandom designs. This again supports the proposition that methods variables must be analyzed to do a comprehensive meta-analysis. The CDATE project also shows that juvenile interventions are typically more effective than adult interventions. However, some of these comparisons rely on very small samples of adult studies. While moderator variables such as type of treatment and type of target population indicate the boundaries of treatment effectiveness, most meta-analyses have been exploratory and unguided by any particular theoretical perspective. One major exception, however, is the work of Andrews et al. (1990).

C. Comparability of Results from Treatment Meta-analyses

An important question is whether the meta-analyses have produced similar results. Unfortunately, it is difficult to compare the meta-analytic studies because they do not always overlap in their inclusion or exclusion of studies. In the juvenile literature, Lipsey's study subsumes all or most other meta-analytic studies of juvenile treatment. Furthermore, the meta-analyses vary in their methodological, theoretical, and statistical rigor. Some are better than others, and it is improper to summarize these studies as if each meta-analysis should be given equal consideration.

We are most interested, of course, in whether certain juvenile and adult interventions are better than others. Comparing the two most comprehensive assessments, Lipsey's and the preliminary results from CDATE, some tentative conclusions stand out. In their preliminary analysis of the CDATE data, Lipton et al. identified the following types of interventions: punishment, community supervision, education programs, cognitive behavioral/social learning programs, substance abuse, and group counseling. Lipsey used the following treatment categories: employment, multimodal (more than one treatment type), behavioral, skill-oriented, institutional, community residential, individual counseling, group counseling, family counseling, vocational training, deterrence, and several kinds of probation and parole interventions.

Unfortunately, thus far, group counseling and behavioral programs are the only treatment categories represented in both meta-analyses. Lipsey's study indicated that the average residualized effect size (after controlling for methods variables) for group counseling conducted within the juvenile justice system was .07. The effect size was .18 in a nonjuvenile justice setting. The CDATE results, so far, indicate that group counseling has had little or no effect on recidivism. Lipton et al. found an average effect size of .01 for juveniles participating in nonrandom studies and an average effect size of .00 for juveniles participating in random assignment studies. It is not clear why the CDATE and Lipsey's results are so discrepant with respect to group counseling.

There is more consistency when comparing studies defined as cognitive-behavioral or social learning interventions. Lipsey found juvenile behavioral studies to have consistently high effect sizes, whether the intervention occurred in a juvenile justice setting (effect size .25) or a nonjuvenile justice setting (effect size .20). The CDATE project indicated average effect sizes for cognitive-behavioral and social learning programs of .18 for juveniles in nonrandom assignment studies and .16 for juveniles in random assignment studies. Despite this apparent similarity in findings, it is difficult to know whether the two analyses use consistent definitions in categorization of studies and thus whether consistency or inconsistency in effect sizes are apparent or real. To examine this question empirically, a public domain data set composed of all of the studies and the variables that have been coded on each study would allow other researchers to compare and contrast these studies as well as conduct their own meta-analyses that build on the previous research. The CDATE project is expected to generate such a public domain data set.

The CDATE analysis also shows that for adults, while effects of treatment have been less pronounced, there seem to be modest effects of education, cognitive skills/social learning programs, substance abuse treatment, and group counseling. If random assignment studies are assumed to be more methodologically rigorous, and more likely to represent the true effect size of a treatment, then the average effect sizes for the adult treatments range between .03 and .06. These are very modest effects.

D. The Substantive Meaning of Effect Sizes

One common way to represent the substantive or practical effects of an intervention is to convert an effect size to a binomial effect size display, or BESD (Rosenthal and Rubin 1982). The BESD represents the change in success (or failure) rate attributable to a treatment procedure. A correlation coefficient of .10 represents a BESD of .10. Thus an experimental manipulation having a BESD of .10 would increase the success rate from 45 percent to 55 percent. A BESD of .05 would increase the success rate from 47.5 percent to 52.5 percent, and a BESD of .20 represents an increase in the success rate from 40 percent to 60 percent.

Based on the juvenile meta-analyses, and especially Lipsey's work, a conservative average effect size for juvenile interventions is .10. Loesel (1995a) has also concluded that .10 is a conservative, yet reasonable effect size for juvenile treatments. This translates into a reduction in recidivism from 55 percent to 45 percent. The magnitude of this effect is substantively quite large. The more modest effect sizes observed in the CDATE adult interventions would represent an average reduction in recidivism from about 52.5 percent to 47.5 percent.

E. The Blueprint Paradigm and the "Preventing Crime" Report

Two other approaches are used to assess interventions. The "blueprints" approach uses a set of criteria that must be met for an intervention to be considered a model program. Similarly, researchers at the

University of Maryland developed a scientific scale to rate programs and used that to identify model programs.

While meta-analysis could be construed as a tool for investigating the principles of intervention, a pragmatic approach is to export exemplary programs with proven track records. Elliot (1997) has attempted to do just that in a series entitled "Blueprints for Violence Prevention." Using a stringent set of program effectiveness criteria, Elliot and his colleagues examined more than 400 delinquency, drug, and violence prevention programs for juveniles. To date, ten programs have met the selection criteria. These programs had a strong research design, showed evidence of significant deterrence effects, produced effects that were sustained well beyond the end of the intervention, and produced effective results at more than one site. Elliot (1997) also looked for evidence of a strong inference design. Although he used different terminology than we have adopted, Elliot expressed surprise that many programs had not collected the data necessary to do a strong inference analysis.

The blueprints approach is atheoretical in the sense that a program must meet primarily methodological rather than theoretical standards. In fact, Elliot emphasizes that blueprint programs are to be adopted without modification. This is because there is no evidence to identify which features of a program make it work. This may be a practical approach to treatment in the absence of good theory and well-supported principles. However, a more theoretically driven approach will eventually result in a more generalizable set of principles and programs. Despite the problems of the rehabilitation and treatment meta-analysis literatures, the blueprints technique is a stopgap, yet sound practical solution in the short run. In the long run, correctional treatment effectiveness must rely on the plodding, conservative, trial-and-error properties of original research.

Another approach to the synthesis of rehabilitation research is a byproduct of an even broader analysis of programs that could reduce crime in different institutional settings such as communities, families, and labor markets, and in places such as businesses. The analysis also covered interventions by police and criminal justice agencies once a defendant had been arrested or convicted. Sherman et al. (1998) developed a scale called the "Maryland Scale of Scientific Methods" to rate different program interventions. The scale is based on research design and methodological criteria and rates studies from one (lowest) to five. Generally, randomized designs achieved the highest rating. Studies that indicated a relationship between a program and crime reduction but had few controls received the lowest rating. Sherman et al. (1998) concluded that two types of programs demonstrated consistent effectiveness: risk-focused interventions and prison residential drug treatment. While we agree with these conclusions, close examination even of these two types of interventions suggests some important qualifications.

F. Summary of Meta-analyses

In a research area as broad as correctional treatment, meta-analysis has provided perspective where, previously, there existed a great deal of confusion. Has it provided the correct perspective? From one point of view, meta-analysis has been used to draw sweeping inferences from a great many studies, many of which were poorly designed. Even if meta-analysis can be used this way, to separate the wheat from the chaff, ultimately meta-analysis should suggest a definitive set of studies. Those studies must be conducted to confirm or repudiate the implications of the meta-analyses. If, through meta-analysis, we learn that interventions must be multimodal, behavior-oriented, and tailored to the client, we should design and implement a series of studies to test these assumptions. These studies should incorporate different staff, multiple treatment sites, and several evaluators in the most rigorous designs possible and have sufficient power and internal and external validity to justify drawing conclusions. Meta-analysis should not be an end unto itself. Cooper and Hedges (1994*b*) make this same point succinctly. "A research synthesis should never be considered a replacement for new primary research. Primary research and its synthesis are complementary parts of a common process" (Cooper and Hedges 1994*b*, p. 524).

The next four sections of this essay summarize findings on specific adult correctional interventions. Several general problems warrant mention apart from the specific studies discussed, since they are endemic to treatment evaluation studies. Too few provide detailed descriptions of the treatment being delivered. Nor do most studies report whether there was any attempt to monitor the quality of the intervention. Few studies use what has been described as a strong inference design (Platt 1964). A strong inference design is one in which the evaluation measures the level of the offender's need or deficit prior to and after the treatment. In such a design, in addition to observing a treatment effect based on differences in mean levels between treatment and comparison subjects, the researcher also analyzes whether treatment reduced the client's needs. A strong inference occurs when there is both a treatment effect for the group and a reduction in a client's deficits related to the client's outcome. For example, cognitive skills could be measured prior to and after cognitive skills training. If offenders in the treatment group were less likely to recidivate after their treatment, that would be taken as evidence of a treatment effect. In addition, if those inmates with the largest increase in cognitive skills ability were the least likely to recidivate, we could draw a much stronger inference that the cognitive skills training caused the observed effect.

Subject selection and attrition is a persistent problem in this literature. In too many studies, inmates were allowed to self-select into treatment, or were selected by another agent, or dropped out of treatment. In this latter case, often there was no attempt to measure the outcomes of dropouts, or their outcomes were analyzed as if they could be considered independently from those of clients who completed treatment. In each of these cases, the selection process may have resulted in a biased outcome. An exposition of this problem is presented by Gaes (1997, 1998) in the context of in-prison drug treatment.

III. Cognitive Skills Training

In the last fifteen years, cognitive-behavioral interventions have been identified as the treatment approach most often associated with reductions in offender recidivism (Gendreau and Ross 1979, 1987; Izzo and Ross 1990; Lipton 1998). Researchers have come to agree on the effectiveness of this treatment approach based on meta-analyses, qualitative analyses, and reviews of the component elements of successful programs. Gendreau and Andrews's (1990) review of meta-analytic studies of correctional treatment led them to conclude that "types of intervention should be behavioral in nature with emphasis on cognitive and skill building techniques" (Gendreau and Andrews 1990, p. 182). More recently, the CDATE meta-analysis confirmed that the cognitive approach produces reductions in criminal recidivism.

A number of cognitive skills-based programs are now delivered in correctional settings. However, no one program seems to have been as widely adopted as the Cognitive Thinking Skills Program (CTSP) developed by Robert Ross and Elizabeth Fabiano. This has become a core program in the federal Canadian correctional system and has been implemented in the United States, Europe, Australia, and New Zealand and throughout the British Prison system and in probation services in the United Kingdom. The CTSP meets all the criteria of effective correctional programs. It is cognitive and behavioral in design. It addresses needs that are empirically associated with criminal behavior. It is multimodal in design, providing a number of behavioral and skill-based treatment techniques to address a range of relevant targets. It is longer in duration than most thinking skills program; thus its dosage or strength is higher than that of many similar treatment programs. Finally, in screening offenders who have significant thinking deficits, the program adheres to the risk principle in that higher-risk offenders are more likely to have these thinking deficits. When properly implemented, therefore, the delivery of the program should test rehabilitation advocates' contention that appropriate cognitive behavioral programs can significantly reduce recidivism. This section briefly describes this program, its development, and implementation. In subsequent sections, we review the cognitive skills program evaluation literature.

The Cognitive Thinking Skills Program, also known as the Reasoning and Rehabilitation Program, was developed by a systematic process that began with a review of all controlled evaluations of correctional programs published between 1973 and 1978 that reduced criminal recidivism (Gendreau and Ross 1979). Ross and Fabiano (1985) identified 100 evaluations of effective programs and found that all applied techniques designed to target offenders' thinking. Ross and Fabiano then engaged in a literature search to identify which cognitive deficits are linked to criminality. Among offenders who demonstrated a repetitive pattern of criminal behavior, the authors identified problems with impulsivity associated with poor verbal self-regulation, impairment in means-end reasoning, a concrete thinking style that impinges on the ability to appreciate the thoughts and feelings of others, conceptual rigidity that inclines people to a repetitive pattern of self-defeating behavior, poor interpersonal problem-solving skills, egocentricity, poor critical reasoning, and a selfish perspective that tends to make people focus only on how their actions affect themselves instead of considering the effects of their actions on others.

Next, Ross and Fabiano scanned the literature for interventions that successfully addressed each of these deficit areas. Those interventions became the core components of CTSP. They found that impulsivity can be reduced by teaching consequential thinking. Fatalistic thinking can be reduced by teaching offenders meta-cognitive skills that enable them to assess the role their thinking has in influencing their actions. Antisocial behavior can be diminished by teaching offenders to replace these behaviors with prosocial ones. Rigid thinking can be minimized by teaching offenders creative thinking skills to provide them with pro-social alternatives in responding to interpersonal problems. Illogical thinking can be modified by critical reasoning skills. Egocentrism can be reduced by teaching offenders social perspective taking and values enhancement. Finally, social adjustment can be improved by training offenders in self-control techniques.

Each skill-training module is delivered over several sessions with considerable overlap in material designed to provide adequate opportunity to overlearn the skills. All of the techniques were selected from programs that had demonstrated a degree of effectiveness in developing the target skills. The authors acknowledge that their final program, consisting of thirty-five two-hour sessions, is an amalgam of content and techniques borrowed from a number of sources. The program is delivered to groups of four to ten offenders two to four times per week. The trainers' manual is highly organized and scripted to maximize the standardization of the program. A key to successful delivery of the program has been the selection of a variety of training techniques that create an enjoyable classroom experience for the participants. The program avoids a didactic presentation of material. Rather, the trainers or coaches, as they are called, use role playing, video-taped feedback, modeling, group discussion, games, and practical homework review to teach the skills. Another important component of the program's success is the careful selection, training, and monitoring of the nonprofessional staff who deliver the program.

A. Outcome Studies

Despite its availability as a program that has been relatively stable now for over ten years, and its delivery in dozens of sites throughout the world, there are suprisingly few controlled outcome studies. The following section reviews the few published studies, some internal reports, and some preliminary findings from sites where the program has been more recently implemented.

The initial evaluation study (Ross, Fabiano, and Ewels 1988) was conducted by the developers who delivered the program to a group of high-risk adult probationers in Ontario, Canada. The probationers were selected based on their high-risk rating on the Level of Supervision Inventory (Andrews 1989), an instrument well validated as a measure of recidivism risk. Probationers were randomly assigned to one of three conditions, CTSP, a life-skills program, and regular probation without any program intervention. The probation officers taught both the cognitive skills and the life skills programs and also supervised the offenders. Recidivism was calculated based on official convictions for new offenses after a period of nine months. The CTSP was significantly more effective in reducing recidivism in the short term compared with either regular probation or the life skills program. Recidivism for the CTSP group was 18.1 percent (4/22). For the regular probation group, it was 69.5 percent (16/23). For the life skills group, it was 47.5 percent (8/17). The differences were statistically significant. The authors also evaluated the program's effect based on the percentage of offenders who received custody sentences following new offenses. While none of the cognitive skills group received a custody sentence, 30 percent (7/23) of the regular probation group were reincarcerated, and 11 percent (2/17) of the life skills group received a sentence of imprisonment. Unfortunately, although the design included a pre- and posttest battery, offenders were not available to complete the posttesting.

In the late 1980s, CTSP was piloted in Correctional Service Canada, Canada's federal correctional service. The service is responsible for the custody and supervision of adult offenders sentenced to two or more years of imprisonment. The initial pilot evaluation involved forty-seven incarcerated offenders who were selected because of deficits in areas targeted by the program. The control group consisted of twenty-six prisoners who met the program criteria, had agreed to treatment, and were on a waiting list (Robinson, Grossman, and Porporino 1991). Analysis of the profiles of the two groups indicated that the program criteria generally screened in higher-risk offenders. The control and treatment groups were not significantly different on important characteristics such as criminal history, risk level, and demographic measures. The correctional staff selected as trainers were themselves trained in the content and delivery of the program by Elizabeth Fabiano, one of the program's developers. Offender recidivism was measured after the inmates had been released to the community. At the time of the initial follow-up, ten offenders in the study had not yet been released from custody. The remaining subjects were followed for an average period of eighteen months. Although the numbers were too small to detect a significant difference, the recidivism rate differences between the two groups imply that a treatment effect may have occurred had a larger sample been selected. Twenty percent (8/40) of the treatment group were reconvicted, while 30.4 percent (7/23) of the control group were reconvicted within the follow-up period. Robinson, Grossman, and Porporino (1991) also measured readmissions without a new conviction. When the data were analyzed using readmissions without a new conviction as the outcome, the effect was in the opposite direction. Twenty-five percent (10/40) of the treatment group, but only 21.7 percent (5/23) of the controls were readmitted without new convictions.

The authors also examined the rates of reconviction based on risk levels that were calculated using the Statistical Information on Recidivism (SIR) scale (Nuffield 1982). Based on the SIR, after 2.5 years the average probability of reconviction for offenders with risk scores similar to the subjects in the treatment and control groups is .52. While the actual probability for the treatment group was much lower at .22., the follow-up period was, on average, one year shorter than the follow-up period used to make the SIR predictions. Robinson, Grossman, and Porporino reasoned, however, that most offenders recidivate within one year of release, so that the rates of return should not be altered significantly after one year. Since the control group also had a substantially lower recidivism rate than that predicted by the SIR risk score, it is probably improper to try to draw any comparison between either the study or control group and a SIR-imputed base rate.

A second pilot study (Porporino, Fabiano, and Robinson 1991) followed a sample of fifty-four offenders (forty-two program completes and twelve dropouts) who had been released to the community for an average follow-up period of twelve months. Although there was no comparison group, the reoffending rate for the treatment group, 4.7 percent, was extremely low. As indicated above, based on the SIR, the expected base rates after 2.5 years would be 52 percent reconvicted. The reconviction rate of the dropout group, however, was 33.3 percent, suggesting again that the offenders who remained in the treatment group may have been among those most predisposed to do well on release.

Following the success of the pilots, the program was implemented nationally. National implementation meant the establishment of a training and monitoring infrastructure that ensured program integrity. Staff awareness training was also held to establish the support required for a well-integrated correctional program. An extensive assessment battery was implemented to measure pre- and postprogram scores on a variety of attitudinal and cognitive skills scales. A great deal of demographic information was also collected on the offenders. An early report (Robinson, Grossman, and Porporino 1991) assessed changes in a sample of 200 treatment participants and fifty-four comparison subjects who were on a waiting list (wait list controls). The treatment group improved on all the attitude tests as well as on the measures of impulsiveness and empathy. The changes were significantly better than those of the wait list controls on four of the nine scales. On the cognitive abilities scales, the treatment group improved significantly on all the relevant scales and improved significantly more than the wait list controls. This report, however, did not provide recidivism data that would have permitted a conclusion that the gains on the program goals were significantly related to reductions in recidivism.

To date, the largest-scale completed evaluation of CTSP was based on a sample of 2,125 released Canadian federal offenders—1,444 program completes, 302 program dropouts, and 379 wait list controls (Robinson 1995). Offenders were randomly assigned to the treatment or wait list groups in the first years of implementation of the program (thereafter, program implementation was expanded allowing for the treatment of all referred offenders). Recidivism outcome data were collected after inmates had been released to the community for a minimum of one year. Overall, the results indicated a small significant difference favoring the treatment group. Of those who completed the program, 44.5 percent were readmitted during the first year in the community compared with 50.1 percent of the wait list controls. When the outcome criterion was reconviction, there was again a small significant difference between the groups. For the treatment group, 19.7 percent received a new conviction, while 24.8 percent of the control group received a new conviction. In both cases, the worst outcomes were for the dropouts, whose readmission and reconviction rates were 58.2 percent and 28.8 percent, respectively. Comparison of the wait list controls with the treatment groups demonstrated that the wait list was composed of significantly more property offenders. To control for these differences in conviction offense, an analysis of covariance was conducted. Regardless of whether outcome was measured as readmission or reconviction, no statistically significant differences between the treated and untreated offenders were found.

Although the overall results were not encouraging, Robinson did a further set of analyses to investigate whether particular subgroups may have benefited more than others from the program. This kind of post hoc analysis should be considered only suggestive. Robinson's analysis of subgroups was based on offense profiles, risk and need levels, and treatment settings. These analyses demonstrated, contrary to the risk principle, that the program was significantly more helpful for lower- rather than higher-risk offenders. However, despite their designation as a "lower-risk" group, these offenders had an average one-year re- admission rate of 36.2 percent, which is quite high. The reanalysis also showed that the medium and high needs offenders, and violent, sex, and drug offenders, were more likely to benefit from treatment than were offenders with fewer deficits and property offenders.

The largest treatment effect was found for offenders who received the program in the community. The study identified 131 subjects who completed their program in the community. However, in the absence of a community-based control group, Robinson compared the commu- nity treatment group with the control group used for the institutional sample. Robinson used statistical procedures to control for the follow- ing offense categories: nonviolent property offenses, robbery offenses, and violent offenses. The results demonstrated a significant treatment effect on both readmissions and reconvictions. He found that 30.5 per- cent of the community treatment completes compared with 50.1 per- cent of the institutional control group were readmitted. He also found that 8.4 percent of the community treatment group compared with 24.8 percent of the institutional control group were reconvicted during the follow-up period. These latter data appear to confirm the evidence from previous reviews of correctional treatment that emphasize greater success of programs delivered in community rather than institutional settings (Andrews et al. 1990; Izzo and Ross 1990; Loesel 1995a).

The conclusions of this study are compromised by several design problems. The outcomes of the treatment completes and dropouts were analyzed separately. This has the effect of biasing the results in favor of finding a treatment effect. The analysis of the community treatment sample had additional problems. Although Robinson applied statistical techniques to control for offense background, the wait list control group was composed of institutional subjects who were likely to be higher-risk offenders, since they had not yet been vetted by a parole board that would have been less likely to release the highest-risk offenders. Robinson's analysis of covariance apparently did not include overall risk level as a control. Thus the comparison between the com- munity treatment group and the institutional control group may not have been an adequate test of the effectiveness of the program.

Second, half of the community treatment population came from one region. In the absence of evidence that the readmission and reconviction base rates from this region were comparable to those in the other four regions, we cannot dismiss the possibility that the treatment effect may actually reflect a generally lower-risk treatment sample that returns to generally less criminogenic communities.

Finally, the dropout rate in the community treatment sample was much higher than that of the institutions (30.6 percent of the community sample compared with 14.2 percent of the institutional sample). This would have the effect of biasing the community-based outcome even more than the institutional outcomes. The high dropout rate was likely to have distilled the most motivated and stable offenders who remained in the treatment group.

In summary, then, the largest-scale outcome study of CTSP to date provided some modest evidence of the effectiveness of the program in reducing returns to custody and reconviction for adult offenders. The study suggested directions for future research. The most resistant offenders to the effects of this intervention were property and nonviolent robbery offenders and offenders under age twenty-five. The report does not provide the results of the pre- and postevaluations. However, Robinson (1998, personal communication) indicated that the treatment completes improved on almost all of the measures of program objectives but that these improvements were not related to their reoffending. On the basis of this result, the Programs Division of the Correctional Service of Canada has redesigned the evaluation framework, developing measures that will more directly assess program content. To date, there have been no outcome studies assessing the new evaluation framework. This effort is consistent with our argument for developing strong inference designs in program evaluations.

Outside of the Correctional Service of Canada, a number of studies have evaluated the effectiveness of cognitive skills training on offenders. The best controlled of these was conducted for the Colorado Judicial Department on a specialized drug offender program (SDOP) (Johnson and Hunter 1992). Prior to data collection, the researchers developed a comprehensive measure designed to assess clients' progress against the program's objectives. The objectives included reduction of drug use and other factors associated with criminal behavior, and improvement in skills and attitudes conducive to a more productive, prosocial lifestyle. All the factors were selected based on their relevance to the goals of the program and their association with subsequent drug use or unlawful behavior.

The study randomly assigned 134 offenders with significant addiction problems to one of three groups: the SDOP with the cognitive skills program, the SDOP without the cognitive skills program, and regular probation. Johnson and Hunter obtained complete pretest batteries from 124 of the clients, while only eighty completed the posttest. After an average follow-up period of eight months, results indicated that cognitive skills training reduced the probability of revocation. Revocation rates were 41.7 percent (15/36) for the regular probation group, 29.4 percent (15/51) for the SDOP/noncognitive group, and 25.5 percent (12/47) for the SDOP/cognitive group. In this study, the risk principle was confirmed. The treatment effect was more significant with the high-risk clients and for those with very high scores on an addictions severity index. The high-risk clients who participated in the SDOP, either with or without the cognitive skills program, had a revocation rate of 35 percent, while the high-risk clients in the regular probation group had a revocation rate of 75 percent. Those clients with high addiction scores who participated in either SDOP treatment group had a revocation rate 60 percent lower than did highly addicted clients in the regular probation group. In this short-term follow-up, the SDOP/noncognitive program option appeared to be most effective with the younger, more disturbed clients. The SDOP/cognitive option was more effective with the older clients (over age thirty) and those with severe substance abuse scores. Diagnostic and survey measures suggest that the cognitive program intervention was not effective with offenders scoring higher on measures associated with psychiatric problems and sociopathy (high normlessness, low empathy, and low belief that criminal behavior is wrong). Posttest results on the measures described above that assessed the extent to which the program met its identified goals indicated that, for the majority of needs, the success rates for clients in the SDOP/cognitive group were higher than success rates in the SDOP/noncognitive group. On sixteen of the eighteen dimensions, the success rates for the two SDOP treatment groups were better than success rates for the regular probation group.

In a later publication, Johnson and Hunter (1995) reported an extension of the study. Examining the survivors of the initial study, 35 percent (8/23) of the regular probation, 30 percent (10/33) of the SDOP/noncognitive group, and 19 percent (6/32) of the SDOP cognitive group were revoked at the end of another year. According to the researchers, this demonstrated that the treatment effect for the SDOP/cognitive group did not diminish over a longer term. Because this was an analysis of survivors, these results could be attributed to characteristics of the remaining clients and not the long-term effect of treatment. A better approach to the survivability of offenders could be addressed with a well-controlled event history analysis that would indicate the hazard of revocation over time.

In the United Kingdom, the cognitive skills program is known as the Reasoning and Rehabilitation program. In the community, the program has been delivered and evaluated in the Mid Glamorgan Probation Service as the Straight Thinking on Probation Program, or STOP (Raynor and Vanstone 1996). Probationers whose risk ratings were high were included in the study. Raynor and Vanstone (1996) compared probationers who completed STOP with offenders referred to other probation options and who had actuarial risk rates similar to the STOP completes. Results from the twelve-month follow-up indicated that the STOP completes' ($n = 59$) actual rate of reconviction was eight percentage points lower than their expected rates (39 percent as opposed to 47 percent, respectively). The actual reconviction rates of the other probationers ($n = 100$) were equivalent to their expected rates. These results, however, appear to have diminished after two years. After two years, the STOP completes' predicted rate of reconviction was 66 percent. Their actual reconviction rate was 68 percent and was closer to the actual rates of the nontreatment comparison groups.

The STOP completes appear to have received relatively lighter sentences on reconviction, suggesting that they engaged in less serious crimes. Only 2 percent (one) of the STOP completes received a custodial sentence after two years, while 15 percent (twenty-five) of the regular probationers received a further custodial sentence. While these results are encouraging, there was very high attrition within the STOP group. Thirty-eight percent of the original group dropped out before completion. This could have produced a biased picture of program success.

The program has been implemented in various other probation sites throughout the United Kingdom. Data collection in almost all of these sites is largely limited to consumer feedback and, in some rarer cases, assessment of the improvement in intermediate variables that could be expected to change with participation in the program. The exception is the Swindon Probation Service where an informal recidivism outcome study was completed. James McGuire (1995a) reported on a follow-up of fifteen offenders involved in the Reasoning and Rehabilitation—R & R program—and a comparison group of fourteen offenders, who were offered an intensive job search service but were not given R & R. In the six-month follow-up, 21 percent of the comparison group were reconvicted and 13 percent of the R & R group. More significantly, in a twelve-month follow-up, 64 percent (9/14) of the comparison group and 38 percent (5/13) of the R & R group reoffended. The results, however, were based on unofficial outcome data collected by the staff at the probation service, and the report does not provide any information on the comparability of the two groups.

For the last five years, the R & R program has been implemented within the British Prison Service. The service has stressed high standards of program implementation, including selection, training, and monitoring of the program trainers. The program has been effectively incorporated into the prison regime. To date, the service has only preliminary outcome data from the first phase of program implementation from October 1993 to March 1996 (Cookson 1998). The implementation of R & R coincided with the development and implementation of the Thinking Skills program, a shorter cognitive program. At the time of the evaluation, the Thinking Skills program was still under development, and staff training and supervision had not reached the same high standard as it had for the R & R program. One-year reconviction rates for the R & R program, the Thinking Skills program, and the comparison group of offenders released from prison at the same time but who had not received programming demonstrated a significant treatment effect. Cookson reported that the standardized reconviction rates for the three groups (adjusted for the effects of the covariates of previous offenses and risk score) were 21 percent for the R & R group ($n = 46$), 38 percent for the Thinking Skills group ($n = 92$), and 40 percent ($n = 857$) for the comparison group. She did not, however, report on the selection criteria or the dropout rates. Although the number of subjects was low, it appears that the program was effective for all offense groups but particularly effective for offenders over twenty-five years old and for nonproperty offenders. In Cookson's opinion, the poorer results achieved with the Thinking Skills program were because the program was not as well developed as the R & R cognitive skills program. This result, she argued, should bolster confidence that the R & R results were due to treatment and not self-selection. However, there is a way in which the different program results could have been due to selection. If the R & R program produced more dropouts than the Thinking Skills program, then the results could have been completely attributable to selection. Thus it is very important to report whether attrition or self-selection is occurring, the extent of that selection, and the results of analyses that include program completes and dropouts.

B. Conclusions

There is modest evidence that the CTSP reduces criminal recidivism in general offender populations. There is stronger evidence that positive results are more likely among certain subgroups. For example, two studies suggest that the program is not effective, or not as effective, with young offenders (under twenty-five) or with property offenders. The largest of the Canadian studies and the evaluation of the SDOP program in Colorado point to poorer results for the highest-risk offenders and offenders with psychopathic characteristics, respectively. Apart from consideration of program effectiveness based on recidivism data, several studies tapping consumers' reports (testimonials from participants and from the staff at the sites where the program has been delivered) are almost uniformly very positive. This is not a negligible consideration for administrators who are looking for initiatives that can contribute to rehabilitation goals by creating a more positive and collaborative correctional environment.

Most of the successes with the program are in probation settings. The one major study of incarcerated adults in the federal correctional system in Canada produced no treatment effect on the incarcerated group until secondary analyses were conducted. These analyses suggest that a further study should be done to assess rigorously the degree to which cognitive skills training may work for some adult incarcerated populations and not others. Although all studies that assessed the outcome of offenders on relevant intermediate variables reported significant improvements, even the best-designed of the studies reviewed here could not satisfy Platt's requirement of a "strong inference" design that demonstrates that the positive change on pre- and postmeasures is linked to reductions in recidivism. Producing significant reductions in criminal recidivism, however, is a particularly rigorous test of an intervention. Criminality is a complex, multidimensional behavior that, among high-risk groups, is persistent and very resistant to change. Many mental health interventions are considered effective if they simply produce improvements on intermediate variables. As Loesel observed, "Meta-analyses in other fields frequently are based on 'softer' outcome criteria, shorter follow-up intervals, less disturbed clients for so-called analog groups, and treatment motivation, the milieu, and the treatment setting are at times more favorable" (Loesel 1995*b*).

Based on the data to date, admittedly less strong than one would like, we can probably conclude that CTSP outcomes could be improved in several ways. Program effectiveness could be enhanced by screening out the most resistant offenders. Since high-risk offenders pose a particular problem, a second approach is to measure and treat their needs by applying some of the recent approaches from the substance abuse field on the readiness model of change (Miller and Rollnick 1991; Prochaska and DiClementi 1986), or by providing more intensive treatment and longer-term follow-up. The CTSP, as designed in Canada, is not expensive to deliver. Nonprofessional staff can be trained within months. If expert monitoring and support are provided, the program can be maintained at a high standard. In Correctional Service Canada, costs per offender for completion of the program are estimated at $1,100 Canadian ($660 U.S.). With costs this low, the treatment effects need not be large to justify implementation of the program in correctional sites. Furthermore, the cognitive skills program could be considered a preparation or foundation course that can be used in conjunction with other intervention approaches. The interaction and cumulative effect of different offender treatment interventions may be the next major research challenge. As Lipsey has shown for juveniles, multimodal treatment can be quite successful. However, to date, the research on multimodal correctional treatment has not been systematic.

IV. Effects of Intensive Drug Treatment in Prison on Postrelease Outcomes

There is compelling evidence that levels of crime are dramatically amplified by use of drugs among a significant number of individuals who commit crime (Anglin and Speckart 1988; Nurco, Kinlock, and Hanlon 1990). For this reason, correctional systems have come under increasing pressure to introduce treatments that reduce or eliminate drug relapse as a way to moderate criminality when offenders are released. Wexler, Lipton, and their colleagues have presented evidence which they claim demonstrates that therapeutic communities or intensive residential substance abuse treatment within prison should be the primary intervention for drug-dependent offenders. Wexler has summarized the evidence on what he believes is a movement toward the use of intensive prison-based drug treatment to reduce recidivism. A panel of experts on corrections, social services, and substance abuse at a meeting sponsored by the Center for Substance Abuse Treatment called for implementation of a therapeutic community "in every federal prison and every state prison system" (Wexler 1994, p. 358). Therapeutic communities partly isolate the drug-dependent offender from the rest of the inmate population. This increases group pressure to commit to the program and decreases peer pressure outside of the group to maintain lifestyles associated with drug use.

On balance, we believe the major studies evaluating residential and in-prison treatment show that residential treatment can moderate drug use when offenders are released to the community (Martin, Butzin, and Inciardi 1995; Pelissier 1997; Wexler et al. 1997). The effect of the intervention is strengthened when prison treatment is combined with community treatment during postrelease supervision.

Our enthusiasm is tempered by problems we have found in this research. We have found misinterpretation of statistical analyses. More than one study has compared the experience of inmates treated in prison who were under postrelease community supervision with untreated inmates who were under supervision for a shorter period. Since community supervision, in this context, is usually associated with lower rearrest rates, such comparisons bias results in favor of finding a treatment effect. We have also found studies that compared the outcomes of treatment clients having shorter postrelease risk periods than did untreated clients. This also biases the results in favor of finding a treatment effect. These problems are discussed in detail in Gaes (1997, 1998).

Selection bias permeates this literature. This usually occurs in one of two ways. Sometimes, procedures select only certain inmates for an intervention program or affect who remains in a program. In either case, researchers are comparing a subset of clients with the ability and motivation to complete a program against comparison groups composed both of clients who also would have completed a program and of clients who would have dropped out of a program. This distorts the picture of in-prison residential treatment outcomes. There is some evidence in some studies that selection produces a pool of higher-risk clients in treatment, while in other studies lower-risk cases were selected into treatment. Treatment dropouts also have characteristics usually associated with a higher likelihood of criminal recidivism than the average subject in a comparison group. The effect of these selection pressures is to distort analyses of treatment effects. Some researchers in this area acknowledge the selection problem and attempt to provide solutions. Because of pressures to place inmates in appropriate prisons, pressure from outside influences (e.g., judges) to place particular inmates in a program, and the constant movement of the inmate population, program providers and researchers often have extreme difficulty maintaining the integrity of an experimental or quasi-experimental design.

We are not convinced that therapeutic communities are the only way to treat drug abusing or dependent incarcerated offenders. There is some evidence, coming from evaluations of nonresidential drug treatment in Canada, that other approaches may also reduce drug relapse and recidivism, if carried out in conjunction with community treatment (Millson and Robinson 1992; Millson, Weeks, and Lightfoot 1995). The Canadian experience may be unique. Correctional Service Canada (CSC) uses a systematic appraisal of inmate needs. This is matched by a very large menu of inmate programs intended to address many different deficits. Since drug abusers often have many deficits other than their dependency, a less intensive drug treatment regimen may work in CSC because it occurs in combination with other interventions. At this point, the CSC data are preliminary, and it remains to be seen whether less intensive drug treatments are successful.

Since residential treatment is the most intensive drug abuse treatment offered in adult correctional settings, we concentrate our review on that small set of studies. Our analysis focuses on six studies that evaluated in-prison intensive drug treatment. These programs are listed in table 2 along with sample sizes, methods of controlling for selection bias, drug and recidivism results, and comments.

One difficulty in comparing these programs is that program content is rarely described in any detail. Most modern residential drug treatment programs emphasize the following program components: knowledge of drug abuse, wellness and fitness, cognitive/behavioral treatments, relapse prevention, lots of practice and role playing, techniques to increase motivation, small group sessions, and individual treatment when necessary. Most programs last six to twelve months. Some researchers advocate use of ex-addicts as models and trainers (Wexler 1994). Even where program training manuals are available on request, it is unusual to find any measurement of program components or any assessment of the extent to which treatment participants internalized what they learned. Such measurements would increase understanding of successful intervention strategies and bolster confidence in the results of quasiexperimental designs.

A. Cornerstone Program

To control for selection effects, Field's (1985) evaluation of the Cornerstone Program attempted retrospectively to adjust for differences in treated and untreated clients by measuring and controlling for their criminal histories. Field used indices of criminal history in an attempt to measure the similarity of individuals in different treatment groups that spent varying amounts of time in the program before dropping out. Although Field's intent was to show that treatment duration was the key to treatment success, the analysis showed that treatment clients were very similar with respect to their criminal histories regardless of when or whether they dropped out of treatment. Presumably there are many different reasons why clients drop out of treatment that are unrelated to the level of their criminal histories. If attempts are made to control for selection effects by measuring background variables, some explanation should be offered as to why these background factors predict why clients remain or drop out of treatment. Field's results, reported in table 2, indicate favorable treatment outcomes. After three years, treatment completes had a 46 percent recidivism rate, compared with an 85 percent recidivism rate for dropouts. However, Field's evaluation was confounded by comparing program graduates with comparison groups composed of dropouts and a group that was chosen retrospectively. The dropout rate was extremely high. In a second study, Field reported an analysis in which he noted that of 220 program admissions over a two-year period, only forty inmates graduated (1992, p. 148). With such high attrition rates and without following the program dropouts, it is difficult to draw any conclusions regardless of how well other factors are assessed that predict recidivism.

B. NewVision Program

Initial results of the New Vision residential treatment program indicated that inmates receiving residential and aftercare treatment were less likely to recidivate (7 percent) within six months of release than were inmates who did not receive treatment (16 percent). A design similar to Field's was used to evaluate the program (Simpson et al. 1994; Knight et al. 1995; and Knight et al., forthcoming). The evaluation compared a control group with a treatment group composed of inmates who participated in a nine-month prison-based therapeutic community, followed by three months of community-based residential treatment, followed by one year of outpatient treatment.

Inmates were selected into treatment by use of a screening mecha-

TABLE 2

Residential Drug Treatment Programs: Sample Size (*N*), Nature of Control Group, Recidivism and Relapse Results, and Comments

Program	*N*	Nature of Control Group	Follow-Up Period	Results: Criminal Recidivism	Results: Drug Relapse	Comments
Cornerstone	567	Dropouts and offenders from another jurisdiction	3 years	Prison Tx: 46% Dropout control: 85% Control group 2: 64%	Not reported	Retrospective design, one treatment site
New Vision	297	Volunteer controls	6 months	Prison Tx: 7% Control: 16%	Prison Tx: 38% Control: 55%	Comparisons based on treatment completes, high attrition rates; one treatment site
Stay 'N Out	1,428	Volunteer controls	Variable, up to 3 years	Prison Tx: 27% Control: 41.5%	Not reported	Multivariate results were ambiguous; one treatment site
Amity Right Turn	715	Volunteer controls	12 months	Prison Tx and aftercare: 6.5% Prison Tx completers/aftercare dropouts: 40% Prison Tx completers: 40% Prison Tx dropouts: 45% Intent to treat controls: 34% Controls: 34%	Not reported	Appeared to be different risk periods for the different groups; one treatment site

Key-Crest	457	Random assignment for the aftercare residential phase	6 months	Prison Tx only: 18% Aftercare only: 15% Prison Tx and aftercare: 5% Control: 28%	Prison Tx only: 30% Aftercare only: 15% Prison Tx and aftercare: 3% Control: 65%	Recidivism and relapse data based on interviews of inmates; prison group consisted of only treatment completers; one treatment site
Bureau of Prisons	1,800	Randomly selected drug abusers in sites where no teatment was available	6 months	Prison Tx: 3% Control: 15%	Prison Tx: 20% Control: 35%	Aftercare provided to most program participants, therefore difficult to disentangle its unique contribution; evaluation included 19 different treatment sites with the same treatment regimen

NOTE.—Tx = treatment.

nism given to all inmates who enter Texas Department of Corrections facilities. A treatment referral committee reviewed the inmate's records, which include self-reported drug use. Inmates who had less than nine months remaining on their sentences or who had committed an aggravated offense were excluded from consideration. Inmates who qualified for treatment had their cases forwarded to the Texas Parole Board for final decision on placement in a drug program. Both comparison and treatment subjects completed the initial referral process. The parole board rejected a certain number of inmates for treatment while still granting parole to these inmates. The reasons for these decisions were not specified by the authors. Thus the initial selection process differentiated treatment and comparison subjects. As it turned out, based on a composite risk assessment, treatment subjects were at higher risk for recidivism than were comparison subjects. Nevertheless, parole board members used their "clinical judgment" to refine further the selection process based on some unknown set of "clinical" criteria.

The attrition process for this evaluation was described comprehensively and provides a good indication of how difficult it is to conduct follow-up interviews for this population once released to the community. Of 482 treatment referrals, 386 (80 percent) graduated; 29 inmates (6 percent) were transferred for medical reasons, outstanding warrants, or inappropriate classification of drug problems; and 67 (14 percent) were terminated for program noncompliance. Unfortunately, no attempt was made to follow up on the program terminations. Also, there was attrition among those who completed the program and those who constituted the control group. At the time of the six-month follow-up, only 222 of the original 386 treatment graduates and seventy-five of 121 control group inmates released to parole could be interviewed. Attrition was due to offenders who moved out of the area accessible to interviewers, who were recommitted to prison, who could not be located, or who refused to be interviewed. While the outcomes of this evaluation are encouraging, the differences may be completely attributable to selection processes.

C. Stay 'N Out and Amity Right Turn Programs

Another technique that has been used to control for selection bias is to offer a program and choose volunteers who have sufficient time remaining on their sentences to complete it. Control groups are chosen from inmates who do not have enough time to complete the program. It is unlikely that there is a relationship between the time remaining on an inmate's sentence, the level of treatment motivation, and the risk of relapse. Under these conditions, the evaluation results will generalize only to treatment volunteers. Nevertheless, the results should be unbiased if no other factors influence program participation and program outcomes.

This technique has been used to evaluate the Stay 'N Out Program in New York State (Wexler and Chin 1981; Wexler and Williams 1986; Wexler, Falkin, and Lipton 1988, 1990; Wexler et al. 1992) and the Amity Right Turn Project funded by the California Department of Corrections (Wexler et al. 1997). A multivariate analysis of the data from the Stay 'N Out program showed that treatment volunteers to a therapeutic community were more likely to recidivate in a postrelease period than were comparison volunteers receiving no treatment or less intensive treatment. Although some of the univariate results may have been more favorable, we believe the multivariate analyses were more appropriate.

The evaluation of the Amity Right Turn Project used a more complicated design (Wexler et al. 1997). Inmates who volunteered to be treated, had a drug problem, and were within nine to fourteen months of their parole release composed a waiting list of eligible participants. From this pool, inmates were randomly selected to participate in the prison therapeutic community. Inmates who were eligible but could not be treated prior to their release composed the control group ($n = 290$). There were four treatment groups consisting of inmates randomly selected for treatment. The composition of the four study groups depended on whether they volunteered for postrelease community-based treatment and whether they completed the prison or community-based program. Thus the first group was composed of inmates who volunteered for the prison program but who were terminated (prison treatment dropouts, $n = 95$). The second group consisted of inmates who completed the prison drug program but did not volunteer for the community-based program (prison treatment completions, $n = 193$). The third group was composed of inmates who volunteered and completed prison drug treatment and who volunteered and were terminated from the community-based program (prison treatment completions/community based dropouts, $n = 45$). The fourth group was composed of inmates who volunteered and completed both the prison and the community-based programs (prison completions/community based completions, $n = 92$).

Wexler et al. reported that the no treatment control group had significantly higher reincarceration proportions at twelve and twenty-four months after release from prison than did all the other study groups combined. The twelve-month comparison indicated that 49.7 percent of the control group recidivated, while the combined recidivism percentage of all four study groups was 33.9 percent. At twenty-four months, these percentages were 59 and 42.6, respectively. When the combined result was separated into the control group and four study groups, the five groups had the following reincarceration percentages at twelve months: control group, 49.7; prison treatment dropouts, 45; prison treatment completions, 40; prison treatment completions/community based dropouts, 40; prison treatment completions/community-based completions, 6.5.[1] A logistic regression of background factors in conjunction with the treatment effect indicated that reincarceration was 42 percent less likely for the combined treatment groups than for the control group.

Wexler et al. acknowledge that their results were confounded because, during the postrelease period, inmates who were receiving treatment in the community-based therapeutic community were at much lower risk than were other study group releasees simply by their residence in the facility. This would also affect the twenty-four-month outcomes. If the risk periods were defined as beginning the day after release from the community-based facility or the day after release from prison for clients who did not participate in the community-based facility, the "risk environment" would have been more comparable for the different groups involved in the evaluation. It is clear from analysis of the individual study groups that the dramatic differences between the combined study group and the control group were primarily attributable to the prison treatment completion/community-based completion group, the same group whose risk environment was much more benign. Although no analysis was presented, there were much more modest differences between the control group and the other three study groups composed of inmates who spent little or no time in the community-based aftercare facility.

Second, as the authors acknowledge, while they were able to control for selection bias during the prison treatment phase, they were unable to control for selection bias during the community-based treatment

---

[1] Wexler et al. (1997) do not provide percentages of inmates who were reincarcerated for the prison dropouts, prison completions, and prison completions/community-based dropouts groups. We estimated these percentages from a bar chart represented as figure 1.

phase. Thus, there was a nonrandom selection process operating during the community phase of treatment.

D. Key-Crest Program

The Key-Crest Program is a drug treatment intervention occurring in three phases (Martin, Butzin, and Inciardi 1995; Martin, Inciardi, and Saum 1995; Inciardi et al. 1997). The Key component is a prison therapeutic community for inmates in the Delaware corrections system. Crest, the second component, involves inmates released to a community work-release center where they maintain jobs in the community but live in a facility where they continue their drug treatment in a modified therapeutic community. In the final component, offenders are released to the community under parole or some other form of supervision.

The results to date suggest that residential treatment in combination with aftercare can significantly reduce drug relapse and recidivism (see table 2). The authors controlled for selection bias by randomly assigning inmate volunteers to treatment and control groups without justifying the decision. Thus, unlike the previous study, which excluded inmate volunteers only if they did not have a sufficient amount of time remaining on their sentence to complete the program, no justification was given to volunteers who were randomly assigned to a no-treatment comparison group in the Key-Crest study. The Key-Crest program used such a technique for two of their four study groups. As noted in DeLeon, Inciardi, and Martin (1995), some of the group receiving drug treatment in a work-release center were clients who did not volunteer for treatment but were motivated by the possibility of an early release. Some of these inmates "displayed negative attitudes toward the treatment program, which generally led to their quitting or being discharged from the Crest program" (1995, p. 88). One can only suspect that inmates who volunteered for treatment and were assigned to a control group viewed this as a capricious decision.

The research design consisted of four groups. The Key group was composed of inmates selected by correctional counselors and who volunteered to participate in the prison-based therapeutic community. Because the Crest program had not yet been implemented, these inmates were the only Key program participants who did not subsequently participate in the Crest stage. The second group consisted of Key-Crest inmates who participated in both stages. Virtually all Key graduates were allowed to participate in Crest after it was implemented. The third and fourth groups were composed of inmates who had drug abuse problems, had not participated in Key, and were given the opportunity to participate in the Crest work-release program. On a random basis, half of these volunteers were provided the Crest program (Crest-only group), while half participated in work release in the absence of residential drug treatment (comparison group). Thus the comparison group were inmates who had drug abuse problems, had volunteered for Crest, and had not received in-prison TC drug treatment but had received AIDS/HIV prevention education.

An eighteen-month follow-up showed that 77 percent of Key-Crest participants reported being arrest-free, while 57 percent of Crest only, 43 percent of Key only, and 46 percent of the comparison group reported being arrest free. While these results are promising, there were two selection biases operating. The first involved selection into the Key and Key-Crest groups. It appears that the selection depended on staff evaluations of candidates for the program. The second selection process occurred as a result of the way baseline data were gathered. These data were gathered just prior to an inmate's release from prison. Baseline data were collected on Key graduates, but not on Key terminations. Thus only Key graduates were followed in the longitudinal design. Data were gathered on Crest and comparison subjects at baseline in the absence of any knowledge about potential future attrition in these two groups. Thus both the Key and Key-Crest groups were composed of inmates who were motivated enough to graduate from the Key component of this program. Even though Key-Crest participants had the opportunity in this design to drop out of the program while they were in the Crest stage, this group already was composed of a very select group of motivated individuals. However, all inmates in the Crest-only group were followed even if they dropped out of the program (Inciardi 1997). Despite these limitations, the data offer further support for the proposition that residential treatment, in combination with aftercare, is an important determinant of drug treatment success.

E. Residential Treatment in the Bureau of Prisons

Another approach that can be used to evaluate inmate programs in the presence of selection bias is to model the selection process and use this information in a simultaneous test of the selection process and the program outcome. This was the approach adopted by Pelissier (1997) to evaluate in-prison drug-treatment programs administered in nineteen federal prisons. The federal residential drug-treatment program consists of all of the components listed at the beginning of this section. However, the program did not use prior inmates who had been drug abusers as trainers or treatment providers. Ninety-six percent of women and 92 percent of men who completed residential treatment in prison also received community aftercare. Thus there was no explicit test of the two components of the program. Pelissier (1997) selected comparison subjects from the nineteen sites where treatment was available as well as sites where there was no treatment available. Inmates with a moderate-to-severe drug abuse problem could volunteer to participate in an intensive in-prison treatment program.

To analyze comparison subjects from treatment sites, Pelissier used statistical procedures to model the selection process in treatment sites while simultaneously testing the effect of treatment on postrelease relapse and recidivism. These procedures have been suggested by Heckman (1979). The analysis demonstrated that there was a selection process, that this process would have biased the results against finding an effect of treatment, and that a treatment effect did occur. Multivariate survival analysis indicated that within the first six months of release into the community, 20 percent of the treated and 36 percent of the untreated inmates had at least one drug relapse (positive urinalysis test). Furthermore, 3.1 percent of the treated and 15 percent of the untreated inmates were arrested on a new charge. The study also showed that one of the most important determinants of postrelease criminal recidivism was whether the offender had a drug relapse. This study suggests that in-prison treatment combined with aftercare may have dramatic effects, at least in the short term. An analysis of long-term findings is forthcoming.

F. Conclusions

There is some evidence that intensive drug treatment in prison may reduce drug relapse and criminal recidivism in the first six to eighteen months after release. The Key-Crest, Amity Right Turn, and Bureau of Prisons studies have the strongest research and analysis designs. Future studies should also measure and report two fundamental characteristics of their treatment and comparison groups—the level of drug dependence and the level of risk of criminal recidivism. Since treatment effects depend on these characteristics, future reviews of drug treatment would benefit from an assessment of the extent to which studies are evaluating interventions with similar or different client pools. A common measurement device for drug abuse/dependence and risk of criminal recidivism would be the best solution. However, even categorical or qualitative measures indicating whether treatment was working for low- or high-drug-dependent clients and low- or high-risk-of-recidivism prisoners would give a better understanding of the effectiveness of drug treatment. The two most compelling determinants of the effectiveness of drug treatment are the nature and intensity of the intervention and the drug dependence and risk of the client. Future work that characterizes the components of treatment will also allow more systematic comparisons between different treatment approaches.

V. Prison Education and Work Programs

Education and work programs are the cornerstones of correctional intervention. Ironically, given the historical prominence of school and work as prison programming, the empirical data on the impact of these activities on offenders' lives is limited. The available evidence, however, is encouraging. Despite methodological shortcomings and challenges, the evidence suggests that carefully designed and administered education and work programs can improve inmates' institutional behavior, reduce recidivism, and promote involvement in prosocial activities after release.

A. Prison Education and Prisoner Behavior

Labor and education programs are the oldest and most enduring of all correctional intervention methods. Educational programs for inmates have been a fixture of American correctional efforts for more than 150 years. The rationale for providing educational services to inmates flows directly from the educational deficits that offenders bring with them to the prison. These educational deficiencies are part of a set of failures and negative experiences that include dysfunctional family relationships, inability to obtain and hold legitimate jobs, pathological relationships with members of the opposite sex, substance abuse histories, and many other criminologically relevant markers (criminogenic needs).

Improving inmates' educational skills may reduce recidivism through several mechanisms. First, providing inmates with sufficient reading and writing skills to enable functional literacy may increase the possibility of lawful employment after release from prison. Since post-release employment is an important factor in enabling ex-offenders to remain crime free, educational programming in prisons may reduce recidivism by improving job opportunities. Second, the education process per se may be helpful in reducing recidivism by facilitating the maturation, conscientiousness, and dedication that educational achievement requires. In this view, education may equip offenders to evaluate their environments and their decisions more thoughtfully and, therefore, make better decisions that will assist them in remaining out of prison when released. A related argument is that through exposure to the worlds of literature, mathematics, science, humanities, and the arts, the offender may develop a broader frame of reference within which to evaluate life choices. The educational setting within the prison also represents an opportunity for inmates to interact with civilian employees in the context of a nonauthoritarian, goal-directed relationship.

Education programs aimed at developing basic literacy and communication skills have been offered in prisons since the earliest U.S. reformatories were established in the 1870s. These programs were often an adjunct to the primary reform program, religious instruction. Academic and vocational education programs began to play a central role in rehabilitative programming in the 1930s, and by the 1960s postsecondary education programs were a feature of most U.S. prison systems (Gerber and Fritsch 1994).

Despite decades of experience with educational programs in U.S. prisons, the research literature on the efficacy of such programming in reducing criminal recidivism is not well developed. In part, this is because for decades no prison programs were formally evaluated. The development of correctional policy in the United States during most of the twentieth century has been guided by intuition, benevolent intentions, and experience rather than by empirical analyses of what works in reducing reoffending. One of the most striking aspects of the famous research survey reported by Lipton, Martinson, and Wilks (1975) was the small number of studies available on nearly every form of correctional treatment. This lack of a solid research base concerning the efficacy of educational programs is the result of many factors, but the design and delivery of educational programs in prisons has commonly violated many of the principles of effective correctional treatment described earlier. That is, educational programs in prison have not been directed to specific criminogenic needs of offenders, have not been part of a multimodal intervention strategy, have not considered responsivity effects, have not been tailored to address the needs of offenders in different risk classifications, and have not been adequately funded to permit the high doses of educational intervention that many offenders require. For Lipton et al., informed public policy requires solid "evidence concerning the differential effects of education programs on postrelease behavior" (1975, p. 363).

Evaluating prison education programs brings the researcher face to face with the thorny problems of selection bias described above in relation to other treatment programs. State legislation or correctional agency policy often dictates assignment to educational programs, so random assignment is impossible. The differential motivation for treatment, and differential attrition from treatment observed in the context of educational programming makes it virtually impossible unambiguously to attribute postrelease recidivism to the effects of educational programming in prison. Researchers have responded to this challenge by using a variety of quasi-experimental designs to assay the effects of educational programming, but these designs often fall short of the kind of empirical evidence that would support rational policy making and program development.

Gerber and Fritsch (1994) conducted a comprehensive assessment of the research literature on correctional education. They divided the studies into three subject areas: academic education (further divided into adult basic/secondary education and college education), vocational education, and social education (often called life skills training). They used three elemental criteria to include studies in their review: the presence of a control or comparison group, use of some form of control (e.g., matching of experimental and control subjects, random assignment to program enrollment, or post hoc statistical control), and reporting of tests of statistical significance. Gerber and Fritsch assigned a "methodology score" to the studies they reviewed. One point each was assigned for each occurrence of the criteria discussed above.

Fourteen studies of *precollege education* programs examined postrelease recidivism as the criterion variable. Measures of program involvement varied across studies, ranging from earning the General Equivalency Diploma (GED) or completion of a prescribed academic program, to "participation" or "enrollment in academic course work" as the measure of program exposure. For example, Anderson, Anderson, and Schumacker (1988) measured educational program exposure by completion of the GED or high school diploma, or higher. Nine of the fourteen studies found educational program participation to be related to reduced recidivism. Of the seven studies that received the highest methodology score, three found no relationship between educational programming and recidivism, and four showed inverse correlations; the more education, the lower the recidivism.

Porporino and Robinson (1992) monitored 1,736 adult basic education (ABE) participants released from Canadian prisons in 1988. Among those who completed the ABE program (equivalent to completion of eighth grade), 30.1 percent were readmitted to prison during the follow-up period. Recidivism was 35.5 percent among those who were released from prison before the ABE program could be completed, and 41.6 percent among those who withdrew from the ABE program. Porporino and Robinson also reported that the effects of ABE program participation were especially effective among higher-risk offenders.

In addition to recidivism measures, Gerber and Fritsch examined four studies that investigated relations between educational program participation and postrelease employment, and two studies that examined postrelease participation in education as criterion variables. Three of the four studies of postrelease employment found that inmates who participated in or completed prison education programming were more likely to be employed after release. Both of the studies that examined postrelease participation in education showed that inmates who participated in educational programming while confined were more likely to continue that participation in the community after release.

Gerber and Fritsch examined fourteen studies of the effect of *college* programs in prisons. Again, measurement of program participation varied across studies, from simple measures of "participation," to completion of twelve college credit hours, to completion of a college degree. Overall, they found that "most studies [ten of fourteen] report an inverse relationship between college education and recidivism" (1994, p. 6). As participation in college programs increased, recidivism rates decreased. Many of the researchers who carried out these studies recognized, however, that confounding effects were substantial. For example, Thorpe, MacDonald, and Bala (1984) reported on a study of New York inmates in which earning a college degree was associated with substantially lower return to prison rates, but the investigators acknowledged that graduates may succeed because of unmeasured attributes such as "motivation" and "competence." As with the studies of basic and secondary education reviewed by Gerber and Fritsch, analyses of college programming found that participants were more likely to be employed after release (three of three studies) and more likely to participate in additional educational opportunities after release, and that college program participants may have more favorable prison disciplinary records than nonparticipants.

Vocational education programming in prisons takes numerous forms, from masonry trades to computer training. Again, the premise of these programs is that the *acquisition* of vocational skills involves commitment, goal-setting and motivation, and learning of technical and nontechnical knowledge, and that the acquisition of vocational skills increases ex-offenders' legitimate employment opportunities after release. Therefore, positive effects on in-prison and postprison rule conformity are presumed. Gerber and Fritsch examined thirteen studies of vocational education programs and found an inverse relationship between participation and recidivism in nine studies. Thus participation in vocational education programs was associated with reduced recidivism rates. As an example, Saylor and Gaes (1992) investigated vocational technical training in the Federal Bureau of Prisons and found that "inmates who received vocational training while in prison showed better 'institutional adjustment' (fewer rule violations) than those who did not receive such training, were more likely to complete stays in a halfway house, were less likely to have their paroles revoked, and were more likely to be employed after release" (in Gerber and Fritsch 1994, p. 8).

Gerber and Fritsch also reported on a small group of studies that probed the effect of "life skills" or *social education training*. These programs are, in many respects, even more difficult to evaluate than traditional academic or vocational education programs. First, the content of these programs varies widely. Some focus on skills needed for daily living, such as hygiene, social interaction norms, and basic financial management. Others focus on skills such as conflict avoidance and verbal communication skills. Second, the measurement of improvement in "coping skills," "problem solving," or "moral development" is itself especially vulnerable to measurement error. Despite these important problems related to reliability and validity, a few studies claim to have documented improvement in these psychosocial dimensions. The relationship between this "personal growth" and reduced recidivism is not documented.

Taken together, Gerber and Fritsch summarized more than ninety studies of various aspects of prison education and behavioral outcomes during and after incarceration. Acknowledging that "without adequate control techniques, it is difficult to speak definitively about the impact of correctional education programs," they concluded that "research shows a fair amount of support for the hypotheses that adult academic and vocational correctional education programs lead to fewer disciplinary violations during incarceration, reductions in recidivism, increases in employment opportunities, and to increases in participation in education upon release" (1994, p. 11).

A multifaceted study of recidivism among more than 14,000 inmates released from Texas prisons in 1991 and 1992 underscored their conclusion (Adams et al. 1994). The study investigated several behavioral outcomes associated with educational programming. Among other findings, this study demonstrated the importance of operationalization of the program "participation" variable. For example, when participation in Texas prison education programs was operationalized as a simple dichotomy, without reference to time spent in the program or measurable educational achievement, there was no relationship with recidivism, defined as reincarceration. When program participation was measured by hours of program participation, however, both vocational and academic education programs yielded reduced recidivism among inmates whose exposure to the programs was greatest. For example, "inmates with fewer than 100 hours in academic programs (at the time of release) had a reincarceration rate of 25 percent compared to 16.6 percent for inmates with more than 300 hours in academic programs and 23.6 percent for inmates who did not participate in academic programs. Similarly, inmates with fewer than 100 hours in vocational programs had a recidivism rate of 22.8 percent, inmates with more than 300 hours in vocational programs had a rate of 18.3 percent, and inmates who did not participate in vocational programs had a rate of 22.4 percent" (Adams et al. 1994, p. 442).

Adams et al. also found an important interaction of program exposure and offenders' needs for educational programming. Confirming the risk principle, the greatest reduction in recidivism was evidenced among inmates whose initial educational achievement levels were low and who received the highest level of exposure to educational programming. "When these two factors [were] combined, the data suggest that the recidivism rate can be reduced by about one third if extensive services are targeted at inmates at the lowest level of educational achievement" (Adams et al. 1994, p. 447). The researchers concluded by echoing the view of many correctional investigators: "correctional intervention works best when programs are matched with offenders' needs and are delivered in a concerted, purposeful manner. This point implies that correctional program administrators must be more successful in assigning inmates to programs so as to maximize the use of resources and minimize the prospect of recidivism" (Adams et al. 1994, pp. 448–49).

B. Prison Labor and Prisoner Behavior

Research on prison labor is also encouraging. It appears that prison work experience operates through several mechanisms to produce better-behaved prisoners during confinement, lower recidivism rates after release, and higher rates of involvement in constructive employment after release.

If education is the oldest prison treatment program, work is the oldest activity within prisons. Indeed, the much chronicled debate between the designers of the Auburn congregate system and the Pennsylvania solitary system of prison organization was essentially a conflict about the most efficient system to organize production under conditions of maximum security. And, just as offenders present deficient educational records on entry to prison, their work histories also reflect sketchy or nonexistent employment records, few marketable skills, and an inadequate work ethic. Thus the purpose of prison labor has always been multifaceted and includes inculcation of positive work attitudes and the development of personal self-discipline and marketable skills. In addition to these offender-focused goals, prison work programs have sought to be economically self-sufficient (if not profitable), and to keep inmates occupied in productive activities that reduce the management dangers associated with inmate idleness. The administration of prison labor programs, and the question whether such programs assist in reducing recidivism is complicated by the multiple goals and objectives that are sought through prison labor (Flanagan 1989). As a research issue, prison labor also suffers from definitional ambiguity; the definition of "prison work assignment" may range from innocuous and unimportant institutional maintenance assignments to forty-hour weeks in industrial shops that approximate real world work practices. Moreover, as prison populations have burgeoned during the last ten years, correctional agencies have not kept pace in providing industry-like jobs for inmates. Thus in examining the effects of prison employment on inmate behavior, the researcher must be very careful to specify the nature of the intervention.

The paucity of empirical evaluations of the effect of prison work is indicated by Lipton, Martinson, and Wilks's (1975) failure to consider institutional employment at all. As recently as 1984, a committee of the Association of the Bar of the City of New York observed that "there is no empirical study showing lower recidivism rates among inmates who have participated in meaningful vocational training and/or prison industry programs" (1984, p. 299). In most studies, to date, the approach has been to compare recidivism rates of prisoners released after having worked in prison industry with rates for a comparison group of nonemployed releasees. Ex post facto control of potential selection bias is usually attempted by disaggregating the work and nonwork groups on recidivism-relevant variables. This is the approach that a Task Force on Correctional Industries of the Utah Department of Corrections took in finding that the one-year return-to-prison rate for all inmates released in 1983 was 29 percent, compared with 13 percent for correctional industry participants released during the same period (State of Utah 1984). To test for selection bias, the researchers compared the industry and nonindustry groups on race, marital status, number of dependents, religion, previous occupation and work record, crime seriousness, prior arrests and incarcerations, and measures of drug and alcohol use. No significant differences were reported on these variables.

Basinger's (1985) research on offenders employed in Ohio Prison Industries employed a similar design but reported modest and nonsignificant differences in recidivism between employed and nonemployed releasees. Similarly, Johnson (1984) found no significant differences between prison industry-employed prisoners and those who were not employed in prison in a two-year community follow-up.

Flanagan et al. (1988) studied the effect of prison industry in a large sample of New York offenders. Industry participants had worked in prison shops for at least six continuous months, and a comparison group was selected from inmates confined in the same facilities during the same time period. However, prison industry participants were older, were serving longer sentences, had served more time in prison, were more likely to have been employed prior to arrest, were less likely to be preprison drug users, and were more likely to be black or Hispanic than were members of the comparison group. Several measures of recidivism were examined. In all but one comparison, there were no significant differences between employed and nonemployed inmates. When controls were imposed for recidivism-relevant differences between the groups, the recidivism rates were virtually identical. In terms of in-prison behavior, however, participation in prison industry was consistently associated with lower rates of disciplinary problems. In evaluating the finding of no significant effect of industry participation on recidivism, one must keep in mind that "employment" among the treatment group in this study lasted an average of eighteen months and was characterized by a typical work week of twenty-six hours.

The most comprehensive and rigorous study of the effect of prison work and vocational training was conducted by the Office of Research and Evaluation of the U.S. Federal Bureau of Prisons (Saylor and Gaes 1992). Unlike previous studies described above, the Post-Release Employment Project (PREP) used a prospective, longitudinal design that featured careful matching of study group participants (those who were employed or received vocational training while imprisoned) and control cases, and followed almost 7,000 subjects through the release experience to twelve months after discharge from prison. The PREP study found that study group inmates were more likely to be employed after release, more likely successfully to complete a halfway house stay, and less likely to have their parole supervision revoked. For example, at twelve months after release, 6.6 percent of study group participants had been revoked, compared with 10.1 percent of comparison group subjects. A study of prison employment in New South Wales (McHutchison 1995) also found that coupling in-prison work experience and work-release transitional programming produced lower recidivism rates.

Saylor and Gaes (1997) also conducted a long-term follow-up of the PREP study and comparison subjects. Bureau of Prisons automated records were searched to determine which inmates had been returned to federal custody for either a new offense or a technical violation of their supervision. In 1995, when these records were searched, if an offender had not been returned to prison, he or she would have been released a minimum of eight years without a federal reconviction. Many of these former PREP study participants had been released for twelve years without a reconviction. A failure time model was used to analyze the possible differences between study group and comparison group releasees. Although there were no significant program effects among women, there were significant differences among the men. Male inmates who had worked in prison industries were 24 percent less likely to recidivate, while those who had participated in either vocational or apprenticeship training were 33 percent less likely to recidivate throughout the follow-up period.

Evaluating the value of prison-based education and work programs in achieving correctional policy goals is a complicated, tenuous undertaking. The prison experience is made up of many diverse elements. In relation to other features of the prison environment, education and work experience may be a small part of the offender's institutional career. The studies reviewed here indicate, however, that public investment in prison work and education programs may be a wise and, considering the total cost of recidivism, a cost-effective investment. When considered as a body of developing scientific work on the impact of prison programs, education and work programs appear able to contribute significantly to increasing offenders' prospects for success. Moreover, the research to date provides correctional authorities with a set of empirically derived guidelines for the design and delivery of such interventions. From a public policy perspective, a retreat from public commitment to investment in prison labor and effective education programs in prison would be misguided.

VI. Treatment of Sex Offenders

Many correctional agencies are being challenged to offer more programming and improved services to sex offenders. Many of these programs are designed to be consistent with the principles outlined at the beginning of this essay. Consistent with the risk principle, Gordon, Holden, and Leis (1991) have argued that sex offender treatment should be concentrated on those who require it the most. Such a recommendation is fraught with ethical and legal questions, not the least of which is trying to decide which category of victim is harmed the most and which type of sex offender is the most at risk to reoffend.

Of the four intervention subdomains we have examined closely, sex offender treatment is the most difficult to summarize (see, e.g., Quinsey 1998). While there are some data to suggest that treatment may reduce recidivism, there are also many qualifications to this conclusion. The sex offender population is heterogeneous, yet many researchers fail consistently to classify and distinguish subgroups of sex offenders. This makes it difficult to know whether treatment failures or successes are comparable across studies.

A. Problems in Sex Offender Classification, Mechanisms of Change, and Treatment Nomenclature

The sex offender literature consists of a diverse collection of studies on exhibitionists, rapists, child molesters, and incest offenders. There is evidence that sex offenders are more likely to "specialize" in certain kinds of deviant sexual behavior than are other offenders, who are classified on the basis of their conviction offense. The extent to which this heterogeneous group of sexual offense "subtypes" overlaps in treatment studies is difficult to determine. Researchers must begin to be more systematic in their classification of sex offender subtypes. Some researchers have been very specific in categorizing client subtype and treatment modality (Lang, Pugh, and Langevin 1988; Knight and Prentky 1990; Marshall and Barbaree 1990; Hagan, King, and Patros 1994), suggesting that different interventions may be more appropriate for different client subtypes. But in general these studies often fail to distinguish offenders by their conviction offense. When researchers do classify sex offenders, they often use different criteria. For example, study participants have been classified not only on the basis of type of conviction but also on the basis of sexual preference or measures of deviant sexual arousal. The absence of uniformity in operational definitions makes comparison of research studies imprecise, since it is not at all clear that different treatment studies are examining the same or even a similar sex offender population.

Another source of confusion arises out of the mechanisms of change proposed in various studies. These include such diverse mechanisms as denial, also called minimization and rationalization (Barbaree 1991), attitudes that are supportive of deviant sexual activity, cognitive distortions (Murphy 1990), social competence skills (Stermac and Quinsey 1986), sexual identity, offender victimization, victim awareness, deviant arousal and fantasy (Laws and Marshall 1990; Quinsey and Earls 1990), anger management/impulse control (Prentky and Knight 1986), and relapse prevention (Pithers 1990). Which of these mechanisms are relevant for which types of sex offenders? Which mechanisms are the most important in sex offending? Are there combinations of mechanisms that act in concert that are highly correlated to sexual offending? These are only some of the questions that researchers will have to address before we can make sense of this treatment area.

It is also important to specify in what setting sex offender treatment is conducted (e.g., residential, outpatient), at what levels of intensity (e.g., duration, focus), employing which treatment techniques (e.g., cognitive-behavioral, pharmacological, psychotherapeutic), and using which modalities (e.g., individual, group). Consequently, any coherent review of the sex offender treatment literature would have to organize studies according to these characteristics. Since many studies fail to report even the most fundamental aspects of treatment, the studies are difficult to review systematically.

B. Problems in Methodology

Within a corrections environment, the random assignment of sex offenders to either "treated" or "nontreated" groups is especially problematic. While some sex offenders who are not motivated to receive
treatment do not willingly participate, many service providers question
the ethics of denying programming to sex offenders who wish to participate but cannot because of the research design (e.g., Marshall
1996). Furthermore, many studies use inappropriate control or comparison groups or lack fundamental matching procedures (Baxter,
Motiuk, and Fortin 1995). For example, studies may compare treatment dropouts to treatment completers, or inmates who deny their sex
offending problems to those who acknowledge them, or incarcerated
sex offenders with those on probation.

Studies of sex offender treatment effectiveness should match treated
offenders with untreated offenders on a set of relevant characteristics
such as release date, age at release, and sentence length (Motiuk, Smiley, and Blanchette 1996). Ideally, the control or comparison group
would also be matched with the treated group on risk factors such as
history of sexual offending and victim age/gender preferences. These
factors have been found to be related to reoffending among sex offenders (Hanson and Bussiere 1996). This presents yet another methodological hurdle to overcome, as selection criteria for treatment could
have adverse impacts on the ability to conduct matching procedures.
This problem is identical to the one we described in detail in our assessment of drug-treatment programs.

Different outcome measures and variable posttreatment follow-up
periods are typical in this area of treatment research. Postrelease outcome studies rarely concur on recidivism rates, in part because of varying definitions of what constitutes "recidivism" (Freeman-Longo and
Knopp 1992). Treatment outcome measures have included self-reports
of new offenses, charges, convictions, or returns to custody. More
stringent definitions of recidivism consider only new convictions for
sex crimes as an outcome measure. Again, the absence of uniformity in
measures makes comparisons difficult.

Because of low base rates of sexual reoffending (Hanson and Bussiere 1996), sample sizes must be exceedingly large. Moreover, reliance
on officially recorded convictions underestimates actual sexual recidivism rates because a great deal of sexual offending goes unreported by
vulnerable or ashamed victims (Weinrott and Saylor 1991). The problem is further compounded by sample attrition since individuals are re-

moved from the study or follow-up for a variety of reasons (Blanchette 1996). Other methodological problems include detailing the therapeutic intervention under investigation, measurement of the service provider's adherence to the treatment protocol, and factoring in the delay between treatment completion and release.

C. Sex Offender Treatment Results

Consistent with the problems that permeate this literature, Quinsey et al. (1993) have questioned whether it is possible to draw any conclusions about the effectiveness of sex offender treatment to reduce sexual reoffending over extended time periods. However, others have argued that some treatments can be empirically demonstrated to be effective with sex offenders and are, in fact, successful in reducing sexual reoffending (Barbaree, Seto, and Maric 1996; Marshall 1996; Robinson 1996). Marques et al. (1994) have reported on an extremely promising evaluation of an experimental sex offender treatment program in California that appears to be methodologically sound. Unfortunately, no conclusive results are available yet.

Hall (1995) produced a meta-analysis of recent sex offender treatment studies that showed a small, but robust, effect size for sex offender treatment. Hall (1995) found that recidivism for untreated sex offenders was 27 percent, compared with 19 percent for treated sex offenders, a relative reduction of 30 percent. Gordon and Nicholaichuk (1996) reported a 24 percent decrease in recidivism for sex offenders receiving cognitive-behavioral treatment. In his study of the Cognitive Skills Training Program discussed in Section III, Robinson (1996) reported a 58 percent reduction in the recidivism of sex offenders who completed treatment while in prison. Although sex offenders appeared to achieve the greatest treatment gains from cognitive skills training relative to other offense groups (violent, drug, property), about one-third had received sex offender treatment before participating in cognitive skills training. While this is suggestive, because of the problems we have noted with this study, future research will have to disentangle whether multiple treatments can enhance the success of intervention and whether there is a particular sequence of treatments that must be followed.

While there is some research that suggests that there may be a modest positive effect of sex offender treatment in prison, we are wary of drawing sweeping conclusions. There is certainly no definitive approach to treatment. Across the many jurisdictions in Canada and the

United States, sex offenders are required to complete a variety of different programs before being considered for release. Then, they may be required to participate in maintenance programs on their release to the community. As yet, the full effects or relative contributions of postprogram efforts (i.e., relapse prevention) to reducing recidivism among sex offenders remain largely untested (Miner et al. 1990).

VII. Future Directions for Correctional Research

There have been major theoretical and methodological advances in the juvenile and adult correctional treatment literature since Lipton, Martinson, and Wilks's (1975) assessment nearly a quarter century ago. We have the rudiments of a theory of intervention that treats criminal behavior as an extension of normative or prosocial behavior. Within the context of psychological learning models, several researchers have proposed a set of principles to be used to extend the social learning model to criminal behavior. Some of these principles need further clarification and empirical assessment.

A. Theoretical Shortcomings

The risk principle, as far as we can tell, has two corollaries. The first is an empirical proposition: "The effects of treatment typically are found to be greater among higher-risk cases than among lower-risk cases" (Andrews et al. 1990, p. 374). The second is prescriptive "and involves the idea of matching levels of treatment services to the risk level of the offender" (Andrews and Bonta 1994, p. 175). As we have shown in several substantive sections of this essay, there are counterexamples to the risk principle as an empirical proposition. There are instances in which lower-risk offenders benefit more from a treatment than do higher-risk offenders. The principle also has been represented as an interaction between the level of risk and the level of treatment. High-intensity interventions work better with high-risk offenders, while low-intensity interventions work better with low-risk clients. To assess this interaction more effectively, more work must be done to classify the intensity of treatments, since several risk scales to predict the likelihood of recidivism are already available.

The needs principle is very intuitive. Specific human deficits directly related to the propensity to commit crime should be addressed. There is a need to specify and classify these needs beyond the level of intuition. Researchers must demonstrate in intervention studies that these human deficits are being treated and that treatment of these deficits leads to reductions in recidivism.

Andrews and Bonta (1994) argue that *the responsivity principle* needs much more development. If this principle is to move beyond the level of tautology—namely, that responsivity is demonstrated by effective treatments—then a great deal of work on the classification of client learning styles and treatment provider techniques must be done.

B. Strong Inference Designs

Too few studies use what Platt (1964) called a "strong inference" design. A strong inference design requires the scientist to articulate clearly both the theoretical reasons and under what conditions a behavioral change (outcome) is expected to occur. The scientist should propose alternative hypotheses or mechanisms of change. A crucial experiment or test should then be conducted. From our perspective, a crucial test includes measurement of the theoretical mechanism that hypothetically causes a change in outcome, development of procedures that ensure the scientific reliability and validity of the measurement of these intervening causal mechanisms, and, finally, proof that changes in these mechanisms are associated with changes in outcomes. Even when a design employs random assignment of clients to conditions, strong inference is bolstered by measurement of the mechanism that mediates change. When the design is quasiexperimental, measuring the mechanism of change is even more important. The principles of correctional treatment help us delineate mechanisms of change. The measurement of risk, treatment intensity, specific needs, and specific treatment styles and techniques will allow stronger inferences to be drawn about the mechanisms of behavior change and the effectiveness of treatment.

Figure 1 represents some of the possible inferences that can be deduced when a strong inference design of a correctional treatment evaluation is used. Three related questions can be asked. Is there a positive change in the pre- to postmeasure of the theoretical mechanism that the social scientist proposes is the source of change in the outcome? Is the magnitude of change in the pre- to postmeasure of the theoretical mechanism correlated with the level of change in outcome? Finally, is the level of outcome for the treatment group better than the level of outcome for the control or comparison group? In Figure 1, we sketched some but not all of the possible paths that lead to different levels of inference depending on the answers to these questions. For

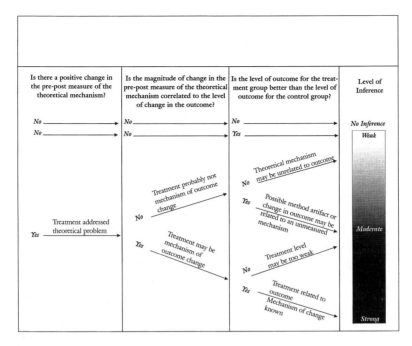

FIG. 1.—Strong and weak inferences

example, the strongest inference comes from an affirmative answer to all three questions. Using these questions also raises other theoretical possibilities. For example, consider the following path: there is an indication that there was a pre- to postdifference in the level of the proposed change mechanism and the magnitude of change in the pre- to postmeasure of the change mechanism was positively correlated to the level of change in outcome; however, there was no significant difference in the outcome levels for treatment and control groups. This may suggest that the researcher was on the right track but that the level of treatment was not strong enough or that something else diluted the effects of treatment. There are many other inferences suggested by the different paths, and we have not considered all of the paths or all of the possible insights suggested by the different paths. However, it is extremely rare for researchers to use strong inference designs in the correctional treatment evaluation literature.

VIII. Summary

We have found support for the effectiveness of some correctional interventions. However, some interventions seem to work better than

others and to work better for juveniles than for adults. Serious definitional, analytical, and methodological problems exist in each of the areas of adult correctional treatment that we have discussed. Are these
problems serious enough to vitiate any general conclusions about these
subdomains of intervention? These were the same conditions encountered by members of the National Academy of Sciences Panel on Rehabilitative Techniques (Sechrest, White, and Brown 1979) and by
Lipton, Martinson, and Wilks (1975). Although their conclusions were
summarily represented as "nothing works," as many others have
pointed out, a closer reading of these publications indicates that authors of these studies thought there were promising intervention programs. We are in a position to make a stronger statement, namely, that
correctional treatment for adults has modest but substantively meaningful effects. Even though the level of recidivism is modest, even
small reductions can produce future reductions in criminality. It is
probably premature to conduct cost-benefit analyses comparing the
gains of treatment against the benefits and costs of alternative crime
reduction policies for prisoners and probationers. Unfortunately, there
is still a great deal of variability in both the quality of the programs
and the quality of the evaluation research.

In more recent years, the results of a number of meta-analyses have
been interpreted to suggest that, despite methodological problems,
some types of interventions can reduce adult postrelease recidivism.
Although most of these studies involve juvenile interventions and the
effects are modest, some types of interventions seem to have a dramatic
impact on postrelease behavior. The next decade of treatment evaluations should capitalize on the results of the best meta-analyses of correctional treatment. Using the principles suggested by meta-analysis
and a coherent theory of treatment, researchers can test these principles under rigorous evaluation conditions, using strong inference designs and insuring that there are sufficient replications. This presents
the greatest opportunity to advance the science of correctional treatment. We would be better positioned properly to assess the evidence
if more of the studies were better designed and executed. Correctional
practice could be improved if the underlying scientific foundations of
correctional intervention research were improved.

We must also come to terms with the unwieldy assortment of programs we currently call treatments. We need a system to classify treatments according to the behavior the intervention is intended to mod-

ify, the mechanism of change, and those factors that mediate, inhibit, or catalyze change. Perhaps theorists can build on the principles of correctional treatment and catalog different interventions according to these principles. The aim of this classification is to get a clearer understanding of essential mechanisms of change and those that are peripheral. For example, are literacy or cognitive skills fundamental to any other intervention? Are there certain emotional or motivational deficits that must be addressed before any program can be successful? The classification of client and treatment characteristics will also benefit future meta-analyses. It is not always clear that researchers are classifying certain treatments into the same categories.

We also need to understand the boundaries and relative effects of individual and collective interventions. Intuitively, it would seem that some programs address behavioral change at the margin while others strike at the heart of the problem. This calls for research designs that include treatment manipulations and the measurement of postrelease contextual factors. For example, training inmates in specific work skills may have little or no impact if they return to economically and socially impoverished conditions. A test of inmate work training should include an analysis of economic and social conditions in different release jurisdictions. If the next decade of correctional treatment research is more imaginative, systematic, and rigorous, the next generation of meta-analyses should produce more demonstrative effects.

APPENDIX

Limitations and Problems of the Treatment Meta-analysis
Literature

This appendix examines some of the problems associated with meta-analysis in the context of the treatment literature. The discussion begins with the interpretation and coding of studies, the most fundamental part of the procedure. We also discuss the possible biased selection of studies and research registers that are a way to ensure that all studies, published and unpublished, will be readily available to the scientific community.

A. The Reliability of Studies Coded for the Purpose of Meta-analysis

Andrews et al. (1990) completed a meta-analysis based on the theoretical formulation of effective treatment outlined at the beginning of this essay and articulated in Andrews and Bonta (1994). In addition to the effect sizes, a moderator variable was coded on the basis of whether a study followed one of four treatment regimens: *criminal sanctions*—the total absence of rehabilitative programs; *inappropriate correctional service*—rehabilitative programs that were not guided by the principles outlined at the beginning of this essay; *appropriate correctional service*—rehabilitation based on delivering services to higher-risk cases, using behavioral programs reflecting responsivity, or nonbehavioral programs that were structured and targeted criminogenic need; and finally, *unspecified correctional service*—treatment that could not be categorized as appropriate or inappropriate. Andrews et al. found that the average effect size for appropriate correctional treatments implied that such treatments could reduce recidivism by 50 percent. The other types of treatment either had a weak influence (unspecified) or were associated with higher recidivism (criminal sanctions, inappropriate treatment). While this meta-analysis was theoretically guided, it had several problems. Unlike the Lipsey meta-analysis, few other methodological or contextual moderator variables were coded. Lipsey has shown that methods variables account for about half of the variation in effect sizes. One would assume that Andrews et al. (1990) would have found a more modest average treatment effect if they had been as comprehensive in their coding.

A second problem with this study points to another caution researchers must observe when they conduct meta-analyses. The treatment regimen variable coded by Andrews et al. which specified interventions as criminal sanctions, appropriate correctional service, inappropriate correctional service, and unspecified correctional service, was subject to too much variation in interpretation. In an attempt to replicate the findings of the Andrews et al. (1990) meta-analysis, Logan et al. (1991) read and evaluated all of the studies considered by Andrews et al. to be exemplars of appropriate correctional treatment. Logan et al. found that many of these studies contained insufficient detail to allow an inference about the study quality. Some arbitrary decisions seemed to have been made in selecting comparisons that demonstrated appropriate treatment. In some cases, effect sizes were based on secondary analyses of the data conducted by the original researchers, when there had been no primary effect of treatment. These post hoc analyses are considered data snooping by most methodologists and statisticians and often result in findings that cannot be replicated. This is because eventually positive results will occur by chance alone if enough post hoc comparisons are done. To understand how difficult it is to code these kinds of moderator variables, the researcher has to examine the minutiae of the methods section of every study. Logan et al. (1991) have shown that a separate set of eyes can come to different conclusions about the interpretation of moderator variables and the effects of treatment. Rather than debate whether Andrews et al. or Logan et al. were more correct in their interpretation of the outcomes of the studies, it is more important to focus on the methods researchers use in approaching the meta-analysis.

There are two primary lessons to be learned. The broader the definition of a variable (as was the case with the Andrews et al. definition of appropriate and inappropriate treatment), the less reliability there will be in the coding of such variables. A second, more subtle lesson, is also evident. If meta-analysis is conducted by advocates or proponents of a particular perspective, the research should have additional safeguards to protect against biased interpretation of the outcomes of a study. Norval Morris calls this "partisan research" (1998). Stephen J. Gould (1981) has demonstrated how subtle bias can be in the interpretation of even physical measurement when the researcher believes in a particular point of view. Researchers with a strong theoretical orientation should have others assess the quality and consistency of their coding, as well as report the reliability of those who have been tasked with coding the studies.

B. Biased Selection of Studies and the Use of Research Registers

Yet another potential problem of meta-analysis is the possibility of bias in the selection of studies. Publication bias can take several forms. Reporting bias results from the failure by authors to report statistically nonsignificant results. There can also be retrieval bias. When the researcher collects studies to synthesize, it is much more difficult to gather unpublished studies or even discarded studies that represent statistically nonsignificant results. We can only speculate whether it is more or less likely that there is more reporting bias in correctional treatment research than in other research domains.

Begg (1994) has examined this issue in some detail using medical research. Citing other studies of publication bias, Begg reported evidence that the odds of having a study published were as high as 3.4 to 1, if the study demonstrated statistical significance, as opposed to nonsignificance. The lowest odds he found were 1.8 to 1 in favor of studies finding statistical significance for an effect. As Begg asserts, "Results of the meta-analysis should be very compelling before we regard them as definitive" (p. 408). One way to begin to address the problem of publication bias is to establish research registers.

A research register is a compilation of all initiated research projects in a particular domain (Dickersin 1994). It can be a data base of planned, ongoing, or completed studies. Dickersin's field is medical research. Her inquiries and analyses seem to be confined to that research domain. Nevertheless, her insights may prove to be equally valuable to the social sciences, and to program and treatment evaluation in particular. As Dickersin indicates, registers are a way to overcome publication bias. She argues that most research syntheses in medicine were based on published studies and estimated that only 50 percent to 80 percent of all studies had been published. She also cites five studies that she claims demonstrated "consistent and persuasive evidence for the existence of publication bias" (p. 75), whether the designs were observational or experimental. Although the existence of research registers may not completely solve the problem of publication bias, if we make registers a common practice in social science research in general and program evaluation research in particular, we can begin to have greater confidence in our coverage of all studies initiated, ongoing, and completed in a particular research domain. Obviously, there are a great many practical difficulties to overcome. Nevertheless, it would seem that if certain social science domains are going to develop, a research register may be a significant step in their maturity. Members of the CDATE project spent a great deal of time and effort to collect published and unpublished studies. Gathering unpublished studies retrospectively is extremely difficult. A treatment research register might make future comprehensive meta-analyses more thorough and perhaps easier to do. Research registers can be updated to include the results of meta-analyses so that there is a common public access data source for everyone to examine the studies that have been started or completed, the calculation of effect sizes, and the coding of moderator variables for a particular evaluation. Such a public domain data set can reduce the level of publication bias and allow different researchers to compare their assessment of a given study against someone else's meta-analytic results.

REFERENCES

Adams, K., K. J. Bennett, T. J. Flanagan, J. W. Marquart, S. J. Cuvelier, E. J. Fritsch, J. Gerber, D. R. Longmire, and V. S. Burton, Jr. 1994. "A Large Scale Multidimensional Test of the Effect of Prison Education Programs on Offenders' Behavior." *Prison Journal* 74:433–49.

Anderson, S. L., D. B. Anderson, and R. E. Schumacker. 1988. *Correctional Education: A Way to Stay Out.* Springfield: Illinois Council on Vocational Education.

Andrews, D. A. 1989. "Recidivism Is Predictable and Can Be Influenced: Using Risk Assessments to Reduce Recidivism." *Forum on Corrections Research* 1(2):11–18.

———. 1995. "The Psychology of Criminal Conduct and Effective Treatment." In *What Works: Reducing Reoffending,* edited by J. McGuire. New York: Wiley.

———. 1996. "Recidivism Is Predictable and Can Be Influenced: An Update." *Forum on Corrections Research* 8(3):42–44.

Andrews, D. A., and J. Bonta. 1994. *The Psychology of Criminal Conduct.* Cincinnati: Anderson.

Andrews, D. A., I. Zinger, R. D. Hoge, J. Bonta, P. Gendreau, and F. T. Cullen. 1990. "Does Correctional Treatment Work? A Psychologically Informed Meta-analysis." *Criminology* 28:369–404.

Anglin, M. Douglas, and G. Speckart. 1988. "Narcotics and Crime: A Multi-sample, Multimethod Analysis." *Criminology* 26:197–233.

Antonowicz, D., and R. R. Ross. 1994. "Essential Components of Successful Rehabilitation Programs for Offenders." *International Journal of Offender Therapy and Comparative Criminology* 38:97–104.

Association of the Bar of the City of New York, Committee on Corrections. 1984. "Can Our Prisons Become Factories with Fences?" *Record of the Association of the Bar of the City of New York* 40(4):299.

Barbaree, H. E. 1991. "Denial and Minimization among Sex Offenders: Assessment and Treatment Outcome." *Forum on Corrections Research* 3(4):30–33.

Barbaree, H. E., M. C. Seto, and A. Maric. 1996. "Effective Sex Offender Treatment: The Warkworth Sexual Behavior Clinic." *Forum on Corrections Research* 8(3):13–15.

Basinger, Aaron. 1985. "Are Prison Work Programs Working? The Impact of

Prison Industry Participation on Recidivism Rates in Ohio." M.P.A. thesis, Ohio State University.

Baxter, D. J., L. L. Motiuk, and S. Fortin. 1995. "Intelligence and Personality in Criminal Offenders." In *International Handbook of Personality and Intelligence*, edited by D. H. Saklofske and M. Zeidner. New York: Plenum.

Begg, C. B. 1994. "Publication Bias." In *The Handbook of Research Synthesis*, edited by H. Cooper and L. Hedges. New York: Russell Sage Foundation.

Blanchette, K. 1996. *Sex Offender Assessment, Treatment and Recidivism: A Review of the Literature*. Research Report. Ottawa: Correctional Service of Canada.

Cookson, H. M. 1998. "Impact of Cognitive Skills Programs on Reconviction Rates." *Living Skills Newsletter*. London: H.M. Prison Service.

Cooper, H., and L. V. Hedges, eds. 1994a. *The Handbook of Research Synthesis*. New York: Russell Sage Foundation.

———. 1994b. "Potentials and Limitations of Research Synthesis." In *The Handbook of Research Synthesis*, edited by H. Cooper and L. Hedges. New York: Russell Sage Foundation.

DeLeon, G., J. A. Inciardi, and S. S. Martin. 1995. "Residential Drug Treatment Research: Are Conventional Control Designs Appropriate for Assessing Treatment Effectiveness?" *Journal of Psychoactive Drugs* 27:85–91.

Dickersin, K. 1994. "Research Registers." In *The Handbook of Research Synthesis*, edited by H. Cooper and L. Hedges. New York: Russell Sage Foundation.

Elliot, D. S. 1997. "Editor's Introduction." In *Blueprints for Violence Prevention*, vols. 1–10, edited by D. S. Elliot. Boulder: University of Colorado, Center for the Study and Prevention of Violence, Institute of Behavioral Science.

Field, G. 1985. "The Cornerstone Program: A Client Outcome Study." *Federal Probation* 49(2):50–55.

———. 1992. "Oregon Prison Drug Treatment Programs." In *Drug Abuse Treatment in Prisons and Jails*, edited by C. G. Leukefeld and F. M. Tims. National Institute on Drug Abuse Monograph 118. Washington, D.C.: Public Health Service, Alcohol, Drug Abuse, and Mental Health Administration.

Flanagan, T. J. 1989. "Prison Labor and Industry." In *The American Prison: Issues of Research and Policy*, edited by Lynne Goodstein and Doris L. Mac-Kenzie. New York: Plenum.

Flanagan, T. J., T. P. Thornberry, K. Maguire, and E. McGarrell. 1988. *The Effect of Prison Industry Employment on Offender Behavior: Final Report of the Prison Industry Research Project*. Albany: University at Albany, State University of New York.

Freeman-Longo, R. E., and H. F. Knopp. 1992. "State-of-the-Art Sex Offender Treatment: Outcome and Issues." *Annals of Sex Research* 5(3):141–60.

Gaes, G. G. 1997. "A Review of Recent Studies of High Intensity Adult Correctional Drug Treatment Programs: The Problem of Selection Bias and Possible Solutions." Unpublished manuscript. Washington, D.C.: Federal Bureau of Prisons.

————. 1998. "Correctional Treatment." In *The Handbook of Crime and Punishment*, edited by M. Tonry. New York: Oxford University Press.

Garrett, C. J. 1985. "Effects of Residential Treatment on Adjudicated Delinquents: A Meta-analysis." *Journal of Research in Crime and Delinquency* 22:287–308.

Gendreau, P., and D. A. Andrews. 1990. "Tertiary Prevention: What the Meta-analysis of the Offender Treatment Literature Tells Us about What Works." *Canadian Journal of Criminology* 32:173–84.

Gendreau, P., and R. R. Ross. 1979. "Effectiveness of Correctional Treatment: Bibliotherapy for Cynics." *Crime and Delinquency* 25:463–89.

————. 1987. "Revivification of Rehabilitation: Evidence from the 1980s." *Justice Quarterly* 4:349–407.

Gensheimer, L. K., J. P. Mayer, R. Gottschalk, and W. S. Davidson. 1986. "Diverting Youth from the Juvenile Justice System—a Meta-analysis of Intervention Efficacy." In *Youth Violence*, edited by S. J. Apter and A. P. Goldstein. New York: Pergamon.

Gerber, J., and E. J. Fritsch. 1994. "The Effects of Academic and Vocational Program Participation on Inmate Misconduct and Reincarceration." Chap. 3 in Sam Houston State University, *Prison Education Research Project: Final Report*. Huntsville, Tex.: Sam Houston State University.

Gordon, A., R. Holden, and T. Leis. 1991. "Managing and Treating Sex Offenders: Matching Risk and Need in Programming." *Forum on Corrections Research* 3:7–11.

Gordon, A., and T. Nicholaichuk. 1996. "Applying the Risk Principle to Sex Offender Treatment." *Forum on Corrections Research* 8(2):36–38.

Gottschalk, R., W. S. Davidson, L. K. Gensheimer, and J. Mayer. 1987a. "Community-Based Interventions." In *Handbook of Juvenile Delinquency*, edited by H. C. Quay. New York: Wiley.

Gottschalk, R., W. S. Davidson, J. Mayer, and L. K. Gensheimer. 1987b. "Behavioral Approaches with Juvenile Offenders: A Meta-analysis of Long-Term Treatment Efficacy." In *Behavioral Approaches to Crime and Delinquency: A Handbook of Application, Research, and Concepts*, edited by E. K. Morris and C. J. Braukman. New York: Plenum.

Gould, S. J. 1981. *The Mismeasure of Man*. New York: Norton.

Hagan, M. P., R. P. King, and R. L. Patros. 1994. "The Efficacy of a Serious Sex Offenders Treatment Program for Adolescent Rapists." *International Journal of Offender Therapy and Comparative Criminology* 38(2):141–50.

Hall, G. C. 1995. "Sex Offender Recidivism Revisited: A Meta-analysis of Recent Treatment Studies." *Journal of Consulting and Clinical Psychology* 63(5):802–9.

Hall, J. A., L. Tickle-Degnen, R. Rosenthal, and F. Mosteller. 1994. "Hypotheses and Problems in Research Synthesis." In *The Handbook of Research Synthesis*, edited by H. Cooper and L. Hedges. New York: Russell Sage Foundation.

Hanson, R. K., and M. T. Bussiere. 1996. "Sex Offender Risk Predictors: A Summary of Research Results." *Forum on Corrections Research* 8(2):10–12.

Heckman, James. 1979. "Sample Selection Bias as a Specification Error." *Econometrica* 47:153–61.

Inciardi, James A. 1997. Personal letter.

Inciardi, J. A., S. S. Martin, C. A. Butzin, R. M. Hooper, and L. D. Harrison. 1997. "An Effective Model of Prison-Based Treatment for Drug-Involved Offenders." *Journal of Drug Issues* 27(2):261–78.

Izzo, R. L., and R. R. Ross. 1990. "Meta-analysis of Rehabilitation Programs for Juvenile Delinquents." *Criminal Justice and Behavior* 17:134–42.

Johnson, C. M. 1984. "The Effects of Prison Labor Programs on Post-Release Employment and Recidivism." Doctoral dissertation, Florida State University, School of Criminology and Criminal Justice.

Johnson, G., and L. Hunter. 1992. "Evaluation of the Specialized Drug Offender Program." Report for the Colorado Judicial Department. Boulder: University of Colorado, Center for Addiction Research.

———. 1995. "Evaluation of the Specialized Drug Offender Program." In *Thinking Straight: The Reasoning and Rehabilitation Program for Delinquency Prevention and Offender Rehabilitation*, edited by R. R. Ross and R. D. Ross. Ottawa: Air Training and Publications.

Knight K., D. D. Simpson, L. R. Chatham, and L. M. Camacho. Forthcoming. "An Assessment of Prison-Based Drug Treatment: Texas' In-prison Therapeutic Program." Fort Worth: Texas Christian University, Institute of Behavioral Research.

Knight, K., D. D. Simpson, L. R. Chatham, L. M. Camacho, and M. Cloud. 1995. "Prison-Based Treatment Assessment (PTA): Final Report on Six-Month Follow-Up Study." Fort Worth, Tex.: Christian University, Institute of Behavioral Research.

Knight, R. A., and R. A. Prentky. 1990. "Classifying Sex Offenders: The Development and Corroboration of Taxonomic Models." In *Handbook of Sexual Assault: Issues, Theories, and Treatment of the Offenders*, edited by W. L. Marshall, D. R. Laws, and H. E. Barbaree. New York: Plenum.

Lang, R. A., G. M. Pugh, and R. Langevin. 1988. "Treatment of Incest and Pedophilic Offenders: A Pilot Study." *Behavioral Sciences and the Law* 6:239–55.

Laws, H. E., and W. L. Marshall. 1990. "A Conditioning Theory of the Etiology and Maintenance of Deviant Sexual Preference and Behavior." In *Handbook of Sexual Assault: Issues, Theories, and Treatment of the Offenders*, edited by W. L. Marshall and H. E. Barbaree. New York: Plenum.

Lipsey, M. W. 1989. "The Efficacy of Intervention for Juvenile Delinquency: Results from 400 Studies." Paper presented at the forty-first meeting of the American Society of Criminology, Reno, Nevada, November.

———. 1992. "Juvenile Delinquency Treatment: A Meta-analytic Inquiry into the Variability of Effects." In *Meta-Analysis for Explanation: A Casebook*, edited by T. D. Cook, H. Cooper, D. S. Cordray, H. Hartmann, L. V. Hedges, R. J. Light, T. A. Louis, and F. Mosteller. New York: Russell Sage Foundation.

———. 1995. "What Do We Learn from 400 Research Studies on the Effectiveness of Treatment with Juvenile Delinquents?" In *What Works: Reducing Reoffending*, edited by J. McGuire. New York: Wiley.

Lipton, D. 1998. "How Do Cognitive Skills Training Programs for Offenders Compare with Other Modalities: A Meta-analytic Perspective." Paper presented at the Stop and Think Conference, York, England.

Lipton, D., R. Martinson, and J. Wilks. 1975. *The Effectiveness of Correctional Treatment*. New York: Praeger.

Lipton, D. S., F. S. Pearson, C. Cleland, and D. Yee. 1998. "Synthesizing Correctional Treatment Outcomes: Preliminary Findings from CDATE." New York: National Development and Research Institutes.

Loesel, F. 1993. "The Effectiveness of Treatment in Institutional and Community Settings." *Criminal Behaviour and Mental Health* 3:416–37.

———. 1995a. "The Efficacy of Correctional Treatment: A Review and Synthesis of Meta-Evaluations." In *What Works: Reducing Reoffending*, edited by J. McGuire. New York: Wiley.

———. 1995b. "What Recent MetaEvaluations Tell Us about the Effectiveness of Correctional Treatment." In *Psychology, Law, Criminal Justice: International Developments in Research and Practice*, edited by G. Davies and S. Lloyd Bostock. Berlin: Walter DeGruyter.

———. 1996. "Effective Correctional Programming: What Empirical Research Tells and What It Doesn't." *Forum on Corrections Research* 8(3):33–37.

Loesel, F., and P. Koferl. 1989. "Evaluation Research on Correctional Treatment in West Germany: A Meta-analysis." In *Criminal Behavior and the Justice System: Psychological Perspectives*, edited by H. Wegener, F. Loesel, and J. Haisch. New York: Springer.

Loesel, F., P. Koferl, and F. Weber. 1987. *Meta-evaluation of Social Therapy*. Stuttgart: Ferdinand Enke.

Logan, C. H., G. G. Gaes, M. D. Harer, C. A. Innes, L. Karacki, and W. G. Saylor. 1991. *Can Meta-analysis Save Correctional Rehabilitation?* Washington, D.C.: Federal Bureau of Prisons.

Marques, J. K., D. M. Day, C. Nelson, and M. West. 1994. "Effects of Cognitive-Behavioral Treatment on Sex Offender Recidivism: Preliminary Results of a Longitudinal Study." *Criminal Justice and Behavior* 21:28–54.

Marshall, W. L. 1996. "Assessment, Treatment, and Theorizing about Sex Offenders: Developments during the Past Twenty Years and Future Directions." *Criminal Justice and Behavior* 23:162–99.

Marshall, W. L., and H. E. Barbaree. 1990. "Outcome of Comprehensive Cognitive-Behavioral Treatment Programs." In *Handbook of Sexual Assault: Issues, Theories, and Treatment of the Offender*, edited by William L. Marshall, D. R. Laws, and H. E. Barbaree. New York: Plenum.

Martin, S. S., C. A. Butzin, and J. A. Inciardi. 1995. "Assessment of a Multistage Therapeutic Community for Drug-Involved Offenders." *Journal of Psychoactive Drugs* 27:109–16.

Martin, S. S., J. A. Inciardi, and C. A. Saum. 1995. "Strengths and Shortcomings of Prison-Based Treatment for Male Drug-Involved Offenders: An Empirical Assessment." Presentation at the annual meeting of the Academy of Criminal Justice Sciences, Boston.

Martinson, R. 1974. "What Works? Questions and Answers about Prison Reform." *Public Interest* 35:22–45.

Mayer, J., L. K. Gensheimer, W. S. Davidson II, and R. Gottschalk. 1986. "Social Learning Treatment within Juvenile Justice: A Meta-analysis of Impact in the Natural Environment." In *Youth Violence: Programs and Prospects*, edited by S. J. Apter and A. P. Goldstein. New York: Pergamon.

McGuire, J. 1995a. "Community-Based Reasoning and Rehabilitation Programs in the U.K." In *Thinking Straight: The Reasoning and Rehabilitation Program for Delinquency Prevention and Offender Rehabilitation*, edited by R. R. Ross and R. D. Ross. Ottawa: Air Training and Publications.

———. 1995b. *What Works? Reducing Reoffending*. New York: Wiley.

McHutchison, Judy. 1995. *Working towards a Better Future: A Study into Inmate Employment in the NSW Correctional System*. Research Publication no. 34. Sydney: New South Wales, Department of Corrective Services.

Miller, W. R., and S. Rollnick. 1991. *Motivational Interviewing: Preparing People to Change Addictive Behavior*. New York: Guilford.

Millson, W. A., and D. Robinson. 1992. *An Assessment of the Offender Substance Abuse Pre-release Program at Drumheller Institution*. Ottawa: Correctional Service of Canada.

Millson, W. A., J. R. Weekes, and L. O. Lightfoot. 1995. *The Offender Substance Abuse Pre-release Program: An Analysis of Pre-release and Post-release Outcomes*. Ottawa: Correctional Service of Canada.

Miner, M. H., J. K. Marques, D. M. Day, and C. Nelson. 1990. "Impact of Relapse Prevention in Treating Sex Offenders: Preliminary Findings." *Annals of Sex Research* 3(2):165–85.

Morris, N. 1998. "Plenary Address at the National Workshop on Assessing the Effectiveness of Corrections Programs." U.S. Department of Justice, Office of Justice Programs, Corrections Program Office, February 10–12, Chicago.

Motiuk, L. L., C. Smiley, and K. Blanchette. 1996. "Intensive Programming for Violent Offenders: A Comparative Investigation." *Forum on Corrections Research* 8(3):10–12.

Murphy, W. D. 1990. "Assessment and Modification of Cognitive Distortions in Sex Offenders." In *Handbook of Sexual Assault: Issues, Theories, and Treatment of the Offender*, edited by W. L. Marshall, D. R. Laws, and H. E. Barbaree. New York: Plenum.

Nuffield, J. 1982. *Parole Decision-Making in Canada: Research towards Decision Guidelines*. Ottawa: Supply and Services.

Nurco, D. N., T. W. Kinlock, and T. E. Hanlon. 1990. "The Drugs-Crime Connection." In *Handbook of Drug Control in the United States*, edited by J. A. Inciardi. Westport, Conn.: Greenwood.

Palmer, T. 1975. "Martinson Revisited." *Journal of Research in Crime and Delinquency* 12:133–52.

———. 1992. *The Re-emergence of Correctional Intervention*. Newbury Park, Calif.: Sage.

Pelissier, B. 1997. "Triad Drug Treatment Evaluation Project: Six-Month Interim Report." Unpublished manuscript. Washington, D.C.: Federal Bureau of Prisons.

Pithers, W. D. 1990. "Relapse Prevention for Sexual Aggressors: A Method for Maintaining Therapeutic Gain and Enhancing External Supervision." In *Handbook of Sexual Assault: Issues, Theories, and Treatment of the Offender*, edited by W. L. Marshall, D. R. Laws, and H. E. Barbaree. New York: Plenum.

Platt, J. R. 1964. "Strong Inference." *Science*, vol. 146, no. 3642 (October 16).

Porporino, F. J., E. A. Fabiano, and D. Robinson. 1991. "Focussing on Successful Reintegration: Cognitive Skills Training for Offenders." Research Report no. 19. Ottawa: Correctional Service of Canada, Research and Statistics Branch.

Porporino, F., and D. Robinson 1992. *Can Educating Adult Offenders Counteract Recidivism?* Ottawa: Correctional Service of Canada.

Prentky, R. A., and R. Knight. 1986. "Impulsivity in Lifestyle and Criminal Behavior of Sexual Offenders." *Criminal Justice and Behavior* 13:141–64.

Prochaska, J. O., and C. C. DiClementi. 1986. "Toward a Comprehensive Model of Change." In *Treating Addictive Behaviors: Processes of Change*, edited by E. E. Miller and N. Heather. New York: Plenum.

Quinsey, V. 1998. "Treatment of Sex Offenders." In *The Handbook of Crime and Punishment*, edited by Michael Tonry. New York: Oxford University Press.

Quinsey, V. L., and C. M. Earls. 1990. "The Modification of Sexual Preferences." In *Handbook of Sexual Assault: Issues, Theories, and Treatment of the Offender*, edited by W. L. Marshall, D. R. Laws, and H. E. Barbaree. New York: Plenum.

Quinsey, V. L., G. T. Harris, M. E. Rice, and M. L. Lalumiere. 1993. "Assessing Treatment Efficacy in Outcome Studies of Sex Offenders." *Journal of Interpersonal Violence* 8:512–23.

Raynor, P., and P. Vanstone. 1996. "Reasoning and Rehabilitation in Britain: The Results of the Straight Thinking on Probation (STOP) Program." *International Journal of Offender Therapy and Comparative Criminology* 40(4): 272–84.

Redondo, S., V. Garrido, and J. Sanchez-Meca. 1996. "Is the Treatment of Offenders Effective in Europe? The Results of a Meta-Analysis." Presented at the forty-eighth annual meeting of the American Society of Criminology, Chicago, November.

Roberts, A. R., and M. J. Camasso. 1991. "The Effect of Juvenile Offender Treatment Programs on Recidivism: A Meta-Analysis of 46 Studies." *Notre Dame Journal of Law, Ethics, and Public Policy* 5:421–41.

Robinson, D. 1995. "The Impact of Cognitive Skills Training on Post Release Recidivism among Canadian Federal Offenders." Research Report. Ottawa: Correctional Service of Canada, Research Branch.

———. 1996. "Factors Influencing the Effectiveness of Cognitive Skills Training." *Forum on Corrections Research* 8(3):6–9.

———. 1998. Personal communication, conversation.

Robinson, D., M. Grossman, and F. Porporino. 1991. "Effectiveness of the Cognitive Skills Training Program: From Pilot to National Implementation." Ottawa: Correctional Service of Canada, Research and Statistics Branch.

Rosenthal, R., and D. B. Rubin. 1982. "A Simple, General Purpose Display of Magnitude of Experimental Effect." *Journal of Educational Psychology* 74(2): 166–69.

Ross, R. R., and E. Fabiano. 1985. "Time to Think: A Cognitive Model of Delinquency Prevention and Offender Rehabilitation." Johnson City, Tenn.: Institute of Social Sciences and Arts.

Ross, R. R., E. Fabiano, and C. D. Ewels. 1988. "Reasoning and Rehabilitation." *International Journal of Offender Therapy and Comparative Criminology* 32:29–35.

Saylor, W. G., and G. G. Gaes. 1992. "PREP Study Links UNICOR Work Experience with Successful Post-Release Outcome." *Research Forum* 1(3):1–8.

———. 1997. "Training Inmates through Industrial Work Participation and Vocational and Apprenticeship Instruction." *Corrections Management Quarterly* 1(2):32–43.

Sechrest, L., S. O. White, and E. D. Brown, eds. 1979. *The Rehabilitation of Criminal Offenders: Problems and Prospects.* Washington, D.C.: National Academy of Sciences.

Sherman, L. W., D. C. Gottfredson, D. L. MacKenzie, J. Eck, P. Reuter, and S. D. Bushway. 1998. *Preventing Crime: What Works, What Doesn't, What's Promising.* Washington, D.C.: National Institute of Justice (http//www.preventingcrime.org/).

Simpson, D. D., K. Knight, L. R. Chatham, L. M. Camacho, and M. Cloud. "Prison-Based Treatment Assessment (PTA): Interim report on Kyle IT evaluation." Report to the Texas Commission on Alcohol and Drug Abuse. Fort Worth: Texas Christian University, Institute of Behavioral Research.

State of Utah, Governor's Task Force on Correctional Industries. 1984. *The Challenge of Correctional Industries.* Salt Lake City: Utah Department of Corrections.

Stermac, L. E., and V. L. Quinsey. 1986. "Social Competence among Rapists." *Behavioral Scientist* 8:171–85.

Thorpe, T., D. MacDonald, and G. Bala. 1984. "Follow-Up of Offenders Who Earned College Degrees while Incarcerated in New York State." *Journal of Correctional Education* 35(3):86–88.

Tobler, N. 1986. "Meta-analysis of 143 Adolescent Drug Prevention Programs: Quantitative Outcome Results of Program Participants Compared to a Control or Comparison Group." *Journal of Drug Issues* 16(4):537–67.

Weinrott, M. R., and M. Saylor. 1991. "Self-Report of Crimes Committed by Sex Offenders." *Journal of Interpersonal Violence* 6:286–300.

Wexler, H. K. 1994. "Progress in Prison Substance Abuse Treatment: A Five Year Report." *Journal of Drug Issues* 24:349–60.

Wexler, H. K., and J. Chin. 1981. "Evaluation of a System to Evaluate Prison-Based Drug Treatment." Paper presented at the Eastern Evaluation Research Society conference, Philadelphia.

Wexler, H. K., G. DeLeon, G. Thomas, D. Kressel, and J. Peters. 1997. "The Amity Prison TC Evaluation: Reincarceration Outcomes." Unpublished manuscript. New York: New York Center for Therapeutic Community Research at the National Development and Research Institutes, Inc.

Wexler, H. K., G. P. Falkin, and D. S. Lipton. 1988. "A Model Prison Reha-
    bilitation Program: An Evaluation of the Stay 'n Out Therapeutic Commu-
    nity." Final report to the National Institute on Drug Abuse. New York:
    Narcotic and Drug Research.
———. 1990. "Outcome Evaluation of a Prison Therapeutic Community for
    Substance Abuse Treatment." *Criminal Justice and Behavior* 17:79–92.
Wexler, H. K., G. P. Falkin, D. S. Lipton, and A. B. Rosenblum. 1992. "Out-
    come Evaluation of a Prison Therapeutic Community for Substance Abuse
    Treatment." In *Drug Abuse Treatment in Prisons and Jails*. National Institute
    on Drug Abuse Monograph 118. Washington, D.C.: U.S. Public Health
    Service, Alcohol, Drug Abuse, and Mental Health Administration.
Wexler, H. K., and R. Williams. 1986. "The Stay 'n Out Therapeutic Com-
    munity: Prison Treatment for Substance Abusers." *Journal of Psychoactive
    Drugs* 18(3):221–30.
Whitehead, J. T., and S. P. Lab. 1989. "A Meta-analysis of Juvenile Correc-
    tional Treatment." *Journal of Research in Crime and Delinquency* 26:276–95.

Douglas C. McDonald

Medical Care in Prisons

ABSTRACT

Until the 1970s, a sentence to imprisonment deprived one not only of
liberty but also put one's health at risk. Medical care was inadequately
available and frequently primitive. This changed when federal courts
intervened, forcing improvements in prisoners' care. Rights to adequate
care were established, standards were promulgated, medical staffs were
expanded, and providers in the surrounding community were called on to
fill gaps. Spending for prisoners' health care consequently rose
dramatically. Prison administrators began adopting various "managed
care" procedures to allocate resources in less costly and more efficient
ways. These include efforts to buy needed goods and services in the larger
health care marketplace at more advantageous prices, establishing controls
and incentives to reduce unnecessary care, and contracting with private
firms to manage and deliver care. Imprisoned criminals are the only
persons in the United States enjoying a constitutional right to adequate
health care. Support for state-funded care of prisoners may become more
precarious if free citizens continue to lack similar legal rights and access
to universal health care.

The provision of medical care in American prisons has been transformed dramatically during the past twenty-five years. For most of the
century and a half prior to the late 1960s, prisoners' health care was
substandard at best, relative to the quality of care available in the larger
society, and appallingly negligent and even brutal at worst. Prisons
were left to operate in a self-contained world largely isolated from the

Douglas C. McDonald is a senior associate at the Cambridge, Massachusetts, offices
of Abt Associates, Inc., a policy research organization. Thanks to John Boston, Carl Pat-
ten, Jr., and Theodore Hammett for their helpful assistance.

surrounding society. Health care was often delivered, if at all, by persons having little or no medical training—sometimes, even other prisoners—or by small numbers of qualified physicians overwhelmed by huge caseloads. As the federal courts began to review the conditions of confinement in prisons and jails in the early 1970s, prisoners' legal rights to medical care were established and extended (Boston and Manville 1996, pp. 37–85). No longer could prisoners be given second-class care. A string of court decisions established, ultimately, that care must be "reasonably commensurate with modern medical science and of a quality acceptable within prudent professional standards" (*Fernandez v. United States*, 941 F.2d 1488 [11th Cir. 1991]). Simultaneously with these legal developments, the wall between prisons and the organized medical profession began to be breached. In the early 1970s, professional medical organizations began to attend to the quality of care in prisons and jails, which resulted in, among other things, the development of health care standards for correctional institutions (American Public Health Association 1976; American Medical Association 1979; American Correctional Association 1981; National Commission on Correctional Health Care 1987).

Since the intervention of the federal courts and the emergence of professional standards pertaining to medical care, correctional authorities have moved away from relying on untrained inmates and unlicensed physicians for primary care. Now, primary care is generally delivered by medical professionals, principally physicians, physicians' assistants, nurses, and pharmacists. These medical professionals generally conduct physical examinations on admission to prison and, in some places, on admission to any new facility following transfer. Prisoners are typically given an opportunity to contact them at daily "sick calls," or at open calls for prisoners who want to see a primary care provider.

The result of these developments has been to integrate prisoner health care into the health care delivery institutions of the larger society to a greater extent than ever before. Even though prisons continue to rely on their own staff to provide most health care, prisons develop relationships with other local physicians, including specialists, who are brought in to hold scheduled "clinics." Prisoners are also taken outside the facilities for consultation, diagnoses, treatment, and hospitalization when needed. Correctional systems have developed specialized facilities to care for prisoners suffering from mental illness and, to a lesser extent, from chronic diseases. Many have contracts with local hospitals to provide needed services; a few have built hospitals with surgical suites inside the walls; and some have even contracted their entire health care delivery system out to privately operated firms to provide all levels and types of care. The general result has been to expand prisoners' access to needed care, and both the amounts and quality of services provided have improved substantially.

Demands on the health care systems in our nation's prisons have grown greatly during this twenty-five year period. The numbers of sentenced persons held in state and federal prisons have grown immensely since 1973. By year-end 1997, there were 1,244,600 prisoners behind bars in state or federal prisons, compared to 204,200 in December 1973 (Langan et al. 1988; Gilliard and Beck 1998). Moreover, the use of imprisonment as the instrument of choice in the war on drugs has brought into prison disproportionately large numbers of persons at high risk of AIDS and other infectious diseases, whose treatment is very costly. Passage of mandatory minimum sentencing provisions, abolition of paroling authorities in many states, and other reforms will result in growing numbers of older prisoners who—like the elderly in the society at large—will consume a disproportionately large share of all health care resources. The demand for mental health services also intensified during the past two and a half decades, a consequence of the widespread "deinstitutionalization" of mentally ill persons from public hospitals during the 1970s. Community-based treatment resources have not been developed enough to support and stabilize mentally ill persons in their communities, and prisons (and jails) have therefore become the principal institutions for housing mentally ill persons (Torrey 1995).

This emergence of the prison as a collecting place for large numbers of unhealthy persons creates what some see as an opportunity (Glaser and Greifinger 1993). That is, prisons could play an important role in monitoring and improving the public health of the larger population, if only because so many people go through them and return to their communities. This would draw the prison health care systems and the public health institutions of the larger society still closer together. Most correctional agencies have not accepted such a mission, however.

This increase in demand for health care services occurred at the same time that health care in the society at large was getting more expensive. Lowering the wall separating prisons from the health care institutions in the larger society therefore had the effect of making prisons more susceptible to the inflationary forces in the larger health care marketplace. In the early 1980s, the cost of medical services throughout the nation began to rise at a faster rate than other services—a trend that has persisted (U.S. Department of Labor 1996, p. 6; 1998). This generalized inflation spurred a vast transformation of American health care, with new organizational forms emerging both to manage care and to control costs. During the 1990s, some of the managed care practices developed by health care insurers and providers in the larger society have been adopted by prison administrators with an eye to controlling spending (McDonald 1995; LIS, Inc. 1997). These include "copayments" or fees paid by prisoner patients, health care utilization management procedures, capitated reimbursement schemes, and more explicit limits on services to be provided, among others.

Prison medical care is consequently being pulled by two opposing tensions. One is to expand access and care, the other is to limit it. Prisoners are the only persons in the United States who have a constitutionally protected right to health care, and the courts show no sign of extinguishing that right, even if they are often hostile to prisoners' assertions of those rights. The threat of lawsuits, as well as the more positive commitment by correctional managers to principles of adequate and humane care, motivate the ongoing professionalization of correctional medicine and the expansion of access to health care. At the same time, however, concerns about rapidly rising correctional health care costs animate efforts, mostly by legislatures or governors, to limit access, diminish use of health care services, limit types of medical services to be provided to prisoners, and control health care spending generally. These opposing dynamics constitute the most powerful tensions within prison health care today.

This essay is organized as follows. The state of prison health care prior to approximately 1970, or what can be seen of it through the lens of court cases and a few observers, is described briefly in Section I. The activist role of the federal courts in forcing improvements in care is discussed (Sec. II), as well as the role of the professional associations in promulgating standards for correctional health care (Sec. III). Section IV surveys some of the principal challenges to delivering care in prisons. Sections V and VI examine whether prisoners get too much health care, relative to nonincarcerated citizens, and whether prisoners are sicker, on the whole, than others in the general population. Subsequent sections discuss rising expenditures for prisoner health care (Sec. VII), whether such expenditures are too high (Sec. VIII), and a brief review of the various managed care strategies that correctional departments are adopting in an effort to control health care costs (Sec. IX).

The final section (Sec. X) speculates on what may be collisions among prisoners' expanding rights to health care (in a nation where nonincarcerated citizens have no such rights), the rising cost of providing such entitlements, and the public's resistance to paying for it.

I. Medical Care prior to the 1970s

The recorded history of medical care in prisons seems to begin in the late 1960s. Written accounts from earlier periods are rare. Although prisoners' medical care prior to this time was probably addressed in the reports of the various public and private monitoring and reformist groups, it was not until the advent of lawsuits in federal courts in the late 1960s and 1970s that the provision of medical care in prisons received focused and systematic attention by outsiders.

The few descriptions of prison health care during this period that exist are not pretty. For example, Thomas Murton, the superintendent of an Arkansas prison, reported that a convict doctor lacking medical or nursing training was responsible for most of the primary care at the Tucker Prison Farm. This person not only ran an illegal drug program and sold medical leaves of absence, but also tortured prisoners by means of hand-cranked electric generators (Murton and Hyams 1969, p. 7). This prison was one of those in Arkansas that was the subject of a series of lawsuits in the 1960s, including the landmark case *Holt v. Sarver* (300 F. Supp. 825 [E.D. Ark. 1969]).

Arkansas was not unique. A U.S. Supreme Court decision in 1972 regarding Alabama's prisons found that prisoners without any formal medical training extracted teeth, dispensed drugs, operated x-ray equipment, and performed minor surgery. Medical services were found to have been withheld by prison staff for purposes of disciplining inmates. One quadriplegic in the hospital unit received no intravenous feeding during the three days preceding his death; another epileptic prisoner died for lack of medical supervision, despite requesting treatment. Hospital facilities had no full-time medical staff and no nursing coverage on weekends or nights, even if critically ill patients were being held in them. Medical supplies were in short supply, and few trained medical personnel were either employed or available to prisoners; medical staff for the entire four-thousand-inmate prison system consisted of no more than three registered nurses. The court characterized these conditions as "barbarous" and found the prisons to be in violation of the Eighth Amendment's prohibition of "cruel and unusual punishment" (*Newman v. State*, 12 Crim. L. Rptr. 2113 [M.D. Ala. 1972]).

Deficient care was not restricted to the southern United States. A 1972 study of medical care in Pennsylvania's prisons by the University of Pennsylvania Law School's Health Law Project (Health Law Project 1972) identified a number of deficiencies. Newly committed prisoners were given only cursory medical examinations, with no provision for ongoing medical surveillance. Access to "sick call," the only point of entry to medical care, was often barred by guards who lacked training in medical triage. Special diets were virtually nonexistent; diabetics were simply told to select their food from regular meals, without instructions or assistance. Provisions for psychiatric services were grossly inadequate. For example, prisoners who tried to hang themselves were simply cut down, given medication, and returned to their cells without psychiatric evaluations. Rudimentary quality controls, such as medical audits, were lacking. Also absent were provisions for informed consent and a mechanism through which prisoners could question care provided or voice their grievances. Allocation of health care personnel and equipment throughout the system was largely unplanned and not reflective of actual needs. Although serious deficiencies were noted at the system's two major medical facilities, other facilities contained equipped but unused operating rooms and laboratories. One major prison had no registered nurses on its staff, and prisoners whose backgrounds qualified them to perform useful health care tasks were often given work assignments as janitors.

The New York State Special Commission on Attica painted a depressing portrait of how health care was delivered in that prison prior to the riot in 1971:

> Most inmate contact with the medical services was through sick call, which began at 8:00 or 8:30 a.m. and lasted for 2 to 2 1/2 hours, Monday through Friday. Any inmate who wished to see the doctor identified himself to the officer supervising his company and was taken to the pharmacy instead of to his morning assignment. Average attendance was 100 to 125. No examinations were given at sick call; there was not enough time and neither doctor felt it was necessary. [Two physicians were employed by the prisons at the time.] A counter topped by a mesh screen which extended to the ceiling divided the pharmacy in two, and separated the doctor from the inmate. At sick call, the doctors asked the nature of the inmate's complaint and either sent him back to his assignment or to his cell after dispensing whatever medication he thought was appropriate. Only in rare cases, the doctors directed

an officer to conduct the man to the examination room. The approach was very businesslike, very direct, and very authoritarian, and usually took but a few seconds. The time and effort necessary to explain, to help provide insight, to gain acceptance, to achieve confidence, were absent. As is often true when the doctor-patient relationship is imposed, not chosen, there was no element of faith and confidence. This was a major complaint by inmates, who further stated that the doctors regularly made disparaging comments, and asked insulting questions, such as "How do you know you have a headache?" or "Pain? I don't see any pain." If an inmate objected to the doctor's disposition of his complaint, he was often threatened with commitment to the psychiatric ward, a threat which Dr. Williams [one of the two prison physicians] confirmed had been carried out. (New York State Special Commission on Attica 1972, pp. 65–66)

In such an environment, it is difficult to imagine how a physician would be able to detect and treat any but the most obvious conditions. The time spent with each patient averaged about one minute. Provision of mental health services was no better:

The paucity of resources and staff also affected how mental health care was provided. It was impossible for the psychiatrists to provide other than an occasional consultation and direct supervision when a true crisis occurred. Some 40 percent of the inmates had requested appointments but it took months before an inmate could be seen, and most were not seen at all unless a crisis arose. . . . Because of the great need among inmates in the area of operational and emotional distress, the medical department has, over the years, developed a procedure in sick call which compensates, but in an eventually damaging way, for the lack of psychiatric availability. Inmates whose complaints were such as might seem indicative of mental or emotional disturbances were given tranquilizers and other support and maintenance drugs in the hope that they would carry the inmates as long as possible without serious or repeated episodes of uncontrollable behavior, with their consequent disturbances. Of course, since the earlier stages were not adequately treated, some inmates tended to become worse than they would have otherwise. This in turn led to increasing numbers of highly disturbed inmates which necessitated a closed ward which was then no longer available for less disturbed persons, who were then merely continued on drugs. In substance the Department of Psychiatry at Attica was overwhelmed and preoccupied with meeting purely technical and legal requirements involved in inmate movement in and out of the prison and with emotional disturbances when those got beyond the level which the correction officers and the general medical personnel could adequately handle. (New York State Special Commission on Attica 1972, pp. 70–71)

One might reasonably wonder if conditions reported in lawsuits and special commissions to investigate prison riots were representative of American prisons at the time. Assessments by several other contemporary observers suggest that they were not atypical. One public health professional concluded as late as 1977 that prison health care is "the furthest removed from any semblance of 'mainstream' medical care" (Newport 1977, p. 565). The medical director of Michigan's state prison health care system declared that this nation's prison health system was two notches below the inner cities (Dr. Jay Harness; Hart 1979, p. 6)—which places it lower than the health care systems found in many developing countries. Studies by the General Accounting Office in the 1970s found that prison health care facilities were frequently old, small, dark, crowded, noisy, and lacking modern or sufficiently available technical equipment and supplies (General Accounting Office 1978, 1981). Reviewing health care in 1983, two authors characterized the existing accounts as portraying many prison health services as "virtually primitive" (Lichtenstein and Rykwalker 1983).

II. The Federal Courts Intervene to Improve Prisoners' Health Care

Presented with cases alleging appallingly unhygienic conditions and inadequate health care services in prisons and jails, the federal courts began in the late 1960s to accept cases and to rule in favor of prisoners' claims. Prior to this, the courts had deferred to the expertise of correctional administrators. Within a few years, the courts established and defined prisoners' constitutional rights to adequate health care. Prison administrators responded by improving procedures and facilities for care, although some of the structural obstacles to providing medical care have persisted.

Prior to the early 1970s, judges in state and federal courts employed common-law, statutory, and administrative law doctrines to guide their responses to complaints by prisoners alleging inadequate medical care

(Neisser 1977, p. 921, n. 2). During the late 1960s, however, federal courts began searching for standards based on the U.S. Constitution. Early decisions focused on gross and "shocking" deprivation of basic hygiene in correctional facilities, in large part because the Eighth Amendment was interpreted by the courts as proscribing torture and other barbarous physical punishments. For example, in *Holt v. Sarver* (309 F. Supp. 362 [E.D. Ark. 1970]), *aff'd*, 442 F.2d 304 (8th Cir. 1971), the court established an imprecise test of what constituted unconstitutional care in a challenge to conditions and practices throughout the entire Arkansas prison system, including medical and dental care: "Generally speaking the punishment that amounts to torture, or that is grossly imposed, or is inherently unfair, or that is unnecessarily degrading, or that is shocking or disgusting to people of reasonable sensitivity is 'cruel and unusual' punishment. And a punishment that is not inherently cruel and unusual may become so by reason of the manner in which it is inflicted" (p. 380).

With respect to medical care, however, the courts had difficulties relying on the barbarous conduct standard for judging its adequacy. Nor was the standard found satisfactory for claims of deprivation of medical treatment, or where prisoners alleged inadequate medical care for serious ailments that were not life threatening, or allegations of misconduct by health care providers. Pressures mounted for reformulation.

In 1976, the U.S. Supreme Court took the opportunity in *Estelle v. Gamble* (429 U.S. 98, 97 Sup. Ct. 285 [1976]) to refine constitutional principles governing the states' obligation to provide medical care to prisoners. Gamble, an inmate in a Texas prison who was injured on a work assignment, alleged that he was not cared for adequately and that the custodial staff interfered with his care. The court concluded that "deliberate indifference to serious medical needs of prisoners constitutes the 'unnecessary and wanton affliction of pain' [citation omitted] proscribed by the Eighth Amendment. This is true whether the indifference is manifested by prison doctors in their response to the prisoner's needs, or by prison guards in intentionally denying or delaying access to medical care or intentionally interfering with the treatment once prescribed. Regardless of how evidenced, deliberate indifference to a prisoner's serious illness or injury states a cause of action" (p. 291).

Later rulings established that because prisoners cannot obtain their own medical services, the Constitution obligates correctional authorities to provide prisoners with "reasonably adequate" medical care

(*Newman v. Alabama,* 559 F.2d 283, 291 [5th Cir.]; *Hoptowit v. Ray,* 682 F.2d 1237, 1246 [9th Cir. 1982]; *Wolfish v. Levi,* 573 F.2d 118, 125 [2d Cir. 1978]; *Langley v. Coughlin,* 888 F.2d 252, 254 [2d Cir. 1989]). "Adequate" medical services have been interpreted to mean "services at a level reasonably commensurate with modern medical science and of a quality acceptable within prudent professional standards" (*Fernandez v. United States; United States v. DeCologero,* 821 F.2d 39, 43 [1st Cir. 1987]; *Tillery v. Owens,* 719 F. Supp. 1256, 1305 [W.D. Pa. 1989], *aff'd,* 907 F.2d 418 [3d Cir. 1990]). In *Tillery v. Owens,* "adequate" services were defined as those affording "a level of health services reasonably designed to meet routine and emergency medical, dental and psychological or psychiatric care" (p. 1301).

Interestingly, in *Estelle v. Gamble,* the court did not rule in the plaintiff's favor, as the plaintiff had not alleged that he was denied treatment, but rather that the treatment he received was inadequate. To the court, this appeared as a malpractice claim rather than a valid federal claim of medical mistreatment. Since then, the courts have continued to see no constitutional issue in arguments about whether the medical provider's professional judgments or techniques were appropriate (Boston and Manville 1996, p. 40). Matters of negligence and malpractice are not generally seen as violating the Constitution, with one important exception: "Repeated examples of negligent acts which disclose a pattern of conduct by the prison medical staff" may be deemed to show "deliberate indifference" (*Ramos v. Lamm,* 639 F.2d 559, 575 [10th Cir. 1980]). Other courts concurred.[1] Fact patterns that have been found to violate this standard include delay or denial of access to medical attention (*Estelle v. Gamble*), denial of access to medical personnel qualified to exercise professional judgment about a medical problem (*Williams v. Edwards,* 547 F.2d 1206, 1216–18 [5th Cir. 1977]), failure to inquire into the essential facts necessary to make a professional judgment (*Tillery v. Owens*), interference with medical

---

[1] *Harris v. Thigpen,* 941 F.2d 1495, 1505 (11th Cir. 1991); *DeGidio v. Pung,* 920 F.2d 525, 533 (8th Cir. 1990) ("consistent pattern of reckless or negligent conduct" establishes deliberate indifference); *Todaro v. Ward,* 565 F.2d 48, 52 (2d Cir. 1977) (acts that appear negligent in isolation may constitute deliberate indifference if repeated); *Williams v. O'Leary,* 805 F. Supp. 634, 638 (N.D. Ill. 1992) (deliberate indifference could be inferred from negligent treatment of long duration); *Diaz v. Broglin,* 781 F. Supp. 566, 564 (N.D. Ind. 1991); *Langley v. Couglin,* 715 F. Supp. 522, 541 (S.D. N.Y. 1988); *Robert E. v. Lane,* 530 F. Supp. 930, 940 (N.D. Ill. 1981) ("A pattern of similar instances presumptively indicates that prison administrators have, through their programs and procedures, created an environment in which negligence is unacceptably likely"); see also *Kelley v. McGinnis,* 899 F.2d 612, 616 (7th Cir. 1990) (noting court has not ruled "definitively" on this "potential theory of recovery").

judgment by nonmedical actors (e.g., *West v. Atkins* 1988, 56, n. 15), and failures to carry out medical orders (*Estelle v. Gamble*, 429 U.S. at 105).

A number of state correctional systems came under federal court supervision, and many were required to make dramatic changes in their health care procedures. By January 1996, thirty-six states plus the District of Columbia, Puerto Rico, and the Virgin Islands were under court order or consent decree to limit population and improve conditions in either the entire state prison system or its major facilities. Thirty-one jurisdictions were under court order for overcrowding or conditions in at least one of their major prison facilities, and eight were under court order covering their entire prison system. By that date, only three states had never been involved in major litigation challenging overcrowding or conditions in their prisons (National Prison Project of the American Civil Liberties Union 1996, p. 1). Challenges to health care provision were parts of the federal cases in the majority of these jurisdictions (National Prison Project of the ACLU Foundation 1995). A survey of 1,375 state and federal correctional facilities conducted at mid-year 1995 by the U.S. Bureau of the Census and the Bureau of Justice Statistics (the most recent of such surveys) counted 139 state facilities under court order or consent decree for inadequate medical care (Stephan 1997, p. 12).

These and subsequent rulings have incompletely defined the medical services to be provided prisoners in a health care system. No single federal court decision, applicable to all prisoners in all prisons, has detailed all the specific services that must be provided. In general, the federal courts have established principles with specific examples, from which standards can be deduced. Moreover, not all court decisions apply equally to all categories of inmates. For example, some pertained only to civil commitments, or detainees, and not to convicted prisoners. Many court decrees were binding only on the specific litigants involved. For more specific guidance regarding the amounts and kinds of care to provide inmates, prison health care administrators have looked to professional standards.

III. The Development of Professional Standards for Prison Health Care

Various professional associations took up the task of developing more precise standards. In 1976, the American Public Health Association issued the first national health care standards for correctional institutions (American Public Health Association 1976). Others followed: the

American Medical Association (for jails [1978] and for prisons [1979]); the American Correctional Association (ACA; 1981); and the National Commission on Correctional Health Care (NCCHC; 1987).

The development of standards has to be seen as a laudable event, but not all have welcomed it. With the emergence of competing standards, some state administrators complained of being confronted with inconsistent demands. For example, Delaware officials argued in 1977 that the promotion of standards and accreditation had resulted in four different sets of medical standards, thereby raising problems of uniform and systematic application of standards (Blindman 1977). During the intervening twenty years, the situation has improved slightly, as there are two competing sets of standards (the ACA's and NCCHC's), but there remains considerable ambiguity regarding how much and what kinds of care prisoners should and should not be given.

IV. The Challenges of Providing Medical Care in Prisons
Developments in the law and in correctional administration have no doubt improved the quality and level of medical care that prisoners receive during the past two decades. But there are a number of difficulties in recruiting well-trained professionals, including physicians, because of prisons' remote locations and generally unappealing conditions, the absence of formally organized health care systems distinct from other functional divisions, inadequate facilities, and inadequate medical record-keeping systems.

A. Difficulties in Recruiting Well-Trained Physicians to Serve Prisoners
A number of observers noted as late as the 1960s and early 1970s that the organized medical profession had largely ignored the health care of prisoners (e.g., Dole 1974; Lindenauer and Harness 1981, p. 56; Anno 1982, p. 2923). Prison administrators may not have been as aggressive as they could have been in obtaining the resources and personnel needed to provide appropriate care, but it was also true that medical professionals did not exactly rush to serve prisoners. Indeed, prison administrators had, and continue to have, difficulties in finding physicians to work in prisons. The reasons are several. Working in prisons is generally perceived to be low-status work, and may carry a stigma (which may be less true today than in the past). The dominance of security considerations in prisons may impinge on the physician's professional autonomy. Prison physicians may sometimes be asked to perform functions that require medical skills but are not conventional

practice outside prisons. These may involve working against the patient's will, such as forced body searches, force feeding, and attendance at or even participation in executions (Thorburn 1981, p. 458). Pay is often extremely low, especially for physicians working under civil service schedules. Prisoners are difficult patients, often seen as disrespectful, distrustful, and uncooperative; since the federal courts' expansion of their rights in the 1970s, they have also become litigious. The threat of violence and fears for one's safety are substantially higher than in the free community. Medical facilities and supplies in prisons are often inadequate. Finally, routines in prisons are rigid, and the types of complaints prisoners bring to health care professionals are quite limited in scope. This tends to create a monotonous medical practice.

Recruiting physicians trained in specialties has typically been even more difficult. Most specialists are needed for consultations or treatments only infrequently, and prisons are therefore unable to provide more than a small fraction of the consumer base needed for their practices. Most specialists also work at higher rates, on average, than do general practice physicians, and are even less likely to agree to prison salary levels for part-time work. A common solution is to hire specialists on a consulting basis to conduct periodic "clinics" at the prisons. Where prisons are located in remote regions, however, needed specialists may not be available at all. An individual primary care physician needs a population base of between three thousand and five thousand persons to support his or her practice. The population base required of certain specialists is much larger. Indeed, for some specialists, the required population exceeds that of many large urban centers (Moran and Wolfe 1991).

An alternative to bringing specialists into the prisons is to take the prisoners to them, either the specialist's office or, more often, to a local hospital where the specialist practices. This is costly and risky, and is generally done only when absolutely necessary.[2]

---

[2] As of May 1997, eighteen departments of corrections reported having operational telemedicine technologies to broaden access to specialist physicians; another ten reported having plans to implement telemedicine (LIS, Inc. 1997, p. 8). Technologies now exist that enable prisoner/patients to be "presented" to specialists working thousands of miles away. Digitized information, including high-resolution video imaging, can be sent to specialists anywhere in the world who have the necessary equipment, thereby enabling remote consultations. The capital costs of such investments are high, as are communications charges, but advances in telecommunications technologies are occurring at a rapid pace, and costs are declining. Indeed, telemedicine can be cost effective in prison settings if significant numbers of trips out for medical services are avoided (McDonald et al. 1998).

Given these difficulties in recruiting physicians and other professionals, or in engaging their services in the community, it was not unusual for prison health staff to be physicians with limited institutional licenses or unlicensed foreign medical graduates, augmented by unlicensed medical corpsmen and untrained inmates serving as "nurses." These inmate nurses administered treatment, gave medication, and in some states even performed suturing and minor surgery. The use of untrained inmate nurses generally disappeared by the 1980s in the wake of lawsuits, as did reliance on unlicensed physicians (Kiel 1983, quoted in Lichtenstein and Rykwalker 1983, p. 590).

An indication of staffing levels during the period before the federal courts' expansion of prisoners' medical rights can be seen in the results of a survey conducted by the President's Commission on Law Enforcement and Administration of Justice in 1965. This surveyed all correctional facilities in the United States and reported the numbers of health care providers. The commission found 358 correctional facilities in state jurisdictions, housing an estimated 201,220 prisoners. A total of 46,680 persons were reportedly employed by these 358 correctional facilities, but only 306 such persons were either physicians, psychiatrists, or dentists—fewer than one per prison. Three hundred twenty-seven were graduate or practical nurses, and another 327 were classified as "paramedical personnel" (The President's Commission on Law Enforcement and Administration of Justice 1967, p. 42). This suggests that the typical staffing patterns at prisons was to have at most one nurse and one other paramedic staff. Whether these ratios of health care providers to prisoners were adequate was not directly assessed.

Some saw no reason for concern in such data, however. For example, Aker's 1970 survey of 110 large state penitentiaries for men concluded that the provision of medical care in these prisons compared favorably or even exceeded, on some dimensions, that available to the general nonincarcerated population (Aker 1970). A study of Nebraska's penal complex concluded that although "medical coverage is less than what is suggested by the ACA Manual, . . . it is sufficient for the needs of the Complex" (Kearney 1970, p. III-43). A study for the New York State Special Commission on Attica (1972, p. 64) concluded that although inadequate medical care was cited by prisoners as one of their principal grievances, the "ratio of doctors to prisoners compares favorably with the norms for small rural communities such as Attica."

Simple ratios of providers to prisoners do not indicate the sufficiency of care, however. Not all staff were employed full-time at the time of these surveys, and the numbers of full-time equivalents were not reported. Moreover, drawing comparisons with ratios observed in the larger society outside the prison is inappropriate. In prisons, most health care staff are primary care providers, and they do nearly all of the work. In the larger society, primary care physicians refer many of their patients to specialists instead of caring for them directly, which enables them to manage a much larger population than would be possible without these resources. Furthermore, ratios cannot be used to infer service quality or sufficiency if no account is made of the demands for service. Utilization rates for health care services are considerably higher in prison than in the general nonincarcerated population. Mere counts of numbers of health care providers do not indicate the extent to which needs are met. For example: even though the consultant hired to evaluate Attica's health care provision judged the physician-to-prisoner ratio to be about the same as in the surrounding rural community, the average time spent with each prisoner in sick call line was approximately one minute. This latter fact speaks more to the quality of care afforded inmates than does a ratio of doctors to patients.

More revealing data about physicians were developed in a 1979 study, well after federal courts forced many prisons to improve health care. Lichtenstein and Rykwalker (1983) surveyed all licensed physicians in the United States who diagnosed or treated patients with non-psychiatric problems on a regularly scheduled basis, for at least twelve hours a month, inside a federal or state prison for adults or adolescents. They identified 382 prison physicians, 58 percent of whom were only part-time. The remaining 42 percent worked full-time in prisons, and physicians in this latter group accounted for nearly three-quarters of the physician hours in the nation's prisons.

A comparison of prison physicians to all physicians in the United States showed them to be similar in age, gender, training, and specialty status. The full-time prison physicians, however, differed significantly from both the part-timers and from the general population of physicians. Among full-time prison physicians, there was a higher percentage having restricted licenses, limited postgraduate medical training, no area of specialization, and no board certification. They were older, on average, and a high proportion (33 percent) were graduates of foreign medical schools. Among physicians in general, licensure, longer periods of training, board certification, specialization, and graduating from domestic rather than foreign medical schools have all been associated with higher quality performance. Given this, Lichtenstein and Rykwalker concluded that "one cannot be sanguine about the quality of care the full-time prison physicians are likely to provide, since their profile indicates that a disproportionate number have characteristics associated with lower quality care" (1983, p. 595).

Whether this conclusion applies to prison health care providers in the late 1990s is difficult to determine, for lack of a more recent survey.

B. *Absence of Specialized Medical Departments in Prisons*

Until recently, medical personnel employed in most correctional institutions did not work in separate departments having specialized lines of authority, led by physician directors. Rather, all such personnel reported to security staff or, ultimately, to the prisons' superintendents. This use of solo practitioners, unsupervised by professionally trained physicians, paralleled the "unmanaged" character of medical care provision in the broader society. Until recently, the majority of all physicians were self-employed, in solo practice, and enjoyed a high degree of professional autonomy. With respect to developing discrete prison health care organizations, the United States lagged far behind England and other countries. In 1794, the English Parliament passed the first model rules for English prisoners, which required doctors to visit the patients every day, examine every person on admission, see every prisoner at least once per week, inquire into the state of his body and mind, and so forth (Sandrick 1981, p. 30). By 1981, the service employed more than one hundred full-time and one hundred part-time physicians (ibid.).

Organized health care units in prisons may counter weaknesses in health care staff. Certain structural attributes of medical practice, such as a high degree of staff organization, extensive use of peer review, medical school affiliation, and group rather than solo practice, have been found to be associated with higher quality of care (Williams and Brook 1975; Rhee 1977; Reidel and Reidel 1979; Lichtenstein and Rykwalker 1983). Prison health care, as of the late 1970s, at least, tended to lack such structural attributes (Weisbuch 1997, pp. 721–22). Since the late 1970s, some correctional agencies have created such health services units, but I have not determined the numbers of such units.

The virtues of distinct health services units, led by a medical director, are not obvious to all correctional managers and, in the eyes of some, are not even virtues. Some correctional agency managers prefer to allocate controlling authority over all matters involving prisoners to each facility's superintendent. This centralization of control in the superintendent's hands no doubt has its many advantages, but this tends to result in placing responsibility for clinical matters with persons having no specialized expertise in health care. In such circumstances, clinicians are more likely to operate in a relatively unmanaged environment. In contrast, physician/managers are more able to review clinicians' performance, to develop and enforce policies and guidelines for clinical practice, and to exercise clinical quality control. Medical directors are not necessary to the performance of such functions, as special committees can be established to advise the superintendents. Which kind of organizational arrangement is most conducive of effective clinical practice is an empirical question that has not been studied systematically.

C. Inadequate Facilities

Provision of adequate health care in prisons has commonly been limited by inadequate facilities. Prisons typically lack sufficient facilities for treating prisoners in other than sick call lines. Most have no ability to isolate infectious patients from the general population. Infirmaries are generally unable to provide skilled nursing round the clock. Prisoners requiring treatment for chronic illnesses are, in many jurisdictions, not separated from the general population and placed in specialized facilities. Diagnostic and testing equipment are rarely available. Consequently, prisons have nearly always relied on hospitals in the surrounding communities to care for prisoners needing treatment not available in the prisons, including specialist consultations, diagnoses, observation, and surgery. Because prisoners must be taken to hospitals under armed guard, which must be posted round the clock for the duration of the prisoner's stay, the costs and risks associated with hospital visits create a high threshold for using such resources. Consequently, access to such services has no doubt been exceedingly limited for the better part of our two-hundred-year experience with prisons.

Diagnostic equipment is limited in prisons because the demand for many types of equipment is too small to justify purchasing it and employing the necessary staff. Some prisons, however, have determined that it is cost effective to buy equipment and to build suites for certain frequently used technologies, such as x-rays or, in women's prisons, mammograms.

The development of specialized facilities to house and care for the seriously ill, isolated from the general population, has also been hampered by the lack of sufficiently large numbers of prisoners to justify the investment. In recent years, however, the increasing numbers of prisoners behind bars have resulted in larger numbers of persons needing specialized treatment. Moreover, health services now consume substantial portions of the correctional agency's budget, and the cost/benefit calculations begin to look different with respect to investments in specialized facilities. Consequently, some agencies have created specialized medical facilities—including fully equipped hospitals—behind prison walls. For example, the Federal Bureau of Prisons has long operated a number of medical centers within selected prisons, the largest of which is at Springfield, Missouri, which has approximately 750 beds for medical/surgical and psychiatric patients (McDonald 1995, p. 30). Georgia's Department of Corrections in 1989 converted an infirmary into a 135-bed hospital, the Augusta Correctional Medical Institution, which provides hospital services to all prisoners in the state (ibid., p. 34). Nevada created surgical capacity in its 120-bed acute care medical facility on the grounds of the state prison in 1994 (ibid., p. 35). In general, the demand for nonemergency surgery has to be strong enough in a state system to justify the considerable investment in building and staffing even a small hospital. All but the largest correctional systems probably lack such demand (indeed, Nevada's surgery suite was abandoned for this reason). In an environment where hospitals in the larger society are underused, it is usually more cost effective to use these facilities on an as-needed basis, even while incurring the high costs of armed escort.

Although most prison systems have not found it cost effective to build hospitals behind the walls, they have been developing specialized facilities to care for prisoners suffering from acute or chronic illnesses that do not require hospitalization. Because both types of patients need close attention, dedicating certain prisons to providing that care relieves other prisons in the state's system from having to provide this specialized capacity. By mid-year 1995, 177 of 1,196 state or federal correctional facilities were dedicated to medical treatment or hospitalization of inmates, double the number that existed only five years earlier (Stephan 1997, p. 7).

D. Inadequate Medical Data Systems

Poorly organized record-keeping practices and data collection procedures also have created obstacles to delivering effective care. Patient information, to the extent that it was collected at all, went into each prisoner's medical records. These records would follow prisoners as they were transferred from prison to prison, but may not follow them in time to inform caregivers at the facilities to which prisoners were reassigned. Rarely were data from these paper records used to assess patterns of service use or to conduct any number of epidemiological studies that could have been useful for improving health care. This primitive level of data collection continues to the present day in most correctional agencies (although most now maintain better medical records for prisoners, if for no other reason than to protect against lawsuits).

V. Do Prisoners Now Get Too Much Health Care?

Prisoners make heavy use, on average, of health care services. The efforts over the past two and half decades to expand access to care have no doubt contributed to this. The question whether such health care utilization levels are appropriate is a controversial one, however, and legislatures and departments of corrections in a number of states have instituted practices and policies to curb prisoners' calls for care. Unfortunately, the debate is occurring without any clear benchmarks as to what constitutes "appropriate" or "excessive" use of services.

The precise nature of prisoners' use of health care services has been little documented. In 1972, Twaddle (1976) examined medical records of 293 randomly selected inmates in a Midwestern U.S. penitentiary as well as aggregate counts of health care encounters for all prisoners. On any given day, approximately 5 percent of all prisoners were seen by a health care provider. Although the form of the data he collected did not allow him to measure utilization rates directly, he estimated that prisoners used health care services approximately four times as heavily as the general U.S. population (which was about 4.3 visits annually to a physician per person). Interestingly, these higher rates were found during a period before the widespread expansion of prisoners' rights to care.

A study of eleven Canadian prisons in 1984 provides another picture, although one cannot assume that it reflects patterns found in U.S. prisons. A study of all prisoners in the Correctional Services of Canada's Pacific Region documented an average of 5.2 health service encounters during a single month (Sheps, Schechter, and Prefontaine 1987). Physician visits occurred at a mean estimated annual rate of 6.7 visits per year, a rate that was 2.4 percent higher than the rate for nonincarcerated men in Canada.

A more recent study of all Washington State's prisons (McDonald, Heliotis, and Hyatt 1997, pp. 31–35) determined that prisoners used medical (not including mental health or dental) services an average of 4.5 times during the first three months of 1996—a rate lower than that measured in the Canadian study. Compared to encounter rates for nonincarcerated persons in the general population, though, prisoners were significantly heavier users of service.

Concluding from such studies that prisoners get too much care, relative to persons who have not committed crimes serious enough to warrant their imprisonment, is premature. Prisoners lack the ability to treat and medicate themselves and are more reliant on the formal health care system than nonincarcerated persons. Free persons go to pharmacies and other retail stores for a wide variety of over-the-counter preparations and supplies. Prisoners have no such alternative, and must stand in sick call lines to receive all but the most trivial medications. (Correctional officers in the cell blocks are authorized in some states to dispense aspirin, but little more.) Moreover, prison authorities control the supply of medication tightly in prisons, and generally do not permit prisoners to bring more than a day's supply back to their cells, if at all. Prisoners suffering from colds and other minor illnesses cannot be cared for by other prisoners, whereas free persons often rely on family members rather than on a physician. Prisoners may also be required to get formal permission from health care providers to skip work assignments—which requires going to sick call.

The high average rates of health care utilization are also misleading because a large proportion of health care is consumed by small numbers of prisoners. Sheps, Schechter, and Prefontaine reported finding that 3.5 percent of the population in eleven Canadian prisons accounted for 25 percent of all encounters during the study period (1987, p. 4). In their study of Washington State's prisons, McDonald, Heliotis, and Hyatt found that although all prisoners paid a visit to a medical care provider during the first three months of 1996, eighty-five inmates out of a population of nearly eleven thousand accounted for 10 percent of all visits (1997, p. 36). These high-rate consumers saw medical providers an average of three times per week; some saw medical staff twice a day. This pattern parallels practice in the general U.S. population: approximately one-fifth of all persons consume about 80 percent of all medical resources (Blue Cross and Blue Shield System 1991, p. 6). Rather than conclude that medical services are abused by prisoners, these patterns suggest that specific approaches designed to serve high-rate consumers of care (e.g., patients with chronic illnesses) might be more appropriate than broad-spectrum remedies prescribed by legislatures, such as requiring prisoners to pay fees for their medical services.

The fundamental difficulty in drawing conclusions about the frequency of prisoners' use of health care is that no benchmarks exist for this particular type of population. Prisoners' opportunities for treating themselves are much more limited than those afforded persons not incarcerated, and one must thereby expect them to make many more calls on the formally organized health care system in the prison. The absence of automated health care record-keeping systems in all but a few states makes it difficult to describe patterns of health care utilization and to develop notions of average, "normal," or expected rates.

VI. Are Prisoners Sicker than Persons Not Incarcerated?
One possible explanation of prisoners' relatively heavier use of health care services is that they are in worse health than persons not imprisoned. It has often been assumed that prisoners are in poorer health than others because of their poverty and high rates of substance abuse prior to being committed to prison, although the health status of inmates has been little studied. Most of what we know is about the incidence of particular specific diseases, such as HIV, or of deaths, rather than their more general health. Most prison systems lack procedures for assessing prisoners' health in ways that can be used for comparisons with other population. Some agencies, such as the Washington State, Florida, and North Carolina departments of correction, have recently initiated use of a screening and classification system adapted from the U.S. armed services but such systems are the exception rather than the rule.[3] Most information about prisoners' health remains in written medical files rather than in computerized data bases, and is not aggregated into broad classifications. Special studies are therefore needed to develop accurate descriptions of prisoners' health.

One such study was conducted during a two-week period in 1975, in which all 1,420 prisoners admitted to the New York City correctional

---

[3] These classification systems are derived from the PULHES scheme used by the U.S. military. They grade the functioning of the prisoners' body systems, distinguishing physical capability (P), upper extremities (U), lower extremities (L), hearing (H), vision (E), mental functioning (S); some also add other functional dimensions, such as dental, general functional capacity, likelihood of needing transportation, and general impairment. (See, e.g., State of Florida 1992.)

facilities were assessed to determine the prevalence of current and past health conditions (Novick et al. 1977). As these facilities serve as jails for the city, findings from the study were indicative of prisoners' status at the time of commitment, and cannot be expected to parallel the status of prisoners in state or federal prisons. They concluded that "prisoners are not a healthy population but have a high frequency of medical complaints, problems and prior hospitalizations, largely associated with substance abuse, psychiatric disorder, and trauma" (p. 215). However, New York City prisoners were not necessarily less healthy than persons not incarcerated. They found 10 percent of all incoming males and 11 percent of females reporting hospitalizations during the six months prior to admission, compared with rates of 8 and 17 percent, respectively, for males and females ages seventeen to forty-four in the general population hospitalized during a twelve-month period (Novick et al. 1977, p. 211). Proportions found to have high blood pressure were approximately equivalent in the jailed and general populations. More recently, the Florida Department of Correction reported that, according to its PULHESDXTI health classification system, 1 percent of all inmates in custody on November 4, 1997, were severely impaired or had one or more severe medical conditions that required continuous monitoring; another 8 percent had a medical condition or physical defect that required certain restrictions in assignments to ensure reasonable availability of care; 35 percent, while meeting acceptable standards of functional capabilities, had some medical or mental condition that might impose limitations on assignments (Burke 1997).

A study of a sample of federal prisons released in 1989 found that the health of most prisoners (89 percent) did not change during the course of their incarceration (Wallace et al. 1991). Seven percent of those sampled worsened—largely older, Hispanic, and higher-security inmates—while 4 percent were deemed to have improved.

As for mortality, one study of deaths in Maryland's state prisons between 1979 and 1987 concluded that male inmates had a 39 percent lower all-cause death rate than the general population of the state after adjustments were made for age and race (Salive, Smith, and Brewer, 1990, p. 1479). (A lower death rate, relative to the general population, was also reported in New York City correctional facilities in 1971–75 by Novick and Remmlinger 1978, p. 753.) The risk of death by injuries was lower, probably because access to weapons is more limited in prison, the authors hypothesized, and the risk of motor vehicle accidents is nearly completely eliminated. The risk of death from most other causes was also lower, perhaps because access to medical care may be greater for these persons than for the general population having similar sociodemographic characteristics, which may lead to early detection and treatment of chronic diseases. Rates of death from infectious diseases and suicide were higher than in the general population, however.

A. HIV/AIDS

At the end of 1996, the rates of confirmed AIDS cases in state and federal prisons were about six times higher than in the general population (Hammett, Maruschak, and Harmon, forthcoming; also see, more generally, Braithwaite, Hammett, and Mayberry 1996). Whereas the rates in the general population were nine in ten thousand persons, fifty-four in ten thousand prisoners were reported as suffering from AIDS. At the end of 1996, state and federal prisons reported holding 5,874 confirmed AIDS patients, which represented 0.5 percent of all prisoners in these facilities. Since 1991, the number of confirmed AIDS cases in these prisons had increased 248 percent. Most were concentrated in a few states; New York, Texas, and California held 55 percent of all AIDS patients. About three out of ten deaths among prisoners during 1996 were attributed to AIDS, making it the second leading cause of death, behind natural causes other than AIDS.

This high prevalence rate should not be surprising (see, e.g., American College of Physicians, National Commission on Correctional Health Care, and American Correctional Health Services Association 1992). Commenting on the fact that injection drug users are at high risk of contracting HIV infections, the National Commission on Acquired Immune Deficiency Syndrome (1991) wrote in 1990: "By choosing mass imprisonment as the Federal and State governments' response to the use of drugs, we have created a de facto policy of incarcerating more individuals with HIV infection. Under the present policy, the percentage of drug offenders in the Federal prison system will rise by 1995 from 47 percent to 70 percent. Clearly, we are thus concentrating the HIV disease problem in our prisons and must take immediate action to deal with it more effectively."

By the end of 1996, state and federal prisons housed 24,881 inmates known to be infected with the human immunodeficiency virus. The number of such known cases has been increasing steadily since 1991, but this appears to be the result of growing prison populations. The proportion of all state and federal prisoners who were known to be

HIV-positive remained nearly unchanged between 1991 and 1996—2.3 percent and 2.4 percent, respectively (Hammett, Maruschak, and Harmon, forthcoming). Prisoners known to be HIV-positive are also concentrated in a few states. New York had the highest proportion—13.2 percent of all state prisoners at the end of 1996.

These HIV prevalence rates may be underestimated. The true proportion of all prisoners infected with HIV is not known for lack of universal testing, and the estimates reported above were obtained from a variety of testing programs, some voluntary and others not. Comparisons in some selected jurisdictions of prevalence rates reported among voluntarily tested prisoners and blinded studies designed to be representative found significant differences. The true rate is likely to be higher than 2–3 percent, but how much higher is difficult to estimate given the limited data.

B. Tuberculosis

Tuberculosis (TB) is significantly more prevalent in prison populations than in the larger society. Prisons draw on those populations which are at high risk of TB infection—those having poor health care before commitment, crowded or itinerant living conditions, prior IV drug use, and compromised immune systems (principally from HIV). In 1996, a survey by the Centers for Disease Control found an incidence rate of 48 per 100,000 prisoners, six times that in the general population (Centers for Disease Control 1997, p. 19). State and federal correctional systems responding to the survey reported a total of almost fifteen thousand TB-infected inmates—that is, those testing positive in purified protein derivative (PPD) skin tests. The incidence of new cases among prison admissions is declining, largely because control measures were strengthened during the 1990s after the resurgence of TB in the general U.S. population was identified.

Especially troubling, however, was the emergence of drug-resistant TB. Drug-resistant TB develops when individuals begin taking medication for TB but do not finish their course of treatment. National estimates suggest that only three-quarters of all persons beginning treatment complete the full twelve months of therapy. Treatment completion rates are far worse in some urban areas: 60 percent in Washington, D.C., 58 percent in Chicago, 54 percent in New York, and a staggering 11 percent among tuberculosis clients at Harlem Hospital, which serves a high-risk, poor, African-American population (Bayer, Dubler, and Landesman 1993).

The available treatment for drug-resistant TB involves risks and takes much longer (up to two years) and treatment efficacy is poor. Among nonimmunocompromised individuals, multidrug resistant strains have a 50 percent cure rate and are not preventable. Among immunocompromised individuals, such as those coinfected with HIV/ AIDS, disease management and control is not even that successful. During 1991, multiple and rapid TB fatalities (mean survival duration after sputum culture diagnosis was twenty-five days) occurred in the New York State correctional system as a result of exposure to and infection with multidrug resistant strains of tuberculosis among immunocompromised (HIV-infected) inmates and staff. Over fifty instances of TB skin test conversions occurred as a result of this brief epidemic among inmates and others who came in contact with these cases (Centers for Disease Control 1992).

Nationwide, the number of drug-resistant TB cases is still relatively small. Nonetheless, TB infection, especially in combination with immunocompromised inmates, amounts to a kind of public health dynamite. Correctional facilities are nearly ideal places for transmitting the disease, and large numbers of prisoners return to the free community to live among others who are already at high risk of infection. Fortunately, correctional systems have instituted TB control procedures, including screening and treatment. During 1997, nine-tenths of all surveyed prison systems required mandatory testing for TB infection at admission and at regular intervals subsequently (Hammett, Maruschak and Harmon, forthcoming, table 8.3).

VII. Rising Expenditures for Prison Health Care

Improving health care provision in the nation's prisons has come at a financial cost. Spending for the health care of prisoners has been increasing rapidly during the past several years—a trend that has alarmed legislatures in several states and has prompted intensified interest in managed care practices or even the "privatization" of prison health care. It is difficult to know precisely how spending has changed at the state or local levels in the absence of uniform accounting and reporting, but comparison of data from three nationwide surveys provides some indication.

Surveys of expenditures for prisoner health care by state departments of correction were conducted by Contact, Inc., in 1982, 1985, 1993, and again in 1995 (Contact, Inc. 1983, 1986; Davis 1993; Wess 1996). In 1990, the NCCHC undertook another survey of state departments and obtained information about 1989 expenditures for health care, employing similar categories (Anno 1991). The latest of these surveys reported state departments of correction budgeting $2.3 billion per year during 1995 for health care, or approximately $2,308 per prisoner. This per prisoner expenditure was 160 percent over 1982 levels (reportedly $883 per year). Although the year-to-year increases varied during this period, the average annual increase in per prisoner spending was 8 percent. Between 1982 and 1989, the average annual rate of increase was higher (about 12 percent), and lower (about 3.5 percent) between 1989 and 1995. Total expenditures for health care rose even faster than per capita amounts during these periods, because the numbers of prisoners under custody increased dramatically throughout the nation.

The surveys also found dramatic differences between states. For example, the 1995 survey reported the highest annual per prisoner expenditure for health care to be $3,740 and the lowest to be $566 (Wess 1996). Although surveys documenting the types of services and the quality of services provided in each of the states do not exist, differences in per prisoner expenditure no doubt reflect differing levels of care provided.

Unfortunately, it is difficult to feel confident about the accuracy of these data. State correctional agencies were asked to report voluntarily, with little guidance in how to classify and report different categories of expense. Most reported not expenditures but planned expenditures (i.e., budgets). Not all jurisdictions reported, and the same states did not respond to each of the surveys. Perhaps most importantly, states vary widely in how responsibilities for health care are divided. In some states, separate state departments of mental health hygiene provide psychological and psychiatric services to prisoners, on their own budgets. In several states, committed prisoners identified as mentally ill are not even under the correctional agency's jurisdiction, and are transferred to other departments. State medical schools may provide services to prisoners, and the cost of these services may not be included in the correctional agency's accounts; state hospitals may also provide hospitalization and other medical or mental health care at no cost to the correctional agency. Chemical dependency/substance abuse programs may or may not be counted. A full accounting of all these shared costs in all states would no doubt raise the cost of correctional health care above the $2.3 billion reported in 1995. Because prison health care costs have been rising at faster rates than prison operations generally, they are consuming progressively larger proportions of the available resources for correctional agencies. In 1982, 7.2 percent of all correctional expenditures were for health care, according to the survey discussed above; by 1995, this had risen to 10.5 percent (Davis 1993; Wess 1996).

These higher levels of spending no doubt reflect, in part, improvements in the amount and quality of care provided to prisoners. Some of these improvements were mandated by the courts, at a substantial cost. In Texas, for example, prison health care expenditures increased 473 percent between 1982 and 1989 (Anno 1991, p. 250), a result in part at least of the U.S. federal district court's demands in *Ruiz v. Estelle* (1980), which found the conditions in the state's prisons, including their health care services, to be unconstitutional. The development of standards for health care provision, the growing importance of accreditation, and the increasing professionalization of prison health care during the past two decades have brought improvements in the quality of services, which no doubt explains some of the increases in per prisoner expenditures.

One effect of federal court attention to prison conditions has been to deepen the dependence of prison systems on community health care providers. Lowering the walls between penal institutions and health care institutions in the larger society has increased prisons' exposure to inflationary tendencies in the broader health care marketplace. Health care in the larger society got more expensive during the 1980s and early 1990s. Between 1982 and 1995, the cost of a fixed "market basket" of medical goods and services used by the U.S. Department of Labor's Bureau of Labor Statistics to track inflation appreciated 124 percent. This rate of increase outpaced the 54 percent increase in the cost of the Bureau's most general index of all goods and services (U.S. Department of Labor 1996, table 25). Prison systems that purchased goods and services in this larger health care marketplace wound up paying higher and higher prices for the same goods and services. In California, for example, the Department of Corrections projected a 29 percent increase in its costs for community hospital contracts alone during fiscal year 1994 (California Department of Corrections 1994). In the Federal Bureau of Prisons, there was a 27 percent increase in per capita spending between fiscal years 1990 and 1993 for inpatient, outpatient, and other services from community providers of care (Waldron, n.d.).

Some of the increase in spending for prisoners' medical care also reflects the growing proportion of female prisoners in our nation's correctional facilities—prisoners whose care is more costly, on average, than men's. The proportion of women to all prisoners has grown larger in recent years. Their care requires the same specialists and providers that men need, as well as gynecological and obstetrical services. Moreover, correctional standards (e.g., National Commission on Correctional Health Care 1987) require that women be given the same level of medical care as men, as well as the additional services that are required to meet their health care needs. Larger proportions of female prisoners therefore result in higher per capita health care costs, in the absence of countervailing cost-containment programs.

VIII. Are Expenditures for Prisoners Too High?

Is $2,300—or even $3,700—too costly an expenditure for prisoners? Are expenditures this high indicative of significant deficiencies in the management of the state prison health care systems? Unfortunately, there exist few benchmarks on which to base an answer to these questions. Health care delivery in prisons is very different from delivery in the world beyond prison walls. Consequently, one must be cautious in comparing expenditures for prisoners with expenditures by health care plans for beneficiaries who are not incarcerated. For example, average annual Medicaid per capita expenditure nationwide was $3,042 in 1993 (Health Care Financing Administration 1995). Medicaid service packages vary by state, but they typically cover prescription drugs, dental services, mental health, and all the usual institutional and home/community-based services. Medicaid does not cover the cost of over-the-counter pharmaceutical supplies, or the labor associated with providing them. It is difficult to know how much larger this expenditure would be if such expenditures were counted.

The other difficulty in using the Medicaid average is that prisoners differ from the population of Medicaid recipients. Indeed, the average Medicaid expenditure varied according to the type of beneficiary, from $1,013 in 1993 for low-income children to $6,168 for low-income aged, many of whom are in nursing homes. Arguably, the most appropriate comparison population is that comprising low-income nondisabled adults; the average per capita Medicaid expenditure for these persons was $1,813 during 1993.

Not all prisoners are free of disabilities, however. Some proportion suffer from significant physical disabilities and mental illnesses. Others are old and suffer from a variety of high-cost acute and chronic conditions. Lacking information that would enable us to characterize the mix of the prisoner/patients according to their health status, we cannot estimate what would be the average per capita Medicaid expenditure for an equivalent population.

Despite these caveats, it is probably fair to conclude that the average annual expenditure for prisoners in the nation's prisons is in the same approximate ballpark as expenditures for Medicaid recipients.

IX. Managed Care Comes to Prison

In the face of rising expenditures for prisoner health care, correctional administrators have become interested in managed care strategies developed in the free community's health care marketplace (McDonald 1995). During the past twenty-five years, and especially in the last decade, government agencies, private insurance companies, and health care providers have developed a number of strategies to control the cost of health care more effectively. Some of these strategies have been pursued because they also appear to promise delivery of better care. Whether these innovations have in fact succeeded either in controlling costs or delivering better care has been the topic of considerable debate. However, even in the absence of clear and compelling research on the effectiveness of these cost-containment procedures in the free community, many correctional managers have begun to adapt them for use in prisons. The importation of these managed care practices into prison systems raises several interesting issues, as well as challenges of implementation. Of special importance is the greater demand in prison systems than in the free community for managed care strategies to improve the quality of care. Whereas cost containment has been the dominant objective animating the development of managed care in the larger society, improving the quality of care is of at least equal importance in prison systems. For this reason, the goals of managed care strategies are perhaps more demanding in prison environments than elsewhere.

Managed care reforms were developed for the purpose of restructuring the decentralized health care market that had existed in this country prior to the 1990s. The essential characteristics of this "unmanaged" system included a predominance of professionally autonomous physicians, a high degree of medical specialization, purchasing choices by individual consumers/patients, fee-for-service payment arrangements, multitiered public and private payment, unregulated pricing by physicians and hospitals, weak controls over the quality of care, and the low priority the medical profession assigns to making cost-effective clinical decisions.

Although the term "managed care" eludes precise definition, it generally refers to the kind of care provided by HMOs and preferred provider organizations. Generally, managed care is a system that integrates the financing and delivery of health care services to covered individuals. The methods employed to deliver managed care include restricting patients' choices; new forms of compensation including negotiated discounts on providers' normal fees or charges; fixed payment rates for specific types of service or for hospitalization; and payments of lump sums in advance to providers for enrolled clients' care; selective contracting to build a network of providers, hospitals, physicians, and ancillary services willing to accept discounted fees or standardized rates in exchange for a promise to channel enrolled clients to them; competitive purchasing and volume discounts; constraints on utilization of expensive care; direct provision of services (the health maintenance organization is, in essence, an insurance plan that "makes" medical care using its own employed staff rather than purchasing care from independent professionals and firms); and global budgets, either in the form of expenditure caps set administratively to limit overall spending for health care services or an overall target for spending for a defined set of services and a defined set of payers.

Some (e.g., Moritsugu 1995) have argued that prisons provide favorable settings for HMO-styled managed care. Conditions supportive of managed care are seen to include the following:

Global Budgets.   Health care divisions within state prison systems are typically given budgets within which to operate. The existence of these fixed budgets in the face of strong demand for services encourages decisions designed to allocate health care resources efficiently.

Universal Coverage and Mandatory Enrollment.   Whereas the provision of health care in the larger community is fragmented by the existence of competing insurance plans and uninsured persons, all prisoners are "enrolled" in a single organization, and enrollment is mandatory.

Limited Patient Choice.   In the free community, competition for enrollees encourages health care plans to enrich their benefit packages and adopt other enticements-approaches that work against cost-effective delivery. Because prisoners have no option but to seek care through the prison's health care system, counterproductive tendencies associated with marketing are minimized.

Ability to Regulate Use of Services.   Because prisoners lack ability to consume all but the least expensive health services without the consent of prison officials, prison administrators have at least the potential of regulating prisoners' use of services very tightly. The ability to accomplish this depends in large part on the prison administration's success in controlling physicians' clinical decisions.

Relatively Fixed Patient Population.   The existence of a relatively stable patient population (over the course of a year, that is) offers the opportunity to negotiate contracts with private physicians or firms who are willing to serve patients at reduced costs in return for the agreement to funnel all patients to them.

Selective Contracting.   Because most prison systems do not provide many types of health care services directly (specialty care, primarily), they are obliged to purchase it from outside providers. This offers the opportunity to contract selectively with high-quality, cost-effective providers—essentially a network of preferred providers seeking to give cost-effective care.

But do prisons really offer fertile grounds for HMO-styled managed care strategies? Several features of prisons may work against the effective implementation of such efforts.

Inability to Bring Most Elements of the Health Care Delivery System under Direct Organizational Control.   Prisons are dependent on outside providers, which may not be in plentiful supply. Prison systems may also be required to use other public facilities, such as public hospitals, the use of which may be "free" but may create other inefficiencies.

Inability to Employ Physicians Directly.   Because of submarket rates and insufficient volume, the efficiencies gained in the free community by employing physicians as salaried staff often are less available in prison systems.

Difficulties in Managing Global Budgets.   Capitating health care costs may be difficult when responsibility for prison health care is fragmented across organizations, individuals, and several outside providers. One solution is to contract with a private health care firm to provide comprehensive care for a fixed per-capita cost.

Managers Not at Risk.   Prison administrators responsible for delivering health care are salaried employees whose salaries are protected, and not dependent on success or failure in meeting cost targets. Lacking the ability to profit directly from instituting cost containment strategies, managerial incentives may be weaker. One way of compensating for the absence of at-risk management is to contract with private providers for comprehensive health care, and to write a contract that puts these managers at financial risk for cost-inefficient care.

Absence of a Competitive Market of Providers in Rural Areas or Small Towns. Managed care strategies work better when there exists sufficient competition among providers. Kronick and his colleagues estimate that a population of 1.2 million persons is needed to support three fully independent staff-model HMOs. A population of 360,000 could support three plans that independently provided most acute care hospital services, but these plans would need to share hospital facilities and contract for tertiary services. A smaller population of 180,000 could support three plans that provided primary care and many basic specialty services but would have to share in-patient cardiology and urology services. They conclude, consequently, that reform of the U.S. health care system through expansion of managed competition is feasible only in medium-sized or large metropolitan areas. In rural areas, where most prisons are located, alternative forms of organization and regulation of health care providers are needed to improve cost efficiency and quality (Kronick et al. 1993). When prisons are dependent on a few providers, they have little or no leverage in negotiating advantageous prices.

Security Constraints. Whereas health care providers in noncorrectional settings can be single minded in their efforts to deliver cost-effective health care, health care in prison systems is constrained powerfully by a more important objective: maintaining security. Meeting this latter objective sometimes requires sacrificing cost effectiveness of health care services. For example, prisoners may be left in hospitals for long stays for security rather than health reasons.

Unpredictable Morbidity. The future rate of growth of AIDS and tuberculosis is difficult to predict. To the extent that prisoners are more likely to come from populations (e.g., drug users) that are susceptible to these diseases, their impact on prison health care costs becomes harder to predict.

Prisoner Suspicion and Expectations. Like all citizens, prisoners may have high expectations that advances in science can work miraculous cures. Prisoners, however, may doubt that the system really wants them to live longer, suffer less, or incur any significant expense in their treatment. Suspicion can result in riots. It can also cause poor compliance with treatments and thus higher long-run expense for the complications of chronic diseases.

Litigious Prisoners. As in the free community, physicians face the threat of lawsuits. Prisoners are now the only category of persons in the United States who have a constitutional right to adequate health care, and many have learned how to file *pro se* lawsuits (or have ready access to "jailhouse lawyers" who have learned). The threat of lawsuits is therefore a real one in correctional facilities. This creates an incentive to practice "defensive" medicine, a practice which is often at war with cost-effectiveness objectives.

Whether or not prisons offer all the conditions well suited to tight HMO-style health care management, correctional administrators in many states are adapting a number of specific managed care approaches to containing costs. Principal among these are various strategies for reducing the costs of goods and services relied on to provide health care services to prisoners, limiting services given to prisoners, and contracting with private correctional health care service firms.

A. Reducing the Costs of Purchased Goods and Services

Until recently, state and federal prisons generally paid suppliers of goods and services full price. Indeed, in many states, this practice continues. In part because correctional agencies have not organized their health service divisions as separate entities, with professional health care managers, purchasers have been unaware of trends outside prisons or have been insufficiently experienced in negotiating prices. Moreover, prisoners are excluded from Medicaid and Medicare eligibility, and the limits that apply to these beneficiaries with respect to payment are absent.

To obtain leverage in the marketplace for pharmaceutical supplies, many departments of correction have joined national purchasing organizations such as the Minnesota Multi-State Government Cooperative Contracting Group, or participate in other consortia. For example, the Federal Bureau of Prisons enhances its buying power by being a participant in the Veterans' Administration Prime Vendor program. In Texas, the Department of Corrections has joined with the state university's medical school hospital to purchase pharmaceutical supplies.

Some state departments of corrections have also sought to negotiate discounts or reduced rates from local hospitals or networks of hospitals—although most have not pursued these opportunities as hard as they might. In return for such discounts or reduced rates, correctional administrators agree to give these hospitals all or most of their business, thereby establishing, in effect, "preferred provider" relationships. In markets where preferred provider networks already exist, prison administrators may be able to contract with network representatives, obtaining agreements with a large number of hospitals in a single transaction. In 1997, there were 983 preferred provider networks operating in the United States (Hoechst Marion Roussel 1997, p. 67). Realistically, the most advantageous rate that can be negotiated is that given to Medicaid patients. The alternative, for hospitals unwilling to accept such low rates, is to negotiate higher per procedure rates—expressed perhaps as a percentage increase over the Medicaid rate—or a specified discount off the usual and customary charge, or a cap on the fee.

Getting preferred provider rates may produce substantial savings. A Federal Bureau of Prisons study compared the actual costs of community-based health care—inpatient, outpatient, and other services, including hospital and physician costs—delivered to inmates at three prisons with the prices that would have been charged if a California-based preferred provider organization had been used instead and had charged the bureau the prices it charged other members of its plan. Bureau analysts estimated that savings in the three prisons would have ranged from 25 percent to 33 percent, with an average of 28 percent across all three (Waldron, n.d.).

Some state departments have developed innovative arrangements with state-supported medical schools to provide care of prisoners at reduced rates. For example, the Utah Department of Corrections arranged with the University of Utah Medical Center to provide the state's prisoners with hospital services. This arrangement combined cost-based reimbursement at a discount with a global budget to minimize unnecessary use of health care services. The department paid the university $200,000 a year to contribute toward its overhead expenses and agreed to pay 63 percent of all usual and customary charges. To protect the medical center against the cost of catastrophic illnesses, the department agreed to cap full liability at $50,000 per year per inmate and agreed to share 50-50 all costs in excess of $50,000. An incentive for the medical center and the department to avoid otherwise unnecessary use was created by establishing a total amount to be spent by the department each year—essentially a global budget. If the department was billed for less than this amount because fewer services had been provided than anticipated, the department and the medical center shared the savings evenly. If the cost exceeded the contracted amount, the university paid for all of the above-budget cost, except for expenditures on catastrophic illness, which were shared according to the formula described above (Worthington 1994).

The same strategy of negotiating with preferred provider networks to obtain discounted prices is also being pursued with respect to physicians. With the emergence of competitive managed care organizations in the larger society, physicians have become increasingly willing to accept payments below their usual and customary levels. For a number of years, many of them accepted discounted payments for treating Medicare and Medicaid patients. With the pervasive growth of preferred provider networks, simple discounts became much less common and were replaced with a variety of other payment arrangements. In 1996, according to a national survey, the most common method of reimbursing physicians participating in preferred provider organizations payment was to pay a fee with a cap (86 percent of all payments that year). Eight percent were reimbursed by paying a discounted fee, 2 percent were paid according to a fixed price per patient (a "capitated" rate), and 1 percent were paid according to a schedule that fixed the price per episode, regardless of the number of visits (Hoechst Marion Roussel 1997, p. 86). However, the willingness to accept reductions is not universal and no doubt depends largely on local market conditions. For example, New York City is home to a large number of psychiatrists, and many may be willing to work at deeply discounted rates. In contrast, no such oversupply exists in many states, and the prevailing rates for psychiatrists are higher. Especially in rural areas where many prisons are located, physicians are in short supply, and specialists are even more so.

The Texas Department of Criminal Justice (TDCJ) has been successful in getting physicians to accept reduced fees. Physicians agree to accept the lesser of the billed charge or the TDCJ maximum allowable fee. This latter computed fee is determined by the use of the Medicare relative value unit (RVU) using the state's specific conversion factors (Riley 1994). Now that Medicare has begun paying all physicians on a relative value scale (RVS) basis, it is possible for states to create a fee schedule for physicians using those relative weights and a state-specific conversion factor (a base price per RVU).

B. Containing Costs by Limiting or Dissuading Prisoners' Use of Services

Common to all managed care strategies are procedures to limit patients' use of services. Some require primary care physicians to act as gatekeepers, permitting patients enrolled in their managed care organizations to see specialists or to obtain diagnostic services only with their approval. All insurance plans issue lists of services that will be covered and those that will be excluded from their "benefit package," as well as procedures for determining whether unlisted services will be covered. Many plans also use financial incentives to limit use, such as cost sharing, ranging from small copayments for all nonemergency visits to full payment for services not covered. Transporting these features into prison health care systems is difficult, however, because prisoners have a right to health care that citizens in the free community lack, and because the courts have been very active in enforcing this right. Moreover, deciding which level of care is both appropriate and constitutional is not easy.

Five broadly different approaches to controlling use of services have been tried by correctional agencies. These include attempts to limit, by means of formal regulatory powers, the use of services deemed unnecessary or inappropriate; "utilization management" procedures developed in free-community managed care programs to gain greater control over patients' use of expensive services; disincentives to discourage prisoners' unnecessary use of services by requiring copayment at the point of service; limits on the use of costly and unnecessary medication; and more expansive use of screening to identify emergent and chronic conditions (such as hypertension and diabetes) that have a potential for high expense.

1. *Limiting Services by Policy.* Prison superintendents and health care managers are often challenged by demands for services that are not easily justified as a reasonable public expenditure. Prisoners on death row have demanded kidney transplants, for example. Case law and professional standards offer relatively little guidance because they have established the minimum standards to be followed—the floor below which service cannot legally fall—but not the upper limits on what the state is obligated to provide. For example, except for stating that cosmetic surgery is not necessary unless there are "important considerations or possible serious psychological impact," the ACA standards are silent on what constitute upper limits (American Correctional Association 1989, p. 79).

Some correctional administrators have sought to establish formal policies, based on a notion of medically "necessary" and "unnecessary" care. For example, in its agreements with free-community hospitals, the Texas Department of Corrections (TDC) commits to reimburse providers for all "covered hospital services," which are defined as "all medically necessary outpatient and inpatient services" (Texas Department of Criminal Justice, n.d.). "Medically necessary" services are defined as appropriate and necessary for the symptoms, diagnosis, or treatment of the medical condition; provided for the diagnosis or direct care and treatment of the medical condition; within standards of good medical practice within the organized medical community; not primarily for the convenience of the TDC inmate patient, the physician or another provider, or the TDC inmate patient's legal counsel whether or not for or in anticipation of litigation; and the most appropriate supply or level of service that can safely be provided. For hospital stays, this means that acute care of an inpatient is necessary due to the kind of services the TDC inmate patient is receiving or the severity of the condition, and that safe and adequate care cannot be received as an outpatient or in a less intensified medical setting.

Implicit in this definition of medical necessity is some notion of an upper limit on health care to be provided. If prisons are to deliver medically necessary care, they need not provide medically "unnecessary" care. Some states explicitly exclude as unnecessary such procedures as elective circumcision, mole removal, and breast surgery for men, cosmetic surgery, and radial keratotomy, among others. However, beyond these explicitly excluded services, the definition of "medically necessary" is probably elastic enough for one physician to deliver procedures to some prisoners that other physicians might term unnecessary. Ambiguity is probably most pronounced with respect to conditions for which new technologies have been developed for diagnosis and treatment.

Improved technologies permit improved and even new approaches to patient care, and the availability of these technologies expands the boundaries of what patients come to expect as part of their "normal" health care service. Organs that fail can be replaced; blocked coronary arteries can be bypassed; bone marrow can be replaced; whole joints—such as knees—can be replaced with artificial replacements; extremely premature babies that once had a very slim chance of making it can be kept alive through intensive care; death can be forestalled for months and years by life-supporting devices; and diagnostic abilities can be enhanced by expensive devices.

In a free market where patients who have money to purchase these often expensive services are able to receive them, there is no need to consider whether these services should be provided—or whether a limit should be placed on their use—although some medical ethicists have found reason to ponder issues raised by the availability of these technologies. Whatever limits exist for these services are generally established either by those who pay for the services (typically commercial insurance companies) or by the providers themselves who elect the menu of services they want to provide to the market. For example, hospitals may choose, as a matter of policy, not to provide heart transplants to persons over a certain age. Third-party payers or the providers themselves generally have the discretionary authority to limit the services they will pay for or provide, and the main constraint on their decision about what to allow and what to exclude is how it will affect their position in the market for services. To be sure, patients do bring suits against insurers and providers for not providing certain services, but this does not invalidate the general point: that consumers in the free community do not have an unrestricted legal right to any type of service from a health care provider.

In prisons, however, where prisoners do not typically pay for their health care services, the availability of "exotic" treatments provokes questions of policy. Should prison systems provide treatments that prisoners would not have received if they were free because they lacked the money to pay for them? Do prisoners have a right to all treatments for "any condition . . . if the denial of care might result in pain, suffering, deterioration or degeneration" (Boney, Dubler, and Rold 1991)? Are "community standards of care" clear enough to enable prison administrators to draw bright lines around treatments that fall within the bounds of "medical necessity" and those that do not? Because of the legal obligation to meet the standards of good medical practice within the organized legal community, the grounds are infirm for limiting expensive or exotic diagnostic tests or treatments that may arguably be medically necessary.

Because general principles defining "medical necessity" and "community standards of care" are not always precise enough to guide prison administrators when faced with considerations of whether to provide treatment, some administrators have looked to upper limit-setting standards established in the larger community. For example, in California prisons, the chief medical officers reportedly rely on application of what they call the "Medi-Cal standard" to guide their decisions about the levels of care to provide prisoners (California Department of Corrections 1994, p. 5). That is, they guide their clinical decisions in part by what they think the state's heath care program for persons living below the poverty line would permit. The logic of this practice is that prisoners, like Medi-Cal patients, for the most part live below the poverty line. However, as a draft version of the California

Department of Corrections document concludes, "In following Medi-Cal, nearly any medical procedure can be justified." Consequently, "[this] really is not a 'standard'" (1994, p. 6).

Another approach to defining explicitly a "benefit package" in the free community are the efforts in Oregon and California to develop lists of diagnostic and treatment procedures to be supported with public funds, restricting access to other services deemed ineffective or not cost effective. The first built on the state's broader work to establish limits on all publicly supported Medicaid services. In California, the Department of Corrections blazed its own trail and aimed to base treatment guidelines and limits on what services are found by "outcomes" research studies to be effective.

However, the ability to develop treatment guidelines from outcomes research has been questioned by some observers (Anderson 1994). Unlike clinical trials, outcomes research typically relies on analyses of claims data and other similar data describing treatments provided to different types of patients and the outcomes of those treatments. Whereas clinical trials involve random assignment to treatment, outcomes research typically compares the treatments prescribed to patients after consideration of their conditions. The likelihood that patients receiving different types of treatment also differed in other ways frustrates our ability to draw strong conclusions about the effects of treatment alone, independent of these other differences among patients and their illnesses. If judgments about cost effectiveness cannot be grounded in strong scientific studies, the choice of "cost-effective" techniques or desirable treatments will continue to be made by informed judgment. As such, they are likely to be subject to dispute and differences in informed opinion.

Given the difficulty of enunciating and defending a formal policy that establishes upper limits, it can be questioned whether such policies are desirable. The alternative is case-by-case review by a correctional manager sitting at a higher level than the medical clinician. Guidelines may be needed to encourage clinicians to identify questionable demands for case and to refer them to high authorities for decision. Such procedures may reduce the risk of having to defend a precisely specified list of services in the legislature and in other public forums where competing constituencies for public expenditure may seek to cut services to the bone.

2. *Utilization Management Procedures to Control Service Provision.* The most commonly followed managed care procedures for case-by-case

review are those collectively termed "utilization management." During the past decade, utilization management has swept the field of health care as a means of managing patients' use of services. The Institute of Medicine's Committee on Utilization Management by Third Parties defines utilization management as "a set of techniques by or on behalf of purchasers of health benefits to manage health care costs by influencing patient care decision making through case-by-case assessment of the appropriateness of care prior to its provision" (Field and Gray 1989). The aim is to match patients' needs to the most cost-effective constellation of services. In principal, utilization management techniques can be employed to accomplish any of several goals—including improvements in service quality and cost containment. In practice, their use may be more focused on the latter, sometimes at the expense of the former, but this is not a necessary consequence of establishing utilization procedures. Thus Florida's Department of Corrections utilization review is considered a part of the department's quality management program, and seeks to "provide a mechanism which monitors the utilization of health care resources while assuring necessary services are provided in a clinically appropriate environment" (State of Florida 1991, p. 2).

The major types of utilization management include hospital preadmission review, concurrent review of length of stay, retrospective review, second surgical opinions, and catastrophic case management. Typically, hospital preadmission certification programs determine if the inpatient care proposed by a physician is appropriate and required. Concurrent reviews are conducted after the patient is in the hospital and are used to determine how long the hospital stay should be extended. Second opinion programs involve referrals to other physicians to confirm if the proposed elective surgical procedures are needed. Case management reviews focus on providing cost-effective care for patients needing high-cost treatments or extended care. Retrospective reviews evaluate the appropriateness of treatment after it is completed. Such reviews are undertaken to educate providers about standards for appropriate care, to identify providers who deviate from the norm, and sometimes to determine if reimbursement should be denied.

Because consultations and procedures performed by specialists and hospitalization are typically the most costly health care services, utilization review procedures are generally designed for these and not for primary care. Consequently, most of the existing research on the effects of utilization management procedures examine their impact on hospitalization practices and the resulting costs, rather than on other medical services. Moreover, the impact of such review programs on the quality of care is undocumented. A report by the Institute of Medicine on utilization management states that physicians' requests for services are infrequently denied, which suggests that savings produced by utilization review programs may stem not from denying coverage or avoiding hospitalization for care deemed inappropriate, but perhaps from an indirect sentinel effect. That is, physicians may be less likely to recommend specialists' care or hospitalization in borderline cases if they know that their recommendations will be reviewed (Field and Gray 1989, p. 103).

Utilization review programs of varying scope have been established in several prison systems, including Georgia's, North Carolina's, and Florida's. For example, in December 1991, the Florida Department of Corrections' Office of Health Services put into effect a utilization management program as part of its broader effort, begun in 1990, to restructure the health care delivery system along the lines of a staff-model HMO (McDonald 1995, pp. 53–54). Important features of this managed care system, which was largely in place by the end of 1992, include a network of providers who offer discounts; consolidation of cases in regions where discounted providers can serve particular types of patients at lower cost; review procedures for monitoring and assessing in an ongoing fashion the delivery of care and its quality; preventive care; and utilization review.

The department believes that this restructuring slowed the growth in spending for health care costs, especially for outside hospitalization. In 1990, before the implementation of the utilization management program, the department averaged 290 hospital inpatient days per thousand inmates. In 1992–93, the use rate declined to 188.2 days. The rate of emergency room visits declined from 91.2 visits per thousand in 1990 to 61.7 per thousand in 1992–93. The department asserts that this lower utilization has reduced the department's expenditures for outside hospitals from $11.9 million in 1991 to a projected $11.3 million in 1992–93, despite an increase of about 20 percent in the average daily population (State of Florida 1994, attachments L and K). It is possible, however, that the reduced number of hospital days during this period declined for reasons other than the implementation of utilization review procedures. Because emergency room visits are not subject to preadmission certification, the decline in these rates may reflect other changes in practice. Moreover, average lengths of stay have been falling in many hospitals across the country. Generally, it is difficult to estimate precisely and isolate the effects of utilization review procedures from other determinants of hospital use.

Another approach especially relevant to primary care is to adopt the HMO practice of assigning primary care physicians to individual patients, so that prisoner/patients deal with single rather than multiple physicians. For example, the State of Utah has restructured its prison health services system along the lines of a staff-controlled (i.e., physician-controlled) health maintenance organization. Inmates are assigned primary care providers who have the responsibility for knowing their patients and for managing their care. Physicians there believe that this system has reduced unnecessary utilization of services and costs.

3. *Disincentives to Use Health Care Services: Prisoner Copayments/Fees.* In the free community, consumers who have to pay for their health care with out-of-pocket funds are less likely, on average, to use services as often as those with full-coverage insurance policies. The Health Insurance Experiment conducted by the Rand Corporation in the 1970s found a significant effect between the size of the copayment and the total expenditure for health care. For example, consumers with a large deductible—up to $1,000 (in 1970s dollars)—reduced total spending for health care by 31 percent, compared with a plan with full coverage (Manning et al. 1987, pp. 251–77). In prisons, without disincentives for overutilizing health care services, inmates may be using health services much more frequently than is necessary. In an effort to control overutilization of health care services by inmates, twenty-four states had instituted requirements for inmates making copayments—or paying fees for services—for health care in prison by May 1997, and another fifteen reported plans to do so (LIS, Inc. 1997, p. 9).

The State of Nevada pioneered prison health service copayments, having passed a law in 1981. This law was enacted to reduce the large number of medical visits to providers that were perceived as unnecessary, to hold inmates partly responsible for their own health care expenses, and to provide a revenue source to address increasing general fund costs for inmate medical care (Nolan 1992). A $4 copayment is charged to an inmate seeking care by institutional physicians, physicians' extenders (physician assistants or nurse practitioners), dentists, optometrists, or psychiatrists for examination or treatment. Follow-ups, referrals, protocols, and emergencies are "nonchargeable." In Nevada, the main effect of copayment has been an apparent reduction in demand for health care services. During fiscal years 1989, 1990, and 1991, the State of Nevada reported an average of 4.39 visits per inmate per year at maximum-security prisons. The department-wide average was 5.99 visits per inmate per year. This represents a substantial reduction relative to the comparison utilization rate when the program began: a 76 percent decrease at the maximum-security level and a 50 percent decrease department-wide (Nolan 1992).

One cannot assume that reducing the number of requests for services by a certain percentage will necessarily produce a proportionate decrease in spending for health care services. Visits to outside providers may not be reduced, because care providers may screen out unnecessary visits because of the security risks and costs associated with these visits. What may most likely be reduced, therefore, are requests for service inside the prison. A large proportion of these costs are fixed—especially if the health care providers are on staff rather than consultants paid on an hourly or daily rate. Fewer prisoners coming for service may enable providers to spend more time with those who do come. In this event, costs will not necessarily decline immediately, but the quality of care might rise—a desirable consequence.

Another possibility is that overall quality of service delivery will decline and that costs will rise if inmates who actually need service are deterred from seeking it because of the copayment requirement. That is, prisoners may not request attention for conditions that could turn worse, which then require more expensive care. If the marginal savings generated by lower utilization rates are small, and if the rate of emergency room visits increases by even a small amount, copayment policies could result in higher expenditures for prison health care services.

C. Contracting with Full-Service Firms to Deliver Health Care

One means of managing prison health care and health care spending is to contract with a private firm and to charge it with the task. Although "privatization" is now often marketed as a means of cost-containment, contracting has historically been pursued for other reasons. Primary among them was the desire to improve the provision and administration of correctional health services—even though the cost of such services would increase. One of the earliest local contracting relationships was struck up between the New York City Department of Correction and Montefiore Hospital in 1973 because it was thought, according to two observers, that "one cause of the riots of 1970 [in the New York City jail system] was the disastrous state of prison health care" (Medvene and Whelan 1976, p. 81). In state prison systems, the common pattern was for a federal court to find the state to be providing inadequate health care, court orders to remedy substandard conditions were then issued, and the government turned to contractors to remedy the deficiencies. For example, in 1978, the first contract to manage and operate an entire prison's health care delivery system was signed in Delaware, under pressure from the federal courts (McDonald 1995, p. 62).

With the rise of interest in privatization during the 1980s, some state legislatures and executives no doubt began considering contracting for the purpose of controlling costs better. The trend has certainly been toward more extensive contracting. By 1989, Alabama, Maryland, Delaware, and Kansas had contractors that were providing all medical services in all prisons in those states (Anno 1991, p. 82). By mid-1998, the number had increased to twenty-two states, and a number of others had extensive contracting relationships in several of their prisons (McDonald et al. 1996, pp. 49–50; Moore 1998).

In principle, contracting offers governments various opportunities to manage health care spending effectively. These include the following.

Hard Spending Limits. The contract can establish a maximum amount to be expended by the contractor for health care during each year of the contract's life. If the contractor is responsible for most or all of the prisoners' health services, the state's ability to control costs will be enhanced.

Allocating Risks. Contracting enables states to shift the risk for cost management to the contractor, which creates powerful incentives for the contractor to identify inefficiencies and to remedy them.

Centralized Management of the Health Care Services in All Prisons (If All the State's Prisons Are Placed under the Contract). This encourages the creation of an integrated "system" as opposed to a collection of nearly autonomous operations in each of the prisons (a condition found in many state systems that deliver services directly, rather than under contract). This may be especially advantageous in departments lacking centralized medical departments directed by professional health care administrators.

Established Goals and Performance Objectives. To develop a request for proposals, the state will be forced to establish clear goals for the health services system and measures against which performance can be monitored. This is an additional benefit of contracting, and contractors can be required to provide the information needed by the department to monitor the performance of the health services delivery system.

Incentives for Good Performance. Contracting permits the state to place somebody at clear financial risk for poor performance—an incentive that is hard to establish in the public sector. Financial rewards also can be designed for good performance.

Quality of Care Requirements. Pressures to underserve the population, or to "cut corners," may be countered by establishing contractual requirements to maintain quality of care at desired levels.

Acquiring the Advantages of Contractor's Techniques and Experience. Contractors can bring their experience and already-developed technologies to bear on managing critically important aspects of health care delivery. These include procedures for controlling prisoners' use (and overuse) of services, procedures for purchasing goods and services in the health care marketplace at discounts, and developed management information systems.

I am not aware of any systematic studies of the cost effectiveness of contracting. Comparisons of relative cost effectiveness would be difficult, if not impossible, in situations where contracting was pursued for the purpose of upgrading care rather than improving cost effectiveness. More importantly, comparisons of cost effectiveness are difficult because measures of health care outcomes, and of service quality generally, are weakly developed. The lack of systematic attention to the outcomes of health care services, whether provided directly or by contractors, is not peculiar to prisons.

X. A Coming Collision between Prisoners' Demands for Health Care, Expanding Rights, and the Public's Support for Prisons?

In American society at large, health care is likely to become a battleground of sorts as the "Baby Boom" cohorts age. Those cohorts represent a huge proportion of the entire American population, and spending for health care by and for these aging boomers will skyrocket. Pressures to intensify cost-containment efforts will mount, which will fuel further conflict between insurers seeking to limit services and consumers demanding them. How scarce and costly health care resources will be allocated in such an environment is exceedingly difficult to predict, but it is certain that the matter will be hotly contested.

It is ironic that incarcerated criminal offenders are the only persons in the United States who have a constitutional right to health care. Free citizens, while some may be entitled to Medicare or Medicaid coverage (the terms of which are subject to change), lack both any rights-based claim to health care and a universal health care insurance plan that would pay for needed care. Instead, the only care that free citizens are entitled to receive, apart from Medicare- and Medicaid-eligibles, is what they contractually elect in employers' benefit plans. In such a situation, one can see the seeds of a conflict between the states' requirement to provide prisoners health care that some free citizens cannot afford and the public's unwillingness to support such care. In an increasingly expensive health care market, in which restrictions on access are becoming tighter, how much support will there be for prisoners' health care entitlements? The public's willingness to support rising expenditures for health care of prisoners will be stretched if it means—as it must—that resources used to care for prisoners will be denied to others who have not committed crimes.

These tensions are likely to be heightened in coming years as the costs of prison health care rise. Numbers of older prisoners will grow larger, partly a reflection of the growing number of old people in the U.S. population at large, and perhaps also a consequence of the passage of mandatory minimum sentencing laws and "three strikes" laws in many states. Older persons in and out of prison are disproportionately heavy consumers of health care services. Approximately 31 percent of all personal health care expenditures nationwide are for persons sixty-five years of age or older (U.S. Special Committee on Aging 1986). In prisons, "older" persons are commonly considered to be fifty years of age or more, in part because the health of the average fifty-year-old prisoner approximates the average health condition of persons ten years older in the free community (Falter 1993, p. 17). These prisoners will require more medical services, including costly long-term care. For example, in 1989, the Federal Bureau of Prisons estimated that 16 percent of its prisoner population will be fifty years or older by 2005 compared with 11.7 percent in 1988. Whereas the cost of providing treatment for cardiac and hypertensive disorders among the population fifty or older was $6.7 million in 1988, the bureau estimated that these treatments will cost $10.1 million in constant 1988 dollars during the year 2000 (Federal Bureau of Prisons 1989).

The heavier burden of HIV/AIDS, tuberculosis, and other infectious diseases in inmate populations will also put powerful pressures on prison budgets. Treatments for HIV are becoming more costly, with the latest combination therapies costing between $600–900 per month per prisoner (*AIDS Policy and Law* 1998, p. 6). Prison officials have little choice whether to support such therapies, as the guidelines from the U.S. Public Health Service establish triple combination therapy as the standard of care, and prisons are obligated to provide care that meets this standard. The impact on prison budgets has already been significant. In Illinois, for example, expenditures for pharmaceuticals increased from $30,000 a month to $300,000 a month after combination therapies began to be prescribed in 1995 (ibid., p. 7).

Faced with new technologies, demands to use them as part of normally prescribed care, and rising expenditures, it is not difficult to imagine that the current trend toward "no frills" imprisonment may be expanded to include a "no frills" prison health care system. The existence of a constitutionally protected right to health care will limit legislatures' cost cutting to some extent, but this may result in attacks on the right and pressure on the courts not to enforce prisoners' claims aggressively. That is possible because what is considered sufficient care is not well defined and is both ambiguous and elastic. Moreover, the courts have already become more cautious in distinguishing between constitutional violations and medical malpractice claims. Pressures to limit prisoners' health care more aggressively might be dampened if all the nation's citizens, and not just those criminal offenders held behind bars (substantial numbers of whom are not American citizens), were at least given access to health care insurance and affordable medical care. However, since the collapse of the Clinton administration's health care reform effort in the mid-1990s, the prospects of such universal coverage seem dim. The conditions are ripe for a few signal incidents—such as a prison official approving a kidney transplant for an aging prisoner serving a life sentence—to trigger a public debate regarding the limits of care in our nation's prisons. Given the current political culture, the public's attitudes toward criminals, and increasingly conservative federal courts, it may be difficult to find defenders of prisoners' claims to health care resources.

REFERENCES

AIDS Policy and Law. 1998. "Prisons Must Adhere to Evolving Standard of HIV Care." 13(3):6–7.

Aker, G. A. 1970. "A National Survey of Medical and Health Facilities in Prisons." In *The Status of Prison Health Care: A Review of the Literature*, edited by Seth B. Goldsmith. *Public Health Reports* 89(6):569–75.

American College of Physicians, National Commission on Correctional Health Care, and American Correctional Health Services Association. 1992.

"The Crisis in Correctional Health Care: The Impact of the National Drug Control Strategy on Correctional Health Services." *Annals of Internal Medicine* 111:71–77.

American Correctional Association. 1981. *Manual of Standards for Adult Correctional Institutions.* 2d ed. Washington, D.C.: Commission on Accreditation for Corrections.

———. 1989. *Certification Standards for Health Care Programs.* Laurel, Md.: American Correctional Association.

American Medical Association. 1978. *Standards for the Accreditation of Medical Care and Health Services in Jails.* Rev. ed. Chicago: American Medical Association.

———. 1979. *Standards for Health Services in Prisons.* Chicago: American Medical Association.

American Public Health Association. 1976. *Standards for Health Services in Correctional Institutions.* Washington, D.C.: American Public Health Association.

Anderson, Christopher. 1994. "Measuring What Works in Health Care." *Science* 263:1080–82.

Anno, B. Jaye. 1982. "The Role of Organized Medicine in Correctional Health Care" (The Jail Program Year). *Journal of the American Medical Association* 247:2923–25.

———. 1991. *Prison Health Care: Guidelines for the Management of an Adequate Delivery System.* Washington, D.C.: National Institute of Corrections.

Bayer, R., N. N. Dubler, and S. Landesman. 1993. "The Dual Epidemics of Tuberculosis and AIDS: Ethical and Policy Issues in Screening and Treatment." *American Journal of Public Health* 83:649–54.

Blindman, M. J. 1977. *Policy Issues Affecting the Provision of Medical Care within Correctional Institutions.* Wilmington: Delaware Governor's Commission on Criminal Justice.

Blue Cross and Blue Shield System. 1991. *Reforming the Small Group Health Insurance Market.* Quoted on p. 87 in John C. Goodman and Gerald L. Musgrave, *Patient Power: The Free Enterprise Alternative to Clinton's Health Plan.* Washington, D.C.: Cato Institute, 1994.

Boney, Jacqueline M., Nancy Neveloff Dubler, and William J. Rold. 1991. "Legal Right to Health Care in Correctional Institutions." In *Prison Health Care: Guidelines for the Management of an Adequate Delivery System,* edited by B. J. Anno. Washington, D.C.: National Institute of Corrections.

Boston, John, and Daniel E. Manville. 1996. *Prisoners' Self-Help Litigation Manual.* New York: Oceana.

Braithwaite, Ronald, Theodore M. Hammett, and Robert M. Mayberry. 1996. *Prisons and AIDS: A Public Health Challenge.* San Francisco: Jossey-Bass.

Burke, John G. 1997. Letter dated November 5. Tallahassee: Florida Department of Corrections, Chief of Health Services Administration.

California Department of Corrections. 1994. *Medical Scope of Services.* Santa Barbara: California Department of Corrections.

Centers for Disease Control. 1992. "Transmission of Multi-drug Resistant Tuberculosis among Immunocompromised Persons, Correctional System—New York, 1991." *Morbidity and Mortality Weekly Report* 41:507–9.

———. 1997. *Reported Tuberculosis in the United States, 1996.* Atlanta: Centers for Disease Control.

Contact Inc. 1983. "Prison Health Care Costs." *Corrections Compendium* 8(2): 5–11.

———. 1986. "Prison Health Care." *Corrections Compendium* 11(1):13–14.

Davis, Su Perk. 1993. "Health Care Costs—10% of the Pie." *Corrections Compendium* 18(5):5–9.

Dole, Vincent P. 1974. "Medicine and the Criminal Justice System." *Annals of Internal Medicine* 81:687–89.

Falter, Robert G. 1993. "Selected Predictors of Health Services Needs of Inmates over Age 50." Ph.D. dissertation, Walden University.

Federal Bureau of Prisons. 1989. "Looking Ahead—the Future BOP Population and Their Costly Health Care Needs." *Research Bulletin.* Washington, D.C.: Office of Research and Evaluation.

Field, Marilyn J., and Bradford H. Gray. 1989. "Should We Regulate Utilization Management?" *Health Affairs,* pp. 103–12.

General Accounting Office. 1978. *A Federal Strategy Is Needed to Help Improve Medical and Dental Care in Prisons and Jails.* GAO no. GGD-78-96. Washington, D.C.: General Accounting Office.

———. 1981. *More than Money Is Needed to Solve Problems Faced by State and Local Corrections Agencies.* GAO no. GGD-81-104. Washington, D.C.: General Accounting Office.

Gilliard, Darrell K., and Allen Beck. 1998. *Prisoners in 1997.* Washington, D.C.: U.S. Department of Justice, Bureau of Justice Statistics.

Glaser, Jordan B., and Robert B. Greifinger. 1993. "Correctional Health Care: A Public Health Opportunity." *Annals of Internal Medicine* 118(2):139–45.

Hammett, Theodore, Laura Maruschak, and Patricia Harmon. Forthcoming. *1997 Update: HIV/AIDs, STDs, and TB in Correctional Facilities.* Washington, D.C.: National Institute of Justice, Centers for Disease Control and Prevention, and Bureau of Justice Statistics.

Hart, William. 1979. "Warning: Prison Medical Care May Be Hazardous to Your Health." *Corrections Magazine* (September), pp. 5–11.

Health Care Financing Administration. 1995. *Statistical Report on Medical Care: Eligibles, Recipients, Payments, and Services.* HCFA Form-2082. Baltimore: Health Care Financing Administration.

Health Law Project. 1972. *Health Care and Conditions in Pennsylvania's State Prisons.* Philadelphia: University of Pennsylvania Law School.

Hoechst Marion Roussel. 1997. *HMO-PPO Medicare/Medicaid Digest.* Kansas City: Hoechst Marion Roussel.

Kearney, A.T. 1970. "Report to the State of Nebraska Department of Public Institutions on Staff Criteria for the Penal and Correctional Complex." Lincoln: Department of Public Institutions.

Kiel, Richard. 1983. Personal communication from the past president of the American Correctional Health Services Association, September 8, reported in Richard L. Lichtenstein and Annette Rykwalker, "Licensed Physicians Who Work in Prisons: A Profile." *Public Health Reports* 98(6):590.

Kronick, Richard, David C. Goodman, John Wennberg, and Edward Wagner.

1993. "The Marketplace in Health Care Reform: The Demographic Limitations of Managed Competition." Special report. *New England Journal of Medicine* 328(2):148–52.

Langan, Patrick A., John V. Fundis, Lawrence A. Greenfeld, and Victoria W. Schneider. 1988. *Historical Statistics on Prisoners in State and Federal Institutions, Yearend 1925–86.* Washington, D.C.: U.S. Department of Justice, Bureau of Justice Statistics.

Lichtenstein, Richard L., and Annette Rykwalker. 1983. "Licensed Physicians Who Work in Prisons: A Profile." *Public Health Reports* 98(6):589–96.

Lindenauer, Marilyn R., and Jay K. Harness. 1981. "Care as Part of the Cure: A Historical Overview of Correctional Health Care." *Journal of Prison Health* 1:56–64.

LIS, Inc. 1997. *Prison Medical Care: Special Needs Populations and Cost Control.* Longmont, Colo.: U.S. Department of Justice, National Institute of Corrections.

Manning, Willard G., et al. 1987. "Health Insurance and the Demand for Medicare Care: Evidence from a Randomized Experiment." *American Economic Review* 77(3):251–77.

McDonald, Douglas C. 1995. *Managing Prison Health Care and Costs.* Washington, D.C.: U.S. Department of Justice, National Institute of Justice.

McDonald, Douglas C., Andrea Hassol, Kenneth Carlson, Jeffrey McCullough, Elizabeth Fournier, and Jennifer Yapp. 1998. *Telemedicine Can Reduce Spending for Prisoners' Healthcare: An Evaluation of a Prison Telemedicine Network.* Cambridge, Mass.: Abt Associates, Inc.

McDonald, Douglas C., Joanna Heliotis, and Raymond R. Hyatt, Jr. 1997. *Health Services Delivery System Study: A Description and Assessment of the Washington State Department of Corrections' Health Services Delivery System.* Report to Office of Financial Management, Olympia, Wash. Cambridge, Mass.: Abt Associates, Inc.

McDonald, Douglas C., Chris L. Pashos, Jacqueline M. Moore, Raymond R. Hyatt, Jr., and Donald H. Moore. 1996. *Health Services Delivery System Study: Policy Options for Restructuring the Washington State Department of Corrections' Health Services Delivery System.* Report to Office of Financial Management, Olympia, Wash. Cambridge, Mass.: Abt Associates, Inc.

Medvene, Louis, and Carol S. Whelan. 1976. *Prison Health Care in New York City: A Historical Perspective.* New York: Community Service Society.

Moore, Jacqueline. 1998. Personal communication from the former executive officer at Prison Health Services, Inc., one of the earliest private correctional health care firms, November 5.

Moran, Donald W., and Patrice R. Wolfe. 1991. "Commentary: Can Managed Care Control Costs?" *Health Affairs* 122:120–28.

Moritsugu, Kenneth. 1995. Personal communication from the assistant surgeon general and medical director of the Federal Bureau of Prisons, November.

Murton, T., and J. Hyams. 1969. *Accomplices to the Crime.* New York: Grove.

National Commission on Acquired Immune Deficiency Syndrome. 1991. *HIV Disease in Correctional Institutions.* Washington, D.C.: National Commission on Acquired Immune Deficiency Syndrome.

National Commission on Correctional Health Care. 1987. *Standards for Health Services in Prisons.* Chicago: National Commission on Correctional Health Care.

National Prison Project of the ACLU Foundation. 1995. *Annual Status Report on States and the Courts.* Washington, D.C.: National Prison Project.

———. 1996. *Annual Status Report on States and the Courts.* Washington, D.C.: National Prison Project.

Neisser, Eric. 1977. "Is There a Doctor in the Joint? The Search for Constitutional Standards for Prison Health Care." *Virginia Law Review* 63:921–73.

Newport, John. 1977. "Review of Health Services in Correctional Facilities in the United States." *Public Health Reports* 92(6):564–69.

New York State Special Commission on Attica. 1972. *Attica: The Official Report of the New York State Special Commission on Attica.* New York: Praeger.

Nolan, M. 1992. "Medical Co-payment System: Nevada Department of Prisons." Presented at the seventeenth annual conference of the American Correctional Health Services Association, Salt Lake City, April.

Novick, Lloyd F., R. Della Penna, M. S. Schwartz, E. Remmlinger, and R. Lowenstein. 1977. "Health Status of the New York City Prison Population." *Medical Care* 15(3):205–16.

Novick, Lloyd F., and Elaine Remmlinger. 1978. "A Study of 128 Deaths in New York City Correctional Facilities (1971–1976): Implications for Prisoner Health Care." *Medical Care* 16(9):749–56.

President's Commission on Law Enforcement and Administration of Justice. 1967. *Task Force Report: Corrections.* Washington, D.C.: U.S. Government Printing Office. Excerpted in *Correctional Institutions*, edited by Robert M. Carter, Daniel Glaser, and Leslie T. Wilkins. Philadelphia: Lippincott, 1972.

Reidel, R. L., and D. C. Reidel. 1979. *Practice and Performance: An Assessment of Ambulatory Care.* Ann Arbor, Mich.: Health Administration Press.

Rhee, S. 1977. "U.S. Medical Graduates versus Foreign Medical Graduates: Are There Performance Differences in Practice?" *Medical Care* 15:568–77.

Riley, James E. 1994. Memorandum from the then executive director, Correctional Managed Health Care, Texas Department of Criminal Justice, August 31.

Salive, Marcel E., Gordon S. Smith, and T. Fordham Brewer. 1990. "Death in Prison: Hanging Mortality Patterns among Male Prisoners in Maryland, 1979–87." *American Journal of Public Health* 80(12):1479–80.

Sandrick, Karen M. 1981. "Health Care in Correctional Institutions in the United States, England, Canada, Poland, and France." *QRB/Quality Review Bulletin*, July, pp. 28–31.

Sheps, Samuel B., Martin T. Schechter, and Real G. Prefontaine. 1987. "Prison Health Services: A Utilization Study." *Journal of Community Health* 12(1):4–22.

State of Florida. 1991. *Quality Management.* Health Services Bulletin no. 15.09.01. Tallahassee: Florida Department of Corrections, Office of Health Services.

———. 1992. *Health Classification of Grades.* Health Bulletin no. 15.13. Tallahassee: Florida Department of Corrections.

―――. 1994. *Office of Health Services: Five Year Needs Assessment*. Tallahassee: Florida Department of Corrections, Office of Health Services.

Stephan, James J. 1997. *Census of State and Federal Correctional Facilities, 1995*. Washington, D.C.: U.S. Department of Justice, Bureau of Justice Statistic.

Texas Department of Criminal Justice. n.d. *Hospital Provider Agreement*. Austin: Texas Department of Criminal Justice.

Thorburn, Kim Marie. 1981. "Croakers' Dilemma: Should Prison Physicians Serve Prisons or Prisoners?" *Western Journal of Medicine* 134:457–61.

Torrey, E. Fuller. 1995. "Editorial: Jails and Prisons—America's New Mental Hospitals." *American Journal of Public Health* 85(12):1611–13.

Twaddle, Andrew C. 1976. "Utilization of Medical Services by a Captive Population: An Analysis of Sick Call in a State Prison." *Journal of Health and Social Behavior* 17:236–48.

U.S. Department of Labor. 1996. *CPI Detailed Report, Data for July 1996*. Washington, D.C.: Bureau of Labor Statistics.

―――. 1998. *Consumer Price Index, All Urban Consumers—(CPI-U)*. Washington, D.C.: Bureau of Labor Statistics.

U.S. Senate Special Committee on Aging, American Association of Retired Persons, Federal Council on Aging, and Administration on Aging. 1986. *Aging America: Trends and Projections, 1985–86*. Rockville, Md.: U.S. Department of Health and Human Services.

Waldron, Ronald. n.d. "Health Care Cost Containment Study (B325): Fact Sheet." Washington, D.C.: Federal Bureau of Prisons.

Wallace S., J. Klein-Saffron, G. Gaes, and K. Moritsugu. 1991. "Health Status of Federal Inmates: A Comparison of Admission and Release Medical Records." *Journal of Prison and Health* 10(2):133–51.

Weisbuch, Jonathan B. 1997. "Public Health Professionals and Prison Health Care Needs." *American Journal of Public Health* 67(8):720–22.

Wess, G. 1996. "Inmate Health Care, Part I: As New Commitments Climb, Health Care Budgets Follow." *Corrections Compendium* 21(10):6–13.

Williams, K. N., and R. H. Brook. 1975. "Foreign Medical Graduates and Their Impact on the Quality of Medical Care in the United States." *Milbank Memorial Fund Quarterly* 53:549–81.

Worthington, David. 1994. Telephone interview, Utah Department of Correction, July.

Joan Petersilia

Parole and Prisoner Reentry in the United States

ABSTRACT

Discretionary parole release and parole field services have undergone major changes as the nation has embraced more punitive policies. Fourteen states have abolished discretionary parole release for all offenders, and twenty-one others severely limit its use. Parole supervision remains, but needed treatment programs are scarce, and parole officers focus on surveillance more than rehabilitation. About half of parolees fail to complete parole successfully, and their returns to prison represent about a third of incoming prisoners. Given an average (median) prison term served of fifteen months, more than half of all inmates now in prison will be in the community in less than two years. Developing programs to reduce parole recidivism should be a top priority, and a few agencies are operating successful job-training and substance abuse programs. Experts argue that a new parole model is sorely needed, one that incorporates advances in technology, risk prediction, effective rehabilitation, and more "active" forms of supervision that incorporate citizens and others who know the offender. Such reforms are more promising than parole abolition, in that they reduce the public safety risks posed by parolees and increase the chances that offenders will succeed.

Public anger and frustration over crime continue to produce significant changes in the American criminal justice system, but reforms focused on parole are among the most profound. Parole, which is both a procedure by which a board administratively releases inmates from prison

Joan Petersilia is professor of criminology, law, and society at the University of California, Irvine. The author particularly thanks Allen Beck, chief, Corrections Statistics Program, Bureau of Justice Statistics, U.S. Department of Justice, for his generous assistance in identifying and interpreting relevant parole data. Edward Rhine, Michael Tonry, Peggy Burke, Frances Cullen, Joe Lehman, Martin Horn, and Gail Hughes made helpful comments on drafts of this article.

and a provision for postrelease supervision, has come to symbolize the leniency of a system in which inmates are "let out" early. When a parolee commits a particularly heinous crime, such as the kidnapping and murder of thirteen-year-old Polly Klaas by California parolee Richard Allen Davis, or the horrifying rape and murder of seven-year-old Megan Kanka in New Jersey by a released sex offender, the public is understandably outraged and calls for "abolishing parole."

State legislatures have responded, and by the end of 1998, fourteen states had abolished early release by a parole board for all offenders, and several others had restricted its use. California still allows discretionary release by a parole board, but only for offenders with indeterminate life sentences (e.g., first-degree murder, kidnap for ransom) (Ditton and Wilson 1999). Even in states that have retained parole, parole boards have become more hesitant to grant it. In Texas, for example, 57 percent of all cases considered for parole release in 1988 were approved; by 1998, that figure had dropped to just 20 percent (Fabelo 1999).

The argument for abolishing parole is that it will lead to longer prison sentences and greater honesty in sentencing decisions. George Allen, former governor of Virginia, made abolishing parole a major campaign issue, and one of his first acts once elected governor in 1994 was to eliminate that state's discretionary parole system for violent offenders. He wrote that: "The principle that has guided our efforts is honesty. Easy-release rules prevented judges and juries from preempting the community's judgement about proper punishment for illegal conduct. Under the new law, judges do not have to play guessing games when imposing sentences. Police officers do not have to see the criminals out on the streets only a year after their last arrest. Criminals know they cannot beat the system. Crime victims and their families are finally seeing that justice is done" (Allen 1997, p. 22).

But correctional experts argue that, while abolishing parole may make good politics, it contributes to bad correctional practices—and ultimately, less public safety. As Burke (1995, p. 11) notes, parole makes release from prison a privilege that must be earned. When states abolish parole or reduce the amount of discretion parole authorities have, they in essence replace a rational, controlled system of "earned" release for *selected* inmates with "automatic" release for nearly *all* inmates. Proponents argue that the public does not understand the tremendous power that is lost when parole is abandoned. Through the exercise of its discretion, parole boards can target more violent and dangerous offenders for longer periods of incarceration. Burke (1995,

p. 11) writes: "The absence of parole means that offenders simply walk out of the door of prison at the end of a pre-determined period of time, no questions asked. No human being asks the tough questions about what has been done to make sure this criminal is no longer a danger before he is released."

The case of Richard Allen Davis is a perfect example. The California Board of Prison Terms (the parole board) knew the risks he posed and had denied him parole in each of the six instances when his case had been reviewed. But once California abolished discretionary parole release, the Board of Prison Terms no longer had the authority to deny release to inmates whose new standard sentence mandated automatic release after serving a set portion of their terms. Release dates were calculated by the computer for thousands of prisoners then in custody, and when it was determined that Davis had already served the amount of prison time that the new law required, he had to be released. Less than four months later, he murdered Polly Klaas. California parole officials suspect that, had the state not abolished parole, Davis would have never been released (Burke 1995). Similarly, the case of the murderer of Megan Kanka was never heard by a parole board; rather, he went out of prison under mandatory release.

Eliminating parole boards also means that several of their important ancillary purposes are also eliminated. Parole boards have the ability to "individualize sentencing" and thus can provide a review mechanism for assuring greater uniformity in sentencing across judges or counties. Parole boards can also take into account changes in the offender's behavior that might have occurred after he or she was incarcerated. Imprisonment can cause psychological breakdowns, depression, or mental illnesses, and the parole board can adjust release dates to account for these changes. Finally, abolishing parole boards also eliminates the major mechanism by which overcrowded prisons can quickly reduce populations. As parole expert Vincent O'Leary once observed: "Most people start out reforming parole, but when you pull that string you find a lot more attached" (Wilson 1977, p. 49).

A few states have not only abolished parole release but have also considered abolishing parole supervision (often referred to as the "other" parole). In Maine, the legislature abolished the parole board and also abolished parole supervision. Similarly, when Virginia abolished parole release, supervision also was abolished. Unless the judge remembers to impose a split sentence with a term of probation to follow prison, when offenders leave prison in Virginia, they have no strings at all. If you abolish parole supervision along with parole release, you lose the ability to supervise or provide services to released inmates when they have the highest risk of recidivism and are most in need of services.

Several states that abolished discretionary parole release have reestablished its equivalent. North Carolina, which placed severe constraints on its parole commission in 1981, has gradually restored some of its previous discretion. Florida, which adopted sentencing guidelines in 1983 and abolished parole, has now returned the function under the new name Controlled Release Authority. Colorado abolished discretionary parole release in 1979 and reinstated it six years later. Elected officials, along with law enforcement and corrections professionals, lobbied to reinstate parole release and supervision after data suggested that the length of prison sentence served had actually decreased following the elimination of parole and the ability to provide surveillance or treatment of high-risk offenders had significantly declined. As Bill Woodward, then director of the Division of Criminal Justice in Colorado, noted: "The problem with abolishing parole is you lose your ability to keep track of the inmates and the ability to keep them in treatment if they have alcohol and drug problems" (Gainsborough 1997, p. 23).

Today, all states except Maine and Virginia have some requirement for postprison or parole supervision, and nearly 80 percent of all released prisoners in 1997 were subject so some form of conditional community or supervised release (Ditton and Wilson 1999). However, some states have changed the name to distance themselves from the negative image that "parole" has. For example, postprison supervision is called "controlled release" in Florida, "community control" in Ohio, "supervised release" in Minnesota and in the federal system, and "community custody" in Washington. Regardless of its name, however, parole supervision has changed significantly during the past decade, as national support for parole-as-rehabilitation has waned.

Parole officers readily admit they have fewer services to offer an ever-growing population of offenders. Safety and security have become major issues in parole services (Lynch 1999), and parole officers are now authorized to carry weapons in two-thirds of the states (Camp and Camp 1997). Parole officers in most large urban areas are now more surveillance than services oriented, and drug testing, electronic monitoring, and verifying curfews are the most common activities of many parole agents (Petersilia 1998b).

Parole was founded primarily to foster offender reformation rather than to increase punitiveness or surveillance. Abandoning parole's historical commitment to rehabilitation worries correctional professionals. The reality is that more than nine out of ten prisoners are released back into the community, and with an average (median) U.S. prison term served of fifteen months, half of all inmates in U.S. prisons today will be back on the streets in less than two years (Beck 1999). The transition from prison back into the community is exceedingly difficult, and recidivism rates are highest in the first year following release. A study by the Bureau of Justice Statistics found that 25 percent of released prisoners are rearrested in the first six months and 40 percent within the first year (Beck and Shipley 1989).

To assist in this high-risk period, parole has historically provided job assistance, family counseling, and chemical dependency programs (although arguably, parole has never provided enough of these services). But punitive public attitudes, combined with diminishing social service resources, have resulted in fewer services provided.

Until recently, the lines were drawn between tough-on-crime "abolitionists" and parole-as-rehabilitation "traditionalists." Politicians continued to shout "abolish parole," while corrections professionals asked for more money to invest in services and surveillance, and the two seemed worlds apart. Over the last year, however, politicians seem to be listening more closely to the professionals, as parole—or more precisely, *failure* on parole—is creating severe fiscal pressures on state prisons' budgets. Greater numbers of parolees are failing supervision and being returned to prison, and, as a result, they are contributing disproportionately to prison crowding and the continued pressure to build more prisons. As New York Assemblyman Daniel L. Feldman recently put it: "Lock 'em up and throw away the key attitudes are coming back to haunt state legislators across the nation" (Carter 1998, p. 2).

In California, for example, where 104,000 adults were on parole in 1997 (one of every seven U.S. parolees), nearly 80 percent are failing to complete supervision successfully (Austin and Lawson 1998). Parole violators accounted for 65 percent of all California prison admissions in 1997, and 41 percent of prison admissions were for violations of the technical conditions of parole rather than for the conviction of new crimes (Austin and Lawson 1998). It should be noted, however, that a technical violation does not necessarily mean the inmate was not engaged in criminal behavior. It may be that the inmate was arrested for a criminal charge but in lieu of prosecution was revoked and returned to custody. The vast majority of these technical violations (82 percent) have an underlying criminal charge (Austin and Lawson 1998).

When revoked to prison, California inmates spend an additional three to four months in prison prior to being rereleased (Little Hoover Commission 1998*b*). Recent analyses suggest that such "high parole revocation rates represents an enormous waste of prison resources and does not fit the mission of a traditional state prison system (i.e., the long-term confinement of sentenced felons)" (Austin and Lawson 1998, p. 13). California has, for the first time since abolishing parole release in 1977, called for a statewide reassessment of the state's parole services and revocation policies (Legislative Analysts Office 1998).

Parole, a system that developed in the United States more by accident than by design, now threatens to become the tail that wags the corrections dog. Prison populations continue to rise, and more offenders are required to be on parole supervision, where fewer services and work programs exist owing to scarcity of resources (often diverted from parole services to fund prison expansion). Greater numbers of parole violations (particularly drug use) are detected through monitoring and drug testing, and parole authorities have diminishing tolerance for failure. Revocation to prison is becoming a predictable (and increasingly short) transition in the prison-to-parole and back-to-prison revolving door cycle. Correctional leaders, joined by many elected officials, are increasingly asking: "Must they all come back?"

Of course, answering that question is exceedingly complex. We would need to know what kinds of programs reduce recidivism for offenders with different needs. Would more intensive surveillance lower recidivism, and how intense must it be to make a difference? What combination of conditions, surveillance, and treatment would get the best results? Once we have identified programs that make a difference, we would have to ask a number of additional questions. For example, should we mandate that parolees participate in needed treatment or simply make it available to those who volunteer? How long should parole last? Should some parolees be kept on "banked" caseloads, with no services or supervision, simply to expedite their return to prison if they commit new crimes? What difference does caseload size make, and which kinds of officers are more successful with which kinds of clients?

These are tough questions, and sound-bite attacks on parole are not very helpful in answering them. We need to begin a serious dialogue aimed at "reinventing" parole in the United States so that it better balances the need to hold offenders accountable with the need to provide services to released offenders. To begin that dialogue, we need first to assemble information on what is known about parole in the United States. That is the purpose of this essay.

Section I begins by describing sources of U.S. adult parole data. I do not describe juvenile data or practices. Section II discusses the early evolution of parole in the United States and its use in modern sentencing practices. This section reviews the dramatic changes in parole release that resulted from the nation's skepticism about the ability of prisons to rehabilitate. Section III describes the current parole population. It presents trend data on the growth of the parole population and what is known about parolees' crimes, personal backgrounds, and court-ordered conditions. It also presents data on the average size of parole caseloads, offender contact requirements, and annual costs of supervision. Section IV is devoted to describing the offender's needs as he or she makes the transition into the community and what services are available to meet these needs. This section also outlines the civil disabilities that apply to ex-convicts. Section V assesses parole outcomes, reviewing parole completion and recidivism rates. Section VI discusses some current thinking on how to reform parole and identifies some of the more promising parole programs. Section VII presents concluding remarks.

I. Sources of Parole Information

Various agencies within the U.S. Department of Justice collect most of the available information regarding current parole practices and parolee characteristics. The National Institute of Corrections has supported periodic surveys since 1990 that describe parole board practices in the United States (Rhine et al. 1991) and whether states currently have discretionary parole release (National Institute of Corrections 1995). The nation's major parole associations, the American Probation and Parole Association, the American Correctional Association, and the Association of Paroling Authorities, International, also have conducted periodic studies (Rhine et al. 1991; Runda, Rhine, and Wetter 1994; Burke 1995). The Bureau of Justice Assistance recently published a survey of state sentencing practices, including information on states' parole practices (Austin 1998).

Most of what we know about U.S. parolee characteristics comes from the Bureau of Justice Statistics (BJS), the statistical arm of the U.S. Department of Justice. Since the early 1980s, the bureau has reported on the numbers of persons entering and exiting parole through its National Corrections Reporting Program. This series collects data nearly every year on all prison admissions and releases and on all parole entries and discharges in participating jurisdictions.

The BJS's National Probation and Parole Reporting Program gathers annual data on state and federal probation and parole counts and movements and the characteristics of persons under the supervision of probation and parole agencies. Published data include admissions and releases by method of entry and discharge. The BJS also sponsors censuses, usually conducted every five to six years, describing the agencies that have control of persons serving a criminal sentence. The Census of State and Local Probation and Parole Agencies, first conducted in 1991, gathers data on the agency organizational location, staffing, expenditures, and programs. Finally, the BJS conducts surveys of jail and prison inmates (usually every five years) that ask offenders whether they were on parole at the time of the arrest that led to their current conviction.

Parole was not always such a minimal topic of data collection and research. Between 1965 and 1977, the National Council on Crime and Delinquency directed the Uniform Parole Reports project, which collected arrest, conviction, and imprisonment data on parolees. Analyses of these data helped researchers to improve methods for predicting parolee behavior (Gottfredson, Hoffman, and Sigler 1975). This data collection effort was discontinued in 1977, and no similar effort replaced it.

At about the same time, the U.S. Board of Parole undertook a major research study to develop parole guidelines, which incorporated offense seriousness and risk of recidivism (Gottfredson, Wilkins, and Hoffman 1978). This research tracked released federal prisoners and used the recidivism data to create an actuarial device, which in turn, was applied to each inmate to create a Salient Factor Score. This score provided the basis for explicit guidelines for release decisions based on a determination of the potential risk of parole violation (Hoffman and DeGostin 1974). The Salient Factor Score was adopted by the U.S. Parole Board in 1972 and remained in use until the abolition of parole at the federal level.

Beyond these early studies and the minimal descriptive data that are now collected, scant attention has been paid parole by the research or scholarly communities. We have very few parole program evaluations or research studies of the parole process and its effects on offenders.

The National Institute of Justice, the research arm of the U.S. Department of Justice, has funded most of what has been conducted, which includes evaluations of drug testing for high-risk parolees in Texas (Turner and Petersilia 1992), intensive parole supervision in Minnesota (Deschenes, Turner, and Petersilia 1995), work release in Washington (Turner and Petersilia 1996a), and the effects of providing work training and day programs to parolees (Finn 1998a, 1998b, 1998c).

Parole has never attracted much scholarly interest, although there are a few notable exceptions (e.g., von Hirsch and Hanrahan 1979; Bottomley 1990; Rhine et al. 1991; McCleary 1992; Simon 1993; Richards 1995; Abadinsky 1997; Cromwell and del Carmen 1999; Lynch 1999).

II. The Origins and Evolution of Parole in the United States

"Parole" comes from the French word *parol*, referring to "word," as in giving one's word of honor or promise. It has come to mean an inmate's promise to conduct himself or herself in a law-abiding manner and according to certain rules in exchange for release. In penal philosophy, parole is part of the general nineteenth-century trend in criminology from punishment to reformation. Chief credit for developing the early parole system is usually given to Alexander Maconochie, who was in charge of the English penal colony at Norfolk Island, 1,000 miles off the coast of Australia, and to Sir Walter Crofton, who directed Ireland's prisons (Cromwell and del Carmen 1999).

A. Early Foundations and Growth of Parole

Maconochie criticized definite prison terms and developed a system of rewards for good conduct, labor, and study. Through a classification procedure he called the "mark system," prisoners could progress through stages of increasing responsibility and ultimately gain freedom. In 1840, he was given an opportunity to apply these principles as superintendent of the Norfolk Island penal settlement in the South Pacific. Under his direction, task accomplishment, not time served, was the criterion for release. Marks of commendation were given to prisoners who performed their tasks well, and they were released from the penal colony as they demonstrated willingness to accept society's rules. Returning to England in 1844 to campaign for penal reform, Maconochie tried to implement his reforms when he was appointed governor of the new Birmingham Borough Prison in 1849. However, he was unable to institute his reforms there because he was dismissed from his position in 1851 on the grounds that his methods were too lenient (Clear and Cole 1997).

Crofton attempted to implement Maconochie's mark system when he became the administrator of the Irish Prison System in 1854. Crofton felt that prison programs should be directed more toward reformation and that "tickets-of-leave" should be awarded to prisoners who had shown definitive achievement and positive attitude change. After a period of strict imprisonment, Crofton began transferring offenders to "intermediate prisons" where they could accumulate marks based on work performance, behavior, and educational improvement. Eventually they would be given tickets-of-leave and released on parole supervision. Parolees were required to submit monthly reports to the police, and a police inspector helped them find jobs and generally oversaw their activities. The concepts of intermediate prisons, assistance, and supervision after release were Crofton's contributions to the modern system of parole (Clear and Cole 1997).

By 1865, American penal reformers were well aware of the reforms achieved in the European prison systems, particularly in the Irish system. At the Cincinnati meeting of the National Prison Association in 1870, a paper by Crofton was read, and specific references to the Irish system were incorporated into the Declaration of Principles, along with such other reforms as indeterminate sentencing and classification for release based on a mark system. Because of Crofton's experiment, many Americans referred to parole as "the Irish system" (Walker 1998).

Zebulon Brockway, a Michigan penologist, is given credit for implementing the first parole system in the United States. He proposed a two-pronged strategy for managing prison populations and preparing inmates for release: indeterminate sentencing coupled with parole supervision. He was given a chance to put his proposal into practice in 1876 when he was appointed superintendent at a new youth reformatory, the Elmira Reformatory in New York. He instituted a system of indeterminacy and parole release, and he is commonly credited as the father of both in the United States. His ideas reflected the tenor of the times—a belief that criminals could be reformed and that every prisoner's treatment should be individualized.

On being admitted to Elmira, each inmate (a male between the ages of sixteen and thirty) was placed in the second grade of classification. Six months of good conduct meant promotion to the first grade—misbehavior could result in being placed in the third grade, from which the inmate would have to work his way back up. Continued good behavior in the first grade resulted in release. Paroled inmates remained under the jurisdiction of authorities for an additional six months, during which the parolee was required to report on the first day of every month to his appointed volunteer guardian (from which parole officers evolved) and provide an account of his situation and conduct (Abadinsky 1997). Written reports became required and were submitted to the institution after being signed by the parolee's employer and guardian.

Indeterminate sentencing and parole spread rapidly through the United States. In 1907, New York became the first state formally to adopt all the components of a parole system: indeterminate sentences, a system for granting release, postrelease supervision, and specific criteria for parole revocation. By 1927, only three states (Florida, Mississippi, and Virginia) were without a parole system, and by 1942, all states and the federal government had such systems (Clear and Cole 1997).

The percentage of U.S. prisoners released on parole rose from 44 percent in 1940 to a high of 72 percent in 1977, after which some states began to question the very foundations of parole, and the number of prisoners released in this fashion began to decline (Bottomley 1990). As shown in figure 1, 28 percent of prison releases in 1997 were from discretionary parole, the lowest figure since the federal government began compiling statistics on this issue (Ditton and Wilson 1999). Mandatory releases—the required release of inmates at the expiration of a certain time period—now surpass parole releases. And if one adds the "expiration releases," where the inmate is released after serving his full sentence, there is even a bigger imbalance between discretionary parole and mandatory release (28 percent vs. 57 percent).

Parole, it seemed, during the first half of the twentieth century, made perfect sense. First, it was believed to contribute to prisoner reform by encouraging participation in programs aimed at rehabilitation. Second, the power to grant parole was thought to provide corrections officials with a tool for maintaining institutional control and discipline. The prospect of a reduced sentence in exchange for good behavior encouraged better conduct among inmates. Finally, release on parole, as a "back-end" solution to prison crowding, was important from the beginning. For complete historical reviews, see Simon (1993) and Bottomley (1990).

The tremendous growth in parole as a concept, however, did not

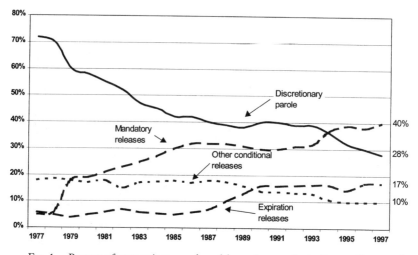

Fig. 1.—Percent of state prisoners released by various methods. Source: Bureau of Justice Statistics (various years–*d*). Note: Discretionary paroles are persons entering the community because of a parole board decision. Mandatory releases are persons whose release from prison was not decided by a parole board, including those entering because of determinate sentencing statutes, good-time provisions, or emergency releases. Other conditional releases include commutations, pardons, and deaths. Expiration releases are those in which the inmate has served his maximum court sentence.

imply uniform development, public support, or quality practices. As Bottomley (1990, p. 326) wrote, "It is doubtful whether parole ever really operated consistently in the United States either in principle or practice." Moreover, Bottomley notes that parole as rehabilitation was never taken very seriously and, from its inception, prison administrators used parole primarily to manage prison crowding and reduce inmate violence.

Despite its expanded usage, parole was controversial from the start (Rothman 1980). A Gallup poll conducted in 1934 revealed that 82 percent of U.S. adults believed that parole was not strict enough and should not be as frequently granted (Gallup Organization 1998). Today, parole is still unpopular, and a recent survey shows that 80 percent of Americans favor making parole more difficult to obtain (Gallup Organization 1998). A comparable percentage is opposed to granting parole a second time to inmates who have previously been granted parole for a serious crime (Flanagan 1996). However, the public significantly underestimates the amount of time inmates serve, so their lack of support for parole reflects that misperception (Flanagan 1996).

Nonetheless, over time, the positivistic approach to crime and criminals—which viewed the offender as "sick" and in need of help—began to influence parole release and supervision. The rehabilitation ideal, as it came to be known, affected all of corrections well into the 1960s and gained acceptance for the belief that the purpose of incarceration and parole was to change the offender's behavior rather than simply to punish. As Rhine (1996) notes, as the rehabilitative ideal evolved, indeterminate sentencing in tandem with parole acquired a newfound legitimacy. It also gave legitimacy and purpose to parole boards, which were supposed to be composed of "experts" in behavioral change, and it was their responsibility to discern when during confinement the offender was rehabilitated and thus suitable for release.

Parole boards, usually political appointees, traditionally were given broad discretion to determine when an offender was ready for release—a decision limited only by the constraints of the maximum sentence imposed by the judge. Parole boards—usually composed of no more than ten individuals—also have the authority to rescind an established parole date, issue warrants and subpoenas, set conditions of supervision, restore offenders' civil rights, and grant final discharges. In most states, they also order the payment of restitution or supervision fees as a condition of parole release.

In the early years, there were few standards governing the decision to grant or deny parole, and decision-making rules were not made public. One of the long-standing criticisms of paroling authorities is that their members are too often selected based on party loyalty and political patronage, rather than professional qualifications and experience (Morse 1939).

In his book *Conscience and Convenience*, David Rothman discussed the issue of discretionary decisions by parole boards. He reported that, in the early twentieth century, parole boards considered primarily the seriousness of the crime in determining whether to release an inmate on parole. However, there was no consensus on what constituted a serious crime. "Instead," Rothman wrote, "each member made his own decisions. The judgements were personal and therefore not subject to debate or reconsideration" (Rothman 1980, p. 173). These personal preferences often resulted in unwarranted sentencing disparities or racial and gender bias (Tonry 1995). As has been observed, "no other part of the criminal justice system concentrates such power in the hands of so few" (Rhine et al. 1991, pp. 32–33).

Regardless of criticisms, the use of parole release grew, and instead of using it as a special privilege to be extended to exceptional prisoners, it began to be used as a standard mode of release from prison, routinely considered on completion of a minimum term of confinement. What had started as a practical alternative to executive clemency, and then came to be used as a mechanism for controlling prison growth, gradually developed a distinctively rehabilitative rationale, incorporating the promise of help and assistance as well as surveillance (Bottomley 1990, p. 325).

By the mid-1950s, indeterminate sentencing coupled with parole release was well entrenched in the United States, the dominant sentencing structure in every state, and by the late 1970s, more than 70 percent of all inmate releases were results of parole board discretionary decision. And in some states, essentially everyone was released as a result of parole board decision making. For example, throughout the 1960s, over 95 percent of all inmates released in Washington, New Hampshire, and California were released on parole (O'Leary 1974). Indeterminate sentencing coupled with parole release was a matter of absolute routine and good correctional practice for most of the twentieth century.

But all that was to change during the late 1970s, and more rapidly in the 1980s and 1990s, as demands for substantial reforms in parole practice began to be heard.

B. Modern Challenges and Changes to Parole

The pillars of the American corrections systems—indeterminate sentencing coupled with parole release, for the purposes of offender rehabilitation—came under severe attack and basically collapsed during the late 1970s and early 1980s. This period in penology has been well documented elsewhere and is not repeated here. For an excellent review, see Reitz (1998).

Attacks on indeterminate sentencing and parole release seem to have centered on three major criticisms. First, there was little scientific evidence that parole release and supervision reduced subsequent recidivism. In 1975, Martinson and his colleagues published the now-famous review of the effectiveness of correctional treatment and concluded that, "with few and isolated exceptions, the rehabilitative efforts that have been reported so far have had no appreciable effect on recidivism" (Lipton, Martinson, and Wilks 1975, p. 20). Of the 289 studies they reviewed, just twenty-five (8.6 percent) pertained to parole, and yet their summary was interpreted to mean that parole supervision (and all rehabilitation programs) did not work.

The National Research Council reviewed the Martinson data and basically concurred with the conclusions reached (Sechrest, White, and Brown 1979). Martinson's study is often credited with giving rehabilitation the coup de grâce. As Holt (1998) notes, once rehabilitation could not be legitimated by science, there was nothing to support the "readiness for release" idea, and therefore no role for parole boards or indeterminate sentencing.

Second, parole and indeterminate sentencing were challenged on moral grounds as unjust and inhumane, especially when imposed on unwilling participants. Research showed there was little relationship between in-prison behavior, participation in rehabilitation programs, and postrelease recidivism (Glaser 1969). If that was true, then why base release dates on in-prison performance? Critics argued that not knowing their release dates kept prisoners in "suspended animation" and contributed one more pain of imprisonment.

Third, indeterminate sentencing permitted authorities to use a great deal of uncontrolled discretion in release decisions, and these decisions were often inconsistent and discriminatory. Since parole boards had a great deal of autonomy and their decisions were not subject to outside scrutiny, critics argued that it was a hidden system of discretionary decision making and led to race and class bias in release decisions (Citizens' Inquiry on Parole and Criminal Justice 1974).

It seemed as if no one liked indeterminate sentencing and parole in the early 1980s, and the time was ripe for change. Crime control advocates denounced parole supervision as being largely nominal and ineffective; social welfare advocates decried the lack of meaningful and useful rehabilitation programs. Several scholars, for example, James Q. Wilson, Andrew von Hirsch, and David Fogel, began to advocate alternative sentencing proposals.

Wilson argued that, if there were no scientific basis for believing rehabilitation worked, then the philosophical rationale for making it the chief goal of sentencing should be abandoned. He urged instead a revival of interest in the deterrent and incapacitative functions of the criminal justice system. He urged abandonment of rehabilitation as a major purpose of corrections, and wrote: "Instead we could view the correctional system as having a very different function—to isolate and to punish. That statement may strike many readers as cruel, even bar-

baric. It is not. It is merely recognition that society must be able to protect itself from dangerous offenders. . . . It is also a frank admission that society really does not know how to do much else" (Wilson 1985, p. 193).

von Hirsch provided a seemingly neutral ideological substitute for rehabilitation (see Holt 1998). He argued that the discredited rehabilitation model should be replaced with a simple nonutilitarian notion that sanctions should reflect the culpability and harm associated with the misconduct. Indeterminacy and parole should be replaced with a specific penalty for a specific offense. He believed that all persons committing the same crimes "deserve" to be sentenced to conditions that are similar in both type and duration and that individual traits such as amenability to treatment or potential for recidivism should be irrelevant to sentencing and parole decisions. He proposed abolishing parole and adopting a system of "just deserts" sentencing, in which similarly situated criminal conduct would be punished similarly (von Hirsch 1976).

Fogel advocated a "justice model" for prisons and parole, in which inmates would be given opportunities to volunteer for rehabilitation programs but that participation would not be required. He criticized the unbridled discretion exercised by correctional officials, particularly parole boards, under the guise of "treatment." He recommended a return to flat time/determinate sentencing and the elimination of parole boards. He also advocated abolishing parole's surveillance function and turning that function over to law enforcement (Fogel 1975).

These individuals had a major influence on both academic and policy thinking about sentencing objectives. Together they advocated a system with less emphasis on rehabilitation and the abolition of indeterminate sentencing and discretionary parole release. Liberals and conservatives endorsed the proposals. The political Left was concerned about excessive discretion that permitted vastly different sentences in presumably similar cases, and the political Right was concerned about the leniency of parole boards. Broad-based support for change resulted, and soon incapacitation and "just deserts" replaced rehabilitation as the primary goal of American prisons.

With that changed focus, indeterminate sentencing and parole release came under serious attack, and calls for "abolishing parole" were heard in state after state. In 1976, Maine became the first state to eliminate parole. The following year, California and Indiana joined Maine in establishing determinate sentencing legislation and abolishing discretionary parole release. By the end of 1998, fourteen states had abolished discretionary parole release for all inmates. In addition, in twenty-one states, parole authorities are operating under what might be called a "sundown provision," in that they have discretion over a small or diminished parole eligible population. Today, just fifteen states have given their parole boards full authority to release inmates through a discretionary process (see table 1).

Likewise, at the federal level, the Comprehensive Crime Control Act of 1984 created the U.S. Sentencing Commission. That legislation abolished the U.S. Parole Commission, and parole was eliminated for offenders sentenced under sentencing guidelines that took effect in 1987 and were kept only for prisoners sentenced under prior laws. Offenders sentenced to federal prison, while no longer eligible for parole release, are now required to serve a defined term of "supervised release" following release from prison (Adams and Roth 1998).

One of the presumed effects of eliminating parole or limiting its use is to increase the length of prison term served. After all, parole release is widely regarded as "letting them out early." Time served in prison has increased in recent years, but that is attributed to the implementation of truth-in-sentencing laws, rather than to the abolition of parole boards. The BJS data reveal no obvious relationship between type of release (mandatory vs. parole board) and length of time spent in prison prior to release. For all offense types combined, the (mean) average time served in prison for those released from state prison in 1996 through "discretionary" (parole) methods was twenty-five months served, whereas for those released "mandatorily," the (mean) average time served in prison was twenty-four months (Ditton and Wilson 1999). Ending parole by itself appears to have had no real impact on time served.

Offenders are, however, spending greater amounts of time in prison and on parole. These longer times may make it more difficult for offenders to maintain family contacts and other social supports, thereby contributing to their social isolation on release. As table 2 shows, the (mean) average time served among released state prisoners, for all types of offenders, has increased from an average of twenty months in 1985 to twenty-five months in 1996. The median prison term served increased from fourteen months in 1985 to fifteen months in 1996. Similarly, the length of time on parole supervision (for those successfully discharged) has increased from an average of nineteen months in 1985 to twenty-three months in 1996. The average time on parole for

TABLE 1

Status of Parole Release in the United States, 1998

	Parole Board Has Full Release Powers	Parole Board Has Limited Release Powers	If Parole Board Powers Are Limited, Crimes Ineligible for Discretionary Release	Discretionary Parole Abolished (Year Abolished)
Alabama	√			
Alaska		√		
Arizona				√ (1994)
Arkansas		√		
California		√	Only for indeterminate life sentences	
Colorado	√			
Connecticut		√	Murders, capital felonies	
Delaware				√ (1990)
Florida		√	Certain capital/life felonies	
Georgia		√	Several felonies	
Hawaii		√	Punishment by life without parole	
Idaho	√			
Illinois				√ (1978)
Indiana				√ (1977)
Iowa		√	Murder 1, kidnap, sex abuse	
Kansas				√ (1993)
Kentucky	√			
Louisiana		√	Several felonies	
Maine				√ (1975)
Maryland		√	Violent, or death penalty sought	
Massachusetts		√	Murder 1	
Michigan		√	Murder 1, 650+ grams cocaine	
Minnesota				√ (1980)
Mississippi				√ (1995)
Missouri		√	Several felonies	
Montana	√			
Nebraska		√	Murder 1/life, kidnap/life	
Nevada	√			
New Hampshire		√	Murder 1	
New Jersey	√			
New Mexico				√ (1979)
New York		√	"Violent felony offenders"	
North Carolina				√ (1994)
North Dakota	√			
Ohio				√ (1996)
Oklahoma	√			
Oregon				√ (1989)
Pennsylvania	√			
Rhode Island	√			
South Carolina	√			
South Dakota		√	None with life sentence	
Tennessee		√	Murder 1/life, rapes	
Texas		√	None of death row	
Utah	√			
Vermont	√			
Virginia				√ (1995)
Washington				√ (1984)
West Virginia		√	No life without mercy	
Wisconsin		√	No life without parole	*
Wyoming	√			
Total	15	21		14

NOTE.—This information is from National Institute of Corrections (1997) and updated with information from Ditton and Wilson (1999).

* Wisconsin abolished discretionary parole release in 1999, to go into effect on January 1, 2000, for crimes committed on or after that date.

TABLE 2

Time Served in Prison, Jail, and on
Parole: All Offense Types Combined,
in Months

	1985	1990	1996
Average time served in jail	6	6	5
Average time served in prison	20	22	25
Time served on parole	19	22	23
Total months	45	50	53

SOURCE.—Data are from the Bureau of Justice Statistics
(various years–c) and include only offenders with a sentence
of more than one year released for the first time on the current sentence. Time served on parole is for "successful"
exits.

"unsuccessful exits" was nineteen months in 1985 and twenty-one
months in 1996 (Bureau of Justice Statistics 1998).

Even in states that did not formally abolish parole or restrict its use
to certain serious offenses, the sentencing reform movement produced
a significant diminution of parole boards' discretionary authority to release. Mandatory minimum sentencing policies now exist in every
state, and the federal government and twenty-four states have enacted
"three strikes, you're out" laws that require extremely long minimum
terms for certain repeat offenders (National Conference of State Legislatures 1996).

Perhaps most significantly, twenty-seven states and the District of
Columbia have established "truth-in-sentencing" laws, under which
people convicted of selected violent crimes must serve at least 85 percent of the announced prison sentence. To satisfy the 85 percent test
(in order to qualify for federal funds for prison construction), states
have limited the powers of parole boards to set release dates or of
prison managers to award good time and gain time (time off for good
behavior or for participation in work or treatment programs), or both.
Truth-in-sentencing laws not only effectively eliminate parole but also
most "good time" (Ditton and Wilson 1999).

Even in the fifteen jurisdictions that give parole authorities discretion to release, most use formal risk prediction instruments (or parole
guidelines) to assist in parole decision making (Runda, Rhine, and
Wetter 1994). Parole guidelines are usually actuarial devices that pre-

dict the risk of recidivism based on crime and offender background information. The guidelines produce a "seriousness" score for each individual by summing points assigned for various background characteristics (higher scores mean greater risk). Inmates with the least serious crime and the lowest statistical probability of reoffending would then be the first to be released. The use of such instruments helps to reduce disparity in parole release decision making and has been shown to be more accurate than release decisions based on the case study or individualized method (Holt 1998). One-half of U.S. jurisdictions now use formal risk assessment instruments in relation to parole release (Runda, Rhine, and Wetter 1994).

III. A Profile of Parolees in the Unites States

While discretionary parole release has declined, parole supervision remains in almost every state. And, as the size of the prison populations has risen, so too has the parole population.

A. Numbers of Parolees under Supervision

The BJS reports that, at year-end 1997, there were 685,033 adults on parole in the United States. Persons on parole represented 12 percent of the total 5.7 million persons who were incarcerated or on community supervision ("under correctional control") at year-end 1997 (Bureau of Justice Statistics 1998).

The growth in parole populations has slowed considerably in recent years, increasing just 1.3 percent in 1997, after growing 24 percent between 1990 and 1992. This is the smallest growth of any of the correctional populations and likely reflects a short-term lull in the growth of the parole population, primarily as a consequence of an increase in the average length of prison term being served as a result of truth-in-sentencing policies (Ditton and Wilson 1999).

Nearly a third (31.2 percent) of all persons on parole in the United States were in Texas or California. Texas led the nation with 109,437 adults on parole in 1997, followed by California with 104,409. In 1997, however, the parole population in Texas declined by 2.8 percent, while the California population increased by 4.9 percent. The District of Columbia has, by far, the greatest percentage of its resident population on parole supervision. In 1997, nearly 1.7 percent of all its residents were on parole supervision (six times the national average of 0.3 percent) (Bureau of Justice Statistics 1998).

B. Selected Characteristics

There is little available information on the characteristics of persons on parole. The BJS reports some basic characteristics of those entering parole as part of its National Corrections Reporting Program series. In 1997, as is true of other correctional populations, males constituted most of the parolee population (89 percent), although the percentage of female parolees increased from 8 percent in 1990 to 11 percent in 1997. Fifty-four percent of the parole population were white, 45 percent were black, and 21 percent were of Hispanic origin. The median age of the parolee population was thirty-four years, and the median education level was eleventh grade (although 13 percent of parolees had an education level below eighth grade, and an additional 45 percent, between ninth and eleventh grade levels) (Bureau of Justice Statistics 1997). These characteristics have remained fairly constant since the early 1980s.

The only parolee characteristic that has changed in recent years appears to be the conviction crime. In 1988, 30 percent of first entries to parole were convicted of violence, but in 1997, that had dropped to 24 percent. In 1985, just 12 percent of those persons released to parole were convicted of drug crimes, whereas in 1997, that was true for 35 percent of first releases to parole (Beck 1999). Today, more than a third of all entrants to parole are convicted of drug-related crimes (see table 3).

Individual states sometimes publish descriptions of their parolees. For example, a recent report by the California Parole and Community Services Division reported that 85 percent of parolees were chronic substance abusers, 10 percent were homeless (but homelessness was as high as 30–50 percent in San Francisco and Los Angeles), 70–90 percent of all parolees were unemployed, and 50 percent were functionally illiterate (California Department of Corrections 1997). Over half of all parolees read below the sixth grade level and therefore could not fill out job applications or compete in the job market; 18 percent have some sort of psychiatric problem.

IV. The Reentry Process and Parole Supervision

Parole consists of two parts: parole boards that have the authority to decide when to release prisoners, and parole field services, whose parole officers supervise offenders after their release. The major criticisms of parole release (e.g., lack of professionalism, unwarranted dis-

TABLE 3

Conviction Offenses of Persons Entering Parole, Selected Years
(in Percent)

Most Serious Offense	First Entries to Parole Supervision*				
	1988	1990	1992	1994	1996
Violent offenses:	30.1	25.2	25.5	23.5	23.6
Homicide	3.8	3.0	2.7	2.3	2.1
Sexual assault	5.4	4.2	4.2	4.4	4.3
Robbery	13.7	11.2	10.7	8.7	8.9
Assault	6.3	5.8	6.6	6.9	6.9
Other violent	.9	1.0	1.0	1.2	1.4
Property offenses:	42.2	37.2	32.7	33.3	31.0
Burglary	20.8	17.5	14.8	14.5	12.9
Larceny/theft	10.2	9.6	8.4	8.5	8.1
Motor vehicle theft	2.9	2.7	2.7	3.1	2.7
Fraud	5.1	4.6	3.9	4.2	4.3
Other property	3.2	2.8	2.9	3.0	3.0
Drug offenses:	19.2	28.2	31.1	31.6	34.7
Possession	6.0	8.6	8.2	7.0	10.0
Trafficking	10.4	15.6	19.3	19.5	19.5
Other	2.8	4.0	3.6	5.1	5.2
Public-order offense:	7.1	8.1	9.8	10.5	10.1
Weapons	1.9	1.8	2.2	2.4	2.7
DWI/DUI	N.A.	3.0	3.7	3.5	3.2
Other	N.A.	3.3	3.9	4.6	4.2
Other offenses	1.4	1.3	1.2	1.1	.6

Source.—Bureau of Justice Statistics (various years–c). Unpublished data are for 1994 and 1996.

Note.—N.A. = not available. All offenses per year sum to 100 percent.

* Based on parole entries who were released for the first time on the current offense and who had a maximum sentence of more than one year.

cretion, and ineffectiveness) were also leveled at field supervision and caused major changes and reforms there as well.

A. Administration of Parole Field Services

One of the first and continuing reforms in parole field services has been to make them more independent of parole boards. Since the mid-1960s, states have increasingly moved parole field services away from being an arm of the parole board and into a separate agency. According to the American Correctional Association, the parole field service agency is housed under a separate agency in forty-one states, usually in the department of corrections. Parole boards have responsibility for supervising parolees in only ten states (American Correctional Association 1995).

Regardless of administrative relationships, parole board directives heavily influence how parole agents carry out their duties and responsibilities. When setting conditions of release, a parole board prescribes the goals it expects parole agents to pursue in the period of supervision. A 1997 survey by the Association of Paroling Authorities International shows that most parole boards are responsible for ordering community service, restitution, supervision fees, sex offender registration, and treatment program participation (Association of Paroling Authorities International 1998). In addition, some parole boards also mandate drug testing, intensified supervision, and participation in mediation programs.

In all states, the decision to revoke parole ultimately rests with the parole board. Parole boards set implicit and explicit criteria about which types of parole violations will warrant return to prison and thereby heavily influence the types of behavior parole officers monitor and record. If, for example, failing a drug test is not a violation that will result in revocation to prison or any serious consequence by the parole board, parole agents will not administer drug tests as frequently since no consequence can be guaranteed (McCleary 1992). In this way, parole boards and parole field services are functionally interdependent.

B. Offenders' Needs for Services and Conditions of Parole Supervision

Persons released from prison face a multitude of difficulties in trying to reenter the outside community successfully. They remain largely uneducated, unskilled, and usually without solid family support systems—and now they bear the added burdens of a prison record and the distrust and fear that inevitably results. If they are African American and under age thirty, they join the largest group of unemployed in the country, with the added handicap of former convict status (Clear and Cole 1997). As Irwin and Austin (1994, p. 133) write: "Any imprisonment reduces the opportunities of felons, most of whom had relatively few opportunities to begin with."

Research has shown that parolees want the same things as the rest of us, although most believe they will not succeed (Richards 1995). Most aspire to a relatively modest, stable, conventional life after prison. "When I get out, I want to have my kids with me and have a good job so I can support them" (Irwin and Austin 1994, p. 126).

The public too would like them to succeed. But what assistance are parolees given as they reenter our communities? Sadly, while inmates' need for services and assistance has increased, parole in some (if not most) states has retreated from its historical mission to provide counseling, job training, and housing assistance.

An excellent ethnographic study of parole officers in California concludes that, while "rehabilitation" remains in parole's rhetoric, as a practical matter parole services are almost entirely focused on control-oriented activities (Lynch 1999). Agents have constructed the prototypical parolee as someone who generally chooses to continue involvement with crime, who needs no more than an attitude adjustment in order to get on the "right track," and who does not need the agent to provide intervention and services to facilitate reform. As Lynch observes: "In this way, while parole may talk of the need and capability for reform among their clientele, the agency can absolve itself of the responsibility to provide it" (Lynch 1998, p. 857). Even when traditional rehabilitative tools are available to agents—for example, drug treatment and counseling—they "are treated as rehabilitative in discourse, but are often used for coercive control in practice" (ibid., p. 860).

1. *Services and Parole Conditions.* Of course, what help parolees receive differs vastly depending on the state and jurisdiction in which they are being supervised. But as states put more and more of their fiscal resources into building prisons, fewer resources are available for parole services. And, as noted earlier, the public has become less tolerant and forgiving of past criminal transgressions and more fearful of particular offenders (e.g., sex offenders). This sentiment has translated into stricter requirements for release and stricter supervision and revocation procedures once released.

In California, for example, there are few services for parolees. There are only 200 shelter beds in the state for more than 10,000 homeless parolees, four mental health clinics for 18,000 psychiatric cases, and 750 beds in treatment programs for 85,000 drug and alcohol abusers (Little Hoover Commission 1998). Under the terms of their parole, offenders are often subjected to periodic drug tests. But they are rarely offered any opportunity to get drug treatment. Of the approximately 130,000 substance abusers in California's prisons, only 3,000 are receiving treatment behind bars. And of the 132,000 inmates released last year in California, just 8,000 received any kind of prerelease program to help them cope with life on the outside. As was recently reported:

Inmates are simply released from prison each year in California, given nothing more than $200 and a bus ticket back to the county where they were convicted. At least 1,200 inmates every year go from a secure housing unit at a Level 4 prison—an isolation unit, designed to hold the most violent and dangerous inmates in the system—right onto the street. One day these predatory inmates are locked in their cells for twenty-three hours at a time and fed all their meals through a slot in the door, and the next day they're out of prison, riding a bus home. (Schlosser 1998, p. 51)

The national picture is almost as disturbing. The Office of National Drug Control Policy recently reported that 70–85 percent of state prison inmates need substance abuse treatment; however, just 13 percent will receive any kind of treatment while incarcerated (McCaffrey 1998).

All parolees are required to sign an agreement to abide by certain regulations. Conditions can generally be grouped into standard conditions applicable to all parolees and special conditions that are tailored to particular offenders. Special conditions for substance abusers, for example, usually include periodic drug testing.

Standard conditions are similar throughout most jurisdictions, and violating them can result in a return to prison. Common standard parole conditions include that one should report to the parole agent within twenty-four hours of release, not carry weapons, report changes of address and employment, not travel more than fifty miles from home or leave the county for more than forty-eight hours without prior approval from the parole agent, obey all parole agent instructions, seek and maintain employment or participate in education/work training, not commit crimes, and submit to search by the police and parole officers.

Some argue that we have created unrealistic parole conditions. Boards were asked in 1988 to indicate standard parole conditions in their state from a list of fourteen items. The most common was "obey all laws." However, 78 percent required "gainful employment" as a standard condition; 61 percent, "no association with persons of criminal records"; 53 percent, "pay all fines and restitution"; and 47 percent, "support family and all dependents." None of these can consistently be met by most parolees (Rhine et al. 1991). Increasingly, drug testing is the most common condition for probationers and parolees. It is estimated that more than a third of all community correctional clients have court-ordered drug testing conditions (Camp and Camp 1997).

In October 1998, Maryland began ordering every drug addict released on parole or probation to report for urine tests twice a week in an ambitious attempt to force about 25,000 criminals statewide to undergo drug treatment or face a series of quickly escalating punishments. The project, known as "Break the Cycle," is based on the theory that frequent drug testing coupled with swift, graduated punishments for drug use will force more addicts off drugs than the threat of long jail terms or treatment programs alone ever could. The state anticipates that more than a million tests annually may be required to make the plan work, compared with the 40,000 tests the state administered the preceding year (Pan 1998).

Seeing that the parolee lives up to this parole contract is the principal responsibility of the parole agent. Parole agents are equipped with legal authority to carry and use firearms; to search places, persons, and property without the constraints imposed by the Fourth Amendment (e.g., the right to privacy); and to order arrests without probable cause and to confine without bail. The power to search applies to the household where a parolee is living and businesses where a parolee is working. The ability to arrest, confine, and in some cases reimprison the parolee makes the parole agent a walking court system (Rudovsky et al. 1988).

2. Parole Classification and Caseload Assignment.   When parolees first report to the parole field office, they are usually interviewed for the purposes of being assigned to a caseload. Most jurisdictions rely on a formal approach to classification and case management. Such systems recognize that not all offenders are equal in their need for supervision. A recent parole survey found that 90 percent of the states use a classification system for assigning parolees to different levels of supervision (Runda, Rhine, and Wetter 1994).

Most often, this assignment is based on a structured assessment of parolee risk and an assessment of the needs or problem areas that have contributed to the parolee's criminality. By scoring information relative to the risk of recidivism and the particular needs of the offender (i.e., a risk/need instrument), a total score is derived, which then indicates the particular level of parole supervision (e.g., intensive, medium, minimum, administrative). Jurisdictions usually establish policy that dictates the contact levels (times the officer will meet with the parolee). These contact levels correspond to each level of parole supervision.

TABLE 4

Parole Caseload Supervision Level, Contacts, and Annual Costs

Caseload Type	Percent of All Parolees	Average Caseload Size	Face to Face Contacts	Annual Supervision Cost ($)
Regular	82	69:1	1.6/month	1,397
Intensive	14	27:1	5.1/month	3,628
Electronic monitoring	.7	25:1	5.7/month	3,628
Specialized	3.7	43:1	4.4/month	4,080

SOURCE.—Camp and Camp (1997).

The notion is that higher-risk inmates and those with greater needs will be seen more frequently (e.g., on "intensive" caseloads). These models are described as "management tools" and are not devices to reduce recidivism directly (Holt 1998).

Larger parole departments have also established "specialized caseloads" to supervise certain types of offenders more effectively. These offenders generally pose a particularly serious threat to public safety or present unique problems that may handicap their adjustment to supervision. Specialized caseloads afford the opportunity to match the special skills and training of parole officers with the specialized needs of parolees. The most common specialized caseloads in the United States target sex offenders and parolees with serious substance abuse problems, although, as shown in table 4, fewer than 4 percent of all parolees are supervised on specialized caseloads.

Cases are then assigned to parole officers and constitute an officer's caseload. Table 4 contains the latest information on these characteristics for U.S. parolees. Over 80 percent of U.S. parolees are supervised on regular caseloads, averaging sixty-nine cases to one parole officer, in which parolees are seen (face-to-face) less than twice per month. Officers may also conduct "collateral" contacts, such as contacting family members or employers to inquire about the parolee's progress. Many parole officers are frustrated because they lack the time and resources to do the kind of job they believe is maximally helpful to their clients. Parole officers often complain that paperwork has increased, that their clients have increasingly more serious problems, and that their caseloads are much higher than the thirty-five to fifty cases that have been considered the ideal caseload for a parole officer. However, there is no empirical evidence to show that smaller caseloads result in lower recidivism rates (Petersilia and Turner 1993).

One important implication of larger caseloads and the reduction in the quality of client supervision is the increased potential for lawsuits arising from negligent supervision by parole officers (del Carmen and Pilant 1994). In a 1986 case, the Alaska Supreme Court ruled that state agencies and their officers may be held liable for negligence when probationers and parolees under their supervision commit violent offenses (*Division of Corrections vs. Neakok*, 721 P.2d 1121, 1125; Alaska [1986]). Thus parole officers are increasingly at risk through tort actions filed by victims harmed by the crimes committed by their offender-clients. Some have argued that this legal threat will eventually force states to invest more heavily in parole supervision.

3. *Parole Revocation.*   If parolees fail to live up to their conditions, they can be revoked to custody. Parole can be revoked for two reasons: the commission of a new crime, or the violation of the conditions of parole (a "technical violation"). Technical violations pertain to behavior that is not criminal, such as the failure to refrain from alcohol use or remain employed.

In either event, the violation process is rather straightforward. Given that parolees are technically still in the legal custody of the prison or parole authorities, and as a result maintain a quasi-prisoner status, their constitutional rights are severely limited. When parole officers become aware of violations of the parole contract, they notify their supervisors, who can rather easily return a parolee to prison.

Parole violations are an administrative function that is typically devoid of court involvement. However, parolees do have some rights in revocation proceedings. Two U.S. Supreme Court cases, *Morrissey vs. Brewer*, 408 U.S. 471 (1972), and *Gagnon vs. Scarpelli*, 411 U.S. 778 (1973), are considered landmark cases of parolee rights in revocation proceedings. Among other things, *Morrissey* and *Gagnon* established minimum requirements for the revocation of parole, requiring boards to conform to minimum standards of due process. Parolees must be given written notice of the nature of the violation and the evidence obtained, and they have a right to confront and cross-examine their accusers.

C. The Changing Nature of Parole Supervision and Services

Historically, parole agents were viewed as paternalistic figures who mixed authority with help. Officers provided direct services (e.g., counseling) and also knew the community and brokered services (e.g., job training) to needy offenders. Parole was originally designed to make the transition from prison to the community more gradual, and, during this time, parole officers were to assist the offender in addressing personal problems and searching for employment and a place to live. Many parole agencies still do assist in these "service" activities. Increasingly, however, parole supervision has shifted away from providing services to parolees and more toward monitoring and surveillance (e.g., drug testing, monitoring curfews, and collecting restitution).

Historically, offering "services" and treatment to parolees was commonplace, but such services are dwindling. A recent survey of twenty-two parole agencies shows that fourteen provide job development help, seven offer detoxification services, and thirteen offer substance abuse treatment, yet all do drug testing (Camp and Camp 1997).

There are a number of reasons for this. For one, a greater number of parole conditions are being assigned to released prisoners. In the federal system, for example, between 1987 and 1996 the proportion of offenders required to comply with at least one special supervision condition increased from 67 percent of entrants to 91 percent (Adams and Roth 1998). Parolees in state systems are also more frequently being required to submit to drug testing, complete community service, and make restitution payments (Petersilia and Turner 1993).

Parole officers work for the corrections system, and if paroling authorities are imposing a greater number of conditions on parolees, then field agents must monitor those conditions. As a result, modern-day parole officers have less time to provide other services, such as counseling, even if they were inclined to do so.

It is also true that the fiscal crises experienced in most states in recent years reduced the number of treatment and job-training programs in the community at large, and given the fear and suspicion surrounding ex-convicts, these persons are usually placed at the end of the waiting lists. The ability to "broker" services to parolees, given the scarcity of programs, has become increasingly difficult. If there is one common complaint among parole officers in the United States, it is the lack of available treatment and job programs for parolees. At the end of the 1960s, when the country had more employment opportunities for blue-collar workers than it does now, there was some movement to reduce employment barriers to ex-prisoners, and studies revealed a full-time employment rate of around 50 percent for parolees (Simon 1993). Today, full-time employment among parolees is rare.

The main reason, however, that "services" are not delivered to most parolees is that parole supervision has been transformed ideologically from a social service to a law enforcement system. Just as the prison system responded to the public's demands for accountability and justice, so did parole officers.

Feely and Simon (1992) argue that over the past few decades a systems analysis approach to danger management has come to dominate parole and that it has evolved into a "waste management" system, rather than one focused on rehabilitation. In their model, those in the dangerous class of criminals are nearly synonymous with those in the larger social category of the underclass, a segment of the population that has been abandoned to a fate of poverty and despair. They suggest that a "new penology" has emerged, one that simply strives to manage risk by use of actuarial methods. Offenders are addressed not as individuals but as aggregate populations. The traditional correctional objectives of rehabilitation and the reduction of offender recidivism have given way to the rational and efficient deployment of control strategies for managing (and confining) high-risk criminals. Surveillance and control have replaced treatment as the main goals of parole.

Newly hired parole officers often embrace the "surveillance" versus "rehabilitation" model of parole and embrace the quasi-policing role that parole has taken on in some locales. Twenty years ago, social work was the most common educational path for those pursuing careers in parole. Today, the most common educational path is criminal justice studies—an academic field spawned in the 1960s to professionalize law enforcement (Parent 1993). Parole agents began to carry concealed firearms in the 1980s. Firearms are now provided in most jurisdictions and represent a major investment of training resources, agent time, and administrative oversight (Holt 1998).

Programming innovations likewise represent a theme of control and supervision rather than service and assistance. Parolees are held more accountable for a broader range of behavior, including alcohol and substance abuse, restitution, curfews, and community service.

As Irwin and Austin (1994, p. 129) put it: "Instead of helping prisoners locate a job, find a residence, or locate needed drug treatment serves, the new parole system is bent on surveillance and detection. Parolees are routinely and randomly checked for illegal drug use, failure to locate or maintain a job, moving without permission, or any other number of petty and nuisance-type behaviors that don't conform to the rules of parole."

In addition to the limitations set out in the parole contract and enforced by the parole officer, parolees face a growing number of legal restrictions or "civil disabilities." Ironically, these civil disabilities often restrict the parolee's ability to carry out one of the most common parole requirements—that of remaining employed.

D. Civil Disabilities and Injunctions of Convicted Felons

While the services available to assist parolees have decreased, the structural obstacles concerning their behavior have increased. Under federal law and the laws of many states, a felony conviction has consequences that continue long after a sentence has been served and parole has ended. For example, convicted felons lose essential rights of citizenship, such as the right to vote and to hold public office, and may be restricted in their ability to obtain occupational and professional licenses. Their criminal record may also preclude them from retaining parental rights, be grounds for divorce, and bar them from serving on a jury, holding public office, and firearm ownership. These statutory restrictions or "civil disabilities" serve as punishments in addition to the conviction and sentence imposed by the court.

A recent survey shows that after a period when states were becoming less restrictive of convicted felons' rights, the "get-tough movement" of the 1980s had the effect of increasing the statutory restrictions placed on parolees. Between 1986 and 1996, state legal codes reveal an increase in restrictions on the rights and opportunities available to released inmates (Olivares, Burton, and Cullen 1996).

A complete state-by-state survey of civil disabilities of convicted felons can be found in Love and Kuzma (1996). These restrictions apply to all convicted felons and not separately to parolees.

1. *Right to Vote.* Fourteen states permanently deny convicted felons the right to vote, whereas most others temporarily restrict this right until the sentence has been fulfilled. Eighteen states suspend the right to vote until the offender has completed the imposed sentence of prison, probation, or parole (and paid all fines). Colorado is typical in this regard and provides that the "right to vote is lost if incarcerated and automatically restored on completion of sentence, including parole." California denies the right to vote to incarcerated offenders and parolees yet allows probationers to vote. Fellner and Mauer (1998) estimate that 1.4 million black males, or 13.1 percent of the black male adult population, are currently or permanently not able to vote as a result of a felony conviction. While most states have procedures for regaining the right to vote, it often requires a gubernatorial pardon.

2. *Parental Rights.*   Nineteen states currently may terminate the parental rights of convicted felons if it can be shown that a felony conviction suggests a parent's unfitness to supervise or care for the child. Oregon and Tennessee require that the parent be incarcerated for a specified length of time (three years in Oregon and two years in Tennessee).

3. *Divorce.*   The use of a felony conviction to permit divorce exists in nineteen states. In twenty-nine jurisdictions, a felony conviction constitutes legal grounds for divorce. In 1996, ten states consider any felony conviction as sufficient grounds, whereas seven jurisdictions require a felony conviction and imprisonment to grant divorce.

4. *Public Employment.*   Public employment is permanently denied in six states: Alabama, Delaware, Iowa, Mississippi, Rhode Island, and South Carolina. The remaining jurisdictions permit public employment in varying degrees. Of these states, ten leave the decision to hire at the discretion of the employer, while twelve jurisdictions apply a "direct relationship test" to determine whether the conviction offense bears directly on the job in question. But the courts have interpreted the "direct relationship" standard liberally; for example, a California case (*Golde vs. Fox*, 98 Cal. App.3d 167, 159 Cal. Rptr. 864 [1st Dist. 1979]) found that conviction of possession of marijuana for sale was substantially related to the business of real estate broker as it shows lack of honesty and integrity.

Each state has its own particular professions that have been restricted to ex-convicts. In Colorado, for example, the professions of dentist, engineer, nurse, pharmacist, physician, and real estate agent are closed to convicted felons. In California, the professions of law, real estate, medicine, nursing, physical therapy, and education are restricted. In Virginia, the professions of optometry, nursing, dentistry, accounting, funeral director, and pharmacy are professions generally closed to ex-felons.

5. *Right to Serve as a Juror.*   The right to serve as a juror is restricted permanently in thirty-two jurisdictions, and the remaining states permit the right with consideration given to varying conditions. For example, ten states restrict the right only during sentence, while four jurisdictions impose an additional delay after sentence completion (e.g., from one year in the District of Columbia to ten years in Kansas).

6. *Right to Hold Public Office.*   Seven states permanently deny elected office to persons convicted of specific crimes including bribery,

perjury, and embezzlement. Twenty states restrict the right to hold public office until the offender has completed his or her sentence of prison, probation, or parole.

7. *Right to Own a Firearm.* Thirty-one of fifty-one jurisdictions permanently deny or restrict the right to own or possess a firearm on "any" felony conviction. In contrast, eighteen states deny the right to own or possess a firearm only for convictions involving violence.

8. *Criminal Registration.* In 1986, only eight of fifty-one jurisdictions required offenders to register with a law enforcement agency on release from prison. By 1998, every state required convicted sex offenders to register with law enforcement on release (Lieb, Quinsey, and Berliner 1998). These state registration schemes, so-called Megan's laws, vary considerably with respect to the crimes for which registration is required, the duration of the registration requirement, and the penalty for failure to register. Illinois, for example, requires sex offenders and those convicted of first-degree murder against a victim under eighteen years old to register. The registration typically lasts for a period of several years but may extend for the life of the offender for certain crimes. In addition, California now requires sex offenders to provide blood and saliva samples for DNA testing.

Simon (1993) notes that these civil disabilities have the effect of creating an inherent contradiction in our legal system. He writes that different laws may serve different purposes, but they must not contradict one another. Yet, in the United States, we spend millions of dollars to "rehabilitate" offenders, convince them that they need to obtain legitimate employment, and then frustrate whatever was thereby accomplished by raising legal barriers that may bar them absolutely from employment and its rewards. He also notes that structural changes in the economy in the United States have taken their toll on the very population from which most parolees come, which have, in turn, affected agents' ability to do their jobs. Most notably, the loss of a solid industrial base over the past few decades, which has traditionally supplied jobs within poorer inner-city communities, has left urban parolees with few opportunities and left agents with fewer venues in which to monitor and supervise their clients (Lynch 1999).

V. Recidivism and Crime Committed by Parolees

The most common question asked about parole is, "Does it work?" By "work," most mean whether persons granted parole refrain from further crime or reduce their "recidivism." Recidivism is currently the primary outcome measure for parole, as it is for all corrections programs.

A. Prisoner Recidivism Rates

The most comprehensive study of state prisoner recidivism tracked 16,000 inmates released during 1983 in eleven states. The study found that, overall, 63 percent of inmates were arrested for a felony or serious misdemeanor offense within three years of release from prison. In unpublished data from that cohort, Beck reports that 62.3 percent of those who were released "conditionally" (i.e., on parole) were rearrested within three years, whereas the figure was 64.8 percent for those who were released "unconditionally." About 47 percent of inmates were convicted of a new offense during the three years after release, and 41 percent returned to prison or jail for a new offense or technical violation of their prison release (Beck and Shipley 1989).

The Beck and Shipley study is the best available to approximate the recidivism rates of parolees, but it has some limitations. Not all persons released from prison were officially on parole; however, in the early 1980s most were, so that these data capture most parolee recidivism. Also, the study tracked inmates for a full three-year period after release, and offenders may or may not have been officially on parole for all of that time period. The study was also conducted more than fifteen years ago, and we know that parole policy has changed considerably since that time. Unfortunately, there are no U.S. record-keeping systems that record the recidivism of parolees and no more recent national prisoner follow-up studies.

B. Successful vs. Unsuccessful Completion of Parole

The BJS, as part of its National Corrections Reporting Program, does collect data each year from every state about its parole population and how many of its parolees successfully complete parole. These data derive from parole agency records, not from the police, and hence they may not capture all arrests. It is possible, for example, for an offender to be arrested (say, for a misdemeanor or low-level felony) and not to be violated from parole and, hence, be recorded as a "successful exit" from parole.

These data reveal a disturbing trend: a majority of those being released to parole will not successfully complete their terms, and the percent of "unsuccessful" parolees is increasing. As Beck (1999) recently reported, annual discharges from state parole supervision reveal a

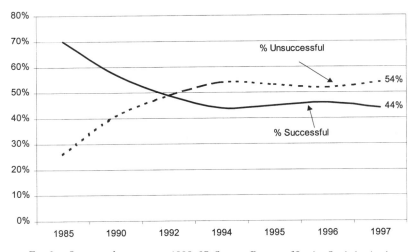

FIG. 2.—State parole outcomes, 1985–97. Source: Bureau of Justice Statistics (various years–*a*).

sharp drop in the percent of parolees who successfully complete their term of community supervision. As a percentage of all discharges from state parole supervision, offenders successfully completing parole declined from 70 percent in 1984 to 44 percent in 1996 (see fig. 2).

C. The Return of Parolees and Other "Conditional Releases" to Custody

Such high parole revocation rates are one of the major factors linked to the growing U.S. prison population. Since 1980, the percentage of conditional release violators—who had originally left state prisons as parolees, mandatory releases, and other type of releases subject to community supervision—has more than doubled, from 16 percent to 33.8 percent (see table 5).

In some states, the figures are even more dramatic. For example, in California in 1997 over two-thirds (64.7 percent) of all persons admitted to state prisons were parole violators. By comparison, in New York, the figure is 23 percent. In Texas, the state most comparable in prison population to California, the figure is also 23 percent. A recent report concluded: "There is no question that California has the highest rate of parole violations in the nation. In terms of total numbers, California accounts for nearly 40 percent of all known parole violators that occur in the nation although it reflects less than 15 percent of the nation's parole population" (Little Hoover Commission 1998, p. 23).

TABLE 5

Percent of Admitted Prisoners Who Were Parole Violators,
Selected Years

State	1980	1985	1992	1997
New York	24.1	13.8	13.9	23.0
Pennsylvania	19.6	26.7	18.6	33.4
Ohio	18.5	21.1	16.6	19.6
Illinois	20.3	29.9	19.7	30.4
Michigan	16.6	23.5	25.8	28.3
North Carolina	10.6	5.8	17.4	23.6
Georgia	8.2	18.3	25.5	23.0
Florida	16.0	6.4	12.7	12.2
Texas	15.8	30.9	39.9	22.7
California	20.7	41.7	56.3	64.7
Average:				
All fifty states	16.09	22.3	28.6	33.8
Federal only	11.09	12.9	*	9.0
State and federal combined	15.8	21.6	28.6	32.3

Source.—Bureau of Justice Statistics (various years–b), and unpublished data from 1997.
* Not reported.

D. *The Contribution of Parolees to Crime*

Another way to examine parole effectiveness is to look at proportions of all persons arrested and in custody who were on "parole" at the time they committed their last crime. The BJS conducts periodic surveys of persons arrested, in jail, in prison, and on death row. These data show that 44 percent of all state prisoners in 1991 had committed their latest crimes while out on probation or parole (fig. 3).

Such high recidivism rates have led to the common perception that community supervision fails to protect the public and that "nothing works." As DiIulio (1997, p. 41) writes: "While formally under supervision in the community, these prison inmate violations included more than 13,000 murders, some 39,000 robberies, and tens of thousands of other crimes. More than a quarter of all felons charged with gun crimes in 1992 were out on probation or parole."

Of course, it is important to remember that more than 80 percent of all parolees are on caseloads where they are seen less than twice a month, and the dollars available to support their supervision and services are generally less than $1,500 per offender per year—when effective treatment programs are estimated to cost $12,000 to $15,000 per

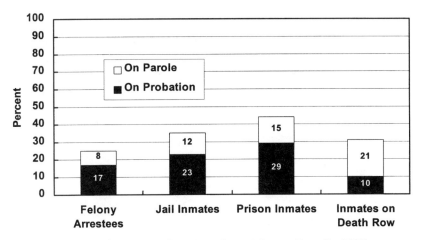

Fɪɢ. 3.—Who is on parole at time of arrest? Source: Petersilia (1997)

year, per client (Institute of Medicine 1990). It is no wonder that recidivism rates are so high. In a sense, we get what we pay for, and as yet, we have never chosen to invest sufficiently in parole programs.

Nevertheless, most view these data as showing that the parole system is neither helping offenders nor protecting the public and that major reform is needed.

VI. Reinventing and Reinvesting in Parole

As Joe Lehman, currently commissioner of the Washington Department of Corrections, said: "We have a broken parole system. Part of the problem is that parole can't do it alone, and we have misled the public in thinking that we can—hence the frustration, and the cries to abolish parole. We don't need to abolish parole, but a new model is sorely needed" (personal communication, September 10, 1998).

Interviews recently conducted with U.S. correctional experts reveal a consensus that parole needs to be "reinvented" (a term commonly used) and that the new parole "model" should incorporate at least four components: the identification of dangerous and violent parolees, for whom surveillance through human and technological means is a top priority; the delivery of quality treatment (particularly substance abuse) and job-training programs to the subgroup of offenders for whom research shows it could be most beneficial; the establishment of intermediate sanctions and other means of diverting technical parole violators to community-based alternatives and away from expensive prison cells;

and committing to a community-centered approach to parole supervision. This approach requires a commitment to manage offender risk in those neighborhoods where parolees live and means forming active partnerships with local police, community members, offenders' families, neighborhood associations, and other indigenous groups. Some refer to this as "neighborhood parole."

A. Greater Monitoring of High-Risk, Violent Parolees

There can be no doubt that the public, aided by private industry, will continue to demand and receive an increase in the level of control over certain violent, predatory offenders in the community. The most visible sign of this is the expanded registration of parolees, originally begun for sex offenses but now expanding in terms of types of crimes, and how accessible the information is to the public. Connecticut recently expanded its parolee registration to include kidnapping for sexual purposes, public indecency, and fourth-degree sexual assault. As of January 1, 1999, Connecticut's entire list is posted on the Internet. Florida and New Jersey also allow citizens to have complete access to inmate release information through an Internet site maintained by each state's department of corrections.

A New York City–based crime victim's advocacy group, using information from the state Department of Correctional Services, now places on the Internet the names of inmates soon to be eligible for parole from New York State prisons. In addition to including inmates' names, criminal backgrounds, and parole eligibility dates, the Internet site includes press clippings of the crime if they are available. The site encourages citizens to contact the New York State Division of Parole with comments.

In California, the State Department of Justice developed a CD-ROM database with the pictures, names, and whereabouts of the state's more than 50,000 registered sex offenders. Visitors to any local police station in the state are able to type in their ZIP codes to find out if a sex offender lives nearby. When the data were first released, many local newspapers published the pictures and addresses of local sex offenders. Los Angeles County just announced that, since few residents are using the CD-ROMs, mass mailings would be made to residents informing them of the location and names of sex offenders living in their neighborhoods. As of January 1, 1999, California school districts also have direct access to the CD-ROM and permission to distribute the information directly to the public.

New York and California both also now have 900-number hotlines set up to allow residents to check whether someone is a registered sex offender. Before that, it was illegal for a law enforcement officer to notify citizens about a sex offender living in the neighborhood.

Sophisticated technology is also assisting police and parole officers to keep better track of parolees once they are in the community. As the cold war wound down, the defense industry, along with the developing computer and electronic industries, saw the community correctional clientele as a natural place to put its energies—a growing market. Electronic monitoring, voice verification systems, cheap on-site drug testing, breathalyzers through the phone (through a mechanism placed in the phone voice piece)—all allowed community corrections the means to become more surveillance-oriented.

Since the mid-1980s, the electronic monitoring industry has continued to expand, and three states (Texas, Florida, New Jersey) now use global-positioning technology to determine when a parolee leaves his or her home or enters a restricted zone, such as an area around a school or the neighborhood of a former victim. The SMART (Satellite Monitoring And Remote Tracking) system was developed by Pro Tech Monitoring, Inc., a company founded by former Florida Governor Bob Martinez. "We integrated technologies proven in military and space applications to serve the citizens here at home," Martinez says. "This new system helps criminal justice and law enforcement officials know where offenders are when the courts release them into our communities" (see http://www.ptm.com/news.html; accessed October 12, 1998). The Florida Department of Corrections began implementing the system in 1997 and has transferred nearly one hundred offenders from the old traditional house arrest systems to the SMART system (see http://www.ptm.com/news.html). New Jersey began using the system in 1997 to monitor high-risk juveniles who have been mainly convicted of violent offenses or sexual assaults. The technology is also being planned for counties in Minnesota and Pennsylvania (Kleinknecht 1997). These initiatives and programs are a far cry from the traditional social work approaches to probation and parole.

B. Delivering Appropriate Treatment and Work Training to Selected Parolees

The public seems to have focused its fear and punitiveness on the violent (particular sexual) offender and seems more willing to tolerate treatment programs for nonviolent offenders, particularly substance abusers (Flanagan and Longmire 1996). Recent research reveals that the public favors both punishing and treating criminals, and punitiveness tends to decline when people are given complex sentencing options and are informed about the high cost of incarceration (Applegate et al. 1996). A recent study found the public unwilling to tolerate regular probation for felons but willing to tolerate, if not prefer, strict community-based alternatives to prison when these sanctions are developed and applied meaningfully. For the crime of robbery with injury, for example, 50 percent of the respondents viewed a sanction between halfway house and strict probation acceptable. When the option of shock incarceration (prison followed by community supervision) is added, this figure rises to a full 63 percent (Sundt et al. 1998). The public seems open to tough community-based sanctions and wants them to include both treatment and surveillance.

This softening of public attitudes seems to have resulted from knowledge about the high costs of prisons, combined with emerging evidence that some treatment programs are effective, for some offenders, under certain empirically established conditions. This research has identified those principles that produce effective correctional interventions. The evidence indicates that well-designed and properly implemented programs incorporating these principles result in significant reductions in recidivism. Those programs that are most successful include a strong behavior and cognitive skills development component (Andrews and Bonta 1994). Some of these programs have been effective in reducing the rearrest rates of parolees.

1. *Drug and Alcohol Dependency Programs.* A recent research summary of drug treatment effectiveness reported that "a growing body of research" shows that voluntary or mandatory drug treatment can reduce recidivism, especially when treatment is matched to offender needs (Prendergast, Anglin, and Wellisch 1995). The most successful programs are based on social learning theory. These programs assume that criminal behavior is learned, so they try to improve offenders' interpersonal relations through vocational and social skill building, peer-oriented behavior programs, role-playing, and interpersonal cognitive skill training. Effective treatment programs must also continue assisting the offender for several months after program completion.

A program that attempts to do this with notable success is San Diego's Parolee Partnership Program, which is part of California's statewide Preventing Paroling Failure Program. The San Diego program, begun in 1992, provides substance abuse treatment for parolees in San Diego County. A private vendor operates the program, using principles of client selection, managed care, case management, and case follow-up. The vendor subcontracts with others for outpatient, residential, and detoxification treatment services and facilities. Support services (e.g., education and vocation training, and transportation) are provided directly by the vendor or through referral to other community resource agencies. Typically, the time limit is 180 days of treatment. The participant is then assigned a "recovery advocate" who motivates the offender to continue in treatment for as long as necessary and keeps the parole agent aware of the parolee's progress. The program served about seven hundred offenders in fiscal year 1995–96 at a total cost of about $1.5 million (about $2,100 per parolee).

An evaluation of the program shows that the Parolee Partnership Program was successful with its target group (which was characterized as a hard-to-treat group, who on average had used drugs for about eleven years). The percentage of parolees placed in the program who were returned to prison was nearly 8 percentage points lower than the return rate for the statistically matched comparison group, and this difference was statistically significant (California Department of Corrections 1997). Los Angeles County operates a similarly successful program. The success of these programs motivated the California State Legislature to increase funding for parole substance abuse programs in 1998–2000.

2. *Employment and Job Training.* Research has consistently shown that if parolees can find decent jobs as soon as possible after release, they are less likely to return to crime and to prison. Several parole programs have been successful at securing employment for parolees.

The Texas RIO (Re-Integration of Offenders) Project, begun as a two-city pilot program in 1985, has become one of the nation's most ambitious government programs devoted to placing parolees in jobs (Finn 1998c). The project has more than one hundred staff members in sixty-two offices who provide job placement services to nearly 16,000 parolees each year in every county in Texas (or nearly half of all parolees released from Texas prisons each year). The RIO Project claims to have placed 69 percent of more than 100,000 ex-offenders in jobs since 1985.

The RIO Project represents a collaboration of two state agencies, the Texas Workforce Commission, where the program is housed, and the Texas Department of Criminal Justice, whose RIO-funded assessment specialists help inmates prepare for employment and whose parole officers refer released inmates to the program. As the reputation of the program has spread, the Texas Workforce Commission has developed a pool of more than 12,000 employers who have hired parolees referred by the RIO program.

A 1992 independent evaluation documented that 60 percent of the RIO participants found employment, compared with 36 percent of a matched group of non-RIO parolees. In addition, one year after release, RIO participants had worked at some time during more three-month intervals than comparison group members had. During the year after release, when most recidivism occurs, 48 percent of the RIO high-risk clients were rearrested compared with 57 percent of the non-RIO high-risk parolees; only 23 percent of high-risk RIO participants returned to prison, compared with 38 percent of a comparable group of non-RIO parolees. The evaluation also concluded that the program continually saved the state money—more than $15 million in 1990 alone—by helping to reduce the number of parolees who would otherwise have been rearrested and sent back to prison (Finn 1998c). These positive findings encouraged the Texas legislature to increase RIO's annual budget to nearly $8 million and other states (e.g., Georgia) to implement aspects of the RIO model.

New York City's Center for Employment Opportunities project is a transitional service for parolees, consisting of day labor work crews. Assignment to a work crew begins immediately after release from prison, and while it is designed to prepare inmates for placement in a permanent job, it also helps to provide structure, instill work habits, and earn early daily income (Finn 1998b). Most participants are young offenders, released from prison boot camp programs, and they are required to enroll as a condition of parole. The descriptive evaluation of this program shows that young parolees associated with the program are more likely to be employed, refrain from substance use, and participate in community service and education while in the program.

3. *Multiservice Centers.* The Safer Foundation, headquartered in Chicago, is now the largest community-based provider of employment services for ex-offenders in the United States, with a professional staff of nearly two hundred in six locations in two states. The foundation offers a wide range of services for parolees, including employment, education, and housing. A recent evaluation shows that Safer has helped more than 40,000 participants find jobs since 1972, and nearly two-thirds of those placed kept their jobs for thirty days or more of continuous employment (Finn 1998a).

Another highly successful program for released prisoners is operated by Pioneer Human Services in Seattle, a private, nonprofit organization. Pioneer Services provides housing, jobs, and social support for released offenders, but it also operates sheltered workshops for the hard-to-place offender. It is different from other social-service agencies in that its program is funded almost entirely by the profits from the various businesses it operates and not through grants. They place a priority on practical living skills and job training. Most of their clients are able to maintain employment either in the free market or for Pioneer Services, and the recidivism rates are less than 5 percent for its work-release participants (Turner and Petersilia 1996*b*).

There are parole programs that work. One of the immediate challenges is to find the money to pay for them. Martin Horn, currently commissioner of the Pennsylvania Department of Corrections, suggests using offender "vouchers" to pay for parole programs. At the end of the prisoner's term, the offender would be provided with vouchers with which he or she can purchase certain type of services on release (e.g., drug and alcohol treatment, job placement, family counseling). Horn suggests giving $2,000 in "service coupons" for each of the two years following prison release. The offender can then purchase the services he feels he most needs. Horn's cost-benefit analysis for this plan for the state of New York shows that it could save about $50 million per year—dollars that he says could then be invested in prevention programs instead of prison (Horn, personal communication, September 10, 1998).

C. Intermediate Sanctions for Parole Violators

States are taking a new look at how they respond to violations of parole—particularly technical violations that do not involve, of themselves, new criminal behavior (Burke 1997). Several states are now structuring the courts' responses to technical violations. Missouri opened the Kansas City Recycling Center in 1988, a forty-one-bed facility operated by a private contractor to deal exclusively with technical violators who have been recommended for revocation. The pilot program proved so successful that the state took over its operation and set aside a complete correctional facility of 250 beds for the program. Mississippi and Georgia use ninety-day boot camp programs, housed in separate wings of the state prisons, for probation violators (for other program descriptions, see Parent et al. [1994]). While empirical evidence as to the effects of these programs is scant, system officials believe that the programs serve to increase the certainty of punishment while reserving scarce prison space for the truly violent. Importantly, experts believe that states with "intermediate" (nonprison) options for responding to less serious parole violations are able to reduce parolees' new commitments to prison, explaining the vast differences shown in table 5.

D. "Neighborhood" Parole

One of the critical lessons learned during the past decade has been that no one program—surveillance or rehabilitation alone—or any one agency—police without parole, parole without mental health, or any of these agencies without the community—can reduce crime, or fear of crime, on their own (Petersilia 1998a). Crime and criminality are complex, multifaceted problems, and real long-term solutions must come from the community and be actively participated in by the community and those who surround the offender. This model of community engagement is the foundation of community policing, and its tenants are now spreading to probation and parole.

This new parole model is being referred to as "neighborhood parole" (Smith and Dickey 1998), "corrections of place" (Clear and Corbett 1999), or "police-parole partnerships" (Morgan and Marrs 1998). Regardless of the name, the key components are the same. They involve strengthening parole's links with law enforcement and the community offering a "full-service" model of parole and attempting to change the offenders' lives through personal, family, and neighborhood interventions. At the core, these models move away from managing parolees on conventional caseloads and toward a more "activist supervision," where agents are responsible for close supervision as well as procuring jobs, social support, and needed treatment.

The "neighborhood parole" model has been most well thought out in Wisconsin, where the Governors' Task Force on Sentencing and Corrections recommended the program. Program proponents realize neighborhood-based parole will be more costly that traditional parole supervision but are hopeful that reduced recidivism and revocations to prison will offset program costs. In 1998, the Wisconsin legislature allocated $8 million to fund and evaluate two countywide pilot projects (Smith and Dickey 1998).

VII. Concluding Remarks

Nearly 700,000 parolees are now doing their time on U.S. streets. Most have been released to parole systems that provide few services and impose conditions that almost guarantee their failure. Our monitoring systems are getting better, and public tolerance for failure on parole is decreasing. The result is that a rising tide of parolees is washing back into prison, putting pressure on states to build more prisons, which in turn, takes money away from rehabilitation programs that might have helped offenders while they were in the community. All of this means that parolees will continue to receive fewer services to help them deal with their underlying problems, assuring that recidivism rates and returns to prison remain high and public support for parole remain low.

This situation represents a formidable challenge to those concerned with crime and punishment. The public will not support community-based punishments until they have been shown to "work," and they will not have an opportunity to "work" without sufficient funding and research. Spending on parole services in California, for example, was cut 44 percent in 1997, causing parole caseloads to nearly double (now standing at a ratio of 82:1). When caseloads increase, services decline, and even parolees who are motivated to change have little opportunity to do so. Job-training programs are cut, and parolees often remain at the end of long waiting lists for community-based drug and alcohol treatment.

Yet crime committed by parolees is a real problem, and there is every reason to be skeptical about our ability to reduce it significantly. Early parole research did not reveal any easy fixes, and the current parole population is increasingly difficult and dangerous. The public is skeptical that the "experts" know how to solve the crime problem and have increasingly taken matters into their own hands. Corrections officials report being increasingly constrained by political forces and are no longer able to use their own best judgments on crime policy (Rubin 1997). State officials feel that even a single visible failure of any parole program could readily become a political disaster for the existing administration. One notorious case was that of Willie Horton and the Massachusetts furlough program. The press often publicizes such cases to feed the public's appetite for news about the failure of the criminal justice system. Such negative news, and the fear of such negative news, often precludes innovative parole reform efforts.

The challenge is to bring greater balance to the handling of parole populations by singling out those offenders who present different public safety risks and different prospects for rehabilitation. The pilot parole programs described in Section VI above are the first step, but it would help considerably if rigorous impact evaluations were always conducted. We do not know with any precision what effect parole has on offenders' recidivism or what supervision conditions are helpful to the reintegration process.

It is safe to say that parole programs have received less research attention that any other correctional component in recent years. A congressionally mandated evaluation of state and local crime prevention programs included just one parole evaluation among the hundreds of recent studies that were summarized for that effort (Sherman et al. 1997). I have spent many years contributing to the evaluation literature on probation effectiveness but know of no similar body of knowledge on parole effectiveness. Without better information, it is unlikely that the public will give corrections officials the political permission needed to invest in rehabilitation and job-training programs for parolees. With better information, we might be able to persuade voters and elected officials to shift their current preferences away from solely punitive crime policies and toward a sanctioning philosophy that balances incapacitation, rehabilitation, and just punishment.

By the year 2000, the United States is predicted to have a record 2 million people in jails and prisons and more people on parole than ever before. If current parole revocation trends continue, more than half of all those entering prison in the year 2000 will be parole failures. Given the increasing human and financial costs associated with prison, investing in effective reentry programs may well be one of the best investments we make.

REFERENCES

Abadinsky, Howard. 1997. *Probation and Parole.* Upper Saddle River, N.J.: Simon & Schuster.
Adams, William, and Jeffrey Roth. 1998. *Federal Offenders under Community Supervision, 1987–96.* Washington, D.C.: U.S. Department of Justice, Bureau of Justice Statistics.
Allen, George. 1997. "Abolishing Parole Saves Lives and Property." *Corrections Today* 59(4):22.
American Correctional Association. 1995. *Probation and Parole Directory.* Lanham, Md.: American Correctional Association.
Andrews, D. A., and James Bonta. 1994. *The Psychology of Criminal Conduct.* Cincinnati, Ohio: Anderson.

Applegate, Brandon, Frances T. Cullen, Michael Turner, and Jody Sundt. 1996. "Assessing Public Support for Three-Strikes-You're Out Laws: Global Versus Specific Attitudes." *Crime and Delinquency* 42:517–34.

Association of Paroling Authorities International. 1998. "APAI Survey of Parole Boards." Washington, D.C.: Association of Paroling Authorities International.

Austin, James, and Robert Lawson. 1998. *Assessment of California Parole Violations and Recommended Intermediate Programs and Policies.* San Francisco: National Council on Crime and Delinquency.

Beck, Allen J. 1999. "Trends in U.S. Correctional Populations." In *The Dilemmas of Corrections,* edited by Kenneth Haas and Geoffrey Alpert. Prospect Heights, Ill.: Waveland.

Beck, Allen, and Bernard Shipley. 1989. "Recidivism of Prisoners Released in 1983." Washington, D.C.: U.S. Department of Justice, Bureau of Justice Statistics.

Bottomley, Keith A. 1990. "Parole in Transition: A Comparative Study of Origins, Developments, and Prospects for the 1990s." In *Crime and Justice: A Review of Research,* vol. 12, edited by Michael Tonry and Norval Morris. Chicago: University of Chicago Press.

Bureau of Justice Statistics. Various years–*a. Annual Parole Survey.* Washington, D.C.: U.S. Department of Justice, Bureau of Justice Statistics.

———. Various years–*b. Correctional Populations in the United States.* Washington, D.C.: U.S. Department of Justice, Bureau of Justice Statistics.

———. Various years–*c. National Corrections Reporting Program.* Washington, D.C.: U.S. Department of Justice, Bureau of Justice Statistics.

———. Various years–*d. National Prisoner Statistics.* Washington, D.C.: U.S. Department of Justice, Bureau of Justice Statistics.

———. 1997. *National Corrections Reporting Program, 1996.* Washington, D.C.: U.S. Department of Justice, Bureau of Justice Statistics.

———. 1998. *Probation and Parole Populations, 1997.* Washington, D.C.: U.S. Department of Justice, Bureau of Justice Statistics.

Burke, Peggy B. 1995. *Abolishing Parole: Why the Emperor Has No Clothes.* Lexington, Ky.: American Probation and Parole Association.

———. 1997. *Policy-Driven Responses to Probation and Parole Violations.* Washington, D.C.: National Institute of Corrections.

California Department of Corrections. 1997. *Preventing Parolee Failure Program: An Evaluation.* Sacramento: California Department of Corrections.

Camp, Camille, and George Camp. 1997. *The Corrections Yearbook.* South Salem, N.Y.: Criminal Justice Institute.

Carter, Beth. 1998. "Harbingers of Change." *Campaign for an Effective Crime Policy Update* (August), pp. 1–2.

Citizens' Inquiry on Parole and Criminal Justice. 1974. "Report on New York Parole." New York: Citizen's Inquiry.

Clear, Todd, and George Cole. 1997. *American Corrections.* Belmont, Calif.: Wadsworth.

Clear, Todd, and Ronald Corbett. 1999. "Community Corrections of Place." *Perspectives* 23:24–32.

Cromwell, Paul F., and Rolando del Carmen. 1999. *Community Based Corrections.* Belmont, Calif.: West/Wadsworth.

del Carmen, Rolando, and James Alan Pilant. 1994. "The Scope of Judicial Immunity for Probation and Parole Officers." *APPA [American Probation and Parole Association] Perspectives* 18:14–21.

Deschenes, Elizabeth, Susan Turner, and Joan Petersilia. 1995. "A Dual Experiment in Intensive Community Supervision: Minnesota's Prison Diversion and Enhanced Supervised Released Programs." *Prison Journal* 75(3): 330–56.

DiIulio, John. 1997. "Reinventing Parole and Probation." *Brookings Review* 15(2):40–42.

Ditton, Paula, and Doris James Wilson. 1999. *Truth in Sentencing in State Prisons.* Washington, D.C.: U.S. Department of Justice, Bureau of Justice Statistics.

Fabelo, Tony. 1999. *Biennial Report to the 76th Texas Legislature.* Austin, Tex.: Criminal Justice Policy Council.

Feely, Malcolm, and Jonathan Simon. 1992. "The New Penology: Notes on the Emerging Strategy of Corrections and Its Implications." *Criminology* 30:449–74.

Fellner, Jamie, and Marc Mauer. 1998. "Nearly 4 Million Americans Denied Vote Because of Felony Convictions." *Overcrowded Times* 9(5):1, 6–13.

Finn, Peter. 1998*a*. *Chicago's Safer Foundation: A Road Back for Ex-Offenders.* Washington, D.C.: National Institute of Justice.

———. 1998*b*. *Successful Job Placement for Ex-Offenders: The Center for Employment Opportunities.* Washington, D.C.: National Institute of Justice.

———. 1998*c*. *Texas' Project RIO (Re-Integration of Offenders).* Washington, D.C.: National Institute of Justice.

Flanagan, Timothy. 1996. "Reform or Punish: Americans' Views of the Correctional System." In *Americans View Crime and Justice: A National Public Opinion Survey,* edited by Timothy Flanagan and Dennis Longmire. Thousand Oaks, Calif.: Sage.

Flanagan, Timothy, and Dennis Longmire, eds. 1996. *Americans View Crime and Justice: A National Public Opinion Survey.* Thousand Oaks, Calif.: Sage.

Fogel, David. 1975. *We Are the Living Proof: The Justice Model for Corrections.* Cincinnati, Ohio: Anderson.

Gainsborough, Jenni. 1997. "Eliminating Parole Is a Dangerous and Expensive Proposition." *Corrections Today* 59(4):23.

Gallup Organization. 1998. *Gallup Surveys Pertaining to Parole (Special Request).* New York: Gallup Organization.

Glaser, Daniel. 1969. *The Effectiveness of a Prison and Parole System.* Indianapolis: Bobbs-Merrill.

Gottfredson, D., P. Hoffman, and M. Sigler. 1975. "Making Parole Policy Explicit." *Crime and Delinquency* 21:7–17.

Gottfredson, Don, Leslie Wilkins, and Peter Hoffman. 1978. *Guidelines for Parole and Sentencing.* Lexington, Mass.: Heath/Lexington.

Hoffman, Peter B., and Lucille K. DeGostin. 1974. "Parole Decision Making: Structuring Discretion." *Federal Probation* (December), pp. 19–28.

Holt, Norman. 1998. "The Current State of Parole in America." In *Community Corrections: Probation, Parole, and Intermediate Sanctions*, edited by Joan Petersilia. New York: Oxford University Press.

Institute of Medicine. 1990. *Treating Drug Problems: A Study of the Evolution, Effectiveness, and Financing of Public and Private Drug Treatment Systems*, edited by D. R. Gerstein and H. J. Harwood. Washington, D.C.: National Academy Press.

Irwin, John, and James Austin. 1994. *It's about Time: America's Imprisonment Binge*. Belmont, Calif.: Wadsworth.

Kleinknecht, William. 1997. "Juvenile Authorities Want Satellite Tracking for Felons." *New York Star Ledger* (November 18), p. 3.

Legislative Analysts Office. 1998. *Reforming California's Adult Parole System*. Sacramento, Calif.: Legislative Analysts Office.

Lieb, Roxanne, Vernon Quinsey, and Lucy Berliner. 1998. "Sexual Predators and Social Policy." In *Crime and Justice: A Review of Research*, vol. 23, edited by Michael Tonry. Chicago: University of Chicago Press.

Lipton, Douglas, Robert Martinson, and Judith Wilks. 1975. *The Effectiveness of Correctional Treatment and What Works: A Survey of Treatment Evaluation Studies*. New York: Praeger.

Little Hoover Commission. 1998. *Beyond Bars: Correctional Reforms to Lower Prison Costs and Reduce Crime*. Sacramento, Calif.: Little Hoover Commission.

Love, Margaret, and Susan Kuzma. 1996. *Civil Disabilities of Convicted Felons: A State-by-State Survey*. Washington, D.C.: Office of the Pardon Attorney.

Lynch, Mona. 1998. "Waste Managers? New Penology, Crime Fighting, and the Parole Agent Identity." *Law and Society Review* 32:839–69.

McCaffrey, Barry. 1998. *Drug Treatment in the Criminal Justice System*. Washington, D.C.: Office of National Drug Control Policy.

McCleary, Richard. 1992. *Dangerous Men: The Sociology of Parole*. New York: Harrow & Heston.

Morgan, Terry, and Stephen Marrs. 1998. "Redmond, Washington's SMART Partnership for Police and Community Corrections." In *Community Corrections: Probation, Parole, and Intermediate Sanctions*, edited by Joan Petersilia. New York: Oxford University Press.

Morse, Wayne. 1939. *U.S. Attorney General's Survey of Release Procedures*. Washington D.C.: U.S. Department of Justice.

National Conference of State Legislatures. 1996. *Three Strikes' Legislation Update*. Denver: National Conference of State Legislatures.

National Institute of Corrections. 1995. *Status Report on Parole, 1995*. Washington, D.C.: U.S. Department of Justice.

———. 1997. *Status Report on Parole, 1996. Results from an NIC Survey*. Washington, D.C.: U.S. Department of Justice.

O'Leary, Vincent, ed. 1974. *Parole Administration*. Chicago: Rand McNally.

Olivares, K., V. Burton, and F. T. Cullen. 1996. "The Collateral Consequences of a Felony Conviction: A National Study of State Legal Codes 10 Years Later." *Federal Probation* 60:10–18.

Pan, Philip. 1998. "Md. Orders Drug Tests for Addicts on Parole." *Washington Post* (November 13), p. A1.

Parent, Dale. 1993. "Structuring Policies to Address Sanctions for Absconders and Violators." In *Reclaiming Offender Accountability: Intermediate Sanctions for Probation and Parole Violators,* edited by Edward Rhine. Laurel, Md.: American Correctional Association.

Parent, Dale, Dan Wentworth, Peggy Burke, and Becky Ney. 1994. *Responding to Probation and Parole Violations.* Washington, D.C.: National Institute of Justice.

Petersilia, Joan. 1997. "Probation in American." In *Crime and Justice: A Review of Research,* vol. 22, edited by Michael Tonry. Chicago: University of Chicago Press.

———. 1998a. "A Decade of Experimenting with Intermediate Sanctions: What Have We Learned?" In *Perspectives on Crime and Justice,* edited by National Institute of Justice. Washington, D.C.: National Institute of Justice.

———. 1998b. "Probation and Parole." In *The Handbook of Crime and Punishment,* edited by Michael Tonry. New York: Oxford University Press.

Petersilia, Joan, and Susan Turner. 1993. "Intensive Probation and Parole." In *Crime and Justice: A Review of Research,* vol. 17, edited by Michael Tonry. Chicago: University of Chicago Press.

Prendergast, Michael L., M. Douglas Anglin, and Jean Wellisch. 1995. "Treatment for Drug-Abusing Offenders under Community Supervision." *Federal Probation* 59(4):66–75.

Reitz, Kevin R. 1998. "Sentencing." In *The Handbook of Crime and Punishment,* edited by Michael Tonry. New York: Oxford University Press.

Rhine, Edward E. 1996. "Parole Boards." In *The Encyclopedia of American Prisons,* edited by Marilyn McShane and Frank Williams. New York: Garland.

Rhine, Edward, William Smith, Ronald Jackson, Peggy Burke, and Roger La-Belle. 1991. *Paroling Authorities: Recent History and Current Practice.* Laurel, Md.: American Correctional Association.

Richards, Stephen C. 1995. *The Structure of Prison Release: An Extended Case Study of Prison Release, Work Release, and Parole.* New York City: McGraw Hill.

Rothman, David. 1980. *Conscience and Convenience: The Asylum and Its Alternatives in Progressive America.* Boston: Little, Brown.

Rubin, Edward. 1997. "Minimizing Harm as a Goal for Crime Policy in California." Berkeley: California Policy Seminar.

Rudovsky, David, Alvin Bronstein, Edard Koren, and Julie Cade. 1988. *The Rights of Prisoners.* Carbondale: Southern Illinois University Press.

Runda, John, Edward Rhine, and Robert Wetter. 1994. *The Practice of Parole Boards.* Lexington, Ky.: Association of Paroling Authorities, International.

Schlosser, Eric. 1998. "The Prison Industrial Complex." *Atlantic Monthly* (December), pp. 51–77.

Sechrest, Lee, Susan White, and Elizabeth Brown. 1979. *The Rehabilitation of Criminal Offenders: Problems and Prospects.* Washington, D.C.: National Academy of Sciences.

Sherman, Lawrence, Denise Gottfredson, Doris MacKenzie, John Eck, Peter

Reuter, and Shawn Bushway. 1997. *Preventing Crime: What Works, What Doesn't, What's Promising.* College Park: University of Maryland.

Simon, Jonathan. 1993. *Poor Discipline: Parole and the Social Control of the Underclass, 1890–1990.* Chicago: University of Chicago Press.

Smith, Michael, and Walter Dickey. 1998. "What If Corrections Were Serious about Public Safety?" *Corrections Management Quarterly* 2:12–30.

Sundt, Jody, Francis T. Cullen, Michael Turner, and Brandon Applegate. 1998. "What Will the Public Tolerate?" *Perspectives* 22:22–26.

Tonry, Michael. 1995. *Malign Neglect: Race, Crime, and Punishment in America.* New York: Oxford University Press.

Turner, Susan, and Joan Petersilia. 1992. "Focusing on High-Risk Parolees: An Experiment to Reduce Commitment to the Texas Department of Corrections." *Journal of Research in Crime and Delinquency* 29:34–61.

———. 1996a. "Work Release in Washington: Effects on Recidivism and Corrections Costs." *Prison Journal* 76(June):138–64.

———. 1996b. *Work Release: Recidivism and Corrections Costs in Washington State.* Washington, D.C.: National Institute of Justice.

von Hirsch, Andrew. 1976. *Doing Justice: The Choice of Punishments.* New York: Hill & Wang.

von Hirsch, Andrew, and Kathleen Hanrahan. 1979. *The Question of Parole: Retention, Reform, or Abolition?* Cambridge, Mass.: Ballinger.

Walker, Samuel. 1998. *A History of American Criminal Justice.* New York: Oxford University Press.

Wilson, James. 1985. *Thinking about Crime.* New York: Basic.

Wilson, Rob. 1977. "Release: Should Parole Boards Hold the Key?" *Corrections Magazine*, pp. 47–55.

Author Index

Subject Index